WARSHIPS
OF THE
WORLD

WARSHIPS OF THE WORLD

AN ILLUSTRATED ENCYCLOPEDIA

GINO GALUPPINI

MILITARY PRESS
NEW YORK

This 1989 edition published by Military Press, a division of Arlington House, distributed
by Crown Publishers, Inc., 225 Park Avenue South, New York, New York 10003.

ISBN 0-517-68252-4

hgfedcba

Library of Congress Cataloguing-in-Publication Data
Galuppini, Gino.
    [Enciclopedia delle navi da guerra. English]
    Warships of the world / Gino Galuppini.
        p.   cm.
    Reprint. Originally published: New York : Times Books, c 1986.
    Translation of: Enciclopedia delle navi da guerra.
    Bibliography: p
    Includes index.
    ISBN 0-517-68252-4
    1. Warship—History.   I. Title.
V750.03513   1989
359.3'25—dc19   89-3249
                                                     CIP

Printed and bound in Italy

INTRODUCTION

The first ships to be used in war operations were not built expressly for that purpose, but were river, coastal, or seagoing vessels used for both trade and warfare. There was no real distinction between warships and merchant ships until Greek and Roman times, when true warships were built. The distinction between the two became blurred again after the fall of Rome, and throughout the Middle Ages it was often difficult to tell whether a ship was designed for trading or warfare. The fact remains, however, that until the sixteenth century, oared ships were used for warfare and sailing ships for trade. The age of steam, the use of iron hulls, technological progress in gun manufacture, the invention of the torpedo, and the use of electrically controlled gun turrets led to the construction of increasingly specialized ships. The result was a subdivision of warships into specific types.

This brief outline brings us to the ships of this century, in which two great wars have put the offensive and defensive capabilities of naval ships to the test, offering the unexpected possibility of gaining experience and enabling rapid improvements to be made.

The use of aircraft in naval warfare further revolutionized operational concepts that had until then prevailed. About forty years have passed since the end of the Second World War, during which time the techniques of warfare have been further developed, especially in terms of armament and propulsion. Armament has progressed in the form of missiles, and propulsion because of the development of nuclear energy and the gas turbine.

The book traces the history of this development, dividing it into various eras. It begins with classical antiquity and goes on to discuss the age of oared and sailing ships. A different pattern has been followed for iron and steel powered ships where the treatment of the material is based on the types of units and, therefore, types of use, rather than on historical periods.

In order to describe and supply information concerning the various units, various sources have been consulted which do not always agree, especially over sailing vessels such as galleons and carracks. Where there has been some doubt, the source regarded as the most reliable has been chosen.

As it is a well-known fact that ships increase their displacement and sometimes change their armament as the years pass, the general rule adopted in the section on modern ships has been to give the dimensions, displacement, and type of armament of a given ship at the time she was commissioned, listing, where possible, subsequent variations. The year, too, is the one when the vessel was commissioned, this being considered more helpful than the year of launching, normally taken to be a warship's "date of birth."

In this book, full-load displacement has as a rule been given, but for some ships, in the absence of other data, the standard displacement has been indicated.

As regards the classification of the various missiles installed on board more modern units, the terms *anti-aircraft, anti-ship,* and *anti-submarine* have been used, which, although not entirely orthodox, are certainly easier for the layperson to understand than the more technical descriptions "surface-to-surface" or "surface-to-air."

The appendix includes a compendium in which the ships are drawn to scale for the purposes of comparison, type by type. These are followed by technical drawings showing a side and plan view of the major classes, providing detailed information on the position and number of weapons, and other features. Lastly we have included tables of the numerical data for the ships referred to in the book.

Gino Galuppini

CONTENTS

In the appendix section of ships drawn to scale two relative proportions are employed:
The first (2.54in = 76.4ft) is used for battleships, aircraft carriers, cruisers, destroyers, frigates and corvettes.
The second (2.54in = 45.9ft) is used for submarines and torpedo boats.

Abbreviations:
a.a. = antiaircraft
a.s. = antisubmarine
GT = gas turbine

CLASSICAL ANTIQUITY
IN THE MEDITERRANEAN
AND THE COUNTRIES TO THE NORTH

The naval battle in ancient times

History has informed us of the affairs of peoples who, many centuries before our time, lived both in the Near East—Babylonians, Medes, and Persians—and around the Mediterranean—Egyptians, Phoenicians, Greeks, Etruscans, Carthaginians, and Romans.

As far as the peoples of the Near East are concerned, very little is known about their navies and naval wars. By contrast, surviving works of poets and writers referring to the ships and wars of the Mediterranean peoples enable us to build up a mental picture of their ships and how they fought their naval battles so many years ago.

Although the Egyptians were a Mediterranean people, they did not play an important role in the naval history of this sea. In fact, Egyptian maritime events about which we have information took place in the Red Sea, such as the voyage of Queen Hatshepsut (1496–1476 B.C.) to the land of Punt (probably present-day Somalia), and that of Pharaoh Rameses III (1200–1168 B.C.) against the "peoples of the sea." The information concerning such expeditions is quite vague, so, with regard to the method of combat in classical antiquity, all we have are documents relating to the other civilizations, handed down to us by Greek and Roman historians and writers.

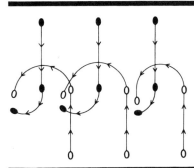

Phormio's Anastrophe. This attacking maneuver, devised by Phormio, entailed facing the enemy in a line abeam formation with the ships so spaced that they could pass between the ships in the enemy formation. Once through the line of enemy ships, the units reversed course by 180° in order to attack the more vulnerable and less well-defended stern area.

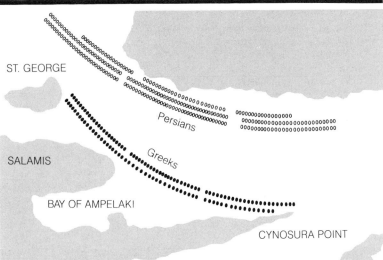

The Battle of Salamis. Fought between the Greek fleet, commanded by Eurybiades and Themistocles, 380 ships strong, and Xerxes' 1000-strong Persian fleet, the battle took place in September 480 B.C. The Greek fleet was stationed in Ampelaki Bay with the Persians opposite, spread out between the Island of St. George and Cynosura Point. The Greeks formed up in front of the Persians as they emerged from the Bay, attacked, and defeated them. Ariabigne, the Persian commander, was killed.

The naval battles of the ancients, as distinct from those of modern times, required a long period of preparation. We read that the fleets of Octavius Caesar and Anthony in the Battle of Actium (August 29–September 2, 31 B.C.) were within sight of each other for four days, waiting for the sea to turn calm. It was not until the fifth day that they actually prepared themselves for battle.

Another important operation preliminary to battle was to disembark the *impedimenta* (heavy baggage) and provisions in a suitable place, to make the ships lighter and more responsive to the action of the oars and rudders. When the ships prepared for battle, the crew had to furl the sails and lower the masts, which were of no use, and prepare the oars, the arms, and the other instruments of war. The fleets then had to be arranged in fighting trim or, as they said, "in order," and finally the propitiatory ceremonies had to be carried out.

In his *Life of Themistocles,* Plutarch tells how the captain made a sacrifice at the stern of his ship, while the seer Euryanthe deduced omens from the way in which the sacrificed victims died. The boatswain, or bard, promised the gods an altar, a temple, or other gifts in exchange for victory implored with sacrifices and prayers. Before the signal to commence battle was given, one last operation had to be performed: the exhortation by the Supreme Commander, to each of his captains, as he passed astern of the ships in a fast boat.

In even earlier times, naval formation was similar to that of an army, comprising a first, second, third, and fourth rank, which were arranged parallel to each other, known to the Romans as first, second, and third class, or acies, the fourth, the *triaria.* Later, there were only two ranks: the first, which was stronger, called *prima classis,* and the second made up of auxiliary ships. Aulus Irzius in his *De Bello Alexandrino* describes how "Caesar...in battle order faces the Alexandrians...and places the auxiliary ships behind, deciding upon and ordering those which he should keep back to assist each of the ones in front..." Sometimes a third rank of light ships was added to the first two, serving as back-up to the auxiliary ships. In addition, outside the formation there were small, fast ships that carried lighted bundles of sticks on their bows to threaten the enemy with fire. With the front line formation, the Commander in Chief had to position his ship in the first position on the right-hand side of the first line, that is, on the right wing.

A variant of this order was the so-called "crescent," where the ends extended like arms, later to close round the enemy and encircle him. With this formation, the Commander in Chief had to place his ship in the middle of the arc. In battle, the wings would attempt to converge toward the center so as to surround the enemy and attack from his flanks, ramming his ships.

Other less common formations were the forceps, the wedge (*cunaeus*), the circle, the oval, and the sickle. The circular formation was taken up for static defense, the ships being grouped in a circle with their bows facing outward and their sterns toward the center, thus presenting their rostra (rams) to the attacking enemy.

When the ships were properly arranged in formation, the signal to commence battle was given by sounding the trumpets and raising a golden shield on the flagship. At this signal, the two fleets would close in on each other, led by their respective flagships. In a frontal attack, the most common maneuver was to ram the enemy ship with the hull to break the oars and supporting structures of the rowlocks (detegere remos), or to try to break the sides with the ram (rostrum), but at the end of the day, the ships would attach themselves to each other with grappling irons and grapnels, and men would leap from one to the other to fight as if on land with swords and spears.

It will be remembered that in the Punic Wars the Romans used the *corvus* on their ships. This was also adopted by Gaius Duilius in the Battle of Milazzo (260 B.C.) and was a sort of gangplank that was laid between his ship and that of the enemy to let the soldiers cross and fight as if on land.

Two of the most interesting maneuvers of the naval battles of classical antiquity were Phormio's *anastrophe* (or *diecplus*) and Aristo's frontal attack. The anastrophe, invented by Phormio, an Athenian commander, consisted in crossing the

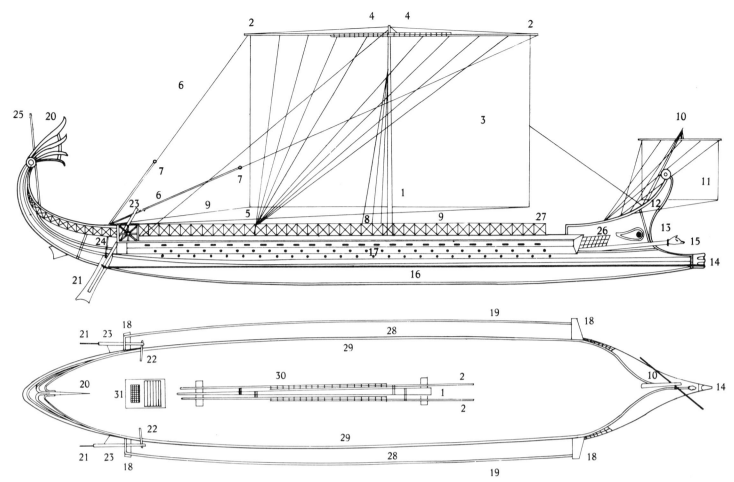

Roman ship and nomenclature of its various parts. (1.) mast (lowered in plan); (2.) yard (in two visible pieces in plan); (3.) sail; (4.) yard lifts; (5.) brails; (6.) yard braces; (7.) brace blocks; (8.) mast rigging; (9.) sail sheets; (10.) bowsprit; (11.) bowsprit sail; (12.) prow ornament; (13.) stem; (14.) ram or rostrum; (15.) counteram; (16.) keel; (17.) sides; (18.) forward and after epotides; (19.) outrigger; (20.) stern ornament;

(21.) rudders; (22.) tiller; (23.) stock; (24.) rope for raising the rudder; (25.) flagpole; (26.) grating to shelter rowers from sea; (27.) quarter boards or bulwark; (28.) starboard and port gangways; (29.) plan of quarter boards; (30.) main deck; (31.) access to lower deck.

---

enemy line, passing ship to ship, and then quickly changing course to attack the enemy units in their less well-defended stern sections. The frontal attack of Aristo, a Corinthian commander, consisted in suitably reinforcing the bows and pounding the enemy ships with them without using the ram; the impact caused damage which, even if it did not sink the ship, made her unfit for combat. This maneuver can be considered a countermaneuver to Phormio's anastrophe.

The Romans' ships were heavier and not as maneuverable as the Greeks'. Although they had a rostrum at the bow, the Romans preferred to come alongside the enemy ship instead of ramming, hook onto her with the corvus or grappling irons, and mount an attack by boarding. The Carthaginians, who by contrast had light, maneuverable ships, tried to avoid being boarded and attacked with the ram.

The ships of classical antiquity

In modern times, when we speak of warships, we use the terms *aircraft carrier, submarine, destroyer, cruiser, minesweeper,* and so on, all terms that indicate very clearly the tasks that the various types of ships must perform. It can be said therefore that ships are defined according to their use. This differentiation dates from almost a century ago, from the period when ships began to be built of iron and to have steam engines.

In the age of sail, descriptions of ships were completely different in that, instead of "ironclad" or "destroyer" people spoke of "three-deckers," "frigates," and "corvettes." Such descriptions continued even in the early years of the age of steam, for example, "steam frigate" and "steam corvette." Sailing ships were defined on the basis of their size or, more precisely, on the basis of the number of (gun) decks, and therefore the batteries of guns that they could carry. Three-deckers (as their name implies) had three continuous gun decks, frigates had two, and corvettes only one. Three-deckers could therefore carry three superimposed bands of guns on either side, frigates two, and corvettes one.

Yet a third system, based neither on ship function nor on size, was used in classical times. Thucydides, a Greek historian, tells us that in the second half of the seventh century B.C., the Corinthian shipwright Ameinokles of Samos built four trieres. Herodotus, another Greek historian, tells us that the Pharaoh Necho II (609–595 B.C.) had trieres built by Greek ships carpenters. Xenophon says that the fleet of Alexander the Great (336–323 B.C.) on the Euphrates River comprised twelve trieres, three tetreres, and four penteres.

In a more recent epoch, Roman historians speak of triremes, quadriremes, and quinqueremes used in the First Punic War (264–241 B.C.), the Second Punic War (212–201 B.C.), and in the Syrian Wars (192–188 B.C.) and Macedonian Wars (171–168 B.C.). Lastly, in Anthony's fleet in the Battle of Actium (31 B.C.), there were "nines," and Anthony's flagship was a "ten." Classification of the warships of classical antiquity was therefore based on the number of oars, or rowers, manning half of one transverse section of the oarage.

Thus, for example, a *triera* (Gk.) or *trireme* (Lat.) had rowers, and oars, arranged along the sides of the ship in three superimposed banks, so that in one transverse section there were six oarsmen who handled three oars on the right-hand side and three oars on the left. On a *quadrireme* or *quinquereme,* and more especially on those with a higher classification, such as an *okteres* (eight) or *dekeres* (ten), this argument is no longer valid: In other words, on an oktera there were not eight rowers manning eight oars per side, but only two or three banks of oars, each oar being handled by more than one rower. A "ten" could, for example, have three banks of oars per side, the longest one (on the highest level) being managed by four rowers and the two shorter ones (on the two lower banks) by three rowers, which brings to ten the number of men manning half of one transverse section of the oarage.

There were no warships bigger than "sixteens," although history tells us of one "twenty" and two "thirties," built for the King of Egypt Ptolemy II Philadelphus (285–246 B.C.), and one "forty," or tesseraconters, built for Ptolemy IV Philopater (221–205 B.C.).

These ships, if in fact they ever existed, were not to be considered as warships but rather floating showpieces, not designed for combat, but only to take the powerful monarchs who had them built for a jaunt at sea.

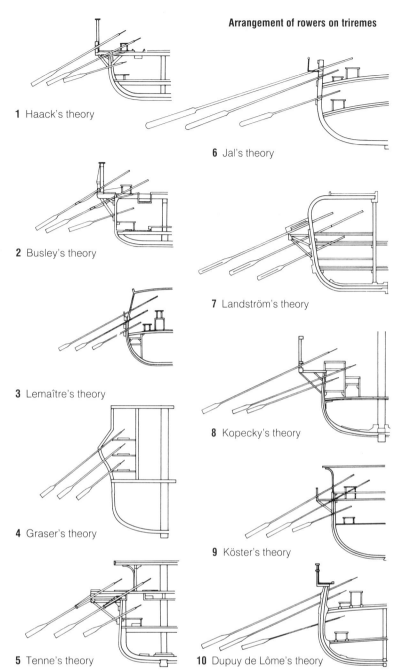

1 Haack's theory

2 Busley's theory

3 Lemaître's theory

4 Graser's theory

5 Tenne's theory

6 Jal's theory

7 Landström's theory

8 Kopecky's theory

9 Köster's theory

10 Dupuy de Lôme's theory

Arrangement of rowers on triremes. The arrangements of the rowers, as postulated by various authors and shown in the figures, are all highly unlikely for various reasons. According to Grazer's theory, triremes would have had three vertical benches one above the other; this would have been difficult to achieve on such small ships. The other theories, with benches on two decks and the rowers of the two longest oars on the upper deck and the rower of the shortest oar on the lower deck, are more acceptable.

The theories of Jal and Dupuy de Lôme, which do not include an outrigger, would make it impossible to handle the longest oar, which would be unbalanced; they are therefore also unacceptable. The other solutions are slightly more likely: these have the tholepins on the outrigger, which is for the longest oar, according to Lemaître, but for the medium-length oar, according to Tenne, Haack, Kopecky, Busley, Köster, and Landström. In effect the various theories can be divided into two groups: one where the longest oar has its blade farther out than the others (3, 4, 6, 9, 10) and one where the blade of the longest oar is between those of the other two (1, 2, 5, 7, 8), with its tholepin on the hull half way between those of the other two oars. Almost all these solutions include rowers' benches of varying height standing on the decks; or, according to Busley, one of the benches would actually be in a well in the planking of the top deck. Theories 5, 9, and 10, with the rowers on two decks, boil down to practically the same thing and are the most acceptable, but the fact that they have three superimposed decks, which would make the ships too tall, still presents a problem.

Since documents referring to dromons and selanders say that these ships had two decks with rowers on the first and second deck, it is highly likely that triremes and other polyremes also had two decks with quarter boards or a gangway either side that jutted out beyond the hull and housed the soldiers, as shown in theories 6, 8, 9, and 10.

Arrangement of the oarsmen on the ships of classical antiquity

We are not in possession of precise information on how the ships of classical antiquity were built. Not one Egyptian, Greek, or Roman warship has survived intact and in a condition to be raised, measured, and reconstructed. However, two Roman ships (not warships) have survived in the Lake of Nemi. They have enabled us to discover the system of construction of both these and other ships. The ships that underwater archeologists have located and studied at various locations in the Mediterranean are merchant ships. Furthermore, their condition has not enabled us to discover the layout of the benches and rowers.

The information we have on classical warships is largely taken from historical reports and stories by writers and poets; in addition, painted depictions have survived in tombs and houses and on vases, as well as in relief decorations on various monuments and on cameos and jewelry. These historians, poets, painters, and sculptors, however, were not naval experts, and they have therefore depicted the ships in an imperfect manner, making it vey difficult to get an exact idea of how the rowers were positioned.

For ships with three banks or oars, we know that the rowers taking the oars in the upper bank were called *thranites*, those who rowed in the middle bank were *zygites*, and those rowing in the lower bank were *thalamites*.

Many scholars have applied themselves to the difficult task of establishing how the rowers were arranged, supporting their ideas with information gleaned from books or monuments. Various theories on seating arrangements of the rowers have evolved from this research, all of which should be considered unacceptable except for the one proposed by Landström, for the following reasons:

1) All require seating arrangements that cannot be put into practice on a ship where the rowers must sit on benches.

2) Most of them have the rower above deck whereas they were in fact positioned below the fighting deck, which accommodated the soldiers.

3) Ships built with their rowers positioned as suggested would have lacked stability since they would have been too tall relative to their beam and draught.

It can be concluded that there were three banks of seats and that the rowers did not sit one below the other but were staggered both lengthwise and widthwise within the ship, especially since the thranites had to pull a longer oar and therefore sit closer to midships while the thalamites had to pull a shorter oar and sit nearer the tholepins (pegs serving as fulcrum). It was therefore certain that the benches were not perpendicular to the centerline. In other words, there was not just one bench from one side of the ship to the other, as on today's small boats; on the contrary, they sloped in a herring-bone pattern, as on medieval galleys.

Assuming that there were only three superimposed banks of oars, ships with more than three rowers could have had the layout shown in the illustration on the page opposite.

An arrangement with more than one rower per oar makes it even more difficult to reconstruct the arrangement on superimposed benches.

The most acceptable solution to this problem, at least for ships with up to five banks of oars, is the one put forward by an Italian scholar, Father Alberto Guglielmotti, in his "Vocabolario Marino e Militare," under the headings "polyreme" and "thwart."

Guglielmotti bears in mind that Vergil, in *The Aeneid*, commands that the oarsmen "*Considite transtris*" and that Phaestos says "*Transtra et tabulae navium dicuntus et tigna, quae ex parietem in pariete porriguntur.*"

The rowers therefore sat on *trasti* which were oblique planks, running from side to side, that is from the ship's side to the gangway, symmetrically positioned on

Classification of warships in Greek and Roman classical antiquity.

Greek name	Latin name	R
	monoremes	
moneres	moneres	1
	polyremes	
dieres, dikrota or dikroton	bireme, bicrota or dicrota	2
trieres	trireme	3
tetreres	quadrieres, quadrireme	4
penteres	quinqueres or quinquereme	5
hexeres	hexeres	6
hepteres	septireme	7
okteres	octeres	8
enneres	enneres	9
dekeres	decereme or deceres	10
hendekeres	undeciremis	11
dodekeres	duodeciremis	12*
triskaidekeres	tredeciremis	13*
pentekaidekeres	quindeciremis	15*
hekkaidekeres	sedeciremis	16*

R: number of rowers in each half section of the oarage.
*The Latin names are not authenticated.

both sides, which means that they were in a herring-bone pattern. Guiglielmotti also says "each thwart had for seats as many planks, nailed higher up, further inwards and further backwards, as the number of banks of the polyreme." To obtain this arrangement, the thwarts had to slant not only in the fore-and-aft direction but also in the top-to-bottom direction: higher where they joined the gangway and lower where they joined the ship's side. According to Guglielmotti, the thwart in a pentera, that is, one that seated five rowers, had to slant six and a half feet (2m) upwards vertically and slant the same measurement toward the bow.

The solution of thwarts inclined and arranged in this way is extremely simple and elegant and solved the complicated problems inherent in layouts with superimposed benches. It also adapts itself perfectly to the simplicity of construction that ships of that period had to have.

According to the reference in the "Attic Tablets," in a pentera (or quinquereme) the rowers bore the following names: *thalamites* for the lowest bank; *zygites* for the second bank; and *thranites* for the third. Then came the *tetrericas* for the fourth and *pentericas* for the fifth bank. The rowers above the third bank were, as a group, called *perinei* (Gk.) and, in Latin, *extraordinari*. The fact that they had both a Greek and a Latin name is further proof that ships with five banks of oars did exist. Father Guglielmotti had a model of a quinquereme built. Examination of the arrangement of the rowers in the model led to the conclusion that, in addition to the arrangement with just one thwart, there could also have been two thwarts since zygites and thalamites could have found room below the penteris and tetraris. With this arrangement the oar ports would have been in two groups: an upper group of three ports and a lower one of two, as shown in representations on some ancient monuments.

This theory would explain the arrangement of rowers in triremes, quadriremes, and quinqueremes, with just one rower per oar. The possibility of having five banks of oars with one rower per oar is historically proven by the fact that in 1529 a galley with five banks of oars, called the Fausto galley, was built in Venice. This galley will be discussed later.

For ships with more than five rowers, it is generally believed and accepted by scholars that there was not one rower per oar but that the oars were pulled by several men sitting on the same bench. In fact, both the arrangement with sloping thwarts and the enormous length and weight of the oars lead us to consider ships of this kind to be impracticable.

So far we have spoken of ships with several superimposed banks of oars with rowers sitting on benches at different heights or superimposed.

In Greek and Roman fleets there were also ships with just one bank of oars which two rowers took turns to manage. In a way they were biremes since there were two banks of rowers, although the tholepins were all at the same, or almost the same, level in the hull, as will be discussed later.

The Romans called ships with rowers and oars arranged in this way "Liburnians." This arrangement had been copied from that used by the Illyrians, a people who lived in present-day Dalmatia. Polybius tells us that in the third century B.C. in the Graeco-Macedonian fleet there were light, fast "Illyrian type" ships. During the Second Punic War (219–201 B.C.), King Philip of Macedonia, an ally of the Carthaginians, built one hundred Illyrian-type warships to operate in the Adriatic against Rome. In classical texts these ships are also called *lembi*, which were light, fast ships with one oar.

The Liburnian galley featured two innovations:

1) The rowers of the two banks of oars sat on the same bench, one next to the

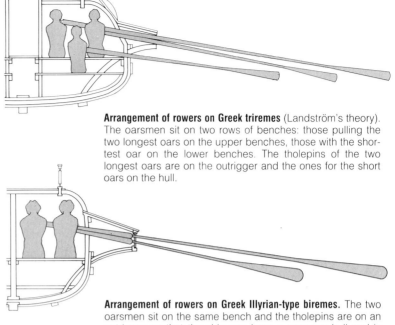

Arrangement of rowers on Greek triremes (Landström's theory). The oarsmen sit on two rows of benches: those pulling the two longest oars on the upper benches, those with the shortest oar on the lower benches. The tholepins of the two longest oars are on the outrigger and the ones for the short oars on the hull.

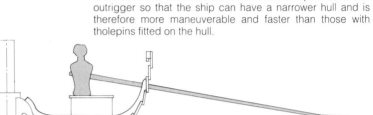

Arrangement of rowers on Greek Illyrian-type biremes. The two oarsmen sit on the same bench and the tholepins are on an outrigger so that the ship can have a narrower hull and is therefore more maneuverable and faster than those with tholepins fitted on the hull.

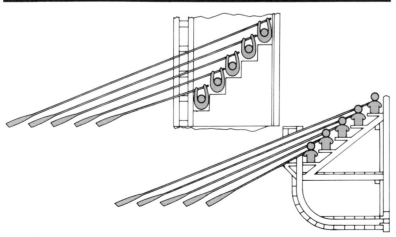

Arrangement of rowers on Viking ships. The rowers sit on benches which rest on the deck. The tholepins are in the hull which has ports from which the oars emerge. These oars are shorter and lighter than those used on Mediterranean biremes and triremes.

other. Obviously the benches were positioned at an angle and not perpendicular to the ship's sides so that the innermost rower, who sat farther aft and pulled the longest oar, could do so without getting in the way of one of the outermost rowers who sat farther forward and pulled a shorter oar.

2) Instead of working on a tholepin fixed to the board of the ship's side, or coming out of a tholepin hole in the side itself, the oars had these tholepins fixed on a longitudinal beam positioned on the outside and at a certain distance from the side. In Venetian galleys this beam was called a *postiza* or gunwale and it meant that the oar could be longer and have a longer arm. The position of the tholepins was therefore similar to that adopted on one of today's racing rowing boats, the "outrigger."

Liburnians therefore had lower and narrower hulls than other polyremes, which meant that, with the same number of rowers, they were lighter. Furthermore, since they had longer oars, they were faster and more maneuverable.

The Greeks also knew of this type of arrangement of oars and rowers. The statue of "Nike of Samothrace," which can be dated at 200 B.C., has a pedestal shaped like the prow of a ship which, although damaged and incomplete, shows the characteristic Liburnian outriggers. Greek biremes with this oar arrangement did not have a special name as did the Roman ones.

Referring to a period around 50 B.C. in his *De Bello Civili*, Julius Caesar says

Arrangement of rowers on a quinquereme (according to Guglielmotti). The rowers sit on benches resting on beams, set at an angle both horizontally and vertically. The tholepins cannot all be at the same level on the outrigger due to the vertical arrangement of the rowers.

Arrangement of rowers

Type of ship	Thranites	Zygites	Thalamites
Quadrireme	2 per oar	1 per oar	1 per oar
Quinquereme	2 per oar	2 per oar	1 per oar
Hexeres	2 per oar	2 per oar	2 per oar
Septireme	3 per oar	2 per oar	2 per oar
Octeres	3 per oar	3 per oar	2 per oar
Enneres	3 per oar	3 per oar	3 per oar
Decereme	4 per oar	3 per oar	3 per oar

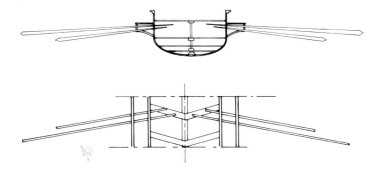

Arrangement of rowers on Roman liburnians. The benches are on one level and arranged in a herring-bone pattern so that the rower on the longest oar is farther aft and farther inboard than the one on the shortest oar. Both oars have their tholepins on the same outrigger. As on the Greek Illyrian-type ships, the hull is much narrower than on ships with the tholepins on the shell.

---

that Marcus Octavius's squadron was made up of Liburnians. In the naval battle of Actium (31 B.C.) in Caesar Octavianus's fleet had about 260 Liburnians while in Anthony's there were only big ships. As the years went by, polyremes were gradually abandoned for ships with only one bank of oars like the liburnians, or even for ships with more rowers but only two banks of oars.

The bow of the Roman ships in the frieze at Praeneste (modern day Palestrina), which appears to have only two banks of oars, was in fact a quadrireme with two rowers per oar; the oars in the top bank are shipped and those in the bottom bank are in the sea. It can also be assumed that this ship was quadrireme with one rower per oar, but with benches arranged as in a Liburnian, that is, a higher bench for the rowers of the two oars in the top bank and a lower one for those of the bottom bank.

As time passed, the number of banks of oars and rowers was gradually reduced until in the Eastern Roman Empire, and even its Western counterpart, there was a return to monoremes with the *triaconters* and *penteconters*.

The oars of the ships of classical antiquity varied in length from 13 to 29½ feet (4–9m) and were therefore made of thick, heavy pieces of wood which, even if handled by several men, had to be properly balanced to make it possible to row. Usually the oar worked on the tholepin and was secured by a strop, a third of the way up the oar, so that the part nearest the rower (the loom) was about half the length of the part nearest the sea (the blade). In order to balance the weight, due to the different lengths of the two parts, the loom was given a large diameter, as is still the case today. Pieces of lead were inserted in it to make it heavier. The loom was so big that it was impossible to grasp, so it was fitted with *manette*, pieces of wood with openings for the rowers' hands to grip.

Sails of the ships of classical antiquity

The many depictions of Egyptian, Greek, and Roman ships that have survived to the present day show that they had only one mast and one large "squaresail," rectangular in shape and suspended from a horizontal yard.

This type of sail was extremely rudimentary and made it impossible to *luff*, which meant it could be used only when the wind was blowing in a favorable direction, that is, from astern.

Some representations of Egyptian and Phoenician ships show us that the sails were unfurled between two yards, one taller than the other; while on the later Greek and Roman ships there was only the taller yard. These sails had the normal "running rigging" still in use today, such as the *halyard* to hoist the yard and sail, the *lifts* to support the ends of the yard, and the braces to guide it. The sail had sheets at its two *clews*, or lower corners, and "spilling line" type *brails* to furl the sail to the top yard.

The sail served as a means of propulsion only for long passages; when the ship was being prepared for combat the sails were not only furled but the masts and sails were actually left ashore so as not to get in the way of the rowers and fighters. This practice was not always followed, however. Plutarch tells us that in the Battle of Actium (31 B.C.) Anthony ordered the commanders of his ships, who wanted to leave the masts and sails ashore, to fight with them on board, while Octavianus's ships disembarked them.

For this reason the masts had to be light and easy to take down: Some representations of Egyptian ships show a bipod mast with counterweights which is raised by rotating round a horizontal spindle. A Greek marble bas relief shows a ship with its mast being raised.

As regards the number of masts, representations of Egyptian, Phoenician, and Carthaginian ships show just one mast. By contrast, some representations of Greek and Roman ships show another, much shorter mast which is raked forward and also fitted with a square sail. This pole and its sail were called *dolonum* (bowsprit) and *dolonum sail* (more commonly, the "artemon"), as mentioned in the writings of Livy, Pollux, and Isidorus. This name continued in use in the late Middle Ages, as proved by a Venetian Statute of 1265:

"*Navis...habeat in prora terzarolium et dolonum....*"

The dolonum mast was used above all on merchant ships. As a result of the development and modification of the shape of the bow, it changed into the bowsprit mast in the age of sail and became known as the "spritsail."

Weapons on the ships of classical antiquity

The most effective weapon of the ships of antiquity was the ram. This weapon was fitted to the ships of the Dorians who, in 3000 B.C., invaded from the North down to the Aegean shores and had their ships depicted on vases of that period. The Phoenician warships in the Assyrian bas reliefs of 700 B.C. also have rams and so too did Phormio's Athenian triremes in the Battle of Patras and Naupactus (429 B.C.). Pliny attributes its invention to the legendary Etruscan navigator Piseus, but little credence can be given to this. Herodotus speaks of it in his *Histories* in a battle, which occurred in 535 B.C. between the fleet of Carthaginian and Etruscan allies against the Greeks in the middle of the Tyrrhenian Sea, between Corsica and the mouth of the Tiber.

The ram had to be directed toward the side of the enemy ship, which demanded great maneuverability on the part of the ship making the attack. Similarly, survival in the face of ramming attacks demanded maneuverability. The ram therefore was best suited as a weapon for small ships that were easy to handle.

Since naval battles in ancient times were normally settled by boarding ships and then engaging in hand-to-hand fighting, the weapon used to hook a ship to an enemy ship to board it was very important.

One such was the *manus ferrea*, composed of a multi-pronged hook attached to a wooden staff. In a more refined form it became the grappling iron which remained in use for boarding ships until the last of the sail-driven naval ships.

A development of the manus ferrea was the *harpago*, or grappling hook, made up of a wooden rod with an iron tip and hooks attached to ropes, which could be hurled at the enemy ship with an "engine of war" such as the crossbow. The iron tip had four blades which, once they had entered the hull, prevented it from coming out. With this weapon the enemy ship could be hooked at a greater distance than was possible with the manus ferrea.

At the time of the First Punic War, the consul, Gaius Duilius, invented and fitted his ships with the *corvus* which, when used in the Battles of Milazzo (260 B.C.) and Ecnomus (256 B.C.) was a determining factor in bringing about his victory. It was a sort of bridge that was lowered onto the enemy ship, enabling the soldiers to pass from one ship to the other, so that the battle was transformed into a land fight. The corvus was abandoned after the Battle of Ecnomus since it was so heavy that it made the ships unstable. By contrast, the manus ferrea remained in use until the end of the sailing ship period. In Roman times its use is documented in the Battle of Naulochus of 36 B.C., during the civil war between Octavius and Pompey.

The other weapons carried on board were catapults, crossbows, and similar weapons designed to fire arrows and stones, or even incendiary arrows (*falaricae*), as used in the Battle of Actium.

These weapons were positioned either on deck or in towers. Originally, the towers were only at the bow and stern but they were later also placed at various points on deck in the larger ships such as the "eights" and "tens." These towers were not an integral part of the hull and could easily be dismantled for long passages, or else, if necessary, thrown in the sea. In fact, Vitruvius writes, "*graviora pelago damna quam bello.*"

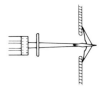

Harpago or **Harpax.** A development of the manus ferrea. It was a wooden rod with an iron tip launched by a machine of war against an enemy ship with the aim of hooking up to her. Once the hull was hit, the iron tip opened and held the ship fast.

The weapons about which we have spoken so far were used in battles between oared ships, in other words, with their masts lowered and sails furled. Roman ships, however, also found themselves fighting against sailing-ships, as Caesar mentions in *De Bello Gallico*; then in 56 B.C. they clashed with the Veneti at Darioritum Venetorum (Vannes, in Brittany), Condivincum (Nantes, on the Loire) and Portus Itius (Boulogne, on the English Channel).

In order to fight against these ships, a special weapon was used, called a *falx,* which was made up of rods with curved blades at the end similar to scythes. These were used to cut down the sail rigging of enemy ships, especially the halyard, with the aim of making the yard crash down onto the deck.

In addition to all this steel weaponry, the ships of classical antiquity also had a firearm that dates from the second century B.C., called a "fire corvus" or "fire pot."

Polybius supplies us with a description of this weapon and Livy and Appian also speak of it. It was made up of receptacles, filled with an incendiary material, which were hung from two booms overhanging either side of the ship's bow and flung onto the enemy ship. A mural graffito found on the island of Pharos, at the entrance to the port of Alexandria, depicts the bow of a ship, on which there is a tower, with a boom carrying the incendiary receptacle. The fire corvus which, according to Livy, was used also in the Battle of Cape Myonnesus (September, 190 B.C.) must not be confused with "Greek fire" used in the navies of the late Middle Ages. Tradition would have it that the Greek fire of the Byzantines was invented by a Syrian architect named Kallinikos and consisted of a mixture of saltpeter, coal, pitch, resin, lime, petroleum, and perhaps phosphor, which, as a suspension of powders in an oil-like liquid, was pumped by siphon onto enemy ships.

A type of flame thrower was also known, however, in more ancient times. It is thought to have been invented by a Greek named Ktesibes who lived in the third century B.C. With this weapon, an incendiary liquid was projected onto the enemy ships, the liquid being oil, or petroleum, or some other ignited mixture.

Another weapon of ancient ships, typically used on merchant ships rather than on warships (or *naves longae*), was the *delphines.* This consisted of a big weight, in the form of a stone or piece of metal, that was hoisted to the end of the sail yard and then dropped on the enemy ship with the aim of smashing the planking or decks. The delphines is mentioned by Thucydides, Diodorus Siculus, and other historians as being a weapon which hung from the sail yard but could not be used in naval battles where, as previously mentioned, the masts and sails were removed.

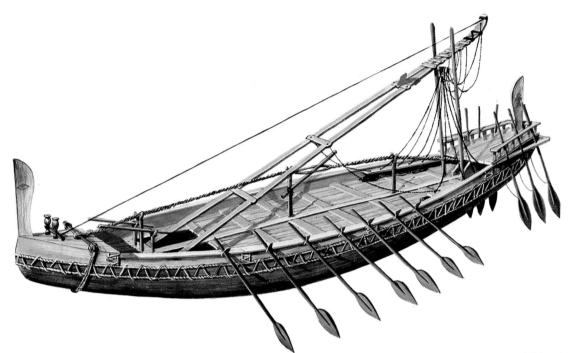

Warship of the Pharaoh Sahu-re (Fifth Dynasty 2540–2421 B.C.). A dignitary for the Pharaoh Sahu-re tells us of a war fought on land and sea against the inhabitants of Syria (probably the Phoenicians). The naval expedition, comprising eight ships, is depicted in a fragment of a bas-relief, which makes it possible to reconstruct the units. Egyptian ships of this period had neither keel nor frames to support the hull planking. The vessel's framework was made up of wide strakes joined together by joints and wooden dowels. In order to achieve the necessary longitudinal strength, there was a thick double rope, stretched between stem and stern and supported by props; it was made taut by twisting the two ends using a piece of wood.

The ship had a bipod mast that could be lowered. When it was lowered it was supported by a beam laid across two posts near the stern. Instead of a rudder there were six oars, three either side of an after platform. The ship did not have a deck as such but only planking along the floor. The rowers sat on benches positioned crosswise and the oars were probably attached to their wooden tholepins or pegs, fixed along the gunwale: "probably" because a terracotta model of a small vessel, found in the tomb of the Pharaoh Mentuhotep IV (Eleventh Dynasty, 2054–2008 B.C.), shows seven rowers either side, using paddles as oars. Furthermore, there are only two steering oars aft instead of six.

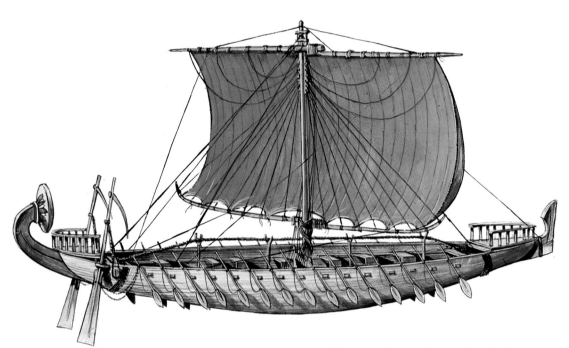

Warship of Queen Hatshepsut (1496–1476 B.C.). Some bas-reliefs in the temple at Deir-el-Bahri, near Luxor, depict the ships that Queen Hatshepsut sent to the land of Punt to bring back precious merchandise. Perhaps they are not warships, but the depictions are very detailed. These ships, too, have just one mast and a huge square sail set on two yards: one at the top and one at the bottom. The mast has no rigging, but only two stays, one forward and one aft, but this could have been a detail left out by the sculptor. The stem is almost vertical, whereas the stern is curved and ends in a lotus flower ornament. There are railed platforms both at the forward and after ends, and there are only two rather than six steering oars, positioned almost vertically on each quarter. Fifteen rowers are shown either side, pulling oars which are fixed to their tholepins. Despite the presence of a stem and sternpost, which would suggest the existence of a keel, there is still the double rope, supported by props, to give longitudinal strength to the hull. The ship did not have a flush deck but only partial coverings fore and aft. These ships were probably 82–88.5ft (25–27m) long with a beam of 13–16ft (4–5m).

Warship of the Pharaoh Rameses III (Twentieth Dynasty 1200–1168 B.C.). There is a bas-relief in the tomb of the Pharaoh Rameses III at Medinet Habu depicting a naval battle that Rameses fought with "the people from the sea"—probably the Philistines mentioned in the Bible. The main innovation on these as compared to previously described ships is the quarter boards on either side of the hull to protect the rowers. It is also clear that the ship has a ram, which is not such a definite feature on ships built 300 years earlier. It would also appear that there is just one after steering oar, although this is not very likely because in much later times Greek and Roman ships always had two. For the first time, a crow's nest is visible on the mast, in the form of a sort of basket; there is also a sail hauled to a yard at the top and fitted with brails, of the "spilling line" type. This is evidence of the disappearance of the bottom yard which earlier ships had had. These ships, too, did not have a flush deck, but only the two fore and aft platforms and perhaps a "corsia" (narrow raised gangway) down the middle to link them together, on which the ends of the rowers' benches rested. From the bas-relief it has not been possible to determine the number of rowers, which, in the reconstruction, have been taken to be twelve per side.

Phoenician warship. Some Assyrian bas-reliefs that date back to the eighth century B.C. show warships that are attributed to the Phoenicians. These ships are particularly interesting because they clearly show two banks of oars, which proves that between 800 and 700 B.C. biremes did exist. The bas-relief shows a ship with a long ram and a hull which seems to be cylindrical in shape. According to a theory put forward by Landström, these ships must have had their central part made of a hollowed out tree trunk; they were therefore dug-outs, or monoxylons. This trunk gave the ship considerable longitudinal strength and, because it was very narrow, it had two light half-hulls which gave the original dug-out considerable stability athwartships especially when under sail. The ship therefore had a long *corsia* (narrow raised gangway) above the central trunk, on which the soldiers stood with their shields hanging either side. The bottom row of oarsmen sat on benches below the corsia while those in the top row sat on benches in the two half-hulls either side. The rudders were in the form of two oars on each quarter. These ships had one mast with a square sail.

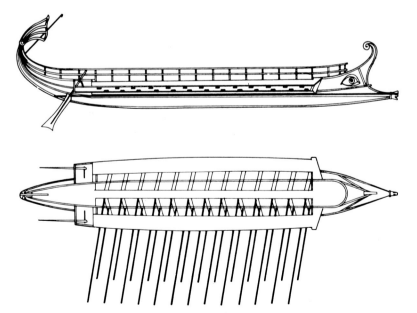

Corinthian bireme of the fourth century B.C. The base of the statue of Nike of Samothrace, in the Louvre Museum in Paris, depicts the prow of a warship in which an outrigger on the starboard side with two oar ports is clearly visible. These openings are staggered: the upper one being farther aft and the lower one farther forward. Examination of the prow of this ship, dated to c. 306 B.C., because it was made to celebrate the naval victory of Demetrius over Ptolemy, has led to the formulation of a different theory about the arrangement of the rowers. Previously it was thought that the rowers on biremes and triremes sat on staggered benches. On these ships, however, both rowers sat on one bench, set at a slight angle, like the upper bench on triremes. The oars had to have their tholepins on the outrigger: the one for the innermost rower with the longest oar positioned further aft, and the one for the other further forward. For a ship with fifty-two rowers and thirteen pairs of oars either side, the dimensions would have been: length 65.5ft (20m); beam 8ft (2.5m); draught 2.5ft (0.8m).

Etruscan bireme. An Etruscan vase, now in the British Museum in London, is decorated with a painting of a bireme which shows us what the ships of this ancient Italic seafaring people were like, around the sixth century B.C. Two banks of oars are clearly visible: the top bank with their tholepins on the wash-board, or perhaps on an outrigger, and the bottom bank emerging from ports in the hull, or with tholepins on the gunwale, hidden by the outrigger, as suggested by the continuous crack visible on the vase. There is a ram at the bow and, particularly interesting, a long forecastle, never before shown as being this tall and long in other pictorial representations. In the reconstruction, the bow has been drawn similar to that of ancient Greek biremes of the same period and is formed by binding together the extensions of the longitudinal members. A mast and sail are also shown. Only one steering oar has been drawn in order to remain faithful to the painting on the vase, but it would be correct to assume that there were two.

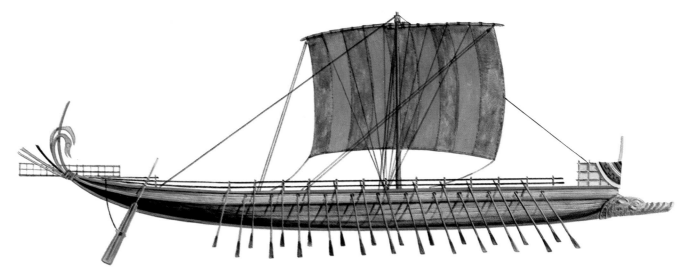

Ancient Greek bireme. Paintings on vases of the period around 500 B.C. depict ships with two banks of oars, one with tholepins on outriggers and one with the oars emerging from round ports in the ship's sides. They are the first depictions of biremes used by the Corinthians in the Peloponnesian Wars (431–404 B.C.). By this time, these ships were no longer monoxylons but had a hull made up of a keel, framework and planking. The hull structure had to be particularly light since it was common practice to sail only during the daytime and beach the ships at night. The illustrations show these ships with a mast carrying a large square sail, a rostrum at the bow and, at the stern, a tall ornament made by joining together the wooden lengths making up the gunwales, rowlocks, outriggers, and the parapet of the after bridge for the helmsman. There were two steering oars, in the normal position on either quarter, and also a gangplank for disembarking. The oarsmen sat on staggered benches athwartships. Amidships, above the benches, was a gangway connecting the fore and after platforms. A vessel with fifty rowers would have been about 80ft (24.5m) long, 10ft (3m) in the beam, and had a draught of 3ft (1m).

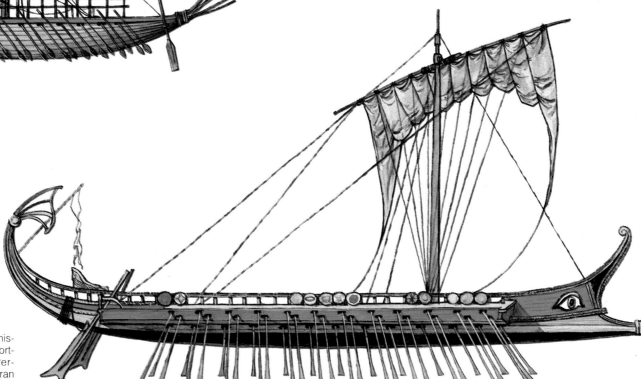

Greek trieres (trireme). The Greek historian Thucydides tells us that "shortly before the wars with the Persians...the Siculan and Corcyran tyrants possessed many triremes," and says that this type of ship had been built since the seventh century B.C. by the ship's carpenter Ameinokles of Samos. Although there are reasons for doubting Thucydides' word, it is clear that in order to achieve greater speed and heavier impact with the ram, the number of rowers on biremes had been increased by adding a third bank. Depictions of the period, and in particular a graffito of a house on the island of Delos, show triremes very similar to the bireme, with a row of shields hanging over the side, beside the rowers. The rowers, according to Landström's theory, sat on two staggered benches. These benches were not perpendicular to the ship's sides but set slightly at an angle, with the ship's side end farther forward than the amidships end. The two rowers on the longest oars both sat on the top benches and the tholepins were on the outrigger. The rowers on the shorter oars sat one per bench, on the lower benches, and the tholepins were on the gunwale. The outrigger was quite rudimentary on ancient biremes; but on these ships, it appears to be much more solid and elegant, as shown on the base of the Nike of Samothrace. The rowers' benches were in the open and, amidships, there was a gangway to link the bow and stern platforms. In a Greek trireme there were thirty-one thranites, twenty-seven zygites, and twenty-seven thalamites per side, making a total of 170 rowers. The longest oars would have been about 13.7ft (4.2m) long. The crew, apart from the rowers, included ten to twelve seamen and twelve to eighteen soldiers. The dimensions were roughly: length 114.8ft (35m); beam 16.4ft (5m); draught 3ft (0.95m), and height of deck above the waterline 8ft (2.45m). Triremes also had one mast and a square sail.

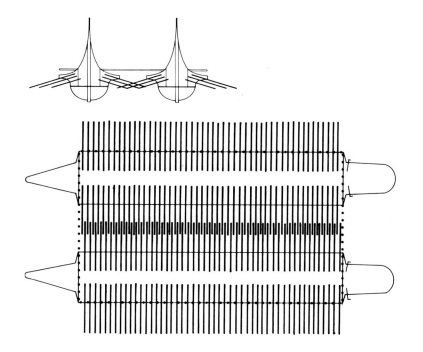

The tesseraconter of Ptolemy Philopater. In 332 B.C. Alexander the Great conquered Egypt. One of his generals, Ptolemy, became crown prince, later assuming the title of king and initiating the Ptolemaic Dynasty, which lasted until the Roman conquest (332–330 B.C.). All the kings of the Hellenistic Dynasty were called Ptolemy, to which a second name was added, such as Euergetes, Soter, or Philopater. Due to the Hellenistic nature of the dynasty, the tesseraconter is included here as a Greek ship. Ships with more than ten banks of oars are mentioned by several historians: Plutarch refers to Demetrius of Macedon's "sixteen" and Diodorus and Polybius describe Hiero of Syracuse's "twenty." According to Plutarch, Ptolemy II Philadelphus, King of Egypt (285–246 B.C.), built one ship with twenty banks of oars and two with thirty and, lastly, Ptolemy IV Philopater built one with forty. This ship would have been 407.87ft (124.32m) long and 55.34ft (16.87m) in the beam, with a 70ft (21.31m) tall super-structure. The end of the *aphlaston* at the stern was 77ft (23.5m) out of the water, the four steering oars were 43.70ft (13.32m) long, and the longest oars, pulled by the thranites, were 55.34ft (16.87m). Where unladen the ship would have drawn about 5.2ft (1.60m) and fully-laden about 11.8ft (3.6m). She carried 4,000 rowers and 2,850 soldiers and had seven rostra, two bows and two sterns. A reconstruction by an American named Casson, shows her as a large catamaran with three banks of oars, the two top banks for the thranites and zygites, having fourteen rowers each, sitting opposite each other, with seven pulling and seven pushing; the thalamite banks had twelve rowers. These ships should be considered more legendary than real, and in fact, the description of the tesseraconter by earlier historians (perhaps Callisthenes) was borrowed by Plutarch and Athenaeus, historians living in the first and second centuries A.D., who, although authoritative, were writing some four centuries later and were hardly in a position to check the facts. We can therefore assume that yarns passed down by word of mouth, recorded by later historians, and borrowed by Plutarch and Athenaeus, were taken to be actual facts. For this reason, many naval scholars have endeavored to convert the measurements given in cubits by these writers into feet and to interpret their descriptions in a logical, or sometimes not so logical, way.

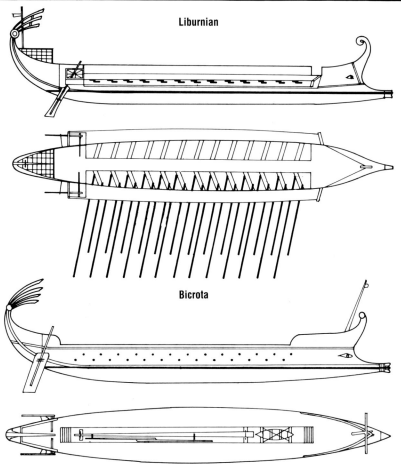

Liburnian

Bicrota

Biremes: bicrota (or dicrota) and liburnian. The bicrota, or dicrota (c. 150 B.C.) was a bireme with two superimposed banks of oars and rowers on staggered benches, as on fifth-century Greek biremes. A bireme had a ram, two steering oars aft, a square-sail mast, and bowsprit forward. The benches were exposed because instead of a flush deck there were just two platforms, one forward and one aft, probably connected by a gangway.

The liburnian was a bireme with a structure similar to that of a fourth-century Greek bireme, that is, with benches all on one level, set at an angle to the ship's sides and with two rowers per bench. The dimensions of a liburnian with fifty-two rowers, that is, thirteen pairs of benches, would have been about: 75.5ft (23m) long, and 14ft (4.3m) in the beam, with a draught of 2.5ft (0.75m). The 14ft (4.3m) beam included 23.6in (60cm) either side for the outriggers. In later times ships with two banks of oars and several rowers for each oar were also called liburnians.

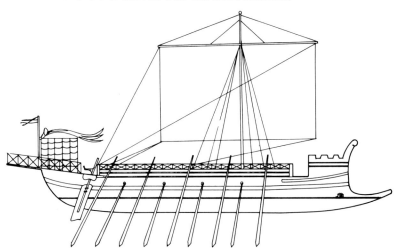

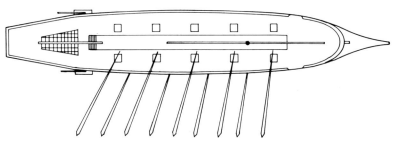

River liburnian

River liburnian. On Trajan's Column there are depictions of triremes and liburnians belonging to the river fleet that operated on the Danube and the Sava at the time of the Dacian Wars (101–107 A.D.). Other liburnians, used by the Romans for troop transport in the wars against the Dacians and in the conquest of Egypt, were probably bigger and had a different structure. The river liburnian had no outriggers for the tholepins which, for the top bank, were on the gunwale, and for the bottom bank took the form of ports in the ship's sides. The reconstruction shows a ship with a rostrum, a platform fore and aft, two steering oars, one square-sail mast, and a landing gangplank, The main deck was complete and the deck rowers sat on seats rather than benches. The dimensions of a river liburnian would have been as follows: length 69ft (21m); beam 10.8ft (3.3m); draught 2.2ft (0.7m), and a freeboard of 6ft (1.8m).

Trireme. Roman triremes were bigger, heavier, and sturdier than their Greek counterparts and the rowers had to sit on three instead of two banks of benches, as is assumed to have been the case on Greek triremes, or else on thwarts set at an angle. In his *De Bello Civili* , Julius Caesar refers to a "*triremis constrata*" (decked trireme), which would lead one to assume that in 50—49 B.C. there were also triremes without a flush deck, as shown in the reconstruction. This, in fact, depicts a ship with a flush fighting deck and a corvus at the bow. There are three banks of oars: the top bank has oval ports in the outrigger while the two bottom ones have round ports in the ship's sides. The leather sleeves that served to prevent seawater from coming in through the ports of the bottom oars are not visible. In Latin these sleeves were called *folliculi* and in Greek *askomata*. As distinct from Greek triremes, Roman triremes had the same number of rowers for each bank. In addition to the rowers there were at least ten to twelve seamen and eighty to ninety soldiers.

The approximate dimensions were: length 111.5ft (34m); beam 18.3ft (5.6m), including 2ft (0.6m) either side for the outriggers; draught 3.2ft (1m).

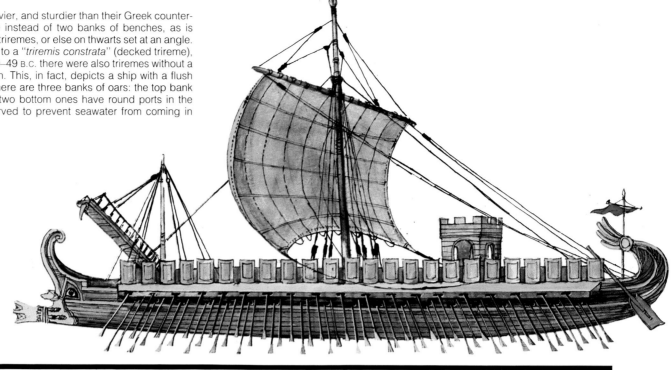

Quadrireme. The quadrireme taken as the model for the reconstruction appears in the frieze in the Temple of Fortune at Praeneste (Palestrina), now in the Vatican Museum. An interesting feature on this quadrireme is that the two top banks of oars are raised and shipped, in other words, laid in. Once the rowers had lifted the blades out of the water, they slid the oars past the tholepins, drawing in the looms until they rested on the opposite wash board or on the gangway. This is still practiced today on navy boats on the command of "ship oars." In the line drawing the ports for the two top banks of oars have been drawn in the outrigger and those of the two bottom banks in the ship's side, assuming that the rowers sat two per bench, as was the case on liburnians, and not on four rows of seats, as is equally possible but less likely. The deck is flush and has railings on either side, with ornaments in the form of round shields. In the colored illustration of the quadrireme only the two bottom banks of oars are shown, not those in the two top banks, as in the Praeneste frieze. In addition, only one tower (*fala*) has been shown forward. As is well known, the towers were constructions which were not part of the hull structure and, if necessary, could be dismantled and thrown into the sea. The historian, Appian, tells us that in the Battle of Naulochus (36 B.C.) Agrippa had to throw his towers into the sea, and Cassius Diodorus says that in the Battle of Actium (31 B.C.) Anthony's ships unfurled their sails, cast their towers into the sea, and fled. In the excavations of the Port of Athens, the remains of the sheds where triremes were kept during the winter season have been uncovered. From their dimensions it has been deduced that the Greek triremes were about 114.8ft (35m) long and 16.4ft (5m) in the beam. Roman quadriremes, which were bigger, can be assumed to have been 131ft (40m) long and 23ft (7m) in the beam. There must have been 200 rowers, plus fifteen to twenty seamen, and one hundred soldiers to complete the crew. According to Polybius the first quadrireme of the Roman Navy was a Carthaginian ship captured in 260 B.C. during the siege of Milazzo (Milae).

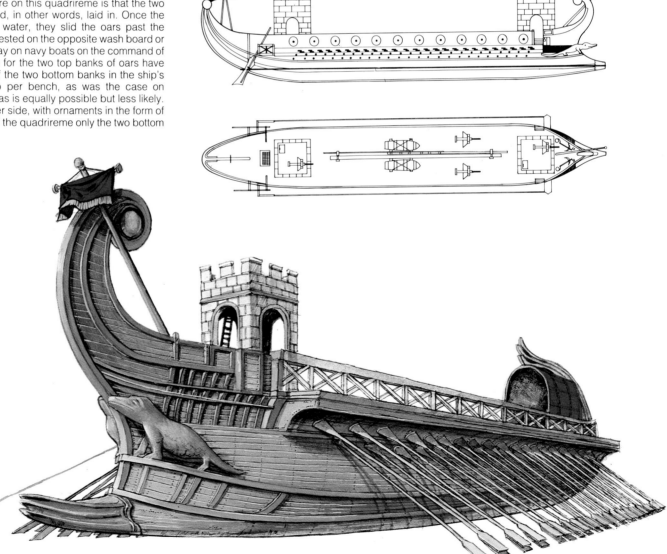

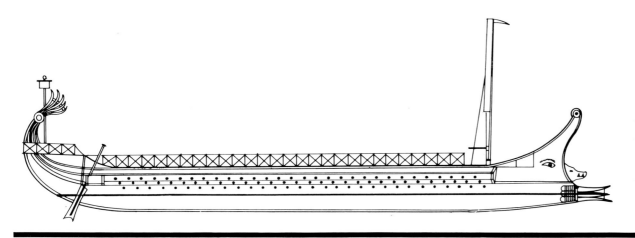

Quinquereme. These were the backbone of the Roman war fleet in the two Punic Wars and the war in Macedonia and Syria. For the prow, the reconstruction is based on the rostral column of Gaius Duilius in the Capitoline Museum and, for the rest, on the ship on the Triumphal Arch in Orange. The ship has three banks of oars, a flush deck, and a corvus at the bow. The rostrum is three-pronged and surmounted by a counter-ram in the form of a boar's head. These ships are assumed to have been 147.6ft (45m) long, 26.2ft (8m) in the beam, and to have had a draught of 4.2ft (1.3m).

Decereme. Probably the biggest ship in the Roman fleets, remaining in commission until the reign of Caligula (37–41 A.D.). The reconstruction is based on the dimensions of the Nemi ships and, for the towers, on a cameo in the Berlin State Museum, on which is engraved a huge warship. The decereme, or deceres, is shown to have two banks of oars, with the rowers arranged as on liburnians. There are thirty-five oars per bank, making a total of 140 oars pulled by five rowers each, thus adding up to 700 rowers. Given the considerable beam of the ship, outriggers have not been drawn, only epotides fore and aft. The customary steering oars are shown on each quarter. The dimensions are the same as those of the Nemi ship with a ram, that is: length 233.9ft (71.3m); beam 65.6ft (20m); draught 6.2ft (1.9m); and freeboard 9.8ft (3m), as quoted by Orosius for Anthony's "ten" in the Battle of Actium.

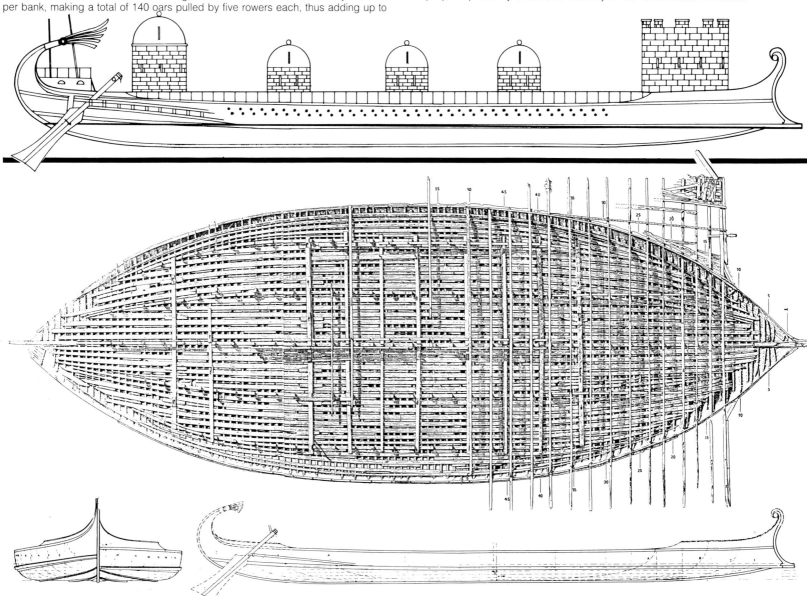

The Nemi ships. These ships were definitely not warships, but since they are the only ones to have survived almost intact and to have been recovered, photographed, and studied, enabling us to assess the skills of Roman shipwrights, we must mention them briefly. The hulls had lain for almost 2,000 years on the bottom of the relatively shallow lake. Their presence was known and, over the years, various attempts were made to recover them. On the whole, this only further damaged their structures, enabling but a few metal objects and pieces of wood to be brought up. These were recovered by lowering the level of the lake. The work lasted from 1927 to 1932; the hulls were then laid out in cradles and transported to a suitable museum. In the wake of the armistice of September 8, 1943, the museum was set on fire by German soldiers and these precious finds were destroyed. Today we have small-scale models of them. The ship with a ram was 234ft (71.3m) long overall and 220.96ft (67.35m) on the waterline. She was 65.6ft (20m) in the beam and had a draught of 6.2ft (1.9m). The ship without a ram was 213.2ft (65m) long between perpendiculars, 77.4ft (23.6m) in the beam, and also had a draught of about 6.5ft (2m). The hulls of these ships, in the submerged part, were covered in felt with lead sheets on top. Roman warships and other vessels had their hulls sheeted in this way to provide protection against the *teredo navalis* (ship worm) and to prevent growth of algae. It has been impossible, however, to learn a great deal about the arrangement and numbers of the rowers, because the outriggers had been practically destroyed in the shipwreck and in earlier recovery attempts. In these ships there was probably one rower per oar, sitting in side galleries, who acted as outrigger. An important find was an anchor (the first to survive intact), with wooden shank and flukes and a lead stock.

Triaconters and penteconters

Early in the Christian era, the development of Roman warships took two forms: the triaconters and the penteconters. The historian Eusebius relates that there were 200 triaconters and penteconters in the Emperor Constantine's navy in 321 A.D. The ships that Marcus Aurelius Carausius, prefect of Britannia, used against the Franks and Saxons at the end of the third century were likewise triaconters. When Constantine left for the conquest of Byzantium in 324 A.D., his fleet, commanded by his son Flavius Valerius Crispus, was made up of eighty triaconters and penteconters. But the fleet of his enemy, Licinius, commanded by Amandus, still numbered 200 triremes and other ships of similar size. While the two fleets were confronting each other, a sudden storm drove many of Amandus' ships onto the rocks along the coast, where 130 of them sank. But Crispus' small, fast, triaconters and penteconters could still maneuver and find shelter in the port of Elaius. The way to Byzantium thus remained clear and Constantine conquered the city in September 324, making it the new capital of the Empire. A Byzantine historian named Zosimus, who lived in the fifth century A.D., says that triremes ceased to be built in the fifth century, while quinqueremes had not been built since the end of the third century. Triaconters had thirty rowers, one per oar, and fifteen oars per side; penteconters had fifty. There was a rostrum at the bow, a tower amidships and instead of a flush deck, they had two platforms fore and aft.

The approximate dimensions of a triaconter were: length 80.3ft (24.5m); beam 14.1ft (4.3m); draught 2.6ft (0.8m) and a crew of forty-five. Penteconters measured approximately 104.9 × 14.7 × 3.2ft (32 × 4.5 × 1m) and had a crew of about seventy.

In classical antiquity, therefore, there was, to begin with, an increase in dimensions resulting in the big multireme ships. Subsequently, from the Battle of Actium (31 A.D.) onwards, dimensions decreased until the third century A.D. when there was a return to monoremes with thirty to fifty rowers. Tacitus says that after the Battle of Actium the big "eights" and "tens" of Anthony's fleet were taken to Forum Julii after capture and broken up. In fact, by then, naval warfare was being waged against barbarians who did not have large ships like those of the Greeks and Carthaginians. So the fleets that operated on the Rhine, the Danube, the Euphrates, the Pannonia, and in the Black Sea were made up of small monoremes. An example was the ship of Quintus Petillius Ceriale, prefect of the Rhine fleet, described as a "trireme," but probably a monoreme with three rowers per bench.

Irish curragh. A very primitive type of vessel with a hull made up of a wooden framework. Instead of the usual wooden planking, this was covered with animal skins, normally cowhide, sewn together and fixed to the boards which were obviously in the form of a complete wooden gunwale. The hull was very light and could be fitted with a central mast, setting a sail which was also made of hide. In order to guarantee some degree of stability, the hull had to be ballasted and fitted with a wooden false keel for beaching.

Ships of Northern European countries

The information we have about the warships of the ancient inhabitants of Northern European countries is far more scarce than that about the peoples of the Mediterranean countries.

For more ancient eras, the main sources of information are cave paintings found in Norway, Sweden, and Denmark, which can be dated between 2000 and 200 B.C. For more recent times, that is, the first centuries of our era, we are in possession of entire vessels and small ships that have survived intact because they were buried and preserved in the mud at the bottoms of rivers and lakes or because they were placed in the tombs of a few chieftains, in conformance with the funeral rites of the time. Last, historians and writers have handed down to us descriptions of warships of the Suione Gauls, as given by Tacitus in his *Germania,* and those of the late Middle Ages, as given by Tropheus in his *Historia Rerum Norvegicarum.* More information can also be found in the sagas, which tell of the exploits of the great conquerors and chieftains.

The oldest crafts were *pirogues* dug out of tree trunks, but even in the Stone and Bronze Ages there must have been boats with frameworks made of wood or the bones of large animals, covered in animal hides stitched together, as continues to be the method by which Eskimos produce their *umiaks.*

Ships were subsequently made of wood, although they never reached the size of the Mediterranean ones, nor did they ever have more than one bank of oars. Moreover, these ships never had a ram. As far as the steering oar was concerned, Nordic crafts had only one, instead of two, as on the Mediterranean ships. This single steering oar was positioned on the starboard quarter. This arrangement was to form the origin of the Anglo-Saxon word *starboard,* which still means the right-hand side of the ship, being derived from "steer board," the side from which the ship is steered. Nordic ships had only one mast but it could not be lowered as on Mediterranean ships. The sail was square and was supported either by one tall yard and one short one or by a single yard. Some pictures of more ancient ships show a sail which appears to be made of squares arranged diagonally to the yard. It is thought that the diagonal lines represent reinforcements made up of double thicknesses of material or hide, sewn onto the canvas of the sails. An anchor discovered at Ladbly, on Fyn Island in Denmark, dating back to the tenth century, had flukes and an iron shank with a wooden stock. It was fitted with a chain about 33 feet (10m) long with a hauser at the end. As mentioned earlier, Nordic ships had no ram or towers. Weapons were spears and swords for close-range combat and stones and arrows for long-range combat. In combat, grappling irons and grapnels were used to hold one's own ship to that of the enemy. Tropheus speaks of a sort of delphines, that he calls a "staf-nliar," which was in the form of a beam hanging from the mast and fitted with metal heads at either end. It was maneuvered by being swung from side to side.

One of the strangest methods of attack was to use a sling to hurl receptacles containing ash or lime at the enemy in an attempt to blind them. This weapon was also used in the Mediterranean in the late Middle Ages.

History has failed to provide us with descriptions of naval battles between the Nordic peoples. It must be concluded that warships, even those of the Vikings and Normans, were used solely to transport warriors and allow them to disembark in the territories to be conquered.

Coracle. A vessel with a wooden framework covered in hide, used in Britain for lake and river fishing.

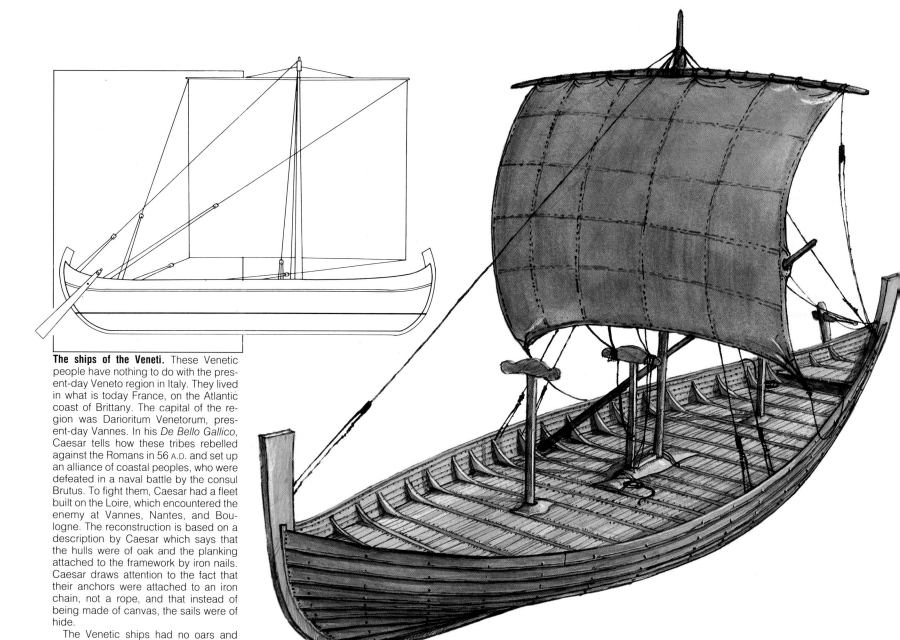

The ships of the Veneti. These Venetic people have nothing to do with the present-day Veneto region in Italy. They lived in what is today France, on the Atlantic coast of Brittany. The capital of the region was Darioritum Venetorum, present-day Vannes. In his *De Bello Gallico*, Caesar tells how these tribes rebelled against the Romans in 56 A.D. and set up an alliance of coastal peoples, who were defeated in a naval battle by the consul Brutus. To fight them, Caesar had a fleet built on the Loire, which encountered the enemy at Vannes, Nantes, and Boulogne. The reconstruction is based on a description by Caesar which says that the hulls were of oak and the planking attached to the framework by iron nails. Caesar draws attention to the fact that their anchors were attached to an iron chain, not a rope, and that instead of being made of canvas, the sails were of hide.

The Venetic ships had no oars and therefore depended solely on sail power, in the form of just one square sail on a single mast. They would have had a flush deck and no ram. Dimensions were about 98–114ft (30–35m) long; 28–29.5ft (8.5–9m) in the beam; 7.5–10ft (2.3–3m) freeboard, and 6.5ft (2m) draught. Their size and weight would certainly have made it impossible to beach them, so they must have stayed moored in harbors. For the second invasion of the British Isles in 54 A.D., Caesar built 600 transport ships that were probably like the Venetic ones.

The Gokstad ship. At Gokstad farm near Sanøy Fjord in Norway, the grave of a Viking chieftain, buried with his ship, was discovered in 1880. The ship had been perfectly preserved under the peat. The grave was that of a queen. In fact, the remains of two women's bodies were found in the ship, which is now in the Oslo Museum and dates back to the tenth century A.D. The dimensions are: length 76.24ft (23.24m), beam 17.06ft; (5.20m); fully laden, she must have displaced about 19.6 tons (20 tonnes). She is fully decked and made of oak; there are no traces of the rowers' benches. The lack of benches would suggest that the rowers sat on removable seats or else that these benches were removed when the ship came to be used as a tomb. Sixty-four round shields were found hanging on the outside of the hull from special supports, thirty-two each side. The ship had a mast for the sail that could be supported by a swinging boom, meeting up with special wooden blocks hollowed out and positioned either side of the deck. In 1893, an exact replica of this ship was built. In twenty-eight days, it crossed the Atlantic under sail, proving that it would have been possible for the ancient Vikings to have reached the American continent before Christopher Columbus.

The drakkar of the Vikings and Normans. The drakkar was the real warship of the Vikings and Normans. No examples have survived but the Gokstad and Oseberg ships show us how they were probably built. Depictions of these ships appear in the Bayeux Tapestry, now kept in Bayeux Cathedral. This tapestry was woven by Princess Matilde and her ladies-in-waiting to celebrate the conquest of England by William the Conqueror (1027–1087), to whom Matilde was married. When referring to warships, the ancient Norse sagas define their size in terms of "spaces," that is, in pairs of oars. The "Ledung" ships had twenty spaces, that is, forty oars, while the Oseberg and Gokstad ships had thirty and thirty-two respectively. Drakkars had thirty-two spaces, or sixty-four rowers; Olaf Tryggvason's had thirty-four spaces and King Canute's is supposed to have had sixty spaces, making it over 262.4ft (80m) long, which throws doubt on the number given in the sagas. Drakkars must have had a hull similar to that of the Gokstad ship and been about 131–137ft (40–42m) long and 16–18ft (5–5.5m) in the beam. They had a single mast with a square sail and, according to the Gotland Stone, there were several sheets at the bottom. They also had bowlines attached to the leech to keep the forward edge of the sail taut instead of pushing it with the swinging boom. Characteristic features of these ships were the heads of fearsome monsters that decorated the end of the stem.

The ships of the Suiones of Gaul. Tacitus' description says that these ships had *"utrimque prora paratam semper appulsui frontem agit"* and that the oars were not in a fixed position, but *"mutabile, utres poscit, hinc vel illinc remigium."* In other words these ships had two bows; by turning round and moving from one bench to the one next to it, the rowers could row in both directions. This swapping of the bow with the stern avoided having to put about and was therefore particularly well suited to fighting in rivers, canals, and narrow waterways. In another passage of his *Annals* Tacitus says that because Germanicus was in the land of the Cauci (Frisians) and was unable to proceed by land against the enemy, he ordered a thousand ships to be built *"augusta puppi proraque,...utrimque gubernaculis, converso ut repente remigio hinc vel illinc adpellerent..."*; he adds that these ships were also used by the Romans. An ancient Scandinavian graffito depicts ships with two rudders—one forward and one aft. The reconstruction is based on the Nydam Boat, built slightly later, found in 1863 in a peat-bog in Schleswig, and thought to date back to c. 300 A.D., about 200 years after the events referred to by Tacitus. The boat is of oak and clinker-built, with fourteen benches for the rowers; to carry out the above-mentioned maneuver, these must have numbered twenty-six, at thirteen pairs of oars. The boat had no mast and her dimensions were: length 75.13ft (22.90m) and beam 10.66ft (3.25m).

The Oseberg ship. The Oseberg ship was found in 1904 on the farm of the same name, in Norway. She too is the grave of a Viking chieftain, whose body was found inside. The ship is now in the Oslo Museum and can be dated to the eleventh century; she is accordingly about one hundred years younger than the Gokstad ship. She is 70.80ft (21.58m) long (about 6.56ft [2m] shorter than the one previously described) but measures the same in the beam—17.06ft (5.20m). The hull is of oak, has a strong bar keel and a framework with twelve strakes per side. The bow structure is the same as the stern and both end in a soaring elegant curve. There are fifteen round ports in either side for thirty oars and slightly forward of amidships, in the keel, a step for the mast. The latter would have been about 42.65ft (13m) long, but only a section of 18.70ft (5.70m) long has been found. The vessel is fully decked and has a sturdy mast partner. On the starboard quarter is a steering oar, pivoted on a ball-and-socket joint and steered from the top by a plaited leather strap. On either side of the ship there are wooden forks to hold the oars when under sail. Fifteen pairs of pinewood oars, ranging from 12.13ft (3.70m) to 13.12ft (4m) in length, were found with the ship. Given her considerable beam, about one quarter of the length, this ship was probably designed for transportation rather than military duties.

OARED WARSHIPS
FROM THE MIDDLE AGES TO MODERN TIMES

The naval battle in the Middle Ages

On August 23, 476 A.D., the barbarian troops that made up virtually the entire army of the Western Roman Empire proclaimed Odoacer as their king. He deposed the last emperor, Romulus Augustulus, and ordered the killing of the Patricians, Orestes and Paulus, who were ruling the government on his behalf. Thus ended the Western Roman Empire.

Historians single out this event as marking the end of the ancient period and the beginning of the Middle Ages, a historical period which lasted for about 1000 years and ended in 1492, with the discovery of America.

In the Middle Ages an extremely important change in the propulsion of ships occurred. As a result of the improvement of sails, the oar was abandoned as a means of propulsion, especially for merchant ships. The sail made possible the great maritime voyages that led to geographical discoveries.

But warships continued to use oars, especially in the Mediterranean, and naval battles were still fought with oared ships, even after the end of the Middle Ages. In fact, whereas the Middle Ages ended in the year 1492, in naval history the oared ship period ended only with the Battle of Lepanto, which occurred on October 7, 1571. Even after this date, however, galleys continued to be part of the war fleets, both in the Mediterranean and in the Nordic countries such as Sweden and Russia, finally disappearing only in the late eighteenth and early nineteenth centuries.

In the French Navy the last Mediterranean galleys remained in service until the latter years of the eighteenth century. In the Papal Navy the last two galleys, the *Santa Ferma* and the *Santa Lucia*, were taken out of commission in 1807. In the Sardinian Navy the galley, *Santa Teresa,* was still in commission in 1812 and the half galley, *Beatrice,* was part of the fleet until about 1820.

As mentioned, the warships of this period continued to be oared like those of classical antiquity and therefore the method of combat did not undergo any significant change. In the Middle Ages and early modern times, too, the element of surprise was of no importance and a battle between two fleets required a long period of preparation. In the Middle Ages, ships appear not to have disembarked equipment before combat, nor to have lowered the masts. Paintings of the Battle of Lepanto, and other battles of the oared ship period, depict galleys with their masts still in position but with the sails furled to their spars.

Preparation for combat underwent a change from the mid-fifteenth century, when the first guns were installed on the galleys. In fact, in addition to furling the sails and securing the spars, the next procedure was to "raise the barriers," in other words, to build shelters arranged crosswise to the hull, out of spare oars, ropes, awnings, and sails, to protect the men from enemy gunfire and grapeshot. Swords, shields, and armor were then handed out to the soldiers, and stands on which to rest the arquebus barrels were fitted to the quarter boards. "Apparatus for fire pots..." and "...trumpets and other similar instruments" were made ready. In most cases, the chains were removed and weapons given to the mercenary galleymen and even the Christian slaves, if they were fighting against Turks, and, lastly, "in order to restore and invigorate the mens' strength...bread, wine, cheese and anything else that could be had at such short notice was placed on the fore and aft gangways" as Contarini relates in his description of preparations for the Battle of Lepanto (*History of Events...*).

Between the Battles of Lepanto (1571) and Salamis (480 B.C.) there was a gap of almost two thousand years, during which time the method of combat on board ships had remained basically unchanged, even though in the last century they were armed with a few guns. In 1571, too, the ships arranged themselves in "sickle formation," and at Lepanto ceremonies were performed to win God's favor, these taking the form of prayers and blessings given by the chaplains on each galley. Lastly, even in the second half of the sixteenth century, there would be an exhortation. In this case, the Commander in Chief of the Christian fleet, Don Juan of Austria, together with Marcantonio Colonna, commander of the Papal galleys, embarked on two fast frigates to inspect the line of galleys, greeting all the commanders by name, and urging the crews to fight well. Returning on board after this "pep talk," Don Juan also performed another propitiatory rite by launching into a frenzied Spanish dance called the *galliard* with two of his knights. At the Battle of Lepanto, a signal was also given to begin combat, but instead of raising a golden shield, it took the more modern form of a shot from a cannon.

The battle formation had remained the same for two thousand years, with the two fleets arranging themselves face to face. At Lepanto, however, the Christian fleet was divided into a left flank of fifty-five galleys, a center, or battalion, of sixty-two, and a right flank of fifty-seven galleys, which faced a Turkish array of fifty-five, ninety-one, and sixty-seven galleys, respectively.

The central squadron was under the command of the Commander of the Fleet, who placed his galley in the central point of the array. By contrast, other commanders placed their galleys at the two outermost ends of the flanks.

The position of the ships in a battle formation was defined by a very specific order of precedence, depending on the rank of their commanders. In the array for the Battle of Lepanto, for instance, where there were ships belonging to an Alliance between the Pope, the republic of Venice, Spain, Malta, Genoa, and the Duchy of Savoy, the position assigned to each galley in the council of war held at Messina, on September 10, 1571, took this "order of precedence" into account.

In arranging the ships for battle, therefore, no account was taken of their fighting power but solely of the rank of the person who hoisted his flag on board, and of the nation it represented. This idea was not totally anachronistic since the superior generals' galleys were usually the largest mainsail galleys, with the best weaponry, and had a greater number of oarsmen in comparison to the light galleys.

The most important innovation at Lepanto, when compared with the ancient naval formation, was the presence of a vanguard made up of six galleasses, and a rear guard, or reserve, one mile behind the main body, ready to intervene, whenever and wherever necessary. The task of the galleasses was to break the line of advancing enemy galleys, with their numerous guns, but it appears that they were not very effective, since the Turkish galleys reached the conflict with the Christian ones almost unscathed.

The actual battle took place as in ancient times, the galleys mounting frontal attacks and attempting to ram each other, but then everything was settled by boarding and hand-to-hand combat with side-arms. At this point, it should be mentioned that the flagship galleys were followed by others bearing nobles and soldiers, who later boarded the flagship to assist its crew in hand-to-hand fighting. At Lepanto, Don Juan of Austria's galley was followed by two galleys with over 400 soldiers and noble warriors.

When discussing the naval battles of ancient times, it was mentioned that one of the offensive tactics used was to ram the gunwale of an enemy ship with the bow so as to break the tholepins and oars (*detegere remos*). By contrast, in the fourteenth and fifteenth centuries the aim was to try to slip a small oared vessel, the size of a

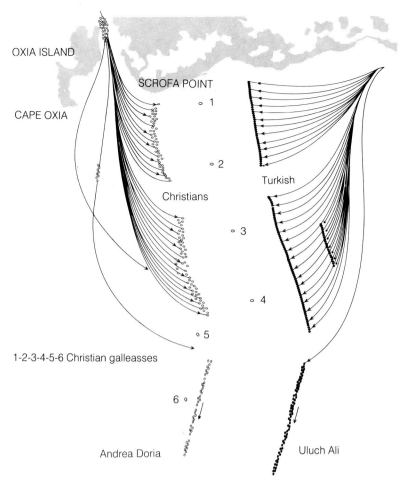

OXIA ISLAND

SCROFA POINT

CAPE OXIA

○ 1

○ 2

Turkish

Christians

○ 3

○ 4

○ 5

1-2-3-4-5-6 Christian galleasses

6 ○

Andrea Doria

Uluch Ali

The Battle of Lepanto (October 7, 1571). The two enemy fleets sighted each other at dawn and took about six hours to array themselves in battle formation, one facing the other along an almost straight line. The Christian fleet had a van of six galleasses and a rearguard; the Turkish fleet had no forward positions. The battle was fought on the basis of a frontal attack between the center and starboard flanks of the Turkish fleet and the opposing Christian squadrons. But the Turkish left flank and the Christian right flank maneuvered in an attempt to encircle each other or to escape being encircled. Only a few Turkish ships managed to escape, all the others being sunk or captured.

The Battle of Meloria (August 6, 1284). Fought between 103 Pisan ships under the command of Alberto Morosini (a Venetian), and eighty-eight Genoese galleys commanded by Oberto Doria, in the waters off Leghorn near the Shoals of Meloria. Oberto Doria went into battle with just fifty-eight galleys, leaving thirty under the command of Benedetto Zaccaria, according to some, hidden by Montenero Point, and to others, at the Shoals of Meloria. The Pisans, who considered themselves superior, attacked head-on and, when fighting was already underway, were taken by surprise by Zaccaria's galleys. Despite the fact that the latter had fewer ships, victory went to the Genoese.

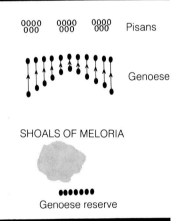

0000 0000 0000
000 000 000   Pisans

Genoese

SHOALS OF MELORIA

●●●●●●●
Genoese reserve

The Battle of Curzola (September 8, 1298). Fought between ninety-six Venetian galleys under the command of Andrea Dandolo and seventy-six Genoese galleys under the command of Lamba Doria. The Venetians were in crescent formation on the seaward side, between the island of Curzola and Meleda, the Genoese in three lines with their sterns towards land. In addition, Lamba Doria had a reserve of fifteen galleys, hidden behind Curzola; these came into action once battle had commenced, and mounted a surprise attack on the Venetian fleet. Eighty-four galleys surrendered and a further twelve managed to reach Venice.

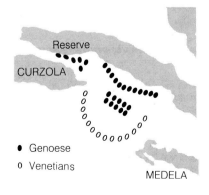

Reserve

CURZOLA

● Genoese
○ Venetians

MEDELA

galliot, beneath the oars on one side of the ship, preventing the men from rowing, and thus immobilizing the enemy.

The main battle maneuver was still the crescent formation of classical antiquity. The aim, in other words, was to try to make the flanks converge toward the center, to collide with the enemy's flanks, and surround him. Of course, this maneuver was not always successful, both for geographical reasons and due to countermaneuvers by the enemy, as occurred at Lepanto.

The left flank of the Christians, commanded by the Venetian Agostino Barbarigo, did not surround the left flank of the Turks. Instead, it attacked from the front (having been prevented from doing otherwise by the proximity of the coast), forcing over fifty Turkish galleys to run aground on the beach where they were abandoned by their crews. The right flank of the Christians, commanded by Gianandrea Doria, spread out to the right to encircle the left flank of the enemy, but was prevented from doing so because the Turks, commanded by Ali Pasha, countermaneuvered by fanning outwards to port.

Another type of maneuver adopted in naval battles between galleys was to keep a group of ships hidden behind an island or headland and then use them to attack the enemy already engaged in battle from the rear. This maneuver was used in the Battle of Meloria, between the Genoese and the Pisans on August 6, 1284, and in the Battle of Curzola, between the Genoese and the Venetians on September 8, 1298.

Nomenclature of oared warships from the tenth to the seventeenth centuries

We have mentioned that in classical antiquity the classification, and therefore the nomenclature of ships, was based on the number of oars, or rowers, manning half of one transverse section of the oarage. Thus, there were the Greek trieres and penteres; the Roman bireme, quinquereme, and "ten"; and the triakonteres and pentekonteres of the Eastern Roman Empire.

In the Middle Ages, the idea of classifying ships according to the number of rowers was dropped, and ships were classified with names which, many centuries later and with no precise definitions, make identification, structure, and rigging complicated. These names have been the object of debate among scholars, who do not always reach the same conclusions.

Even in the Middle Ages, however, the number of rowers or oars continued to be mentioned, not to classify a type of ship, but to define the size of ships of the same type: such as the 230-rower dromon, the 180-rower dromon, or the 100-oar selander and the eighty-oar selander. In the centuries that followed, it was more common to refer to the number of benches, and so there was the twenty-five-bench galley and the eighteen-bench galliot.

Since Latin was the language used by the learned up until 1700, it is quite common to find in texts written in this language the words *triremis*, *quadriremis*, and even *quinqueremis*, but these words no longer have the meaning they had in classical antiquity and have been used to indicate the number of rowers per bench. Thus, triremis was a galley with three men per bench. When the *zenzile* system was replaced with the stepped tiers system, namely with several rowers pulling one oar, Latin nomenclature was abandoned.

The main sources of information about the ships of the early Middle Ages are found in various documents, the oldest being the Byzantine ones, such as the treatise *Naumachia* by the Eastern Emperor Leo VI (Leo the Wise, 886–912) and the book *De Caerimoniis Aulae Byzantinae* by Constantine VII (Porphyrogenitus, 912–959); a story in Latin, "*Richardi Regis Iter Hierosolymitanorum*," by the chronicler Galfrid Winesalf, who followed Richard the Lionhearted on the 1191–1192 Crusade, the "*Gazaria Statutes*" of the Republic of Genoa, Venice's 1255 "*Capitolare Nauticum*," and other works.

More extensive and complete documentation is available for the galleys of early modern times, and we shall mention only a few of the better known works, such as *Nautica Mediterranea* by the Roman, Bartolomeo Crescenzio (1607), and *Armata Navale* by Pantero Pantera (1614), as well as *Naval Art* by a Frenchman named Paul Hoste (1697), and many other Venetian documents, among which, out of curiosity, we should mention the manuscript by the Venetian, Pico della Mirandola "*Intorno alla fabbrica dei legni marittimi da guerra*" (Concerning the Building of Naval Warships), dedicated to "the Most Serene Prince of Venice," in which he proposed the construction of a galley with two banks of oars.

Examination of this document supplies us with a series of names, but not always adequate descriptions of the types of ships that they were meant to indicate. Moreover, it is to be expected that, as the centuries passed, ships of decidedly different types were referred to by the same name. The documents dating back to between the sixth and tenth centuries refer to dromons, selanders, yachts, visser selanders, and even galleys. Those from the twelfth to the seventeenth centuries, however, do not contain these names and refer almost exclusively to the galley, with its derivatives: the galliot, galleass, fusta (small galley) brig, and frigate.

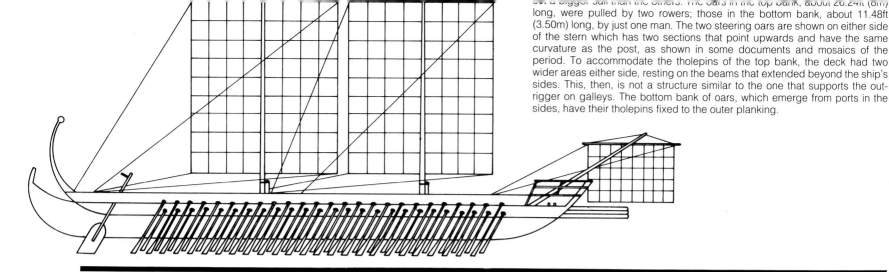

a bigger sail than the others. The oars in the top bank, about 26.24ft (8m) long, were pulled by two rowers; those in the bottom bank, about 11.48ft (3.50m) long, by just one man. The two steering oars are shown on either side of the stern which has two sections that point upwards and have the same curvature as the post, as shown in some documents and mosaics of the period. To accommodate the tholepins of the top bank, the deck had two wider areas either side, resting on the beams that extended beyond the ship's sides. This, then, is not a structure similar to the one that supports the outrigger on galleys. The bottom bank of oars, which emerge from ports in the sides, have their tholepins fixed to the outer planking.

Summing up, it is possible to make a rough distinction and conclude that up to about 1100 oared warships belonged to the dromon family, whereas from 1100 onward oared warships belonged to the galley family.

The *galley* family had one bank of oars, handled by several rowers seated on the same bench. Usually the light galley, with one rower per oar, had three rowers per bench, each handling his own oar. All the oars, however, had their tholepin at the same level on a wooden beam called the *gunwale*.

The *dromon* family had two banks of oars, the top one handled by rowers who sat on benches arranged under the same deck.

The dromons were the most common warships, having one hundred oars and were therefore also called "hekatonteres." The oars were in two banks of twenty-five per side. As a rule, those on the top bank, which were longer and heavier, were pulled by two rowers, and those on the bottom bank, by just one.

In his *Vocabolario Marino e Militare*, Guglielmotti says that dromons were 197ft (60m) long and had a beam of 33ft (10m). These measurements seem excessive, since the largest galleys, built four or five centuries later, were only about 164ft (50m) long, with a beam of 16½ft (5m). Calculating that they had twenty-five oars per side, handled by a maximum of two rowers, it can be assumed that they were about 131ft (40m) long, more or less like a twenty-five-bench galley. After pointing out that there is very little information about this type of ship, Landström produces a reconstruction, which has twenty-five oars per side, arranged in two banks: the upper one having twelve and the lower one thirteen oars, while from the above-mentioned texts it is very clear that there were twenty-five oars in each bank.

Where sails are concerned, Guglielmotti opts for square sails. Landström puts a lateen sail on his model, but it is more likely that the sails were square, as will be explained when we discuss rigging.

Yachts are referred to by Leo the Wise in his *Naumachia*. He writes that a squadron commander must embark on a type of dromon called a yacht and says that this yacht must be larger, faster, and better-armed than other dromons. This description would lead us to picture a dromon with at least thirty oars per bank, rather than twenty-five. But a few years before, in his *De Cerimoniis Aulae Byzantinae*, Constantine Porphyrogenitus writes: "The Imperial Fleet numbered 60 dromons, each with 230 rowers and 70 soldiers. In addition to the dromons there were 40 yachts, twenty of which carried 160 men and twenty only 130." In his *De Thamate Sami*, another contemporary author, Mersius, talks of ". . . 12 yachts with 160 rowers and 8 with 130:"

From this it would seem that yachts would have been smaller, faster dromons, having the same arrangement of two banks of oars, with a maximum of twenty-five oars per bank. They probably had only one mast and one square sail. It should be pointed out that in the Gazaria Statute of March 17, 1340, yachts are listed together with galleys as "merchant ships with only one deck," which shows that in 300 years the meaning of the word had already changed. In much more recent times, the word yacht has been used exclusively to describe pleasure craft, especially luxury ships both sail- and motor-powered.

There is also some mystery surrounding the form of selanders, but they certainly belong to the dromon family. Tenth century documents (Ditmar—Book III) describe them as "a ship of extraordinary length and amazing speed, with two banks of oars and 150 rowers." When describing the expedition against Crete in 949, Constantine Porphyrogenitus writes: "The Imperial Fleet was made up of 150 vissers, including six yachts . . . a hundred selanders converted into vissers . . . ." Elsewhere he says: "The Strategus of Samos was sent to Crete with 6 visser selanders, each of which carried 100 men" and "6 yacht selanders, each with 120 men, and 4 visser selanders with 108 men were left to guard the city."

In his *Vocabolario Marino e Militare*, Guglielmotti says that the selander derived its name from the Greek word for tortoise, due to the shape of its castle, and that it had only one bank of oars, one or two masts with lateen sails, and, as its main feature, a flat bottom and small draught, so as to be able to sail in shallow waters. Since all this is not documented and disagrees with the works of tenth- and eleventh-century writers, there are doubts as to its accuracy.

We have a depiction of a selander, but it is of little value since it appears on a medal struck for Doge Pietro Candiano. There were four doges who bore this name: the first from 887 to 888, the second from 923 to 939, the third from 942 to 959 and the fourth from 959 to 976. Since the medal bears no date, it must be assumed that it was struck to celebrate Pietro Candiano I's exploits against the Narentine pirates, and can therefore be dated to 888. The selander depicted is a ship with just one bank of oars, six oars per side, three before and three abaft a large tower amidships, and a mast forward.

We can therefore conclude that a selander was a dromon with a tall rounded castle forward and two banks of oars with 100 or 150 rowers. When the selander was combined with other ships, it became a yacht selander, faster and better-armed, or a visser selander, with fewer rowers, since it was not required to be fast. We conclude by citing Jal's theory, according to which the term selander was used to describe a slower ship than the fast dromon.

The galley was the smallest of the dromons referred to by Leo the Wise. He specifies that it had only one bank of oars, which could number twenty-five per side. The number of twenty-five benches per side remained the same also for the

---

The selander

This ship belonged to the dromon family and was also very fast. She incorporated features of other ships, thus becoming a yacht selander and a visser selander. It seems likely that the yacht selander was the selander proper, in other words, a warship with 150 rowers. By contrast, visser selanders, used to transport horses, were slower and had fewer rowers. The selander proper had two banks of oars with twenty-five oars per bank, making a total of 150 rowers. She had two steering oars aft and two "horns," like dromons. She probably had only two square-sail masts and the usual raked mast forward, as on Roman transport ships. The probable dimensions are: length 155.83ft (47.50m); beam 24.93ft (7.60m); height 15.58ft (4.75m); crew 150 rowers plus eighty soldiers, making a total of 230 men.

galleys of the fourteenth and fifteenth centuries, but on each bench there were three rowers, each with his own oar; so the oars that in the tenth-century galley numbered fifty in all, in the Venetian "zenzile galley" or the fourteenth- and fifteenth-century Genoese "galera ad tre remos per banchum" were increased to 150. In sixteenth- and seventeenth-century galleys, after the "stepped tier" system of rowing was adopted, the oars went back to being one per bench, reaching a maximum of thirty-six benches.

Continuing with the nomenclature of the tenth and eleventh centuries, we still find mention of the "cat," the "bucentaurum," the "ligna de teriis," and the "large galley."

The term cat perhaps derives from a corruption of the Gallic word into cattus and cat: According to a Venetian law, the cat was a large galley, among those that had "ducentorum hominum."

Archbishop William of Tyre, in his Gesta Dei per Francos, says that in 1121 Doge Domenico Michele left for Syria with a fleet made up of forty galleys, twenty-eight cats and four large freighters, later explaining that the "naves rostratae quas gatos vocant" were larger than the galleys and had one hundred oars each handled by two men. In sailing order, the cats were with the four large freighters and the galleys brought up the rear; cats were therefore ill suited to combat. One of their characteristics, which they shared with the galleys of the late fourteenth century, was their two steering oars. Another chronicler, Albert d'Aix (Albertus Aquensis), says, "In galeidis...in triremibus, dictis vulgariter cattis..." which would confirm that the term cat refers to a large galley.

The bucentarum, the doges's state barge, was not a warship but fourteenth-century documents refer to these vessels as being a variety of large galley.

A Venetian decree of December 30, 1337 states, "armentur sex galeae quarum quatuor sint de mensuris bucentaurum..." from which it is possible to assume that bucentaurum is a corruption of ducentorum, and therefore bucentaurs and cats were the same type of ship.

The ligna de teriis, mentioned almost solely in the Ufficio di Gazaria Statutes of Genoa in the years between 1300 and 1350, were smaller ships than galleys with three and two oars per bench (ligna de duabus teriis). We can deduce that these ships were smaller than galleys from one of the Genoese Statutes which is dated October 14, 1316 and entitled "Ordinamentum factum in galeis navigaturis ad Aguas Mortuas," in which it was stated that when sailing from Genoa to Aigues Mortes, near Montpellier in France, the ships could not sail alone, but each galley had to be accompanied by another galley or a "lignum de teriis" with eighty to one hundred oars. The "ligna de teriis" could not sail in pairs, but only when accompanied by a larger and better-armed galley.

The "large galley" was not normally a warship but a mercantile vessel. The large war galleys were given special names, such as the above-mentioned cat, bucentaur and, from the sixteenth to the seventeenth century, other names.

The galley from the fifteenth to the eighteenth century

Moving on to the nomenclature of oared warships, built after the fifteenth century, in Pantero Pantera's Armata Navale we find a list of the following types: galleys (and subtypes), galliots, brigs, frigates, feluccas, and castaldellas, to which we should add galleasses and fustas. The galley, as mentioned previously, was used in the navy of the Eastern Roman Empire. Leo the Wise refers to "galaias moneres," and says that "dromonis minores fabricabis...unum remorum ordines habentes." Moreover, Winesalf tells us that "what the ancients called Liburnian, the men of our time call a galley."

In the tenth century, however, galleys were not the backbone of the fleets. This role was filled by dromons, selanders, and yachts, and galleys were used for exploration and other tasks which required speed. Obviously, the galleys of the twelfth and thirteenth centuries were no longer the same as the galleys of the tenth century, but a converted version of a dromon that had lost one bank of oars, had all their oarsmen sitting on deck, one or two masts with lateen sails, and, later on, just one rudder aft. In other words, the large dromons with 230 oarsmen and seventy soldiers were roughly the same size as the light galleys of the twelfth and thirteenth centuries, which were much bigger than the "galaia moneres" of the previous centuries.

Whereas, in order to describe the various types of ships built before 1300, a great many theories had to be formulated to resolve a few problems of shipbuilding and arrangement of the men at the oars, this is not the case for galleys. These are reasonably modern ships for which we have descriptions, body plans, and a wealth of pictorial documentation.

The chief characteristic of a galley is that it is a ship made up of two separate parts: the hull, which serves as a load-bearing structure, as in all other ships, and the gunwale, or frame, an enormous wooden rectangular structure, shorter but much wider than the hull, which serves as a rest for the tholepins and a support for the weapons and soldiers at the forward end on the "bow platform" and along the two side corridors above the tholepins. In pictorial representations, the hull is not normally visible, but it is possible to see the gunwale, oars, masts, sails, and the small poop deck, usually covered by a sumptuous awning that the Venetians call a celega. At the bow, the hull had a sturdy ram and a very rounded deck, sloping steeply at the sides so as to allow the water, which could easily wash over so low a deck, to drain back into the sea. Inside the hull, the following spaces were arranged fore to aft:

1) The bow- (or doctor's) space, with a way down from a hatch at the twenty-third bench on the starboard side. It housed the ropes and the surgeon's instruments, and served as a hospital for the sick.

2) The sail space, adjacent to the powder space, with a way down from the fourteenth bench on the port side, near the mainmast. It housed the awnings and sails and, in the powder room, the ammunition for the guns. The boatswain distributed and sold wine from here.

3) Middle (or dunnage) space which housed the dry provisions, such as biscuits, salted meat, and so on.

4) Storeroom for water, wine, salami, cheeses, and so on, which contained barrels for the liquids and shelves for the rest. The way down was from the tenth bench on the port side.

Bucentaur. This term described a state barge built specially to celebrate the "sea wedding" ceremony in which Venetian doges symbolically married the sea by throwing a ring into the water. The ceremony originated in 998, under Doge Pietro Orseolo II, and was celebrated on Ascension Day. The barge was a huge pontoon with an enormous superstructure sumptuously decorated with gilded sculptures, and propelled by twenty-one oars either side, pulled by three to four rowers each. After the fall of the Republic of Venice, the last bucentaur had her top part broken up and her hull used as a working pontoon.

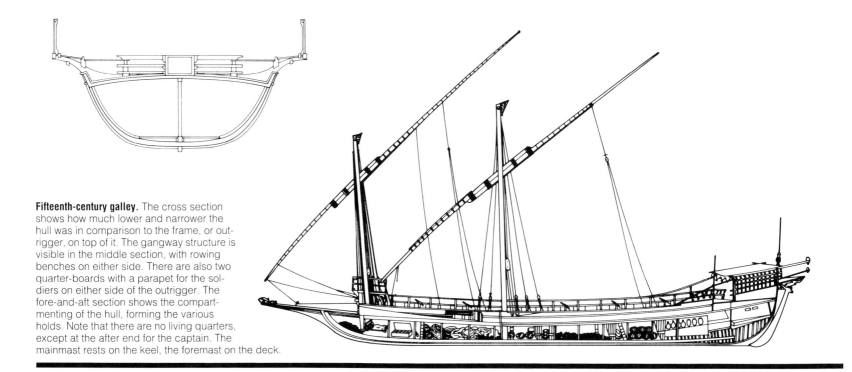

Fifteenth-century galley. The cross section shows how much lower and narrower the hull was in comparison to the frame, or outrigger, on top of it. The gangway structure is visible in the middle section, with rowing benches on either side. There are also two quarter-boards with a parapet for the soldiers on either side of the outrigger. The fore-and-aft section shows the compartmenting of the hull, forming the various holds. Note that there are no living quarters, except at the after end for the captain. The mainmast rests on the keel, the foremast on the deck.

5) Stern cabin, or victualling store, for the captain, which also contained the armor and weapons of the nobles. The way down was from the sixth bench on the starboard side.

6) Afterpeak, containing the captain's quarters with a way down from a hatch next to the bridge platform on the port side.

The hatchways down to the various holds were positioned alternately on the starboard and port side of the ship. According to Hobier, light entered the peak through round scuttles called "*cantanettes*," but for all the other spaces air and light entered only through the entrance hatch on the deck.

As can be seen from the above list, there was no space set aside to house the very large crew. Only the commander, and perhaps a few noblemen, could bed down for the night in the afterpeak. But on light galleys this was usually so small that there was only room for the captain's bed and the noblemen slept under the "celega" on deck.

All the rest of the crew slept as best they could, whether free men, or slaves, and convicts, the oarsmen sitting on their rowing benches to which slaves and convicts would be chained by one foot. The sailors and soldiers slept on the bow platform and in the side gangways which were about 31½in (80cm) wide; the soldiers propped on their seabags "in a very uncomfortable position."

The only shelter from the sun and rain was a large awning which was spread over the middle part of the galley and covered the frame, that is, the part between the bow platform and stern, where the oarsmen sat and the soldiers and sailors were positioned. For this reason, galleys were normally used for combat only in good weather and "wintered' in port. Naval campaigns, therefore, took place in seasonal cycles.

The nonexistent accommodation arrangements also forced the galleys to call in at port or beach every night so that the crew could rest. Only when under sail with the oars lifted out of the water and secured to the gangway (oars laid in), was it possible to remain at sea, since propulsion by sail required the use of only a small number of sailors.

Galleys were classified according to their size or the number of benches, or by the use of special names, such as mainsail galleys, flag ships or superior generals' galleys, galliots, and galleasses.

The normal light galley had twenty-five or twenty-six benches per side, but the number could vary according to the period and the type of galley.

The Genoese Statutes of February 16, 1340, and June 21, 1441, refer to galleys with seventeen benches and ninety-nine rowers, due to the presence of the touch-hole bench on the port side. The French galleys that Philippe de Valois prepared in 1335 for a crusade had twenty-nine benches with two rowers per bench, making a total of 116 oars. In Spain, the galleys of King Don Pedro of Aragon, according to a statute of 1354, could have twenty-five benches with two oars per bench and, therefore, one hundred rowers, or twenty-nine benches, still with two rowers, making a total of 116 oars.

Both the Genoese Statutes and the Spanish and French ones laid down that, in addition to rowing oarsmen, there should be a certain number of reserves; to be precise, sixty-three on the Genoese galleys, fifty-eight on the French, and fifty-four

or forty-four on the Spanish. This incidentally was already an established practice on the dromons of the Byzantine era.

This shows great foresight on the part of the rulers, since, on a fairly long naval expedition, the number of rowers could be whittled down, as a result of a few individuals dying or becoming incapacitated. So just as today spare fuel and engine parts are carried on board ship, in those days reserve rowers were carried.

After the fifteenth century, when the "zenzile" system was replaced by the "stepped tiers" system, that is, with several rowers at the same oar, those galleys that had two different manning levels for each side of the oarage (five men per oar in the benches in the forward half and six men per oar in the after half, to be precise) were called mainsail galleys. They were larger than the light galleys and were reserved for those whom the Venetians called "Capi da Mar," that is, the commanders of galley fleets or squadrons. For a mainsail galley with twenty-six benches, taking into account that there was one bench less due to the touch-hole, there were 25 × 5 men in the forward section and 26 × 6 in the after part, making a total of 281 oarsmen.

The flagships, or superior generals' galleys, were even bigger than the mainsail galleys, and earmarked for the captain generals, in other words, for the command-

The Fausto quinquereme

When discussing the number and arrangement of the rowers on a galley it was said that on those with *zenzile* manning there were usually three rowers per bench, each with his own oar. History provides us with evidence of a galley with five oars per bench that enjoyed its hey-day in Venice in the mid-sixteenth century. She is known as the Fausto galley, after the name of the man who built her. Vettor Fausto was not a master shipwright at the Arsenale (naval dockyard), but a professor of Greek who, in September 1526, made a proposal to the Senate to build a galley with five oars per bench based on the measurements found in books on ancient Greece; he also proposed modifying a mainsail galley by fitting her out with benches and oars to his own design. The quinquereme, details of which are not known, was launched on April 24, 1529, and immediately put to the test by having to race with a galley with three oars per bench, commanded by Captain Marco Corner. An account of this trial is given by Martin Sanudo who tells us that the galleys started at Malamocco and finished at St. Mark's. The Fausto galley was slightly in the lead, then went down the grand Canal to Ca' Foscari where she turned round with some difficulty, being 159.38ft (28 paces [48.58m]) long. This galley was given as a flagship to Ser Girolamo Canal in August 1529, who praised her highly and advised the doge to build ten more. But a year later the galley was taken out of commission and it appears that she was broken up in 1544. Other sources say that she was still in service in 1571 (which is highly unlikely). After the Battle of Lepanto she was given as a flagship to Marcantonio Colonna who had lost his own ship. She was later set afire by lightning. From her length it can be assumed that she had only nine or ten benches each side, with ninety or one hundred oars. Since Fausto maintained that the fifth oar would row better than the third, it can be suggested that instead of having their tholepins on the outrigger, the two shortest oars had them farther down, on a beam that ran parallel to the outrigger and was supported by the timber extensions.

ers of the fleets. They usually had six men per bench and it is said that the sixth oarsman was added by Andrea Doria. The French seventeenth century galley *Réale* had thirty-two benches and, therefore, 384 oarsmen. The flagship galley with the greatest number of benches was the one built by the Turkish Pasha Captain, Uluch Ali, after the Battle of Lepanto, which had thirty-six benches with 432 oarsmen. These huge galleys (the French galley *Réale* 170.6ft [52m] long and that of Uluch Ali 179ft [54.57m] long) were slow and difficult to handle and were therefore less suitable for maneuvering and combat.

Galliots were smaller than galleys. In many Genoese documents they are referred to by the term "*ligna de teriis*" and in other Venetian ones as "*lignum de remis centum...de remis octoginta....*" These ligna, which were different from galleys, have not been described by the writers of the day but there is no doubt that they must have been structurally similar to light galleys, from which they differed in size and number of rowers. Whereas on a galley with twenty-five benches and three men per bench there were 150 oars, the ligna had one hundred and eighty, according to a decree proclaimed in Venice on March 12, 1334, and twenty to one hundred, according to an *Imposicio Officii Gazariae* of 1313.

Probably, as the years went by and Latin (still the official language in 1300) was abandoned, the term *ligna* was replaced with *galliot*. In his *Armata Navale*, Pantero Pantera refers only to galliots and says that they are built like galleys but do not have the bow platform and not always the foremast. They were sometimes to twenty-three benches with only two oars per bench. Pantera adds that in Barbary there were galliots as big as ordinary galleys, but without the bow platform and foremast, explaining that the Turks made use of this expedient to avoid having their ships requisitioned by the state in the event of war. In this regard it will be remembered that in the Battle of Lepanto (1571), while in the Christian fleet there were only galleys, mainsail galleys, flagships, and galleasses, in the Turkish fleet there were thirty-eight ships classified as galliots and seventeen as fustas.

Below galliots, the navy included *brigs*, structurally similar to galliots, but without the gangway between benches and with eight to sixteen benches, each seating one rower, which meant sixteen to thirty-two oars. These oars were very long and light so as to be easier to handle than the big, heavy oars of the sixteenth century and subsequent *stepped tier* galleys. Pantero Pantera says that they were very fast and for this reason widely used by Turkish pirates.

Frigates were smaller ancestors of brigs, some without a deck, but all with a gangway between the benches. Their stern was lower than that on a brig and in addition they had no outrigger, the oar tholepins being on the edge of the hull. They had six to twelve benches with only one rower each, therefore twelve to twenty-four oars, of the same type as those used on brigantines. They had only one mast with a lateen sail. According to Jal, the name frigate is a corruption of *afracta*, which means without a deck.

The *felucca* was smaller than the frigate. It had no deck and only one mast and three or five benches, which means six to ten oars. A subtype of the felucca was the *castaldella* mentioned by Pantero Pantera. According to Aubin, feluccas had a bow which was interchangeable with the stern, both of which were fitted with rudder gudgeons.

The *lateener* was a very common ship in the twelfth and thirteenth centuries and is mentioned in the history of Pisa and Caffaro's Annals as a ship used by pirates. From documents of that period, it seems to have had twelve oars. In the seventeenth century, however, this term was used to mean a three-masted sailing ship with lateen sails, suitable both for combat and trade.

The deckless *coaster* was another small warship fitted with a ram. It was perhaps a subtype of frigate with fewer benches. One special type of ship, widely used by Barbary pirates up to the eighteenth century, was the *fusta*. It is referred to by Lazarus Baif in his *De Re Navali,* where he says that the Venetian fusta had two oars per bench from the stern to the mainmast and only one oar per bench from the mainmast to the bow. A fusta with twenty benches and the mainmast at the eleventh bench could have had sixty-two oars, therefore about twenty oars more than a brig with the same number of benches. In the thirteenth-century *Book of the Consulate* (code of maritime law in use in the Mediterranean), the fusta is listed after the galley and before the lateener, which is proof of its size and oar arrangement. The biggest of the larger galleys, even bigger than the flagships with six rowers per bench, was the *galleass*. The galleass belongs to the galley family and has nothing in common with the galleon, very different in hull structure, sails, and armament. The galleass was invented after the adoption of firearms so as to be able to equip a ship with more guns than could be carried on a galley. This ship is of Venetian origin, since it was designed and built by the "*Proto dei Marangoni*" (master shipwright) of Venice's Naval Dockyard, Francesco Bressan. Galleasses were used in the Battle of Lepanto, where it appears that they were not very successful. There were five galleasses in Philip II's invincible Spanish Armada, which was destroyed by the British at Calais on July 27, 1588. From that date, the galleass practically disappeared from European navies; only the Republic of Venice kept them until the eighteenth century. In fact, there were galleasses in Lorenzo Marcello's fleet in 1656, and in Francesco Morosini's in 1684, and again in 1714. Having emerged in about 1530, when the zenzile system had been replaced by the "stepped tiers" system, it had one oar per bench, handled by seven rowers, and normally twenty-five or twenty-six benches, like an ordinary galley, but obviously more spaced out. According to Crescenzio's description in his *Nautica Mediterranea*, the galleass was about a third longer than a galley and proportionately beamier. It had three masts with lateen sails, a rudder aft, plus two "steering oars" on each quarter to assist in going about, given its great size. It differed from galleys in that it did not have a ram at the bow.

There were two platforms fore and aft, not yet proper castles, which housed the artillery. Down the sides were the two quarter boards, much taller than on galleys, and the two side gangways, where the arquebuses and stone-throwing cannons could be arranged. Down the middle of the benches was the normal gangway running fore and aft; the rowers' benches rested on the deck planking of the hull, which, as on galleys, was narrower than the gunwale frame, and the sides were open between the two above-mentioned parts. At the after end of the galleass was a deck for the commander and soldiers. Like the other types of ships, galleasses also underwent modifications over the years. In the more modern ones, the forecastle and poop deck had taken on the form of proper superstructures with two banks of

The French royal galley. This seventeenth-century galley, built for the Captain General of the Galleys, was one of the largest in the Mediterranean. She had thirty-one benches with seven rowers per bench; including the touch-hole bench, there were, in all, sixty-one oars and 427 rowers. There were two lateen-rigged masts and at the forward end the bow platform was surmounted by a castle with bulwarks where the soldiers could position the stands on which to rest their muskets and arquebuses. Artillery was made up of a gangway cannon that fired thirty-six-pound balls and, on either side, a twenty-four-pounder, called a "bastard cannon," plus an eighteen-pounder called a "demi-cannon." There were five cannons in all, but they could not be trained; so during combat the galley had to be positioned with her bow facing the enemy. Muskets were mounted on the two side gangways that ran above the tholepins and were sometimes called "loop-holes," because the crossbowmen once took up their positions there. At the stern, on the after superstructure, there were no muskets as a rule, but men armed only with swords for hand-to-hand fighting, which usually settled the outcome of the battle. Dimensions were: length on the waterline 170.60ft (52m); overall length including the ram and the stern overhang 203.41ft (62m); hull breadth 21ft (6.40m); crew 427 rowers plus 120 seamen and soldiers.

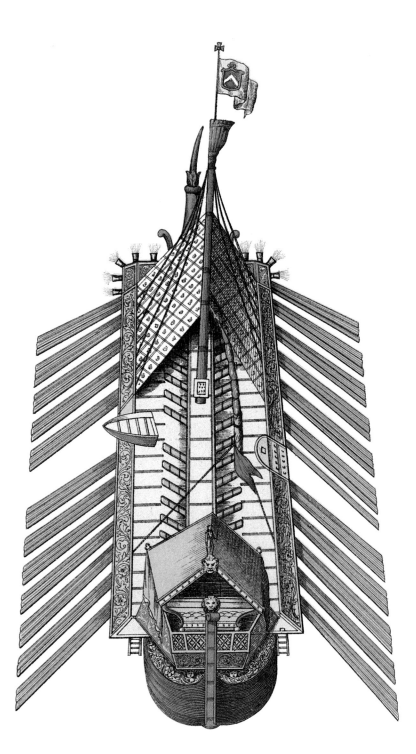

Fourteenth-century zenzile galley. The light galley, the war-galley par excellence, was not an adaptation of the tenth and eleventh-century dromons, but a new design of ship with a completely different arrangement of oars and rowers. In order to have ships that were faster than dromons, the hull was reduced to the minimum dimensions possible while, to have longer oars, a wide frame enabling the tholepins to be much further away from the rowers, was placed on top of this hull. As regards the arrangement of the oars on the same bench, there was a return to the old method, copying that used on Roman liburnians, no longer using several men on the same oar, as on the Roman polyremes and on dromons. The galley shown here has twelve benches with three rowers per bench, an arrangement that allowed the maximum number of oars without making the galley too long. There were only eleven groups of oars on the starboard side because of the touch-hole bench. Dimensions are: length 124.67ft (38m); beam 17.06ft (5.20m); hull height 6.23ft (1.90m); crew 150 rowers plus forty soldiers and seamen (from a contemporary Venetian manuscript).

guns; the two steering oars had disappeared; and, lastly, the two after ladders were no longer present, but the gunwale extended into a gallery round the stern, similar to the more modern quarters.

Despite the great number of rowers on each bench, galleasses were slow and difficult to maneuver, so much so that, as can be read in the story of the Battle of Lepanto, when the ships arranged themselves in battle formation, the six galleasses of the fleet had to be towed into the position that they were to occupy.

Arrangement of the rowers on tenth to seventeenth-century oared warships

When we discussed the Battle of Actium (31 B.C.), we said that the large ships with several banks of oars were abandoned after the battle and there was a move toward simpler ships with only one bank of oars.

The arrangement of the rowers on the ships of the Middle Ages is much less problematic than the theories put forward for the polyremes of ancient times, especially since surviving documents explain more clearly how many oarsmen there were and how they were positioned on their benches.

We thus know that on ships of the dromon family there were two banks of oars, as Leo the Wise says, "each bank of rowers would have at least 25 benches on which the rowers would sit: one on the starboard and one on the port side . . . fifty in the bottom bank and from 150 to 200 in the top bank." He tells us that in addition to the fact that there were 150 to 200 men, two per oar, on the deck there must have been other men who were probably used as reserves or soldiers, ready for combat.

A *Chrysobull* or Golden Bull, as the decrees of the Eastern emperors were called, promulgated by Emperor Isaac II Angelus (1185–1195) in 1188, in setting up an alliance with the Republic of Venice, states, among other things, that Venice had to supply galleys manned by 140 rowers. The surviving translation speaks of galleys, but they must have been dromons with two banks of rowers and forty-eight oars, twenty-four per side in the bottom bank, and ninety-two at forty-six oars in the top bank. On the ships of the dromon family, however, there was a deck, so half of the benches were above this deck and half below; in this way the two different banks of rowers did not hinder each other. Doubt still remains, however, regarding what system was used to achieve synchronization of movement between the two banks of rowers who could not see each other.

It has already been mentioned that the rowers on the upper deck sat two per oar, since the oars of this bank were longer and heavier. This meant that the benches were arranged in a herring-bone pattern, whereas the benches of the lower bank could even have been positioned crosswise.

Moving on to the ships of the galley family, that is, to around 1200, the two superimposed banks of oars disappear and only one is left, but instead of there being only one per bench, the oars increase to two, three, four, and even five per bench with an oar arrangement which, to use a Venetian term, is called the *zenzile system*. In classical antiquity, ships with two oars and two oarsmen per bench already existed. The Romans called them Liburnians and had copied them from the Illyrians. The zenzile system adopted on galleys from 1200 to 1500 thus represents a return to the old method.

We have already shown that the rowers' benches had to be arranged in a herring-bone pattern and that the oars had to be of different lengths, each working on its own tholepin on the gunwale. Let us examine the arrangement of the oars in more detail, beginning with that of a galley with two rowers per bench.

In order to have the space necessary for the two rowers to be able to row without getting in each other's way, the bench had to be inclined at 37.4in (95cm) and be 8.8ft (2.70m) long. The two rowers sat 37.4in (95cm) apart, and the same distance from the gunwale and gangway. The innermost rower had to handle an oar 21.6ft (6.60m) long, a third of which came before the tholepin and two-thirds beyond it. The outermost rower handled an oar 12.4ft (3.80m) long, also balanced with one-third before the tholepin and two-thirds beyond it. By arranging the oars of subsequent benches in a similar fashion, it can be seen that they must have emerged from the sides of the galley in groups of two through ports 19.6in (50cm) long and 37.4in (95cm) apart.

The inclination of 37.4in (95cm) for the bench with two oars is not sufficient for a bench with three rowers, for whom 5ft (1.55m) is needed. The bench must also be longer, even supposing that the rowers sat 23.6in (60cm) apart, but still 37.4in (95cm) from the gunwale and gangway. It is assumed that the longest oar was the same length as that of the galley with two oars per bench, namely 21.6ft (6.60m); the second was 14.7ft (4.50m) and the third 9.1ft (2.80m). The tholepins were probably 11.8in (30cm) apart. With this oar arrangement, a galley with three benches must have had ports 31.4in (80cm) long, spaced 3.7ft (1.15m) apart.

The addition of a fourth oarsman brings the inclination of the bench to 7.8ft (2.40m) and its length to 14.7ft (4.50m). The longest oar is 23.6ft (7.20m) long, the second 21.6ft (6.60m), the third 15.7ft (4.80m), and the fourth 11.4ft (3.50m). The oar ports must have been 5.5ft (1.70m) long, and the distance between the next two must have been 4.2ft (1.30m).

Stepped-tier galley. In the sixteenth century, galleys had one oar per bench with the number of rowers ranging from three to seven per oar. This method of manning was called the "stepped-tier" system. Stepped-tier rowing was tried out for the first time in Venice, by order of a decree dated July 30, 1534, which laid down that "60 large oars of the type to be rowed by three men per oar" should be built and tried out on a galley. The number of rowers depended on the size of the galley and its use. For example, the Spanish galleys of Philip II, to be used to transport army units between the ports of Italy and Spain, had three rowers per oar, since they were not required to be fast. Galleys used for privateering, however, or those used to put off the enemy or Berber pirates, had to have five men per oar. Mainsail galleys and flagships, which were larger and heavier than the light galleys, had, if they were mainsails, six men per oar in the after half of the oarage and five in the forward half. Flagships had six men for the entire oarage. The galley shown here has her sails furled, ready for battle, and twenty-six benches with four men per oar; making a total of 208 rowers. There is only one rudder and the cannons on the bow platform are not visible. Dimensions are: length 131ft (39.93m); beam 16.50ft (5.03m); deck height above the keel 9.94ft (3.03m). In the cross section, there are seven rowers per oar.

A galley with five oars per bench must have had benches inclined at 10.4ft (3.20m) and 17ft (5.20m) long. The longest oar must therefore have been 23.6ft (7.20m), the second one 21.6ft (6.60m), the third 16ft (4.90m), the fourth 12.7ft (3.90m), and the fifth 9.8ft (3.00m). The port for five bars must have been 6.2ft (1.90m) long and 4.2ft (1.30m) from the next one.

From these proportions it can be deduced that by increasing the number of oars for each bench, it would have been necessary to reduce the number of benches in order to keep the length of the galley within reasonable limits.

The most logically acceptable arrangement for oars and rowers is shown in the diagram.

Comparison of the various documentation leads us to conclude that the best number of oars to use per bench was two or three; while increasing them to four, five, or six led to a gradual reduction in the total number of oars, without taking into account that the latter had to become increasingly longer and heavier, making them ever more difficult to handle.

Documentation from the thirteenth to fifteenth centuries tells us that the word galley meant a ship with three oars per bench, whereas the words ligna or ligna de teriis meant those with fewer men.

galley with 2 oars per bench: 25 benches with 100 oars;
galley with 3 oars per bench: 19 benches with 114 oars;
galley with 4 oars per bench: 12 benches with 96 oars;
galley with 5 oars per bench: 9 benches with 90 oars;
galley with 6 oars per bench: 7 benches with 84 oars.

Toward the middle of the fifteenth century an extremely important innovation occurred regarding the rowing of galleys: instead of having two, three, or four oars per bench, each pulled by one rower, there was just one big oar pulled by three, four, and even seven rowers. This type of rowing, called the *stepped tiers* system, was adopted on galleys and galleasses. The oars were really wooden beams up to 50.8ft (15.5m) long with about 16.4ft (5m) before the tholepin (the part known as the *loom*) so as to balance the part beyond it which was about 36ft (11m) long. In order to achieve balance, the loom had to be so big that it could not be gripped by the rowers. It was therefore fitted with wooden *manette,* which the rowers would grasp. The rower nearest the gangway was called the "vogavanto"; then came the "gunwale oarsman," the "third rower," the "fourth rower," and so on.

The big oars of the stepped tier galleys had to be built of special tree trunks and were much more expensive than those used on the galleys adopting the zenzile system. Pantero Pantera says that one stepped tier galley oar costs twice as much as the three oars for a zenzile bench.

Unfortunately, not one original galley oar has survived to the present day, and the only example of a seventeenth-century stepped tier galley oar is in a Swedish museum.

Having dealt with the oars we must now discuss the rowers. Until around 1350, galley rowers were free men, taken on for this task by fleet commanders. After 1350 prisoners of war and slaves bought in public markets were used as rowers. Men convicted of common crimes were also sent to row on the galleys.

In the Republic of Venice, only about two centuries later, in 1542, the "Colegieto dei Condannati" was set up to administer the convicts condemned to the galleys. There were still some free rowers, however, especially for the galleys of the "Capi da Mar," whereas the "convict" galleys were grouped together in a squadron commanded by the "Governor of Convicts."

Around 1500, as revealed by documents of the period, almost all galliots were

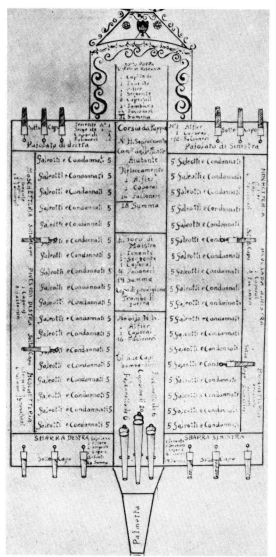

Seventeenth-century Venetian galley

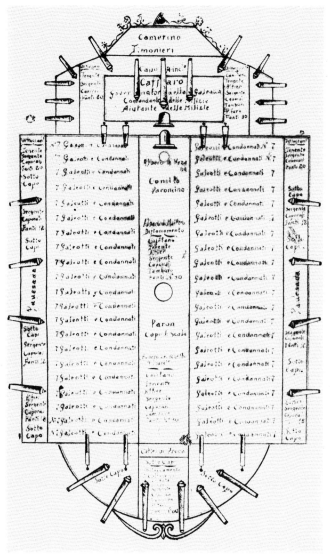

Seventeenth-century Venetian galleass

Arrangement of the rowers in combat

These two drawings are from a manuscript in the Querini Stampalia Library in Venice. In the one showing a galley, the rowers are positioned in the stepped-tier system: five per bench with eighteen oars per side. She is therefore a senior general's galley. The combat positions of all the ship's personnel are shown in detail. It will be noted that the captain and the army commander were positioned aft on the gangway, with the soldiers on the bulwarks. This galley had three gangway cannons (one cannon and two falconets), six cannons forward on the starboard and port rails, six cannons aft on the starboard and port mountings, and four cannons, two either side, on the bulwarks.

In the drawing depicting the galleass, note the heavy batteries forward (ten cannons) and aft (seventeen cannons) plus a further eight cannons, four on either side, on the bulwarks. On galleasses, the captain and the army commander were not positioned on the gangway but on the quarter deck. The galleass shown here has three masts and twenty-one oars per side, each handled by seven rowers. It will be noted that whereas the galley has three gangway cannons and six falconets (three per side), the galleass has two gangway cannons and two cannons per side, as well as a good number of after cannons, all of the fixed type.

manned by convicts and divided into three categories, which Crescenzio lists in his *Nautica Mediterranea:*

1) The convicts sentenced to hard labour, i.e. those condemned by the courts to a fixed period or life, were chained to the bench, by their right foot if they occupied the benches on the port side, and their left foot if they occupied the benches on the starboard side. Their heads and beards were completely shaved.

2) The slaves or ''Turks,'' in other words Mohammedans, who were prisoners of war or bought in the markets, were also used for onshore work, to stock up with wood and water, and to work on board. They were also chained to their benches and identifiable by a tuft of hair on their heads.

3) Mercenary galleymen, or free men, were convicts who, after serving their sentence, stayed on the galleys of their own free will, or else were vagrants and adventurers who accepted being chained to the benches. Crescenzio says that the largest and best groups were the Spaniards and the Neapolitans. Although they were chained, the mercenary galleymen were paid a wage, which was used partly to cover board and supplement rations, and partly to pay for galleymen's clothing, handed out free of charge to the convicts and slaves. They could be ''unchained'' and go freely about the galleys, with only an iron ring, or shackle, around their ankle. They could be told apart from the others because they wore beards. The stroke oars were recruited from among the mercenary galleymen.

After the fourteenth century, the rowers were, for the most part, convicts and slaves. On normal voyages, only a third of the oarsmen rowed while the other two-thirds rested, taking turns to row. For this reason, on one galley there were six stroke oars, two on the stern bench, two on the eighth bench, and two on the sixteenth, in order to lead the rowing in the respective sectors. Only during combat and entering or leaving port were all the oars used, just as multi-boilered steamships would fire all their boilers in similar circumstances, leaving some cold during normal steaming at economic speed.

Zenzile galleys did not always have all their oars manned. When the Republic of Venice had to send galleys to the Eastern Mediterranean, it normally made them leave with two oars per bench, and the galleys were then ''made up to three'' by

completing the number of rowers in Albania or Greece with galleymen hired on the spot. This practice was no longer followed when stepped tier oars began to be adopted, both because the oars could not be handled by fewer men than the prescribed number, and because slaves and convicts were used in place of free galleymen.

Sails and rudders of oared warships from the tenth to the seventeenth century

It was said earlier that very little is known about ships belonging to the dromon family. It is possible, however, to formulate likely theories. Winesalf notes that King Richard's fleet encountered an enormous enemy dromon with three masts and three sails, an encounter which is also referred to by the chronicler, Matthew of Paris in his *Chronica Mayor,* which sets the date at June 8, 1191. This ''enormous'' dromon had three masts and three sails, so it can be assumed that a normal dromon had only two sails and probably also a raked mast setting a bowsprit sail forward. The sails must have been square, just as the Roman warships had square sails; it is highly unlikely that they had lateen sails, although some writers give dromons and selanders this type of sail.

Some mosaics in St. Mark's Basilica, depicting twelfth century Venetian ships, show sails which are more easily identified as square sails, although the lateen sail appeared in the Mediterranean at the end of the nineth century—though only for small craft. It will also be remembered that in the Middle Ages warships did not use sails in combat, so they were only used for long passages, and it was therefore more likely that they were square sails since these were less difficult to handle.

Ships belonging to the galley family, however, did have lateen sails: The light galley normally had one mainmast and one foremast. The mainmast was positioned a third of the way along from the bow and wedged up against the bar keel. The foremast, smaller and lighter, did not rest on the keel but was stepped to the main deck. The mainmast was about 65.6ft (20m) long; the yard, or lateen yard, was made up of two main pieces and a third smaller one. The two main pieces—the bottom one was called a *truck* and the top one a *peak*—were joined together by doubling and sturdy binding. The third piece, called the *lengthening pole*, was attached by the same method to the top part of the peak. On mainsail and flagship galleys, there was usually a third mast called the *mizzenmast*, at roughly two-thirds of the ship's length from the bow.

Galleys had four types of sail for the mainmast, one square sail, called a *course*, which obviously had to be bent on with the lateen yard positioned horizontally and was used when running before the wind, and three lateen sails called *bastarda* (mainsail), *borda* (short-luffed lug), and *marabutto* (storm-sail). The bastarda was the largest and was hoisted when the sea was calm, the borda when there was a fresh wind, and the marabutto in bad weather. For the foremast, however, there was only one sail, whose area could be reduced in case of bad weather by *reefing*, in other words by folding the strip of sail nearest the lateen yard against the yard itself, and tying it down with reef points through holes made in the sail. A similar procedure was carried out for the mizzen sail if the galley was three-masted: In order to perform the above-mentioned operations, the lateen yards had to be lowered and laid on the gangway.

The names referred to above are taken from *Armata Navale*. In Venetian documents, however, the square sail is called the *cochina* and the three lateen sails are called the *artemon*, *reef*, and *papafico*, or *mizzen*.

The sails of normal galleys were all the color of raw hemp. Flagships, however, had two-color sails, usually white and red, which made them easily distinguishable even from far off. Similarly, during the night, flagship galleys put a light aft, and so were known in Venetian as *fano* (light) galleys. Instead of just one light, the captain general's galley had three.

Galleasses also had three masts and lateen sails plus, as shown by pictures of galleasses at Lepanto, a raked mast forward setting a square sail.

As regards rudders, dromons certainly had steering oars on each quarter; these were retained on galleys until the fourteenth century. The stern rudder, which appeared on Scandinavian ships during the twelfth century, was not adopted on Mediterranean oared ships until two centuries later. An oared ship with a rudder is depicted in the *Atlas Catalan*, which dates from 1370, from which it is possible to deduce that galleys had Navarre-type stern rudders in the first decades of the 1400s. Steering oars were not totally abandoned, however, but retained as back-ups for the central rudder even on fifteenth-century galleys and on galleasses (sixteenth-century ships).

The single rudder and stepped tier rowing system were the most important structural changes for the galley throughout its lifetime of about 600 years.

The armament of oared warships from the tenth to the seventeenth century

Like the ships of classical antiquity, those of the Middle Ages and even up to the end of the oared ship period were fitted with a ram: The chief exceptions were galleasses, which were ramless. This weapon was retained even after firearms were adopted, although it had lost much of its importance.

In his *Nautica Mediterranea*, Crescenzio says that a ram had to be as many spans long as there were benches, so a twenty-five-bench galley had to have a ram about 19½ft (6m) long. The ram was no longer at the water line as it was on the ships of classical antiquity, but quite high up and reinforced with a metal tip.

Dromons and selanders could have towers on deck (the "*lignea castra*" shown in Doge Pietro Candiano's medal) on which there were soldiers with projectile-launching weapons, such as crossbows and long-bows. In addition, they were certainly armed with a *mangonel* in the bows for hurling stones, and syphons for pumping out Greek fire.

When in the thirteenth century dromons disappeared and galleys appeared, the latter were also armed with a mangonel in the forward part of the gangway, in addition to smaller projectile-launching weapons. After the introduction of the cannon, galleys also had their own artillery. The main weapon was the gangway cannon, positioned on the bow platform in place of the old mangonel. On either side of the gangway cannon were the smaller pieces, called *falconets*, ranging from one to three per side depending on the size of galley. Wooden reinforcements, between the bow platform and deck, served to support these cannons. Other small firearms were positioned along the side gangways, behind the quarter boards, such as arquebuses and stone-throwing cannons or large muskets, resting on iron brackets.

On a French galley, in 1538, ammunition and personal arms consisted of the following: "15 quintals of powder, 50 cannon-balls, 100 balls for smaller cannons 6 flamethrowers, 50 fire-pots, 24 arquebuses with powder and lead pellets, 24 crossbows with arrows, 12 pikes, 12 partisans or halberds, 50 morions, 50 swords, 24 round shields and 20 scaled cuirasses."

Another type of weapon, mentioned in various statutes of the Republics of Genoa and Venice, was the sickle, used to cut down the sails and their rigging.

From the above, it is possible to deduce that even after the adoption of firearms naval battles were won or lost by boarding and hand-to-hand fighting, as evidenced by the account of the Battle of Lepanto fought in 1571.

Galleass. This type of ship is a development of the galley, with the same lines but larger all round. The early galleasses built by Francesco Bressan were therefore simply large galleys with a deck at the waterline and a frame for the outrigger and quarter boards. The galleass later changed her form and had a complete hull, like that of the large oared ships; there was no ram, but she kept her old name and was still driven by oar, with seven men per bench. Sixteenth-century galleasses had three lateen-rigged masts (due to the addition of a mizzenmast aft), a conventional rudder, and two steering oars to assist when going about. At the forward and after end there were two decked areas for the soldiers and cannons; other smaller firearms were positioned on the quarter boards. All in all, a galleass had about seventy cannons of varying sizes. The heaviest were the gangway cannons and the four either side of them. The others were on the fore and after castles and the smallest, stone-launching cannons, were on the quarter boards in the gaps between the rowers' benches. Seventeenth-century galleasses outwardly resembled large sailing ships with a forecastle and poop deck that extended far beyond the rudder. A model in the Naval Museum in Venice shows that the two steering oars aft had been abandoned. The dimensions calculated from this model are: length 193.89ft (59.10m); beam 29.56ft (9.01m); height of the deck above the keel 11ft (3.35m); height of the parapet above the keel 21.39ft (6.52m). For a galleass with twenty oars per side and seven men per oar, the rowers numbered 140. The crew can be estimated to have been 250 to 300 men.

SAILING WARSHIPS
FROM THE MIDDLE AGES TO MODERN TIMES

The naval battle of sailing warships

Oared ships had their own motive power and could maneuver independently even in unfavorable and adverse wind conditions. By contrast, a sailing ship was totally dependent on the wind for headway and maneuvering. This factor obviously conditioned and changed tactics and combat formations.

The possibility of maneuvering independently was the reason why the oared galley continued to be used as a warship in the Mediterranean until the eighteenth century, at a time when the navies of oceanic nations already had war fleets made up entirely of sailing ships and had developed their fighting tactics accordingly.

There was a period of transition during which there were fleets made up of both sailing and oared ships. In the Republic of Venice, the fleet of sailing ships was called the "Heavy Fleet," and the one made up of galleys the "Light Fleet." Naval battles between mixed fleets of three-decked sailing ships and galleys occurred in the Mediterranean until 1714, when Venice mounted a fleet of twenty-two three-decked sailing ships, two galleasses, and thirty-three galleys against the Turks while the latter's fleet comprised fifty-eight three-decked sailing ships and thirty-four galleys. By 1716 and 1717, the Venetian fleet still combined three-decked sailing ships and galleys, whereas in France, England, Holland, and Spain, oared ships had disappeared almost a century before. In 1700, only in the Swedish and Russian fleets and in some Mediterranean navies were there still galleys and this was because of the special conditions under which they had to operate, on inland seas and lakes.

One of the first naval battles fought in the Mediterranean between sailing ships was the one which took place on August 5, 1435 off the Island of Ponza, between the Spanish fleet of Alfonso of Aragon and the Genoese fleet commanded by Biagio Assereto. In this battle, the fleet from Aragon, made up of fourteen ships and eleven galleys, was attacked by nine Genoese (sailing) cogs and three galleys. The conflict was conducted solely between the sailing ships, attacking with grapnels, whose crews fought fiercely in an attempt to board each other's ships. Galleys played a secondary role. The Genoese were victorious and the outcome was the capture of King Alfonso.

From this naval battle, and from others of the same period, it is not possible to draw any conclusions regarding the tactics used. Pantero Pantera, in the early seventeenth century, tells us that the crescent formation, which was the most widespread battle array for galleys, was not suitable for sailing ships since a wind which the ships in one flank found favorable was unfavorable for those in the opposite flank. He therefore advises that the largest and strongest ships be positioned on the windward flank, the medium ones in the center, and the smallest and weakest ones in the leeward flank.

The crescent battle formation was also retained, however, in ocean-going navies, as evidenced by documents describing the formation taken up by the French fleet of King Francis I on July 19, 1545, off the Isle of Wight, to fight the English fleet. There were thirty-six ships in the right wing, thirty in the middle, and thirty-six in the left wing. The galleys had been sent ahead to harass enemy sailing ships.

Not until the mid-seventeenth century is it possible to find the first examples of different battle formations and tactical maneuvers by the squadrons, performed mostly by the squadron that had the wind in its favor.

It should be noted that, whereas on galleys the small amount of artillery that each ship had was all concentrated at the bow, on sailing ships most of the guns were positioned down the sides and only a few pieces could fire fore and aft. Instead of being concentrated at the bow, the fire power was thus equally distributed along the sides.

For this reason, ships adopted the single line ahead battle formation, to make their maximum offensive power available, that is, one side battery against the other. Combat tactics had become completely different from those adopted by galleys, and instead of encountering each other face to face and settling the conflict by boarding and skirmishes with side arms, the fleets fought each other by sailing in parallel, at a distance equal to the guns' range, or by passing astern on the opposite tack. Even on sailing ships, however, the practice of boarding as a means of settling the fighting was not completely abandoned.

The great warships were called "ships of the line," an expression which appeared for the first time in the British Admiralty's "Fighting Instructions" of 1653. The line ahead formation led to a tactical maneuver called "cutting the line," a maneuver by which a fleet cut through the enemy line at one or two points, separating the ships into small groups that were attacked separately, before giving the ships cut off at the head of the line time to maneuver and come to their assistance.

One of the first examples of cutting through the line was at the Battle of Yarmouth on June 2, 1653, between the Dutch fleet, commanded by Maarten Tromp, and the British one, commanded by Admiral Monk. As usual, the fleets were divided into three squadrons: the Dutch van was commanded by Admiral Evertszoon, the middle by Maarten Tromp, and the rearguard by Admiral Ruyter. The British fleet had Admiral Lawson at the van, Monk at the center, and Deane at the rearguard.

The British fleet was 125 ships of the line strong and had the wind in its favor. The Dutch had ninety-eight ships plus a few fire ships. On the first day of fighting, the British van crossed the enemy line cutting off the Dutch rearguard, which was

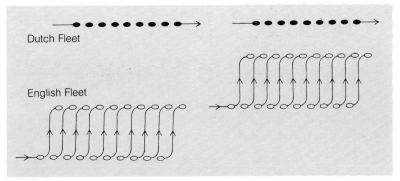

Dutch Fleet

English Fleet

The Battle of Lowestoft (June 3, 1665). Fought between the Dutch fleet under the command of Admiral Jacob van Wassenaer, Baron of Obdam, and the British squadron under the command of the Duke of York. The two squadrons proceeded in a line ahead formation in the same direction, the British to windward. The British fleet made two changes of course to get closer to the enemy line and then closed in to fire its artillery.

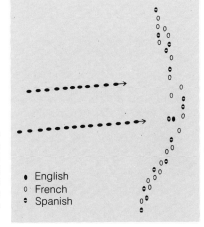

• English
○ French
◉ Spanish

The Battle of Trafalgar (October 21, 1805). Fought between the combined French and Spanish fleet, under the command of Admiral Villeneuve, and the British, commanded by Nelson. The combined French and Spanish fleet was in line ahead formation. Running before the wind, the British attacked in two parallel lines, breaking the enemy formation at the rear of the van and where the twelfth ship from the center was positioned, so that the British ships engaged only the middle and rear of the enemy line.

surrounded, but with a timely maneuver, Tromp came to his aid and freed him. On the second day a British reinforcement of eighteen ships arrived, commanded by Admiral Blake, who settled the battle in Britain's favor.

We saw that in the oared ship period, one of the maneuvers in battle was to keep a certain number of reserve ships hidden close by the area in which the battle was to take place, so as to bring them in, possibly behind the enemy, at the most appropriate moment. This was no longer done in the sailing ship period. Since the wind was depended upon for maneuvers, it was unwise to space out the ships which, if the wind later changed or dropped, would have been unable to catch up again. The admirals commanding-in-chief, who usually positioned their ships at the head of the squadron in the middle of the line, considered it a debt of honor, when battle occurred on parallel courses, to fight each other, just as the captain generals' galleys of the oared ship fleets had done.

We have stressed the importance of occupying a windward position, which offered the advantage of deciding the moment of attack, made it easy to send fire ships against the enemy line, made it possible to regain visibility more quickly because the wind blew away the gun smoke, and lastly because the ships, leaning towards the enemy as the wind was filling their sails, had more of their hulls submerged, and so offered less of a target for gunfire. But the leeward position also had its advantages, such as the fact that those ships damaged in combat could leave the line by dropping even further to leeward, and thus be protected by the others. Moreover, the ships that were leaning in the opposite direction to that of the enemy could also fire their lower deck (most powerful) guns. Lastly, the leeward squadron could force that of the enemy to accept battle in a narrow strait, against its will. In general, the windward position favored offensive action, whereas the leeward position favored defensive maneuvers.

In the Battle of Lowestoft of 1665, between the British and Dutch navies, there was a new maneuver: Two successive British changes of course towards the enemy, the first, to put the squadron at a distance for long-range use of the artillery, and the second, to bring it back to short-range and settle the battle with smaller weapons.

Cutting through the line, which probably occurred by chance in Yarmouth in 1653, became an intentional, planned tactical maneuver at the Battle of Saintes on February 12, 1782, in which thirty-six British three-deckers, commanded by

Admiral Rodney, faced thirty-four French three-deckers, commanded by Admiral De Grasse. The two fleets first passed by on an opposite tack, then Rodney cut through the French line behind De Grasse's ships, followed by six three-deckers, which he used to attack the ships at the end of the French line, causing them to surrender and be captured.

The theory of cutting the line was worked out by Nelson in his two famous "Memoranda" and applied by him and Collingwood in the Battles of Cape St. Vincent on February 14, 1797 and Trafalgar on October 21, 1805. These "Memoranda," the second of which bears the date October 9, 1805, just over ten days before Trafalgar, mark the peak of sailing ship tactics.

In his second memorandum, showing the difficulties of maneuvering with just one line ahead, Nelson recommended, among other things, for long passages and attack, a formation consisting of two parallel lines with a van of eight to ten of the fastest three-deckers to reinforce one or the other of the two lines.

The tactic of attacking on two lines was applied at Trafalgar and proved to be extremely effective.

When treating the ships of classical antiquity and oared ships, we said that before battle, as a rule, the commanders-in-chief of the fleets gave a "pep talk." This practice was preserved on sailing ships, too, although clearly in a different form: To be precise, a report was given to the subordinate admirals and commanders. Instead of the supreme commander going on a small boat to inspect the ships, as had occurred at Lepanto, the commanders of the ships gathered on board the Admiral's ship to hear personally from their leader, who called upon their sense of honor and patriotism. Another form of pep talk, which continued for many years, was to send a message of incitement to all the ships, by semaphore. Thus, did Nelson, at Trafalgar, with his famous phrase: "England expects every man will do his duty."

Nomenclature of tenth to seventeenth century sailing warships

The distinction between warships and sailing merchant ships is not as clear-cut and simple as the distinction between the oared warships and sailing merchant ships of ancient times. In the time of oared ships in the Middle Ages, apart from light galleys, or war galleys, there were also "Flemish galleys" and "Rumanian Galleys," which were designed to transport goods, although they were armed and fitted out like combat ships.

Mercantile sailing craft, like the Flemish and Rumanian galleys, had to make long voyages and were liable to enemy or pirate attack. They, therefore, had to be well armed, and able to defend themselves effectively. This was especially true after the great geographical discoveries, when the carracks and galleons bringing back their valuable cargoes were tempting prey, and therefore had to be in a position to defend themselves from attacks by ships of the same size and armament.

The documentation we have does not make a clear distinction between a war galleon and a merchant galleon, and even at the end of the sailing ship period, in the first half of the nineteenth century, there were no differences in hull structure or composition and arrangement of the sails between a three-decker, a war frigate, and a similar merchant ship. Such structural differentiation was present, however, after the introduction of steam propulsion.

The oldest sailing warship of the Mediterranean was the *cog*, used primarily as a freighter but also as a warship as it was, for instance, in the fleet fitted out by the Republic of Venice for the 1202 crusade. In this fleet there were 480 ships, including 120 vissers and a vast number of cogs, suitably equipped with towers and drawbridges to storm the walls of the cities to be conquered. These ships played an active part in the conquest of Constantinople: In the attack on the city they were preceded by galleys that disembarked their soldiers with ladders for scaling the walls, and then withdrew to leave room for the cogs, which, with their towers and drawbridges, came alongside the walls so that the soldiers were practically at the same level as those defending the city. As is well-known, Constantinople was conquered on July 17, 1203, by the crusaders who ousted the Byzantine emperors of the Eastern Roman Empire, creating a fleeting Latin Empire.

When Jean de Brienne, a crusader commander, beseiged Damietta in 1218, he used cogs tied together in pairs, which supported a tower or castle for storming the walls, as recorded by the chronicler, Oliviero da Colonia.

Cogs made up part of Biagio Assereto's fleet at Ponza in 1435, but they were probably no longer the same type of ship, even though they bore the same name.

In the thirteenth century, in addition to cogs, there were other quite sizeable vessels simply called ships. We can get a fairly accurate picture of a sailing ship in the year 1268 from the "Contractus Navigiis Dominis Regis cum Venetis" that King Louis of France signed with the Republic of Venice to supply ships for the crusade. This contract lists the size and specifications of some ships, particularly those named *Sainte Marie*, *Roquefort*, and *Saint Nicolas*. *Roquefort* had a 103.34 ft (31.50m) long keel and an overall length of 162.4 ft (49.50m), a beam of 46.94 ft

Thirteenth-century Mediterranean cog. A mosaic in Ravenna shows a thirteenth-century merchantman which can be described as a cog: a ship used both as a merchantman and a man-of-war. The reconstruction shows a ship with a high freeboard and a rounded hull, with a length three times the beam. There were two lateen-rigged masts with round crow's nests and also the two conventional steering oars aft. The poop deck is almost completely within the stern while the forecastle overhangs the bow. The conversion of the cog into a warship probably involved replacing the poop deck and forecastle with towers, or *lignea castra*, to accommodate the soldiers. Very approximate dimensions are: length 131ft (40m); beam 42.5ft (13m); height of the deck above the keel 17ft (5.30m); draught 11.5ft (3.50m).

Fourteenth-century Northern cog. The Northern cog was smaller than her Mediterranean sister and also was used mostly for trade. Highly stylized versions appear on the seals of many towns and cities. She had only one mast amidships, setting a big square sail with a bonnet. The hull, with almost straight stem- and sternposts, had a quarterdeck extending a good third of its length, fitted with battlements. By contrast, the forecastle was quite small. Note the single rudder aft, instead of the two steering oars of the Mediterranean cogs, and the long raked pole at the bow for the bowline blocks of the big sail. Estimated dimensions are: length 91–98ft (28–30m); beam 26–29ft (8–9m); deck height 13ft (4m); draught 8ft (2.5m).

Santa Caterina do Monte Sinai (Portugal c. 1520). In 1520 the Portuguese Navy included this huge war carrack, the subject of a painting now in the National Maritime Museum in Greenwich. This carrack had two square-rigged masts, a tall mainmast amidships and a foremast forward, almost on the stem. There is a second lateen-rigged mast aft called the bonaventure mast, as well as a topsail on the foremast. The after superstructure, which runs from the mainmast to the stern, has three levels: quarterdeck, half deck, and stern bridge. The forecastle extends well out beyond the bow, with two superimposed batteries of cannons. Due to their number and their raised position, the quarterdeck and forecastle cannons were not large caliber. In fact, they were large muskets and small rail cannons. Only amidships on the deck was there a battery of mounted cannons that fired shot of considerable weight. The stern is round but the quarterdeck above it is square and has ports as well as cannons to fire astern. Note also that there are no ports or "sabords" for the broadside cannons, since there is only one battery of cannons on deck with pieces that fired through openings in the parapet. We know that the ship had 140 cannons but we do not know how they were subdivided into types. Estimated dimensions are: length 124.5–131ft (38–40m); beam 39–46ft (12–14m); height of the main deck 18–19.5ft (5.5–6m); draught 13–14.5ft (4–4.5m).

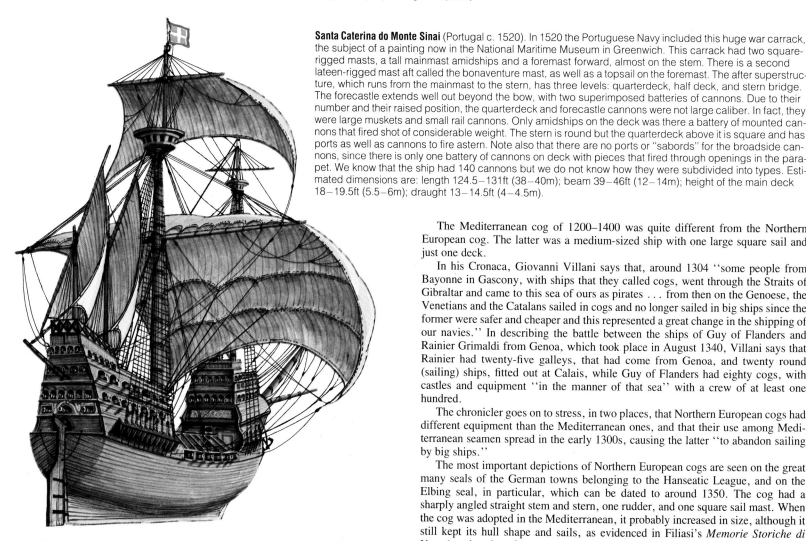

The Mediterranean cog of 1200–1400 was quite different from the Northern European cog. The latter was a medium-sized ship with one large square sail and just one deck.

In his Cronaca, Giovanni Villani says that, around 1304 "some people from Bayonne in Gascony, with ships that they called cogs, went through the Straits of Gibraltar and came to this sea of ours as pirates . . . from then on the Genoese, the Venetians and the Catalans sailed in cogs and no longer sailed in big ships since the former were safer and cheaper and this represented a great change in the shipping of our navies." In describing the battle between the ships of Guy of Flanders and Rainier Grimaldi from Genoa, which took place in August 1340, Villani says that Rainier had twenty-five galleys, that had come from Genoa, and twenty round (sailing) ships, fitted out at Calais, while Guy of Flanders had eighty cogs, with castles and equipment "in the manner of that sea" with a crew of at least one hundred.

The chronicler goes on to stress, in two places, that Northern European cogs had different equipment than the Mediterranean ones, and that their use among Mediterranean seamen spread in the early 1300s, causing the latter "to abandon sailing by big ships."

The most important depictions of Northern European cogs are seen on the great many seals of the German towns belonging to the Hanseatic League, and on the Elbing seal, in particular, which can be dated to around 1350. The cog had a sharply angled straight stem and stern, one rudder, and one square sail mast. When the cog was adopted in the Mediterranean, it probably increased in size, although it still kept its hull shape and sails, as evidenced in Filiasi's *Memorie Storiche di Venezia*, where he refers to cogs that carried 700 to 800 men. A decree, proclaimed by Don Pedro of Aragon in 1340, lists cogs together with big ships "*Que si alguna nau, cocha o altro vexel gros . . .*" ("That if any ship, cog or other large vessel . . .").

After the cog, the next development was the *carrack*, a type of ship whose use became widespread in the Mediterranean and Atlantic Ocean at the beginning of the fifteenth century. A characteristic of the carrack was that it had a square-rigged mast slightly forward of amidships and a lateen-rigged aftermast.

An early portrayal of a carrack can be found in a painting by Gentile da Fabriano, kept in the Vatican Museums. The carrack depicted has its mainsail fitted with a "bonnet," that is, a strip of canvas applied below the gore to increase the sail area. It is a small carrack with just one square-rigged mast and one lateen-rigged mast. Another characteristic of this type of ship is its forecastle jutting well out beyond the stem, normally above the bowsprit, this forecastle always being two or three 'tween decks tall.

In the fifteenth and sixteenth centuries, the carrack increased in size and its sails

(14.31m), two complete decks, plus a main deck and castles three 'tween decks high, both fore and aft. The crew numbered 110 but the ship could carry 700 to 800 men and fifty horses.

From the contract drawn up with Genoa, which in fact supplied the ships described as "*Litteris Comunis Januae . . . pro passagio Domini Regis ultra mare,*" it appears that the Genoese ships had two masts (the tallest one forward), setting lateen sails and two steering oars aft. These ships are defined as ships and not cogs, probably because they were larger and had rigging on two lateen-sail masts. Chapter XI of the *Imposicio Officii Gazariae* of 1441 distinguishes between ships and cogs but, being the same size, gives both the same war apparel. When discussing the ship, it says that it must have a mainsail with a bonnet, therefore a square not a lateen sail, and a second smaller mast. The ships of 1441, therefore, had two square sail masts.

Henry Grâce à Dieu or **Great Harry** (England 1514). This great carrack, built in 1514 by order of Henry VIII of England originally had a rigging system with courses, topsails, and main-topgallant sails set on the two aftermasts. Armament comprised 184 cannons; 130 small-caliber iron ones, and fifty-four larger bronze guns. Unlike the *Ark Royal,* the after superstructure is on two levels only, a quarterdeck and a half deck. The stern bridge is exposed and protected only by an awning or grating. The forecastle has three levels, the highest being covered only abaft the foremast. This carrack has two rows of ports for the broadside guns. There were seven cannons per side on the lower level, seven on the top one, six at main deck level, four above the quarterdeck and three on the forecastle deck. The other 130 small cannons were on the higher decks. Note that the stern is square and the sides have a pronounced tumble home, in other words the hull gradually narrows toward the higher decks, according to an old concept of defense, making it more difficult for the enemy to board. The ship was refitted between 1536 and 1539, but destroyed by fire in 1552. Assumed dimensions: length 131.23ft (40m); beam 29.52ft (9m); deck height 26.57ft (8.10m); draught 18.04ft (5.50m).

Ark Royal (England 1587). Not a carrack, but a galleon, identifiable by the shape of her forecastle, which did not extend beyond the bow, by the cutwater, and by the superstructures on the upper decks which were lower and curved-in less. Sails were the same as on the large carracks: the illustration shows the two aftermasts setting just one lateen sail each. The spritsail is furled and can be seen below the bowsprit. Note that the stern is flat and there are gunports on the transom, too. Armament comprises fifty big-caliber cannons on two gallery decks and the main deck: seven per side in the bottom battery, eight per side in the top one, and eight on the main deck, below the quarterdeck and forecastle. There were also four cannons on the transom stern. In addition to the large cannons, there was also a number of smaller ones. The crew numbered 425 men. The bindings to hold together the various staves of the masts can be seen as well as the large round crow's nests that hide the double-joint between the lower mast and main top-mast. Note also the gallery running round the stern, which is not a feature on carracks. *Ark Royal* was Lord Howard of Effingham's flagship during the naval operations against the Invincible Armada of Spain in 1588.

Dimensions are: length above the waterline 120.73ft (36.80m); beam 28.70ft (8.75m); draught 15.91ft (4.85m); displacement 787t (800 tonnes).

35

were set on four masts, the two foremasts being square-rigged, and the two aftermasts lateen-rigged. In addition, another square sail was fitted below the bowsprit, similar to the "*dolonis*" sail on Roman ships, which became known as the *spritsail*. Whereas in the older carracks the two square-rigged masts had only one yard and one sail, around 1500 to 1520, a second yard was used for the topsail. This sail is depicted in a painting kept at the Greenwich Naval Museum which shows the Portuguese carrack *Santa Caterina do Monte Sinai*, which can be dated to about 1520.

A further increase in sails was achieved by adding main-topgallant yards to the two square-rigged masts and two lateen sails to the two aftermasts, as can be seen on the great English carrack, *Henry Grâce à Dieu* of 1514.

Galleons and carracks had similar sails but differently shaped hulls: Instead of jutting out beyond the bow, the castle rose up much further back, leaving a projecting part in front called a cutwater, an extension of the deck, clearly visible on the English galleon, *Ark Royal*, built in 1587, shown in a painting depicting the destruction of Spain's Invincible Armada at Dover in 1588. The cutwater is shown even more clearly in a painting of the Dutch-built French galleon, *Saint Louis*, of 1626. An interesting feature is a vertical pole at the end of the bowsprit, with a square sail called the spritsail topsail, while below the bowsprit is the normal spritsail. The sails of this galleon are on only three masts, since there is just one lateen-rigged mast aft. The third sail, or main-topgallant sail, on the two foremasts should also be noted. On the great English galleon, *Sovereign of the Seas* of 1637, there is a third and fourth square sail on the two foremasts and two square sails above the lateen sail of the mizzen-topmast.

While sails became ever more complicated on the huge English galleons, in

Holland they were beginning to build ships with much simpler sails, with the aim of reducing the number of crew members needed for maneuvers. These ships, called *fluyts*, had two square-rigged masts, one lateen-rigged mast, a spritsail and spritsail topsail on the bowsprit, and, a feature common to other ships of the sixteenth and seventeenth centuries, a topsail that was bigger than the lower sail.

In the second half of the 1600s the galleon underwent a development which transformed it into the *three-decked warship*. This transformation saw the disappearance of the large multi-deck superstructures fore and aft that were reduced to a poop deck and forecastle just one 'tween deck high and normally not visible, since they were at the same level as the quarter boards of the main deck. A feature of seventeenth- and eighteenth-century three-deckers was the shape of the stern, which in the part out of the water was square, and had elaborate ornaments, and gilt work, as well as rows of wide glass windows for the quarters of the officers, commanders, and high-ranking passengers. In the sails of these three-deckers, it is possible to see the gradual disappearance of the spritsails and the adoption of jibs and stay-sails.

With the adoption of a rounded stern out of the water, the reduction of ornaments and carving, and the complete disappearance of the spritsails, the three-decker took on its final form, which was one that it retained until the middle of the nineteenth century.

Three-deckers were the largest of the warships and up until around the end of the eighteenth century their size and fighting power were indicated by the number of guns. Thus, for example, reference was made to *Vasa*, a sixty-four-gun Swedish three-decker, or *Couronne*, a seventy-two-gun French three-decker. Another type of classification was by "ratings," still based, however, on the number of guns: A

Sovereign of the Seas, later **Royal Sovereign** (England 1637). *Sovereign of the Seas* was a huge galleon built on the orders of Charles I of England, to a design by the famous shipwright, Phineas Pett, at the Woolwich Naval Dockyard. She was intended to be the largest ship in the world, which caused various senior naval authorities to express doubtful opinions about the wisdom of building such a giant. The ship was built all the same and launched in 1637. She was elaborately decorated with ornaments and gilded figures, especially on the cutwater and transom stern.

Three masts were rigged: fore and mainmasts with square sails and a mizzen with mixed lateen and square sails. Both square-rigged masts had four sails, that is, courses, topsails, topgallants, and royals; one more than the British carrack *Henry Grâce à Dieu* (1514) and the galleon *Ark Royal* (1587). Apart from a lateen sail, the mizzenmast had two square sails at the top, like France's *Soleil Royal* (1669) and Sweden's *Wasa* (1627) whereas on her two aftermasts the previously mentioned *Henry Grâce à Dieu* had three and two lateen sails respectively. At the bow, on the bowsprit, were the sprit and spritsail topsail, also present on the *Soleil Royal* and the *Wasa*. Armament was made up of twenty-four twenty-four-pounders in the lower battery, twenty twenty-four-pounders in the top battery and twenty-two eighteen-pounders on the main deck, plus various smaller pieces ranging from nine- to twelve-pounders, on the fore- and quarterdeck. Note that in the illustration showing a side view of the ship, the national flag is blue with a red cross on a white background in the top right-hand quarter; whereas the one on the bowsprit is a Union Jack, used in the period from May 5, 1634, and February 23, 1649; in the two figures showing a stern view of the ship, on the other hand, the national flag is red with the cross against a white background quartered at the top, a flag that was used from February 23, 1649, until 1864, when the White Ensign flag was adopted on warships. Between 1654 and 1660 the ship was modified by Peter Pett, son of Phineas, he cut it down from a three- to a two-decker, thus making it lighter and more maneuverable; but this also reduced the number of cannons. In the Battle of Beachy Head on July 10, 1690, the ship was under the command of Arthur Herbert, Earl of Torrington. The enemy French fleet was under the command of Admiral Conte de Tourville. In the battle *Sovereign of the Seas* encountered the French ships *Content, Entreprenant,* and *Apollon,* carrying sixty cannons. The English squadron had to withdraw and Admiral Herbert was court-martialed, and stripped of his command. After this engagement the ship's name was changed to *Royal Sovereign* and served for another six years; she was destroyed by fire in 1696. Her dimensions were: length 233ft (71m); beam 48ft (14.75m); draught 23.5ft (7.16m); displacement 1,516t (1,541 tonnes); 780 crew.

three-decker with seventy to eighty guns, for instance, was a first rate vessel, one with fifty to sixty was second rate, and so on. In 1700 this rather crude classification was replaced by another which, in addition to the number of guns, also took into account the number of batteries they were arranged in, down the sides of the ship. Thus there was the three-decker which had three superimposed batteries of guns, including the battery on the main deck and therefore (as its name implies) had three decks, the *frigate,* which had two superimposed batteries and therefore two decks, and lastly, the *corvette,* which had just one battery and therefore one deck.

As for sails, three-deckers, frigates, and corvettes had three square-rigged masts, a bowsprit, and jibs. Obviously, as the size of the hull decreased, so too did the masts and sails.

Generally speaking, three-deckers were defined as battleships or ships of the line, whereas frigates and corvettes, less well-armed, did not make up part of the main fighting squadrons.

Ships which had only two instead of three square-rigged masts, still with bowsprit and jibs, were known as *brigs.* If, instead of square sails, they had two or three fore-and-aft rigged masts, in other words, spankers and gaff sails but never lateen sails, they were called *schooners.* A ship that had a square-rigged aftermast and fore-and-aft-rigged mainmast was classified as a *brigantine.* These ships usually had only one deck and one battery of guns.

Sails of tenth to eighteenth century sailing warships

Mediterranean cogs of the tenth, eleventh, and twelfth centuries probably had only one square-rigged mast amidships, and in all probability a raked mast forward with a spritsail, as well—a rig similar to that on Roman freighters. By contrast, Northern European cogs had only one square-rigged mast, as can be seen in the great many examples depicted on seals of that period.

In the depictions on the seals, it will be noted that the masts of cogs had shrouds. Furthermore, at the bow there was a raked pole or boom, not intended to carry stays or sails, but to support two blocks for bowline tackle, required to hold the front edge of the sail taut ahead when sailing close-hauled, in other words, when it was necessary to luff.

The advent of the carrack led to the adoption of mixed sails; a small lateen sail set on the mast positioned aft on the quarter-deck, was added to the large square sail on the central mast. In the sails of the square-rigged masts, apart from shrouds, stays begin to be used in order to give longitudinal stability to the mast. These staysails ended up, for the foremast, on the bowsprit.

One feature of the large square sails on carracks was the *bonnet,* a strip of canvas which served to increase the sail's surface. Whereas on ships in later centuries it was normal to have sails with *reefs* to reduce the area if need be, ships of the fourteenth and fifteenth centuries had this bonnet which served to increase the sail area when there was little wind. The bonnet was ''laced'' to the bottom of the mainsail gore, and for this purpose both the sail and the bonnet had to have a series of holes along their joining edge through which the laces could be threaded.

In the *Imposicio Officii Gazariae* of 1441, mentioned several times above, it was made compulsory for Genoese ships and cogs to have two spare mainsails and a bonnet in addition to the one on the mast.

The sprit and spritsail topsails were held taut in a peculiar manner: The sails of normal masts are held taut by sheets attached to the bottom clews, which pull the canvas toward the end of the bottom yard or toward the deck, but these sails could not be equipped with similar

sheets. They were, therefore, fitted with two heavy weights at the clews so as to keep hauled whatever the circumstances. Since the spritsail could be submerged in the water, it also had holes at the bottom to let the water run out.

The older carracks, with just one square sail, had their masts made in either one piece or several pieces of the same length slotted together and held in place with rope bindings. These masts usually had a round top at the end. When a second sail was used, the mast had to be extended by means of a second mast attached to the first by doubling level with the top. The bottom mast was called ''lower mast,'' the second ''mast'' and, if there was a third, ''pole.'' The lateen sails of the two aftermasts on carracks and galleons, known as mizzen and bonaventure (aftermizzen) masts, respectively, were replaced by a spanker on three-deckers built after 1750.

A further change in sails was the adoption of jibs and staysails: the jibs being arranged on the stays between the aftermast and bowsprit, and the staysails on the stays between the main, mizzen, and after masts. It has already been pointed out that on sixteenth-century galleons and seventeenth-century three-deckers, the topsail was very often bigger than the bottom sail. Usually these large sails had several rows of reefs to reduce their area. As the years went on, the single large topsail was split in two: the bottom half being a fixed topsail and the top half an upper main topsail. These sails were easier to handle and were used on three-deckers and frigates in the late eighteenth and early nineteenth centuries.

The armament of sailing warships from the tenth to the eighteenth century

Up until the end of the fourteenth century, cogs and ships had the same weapons as ancient ships, but even after the introduction of firearms, the armament continued to be of a traditional type.

The *Imposicio Officii Gazariae* of 1441 stipulated that a ship or cog with cargo of 20,000 cantaros (an old measure of weight, varying from fifty to eighty kg., or about 1500 tons) had to be equipped with eight bombards with 200 stones (cannonballs) and three barrels of powder, but added that on board there had to be twenty-two cuirasses, twenty-two breast plates, six billhooks to cut sails and rigging, three grapnels with chain, tacks, vessels full of lime and liquid soap, spears, and arrows.

The weaponry clearly included the usual side arms. It should be explained that tacks were pointed objects thrown onto the decks, together with the liquid soap, to make walking difficult; the lime was used to blind and choke the enemy; and, lastly, the fact that it was compulsory to have cuirasses and spears on board ship shows that a naval battle was normally settled by hand-to-hand fighting. As a matter of curiosity, in a book entitled *Juvincel introduit aux armes,* written by a French admiral named Jean de Beuil in 1439, Greek fire, delphines, and even divers, trained to sabotage the bottoms of enemy ships, are still included among ships' weapons.

In sixteenth-century galleons, armament was made up almost exclusively of firearms. A proclamation made by King Henry III of France in 1584 stating which armament certain sizes of ships had to have (these were mercantile, not war, ships), laid down that ships with forty-five crewmen had to have two ''cardinal'' cannons, four ''long-range culverins,'' twelve ''brace'' cannons, and twelve flamethrowers, but still had twenty-four pikes, and two sickles to cut the rigging and twelve crossbows.

When describing oared ships, we mentioned that on galleys all the artillery was at the bow, while galleasses also had cannons aft, plus a few large muskets and

La Couronne (France 1636). The distinction between a galleon built in the first half of the seventeenth century and a three-decker built in the latter half is a somewhat theoretical one because some ships called galleons had two batteries below the main deck; and the shape of the hull and the sails were not much different from each other, either. A good example is La Couronne, also classified as a galleon, and the first ship built in France by the shipwright Charles Morieur of Dieppe. Hull and sails were similar to those of the Saint Louis, which was probably used as a model. The cutwater at the bow was very wide and long, the forecastle and quarterdeck were the same height as the quarter boards, and the half deck and stern deck were quite high, accentuated by the marked sheer of the deck at the after end. The channels of the two lower masts were level with the gallery deck instead of the main deck. The after gallery, which was flat, was very cumbersome and extended well out beyond the rudder. The armament was on three decks: in the lower battery there were twenty-four eighteen-pound cannons (or culverins), in the top battery twenty eighteen- and nine-pound culverins, and on the main deck twelve nine-pound and sixteen six-pound culverins, some of these on the superstructures as well. There were two cannons below the forecastle that fired ahead and four below the quarterdeck that fired astern. On this ship, too, the topsails were bigger than the courses. Dimensions were: length 131.23ft (40m); beam 49.21ft (15m); deck height 39.37ft (12m); draught 22.96ft (7m); displacement 1,063t (1,080 tonnes); 638 crew.

Gunport or **"sabord."** On sailing ships the guns were arranged on the various decks along the ship's sides. So that the guns on the lower decks could fire, their barrels had to be fired through an opening in the side. In order to prevent the entry of water in high seas or when the ship was heeling, the openings were protected by wooden ports, hinged at the top, that opened outwards.

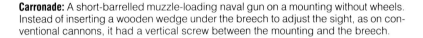

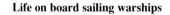

Carronade: A short-barrelled muzzle-loading naval gun on a mounting without wheels. Instead of inserting a wooden wedge under the breech to adjust the sight, as on conventional cannons, it had a vertical screw between the mounting and the breech.

Naval cannon. Naval cannons had a bronze (later iron) barrel, supported by two pivots on a wooden mounting with four wooden wheels. When the cannon was fired, the mounting was pushed up to the ship's side so that the barrel poked out of the port. When the cannon had to be reloaded, it was pulled backwards to be primed with gunpowder, and the ball was placed in the muzzle (muzzle-loading guns).

arquebuses on either side on the quarter boards above the oar tholepins. By contrast, on carracks, galleons, and more modern ships, the main artillery was arranged along the sides and only a few cannons could fire ahead and astern. This was due to a structural feature: Galleys and galleasses did not have a deck on which cannons could be arranged, whereas all sailing ships had one, two, or three decks that were part of the ship's structure and therefore were able to withstand the weight of a great many large caliber cannons. It should be emphasized that, for reasons of stability and structural sturdiness, the larger, heavier cannons were positioned on the lowest deck and progressively lighter ones on the upper decks. The cannons on the main deck and fore and after castle could fire through openings in the quarter boards and railings. These openings did not have to be closed when the ship was underway. The cannons on the lower decks, however, had to fire through portholes in the ship's sides. For safety reasons it had to be possible to close these portholes when the ship was underway. They were rectangular, almost square, in shape and appeared on carracks around 1450. They are said to have been invented by a French carpenter named Deschardes, in 1410, and known in French as *sabords*. On galleasses, arquebuses and other small firearms had already been arranged on the quarter boards, but since the supporting framework of the gunwale was weak, it was not possible to load it with weapons that were bigger than those that could be held by a man, with the help of an iron bracket to rest the barrel on.

The small guns arranged on galleys at the forward end, such as falconets and culverins, had a wooden, wheelless mounting, and to be able to load them, the gunners had to have access to the mouth or muzzle end. By contrast, the cannons on carracks and galleons, as well as on men-of-war and frigates, were mounted on wheels. Reloading involved pulling them back on board and they were drawn backwards and forwards by tackle fixed to the decks and sides.

Cannons improved with time, changing from objets d'art decorated with elaborate relief ornaments to simple bronze or iron tubes. The projectiles, too, originally stone balls, were replaced by iron balls. Iron balls could also be fired chained together in pairs so as to cause greater damage to the masting, or else heated (fireballs), so as to start fires. By the middle of the nineteenth century, however, when the age of steam began, ships' cannons still fired spherical projectiles, did not have rifled barrels, and were all muzzle-loading. The only notable improvement was the introduction of *carronades*, cannons which instead of being mounted on wheels, had a fixed mounting, and instead of having their sights adjusted by inserting a wooden wedge under the breech, had a vertical interrupted-screw breechblock mechanism, placed between the mounting and the breech.

The name derives from the town of Carron, near Falkirk (Firth of Forth) in Scotland, where the first guns of this type were cast in 1774.

One special type of weapon, introduced in the sixteenth century, was the *fire ship*. It was not a weapon, as such, but a small ship (or large boat) loaded with flammable material that was launched in a following wind against enemy ships, with the aim of starting off fires and destroying units.

Life on board sailing warships

When discussing galleys, we spoke of the crew's terrible living conditions. On sailing ships, habitability was decidedly better. First of all there were not huge numbers of oarsmen, freemen, or convicts; secondly, all sailing ships had a main deck and other decks and superstructures in which living quarters could be made, therefore people no longer had to sleep as best they could, but had mattresses and hammocks. It is not exactly clear when the hammock was introduced. It could be taken down during the daytime since it hung on hooks below decks. We know for certain that in the fourteenth century, ships that carried pilgrims to the Holy Land had one hammock shared by two people. One slept with his feet where the other rested his head: *"uno tenente pedes versus caput alterius,"* as described in the "Statuta Massiliae" which refers to *"de placis peregrinorum constituendi."* Venice's *Capitolario Nautico* tells us that the seamen could take a woollen mattress on board weighing seven rotolos (old measure of weight equaling 891g in Naples, 793g in Palermo), and pay a rental for a bed, which would suggest that those who did not pay could lay out their mattresses on deck.

There is no doubt that in seventeenth-century ships the seamen slept in hammocks, and that the officers had cabins in the large after superstructure. As regards toilets and washing facilities, for the officers these were set up in the after balconies or stern-walks, while for the crew, the cutwater, forward, was set aside for this use (hence the modern term "heads").

It was possible to wash with fresh water but always in extremely small amounts, with eight to ten men washing together in the same bath, a practice which continued in the Italian navy, even after the First World War. The ship's kitchen was no longer the rudimentary cook-house that it was on the galleys, but a room usually positioned below the forecastle. It had only one cauldron, however, in which everything was cooked for everyone, except the officers. Meals were therefore somewhat rudimentary, consisting of soups and boiled meat. Lastly, it was impossible to keep perishable foodstuffs on long journeys, so when the fresh supplies, in the form of a few oxen taken on board alive and slaughtered after a few days, were used up, the crew went on to eat salted meat and ship's biscuits, which caused vitamin deficiency and scurvy.

The lack of any form of mechanical energy meant that the various maneuvers had to be carried out with sheer human strength. In particular, a great deal of strength was required to raise the yards of the large sails or to weigh anchor. These operations were performed with the help of windlasses, the most rudimentary having a horizontal shaft and the more advanced type a vertical one, fitted with eight to ten reels which were manned, thus combining the force of forty to fifty people. The capstan was usually positioned below the main deck and its shaft went right down to the keel on which it was pivoted in order to provide the strong base necessary for it to work. Clearly, to weigh the anchor or hoist the yards, it may have been necessary to use pieces of rope to extend those which had to be hauled.

The Matarò ship (Spain c. 1460). The main features of a carrack were her sails and rigging, consisting of partly square-rigged and partly lateen-rigged masts, the latter being smaller and in the after area. The ship shown here is a small carrack reconstructed from a model known as "the Matarò ship," now in the Prins Hendrik Museum in Rotterdam. The hull is rounded and about three times as long as it is wide. At the after end is a quarterdeck that extends up to the mainmast, and at the forward end a tall forecastle. The mainmast is amidships and the yard for the square sail is made up of two partially overlapping sections lashed together with binding. Note the stay that runs from the top of the mast to the forecastle. The second lateen-rigged mast is on the quarterdeck, very near the stern, and also has its spar made of two sections tied together. The three large vertical timbers on the outside of the hull below the quarterdeck and the one at the end of the forecastle are fenders to protect the planking from collisions with quays or other ships. As this ship can be dated to around 1450, there are no firearms. Dimensions would have been: length 98.42ft (30m); beam 29.52–32.80ft (9–10m); height of the main deck 11.48ft (3.50m); draught 8.85ft (2.70m).

Santa Maria (Spain 1480). This was the largest ship in the expedition mounted by Columbus. She was not a caravel like the other two, *Niña* and *Pinta*, but a carrack; Columbus defined her as a "nao" or ship. Her rigging differed from that of the Matarò carrack by including a second square-sail mast (the foremast on the forecastle), a second sail on the main-mast (the topsail), and a spritsail beneath the bowsprit. The lateen-rigged after-mast is typical of a carrack. Dimensions: length 78.66ft (23.60m); beam 26.4ft (7.92m); draught 7ft (2.10m); displacement approximately 250 tons; crew thirty-nine men.

Sparrow (England 1470). The sails were set on two masts, each with just one square sail, and a third mast aft with a lateen sail. Note the forecastle extending well out beyond the bow and the absence of a quarterdeck of any size. Armament comprised eight to ten cannons, all amidships on the main deck. Length was about 114.82ft (35m) and displacement about 344½t (350 tonnes); seventy crew.

La Grande Françoise (France 1535). A typical example of a large four-masted carrack. The foremast had only a main and a topsail; the mainmast had main, top, and topgallant sails; the mizzen two lateen sails; and the bonaventure mast just one lateen sail. Although a large ship, she does not appear to have had ports and guns on the lower decks. Dimensions: length 134.51ft (41m); beam 23.62ft (7.20m); draught 19.35ft (5.90m); displacement 1,106.24t (1,124 tonnes).

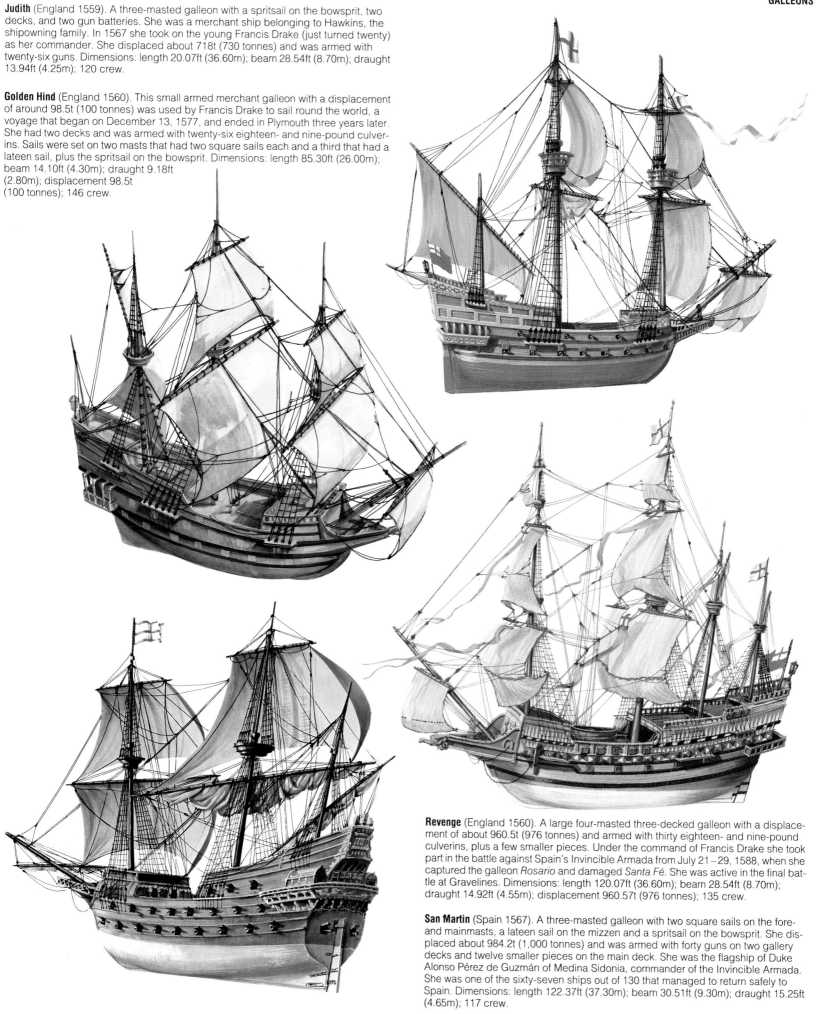

Judith (England 1559). A three-masted galleon with a spritsail on the bowsprit, two decks, and two gun batteries. She was a merchant ship belonging to Hawkins, the shipowning family. In 1567 she took on the young Francis Drake (just turned twenty) as her commander. She displaced about 718t (730 tonnes) and was armed with twenty-six guns. Dimensions: length 20.07ft (36.60m); beam 28.54ft (8.70m); draught 13.94ft (4.25m); 120 crew.

Golden Hind (England 1560). This small armed merchant galleon with a displacement of around 98.5t (100 tonnes) was used by Francis Drake to sail round the world, a voyage that began on December 13, 1577, and ended in Plymouth three years later. She had two decks and was armed with twenty-six eighteen- and nine-pound culverins. Sails were set on two masts that had two square sails each and a third that had a lateen sail, plus the spritsail on the bowsprit. Dimensions: length 85.30ft (26.00m); beam 14.10ft (4.30m); draught 9.18ft (2.80m); displacement 98.5t (100 tonnes); 146 crew.

Revenge (England 1560). A large four-masted three-decked galleon with a displacement of about 960.5t (976 tonnes) and armed with thirty eighteen- and nine-pound culverins, plus a few smaller pieces. Under the command of Francis Drake she took part in the battle against Spain's Invincible Armada from July 21 – 29, 1588, when she captured the galleon *Rosario* and damaged *Santa Fé*. She was active in the final battle at Gravelines. Dimensions: length 120.07ft (36.60m); beam 28.54ft (8.70m); draught 14.92ft (4.55m); displacement 960.57t (976 tonnes); 135 crew.

San Martin (Spain 1567). A three-masted galleon with two square sails on the fore- and mainmasts, a lateen sail on the mizzen and a spritsail on the bowsprit. She displaced about 984.2t (1,000 tonnes) and was armed with forty guns on two gallery decks and twelve smaller pieces on the main deck. She was the flagship of Duke Alonso Pérez de Guzmán of Medina Sidonia, commander of the Invincible Armada. She was one of the sixty-seven ships out of 130 that managed to return safely to Spain. Dimensions: length 122.37ft (37.30m); beam 30.51ft (9.30m); draught 15.25ft (4.65m); 117 crew.

Triumph (England 1576). A four-masted galleon with two square-sails on the fore- and mainmasts, two lateen sails on the mizzen, and one on the bonaventure mast. She made a name for herself under the command of Martin Frobisher in the Battle of Gravelines on July 29, 1588, when Spain's Invincible Armada was destroyed. Dimensions: length 120.73ft (36.80m); beam 30.83ft (9.40m); draught 15.94ft (4.86m); displacement 875.9t (890 tonnes); 189 crew.

Victory (England 1571). A three-masted galleon with a spritsail and spritsail topsail on the bowsprit. She had three gun batteries with eighteen eighteen-pound culverins in the lower battery, twenty in the upper one, and smaller pieces on the main deck. She took part in the battle against Spain's Invincible Armada and on July 29, 1588, off Gravelines, mounting an unsuccessful attack on the Spanish ship *Gran Grifon*. Dimensions: length 105.15ft (32.05m); beam 41.66ft (12.70m); draught 13.38ft (4.08m); 120 crew.

Roter Löwe (Holland 1597). A galleon built for the Elector of Brandenburg. She had only two decks and one battery of twelve twenty-four-pounders plus another twelve guns on the main deck and quarterdeck. There were two square-rigged masts, both of which had a course and topsail, and one lateen-rigged mast, plus a spritsail on the bowsprit. She was smaller than Spain's *San Martin* and England's *Triumph*. Dimensions: length 131.23ft (40.00m); beam 26.24ft (8.00m); draught 13.12ft (4.00m).

Brederoe (Holland 1650). A galleon with conventional sails on three masts and a sprit-sail. Although she was built fifty to ninety years after the other galleons just described, her lines were much the same. She had only one battery of twelve nineteen-pounders, plus twelve small guns on the main deck. She was the flagship of Maarten Tromp, who died on board in the battle of Scheveningen against the English in 1653. Dimensions: length 127.95ft (39.00m); beam 29.92ft (5.35m); displacement 1,094t (1,112 tonnes); 366 crew.

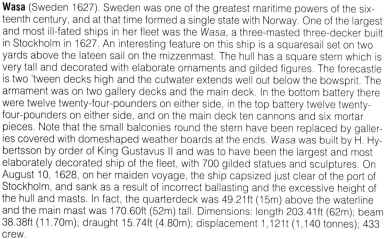

Wasa (Sweden 1627). Sweden was one of the greatest maritime powers of the six-teenth century, and at that time formed a single state with Norway. One of the largest and most ill-fated ships in her fleet was the *Wasa,* a three-masted three-decker built in Stockholm in 1627. An interesting feature on this ship is a squaresail set on two yards above the lateen sail on the mizzenmast. The hull has a square stern which is very tall and decorated with elaborate ornaments and gilded figures. The forecastle is two 'tween decks high and the cutwater extends well out below the bowsprit. The armament was on two gallery decks and the main deck. In the bottom battery there were twelve twenty-four-pounders on either side, in the top battery twelve twenty-four-pounders on either side, and on the main deck ten cannons and six mortar pieces. Note that the small balconies round the stern have been replaced by galler-ies covered with domeshaped weather boards at the ends. *Wasa* was built by H. Hy-bertsson by order of King Gustavus II and was to have been the largest and most elaborately decorated ship of the fleet, with 700 gilded statues and sculptures. On August 10, 1628, on her maiden voyage, the ship capsized just clear of the port of Stockholm, and sank as a result of incorrect ballasting and the excessive height of the hull and masts. In fact, the quarterdeck was 49.21ft (15m) above the waterline and the main mast was 170.60ft (52m) tall. Dimensions: length 203.41ft (62m); beam 38.38ft (11.70m); draught 15.74ft (4.80m); displacement 1,121t (1,140 tonnes); 433 crew.

De Zeven Provincien (Holland 1665). *De Zeven Provincien* was a famous Dutch three-decker whose structure closely resembled that of a galleon. Her name refers to the seven provinces which, after the Peace of Westphalia (1648), formed the new state of the Netherlands, now independent of Spain. This ship, with her three decks, one more than the *Saint Louis,* had the same rigging, that is, two square-rigged masts and one lateen-rigged, in addition to the spritsail amd spritsail topsail. It should be stressed that the topsails were much bigger than the courses and that the crow's nests were no longer in the form of round baskets. Another interesting feature is that the shrouds of the three masts are fixed to chainwales outside the ship's sides, as had already been done on carracks and galleons. The armament consisted of thirty forty-two-pounders, fifteen per side in the bottom battery, thirty twenty-four-pounders in the top battery and twenty twelve-pounders on the main deck and castles. The quarterdeck was much lower than it was on galleons and the forecastle was the same height as the quarter boards of the main deck, making it almost invisible from the out-side. The *De Zeven Provincien* was De Ruyter's flagship in the Battle of Sole Bay fought on June 7, 1672, in which the Dutch defeated the allied fleets of England and France. Estimated dimensions: length 203.41ft (62m); beam 42.65ft (13m); height 22.63ft (6.90m); draught 14.76ft (4.50m); 743 crew.

Soleil Royal (France 1669). The French Navy built this three-decker in answer to England's *Sovereign of the Seas*, although she was smaller and had less canvas. Her sails differed from those on the English ship in that she had no topgallants on the two square-rigged masts. The hull profiles were similar and so too was the very high stern with three superimposed galleries, all topped by a gigantic panel on which were placed the three impressive lanterns, signifying that she was flagship. The armament consisted of thirty-six forty-two-pounders, twenty-eight of which were in the lower battery and eight, four per side, in the middle of the top battery, which had ten twenty-four-pounders either side at the ends. Similarly, there were eight twenty-four-pounders amidships on the main deck, plus ten eighteen-pounders either side. There were another four eighteen-pounders aft and two forward above the cutwater below the forecastle, in addition to ten smaller guns on the superstructures. This was the first three-decker to be built according to the technical regulations issued by the French Admiralty concerning the building and fitting-out of warships. She took part in naval operations against the British fleet at Bévéziers (Beachy Head) on July 10, 1690, and at Barfleur on May 29, 1692, when she was so seriously damaged that she ran aground on the coast near Cherbourg where the English fireship, *Blaze,* attacked and destroyed her. Dimensions: length 199.63ft (60.85m); beam 42.91ft (13.08m); draught 20.83ft (6.35m); displacement 1,292.25t (1,313 tonnes); 836 crew.

Saint George (England 1690). A three-decker with sails on three masts, main and fore-masts with three square sails each, and mizzen with a lateen sail and, at the top, a square sail set between two yards (one at the top and one at the bottom). The spritsail and spritsail topsail yards, without sails bent to them, can be seen at the bowsprit. The main and foremasts were of a composite structure, made up of several sections held together by clearly visible joints and bindings. Note that the topsails are larger than the courses, a typical feature of sails of that time. The hull is fairly well developed in the part underwater, but once out of the water has a large transom stern with three superimposed galleries extending into short side galleries. All this was lavishly deco-rated with gilded figures and ornaments and surmounted by the three lanterns, iden-tifying the admiral's flagship. Armament was split onto three decks: twenty-eight thir-ty-two-pounders in the bottom battery; fourteen twenty-four-pounders in the top one and eighteen guns and twenty-six smaller pieces on the main and quarterdecks. The reconstruction is based on a model in Great Britain. Dimensions: length 195.53ft (59.60m); beam 38.71ft (11.80m); draught 17.71ft (5.40m); displacement 1,275.52t (1,296 tonnes); 657 crew.

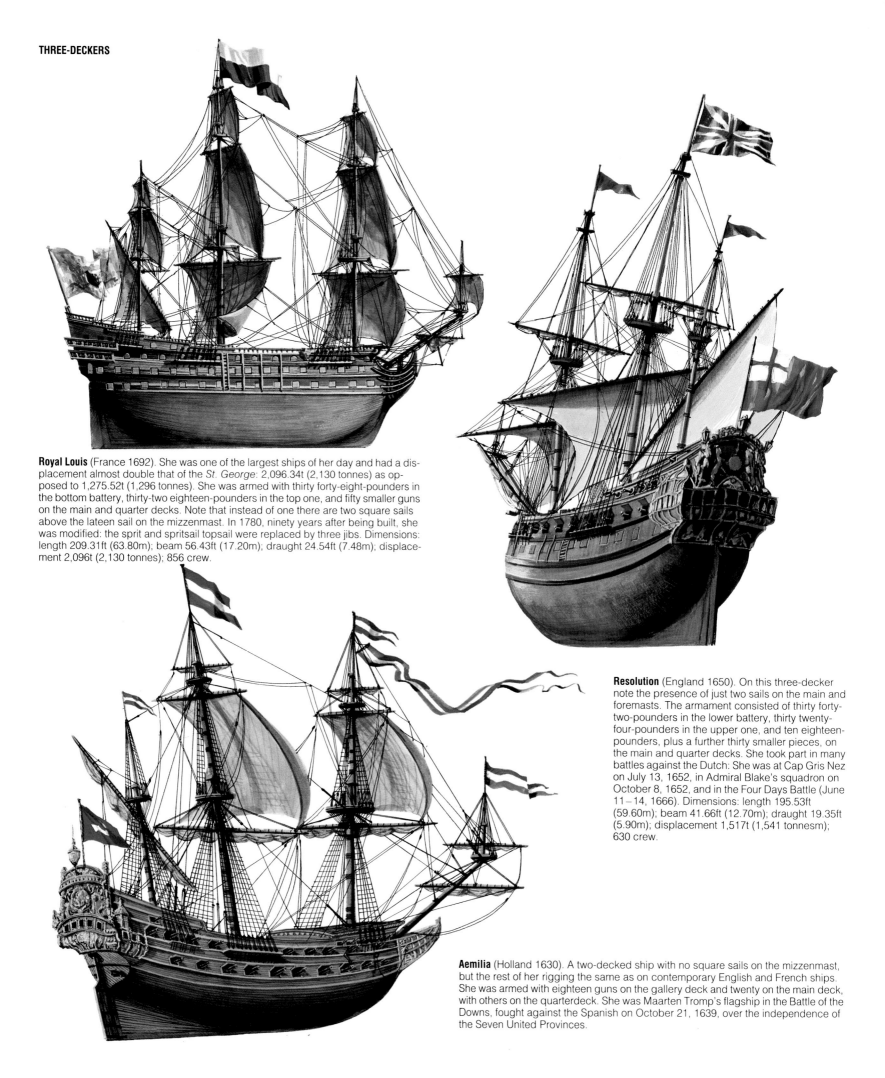

Royal Louis (France 1692). She was one of the largest ships of her day and had a displacement almost double that of the *St. George*: 2,096.34t (2,130 tonnes) as opposed to 1,275.52t (1,296 tonnes). She was armed with thirty forty-eight-pounders in the bottom battery, thirty-two eighteen-pounders in the top one, and fifty smaller guns on the main and quarter decks. Note that instead of one there are two square sails above the lateen sail on the mizzenmast. In 1780, ninety years after being built, she was modified: the sprit and spritsail topsail were replaced by three jibs. Dimensions: length 209.31ft (63.80m); beam 56.43ft (17.20m); draught 24.54ft (7.48m); displacement 2,096t (2,130 tonnes); 856 crew.

Resolution (England 1650). On this three-decker note the presence of just two sails on the main and foremasts. The armament consisted of thirty forty-two-pounders in the lower battery, thirty twenty-four-pounders in the upper one, and ten eighteen-pounders, plus a further thirty smaller pieces, on the main and quarter decks. She took part in many battles against the Dutch: She was at Cap Gris Nez on July 13, 1652, in Admiral Blake's squadron on October 8, 1652, and in the Four Days Battle (June 11–14, 1666). Dimensions: length 195.53ft (59.60m); beam 41.66ft (12.70m); draught 19.35ft (5.90m); displacement 1,517t (1,541 tonnesm); 630 crew.

Aemilia (Holland 1630). A two-decked ship with no square sails on the mizzenmast, but the rest of her rigging the same as on contemporary English and French ships. She was armed with eighteen guns on the gallery deck and twenty on the main deck, with others on the quarterdeck. She was Maarten Tromp's flagship in the Battle of the Downs, fought against the Spanish on October 21, 1639, over the independence of the Seven United Provinces.

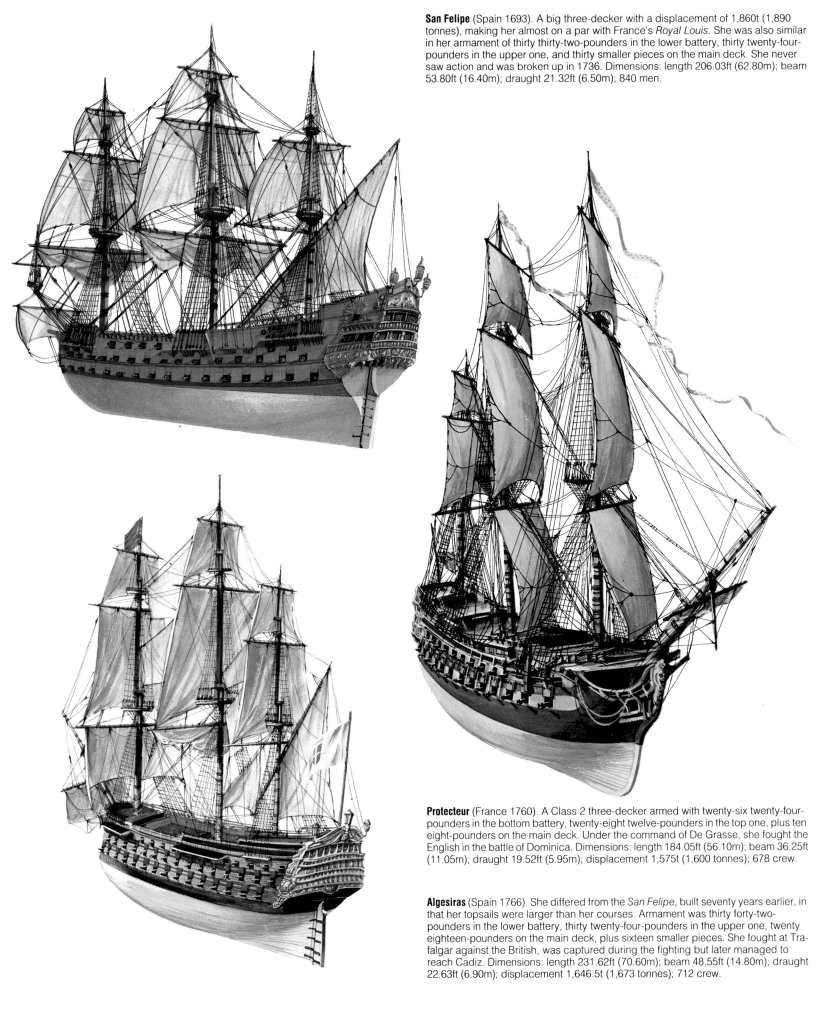

San Felipe (Spain 1693). A big three-decker with a displacement of 1,860t (1,890 tonnes), making her almost on a par with France's *Royal Louis*. She was also similar in her armament of thirty thirty-two-pounders in the lower battery, thirty twenty-four-pounders in the upper one, and thirty smaller pieces on the main deck. She never saw action and was broken up in 1736. Dimensions: length 206.03ft (62.80m); beam 53.80ft (16.40m); draught 21.32ft (6.50m); 840 men.

Protecteur (France 1760). A Class 2 three-decker armed with twenty-six twenty-four-pounders in the bottom battery, twenty-eight twelve-pounders in the top one, plus ten eight-pounders on the main deck. Under the command of De Grasse, she fought the English in the battle of Dominica. Dimensions: length 184.05ft (56.10m); beam 36.25ft (11.05m); draught 19.52ft (5.95m); displacement 1,575t (1,600 tonnes); 678 crew.

Algesiras (Spain 1766). She differed from the *San Felipe,* built seventy years earlier, in that her topsails were larger than her courses. Armament was thirty forty-two-pounders in the lower battery, thirty twenty-four-pounders in the upper one, twenty eighteen-pounders on the main deck, plus sixteen smaller pieces. She fought at Trafalgar against the British, was captured during the fighting but later managed to reach Cadiz. Dimensions: length 231.62ft (70.60m); beam 48.55ft (14.80m); draught 22.63ft (6.90m); displacement 1,646.5t (1,673 tonnes); 712 crew.

THREE-DECKERS

Victory (England 1765). *Victory* was Nelson's flagship in the Battle of Trafalgar. She is the most famous three-decker of all, and survives to this day in her original condition. She was built at the Naval Dockyard in Chatham and launched on May 7, 1765. Her rigging had undergone some changes in comparison to earlier ships, with the introduction of jibs (triangular sails set on the stays between the bowsprit and foremast) and the removal of the lateen sail on the mizzenmast, replaced by a spanker. The hull had a simpler line achieved by the removal of the half deck and stern bridge above the quarterdeck, and the galleries round the stern were smaller, although the shape of the cutwater at the bow had not changed. The chainwales of the main and foremasts had been raised to main deck level. In 1805, *Victory* was armed with thirty thirty-two-pounders in the lower battery, twenty-eight twenty-four-pounders in the upper battery, thirty twelve-pounders on the main deck, ten twelve-pounders on the quarterdeck and two twelve-pounders and two sixty-eight-pound carronades on the forecastle. Note that on top of the main deck amidships there were beams that supported both the boat chocks, and two gangplanks connecting the quarterdeck with the forecastle. She was taken out of commission in the early nineteenth century, dismasted, and converted into a depot ship; but at the beginning of this century she was restored to her original condition, and to this day is in commission with a commander and a crew made up, not of sailors and gunners, but tourist guides. On the anniversary of the Battle of Trafalgar, Nelson's flag signal is hoisted: "England expects that every man will do his duty." Dimensions: length 226.24ft (68.96m); beam 51.41ft (15.67m); draught 25.09ft (7.65m); displacement 3,174t (3,225 tonnes); 850 crew.

Berlin (Brandenburg 1674). The frigate *Berlin* was built in Holland and had the same outward appearance as a galleon, with her forecastle curved inwards in relation to the cutwater and a quarterdeck with a half deck aft. The basic difference is not easy to see from the outside since the frigate has only one covered gun deck instead of two, like three-deckers, and therefore can have only two broadside batteries. The rigging is like that of carracks, galleons, and three-deckers, that is, two square-rigged masts and one lateen-rigged aft, plus the sprit and spritsail topsail on the bowsprit. There are three square sails per mast, the topsails being bigger than the courses in this case too. *Berlin* carried twelve seven-pounders, six per side on the gallery deck, and six five-pounders, three per side on the main deck, which was very modest in comparison to that carried on the big three-deckers. Towards the end of 1676, *Berlin* captured the Swedish mail schooner, *Maria,* which was carrying important military documents. In November 1675, she engaged the French frigate *Royal de Dunkerque,* forcing the latter to withdraw. She then fought against Spanish ships in Flanders. After being detached to the West Indies, she was captured by Dutch ships from the East India Company in 1688.

Dimensions: length 74.14ft (22.60m); beam 20.34ft (6.20m); draught 18.70ft (5.70m); 100 crew.

Winchester (England 1695). One of England's first frigates, she was still classified as a "6th rater"; in other words, she had only one gun deck. Sails and hull lines were like those of the three-deckers, although frigates were smaller. Both frigates and three-deckers were "ships of the line," included in the battle formation. Armament was in the form of twenty thirty-two-pounders in the battery and eighteen nine-pounders on the main deck. Dimensions: length 181.98ft (55.47m); beam 38.71ft (11.80m); draught 18.37ft (5.60m); displacement 1,545t (1,570 tonnes); 456 crew.

Bounty (England 1787). *Bounty* was not a real warship but an armed merchantman with a crew supplied by the navy. The large English, Dutch, and French merchantmen that voyaged to India and the Far East were, however, armed and crewed like warships. *Bounty* was a conventional frigate with a rounded hull (at the stern too), a quarterdeck and a forecastle just one 'tween deck high and not visible because it was hidden by the high quarter boards. There was still a cutwater below the bowsprit. Interesting features of the rigging include the three jibs on the bowsprit and the spanker on the mizzenmast. The ship was armed with twenty-four eighteen-pounders positioned on the main deck and below the quarterdeck; being a merchantman, there were no guns on the covered deck because it was here that the cargo was stowed.

In December 1787, *Bounty* left Spithead bound for the company's islands with a cargo of breadfruit trees. There was considerable animosity between the commander, William Bligh, and the Second Mate Christian Fletcher. But they reached Tahiti and stayed there for five months; when it was time to leave; some of the crew, led by Fletcher, mutinied; they put Bligh and eighteen men in the lifeboat with provisions and water and abandoned them. After some exceptionally skillful navigation, Bligh reached the island of Timor. Some of the mutineers returned to Tahiti, while others went to the island of Pitcairn. The men on Tahiti were captured and three of them were condemned to death.

Dimensions: length 179.78ft (54.80m); beam 44.29ft (13.50m); draught 21ft (6.40m); dfisplacement 964.5t (980 tonnes); 46 crew.

Constitution (United States 1797). *Constitution* and six other frigates were built by the United States Navy with the aim of protecting the merchantmen trading in the Mediterranean from being attacked and preyed upon by pirates from North Africa. In the building specifications it was requested that these ships should not be forced to engage themselves in combat unless conditions were to their advantage. They therefore had to be extremely fast so that they could disengage themselves at will from contact with an enemy. Like all late eighteenth-century frigates, she had a handsome line and a rounded stern. She had "ship's" sails, that is, three square-rigged masts, although the mizzenmast had a spanker instead of a course. The bowsprit had a jib boom and three jibs. All the masts had a topgallant and royal. Armament consisted of thirty twenty-four-pounders in the battery and twenty-two forty-two- and thirty-two-pound carronades below the quarterdeck, foredeck, and main deck. *Constitution* was important in various battle operations: on December 29, 1812, under the command of Captain William Bainbridge, she sank the forty-nine gun British frigate *Java,* off Bahia on the coast of Brazil. She was then posted to the North African coast, to pursue pirates. She remained in service until 1881, and during her eighty-four years of life underwent many changes, including some to her rigging. Restored to her original condition, she is now in the Boston Navy Yard. She remains on the Navy List, even though she has been converted to a museum. Dimensions: length 172.90ft (52.70m); beam 44.29ft (13.40m); draught 22.63ft (6.90m); displacement 1,650t (1,677 tonnes); 540 crew.

Independence (United States 1798). Unlike the *Havfruen,* this frigate no longer has a spritsail, but "studding sails," in other words, two narrow sails set on two extensions to the yard, in addition to the sails carried on the yard, itself, bent to the fore and topmast yards. All three masts had topgallants. She carried thirty twenty-four-pound carronades on the gallery deck and twenty-two thirty-two-pounders on the main deck. She was one of the first ships to have copper sheeting on her keel to prevent the growth of algae. Dimensions: length 168.30ft (51.30m); beam 43.96ft (13.40m); draught 22.24ft (6.78m); displacement 1,159t (1,178 tonnes); 356 crew.

Havfruen (Denmark 1789). A frigate which, like England's *Bounty* and America's *Constitution,* has sails on three masts with a spanker on the mizzen (instead of a lateen sail), jibs, and staysails—sails not used on the frigates and three-deckers of 1650–1680. Note the studding sails on the main topsail. Armament was twenty-six eighteen-pounders on the gallery deck and fourteen eight-pounders on the main deck. Dimensions: length 213.25ft (65.00m); beam 45.60ft (13.90m); draught 22.96ft (7.00m); displacement 1,279t (1,300 tonnes); 326 crew.

La Pomone (France 1794). The frigate *Berlin* of 1674 was one of the prototypes for this type of ship while *La Pomone,* built in 1794, represents its most developed form. The hull has become sleeker and the bulky after superstructures have been replaced by a one 'tween deck-high quarterdeck. The sails, too, have changed, with the removal of the spritsails at the bow, although the bowsprit is extended by the jib boom and the jib; flying jib and foretopmast staysail are on the three stays that run from the bowsprit to the foremast; furthermore, the lateen sail on the mizzenmast has also been replaced by a spanker. Armament was made up of twenty-six thirty-six-pounders on the gallery deck and twenty-six twenty-four-pounders, sixteen of which were below the quarterdeck and ten on the main deck. There were also eight nine-pound demi-culverins on the quarter- and fore decks. Below the quarterdeck, as usual, were the officers' quarters, sectioned off by simple movable partitions which were removed during combat, when the guns had to be maneuvered. This ship was decorated in a very simple fashion and only on the raised part of the stern. In the early nineteenth century, ships were usually painted black with a white band level with each battery of guns. Dimensions: length 179.95ft (54.85m); beam 39.37ft (12m); draught 20.01ft (6.10m); displacement 1,518t (1,543 tonnes); 342 crew.

La Belle Poule (France 1834). This was the third French frigate to bear this name: The first was in service from 1755 to 1781, the second built in 1801–1805, with *La Belle Poule* in service from 1834 to 1868. She had the simple lines common to nineteenth century ships, with no gilt work or large galleries round the stern. The armament consisted of sixty thirty-pounders (or thereabouts), half on the gallery deck and half on the main deck, plus a few eighty-pound howitzers. She was used as an escort for the ships of the French India Company. In 1859, during the Italian War of Independence, she was detached to Genoa. Dimensions: length 177.16ft (54.00m); beam 49.21ft (15.00m); draught 18.70ft (5.7m); displacement 1,476t (1,500 tonnes); 465 crew.

The corvette

The corvette was the smallest of the warships in the man o'war family. Like ships and frigates, she had three square-rigged masts, bowsprit, and jibs, with a spanker on the mizzenmast. A distinguishing feature of the corvette was that she had only one deck and therefore only one battery of guns on the main deck. In actual fact, some corvettes had two decks, a structurally strong lower deck to support the weight of the guns, and an upper deck of a much less sturdy structure for the crew and rigging operations. Ships of this type were called "covered-battery corvettes" or "decked corvettes."

General Pike (United States 1813). She took part in the War of 1812 (1812–1815), operating against the British fleet on Lake Ontario. She had three square-rigged masts, jibs, and spanker on the mizzen. (It is worth noting the five sails on the foremast and mainmast, a fairly unusual type of rigging. She was armed with twenty-six twenty-four-pound guns, all under cover.) While under construction, she was damaged, on May 29, 1813, by the British, but went into service anyway and was stricken in 1825. Dimensions: length 144.98ft (44.19m); beam 36.97ft (11.27m); draught 14.76ft (4.50m); displacement 861t (875 tonnes); 300 crew.

Astrolabe (French 1811). She was originally called *Coquille*. She had the normal three square-rigged masts, bowsprit, and jibs. She went on hydrographic expeditions in the Mediterranean, then on August 11, 1822, set off to sail round the world under the command of Lieutenant Duperrey, with Jules Dumont D'Urville of the same rank as second in command. In 1826, the ship was renamed *Astrolabe*. On April 25, she set sail for a second voyage round the world under the command of D'Urville, now a commander. From 1837 to 1840, still under D'Urville's command, she explored Tierra del Fuego and the South Pacific. She made a second voyage into the polar regions off South America in 1847–1850. She was armed with fourteen six-pounders. She was withdrawn from service in 1851. Dimensions: length 101.04ft (30.80m); beam 28.54ft (8.70m); draught 11.97ft (3.65m); displacement 374t (380 tonnes).

The brigantine

The brig differed from the corvette in its rigging, with sails set on two masts instead of three. The hull had just one deck and, therefore, just one battery of guns. Brigs were used to provide fast connections with distant ports, for maritime policing operations and, in combat, as "order repeaters." In fact, in a line ahead formation of forty to fifty ships, it was impossible for the commanders of the ships at the head or end of the line to see the flag signals hoisted by the flagship, which was usually in the middle of the line. Similarly, the ships at the tail end of the line could not see the signals if the flagship was at the head of one of the lines, in the formation prescribed by Nelson. For this reason two or three brigs, positioned alongside the line of ships, raised the flag signals being transmitted by the flagship (which they could easily see from their position outside the formation) and these could then be seen by the other units in the line.

Daino (Kingdom of Sardinia 1844). *Daino* was built in Genoa at the Foce Dockyard for the navy of the Kingdom of Sardinia. She had two square-rigged masts, bowsprit, jibs, and spanker on the main mast. The hull profile now lacked the old cutwater which had been replaced by a new streamlined one. The battery was made up of fourteen 3in (80mm) guns arranged seven per side on the main deck. During her time in the Sardinian Navy she took part in the 1848 war against Austria, under Persano's command. In 1861 she was transferred to the Italian Navy, where she served as a cadet training ship until 1869. She was then handed over to the Garaventa Foundation in Genoa and used for the purposes of recreation. Dimensions: length 108.13ft (32.96m); beam 29.65ft (9.04m); draught 14.04ft (4.28m); displacement 492t (500 tonnes); 135 crew.

La Tactique (France 1792). A twenty-gun brig, built at St. Malo. She had brig sails on two masts with four square sails each, a spanker on the main mast, jibs on the bowsprit, and various staysails set on the stays between the main and fore masts. The twenty-gun battery was on the main deck, the four after pieces, interestingly enough, two per side below the quarterdeck. Her dimensions are not known.

Sealark (England 1843). A brig armed with twelve thirty-two-pound carronades in a single battery on the main deck. She had a short forecastle and a quarterdeck aft, both of which could not be seen from the outside because the sides amidships were as tall as the superstructures. The masts were very tall with four square sails each. The topsails are of interest since they are very large and have four reefs. She was taken out of commission and sold in 1898. Her dimensions are not known.

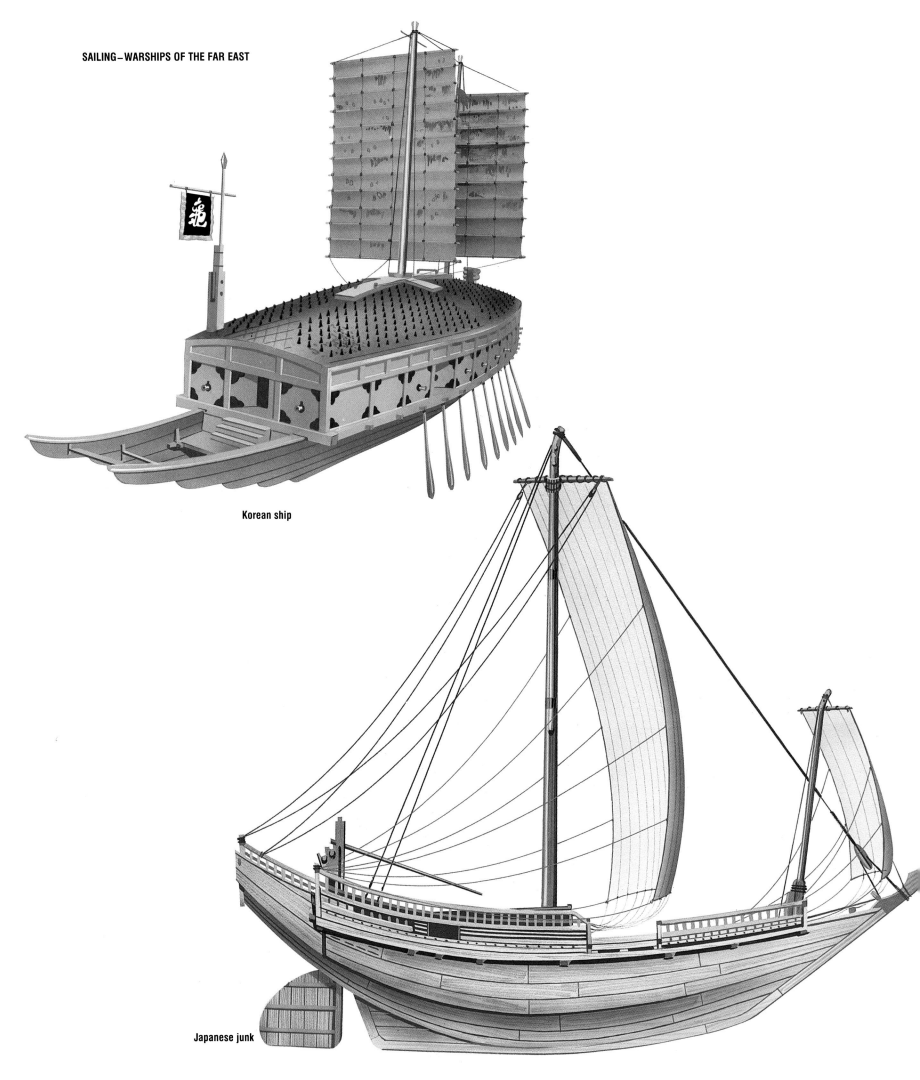

Korean ship

Japanese junk

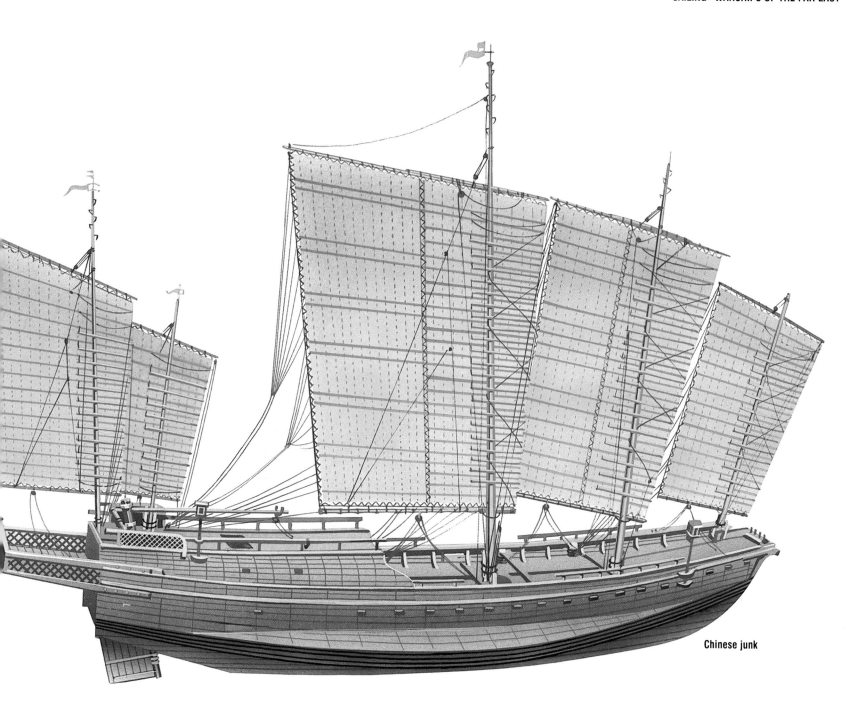

Chinese junk

Sailing—warships: China, Japan, Korea. China is a country with a civilization that is thousands of years old, and we have information about her ships from Marco Polo's *Milione,* although it is not very detailed. But because sailing—warships and merchantmen in the West were more or less the same, we can assume that the same goes for those in the Far East. The Chinese junk, which was still in use up to the end of the Second World War, was about 164ft (50m) long, 46–49ft (14–15m) in the beam, and had five masts with rectangular mat-sails. The foremasts and the mast second from the stern could be lowered to reduce the sail area and there was also a system for reefing the other sails. The hull was in the form of a pontoon, and rectangular in shape (hardly pointed at all at the bow and stern, which both had transoms). The junk had a long quarterdeck and a single large rudder. In order to maneuver the sails on the sternmost mast, there was a stern walk that overhung the transom stern. To judge from a sixteenth-century engraving, the war junk of that time had only two masts with sails set on two booms (lug sails), high quarter boards either side, a poop deck, and a sort of ram at the bow.

Unlike the Chinese junk, the Japanese junk had a more compact hull with a greater sheer, although it did have a straight, sharply raked stem and a stern very high out of the water. The latter extended beyond the rudder with a structure forming part of the hull, unlike the small balcony on the Chinese junk. The hull had only one deck with neither quarter- nor fore deck, like contemporary European ships. The rigging was very simple, and did not entail the five masts of Chinese junks. There was only one tall mast amidships, setting a narrow rectangular sail secured by one sturdy stay forward

and two aft. Later on, there was also another small raked mast forward, which, as on galleys, was not stepped in the keel but had only one support on the deck, which would suggest that it could be lowered. Note that the main deck beams overhang either side of the hull in order to make the deck wider and thus provide more cargo space. There is only one rather large rudder, which was maneuvered by a long tiller. The sails are made of cloth, not matting.

Korea had mixed sail- and oar-powered warships of which we have descriptions that are sufficiently detailed to enable a reconstruction to be made. They are known as the "armored ships" or "turtle ships" of Admiral Li Sun Chin, who used them in the 1592–1598 war against Japan.

These ships had a raft-like hull, with a transom bow and stern, and a strange structure aft comprising an extension of the ship's two sides. There were two sails, of the same type as those used on junks. In addition, there were nine or ten oars either side, arranged in an almost vertical position and lacking the Western-style tholepins that were handled differently than the oars on Mediterranean galleys. The most striking feature of these units, and that gives them their name, is that they have a protective turtleback structure over the main deck which extended along the entire hull, except for the after extension. This structure was covered by a metal sheet with iron spikes to prevent the enemy from boarding the ship since he would have been unable to walk on them. Armament consisted of 4in (10cm) caliber bronze broadside guns and four smaller guns, two forward and two aft in the flat area above the transom. These ships were 116.4ft (33.5m) long and 27.8ft (8.5m) in the beam.

THE AGE OF STEAM

The development of warships in the nineteenth and twentieth centuries

The history of warships up to the eighteenth century can be split into three periods: antiquity, the age of oared ships, and the age of sailing ships. By contrast, their history from the mid-nineteenth century to the present day cannot be divided in a similar fashion. We have therefore considered it more appropriate to outline a brief history of the development of the various types of ships that existed in the period between the latter years of the nineteenth century and post-World War II.

Warships changed slowly until they took on the form of three-deckers, frigates, and corvettes (ships that made up the world's fleets until around 1850). Then, in the short space of a few decades, they completely changed their appearance, means of propulsion, armament, and method of combat. This is not due solely to the adoption of steam propulsion, but also to the technological progress in other areas that occurred in the final years of the last century and has continued at an even faster pace in this century.

The great three-deckers of 1850 were no different from the carracks of 1450 except for slight modifications in hull shape, a few sail changes, and a certain amount of improvement in the making of firearms. By contrast, a three-decker of 1850 was a completely different vessel from an ironclad of 1880–1890, both in external appearance and hull shape, but above all in armament. This was due to the enormous progress that had been made in weaponry. The use of steam for propulsion and for operating the various pieces of machinery on board is almost of secondary importance in this transformation. What would have been the advantages, indeed, for naval ships had they been limited to achieving propulsion independent of the wind, had their hulls continued to be made of wood, had their guns still limited to a range of close on 3,000ft (800–900m), and had candlelight and semaphore continued to be used?

The great Industrial Revolution, which occurred during the nineteenth century, had an enormous influence on the development of the warship. In the first place, progress in metallurgy made it possible to move from wood to iron and on to steel in hull construction, which made possible the construction of ever larger and stronger hulls, weighing only a third or a quarter as much as similar hulls of wood. This same progress in metallurgy, combined with that in ballistics, led to the manufacture of guns that, instead of firing spherical balls over a distance of less than a mile, fired pointed projectiles over a distance of three or 3.7 miles (5–6km), later increasing to eleven or twelve miles (19–20km). Progress in mechanics made it possible to equip ships not only with power units but also with machinery that replaced human strength in the various ship's maneuvers such as the sailors' tasks of weighing the anchor and hauling the mooring ropes, but above all in maneuvering the large turret guns which would have been impossible to do by hand. Lastly, the development of electricity in its various applications for lighting, motive power, and telecommunications greatly increased the fighting capability of all ships. This progress, however, was blocked by a still insurmountable natural obstacle which was the fact that, both in normal sailing and in combat, men had to depend exclusively on their own sight to get their bearings, fire the guns, and direct maneuvers. For this reason it was impossible to fight at night, submarines became invisible when they were submerged, ships had to lay low in the water, camouflaged so as to be less distinguishable from a distance, even with a telescope, and the visible horizon was the maximum range at which a naval battle could be contemplated.

The use of radar, sonar, and aircraft broke down even these last barriers, as was clearly shown during the 1939–1945 war.

Nomenclature of warships from 1850 to 1945

The disappearance of special names for sail-powered warships was due not so much to the use of steam propulsion, but to the use of iron and steel in hull building and to the improvement of weapons, that was occurring at the same time.

Steam propulsion had not changed the situation to any great extent; in fact in the decade of 1860–1870 there were still ships classified as "screw ships," "paddle frigates," or "steam corvettes." Even the use of armor did not lead to any substantial changes because there were "armored frigates," "armored corvettes," and "armored batteries."

With the passing of time, the abolition of masts and sails, and above all, the abandoning of guns in a battery down both the ship's sides, came a new name for large warships which, around 1870, simply were known as ironclads or battleships. Those units which, in terms of size and armament, came after ironclads, were called cruisers. These, too, could be armored and on the basis of the arrangement of the armor, they were separated into armored cruisers and protected cruisers. In more modern times, around 1910–1915, due to an increase in speed and armament, the armored cruiser developed into the battle cruiser and the distinction between armored and protected cruisers was dropped and replaced by a single type known as the light cruiser. After the First World War, cruisers were subdivided into two types: heavy and light.

The use of the steam engine reintroduced an ancient weapon: the ram, which had had a fleeting success in the Battle of Lissa (1866). Both ironclads and cruisers therefore had rams, but so too did smaller specialized ships, such as the Italian *Affondatore*.

The development of a new weapon, the torpedo, introduced a new type of ship into the world's navies: the torpedo boat.

Since the large battleships and cruisers were not sufficiently fast and maneuverable to fight and defend themselves against these small torpedo boats, a new type of ship emerged: the torpedo-boat destroyer or simply "destroyer"; it was originally designed to fight torpedo boats but has retained its name even though its duties have changed completely.

Torpedo boats and destroyers were called collectively torpedo craft or light craft, in contrast to battleships and cruisers which are heavy ships.

In the early 1900s, the first submarines began to be included in navies. As the years went by they were subdivided into various types: short-range, sea-going, and fleet types.

During the First World War, another very small warship was introduced: the motor torpedo boat or motor gunboat (abbreviated to MTBs).

In the First World War the British and German Navies had used a few ships to transport, lower into the sea, and recover seaplanes, but only after the end of the war did a real aircraft carrier become operational. This type of unit was to develop in the twenty-year period between the two world wars until it became the most important ship of the Second World War.

The first ships equipped as minelayers and minesweepers also began service in the First World War, improving, along with the development of mines, even after the Second World War. Lastly, in the Second World War, the terms frigate and corvette were brought back into use, no longer to indicate ships with one or two batteries of guns, but to describe a type of escort ship especially equipped for anti-aircraft and anti-submarine defense.

After the 1939–1945 war, battleships and torpedo boats disappeared from the fleets, and so now war vessels are classified as submarines, aircraft carriers,

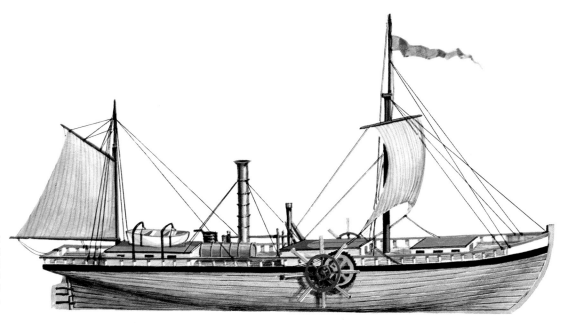

Clermont (United States 1806). Built by Robert Fulton, she was the first steamship to operate a regular passenger service between New York and Albany. She had elegant lines and a flat-bottomed hull. Her steam engine drove two paddle-wheels and developed a speed of 4.7 knots.

cruisers, destroyers, frigates and corvettes, motor torpedo boats, and motor gunboats and minesweepers, plus a few other types of special ships such as amphibious craft.

The power plants of ships from 1850 to 1945

The use of steam propulsion on warships did not result in rapid transformation of ships; on the contrary, it was opposed for many years and masts and sails were retained even on ships built around 1880. Although the early merchant steamships, such as Robert Fulton's *Clermont*, dated back to 1807, in fleets the first steamships were small despatch boats or paddle corvettes that came into service about twenty-five years later, around 1830. The first units were perhaps the 177-ton French despatch boat *Sphinx*, with a 158hp (160CV) engine, and the French steam corvette *Archimède*, both built in 1830. In Italy, the first two steamships were the despatch boats of the Bourbon Navy, followed by the despatch boat *Gulnara*, bought from England in 1835 by the Sardinian Navy.

The first ninety-gun screw ship of the line was the French vessel *Napoléon*, built in 1850. She had an 888hp (900CV) engine and a speed of 13.5 knots. The first two ironclad frigates in the world were also screw ships: the French *Gloire* of 1861, with a 2,502hp (2,537CV) engine and speed of 12.85 knots, and the British *Warrior* of 1862, with a 5,395hp (5,470CV) engine and speed of 14.35 knots.

After the favorable experiment carried out with these prototypes, the various navies even fitted out ships already in commission and built solely as sailing ships with a propeller power plant.

A ship's power plant comprises two separate components: the steam generator, made up of one or more boilers in which the working fluid (steam) is produced, and the engine, where the steam's energy is converted into mechanical power and turns the shaft of the propeller or paddlewheels.

In the early stages, boilers were very rudimentary, cylindrical in shape, and built of copper or iron sheets, which meant that the steam could only reach very low pressures of around 7.1 lb/in^2 (0.5kg/cm^2). At first, wood was used as fuel, replaced around 1830–1835 by coal and only in 1905–1915 by fuel oil.

For paddle ships, the most widely seen engine was the ''rocker arm'' type, usually having just one vertical cylinder; the rod worked a rocker arm, at the other end of which was a connecting rod that drove the crank fixed to the paddle wheel axles. Another type of engine for paddle and screw ships was the ''oscillating cylinder'' type, which had one or two cylinders free to oscillate round a horizontal shaft so that the piston rod could be attached directly to the crank. They were known as ''Penn'' engines after the name of the English firm that built them. For screw ships, the older type of engines had one or more horizontal cylinders, since on single screw ships the shaft was down the center line and the cylinder, or cylinders, had to be positioned laterally; this limited the piston stroke and the engine's power. This problem was overcome by using engines with reverse connecting rods where instead of being placed after the piston rod, the connecting rod reversed towards the cylinder and the crankshaft was positioned between the cylinder and the cross-head sliding block. The piston stroke was thus doubled in comparison to that of an engine with a normal connecting rod.

Horizontal engines with an oscillating cylinder were double-acting, in other words the steam acted alternately on the two sides of the piston. A subsequent improvement led to the double-expansion engine where the steam worked first in a high-pressure cylinder and then in a low-pressure one, thus giving increased efficiency.

After having served its usefulness in the cylinders, the steam passed into a condenser, the oldest of which were mixture types. In these condensers the steam was condensed by cooling, using jets of sea water, and the boilers were also fed with sea water. The salt contained in this water deposited on the walls of the boilers and condensers causing dangerous scale. When mixture condensers were replaced by surface condensers, where the cooling water circulated inside tubes and did not come into contact with the steam, boilers were no longer fed with sea water but with fresh water instead. Thus, sea salt scale was avoided but scale from the calcareous salts in the drinking water was not; so, as boilers improved, they began to be fed with distilled water, and this system is still in use today.

Between 1870 and 1875 cylindrical boilers were replaced by shell boilers, operating at higher pressures. Engines developed from being horizontal to vertical (also known as ''inverted cylinder'' engines). The latter were better balanced than horizontal engines and so the piston could travel faster, which meant a greater number of revolutions per minute for the propeller.

Two of the first ironclads to be fitted with vertical engines were the Italian *Duilio* and the British *Inflexible*, both launched in 1876.

The early screw ships had had just one propeller: then in 1869 there were two on the British ironclad *Captain*, (cruisers already had two propellers) and in 1862 on the Confederate States of America (Southerners') ship *Tallahassee*.

It should be mentioned that in order to limit engine size and at the same time increase motive power, many ships had two low-power engines on just one propeller shaft. The British ironclad *Devastation* of 1871, for example, had four engines on two propellers and so too did Italy's ironclads *Italia* and *Lepanto* of 1880. One of the first cruisers to have two engines per propeller was Britain's *Shannon* of 1876. Among the first ironclads to have three propellers were the French *Henry IV* of 1899 and the German *Nassau* Class vessels of 1908; the first cruisers were the U.S. *Columbia* and *Minneapolis* of 1894, the German *Fürst Bismarck* of 1897 and *Scharnhorst* of 1906, as well as the French *Dupuy de Lôme* of 1890 and *Jeanne d'Arc* of 1899. There were a great many smaller ships with three propellers.

The maximum number of propellers on normal naval ships was four. The first battleships with four propellers were the British *Dreadnought* of 1906 and the Italian *Dante Alighieri* of 1910 and the four *Conte di Cavour* Class ships of 1911–1915, all fitted with turbines instead of reciprocating (piston) engines.

The only examples of six-propeller ships with reciprocating engines were the Russian circular ironclads *Vize Admiral Popov* and *Novgorod* of 1876.

Returning to the subject of boilers, around 1885–1890 fire-tube shell boilers began to be replaced by water-tube boilers which were lighter and produced steam at a higher pressure. Double-expansion engines developed into triple-expansion ones and they had up to four cylinders. The huge reciprocating triple-expansion four-cylinder engine represents the peak in the development of this type of engine, reached in 1895 and remaining as such until 1905–1910 when the old piston engine was replaced on naval ships by the turbine.

The steam turbine could be used on land-based plants but some of its characteristics prevented its use on ships. In the first place, in order to give good performance a turbine had to rotate very rapidly, whereas propellers rotated most efficiently at only eighty to one hundred rpm. In the second place, a turbine had only one direction of rotation and therefore could not operate in reverse.

The problem of the speed of rotation was resolved by a few manufacturers, such

Napoléon (France 1850). She was the first steamship of the line and was built by Stanislas Dupuy de Lôme. She was armed with ninety guns, had a displacement of 1,840t (1,870 tonnes) and could reach a speed of 13.5 knots, which was truly remarkable for that time.

as Parsons of England with their reaction turbines, and Curtiss of America with their multi-stage impulse turbines. The turbine was first tried out in England in 1894 on an experimental ship named *Turbinia*; then it was installed on small torpedo boats and, in 1903, on the cruiser *Amethyst*. Among the first battleships to as Parsons of England with their reaction turbines, and Curtiss of America with their multi-stage impulse turbines. The turbine was first tried out in England in 1894 on an experimental ship named *Turbinia*; then it was installed on small torpedo boats and, in 1903, on the cruiser *Amethyst*. Among the first battleships to have turbine engines were Britain's *Dreadnought* (1906), Italy's *Dante Alighieri* (1910), Russia's *Gangut* (1911), and Austria's *Viribus Unitis* (also 1911). As for cruisers, apart from the previously mentioned *Amethyst* and the other British ships, there were also the German *Lübeck* of 1904, the Austrian *Saida* of 1912, the Brazilian *Bahia* of 1909, and the Italian *San Marco* of 1908. All battle cruisers built between 1907 and 1918 had turbine power units.

On all turbine ships, the problem of reversing was solved by fitting a special engine separate from the forward speed one.

Just as with alternating engines there was a move from those with one cylinder to those with two, three, and four cylinders, so too with turbines where an engine with just one turbine was replaced by one with a set of two turbines, one high- and one low-pressure, or three turbines, one high-, one medium- and one low-pressure. On the early ships with turbines directly linked to the propeller shafts, the high-pressure turbine usually drove one propeller and the low-pressure another. Britain's *Dreadnought* thus had two sets of turbines on four shafts and so too did France's *Jean Bart*, Japan's *Kongo* Class ships, and others. On the Italian battleships *Dante Alighieri* and the four *Conte di Cavour* Class, however, there were three sets of turbines on four shafts, the two side propellers being driven by one high- and one low-pressure turbine (one behind the other on the same shaft), and one of the two middle propellers by the high-pressure turbine and the other by the low-pressure turbine of the third set.

During and after the First World War reduction gears were introduced, allowing turbines to run at much higher speeds, and therefore more efficiently. (Note that the U.S. Navy tried to achieve much the same result by using turbo-electric drive, in which the turbines ran electric generators, which in turn ran the electric motors turning the propellers. This system was used in the four battleships and two aircraft carriers, but was abandoned because it was too heavy, compared to reduction gearing.) As a result, the turbines themselves could be reduced in size. Beyond this, the other main improvements in steam plants have come from the use of a more efficient fuel, oil, and from increases in operating temperature and pressure.

Coal had been the fuel used for boilers until up to about the First World War, when it was generally replaced by fuel oil. As early as the 1890s, oil had been tried out in boilers on small torpedo boats. In the Italian Navy, the Chief Naval Engineer, Vittorio Cuniberti, designed oil burners which were fitted to torpedo boat boilers of the day and became prototypes that were copied all over the world. The transition from coal to fuel oil was quite slow, and it is a significant fact that many ships built between 1900 and 1910 had partly coal-fired and partly oil-fired boilers. In addition to making it easier to operate the boilers, fuel oil also gave a higher rate of steam production, about 20 to 25 percent more, which made it possible to vary speed rapidly, a very important requirement at sea.

The major drawback to oil was that, whereas coal was plentiful, few major nations had large oil supplies on their own territory. The United States, which adopted oil in 1911, was the major exception. For Britain, adopting oil fuel in 1912 required a political effort to control the source of that oil, in the Persian Gulf. Germany deliberately avoided adopting oil fuel during World War I because she had no ready source of oil. The problem was very real: When oil supplies to Britain were cut off by submarines during World War I, the oil-burning battleships were nearly immobilized. Similarly, the Italian fleet was immobilized in 1942–1943 for lack of oil.

Up to the Second World War, all large ships had steam engines, the only exception being the German *Deutschland*-type battleships which had diesel engines, quite widespread on warships built after 1950–1960. The German *Deutschland*-type battleships, also called pocket battleships, were built in Germany in 1931, still within the limits laid down by the Versailles Peace Treaty, and were fitted with diesel engines both to remain within the displacement limit of 10,00 tons and to achieve extremely long range, for commerce raiding. The Germans abandoned this type of engine when they rejected the Versailles limits, and began to build much larger ships.

However, they continued to value the long range the diesel promised, and planned diesel plants for several classes of capital ships. The temporary abandonment of diesels can be laid to what the Germans hoped were temporary limits on maximum output per engine.

Ships' weapons from 1850 to 1945

The main weapons used on ships up to the Second World War were: the gun, torpedo, anti-aircraft weapons, and aircraft.

The early steamships were built and armed like the sailing ships that came before them: They had iron or bronze guns with a smooth-bore barrel and a wooden mounting on wheels and were muzzle-loading. The first ironclad ship in the world, the French *Gloire* of 1861, had breech-loading guns, however, with a breech-block designed for land guns by Treuille de Beaulieu, an artillery colonel. These guns fired spherical balls; aiming was very approximate and the rear sight was adjusted by means of a wooden wedge pushed under the breech to the desired degree.

The first great step forward came with the rifled-bore barrel and the cylindrical ogival-shaped shell. A rifled barrel gives its shells a spin that results in greater stability of the trajectory and therefore greater firing accuracy. As guns became larger and heavier, their number decreased. Hence the sailing ship arrangement in a battery down either side of the ship gave way to a central citadel. In the most extreme case, guns were mounted, singly or paired, in revolving turrets. The U.S. *Monitor* (1862) was the prototype. From about 1865 through about 1885 navies built both turret and central-battery ships. In all of these vessels, instead of being mounted on wheels, guns were trainable. The key development was in recoil braking systems (initially using friction brakes and later hydraulic brakes). By the 1880s, it was standard for guns to be mounted in barbettes or turrets. The guns in barbettes were uncovered and positioned inside a low armored ring intended to protect the rotating platform and its mechanisms. Guns in turrets, however, had their breeches and mechanisms enclosed in an armored box, normally the same thickness as the side armor. The older ships had extremely large-caliber guns, reaching 17.7in in the Italian *Duilio* and *Dandolo*. Around 1880, the caliber was reduced, as improved powders made for higher muzzle velocities. Armor penetration depends on shell energy, which is not proportional to the weight of the shell but to the square of the velocity. Lighter shells were also easier to handle, and lighter guns were easier to maneuver. In the Royal Navy, for example, the standard fell from 16.25in to 13.5in and then to 12in. After 1910, calibers began to increase again and in the First World War reached 15in (381mm) and 16in (406mm) for battleships, and 18in (457mm) on the British battle cruiser *Furious*. The weight of a 15in (381mm) gun shell is around 1920lb, and that of an 18in (457mm) one 3600lb.

After the First World War, the Washington Naval Arms Limitation Treaty (1922) restricted gun caliber to 16in (406mm) for battleships and to 8in (203mm) for cruisers. These limits were exceeded only by the Japanese for their *Yamato*-type battleships, which had 18in (460mm) guns.

The First World War saw the first bombings of ships and installations by airplanes and seaplanes. In the interwar years, weapons were therefore developed to resist air attack, which usually took the form of a combination of medium-caliber rapid-fire guns (3in to 6in caliber) and of machine guns. The machine guns were usually arranged with two to four barrels on the same mounting so as to achieve a greater concentration of fire. In the Second World War, large battleships had anti-aircraft armament comprising over one hundred machine guns. On the American *Missouri* types, for example, there were eighty 1.57in (40mm) and forty-nine 0.78in (20mm) machine guns, making a total of 129.

Medium-caliber was adopted for the heavier anti-aircraft weapons to achieve a high rate of fire and also so that the barrels could easily be maneuvered to follow fast targets. Navies began the Second World War with what proved grossly insufficient anti-aircraft armament, and during the conflict the number of weapons, especially machine-guns, was greatly increased.

Another ships' weapon of this period was the torpedo, a weapon which is not fired like a gun shell but is self-propelled, like a small submarine, by motors that at first were compressed-air ones and more recently electric.

Torpedoes were first tried out in Austria in 1864 by an Englishman named Robert Whitehead. In 1868, Whitehead put forward a second model of his torpedo. It was 13ft (4m) long, covered a distance of 1,968.5ft (600m) at a speed of six knots and carried a 59.5lb (27kg) charge.

Progress and improvements were made on the torpedo and in the First World War its range was 3560yds (6000m) and warhead 330.6lb (150kg). In the 1939–1945 war this increased to 13,120 yds (12,000m) with a warhead of 661.2lb (300kg). It was the major weapon of submarines and torpedo boats. In the period preceding the First World War, battleships were also armed with torpedoes, but this weapon was abandoned, although it did remain on cruisers and smaller ships. A special type of torpedo was designed and used on torpedo planes.

The most important naval weapon of the Second World War was the airplane, although only one special type of unit was equipped with it. This was the aircraft carrier, with her flight deck for take-off and landing of the various types of aircraft which, depending on the armament they carried, were classified as bombers, dive bombers, and torpedo planes, plus fighter planes needed to stand up to enemy aerial formations on the attack.

In the period between the First and Second World Wars, almost all battleships and large cruisers were equipped with reconnaissance seaplanes that could be launched by catapults but on their return had to land in the sea. These planes were used for reconnaissance and for spotting the fall of shot. In the latter role they could considerably extend the effective range of gunfire. They were abandoned after World War II, when carrier aircraft provided better reconnaissance and helicopters could be used for spotting.

The naval battle at the end of the nineteenth century

One of the first battles fought by fleets made up of steam-powered ships was the Battle of Lissa which took place on July 20, 1866, between Italy and Austria. This was, in fact, the first battle to be fought by screw ships and did not lead to tactical innovations in comparison with those in use in the sailing ship navy: the Italian ironclad fleet presented itself in a line-

Ferdinand Max (Austria 1865). An armored battery with a wooden hull. She was Tegetthoff's flagship in the Battle of Lissa and sank the ironclad *Re d'Italia* with her ram. She still carried masts and sails, although these were removed in 1875. In 1895, after thirty years of service, she became a Gunners Training Ship at Pola. She was stricken in 1916.

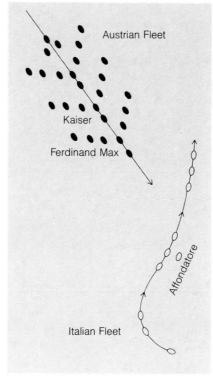

The Battle of Lissa (July 20, 1866). The diagram shows the positions taken up by the Italian and Austrian Fleets at the beginning of the Battle of Lissa. The Italian squadron, ordered by Admiral Persano to move from Ancona towards Lissa, was made up of eleven ironclads and an armored-ram, *Affondatore*.

The Austrian squadron, under the command of Admiral Tegetthoff, had taken up positions in the port of Pola, which it left on July 19, to engage the enemy formation. Tegetthoff could count on seven ironclads and seven wooden ships.

In the Battle of Lissa, the main weapon was the ram, because of the poor range of the guns (which fired round shot).

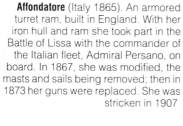

Affondatore (Italy 1865). An armored turret ram, built in England. With her iron hull and ram she took part in the Battle of Lissa with the commander of the Italian fleet, Admiral Persano, on board. In 1867, she was modified, the masts and sails being removed; then in 1873 her guns were replaced. She was stricken in 1907

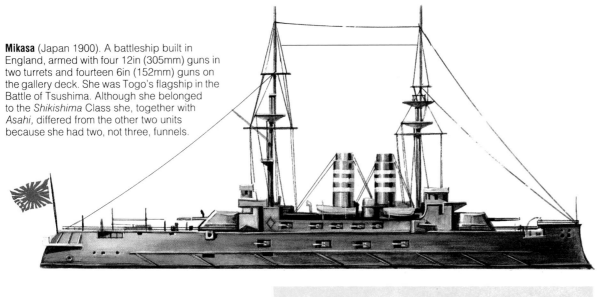

Mikasa (Japan 1900). A battleship built in England, armed with four 12in (305mm) guns in two turrets and fourteen 6in (152mm) guns on the gallery deck. She was Togo's flagship in the Battle of Tsushima. Although she belonged to the *Shikishima* Class she, together with *Asahi*, differed from the other two units because she had two, not three, funnels.

Shikishima (Japan 1900). With *Hatsusé, Asahi,* and *Mikasa*, she was one of a class of four ships built in England for the Japanese Navy. She took part in the Battle of Tsushima. She was then downgraded in 1912 to a coast defense ship, and in 1923 was taken out of commission and became a training ship. She was sold in 1945 and broken up in 1948.

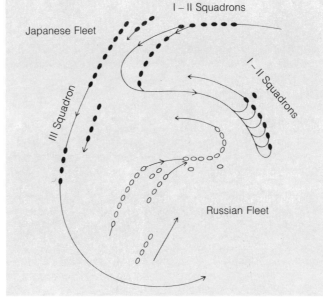

The Battle of Tsushima (May 27, 1905). Fought during the 1904–1905 Russo-Japanese War, this battle marked a significant development in naval tactics and highlighted the uselessness of the ram. The diagram shows the initial stages of the battle. The first and second Japanese Squadrons were proceeding in the same line, the third in a parallel line. The Russian Squadron was advancing in a single line. It sighted the enemy on the port side and took advantage of the fog to change formation and confuse the enemy; but when the fog lifted, the first and second Japanese Squadrons were on the starboard side. Fighting took place at maximum gun range and demonstrated the superior fire power of the Japanese.

Petropavlovsk (Russia 1898). A battleship that had both main and secondary armament in turrets. In the Russo-Japanese War (in which the Battle of Tsushima took place), she was the flagship of Makarov, commander of the Russian Pacific Squadron. She was sunk by a mine on April 13, 1904.

ahead formation whereas the Austrian navy took on a wedge formation, collided with the Italians, and succeeded in cutting through the line, breaking up the ships into small groups and, in the skirmish that followed, Admiral Tegetthoff, with his ship *Ferdinand Max*, rammed and sank the Italian ironclad, *Re d'Italia*. The Austrian ironclad *Kaiser* also tried to ram *Re di Portogallo* but the attempt was unsuccessful. The Battle of Lissa brought naval tactics back to those used in the age of oared ships, when the ram was the main weapon, while artillery fire was not exploited to the full due to the poor range of the guns that still fired ball-shaped projectiles.

A naval battle employing completely different tactics was the Battle of Tsushima, May 27, 1905, where the outcome was not settled by the ram but by artillery.

This battle was fought between the Russian fleet, commanded by Admiral Rozestvenskij, and the Japanese, commanded by Admiral Togo.

The Russian fleet, which left the Baltic ports on October 14, 1904, after having sailed round Africa and across the Indian Ocean, reached the China Sea after over seven months, on May 20, 1905. It was Rozestvenskij's intention to reach Vladivostok, Russia's Far East naval base, by going through the Korea strait, but on the night of May 26th he was sighted by Japanese ships. The Battle of Tsushima was fought on the line-ahead formation and emphasized the importance of long-range artillery. It also made it perfectly clear that, in order to fight, the ships had to be able to see each other and that just a little fog or cloud and, needless to say, nightfall, were enough to put a stop to fighting.

The Russians' first sighting of the Japanese was on the port side and when taking up battle formation Rozestvenskij took this into account. But when the fog cleared, he found that he had the main body of the Japanese forces on his starboard side. The Japanese immediately opened fire at maximum range, sinking and damaging many Russian ships which, shortly before sunset, were attacked also by torpedoes from destroyers. As night fell, the surviving Russian units, under the command of Admiral Nebogatov, made their way northwards unchallenged. But at daybreak they were again attacked by superior Japanese forces and forced to surrender.

The naval battle in the First World War

In the ten years between the Battle of Tsushima and the First World War, warships were improved, submarines became a powerful weapon, and improved radio communications made it possible for ships at sea to link up with their land-based commands and to communicate with each other, even though there were

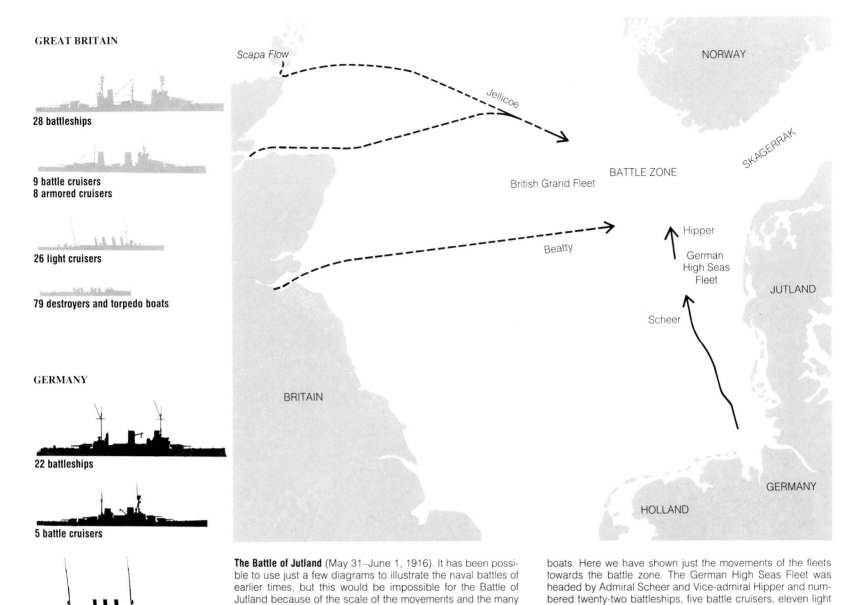

GREAT BRITAIN

28 battleships

9 battle cruisers
8 armored cruisers

26 light cruisers

79 destroyers and torpedo boats

GERMANY

22 battleships

5 battle cruisers

11 light cruisers

62 destroyers and torpedo boats

Scapa Flow

Jellicoe

NORWAY

SKAGERRAK

BATTLE ZONE

British Grand Fleet

Beatty

Hipper

German
High Seas
Fleet

JUTLAND

Scheer

BRITAIN

GERMANY

HOLLAND

The Battle of Jutland (May 31–June 1, 1916). It has been possible to use just a few diagrams to illustrate the naval battles of earlier times, but this would be impossible for the Battle of Jutland because of the scale of the movements and the many maneuvers carried out by the two opposing fleets during the long drawn-out fighting. A British publication describing this battle runs to five volumes and contains over a hundred maps and insets showing the various stages, starting with the reconnaissance divisions first sighting each other and engaging, and ending with the nighttime engagement between the German High Seas Fleet and the British *Black Prince* and torpedo boats. Here we have shown just the movements of the fleets towards the battle zone. The German High Seas Fleet was headed by Admiral Scheer and Vice-admiral Hipper and numbered twenty-two battleships, five battle cruisers, eleven light cruisers, and sixty-two destroyers and torpedo boats. The British Grand Fleet, commanded by Admiral Jellicoe and Vice-admiral Beatty, advanced in three columns towards the agreed meeting place, and was made up of twenty-eight battleships, nine battle cruisers, twenty-six light cruisers, eight armored cruisers, and seventy-nine destroyers and torpedo boats.

certain limitations. One of the basic conditions to be able to fight, however, was still to sight the enemy, since every action and maneuver was decided by the commanders after having seen the situation with their own eyes. For this reason the "admiral's bridge" on ships of that period, and today's ships too, was in an elevated position, usually inside an armored conning tower, above the ship's navigating bridge.

The most important naval battle to take place in the 1914–1918 war was the one known to the British as the Battle of Jutland and to the Germans as the Battle of Skagerrak, fought from May 31 to June 1, 1916, between the German High Seas Fleet and the British Grand Fleet. This battle, in which practically the entire fleets of the two contending nations were engaged and which involved battleships, battle cruisers, and destroyers was, to all practical purposes, history's last great naval battle.

Fighting commenced through the initiative of the Germans, whose fleet put to sea on the night of May 30th. The British, informed by their intelligence network, left that same night, ahead of the Germans. The first contact came on May 31, at 14.48 between the opposing cruiser squadrons heading the main body of battleships. They opened fire at a distance of nine miles (14.5km). Later on, at 18.15, the German fleet came into gun range with the bulk of the British Home Fleet. The encounter lasted for a few minutes because the German High Seas Fleet reversed course and the British lost sight of it.

Noticing that his ships were not very badly damaged, Scheer decided to change course again and at 19.05 gunnery contact with the enemy forces was renewed. The German fleet immediately found itself in difficulty due to poor visibility. It therefore reversed course again (at 19.13) and fighting practically ceased, with just the odd encounter between destroyers and light craft, although the two fleets were both looking for each other.

The German fleet passed unseen astern of the British and reached its bases unchallenged. There were heavy losses in this naval encounter: British ships sunk numbered three battle cruisers, three armored cruisers, and eight destroyers; 6097 dead; German ships sunk numbered one battleship, four light cruisers, and five destroyers; 2551 dead. But more than the losses, this battle, like Tsushima, shows us how, at that time, the lack of aerial reconnaissance and modern electronic detection equipment could have led to situations that nowadays would be inconceivable. The lack of aerial reconnaissance meant that the two opposing fleets were searching for each other without knowing each other's movements. The information on which the admirals had to make their decisions was based on sightings by scout ships, such as cruisers, which often conflicted with each other due to errors in assessing the positions and types of ships detected. The first examples of cooperation between aircraft and shipping came in the Battle of Jutland. Admiral Beatty, on the British side, ordered the seaplane carrier, *Engadine*, during the initial search stage, to send out scouts, but the only aircraft to take off and report that the Germans had reversed course had to make a sea landing after half an hour due to breakdown. Scheer, for the Germans, ordered airship reconnaissance on June 1st at

61

THE HOME FLEET AGAINST BISMARCK

The sinking of Bismarck (May 27, 1941). The map shows the route taken by the battleship *Bismarck* from May 18–27, 1941, the latter date when she was sunk. The battleship *Bismarck* and the cruiser *Prinz Eugen* left Gdynia (Danzig) on May 18, 1941, hugged the Norwegian coastline, then sailed north of Iceland, and headed for the Atlantic. Practically all the ships of the British fleet set off in search of them. On the evening of May 23, after five days under way, the two German ships met with the British battle cruiser *Hood* and the battleship *Prince of Wales* in the waters off Iceland. In the gun battle that followed (which raged through the night), *Hood* was sunk and the *Prince of Wales* damaged. After this encounter, *Prinz Eugen* broke away from *Bismarck* and continued southwards. *Bismarck*, however, headed for the middle of the Atlantic. The British Home Fleet, which had set off from Scapa Flow on May 22, and the *Rodney* Group, which set out on May 23, patrolled the central Atlantic region in search of the enemy.

Bismarck was sighted by an aircraft on the morning of May 26, and attacked by torpedo planes from the *Ark Royal*. That same evening she was reduced to a floating wreck which was shelled by *King George V* and *Rodney* on the morning of May 27, and sunk by a torpedo from the cruiser *Dorsetshire*. *Prinz Eugen* managed to reach a French port. This action, which was not a naval battle as such, did not take place in a restricted area of water, like the Battle of Lissa and the Battle of Jutland, but was spread out across an entire ocean.

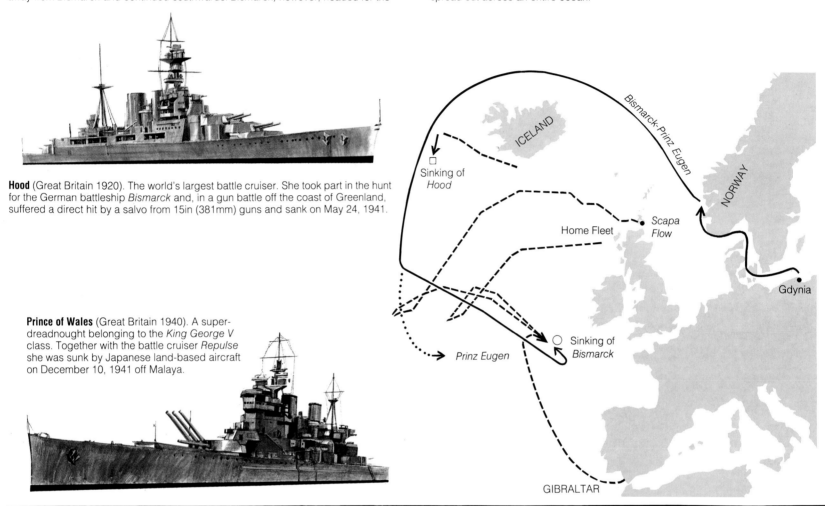

Hood (Great Britain 1920). The world's largest battle cruiser. She took part in the hunt for the German battleship *Bismarck* and, in a gun battle off the coast of Greenland, suffered a direct hit by a salvo from 15in (381mm) guns and sank on May 24, 1941.

Prince of Wales (Great Britain 1940). A super-dreadnought belonging to the *King George V* class. Together with the battle cruiser *Repulse* she was sunk by Japanese land-based aircraft on December 10, 1941 off Malaya.

daybreak. One of these sighted Admiral Beatty's cruisers, as well as the ships of the Grand Fleet, and reported as much, but Scheer did not consider this sighting reliable and acted accordingly. The lack of electronic monitoring and detection equipment meant that fighting was almost by guesswork, between squadrons of battle cruisers and battleships that were searching for each other and assessing their respective positions and strength only by sightings.

This was how, at Tsushima, Admiral Nebogatov's ships could leave the battle area unchallenged and, at Jutland, the entire German High Seas Fleet could pass just a few miles astern of the British Grand Fleet that was searching for it and reach its bases unchallenged.

The naval battle in the Second World War

The most important innovation in naval combat in 1939 was the presence of aircraft at sea, not only as they were used in 1916 for reconnaissance and scouting, but also as bombers and torpedo planes—in other words, as carriers of arms for use against the enemy. In the First World War the combat distance was dictated by the range of the guns (about 11–12mi [18–20km]); but in the Second World War it was dictated by the much greater distance that the aircraft could fly, in other words, ships could fight without seeing each other.

Two classic examples of this new method of naval combat are the British attack on the base at Taranto on November 12, 1940, and the Japanese attack on Pearl Harbor on December 7, 1941.

The British attack on Taranto was carried out by aircraft that had taken off from the aircraft carrier *Illustrious* which was in the Adriatic 170 miles off Taranto, forty miles off Cephalonia. The Japanese attack on Pearl Harbor was by aircraft that had taken off from the aircraft carriers *Akagi, Kaga, Hiryu, Soryu, Shokaku,* and *Zuikaku* at a point in the Pacific 230 miles off the island of Ohau.

The attack of aircraft against ships could also have been carried out with units based on land rather than on aircraft carriers. The most sensational and convincing example was the sinking of Britain's battleship *Prince of Wales* and the battle cruiser *Repulse*, which occurred on December 10, 1941, off Malaya as a result of Japanese bombing from airports in Indochina. Another less important example was when German aircraft of the Luftwaffe from airports in Sicily inflicted heavy losses on convoys of the British naval forces bound for Malta. Particularly memorable was the operation that took place from August 12 to 15, 1942, in which a convoy bound for Malta was escorted by the aircraft carriers *Victorious, Indomitable,* and *Eagle*. *Eagle* was sunk by a German submarine, *U 73,* on August 11th and *Indomitable* had her flight deck destroyed by aerial bombing on the evening of August 12 by aircraft from Sicily.

The most extensive air and sea battles took place in the vast waters of the Pacific Ocean between American and Japanese task forces, still made up of a great many aircraft carriers.

The first battle in which the ships of the two opposing fleets neither saw nor

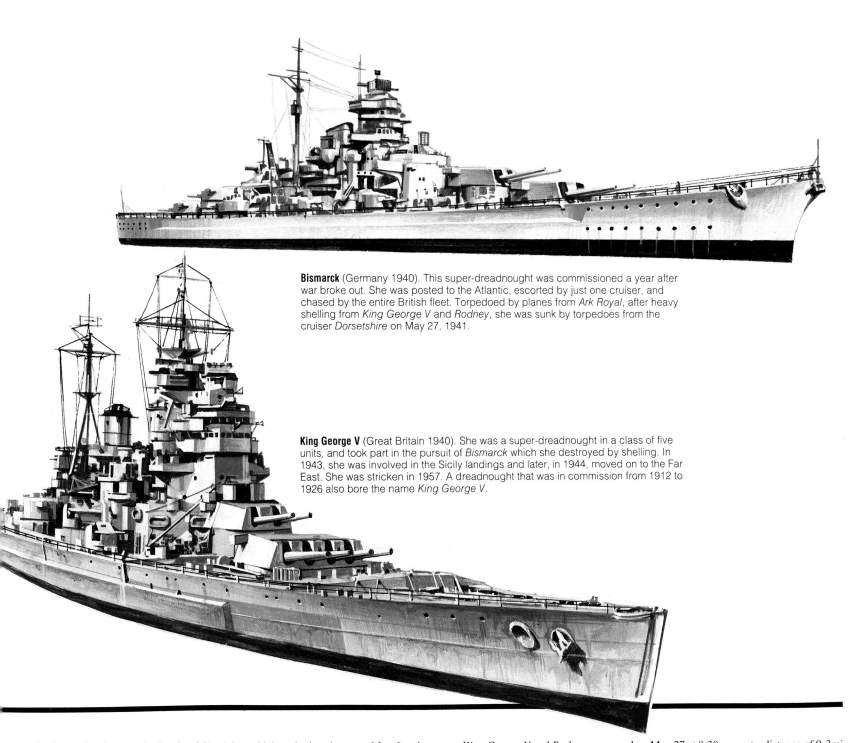

Bismarck (Germany 1940). This super-dreadnought was commissioned a year after war broke out. She was posted to the Atlantic, escorted by just one cruiser, and chased by the entire British fleet. Torpedoed by planes from *Ark Royal*, after heavy shelling from *King George V* and *Rodney*, she was sunk by torpedoes from the cruiser *Dorsetshire* on May 27, 1941.

King George V (Great Britain 1940). She was a super-dreadnought in a class of five units, and took part in the pursuit of *Bismarck* which she destroyed by shelling. In 1943, she was involved in the Sicily landings and later, in 1944, moved on to the Far East. She was stricken in 1957. A dreadnought that was in commission from 1912 to 1926 also bore the name *King George V*.

fired at each other was the Battle of Coral Sea which took place between May 6 and 8, 1942 and during which the American and Japanese aircraft carriers *Lexington* and *Shoho* were sunk. The Japanese aircraft carriers *Shoho, Shokaku,* and *Zuikaku* and the American *Yorktown* and *Lexington* took part in this battle. The distance between the opposing fleets was about 200 miles. Perhaps the greatest air-sea battle of the Pacific was the so-called Battle of Midway, which took place on June 4 and 5, 1942, during which the Japanese aircraft carriers *Soryu, Kaga, Akagi,* and *Hiryu* and the American *Yorktown* were sunk. The Japanese also lost the cruiser *Mogami,* and four aircraft carriers, 250 naval aircraft, and a large number of technical and air group personnel which caused serious replacement problems. In this battle, too, the Japanese aircraft carriers sent out their planes at a distance of 240 miles from their targets on the Midway Islands and the Americans reacted by sending out theirs at a distance of over 200 miles from the Japanese ships.

The 1939–1945 war was chiefly an air-sea war, but there was also action involving ships alone which, however, was not as important as action between entire fleets, as in 1916 at Jutland. A typical example was when the British fleet gave chase to the German ships *Bismarck* and *Prinz Eugen*. These two ships had left Gdynia on May 18, 1941, and, passing north of Iceland, headed for the Atlantic. The British sent out the battle cruiser *Hood* and the battleship *Prince of Wales* from Scapa Flow, plus the entire Home Fleet which also included the battle cruiser *Repulse*. In an early encounter, on a level with Iceland, *Bismarck* sank *Hood* (6 A.M. on May 24, 1941) simply by using her guns at a distance of 11.18mi (18,000m). A second exchange of gunfire, between *Bismarck* and the battleships

King George V and *Rodney,* occurred on May 27 at 8:30 A.M. at a distance of 9.3mi (15,000m). *Bismarck,* already damaged on the evening of May 26 by torpedo planes from the aircraft carrier *Ark Royal,* was reduced practically to a floating wreck and two hours later was sunk by torpedoes from the cruiser *Dorsetshire* (10:36 A.M. on May 27, 1941). Although there was naval action where aircraft had only been used for marginal attacks, the experience gained from the 1939–1945 war proved the uselessness of large battleships and the extreme importance of aircraft carriers. Apart from the use of aircraft, in the Second World War, it was possible to see and locate the enemy even at night and in dreadful conditions of visibility during the day. It was the use of radar by the British Navy that caused the loss of three cruisers: *Pola, Zara,* and *Fiume* on the night of March 28, 1941. *Zara* and *Fiume* had been sent to assist *Pola,* which had been hit by two torpedoes during an air raid. The Italian cruisers were unprepared for combat because Italian ships were not equipped to fire at night; without hesitation, they placed themselves within range of the guns of the British battleships which had pinpointed their position by radar and which calmly waited for them to reach the best position for opening fire. The use of radar was also one of the reasons for the failure of the war on traffic by German submarines in the Atlantic. In fact, before the advent of radar, submarines were practically invisible. They were submerged by day and surfaced only at night, to recharge their electric batteries, when the human eye could not see them. By contrast, radar could see and detect them so it was relatively easy to attack from the air, especially on their return routes, a short distance from the Atlantic coasts of France and Germany.

BATTLESHIPS

The development of battleships from 1855 to 1945

The great sailing ships of the first half of the nineteenth century were armed with guns arranged in two or three batteries down the sides that fired solid round iron balls. In 1819, a French artillery officer, Major Paixhans, designed and introduced fragmentation shells for landguns. These shells were made up of a hollow envelope containing a charge which was exploded by a detonating fuse when the latter received a blow as a result of the shell hitting a target, such as the wall of a fortification. The explosion of the inner charge caused the envelope to break, its fragments being hurled in all directions, damaging men and weapons far more than a one-piece shell would have done. Paixhan's shell was also used for naval guns as a result of experiments carried out in 1834 in France to check the resistance to penetration of these shells into structures of various types, including structures simulating ships' sides. As a result of these experiments, Paixhans suggested increasing the resistance of the ships' sides' resistance to penetration of his shells by covering the wood with iron plates: Thus the idea of ships' armor was born, although it was not put into practice until fifteen years later. Other experiments involving firing at structures, some of which simulated a ship's sides, were carried out in 1843–1845, covering the wood with one or more layers of sheet iron 0.47 and 0.19in (12 and 5mm) thick, but these thicknesses were well under the 3.93–4.72in (10–12cm) of the armor of the first ships. Final and decisive tests were performed in 1854 on a target made up of a 4.33in (11cm)-thick iron plate on a 16.53in (42cm)-thick wooden structure. These led to the construction of the first armored ships, namely the five batteries *Dévastation, Tonnante, Lave, Foudroyant,* and *Congrève,* commissioned in 1855. These ships were used in the Crimean War, during which two episodes occurred that had a great influence on ships' armament and armor. The first occurred in fighting at Sinop on November 30, 1853, between a Turkish naval squadron, armed only with round ball twenty-four pounders, and a Russian squadron armed with guns and fragmentation shells. It showed the effectiveness of explosive shells in naval action. The Russian units, although fewer in number, practically annihilated the Turkish squadron by firing Paixhans' shells, without being damaged by the round balls of the Turkish guns. The second episode was the bombardment of Russia's Kinburn Forts, on October 17, 1855, showing the effectiveness of protecting ships' sides with armor. In four hours of bombardment the French naval squadron, which included the armored batteries, *Dévastation, Lave,* and *Tonnante,* destroyed Russia's Kinburn Forts. The three armored batteries emerged unscathed even though *Dévastation* had been hit sixty-four times, twenty-nine hits on her side armor and thirty-five on her deck, and *Tonnante* sixty-five times, fifty-five hits being on her sides. There were three hits on *Dévastation's* battery, which wounded eight men, and *Tonnante* received two in the same place wounding nine men.

Learning the lesson of the Crimean War, a French commander named Dupré, who had commanded the *Tonnante* at Kinburn, suggested building two types of armored ships, one of which would be equipped to operate against ships of the line fleets, and the other of a type similar to the armored batteries, for use against land fortifications. Although the idea of placing armor on ships' sides must be attributed to Paixhans, it was Commander Dupré who suggested building armored fighting ships. The French Navy welcomed Dupré's suggestion and ordered the armored frigate *Gloire* to be built. She was laid down in Toulon Dockyard on March 4, 1858, following a design by an engineer named Dupuy de Lôme. This, the first armored ship, was modeled on unarmored ships in commission at that time and had her guns in batteries down either side, totalling thirty-six 6.3in (160mm) breech-loading guns, all in a battery, eighteen on each side.

The gun arrangement of the first armored ships presented two serious problems: The first was an operational weakness, since the ship could fire only if the enemy was coming broadside on, while screw propulsion meant that he could be approached from any direction, particularly ahead or astern. The second problem affected the armor's ability to protect the ship, since it was weakened by a great many gun ports, all of which were of a considerable size.

An early development of the ''full-battery ironclad'' was the ''central-battery ironclad.'' She still had the shortcomings of her predecessor, but reduced the area where the guns were positioned and therefore the weight of the armor. The first example of an ironclad with a central battery was Britain's *Warrior* of 1860, armed with twenty-eight 7in (178mm) and four 8in (203mm) guns, twenty-six of the 7in (178mm) ones arranged thirteen per side in a battery in the central part of the hull, which was protected along about two thirds of its length.

The progress in artillery made it possible to build trainable guns, in other words, guns that could fire in an arc of 90–100° and were normally of a larger caliber than nontrainable guns.

The second stage of development was a further reduction in the length of the battery which was transformed into a ''central citadel'' inside which were a smaller number of guns (the ones at the four highest points being trainable), which could also fire in the fore and after quarters. Examples of ironclads with a central citadel are Germany's *Kaiser* of 1874, Britain's *Alexandra* of 1875, Austria's *Tegetthoff* of 1878, France's *Dévastation* of 1879, and others.

Guns became even bigger and, instead of being placed on pivot and rail mountings, were arranged on trainable platforms which also accommodated twin guns.

The next development was toward ships with barbette citadels, hybrid vessels with some of their guns in a battery and some in barbettes on the main deck. There are few examples of such ships: Britain's *Temeraire* of 1876 and France's *Amiral Duperré* of 1879.

Amiral Duperré should be described not as a ship with a central citadel, but rather as an ironclad with a central battery and barbettes, since she had seven 5.5in (140mm) guns per side in the after end of the midships area, and four 13.3in (340mm) barbette guns on the main deck, two of which were aft (one between the main and mizzen masts and one abaft the mizzen mast), the other two being symmetrically placed on either side between the fore- and main mast.

The increase in the caliber of the main guns led to the disappearance of guns in a battery and armament comprised solely of four big guns, usually twinned, in either a barbette or turret. Perhaps the only examples of ironclads with diagonal barbettes were the two Italian ships *Italia* and *Lepanto* of 1880, armed with four 16.9in (431mm) guns arranged in pairs on two platforms within a large diagonal barbette with 18.9in (480mm) of thick armor plating.

The first ship to have guns in a turret was *Monitor,* built in 1861 by a Swede named Ericsson for the United States Navy and armed with two 11in (280mm) guns in a single turret. Ericsson's ideas were taken up by Captain Cowper Coles of the British Navy who, in 1864, designed and built the *Rolf Krake,* and armored gunboat for the Danish Navy, armed with four 8in (203mm) guns in two twin turrets. The first ironclads with guns in turrets were Britain's *Monarch* (1868) and *Captain* (1869), and Germany's *Preussen* (1873). All three of these ships still had masts and sails and their artillery turrets down the center line. *Monarch* had two turrets with four 12in (305mm) guns, one behind the other, between the main and fore masts, level with the superstructure top. *Captain* also had two turrets with four

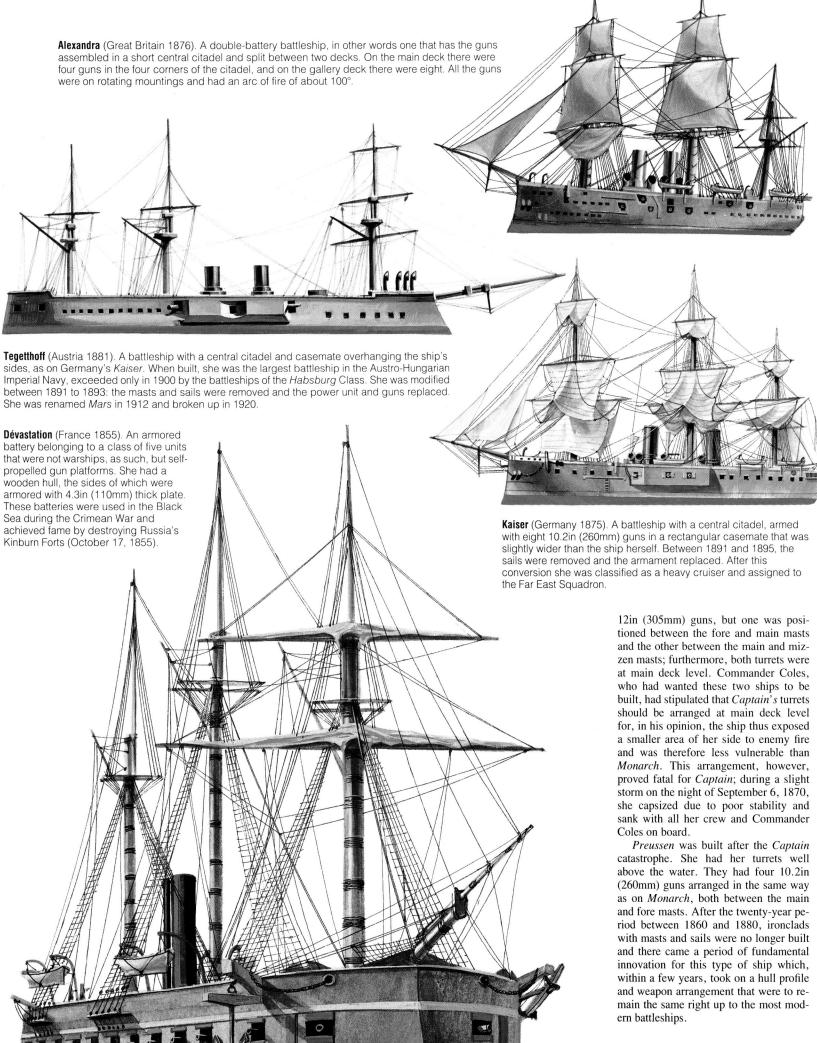

Alexandra (Great Britain 1876). A double-battery battleship, in other words one that has the guns assembled in a short central citadel and split between two decks. On the main deck there were four guns in the four corners of the citadel, and on the gallery deck there were eight. All the guns were on rotating mountings and had an arc of fire of about 100°.

Tegetthoff (Austria 1881). A battleship with a central citadel and casemate overhanging the ship's sides, as on Germany's *Kaiser*. When built, she was the largest battleship in the Austro-Hungarian Imperial Navy, exceeded only in 1900 by the battleships of the *Habsburg* Class. She was modified between 1891 to 1893: the masts and sails were removed and the power unit and guns replaced. She was renamed *Mars* in 1912 and broken up in 1920.

Dévastation (France 1855). An armored battery belonging to a class of five units that were not warships, as such, but self-propelled gun platforms. She had a wooden hull, the sides of which were armored with 4.3in (110mm) thick plate. These batteries were used in the Black Sea during the Crimean War and achieved fame by destroying Russia's Kinburn Forts (October 17, 1855).

Kaiser (Germany 1875). A battleship with a central citadel, armed with eight 10.2in (260mm) guns in a rectangular casemate that was slightly wider than the ship herself. Between 1891 and 1895, the sails were removed and the armament replaced. After this conversion she was classified as a heavy cruiser and assigned to the Far East Squadron.

12in (305mm) guns, but one was positioned between the fore and main masts and the other between the main and mizzen masts; furthermore, both turrets were at main deck level. Commander Coles, who had wanted these two ships to be built, had stipulated that *Captain's* turrets should be arranged at main deck level for, in his opinion, the ship thus exposed a smaller area of her side to enemy fire and was therefore less vulnerable than *Monarch*. This arrangement, however, proved fatal for *Captain*; during a slight storm on the night of September 6, 1870, she capsized due to poor stability and sank with all her crew and Commander Coles on board.

Preussen was built after the *Captain* catastrophe. She had her turrets well above the water. They had four 10.2in (260mm) guns arranged in the same way as on *Monarch*, both between the main and fore masts. After the twenty-year period between 1860 and 1880, ironclads with masts and sails were no longer built and there came a period of fundamental innovation for this type of ship which, within a few years, took on a hull profile and weapon arrangement that were to remain the same right up to the most modern battleships.

The prototypes of this development were the Italian ironclads *Duilio* and *Dandolo* and Britain's *Inflexible*, all dating back to 1876. These ships had main armament of just four very large-caliber guns: 17.7in (450mm) on *Duilio* and 16in (406mm) on *Inflexible*, still the muzzle-loading type, arranged in two turrets amidships, which instead of having their axes down the center line like those on *Monarch*, *Captain*, and *Preussen*, had them offset on either side. On the Italian ships the one farthest forward was to the starboard side and on *Inflexible* the one farthest forward was to the port side. These ships were called "diagonal turret" ships and they had a central citadel below the turrets, which was protected by 16.9in (430mm) armor plating on the Italian ships and 12 + 8in (305 + 203mm) on the British one. The armor plating on the turrets was of a similar thickness. The diagonal turret arrangement was short-lived: the British Navy had *Colossus* and *Majestic* of 1882, the Italians had *Ruggero di Lauria*, *Andrea Doria*, and *Francesco Morosini* of 1885, copied by the United States Navy in the form of *Texas* of 1892.

By the late 1880s, the arrangement of the big guns had become standardized, with turrets with their axes down the center line with one forward and one aft. This arrangement was first seen on the barbette ironclads and was repeated on other ships with turrets. As early as 1882, the six British ironclads of the *Collingwood* Class had had a main armament of four guns in barbettes, consisting of two twin 12in (305mm) guns, one before and

Italia (Italy 1885). A battleship with diagonal barbettes. She had no armor on her sides, just an armored deck and barbettes, 18.8in (480mm) thick, that protected the base of the 17in (431mm) guns in two twin mountings arranged diagonally amidships. An outstanding feature of this ship was that she had six funnels, in two groups of three. This type of ship was not repeated except for her sister *Lepanto*. In 1909–1910 she became a torpedo boat training vessel at La Spezia and she was stricken in 1914.

Amiral Duperré (France 1881). A battleship with a central battery and barbettes, armed with fourteen 5.5in (140mm) guns on the gun deck amidships and four 13.3in (340mm) guns in four barbettes on the main deck: two (on either beam) before the funnels and two on the centerline aft. She was armored only round the belt (21.6in [550mm]) and on the upper deck (2.3in [60mm]). One particularly interesting feature was that she had two funnels abreast.

one abaft the ship's superstructure. In 1883, France's four battleships of the *Indomptable* Class had had two 16.5in (420mm) guns in two barbettes with their axes down the center line, one forward and one aft. In 1891, Britain's seven ironclads of the *Royal Sovereign* Class had had four 13.5in (343mm) guns in two barbettes, one forward and one aft.

Open barbettes did not protect gun crews from light weapons, which were increasingly important from about 1880 on. The guns' breeches were, therefore, enclosed in a metal structure which did not need to be as strong as a turret. Still later, this structure was reinforced to the point of matching the barbette armor, to form the modern turret. Ships of this type were called ''barbette turret'' ironclads. Barbette turrets were also arranged with their axes down the center line, one forward and one aft. Examples of barbette turret ironclads are the two French *Amiral Baudin* Class of 1883, armed with two 14.5in (370mm) guns; France's *Magenta, Marceau,* and *Neptune* of 1890, armed with four 12in (305mm) guns in four barbette turrets, one forward and one aft with their axes down the center line and two symmetrically placed either side amidships; and the three Italian ships *Re Umberto, Sicilia,* and *Sardegna,* with four 13.5in (343mm) guns in two twin mounts, one forward and one aft. Lastly, Germany's four *Brandenburg* Class ships of 1891 had six 11in (280mm) guns in three barbette turrets, one forward, one aft, and one amidships, all with their axes down the center line.

Preussen (Germany 1876). A turret battleship with masts and sails and a similar armament arrangement to that of *Monarch* and *Captain*. In 1890 she was modified: During the refit, the masts and sails were removed and new superstructures built. During the First World War, she was used as a floating coal depot. She was broken up in 1920.

Inflexible (Great Britain 1880). A battleship with diagonal turrets, built at the same time as *Duilio*. She differed from the Italian ship in that she was armed with four guns of a caliber of 16in (406mm) rather than 17.7in (450mm). Originally she had two square-rigged masts that were removed four years later. She also served in the Mediterranean and was stricken in 1903.

Monarch (Great Britain 1869). One of the first turret battleships, still fitted with masts and sails. She had a freeboard of 14ft (4.3m), so the main deck was well above the waterline.

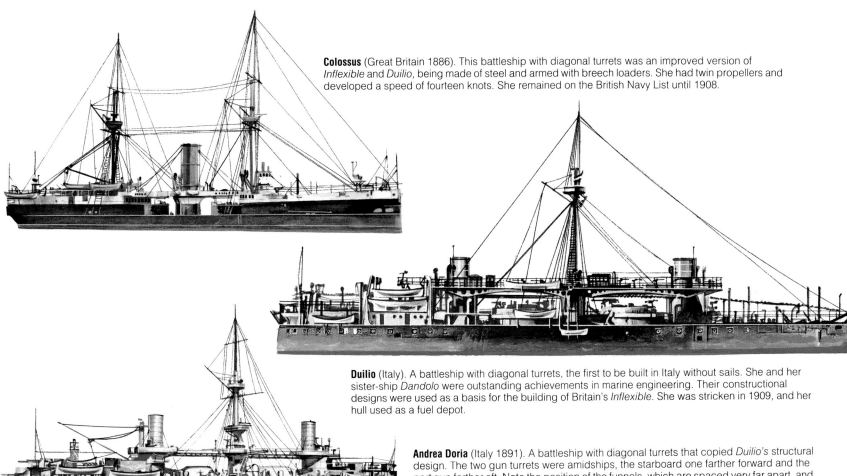

Colossus (Great Britain 1886). This battleship with diagonal turrets was an improved version of *Inflexible* and *Duilio,* being made of steel and armed with breech loaders. She had twin propellers and developed a speed of fourteen knots. She remained on the British Navy List until 1908.

Duilio (Italy). A battleship with diagonal turrets, the first to be built in Italy without sails. She and her sister-ship *Dandolo* were outstanding achievements in marine engineering. Their constructional designs were used as a basis for the building of Britain's *Inflexible*. She was stricken in 1909, and her hull used as a fuel depot.

Andrea Doria (Italy 1891). A battleship with diagonal turrets that copied *Duilio's* structural design. The two gun turrets were amidships, the starboard one farther forward and the port gun farther aft. Note the position of the funnels, which are spaced very far apart, and the single mast. *Andrea Doria* was stricken in 1911 when work began on a new battleship of the same name.

At the end of the century all the battleships, later defined as ''pre-dreadnought'' types, had their guns in turrets. In addition to having their large-caliber guns in turrets, many of these ships had turrets for their middle-caliber guns which, on many other ships, however, were in casemates in a battery or on the superstructure.

The three Russian *Petropavlovsk* Class ships of 1894, for example, apart from having four 12in (305mm) guns in two twin turrets (one forward and one aft), had eight 6in (152mm) guns in four twin turrets, two per side amidships. America's *Kearsage* type ships of 1898, in addition to four 13in (330mm) guns in two twin turrets, had four 8in (203mm) ones in two twin turrets above the 13in (330mm) guns. Japan's *Shikishima* types of 1898, apart from four 12in (305mm) guns in two twin barbette turrets, had their fourteen 6in (152mm) secondary-caliber guns in casemates down the ship's sides, eight on the gallery deck and six in the superstructure on the main deck. The Russian *Kniaz Potemkin Tavricheskey* ironclads, the Austrian *Hapsburgs*, and the Italian *Brins* of 1901 also had their secondary-caliber guns in casemates in a battery and in the central citadel.

The great change that followed in the armament of battleships brings us to the

dreadnought types which, together with battle cruisers, played a major role in the First World War.

We have mentioned that the ironclads of the late 1800s had an armament comprising a small number of large-caliber guns, usually four, which served as the main armament for long-range fighting. Apart from these guns there were many others of so-called secondary-caliber, for close-range combat with other armored ships or cruisers. There were even guns of smaller caliber, called anti-torpedo guns, for fighting torpedo crafts that attacked large ships at very close range, given the poor operating range of torpedoes, which, in order to strike effectively, had to be launched from a distance of about a thousand yards or even less. All these guns and their ammunition created serious stowage problems. Furthermore close-range combat between big ships proved, in practice, to be something of a pipe-dream. In fact, in the Battle of Tsushima, Russian and Japanese ironclads fired at each other from the maximum range of their heaviest guns, proving that it was pointless to have middle-caliber guns.

Texas (United States 1894). One of the last examples of a battleship with diagonal turrets. She had a 12in (305mm) thick quadrangular barbette, similar to that of the Italian ships *Italia* and *Lepanto*. She was the second battleship to be built by the United States Navy. In 1911, she was used as a target ship and her name was changed to *San Marco*.

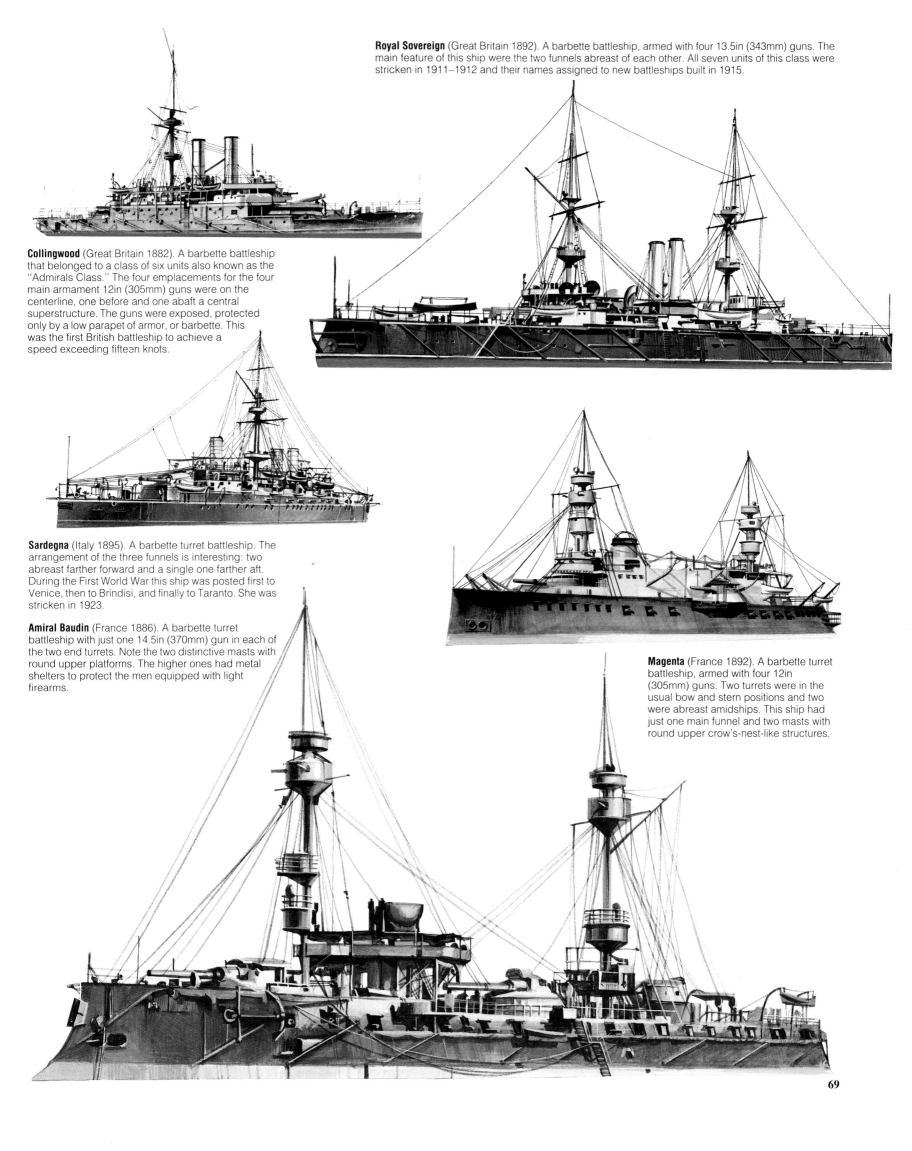

Royal Sovereign (Great Britain 1892). A barbette battleship, armed with four 13.5in (343mm) guns. The main feature of this ship were the two funnels abreast of each other. All seven units of this class were stricken in 1911–1912 and their names assigned to new battleships built in 1915.

Collingwood (Great Britain 1882). A barbette battleship that belonged to a class of six units also known as the "Admirals Class." The four emplacements for the four main armament 12in (305mm) guns were on the centerline, one before and one abaft a central superstructure. The guns were exposed, protected only by a low parapet of armor, or barbette. This was the first British battleship to achieve a speed exceeding fifteen knots.

Sardegna (Italy 1895). A barbette turret battleship. The arrangement of the three funnels is interesting: two abreast farther forward and a single one farther aft. During the First World War this ship was posted first to Venice, then to Brindisi, and finally to Taranto. She was stricken in 1923.

Amiral Baudin (France 1886). A barbette turret battleship with just one 14.5in (370mm) gun in each of the two end turrets. Note the two distinctive masts with round upper platforms. The higher ones had metal shelters to protect the men equipped with light firearms.

Magenta (France 1892). A barbette turret battleship, armed with four 12in (305mm) guns. Two turrets were in the usual bow and stern positions and two were abreast amidships. This ship had just one main funnel and two masts with round upper crow's-nest-like structures.

Kearsage (United States 1900). Together with the *New Jersey* Class, this ship was typical of the superimposed-turret type of battleship. The lower turrets were armed with two 13in (330mm) guns each; the upper ones with two 8in (203mm) guns each. These turrets were joined in a single structure and trained together. *Kearsage* was the flagship of the North Atlantic Fleet until 1904 and was stricken in 1955 after having been used as a crane ship for thirty-five years.

Brandenburg (Germany 1892). A barbette-turret battleship, in other words a ship with guns protected only by a metal shield, not an armored turret. In 1900, in the wake of the Boxer Rebellion, she was sent to China. In 1915, she was used for coastal defense before being stricken in 1920.

Kniaz Potemkin Tavricheskey (Russia 1903). A turret battleship, built in 1898 at the Nikolayev Naval Dockyard. She was armed with four 12in (305mm) guns in two twin turrets, sixteen 6in (152mm) and fourteen 3in (76mm) guns, some of which were on the battery deck and some on the superstructures. A famous mutiny took place on board this ship on May 26, 1905, when the crew raised the red flag and took the vessel first to Odessa and then to Constance, where they surrendered. After this, the ship's name was changed to *Panteleimon*. She was renamed *Potemkin* after the 1917 revolution.

Thus, the idea of the "single-caliber" ship was formulated, in other words, a battleship that, instead of having a small number of large-caliber guns and others of medium-caliber, had a main armament made up of a considerable number of large-caliber guns, eight or ten pieces, plus some anti-torpedo guns.

This theory was put forward by Italy's Director (Colonel) of Naval Engineers, Vittorio Cuniberti in an article published in the 1903 edition of *Jane's Fighting Ships*. In those days the publishers of this annual put forward each year a topic of discussion for the leading naval engineers of the various countries. In 1903, the topic concerned the characteristics that the ideal warship for the British Navy should possess.

Cuniberti suggested an armored ship with twelve 12in (305mm) guns, protected by 12in (305mm) armor and capable of achieving a speed of twenty to twenty-two knots, faster, in other words, than the eighteen to nineteen knots of the pre-dreadnoughts. The fact that this ship was faster would enable her to close in on slower enemy battleships and attack them with her twelve guns giving almost triple the fire power of the four guns on conventional battleships. If the situation then became untenable, this new battleship, with her superior speed, could easily distance herself, breaking gunnery contact whenever she wished, ready to move in again at a moment's notice if the situation turned back to her advantage. Naval squadrons would always fight solely with their main guns and at the maximum range possible so that all the weight saved in secondary armament could be used to increase the main armament. Admiral Fisher, commander in chief of the British Navy, welcomed Cuniberti's idea with great enthusiasm and laid down a prototype single-caliber ship named *Dreadnought* which was commissioned on December 31, 1906.

This ship was armed with ten 12in (305mm) and twenty-three 3in (76mm) guns. The middle caliber, which, on earlier British battleships such as the *King Edward VII* Class, commissioned just a year before in 1905, had comprised four 9.2in (234mm) and ten 6in (152mm) guns, had disappeared.

This elimination of the secondary-caliber was very incomplete on the *Dreadnought*s built immediately after the prototype. In addition to the ten to twelve main-caliber guns there were generally twelve to twenty middle-caliber guns. In some cases these were anti-torpedo weapons, their increased caliber reflecting increased torpedo ranges and destroyer size. The Germans and Austrians, however, kept intermediate guns *in addition* to anti-torpedo weapons of lesser caliber. The German *Nassau* types of 1908, for example, had twelve 11in (280mm) guns as main-caliber and twelve 5.9in (150mm) middle-caliber guns. The Russian *Gangut* types of 1911 had twelve 12in (305mm) and sixteen 4.7in (120mm) guns, and the Austrian *Viribus Unitis* types of 1911 had twelve 12in (305mm) and twelve 5.9in (150mm) guns. Even the British battleships built immediately after the *Dreadnought*, namely the three *Bellerophon* Class of 1907 and the three *Saint Vincent* Class of 1908, had ten 12in (305mm) guns as their main-caliber, plus sixteen and eighteen 4in (102mm) guns respectively as their secondary-caliber.

Benedetto Brin (Italy 1905). A turret battleship armed with four 8in (203mm) guns in two twin turrets and twelve 6in (152mm) guns in a central citadel below the main deck. Note the three funnels, the two forward ones being symmetrically placed abreast. This ship was sunk by an act of sabotage on September 27, 1915 in the port of Taranto.

Cornwallis (Great Britain 1903). A contemporary of the Italian *Brin* Class, with the same displacement. She was armed with much more powerful 12in (305mm) guns in two twin turrets, and twelve 6in (152mm) guns in casemates either side of the citadel, plus other smaller guns. She still had a ram and a small captain's walk overhanging the stern. She was torpedoed by a German submarine in the Mediterranean and sank on January 9, 1917.

Viribus Unitis (Austria 1912). A dreadnought-type battleship belonging to a class of four units that were the last battleships of the Austo-Hungarian Navy. She was sunk in the port of Pola on November 1, 1918 by Italian assault craft commanded by Major of the Engineer Corps Rossetti and Medical Officer Paolucci, both decorated with a gold medal for this action.

Jean Bart (France 1911). A dreadnought-type battleship belonging to a class of three units armed with twelve 12in (305mm) guns in six twin turrets, two at the bow and two at the stern and two symmetrically placed amidships. This ship had a four-shaft turbine powerplant; side armor was a maximum thickness of 11.8in (300m) in the belt and 7in (178mm) in the citadel. She was modernized in 1926–1929, and took part in the initial phase of the Second World War. She was scuttled at Toulon in November 1942.

Dreadnought's ten 12in (305mm) guns were in five twin turrets, three with their axes down the center line, one forward and two aft, plus two more symmetrically placed on either side amidships.

Side turrets also appeared on the German *Nassau* battleships which instead of having two as on the *Dreadnought*, had four, two per side, plus another two twin turrets (one forward and one aft). But the arrangement of the main armament soon settled at turrets which had their axes down the center line and usually with two forward and two aft; but in certain cases there were even one or two turrets amidships, such as the British *King George V* Class of 1911, and the French *Bretagnes* of 1913 and German *Koenigs* of 1913. The Italian *Conte di Cavour* Class of 1911 also had five turrets.

The first battleship to have three guns per turret was the Italian *Dante Alighieri* of 1910, armed with twelve 12in (305mm) guns in four triple turrets, one forward, one aft and two amidships, all with their axes down the center line. A similar four triple-turret arrangement was used on the Russian *Gangut* types of 1911, the Austrian *Viribus Unitis* of 1911, and the American *Pennsylvania, New Mexico,* and *Tennessee* types. The American *Arkansas*-type battleships of 1911, the Japanese *Fusos* of 1914, and the French *Jean Barts* of 1911 had their twelve main-caliber guns in six twin turrets. The *Arkansas* and *Fuso* types had two turrets forward, two amidships and two aft, all with their axes down the center line, whereas the *Jean Barts* had their two middle turrets positioned symmetrically on either side. The ship with the record number of large-caliber gun turrets was Britain's *Agincourt* of 1913

which had seven, two forward, two amidships, and three aft, making a total of fourteen 12in (305mm) guns. The number of turrets was later settled at just four, two forward and two aft. On some types, the end turrets, in other words the lowest ones fore and aft, had three guns each, whereas the higher ones had only two, making a total of ten guns, such as the Italian *Conte di Cavour* Class after modifications made in 1935-1938.

The only ships with four twin turrets were America's *South Carolinas* and Spain's *Españas* with eight 12in (305mm), Germany's *Badens* with eight 15in (381mm), Japan's *Kongo* types with eight 14in (356mm), Britain's *Queen Elizabeths, Royal Sovereigns,* and *Hood* with eight 15in (381mm), Japan's *Nagatos,* and America's *West Virginias* with eight 16in (406mm) guns.

After the First World War, the Washington Treaty stipulated that battleships should be limited to 35,000 tons displacement and a maximum of 16in (406mm) caliber guns. It was also stipulated that each of the great naval powers would have a tonnage "quota" for the battleships in their possession. These limitations applied to the signatories to the Treaty: Great Britain, the United States, Japan, France, and Italy. For Germany, the defeated nation, the limitations were set by the Peace Treaty: The Austrian Navy had disappeared as a result of carving up the territory which, by depriving Austria of Yugoslavia and Venetia Julia, made her a land-locked power. The Russian Navy, too, a great Imperial Navy until 1917, went through a sharp decline after the Revolution, during which time it became very insignificant and was to remain so until after the Second World War.

Nassau (Germany 1909). A dreadnought-type battleship belonging to a class of four units. At the end of the First World War she was assigned by a Peace Treaty to Japan, but was sold and broken up in England instead.

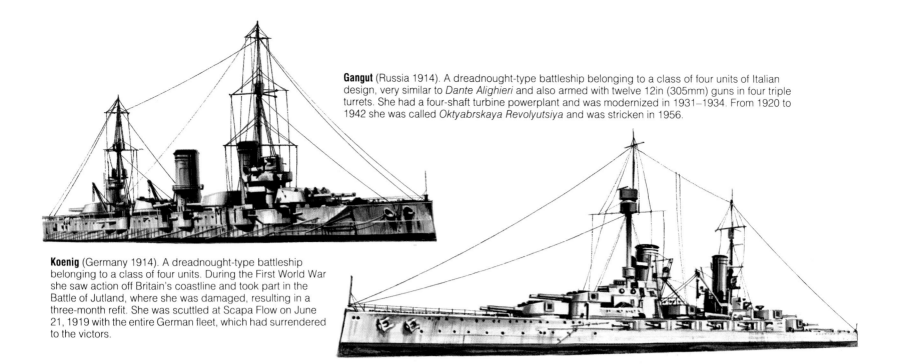

Gangut (Russia 1914). A dreadnought-type battleship belonging to a class of four units of Italian design, very similar to *Dante Alighieri* and also armed with twelve 12in (305mm) guns in four triple turrets. She had a four-shaft turbine powerplant and was modernized in 1931–1934. From 1920 to 1942 she was called *Oktyabrskaya Revolyutsiya* and was stricken in 1956.

Koenig (Germany 1914). A dreadnought-type battleship belonging to a class of four units. During the First World War she saw action off Britain's coastline and took part in the Battle of Jutland, where she was damaged, resulting in a three-month refit. She was scuttled at Scapa Flow on June 21, 1919 with the entire German fleet, which had surrendered to the victors.

Despite the limitations of the Washington Treaty, technological progress brought the battleship to the peak of her development, and as the Washington Treaty had stipulated that new battleships could not be built for ten years, the new types were laid down from 1930-1935, during the period of rearmament that preceded the Second World War.

The ships built between 1930 and 1945 were called ''super-Dreadnoughts'' or fast battleships. The description implies that they had superior fighting qualities to the *Dreadnoughts* built between 1905 and 1925. The word ''fast'' means that they could go faster than the twenty to twenty-two knots of ships of the previous period which, according to Cuniberti's theories, were already faster than the *pre-Dreadnoughts*. The French *Dunkerque* types of 1935 developed 29.5 knots; the German *Scharnhorst* types of 1936, 31.5 knots; the Italian *Littorios* of 1937, thirty knots; the French *Richelieus* of 1939, thirty knots; the American *North Carolinas* of 1941 and *South Dakotas* of 1942, 27.5 knots; and the Japanese *Yamato* types of 1940, being the largest battleships in the world and therefore also the slowest, developed only twenty-seven knots. The fastest were the U.S. *Iowas*, at 32.5 knots.

As regards the arrangement of the guns, the balanced layout of half the armament forward and half aft on the *Dreadnought* types was replaced by having most of the armament in the forward firing area.

Britain's battleships *Nelson* and *Rodney* of 1925, armed with nine 16in

(406mm) guns, therefore had all three of their triple turrets forward. Due to their construction date, however, these ships can be considered transitional types. The French ships *Dunkerque* and *Richelieu* of 1935–1939 also had all their armament forward, each having eight 13in (330 mm) and eight 15in (380mm) respectively, in two quadruple turrets. But the most common arrangement was to have three triple turrets, two forward and one aft. All the *Super-Dreadnoughts* had quite a well-developed anti-aircraft armament which, however, when tried and tested in the war proved insufficient and had to be increased. The French *Dunkerque* types of 1935 had sixteen 5.1-inch dual-purpose guns as well as forty anti-aircraft machine guns; the German *Scharnhorsts* and the Italian *Littorios* of 1937 had single-purpose (anti-destroyer) secondary guns plus specialized medium-caliber anti-aircraft guns, as well as machine guns; to be precise, the Germans had fourteen 4in (105mm) and the Italians twelve 3.5in (90mm) guns. The French *Richelieu* types of 1939 had twelve 3.9in (100mm) guns and the American *North Carolina, Alabama,* and *Missouri* types had twenty 5in (127mm) dual-purpose guns. The later *Missouris* (1944) were also armed with a total of 130 anti-aircraft machine guns.

Usually, none of the fast battleships was armed with torpedoes (the only exceptions were the German *Scharnhorst, Gniesenau,* and *Tirpitz*) whereas they were all equipped with one or even two catapults and a certain number of reconnaissance seaplanes.

Agincourt (Great Britain 1914). A dreadnought-type battleship of particular interest because fitted with a large number of turrets: seven twin turrets, all on the centerline, two forward, two amidships, and three aft, an arrangement never again repeated. She was broken up in 1924.

King George V (Great Britain 1912). A dreadnought-type battleship not to be confused with the super-dreadnought of 1940. She belonged to a class of three units armed with ten 13.5in (343mm) guns in five twin turrets, all on the centerline, two forward, two aft, and the fifth behind the funnels. She was part of the Home Fleet until 1916. From 1919 to 1923 she was detached to the Mediterranean and was stricken in 1926.

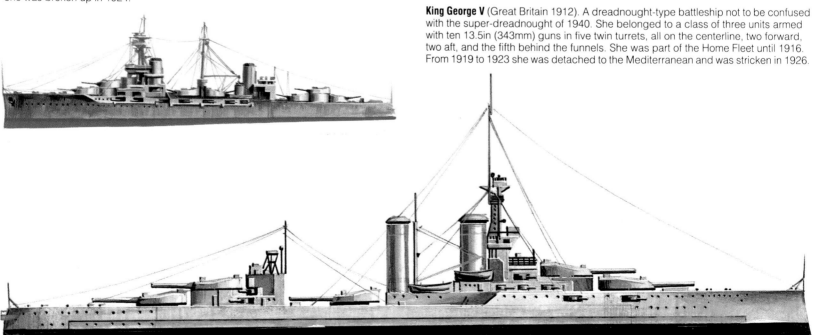

Mixed propulsion ironclads from 1850 to 1875

The ironclads built between 1850 and 1875 continued to be fully rigged, usually having three square-sail masts, a bowsprit, and jibs. They are particularly interesting because they were used to try out various forms of armor which led to the final arrangement achieved only by sailless battleships of the following period.

The first armored frigate, the French *Gloire* of 1859, like her sister ships *Invincible* and *Normandie*, had a wooden hull and the usual foremast with square sails, whereas the main and mizzen masts had spankers. There was armor plating on the sides that extended from just below the water line up to main deck level, along the entire length of the ship. The plates were 4.75in (121mm) thick at the water line, tapering to 4.5in (114mm) in the part above the gun deck. There were eighteen rectangular openings in these plates, on either side of the ship, for the gun barrels. The plates were still made of mild rather than hard steel.

Britain's first two armored frigates, *Warrior* and *Black Prince* of 1860, had a different form of protection. These two ships, as distinct from the French ones, had an iron hull and their armor protected only the middle area, leaving the extreme bow and stern parts (where there were no guns) unprotected. At each end of the two side armored areas was an armored bulkhead, making a rectangular citadel.

Gloire (France 1861). The armored frigate *Gloire* was the first fighting ship to have armor plating on the sides. She had a wooden hull, a small 2502hp (2537CV) engine and a speed of less than thirteen knots. She had to use sails for making long passages.

Re d'Italia (Italy 1864). A battery ironclad with a wooden hull completely covered by iron plates. Two interesting features were the ram at the bow and a funnel. She was the flagship of the Italian Fleet for the operations in the Adriatic in 1866. On July 20, of the same year, during the Battle of Lissa, she was rammed by the Austrian ironclad *Ferdinand Max* and sank, claiming the life of Captain Faà di Bruno.

Warrior (Great Britain 1862). The first armored frigate to have an iron rather than a wooden hull, like her contemporary *Gloire*. The armor did not extend the entire length of the ship but was only fitted amidships on a level with the thirteen battery gunports.

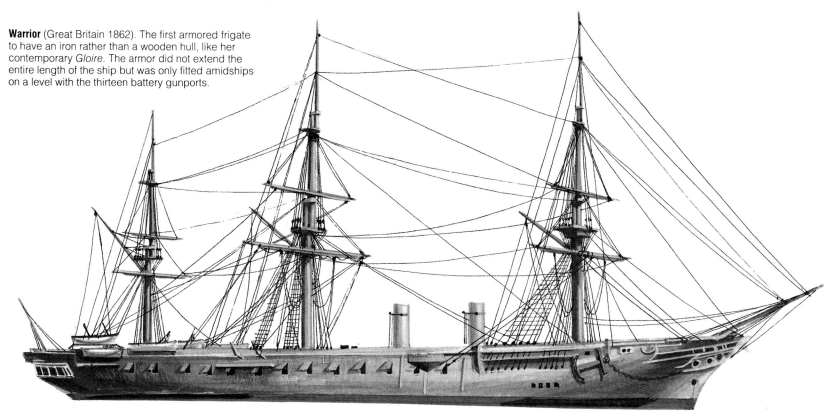

Northumberland (Great Britain 1867). A battery ironclad belonging to a class of three units characterized by having five masts, three square-rigged in the forward-to-midships area, and two with spankers in the after area. They had iron hulls and belt armor 5.5in (140mm) thick. They had only one propeller and developed a speed of 15.5 knots. The *Northumberland* remained in service until 1898, then was used as a training ship, and finally as a coal depot. She was stricken in 1928.

Bellerophon (Great Britain 1866). An ironclad with a central citadel, iron hull, and belt armor in the citadel. One of the first ships to have an armored deck. In 1881–1882 the masts and sails were removed and the superstructures modified. In 1892 she was used for harbor defense, and in 1904 as a stokers' training ship. She was stricken in 1922.

Ancona (Italy 1866). A battery ironclad of a class of four units with a wooden hull and 4.7in (120mm) thick belt armor. During her refit, carried out from 1878 to 1881, the masts and sails were removed. She was stricken in 1903.

Koenig Wilhelm (Germany 1869). A battery ironclad built in England. She had an iron hull and 8in (203mm) thick armor in the belt and above the gallery deck. Armament was eighteen 9.4in (240mm) guns on the gallery deck and five 8.2in (210mm) guns: four in side turrets on the main deck and one right aft on the gallery deck. Originally she had three square-rigged masts but these were later removed. She was used as a training ship and then stricken in 1921.

The armor plates on *Warrior* were also made of mild steel. They had a uniform thickness of 4.5in (114mm) and, as there were only twenty-six battery guns, there were thirteen openings on each side that were spaced farther apart than on the *Gloire* types so as not to weaken the protection so much.

There were other ironclads with wooden hulls and complete protection, such as Italy's *Re d'Italia* and *Re di Portogallo* of 1863 and Austria's *Habsburg* and *Ferdinand Max* of 1865, which took part in the Battle of Lissa. By contrast, Britain's *Minotaur* and *Agincourt* of 1866 had iron hulls and complete armor plating, but the third ship, *Northumberland*, had a citadel and belt instead.

A combination of complete armor and armor on the central battery only led to a type of mixed protection comprising a complete belt of armor at water line level with armor plating extending up to the main deck only in the middle part of the hull.

Ships with this type of armor were Italy's *Ancona* types of 1864 which had a wooden hull and belt armor 4.7in (120mm) thick in the middle and 3in (78mm) at the edges. This belt extended 6.5ft (2m) below the water line and 4.92ft (1.50m) above it. The central citadel, made of 4.3in (110mm) thick plates both on the sides and beams, extended about two-thirds of the ship's length. There were twenty battery guns and therefore ten ports per side in the armor.

Another ship with a battery belt was Britain's *Bellerophon*, remarkable for being the first to have armor plating on her decks too. The main deck had 1in (25.4mm) thick plates and the upper deck 0.5in (12.7mm) thick plates restricted to the part above the citadel. The belt extended 4.9ft (1.50m) below and 5.9ft (1.80m)

above the water line and had a maximum thickness of 6in (152mm). The armor on the citadel was 5in (127mm) thick both on the sides and beams. There were only ten battery guns and therefore five ports in the armor on either side that were larger than those on previous ships. The guns were trainable and could fire up to about 45° ahead and astern.

The German Navy also had a ship with a belt battery, the *Koenig Wilhelm* of 1868, ordered by Turkey and later sold to Prussia. The 8in (203mm) thick belt extended 6.9ft (2.13m) below the water line and up to the third deck. The battery also had sides and bulkheads of the same thickness. There were eighteen 9.4in (240mm) guns and so there were nine ports on either side.

There was a further reduction in the armor plating above the belt when the number of guns decreased. Because their caliber had increased and they could be trained, they were no longer arranged in a battery but in a central citadel.

Examples of ironclads with a belt and central citadel were Britain's *Hercules* type of 1868, whose belt extended from 4.92ft (1.50m) below to 8.98ft (2.74m) above the water line, having a maximum thickness of 9in (229mm). The citadel was protected by 8in (203mm)-thick armor on the sides and 6in (152mm) and 5in (127mm) thick on the forward and after bulkheads respectively. The four guns on the highest points of the citadel were on pivot and rail mountings so they could be trained to fire ahead and astern.

France's *Marengo, Océan,* and *Suffren* of 1868 were yet more examples of ironclads with a belt and citadel plus a special arrangement of some guns in barbette. The belt was 7.8in (200mm) thick and at the forward end extended downwards to strengthen the ram. The citadel was 65.6ft (20m) long and protected by armor 6.2in (160mm) thick. Inside the citadel were four nontrainable 10.6in (270mm) caliber guns, two either side. Apart from these guns, above the citadel top there were four barbettes, one at each high point with 9.4in (240mm) guns on trainable platforms. As a final example, we should mention Britain's *Temeraire* of 1876, protected by a belt of armor 11in (280mm) thick in the middle and 7in (178mm) at the edges, with a casemate covered by plates 10in (254mm) thick on the sides and 8in (203mm) thick where it joined the deck and on the forward beam. Inside the citadel there were four 12in (305mm) nontrainable guns and two 10in (254mm) trainable ones on the two forward high points. Another two 10in (254mm) guns were in two barbettes on the main deck, one forward and one aft with their axes down the center line.

The most outstanding mixed propulsion ironclads were those with their guns in turrets. One such ship was Italy's *Affondatore* of 1865. She was a small ram with a displacement of just 4,468 tons (4,540 tonnes) and armed with two 8.6in (220mm) guns in two turrets, one forward and one aft, with their axes down the center line. There were very few sails: two spanker masts and a jib, which were removed during a refit after she was sunk (then raised) off Ancona in 1866. *Affondatore's* armor comprised a belt that extended from 4.16ft (1.27m) below to 3.93ft (1.20m) above the water line, with a uniform thickness of 5in (127mm). Instead of a citadel, she had 1.9in (50mm)-thick armor plating on the main deck.

Russia's *Admiral Lazarey* Class of 1867 were further examples of turret ironclads. They were armed with six 9in (229mm) guns in three twin turrets. But the most famous turret ironclads were the British *Monarch* and *Captain* of 1868–1869. They both had a complete belt; *Monarch* had a citadel and *Captain* did not.

Pre-Dreadnought battleships from 1875 to 1900

Only very few mixed propulsion ironclads were armed with guns in turrets and protected on their decks as well as their sides. By contrast, sailless battleships, built between 1875 and 1900, all had their big guns in turrets and at least one armored deck.

The first ironclads, like *Gloire* and *Warrior* and almost all those built between 1850 and 1875, had had mild steel armor plating since the metallurgical industry was unable to build steel plates of the necessary size. A plate of armor must have a very hard outer surface so as to prevent shell penetration. Its inner part, however, must not be so hard as to be brittle and break from the impact of a

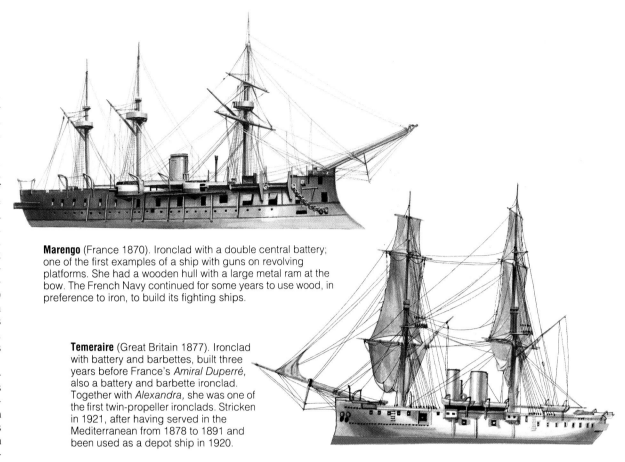

Marengo (France 1870). Ironclad with a double central battery; one of the first examples of a ship with guns on revolving platforms. She had a wooden hull with a large metal ram at the bow. The French Navy continued for some years to use wood, in preference to iron, to build its fighting ships.

Temeraire (Great Britain 1877). Ironclad with battery and barbettes, built three years before France's *Amiral Duperré,* also a battery and barbette ironclad. Together with *Alexandra,* she was one of the first twin-propeller ironclads. Stricken in 1921, after having served in the Mediterranean from 1878 to 1891 and been used as a depot ship in 1920.

Admiral Lazarev (Russia 1868). An ironclad with unusual turrets and belonging to a class of coastal ironclads. She had three turrets, each with two 9in (229mm) guns, whereas the other two units of the class had three turrets with just one 11in (278mm) gun. These ships were unstable and handled badly in heavy seas.

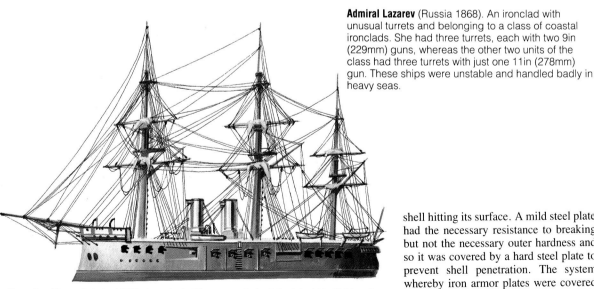

Hercules (Great Britain 1868). Ironclad with a central citadel, eight 10in (254mm) guns in the gallery deck citadel, and two 9in (229mm) guns: one forward and one aft, also on the gallery deck. From 1905 to 1914 she was used as a depot ship at Gibraltar and then stricken.

shell hitting its surface. A mild steel plate had the necessary resistance to breaking but not the necessary outer hardness and so it was covered by a hard steel plate to prevent shell penetration. The system whereby iron armor plates were covered with a steel one was called "sandwich" or compound plating. But heat treatments were developed in the 1890s, making

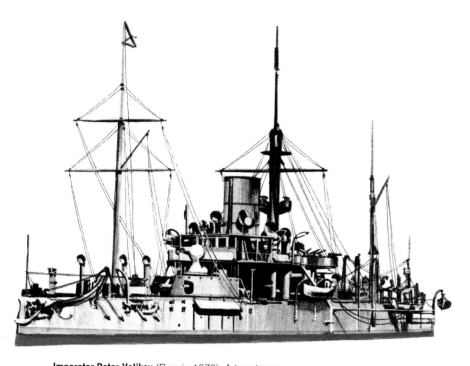

Imperator Peter Velikey (Russia 1876). A turret pre-dreadnought ironclad without masts or sails. She had two engines and two propellers and developed a speed of 12.5 knots. In 1880 the engines were removed and replaced with more modern ones. In 1907 she was converted into an artillery training ship and the 12in (305mm) gun turrets were removed. After 1917 she was renamed *Respublikanets* and stricken in 1922.

it possible to surface-harden steel plates, resulting in single-plate armor where the plates are called "harveyized," after the surface hardening process used, or Krupp cemented, after the first major manufacturer. Depending on its arrangement on the hulls, armor plating is either vertical, if on the bulkheads and sides, or horizontal, if on the decks. All the pre-dreadnought ironclads and those that followed usually had vertical armor in the form of a belt and a citadel with armored ends. The citadel was about two-thirds of the ship's length and housed the engines, boilers, artillery turrets, and magazines, in other words, all the vital parts that required greatest protection.

Apart from being on the deck which formed the top of the citadel box, and on any other decks or parts of decks, horizontal armor was always in the form of a "protective deck" shaped like a turtle's back, meaning that it was higher in the middle and lower at the ends and sides so as to be above the water line in the middle part and below it at the edges. The protective deck usually connected at the forward end to the ram structure to provide the latter with extra strength, and on the sides joined to the lower part of the belt armor.

In chronological order, the first sailless sea-going ironclads were the two British ships *Dévastation* and *Thunderer* of 1871 and the Russian *Peter Velikey* of 1872, whose main armament comprised four guns in two twin turrets, one before and one abaft of the central superstructure. Protection was in the form of a belt and citadel 12in (305mm) thick on the British ships and 13.9in (355mm) on the Russian ships. Horizontal armor was simply a protective deck.

Another ship whose name was to become famous since it was given to her successor built in 1905, was the *Dreadnought* of 1875, also armed with four 12.5in (317mm) guns in two twin turrets, one forward and one aft.

After these early types came ironclads with their artillery in diagonal turrets, the prototypes being Britain's *Inflexible* and Italy's *Duilio* and *Dandolo*, all commissioned in 1876. Few other ironclads had diagonal turrets; examples were Britain's *Colossus* and *Majestic* of 1882 and Italy's three *Ruggero di Lauria* types of 1885, as well as America's *Texas* of 1892.

When building the first units, the hulls had been made of iron, whereas subsequent units had steel hulls, which was a great saving in weight, enabling the embarkation of extra fighting equipment.

Italy's *Italia* and *Lepanto* of 1880, of similar configuration, were traditionally classified as battleships but were in fact large protected cruisers for they had no side armor and their horizontal protection was limited to a protective deck with a maximum thickness of just 3in (76mm). The four Russian *Sinop* Class were armed with six 12in (305mm) guns in three twin mounts positioned two abreast forward and one on the center line aft. These mounts were protected by a triangular barbette with 11.8–14in (300–356mm) thick plates. Hull armor was in the form of a belt 18in (457mm) in the middle, 9.8in (250mm) forward, and 9in (230mm) aft, above which was a rectangular citadel with 12in (305mm)-thick armor both on the sides and beams. This citadel supported the triangular barbette of the three gun mounts.

Dévastation (Great Britain 1872). The British Navy's first sailless pre-dreadnought turret ironclad. Armed with four 12in (305mm) guns in two twin turrets, one before and one abaft the central citadel, and stricken in 1907.

The French *Magenta*-type battleships of 1890 and *Jaureguiberry* types of 1893 had a similar gun arrangement. On these ships the four main-caliber guns were in single turrets instead of in two twin mounts, one of which was forward, one aft, and two symmetrically placed amidships. On the *Magenta*s all four guns had a caliber of 12in (305mm) but the two in the symmetrically placed side turrets on the *Jaureguiberry*s had a caliber of 10.7in (274mm). In the decade 1890–1900 the artillery distribution and profile of the ships settled on a single type, whether the main-caliber guns were in turrets or barbette turrets.

Fore and aft were two turrets, single or twin, main-caliber guns, while amidships were the secondary-caliber guns, usually in a containing casemate but in a few cases, in turrets.

Kansas (United States 1907). A pre-dreadnought of a class of six units armed with turrets arranged as on the Russian *Petropavlovsk* types of 1894. *Kansas* took part in the round-the-world voyage by the Great White Fleet in 1908–1909 and was stricken in 1923.

Jaureguiberry (France 1895). A pre-dreadnought with an unusual armament arrangement. In fact, there were two 12in (305mm) guns in two single turrets, one forward and one aft, and two 10.7in (274mm) guns in another two single turrets, symmetrically placed either side amidships, plus eight 5.5in (140mm) guns in symmetrical twin turrets, two either side, a quarter of the length from the bow and stern.

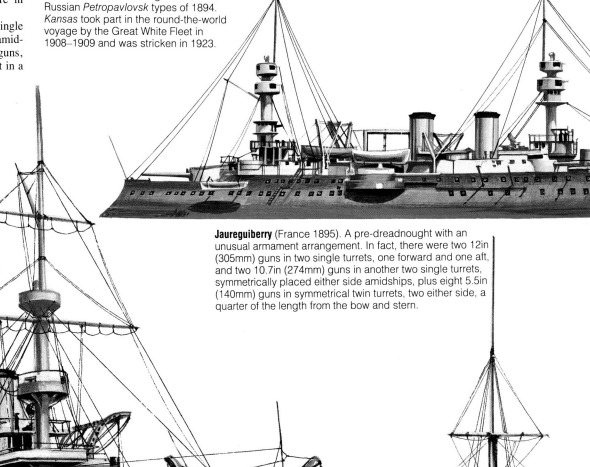

Sinop (Russia 1889). A pre-dreadnought of a class of four units with a special armament arrangement in three twin 12in (305mm) gun turrets, two abreast in the after area and one on the centerline in the forward area, all in a triangular-shaped citadel. The walls of this citadel were armored with plates 14in (356mm) thick on the sides and 11.8in (300mm) thick on the bottom. She was hit and put out of action in 1919 in the port of Odessa and broken up in 1922.

Dreadnought (Great Britain 1879). This unit bore the same name as the one that was to be built in 1905 and from which a type of battleship was derived. Despite the name, she was not a dreadnought but a turret ironclad like *Devastation* and *Peter Velikey*, armed with four 12.5in (317mm) guns in two twin turrets, one forward and one aft, and six small 2.2in (57mm) and twelve 1.8in (47mm) guns. Originally she belonged to the *Devastation* Class but was modified during construction. She was taken out of commission in 1902, then served for six years as a depot ship before being broken up in 1908.

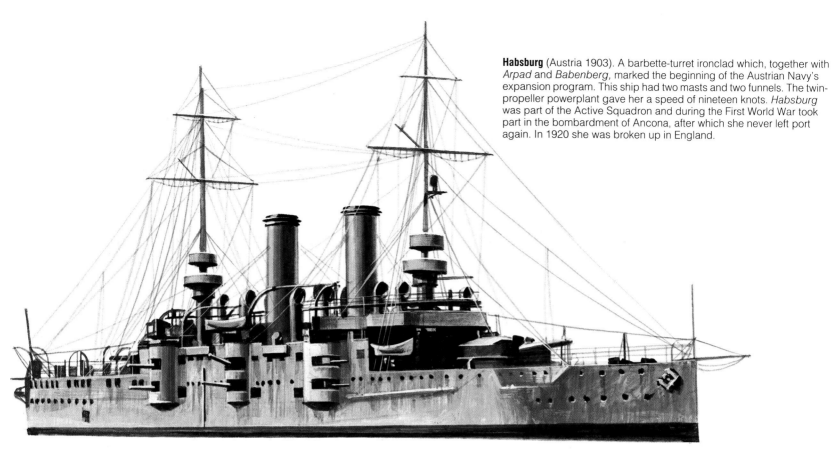

Habsburg (Austria 1903). A barbette-turret ironclad which, together with *Arpad* and *Babenberg,* marked the beginning of the Austrian Navy's expansion program. This ship had two masts and two funnels. The twin-propeller powerplant gave her a speed of nineteen knots. *Habsburg* was part of the Active Squadron and during the First World War took part in the bombardment of Ancona, after which she never left port again. In 1920 she was broken up in England.

On the superstructures and in the tops were the small-caliber and anti-torpedo weapons. Most ships were also armed with torpedo tubes, often firing underwater. An example of a battleship with secondary-caliber guns in turrets was the Russian *Petropavlosk* Class of 1894. Examples of units with their main guns in barbette turrets and secondary-caliber guns in a battery were the British *Majestic*s of 1895, the Japanese *Shikissima*s of 1898, and the British *Cornwallis* types of 1901. Examples of units with their main guns in turrets and secondary guns in casemates were the Italian *Benedetto Brian* types of 1901, the Russian *Kniaz Potemkin Tavrichesky* types, and the Austrian *Habsburgs* of 1900. The latter's main armament comprised a forward turret with two guns and an after turret with just one. Furthermore they had their twelve 6in (152mm) secondary-caliber guns in six casemates arranged on two levels, three per side, so that one gun was higher than the other.

The battleships with the most unusual main- and secondary-gun arrangement were the American *Kearsage* Class of 1898 and the *New Jersey* Class of 1904. They had their main armament of four heavy guns (13in and 12in, respectively) in two twin turrets, one forward and one aft. The four 8in (203mm) guns were also in two twin turrets, coaxial with the main guns and mounted directly over them. In the *Kearsage*, the secondary armament of fourteen 5in (127mm) and twenty 2.2in (57mm) guns were arranged in two batteries either side, the bigger guns being in the lower one. The two raised turrets were rigidly connected to the lower ones so that they trained together; if the main-caliber guns were firing, others could not, and vice versa.

As regards torpedo tubes, pre-dreadnought battleships usually had from two to four, all underwater and of the fixed type. If there were two, one was forward and the other aft. If there were four, either all were situated down the sides or else there was one each side, one forward and one aft.

Majestic (Great Britain 1896). A barbette-turret ironclad whose main armament was no longer diagonally arranged but in two emplacements on the centerline, one forward and one aft. She was sunk in the Dardanelles in May 1915 by a German submarine. The two funnels abreast were a distinctive feature.

Brétagne (France 1915). She belonged to a class of three ships armed with ten 13.3in (340mm) guns in five twin turrets, the fifth being amidships between the two funnels. She served in the First and Second World Wars, but sank during the British bombardment of Mers-el-Kabir, on July 3, 1940, after shelling by the British battleships *Hood, Barham,* and *Resolution.*

Dreadnoughts from 1905 to 1925

At the beginning of the century, an Italian engineer named Cuniberti had formulated the theory of drastically changing the number of large-caliber guns on battleships by increasing the number of main-caliber guns and reducing those of the middle-caliber.

The first ship to be built along the lines of these new ideas was Britain's *Dreadnought* of 1905. Whereas the ship Cuniberti described in the 1903 edition of *Jane's Fighting Ships* was armed with twelve 12in (305mm) guns in four twin and four single turrets, *Dreadnought* had only ten in five twin turrets. The ship's profile was the same as that of the pre-dreadnoughts which, however, had only two large-caliber turrets: one forward and one aft of the central superstructure. In addition to the two fore and aft turrets, *Dreadnought* had a second turret aft on the center line and two on either side amidships, symmetrically placed, in the space between the two funnels. On this first version, there was no secondary-caliber armament whatsoever and there were only twenty-three 3in (76mm) anti-torpedo guns on the superstructures and roofs of the large-caliber turrets. The symmetrical arrangement of the large-caliber turrets amidships was not very popular. Examples were the four

German *Nassau* types of 1908 which had twelve 11in (280mm) guns in six twin turrets: one forward, one aft, and four abreast amidships. On these units secondary-caliber armament were twelve 5.9in (150mm) guns in casemates in the central citadel. Another example of ships with turrets abreast were France's *Jean Bart, Paris,* and *Courbet* of 1911 which displaced 25,495t (25,850 tonnes) against *Dreadnought*'s 17,654t (17,900 tonnes), and the *Nassaus*' 18,207t (18,500 tonnes). Main armament comprised twelve 12in (305mm) guns in six twin turrets, two forward and two aft on the center line, side by side in between two of the ship's three funnels (two of which were close together farther forward, and one farther aft.) Secondary armament consisted of twenty-two 5.5in (138mm) guns in casemates, eighteen at main deck level and four on the gallery deck.

It will be remembered that the symmetrical arrangement of the turrets amidships had already been adopted by the French Navy for its pre-dreadnoughts *Magenta* and *Jaureguiberry.*

Other ships that had their turrets amidships, but not in a symmetrical position, were Brazil's *Minas Gerais* and *São Paulo,* built in England in 1908 and Spain's *España* types, built at El Ferrol in 1912. The latter battleships had their middle turrets diagonally positioned like the old *Duilio* and *Inflexible* of 1876. The main

Minas Gerais (Brazil 1910). Built in Britain, together with her sister ship *São Paulo,* for the Brazilian Navy. Originally there were two tall funnels, but in 1934-1937 the eighteen original coal-fired boilers were replaced with six oil-fired ones, so the forward funnel was removed. She served in the 1939-1945 war, was stricken in 1953, and broken up in 1954.

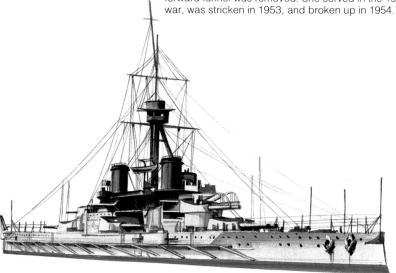

España (Spain 1913). She belonged to a class of three ships and had two very tall tripod masts and one funnel. After running aground on the coast of Morocco, in August 1923, she was wrecked by a storm. Her name was given to her sister-ship *Alfonso XIII,* which was sunk on April 30, 1937, during the Spanish Civil War.

Bayern (Germany 1916). A dreadnought battleship belonging to a class of two units armed with eight 15in (380mm) guns, which was a considerable increase in comparison to the 12in (305mm) guns on the majority of the single-caliber battleships. Like other German ships, she had three propellers driven by turbines. During the First World War she was operated in the North Sea and the Baltic, and was scuttled at Scapa Flow in June 1919.

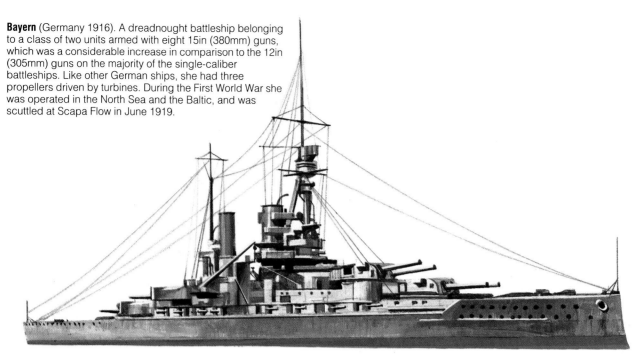

armament of the Brazilian ships was twelve 12in (305mm) guns in six twin turrets. The Spanish ships had eight 12in (305mm) guns in four twin turrets, the two central ones not symmetrical, the starboard one being further forward. The secondary-caliber guns were in casemates on the gallery deck and in the central citadel.

The various navies copied the British and large numbers of dreadnought battleships were built between 1905 and 1920. Usually their main armament was made up of eight to twelve guns of calibers varying from 11in (280mm) to 16in (406mm).

America's *South Carolina* battleships of 1908 had eight 12in (305mm) guns in four twin turrets. Britain's *Queen Elizabeth* Class of 1913 and the five *Resolution* Class of 1915 also had eight guns, although they were of the larger caliber of 15in (381mm). The caliber increased to 16in (406mm) on the American *West Virginia* Class of 1921 and the two Japanese *Nagatos* of 1919.

The increase in the number of main-caliber guns brought with it two different trends: The first was to keep the twin turrets and increase their number; the second was to keep the number of turrets at four and convert all or some of them into triples. Britain's *King George V* Class of 1911 had five twin 13.5in (343mm) turrets; Germany's *Koenig* Class of 1913 had five twin 12in (305mm) turrets and France's *Brétagne* Class had five twin 13.4in (340mm) turrets. These turrets were arranged as follows: two forward, two aft, and one amidships, either behind the funnels as on the *King George V*s, or else between the funnels as on the *Koenigs* and *Brétagnes*.

America's *Arkansas* and *Wyoming* of 1911 had six twin 12in (305mm) turrets; Japan's *Yamashiro* and *Fuso* of 1914 had the same number of turrets with 14in (356mm) guns, and finally came the seven twin 12in (305mm) turrets of Britain's *Agincourt* (1913), a ship which had a complicated arrangement of turrets, some higher and some lower so as not to block each other's fire.

South Carolina (United States 1910). Along with *Michigan,* this was the United States Navy's first dreadnought, or single-caliber battleship. They had the first superfiring turrets in the world. The two cage masts typical of American ships of this period, and the two tall funnels are worth noting. She was stricken in 1924, after having served in the First World War with the Atlantic Squadron.

Tennessee (United States 1920). This battleship was commissioned when the First World War was over and modernized in 1929–1930. She had a four-shaft turbo-electric drive. She was damaged in the attack on Pearl Harbor on December 7, 1941, but refitted, with changes to the armament and superstructures. She took part in the War in the Pacific, was taken out of commission on February 14, 1947, and broken up in 1959.

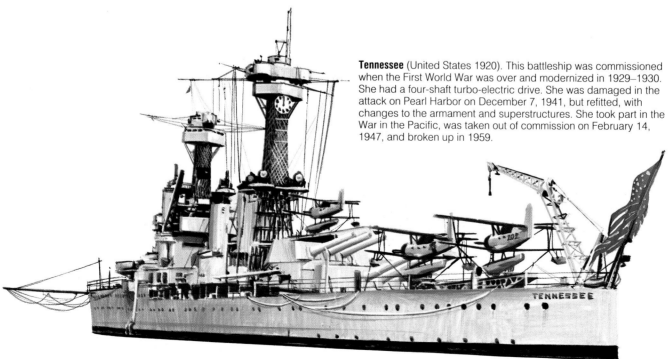

Still keeping the number of turrets at four, Italy's *Dante Alighieri* of 1910, Russia's four *Gangut* types of 1911, Austria's four *Viribus Unitis* of 1911 and Russia's four *Imperator Alexander III* of 1914 all had twelve 12in (305mm) guns while America's *Pennsylvania* and *Arizona* of 1915, *New Mexico, Mississippi,* and *Idaho* of 1917, and *Tennessee* and *California* of 1919 had twelve 14in (356mm) guns.

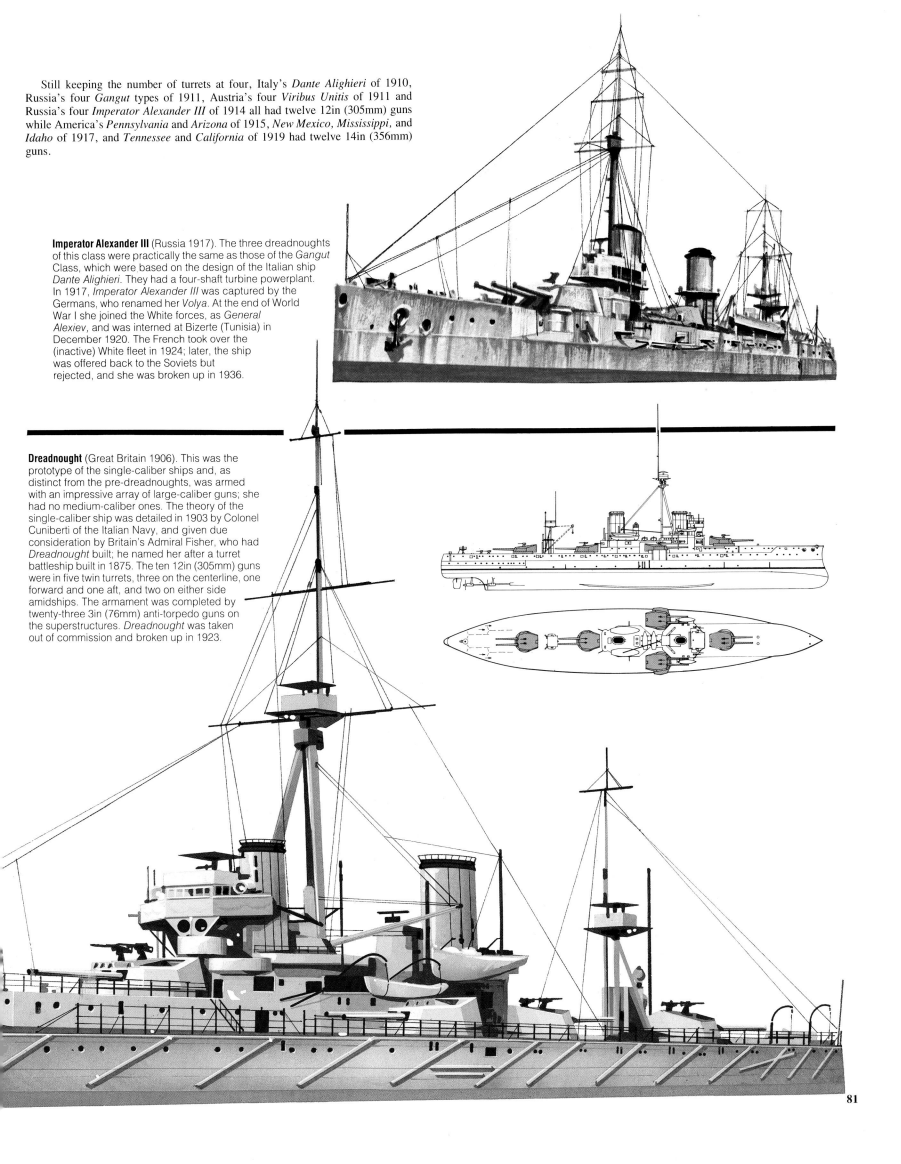

Imperator Alexander III (Russia 1917). The three dreadnoughts of this class were practically the same as those of the *Gangut* Class, which were based on the design of the Italian ship *Dante Alighieri*. They had a four-shaft turbine powerplant. In 1917, *Imperator Alexander III* was captured by the Germans, who renamed her *Volya*. At the end of World War I she joined the White forces, as *General Alexiev,* and was interned at Bizerte (Tunisia) in December 1920. The French took over the (inactive) White fleet in 1924; later, the ship was offered back to the Soviets but rejected, and she was broken up in 1936.

Dreadnought (Great Britain 1906). This was the prototype of the single-caliber ships and, as distinct from the pre-dreadnoughts, was armed with an impressive array of large-caliber guns; she had no medium-caliber ones. The theory of the single-caliber ship was detailed in 1903 by Colonel Cuniberti of the Italian Navy, and given due consideration by Britain's Admiral Fisher, who had *Dreadnought* built; he named her after a turret battleship built in 1875. The ten 12in (305mm) guns were in five twin turrets, three on the centerline, one forward and one aft, and two on either side amidships. The armament was completed by twenty-three 3in (76mm) anti-torpedo guns on the superstructures. *Dreadnought* was taken out of commission and broken up in 1923.

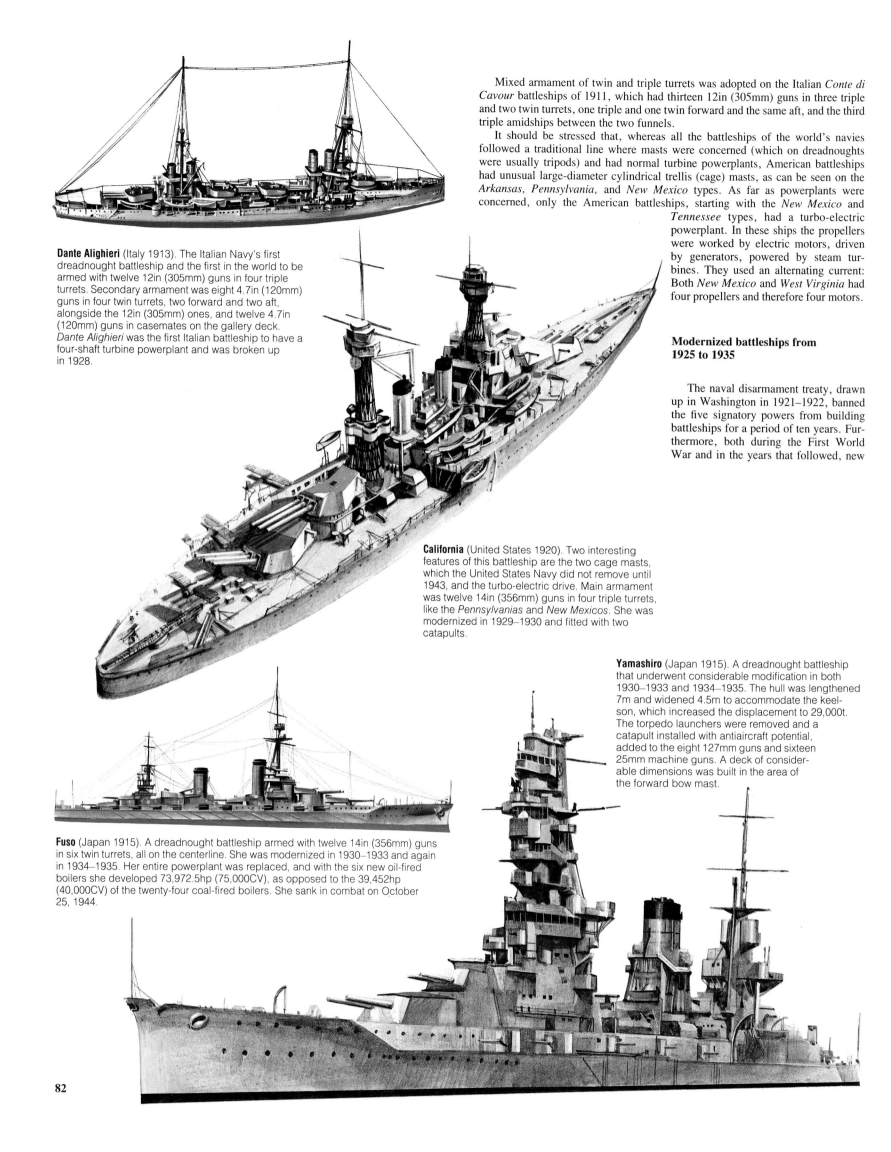

Mixed armament of twin and triple turrets was adopted on the Italian *Conte di Cavour* battleships of 1911, which had thirteen 12in (305mm) guns in three triple and two twin turrets, one triple and one twin forward and the same aft, and the third triple amidships between the two funnels.

It should be stressed that, whereas all the battleships of the world's navies followed a traditional line where masts were concerned (which on dreadnoughts were usually tripods) and had normal turbine powerplants, American battleships had unusual large-diameter cylindrical trellis (cage) masts, as can be seen on the *Arkansas, Pennsylvania,* and *New Mexico* types. As far as powerplants were concerned, only the American battleships, starting with the *New Mexico* and *Tennessee* types, had a turbo-electric powerplant. In these ships the propellers were worked by electric motors, driven by generators, powered by steam turbines. They used an alternating current: Both *New Mexico* and *West Virginia* had four propellers and therefore four motors.

Dante Alighieri (Italy 1913). The Italian Navy's first dreadnought battleship and the first in the world to be armed with twelve 12in (305mm) guns in four triple turrets. Secondary armament was eight 4.7in (120mm) guns in four twin turrets, two forward and two aft, alongside the 12in (305mm) ones, and twelve 4.7in (120mm) guns in casemates on the gallery deck. *Dante Alighieri* was the first Italian battleship to have a four-shaft turbine powerplant and was broken up in 1928.

Modernized battleships from 1925 to 1935

The naval disarmament treaty, drawn up in Washington in 1921–1922, banned the five signatory powers from building battleships for a period of ten years. Furthermore, both during the First World War and in the years that followed, new

California (United States 1920). Two interesting features of this battleship are the two cage masts, which the United States Navy did not remove until 1943, and the turbo-electric drive. Main armament was twelve 14in (356mm) guns in four triple turrets, like the *Pennsylvanias* and *New Mexicos*. She was modernized in 1929–1930 and fitted with two catapults.

Yamashiro (Japan 1915). A dreadnought battleship that underwent considerable modification in both 1930–1933 and 1934–1935. The hull was lengthened 7m and widened 4.5m to accommodate the keelson, which increased the displacement to 29,000t. The torpedo launchers were removed and a catapult installed with antiaircraft potential, added to the eight 127mm guns and sixteen 25mm machine guns. A deck of considerable dimensions was built in the area of the forward bow mast.

Fuso (Japan 1915). A dreadnought battleship armed with twelve 14in (356mm) guns in six twin turrets, all on the centerline. She was modernized in 1930–1933 and again in 1934–1935. Her entire powerplant was replaced, and with the six new oil-fired boilers she developed 73,972.5hp (75,000CV), as opposed to the 39,452hp (40,000CV) of the twenty-four coal-fired boilers. She sank in combat on October 25, 1944.

theories had been formulated for the armament of large ships which made the great dreadnought battleships, built only five to ten years before, obsolete. Lastly, the use of geared turbines and oil-fired boilers made powerplants capable of reaching speeds in the order of twenty to twenty-two knots obsolete. This was the average speed that dreadnought battleships could maintain.

For these reasons, all the major maritime powers called in some of their classes of battleships for extensive modification and modernization work. This did not turn these ships into super-dreadnoughts, but it did greatly increase their fighting capability by considerably prolonging their operational life.

Among the numerous dreadnought battleships that were modernized was the Brazilian *Minas Gerais*, originally equipped with eighteen coal-fired boilers and two funnels which were changed in 1934–1937 to six oil-fired boilers, and just one funnel, increasing the original 23,178hp (23,500CV) to 29,589hp (30,000CV). The bridge superstructures were also modified and the eight secondary-caliber guns removed.

Giulio Cesare (Italy). This ship belonged to the first class of four Italian dreadnoughts, armed with thirteen 12in (305mm) guns in five turrets, three of which were triples and two twins. One of the triples was amidships between the two funnels. This ship had a four-shaft turbine powerplant. During a refit in 1932, the amidships turret was removed and the number of guns reduced from thirteen to ten (although the latter had a caliber of 12.5in [320mm]). The powerplant was replaced with a two-shaft one and the foremast removed. *Giulio Cesare* was handed over to the Soviet Union in 1948 as stipulated by the Peace Treaty.

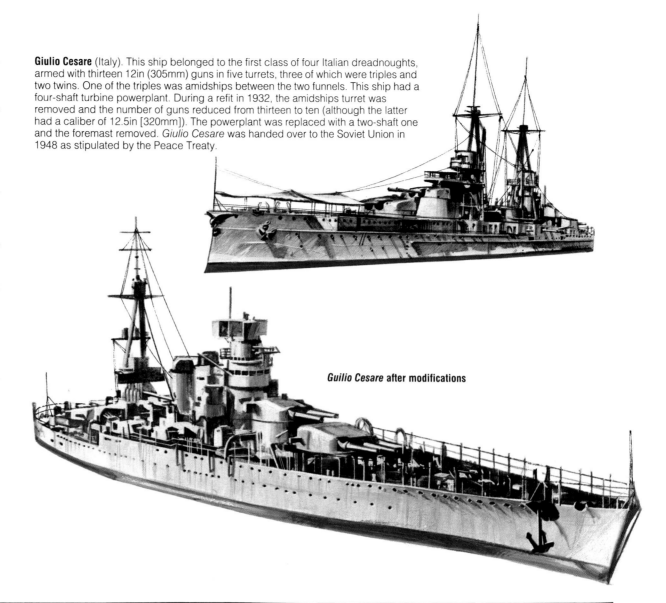

Guilio Cesare **after modifications**

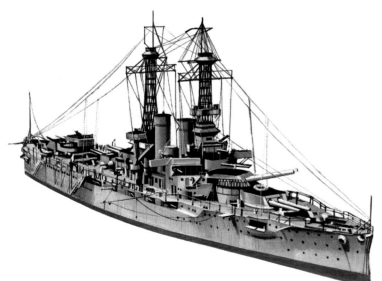

Arkansas (United States). She was built in 1910–1912 together with *Wyoming*, and modernized in 1925–1927. The modifications did not affect the powerplant, since the original one was kept. The twelve coal-fired boilers were replaced with four oil-fired ones, and one of the funnels was removed as a result. The cage mast aft was replaced by a tripod mast. In 1942 the ship was further modified: the main armament remained the same but the secondary armament was stepped up with antiaircraft guns and machine guns. The second cage mast (forward) was also removed. *Arkansas* was sunk at Bikini during the atomic bomb experiments on July 25, 1946.

Arkansas **after modifications.**

Pennsylvania (United States). *Pennsylvania* and *Arizona* were built in 1915 and modernized in 1930–1931. On both these ships the boilers were replaced and reduced in number from twelve to four while the armament remained unchanged. The old cage masts were removed, the bridge superstructure modified, an aircraft catapult added, and the secondary armament replaced. *Pennsylvania* was damaged in the attack on Pearl Harbor and was refitted and further modernized in 1942–1943. The following were installed: eight twin turrets for 5in (127mm) anti-aircraft guns; forty-five 1.5in (40mm) and fifty 0.7in (20mm) machine guns; and radar. This ship was used in the Bikini experiments but emerged only lightly damaged. She was sunk as a target on February 10, 1948.

Italy's four battleships *Giulio Cesare, Conte di Cavour, Andrea Doria,* and *Caio Duilio,* were much more extensively modified between 1932 and 1940. On these ships, the main armament changed from thirteen 12in (305mm) guns to ten 12.6in (320mm) guns, eliminating the triple turret amidships. Secondary armament of eighteen 4.7in (120mm) guns in casemates was replaced with twelve 4.7in (120mm) guns in six twin turrets on either side of the superstructure abreast of the funnels. The nineteen 3in (76mm) anti-torpedo guns were replaced by anti-aircraft armament of eight 3.9in (100mm) guns and twenty machine guns. Lastly, the three underwater torpedo tubes were removed. A modern fire-control system was installed in the large armored tower mast which had replaced the original bridge superstructure. The powerplant was completely changed and reduced from a four to a two-shaft unit; the twenty-four coal-fired boilers were replaced by eight oil-fired ones, power tripled from 30,575hp (31,000CV) to 91,726hp (93,000CV), and speed increased from 21.5 to 28 knots. The hull was lengthened at the bow (the old ram-bow was actually buried in the new structure) and a new Pugliese underwater protection system installed; the ships had been built essentially without underwater protection.

America's *Arkansas* Class underwent a less radical modification from 1925 to 1927 and from March to July 1942. The cage mainmast was removed, the two funnels were reduced to one, and the twelve coal-fired boilers changed for four oil-fired ones. The secondary armament was reduced from twenty-one 5in (127mm) to sixteen. Anti-aircraft weapons installed at this time were eight 3in (76mm) guns. The two submerged torpedo-tubes were removed and a catapult with three seaplanes added. Main armament remained unchanged: twelve 12in (305mm) guns in six twin turrets. Japan's fast *Kongo*-type battleships were also modernized, between 1927 and 1931 and again in 1934–1937. During the latter period, the main armament of eight 14in (356mm) guns had their elevation (maximum range) increased. The hull was lengthened and was given bulged sections for underwater protection and the powerplant replaced with a much more powerful one made up of four reduction gear turbine units, powered by eight oil-fired boilers. It replaced the old powerplant of

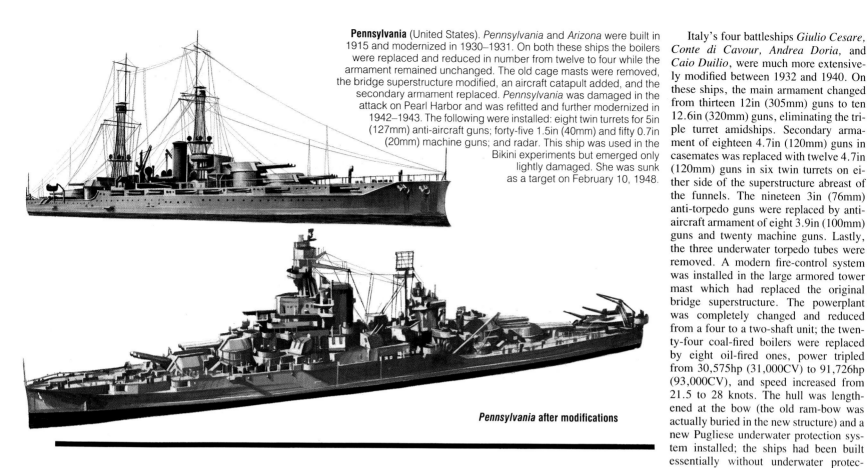

Pennsylvania after modifications

Kongo (Japan). The four fast *Kongo* Class battleships were built in 1911–1913 and modernized in 1927–1931 and 1934–1937. While making these changes the powerplant was replaced, the thirty-six boilers were reduced to eight, and the horsepower was raised from 64,000 to 136,000. The three funnels reduced to two, and the deck superstructure underwent some changes. The hull was lengthened by 26.2ft (8m). The main armament of eight 9in (356mm) guns remained unchanged, while the secondary armament was altered, in particular, by the installation of eight 5in (127mm) anti-aircraft guns. During the war, 118 .10in (25mm) machine guns were added. She was used in the war in the Pacific, and was sunk by the American submarine *Sea Lion* during November 1944 in the Straits of Formosa.

Kongo after modifications

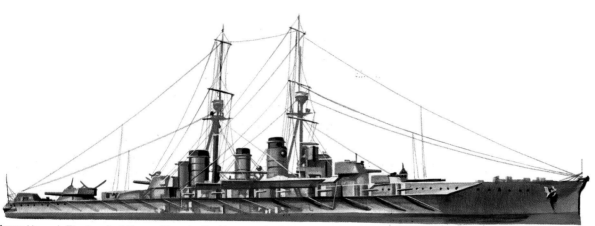

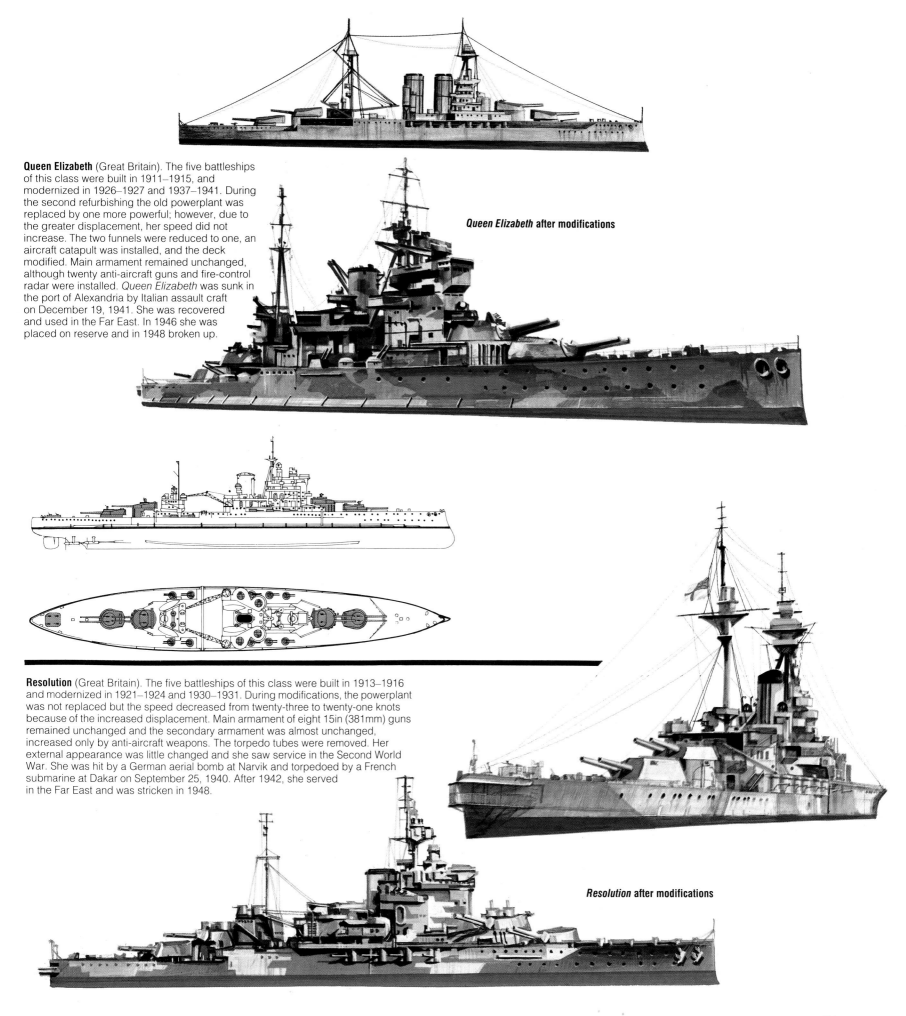

Queen Elizabeth (Great Britain). The five battleships of this class were built in 1911–1915, and modernized in 1926–1927 and 1937–1941. During the second refurbishing the old powerplant was replaced by one more powerful; however, due to the greater displacement, her speed did not increase. The two funnels were reduced to one, an aircraft catapult was installed, and the deck modified. Main armament remained unchanged, although twenty anti-aircraft guns and fire-control radar were installed. *Queen Elizabeth* was sunk in the port of Alexandria by Italian assault craft on December 19, 1941. She was recovered and used in the Far East. In 1946 she was placed on reserve and in 1948 broken up.

Queen Elizabeth after modifications

Resolution (Great Britain). The five battleships of this class were built in 1913–1916 and modernized in 1921–1924 and 1930–1931. During modifications, the powerplant was not replaced but the speed decreased from twenty-three to twenty-one knots because of the increased displacement. Main armament of eight 15in (381mm) guns remained unchanged and the secondary armament was almost unchanged, increased only by anti-aircraft weapons. The torpedo tubes were removed. Her external appearance was little changed and she saw service in the Second World War. She was hit by a German aerial bomb at Narvik and torpedoed by a French submarine at Dakar on September 25, 1940. After 1942, she served in the Far East and was stricken in 1948.

Resolution after modifications

Nagato (Japan). *Nagato* and *Mutsu* were built in 1917–1920 and modernized in 1934–1936. The hull was made 16.4ft (5m) wider, the powerplant replaced with another more powerful and modern one and the twenty-one boilers reduced to ten, with the removal of one funnel. The bridge was totally replaced and a catapult with three seaplanes installed. The armament remained unchanged; only the 5.5in (140mm) pieces were cut from twenty to sixteen. Eight 5in (127mm) anti-aircraft guns and ninety-eight 1in (25mm) machine guns were installed and the torpedo tubes removed. *Nagato* was seriously damaged in an air raid on July 18, 1945, and after being captured by the Americans was sunk in the Bikini experiments on July 25, 1946.

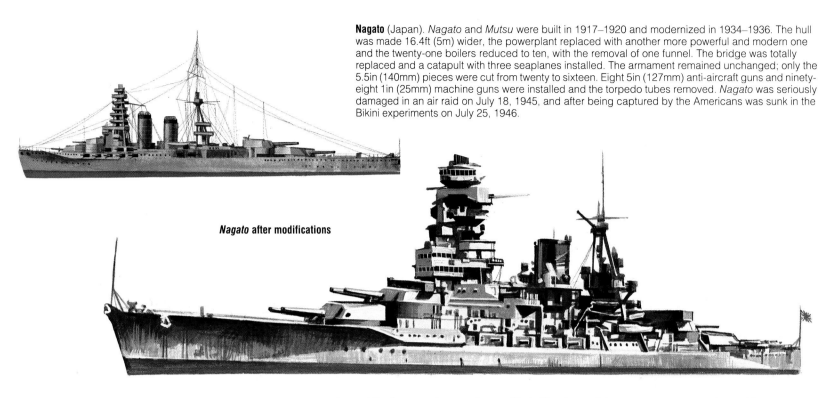

Nagato after modifications

four turbines directly linked to the shafts and powered by thirty-six coal-fired boilers. After this modification the three funnels were reduced to two, the bridge superstructure was replaced by an armored tower mast and secondary armament was replaced by twelve 5in (127mm) anti-aircraft guns. The torpedo tubes were removed and a catapult with three seaplanes installed. Speed increased from twenty-six to thirty knots, and deck armor was added. Britain modernized her *Queen Elizabeth* Class, first in the late 1920s and then (except for *Barham* and *Malaya*) between 1937 and 1941. The work consisted mainly in replacing the powerplant: Four turbines, directly linked to the shafts and powered by twenty-four boilers, became four reduction gear turbine sets powered by eight oil-fired boilers. Speed was not increased, however, because the hull was widened by about 13ft (4m) to accommodate the bulges for underwater protection. In *Queen Elizabeth* and *Valiant*, the sixteen 6in (152mm) guns of the secondary caliber were replaced by twenty 4.5in (114mm) anti-aircraft guns, in ten twin turrets either side of the central superstructure. The four torpedo tubes were removed and a catapult and

four seaplanes added. The shape of the superstructure was changed because a new bridge was added, the masts were lowered, and one of the two funnels removed.

More sweeping modifications were carried out on the Japanese *Negato* types and American *New Mexicos*, especially to the power-plants. The Japanese *Nagato* and *Mutsu* battleships had four turbines linked directly to the shafts and powered by twenty-one coal-fired boilers. From 1934 to 1936 this powerplant was replaced by one made up of four reduction gear turbine sets, powered by ten oil-fired boilers. The rating rose from 78,904hp (80,000CV) to 80,876hp (82,000CV) but the speed stayed around twenty-five knots because the hull had been made about 29.5ft (9m) longer and about 16ft (5m) wider due to the application of bulges for underwater protection, thus increasing the displacement from 33,577t (34,116 tonnes) to 45,617t (46,350 tonnes).

Main and secondary armament remained almost unchanged but elevations were increased: Eight 16in (406mm) guns in four twin turrets and sixteen (instead of twenty) 5.5in (140mm) guns in casemates in the middle of the gallery deck. Anti-aircraft armament was eight 5in (127mm) guns. A new "pagoda" tower mast was installed, one of the two funnels removed along with the eight torpedo-tubes, and a catapult with three seaplanes added.

The American *New Mexico* battleships had their engines replaced in 1931–1933 by four reduction gear turbine units. The power rating rose from 27,500shp to 40,000shp but the speed stayed almost the same because bulges had been applied to the hull, increasing the displacement from 32,970t (33,500 tonnes) to 35,431t (36,000 tonnes). The two cage masts were removed, an armored tower bridge

New Mexico (United States). *New Mexico* belonged to a class completed by *Mississippi* and *Idaho* but had a turbo-electric drive, whereas the other two had direct-drive steam turbines. In 1931–1933 the electric drive was replaced by a geared steam turbine power plant, the hull made 4.4ft (1.35mm) wider and the cage masts removed. The main armament of twelve 14in (356mm) guns remained unchanged. In a second refit in 1942, anti-aircraft armament was stepped up by adding sixteen 1.5in (40mm) and forty-four 0.7in (20mm) machine guns. In 1944 radar was installed. *New Mexico* was attacked twice by kamikaze aircraft and was badly damaged but she never failed to return to the line. She was stricken in 1947.

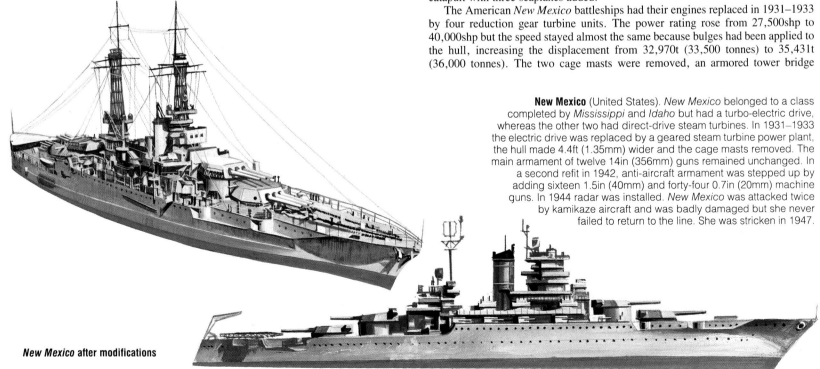

New Mexico after modifications

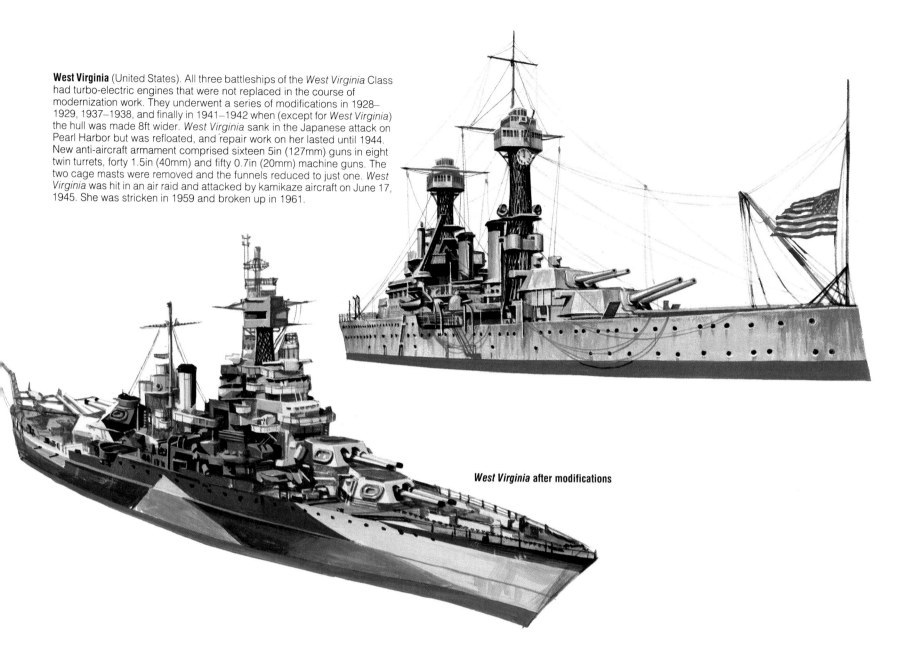

West Virginia (United States). All three battleships of the *West Virginia* Class had turbo-electric engines that were not replaced in the course of modernization work. They underwent a series of modifications in 1928–1929, 1937–1938, and finally in 1941–1942 when (except for *West Virginia*) the hull was made 8ft wider. *West Virginia* sank in the Japanese attack on Pearl Harbor but was refloated, and repair work on her lasted until 1944. New anti-aircraft armament comprised sixteen 5in (127mm) guns in eight twin turrets, forty 1.5in (40mm) and fifty 0.7in (20mm) machine guns. The two cage masts were removed and the funnels reduced to just one. *West Virginia* was hit in an air raid and attacked by kamikaze aircraft on June 17, 1945. She was stricken in 1959 and broken up in 1961.

West Virginia **after modifications**

added, the torpedo-tubes removed, and a catapult with three seaplanes installed. Main armament remained unchanged, at twelve 14in, twelve 5in/51, and eight 5in AA guns.

The *West Virginia*s did not undergo any powerplant modification and retained their turbo-electric drive. Damaged in the attack on Pearl Harbor, *West Virgina* was rebuilt. Her hull was bulged, her superstructure and masts replaced by a low structure with a tower mast. The two cage masts were removed. The mixed secondary battery of single-purpose and anti-aircraft guns was replaced by sixteen 5in (127mm) anti-aircraft guns. Furthermore, forty 1.5in (40mm) and fifty 0.7in (20mm) machine guns were installed, plus a catapult and three seaplanes. The sixteen 5in (127mm) guns were in eight twin turrets either side of the central superstructure. The 1.5in (40mm) machine guns were in quadruple mountings. *West Virginia* had been fitted with radar but on December 7, 1941, at the moment of the Japanese attack on Pearl Harbor, a Sunday, the system was not in operation and so could not detect the enemy aircraft. The battleships *Tennessee* and *California* were similarly modified; *Tennessee* had been damaged at Pearl Harbor.

Super-dreadnoughts from 1935 to 1945

The final development of battleships led to the construction of the super-dreadnoughts. In 1930–1932, after abiding by the conditions of the Treaty of Washington stipulating the ten-year "naval holiday," France laid down the *Dunkerque* and *Strasbourg*; then in 1934 Italy built *Littorio* and *Vittorio Veneto*, and in 1935–1936 came Germany's turn with *Scharnhorst* and *Gneisenau*. Britain began building the super-dreadnoughts in 1937, starting with the five *King George V* Class. The United States, too, started building the *North Carolina* Class in 1938, followed before long by the *South Dakota*s. In 1937, the Japanese Navy laid down

the keels of the two battleships, *Yamato* and *Musashi* which, with their displacement of 71,748t (72,900 tonnes), were the largest in the world. While all the major naval powers kept more or less to the 35,000-ton displacement limit laid down by the Washington Treaty, the Japanese had withdrawn from the Treaty in March, 1934, and therefore built ships double this displacement. Moreover, they were the only ones to equip their ships with 18in (460mm) guns, while the Treaty limit was 16in (406mm), a limit respected by all the other powers.

It is appropriate here to point out that the 35,000-ton limit referred to a "Standard" displacement, that is, the displacement of a ship without fuel and reserve water supplies for the boilers. Italy's *Littorio*-Class battleships with a full-load displacement of 45,236t (45,963 tonnes), including 3,936t (4,000 tonnes) of fuel therefore came to about 40,000 tons Standard displacement. Designed in the Mediterranean, they had relatively little fuel oil. Germany's longer-ranged *Bismarck* Class, of 50,095-tons (50,900-tonne) full-load displacement, exceeded the set limit by about 6,700 tons.

Typical features common to all the super-dreadnoughts were high speed, heavy armor, extensive underwater protection, and relatively few turrets, usually only three, each turret containing a large number of guns. Speed ranged from twenty-seven to thirty-three knots, the slowest being Japan's *Yamato*s, followed by Britain's *King George V*s with 27.5 knots and America's *North Carolina* and *Alabama* with twenty-eight knots. France's *Dunkerque*s, Germany's *Bismarck*s, and Britain's *Vanguard*s developed twenty-nine knots. Italy's *Littorio*s and France's *Richelieu*s managed thirty knots and Germany's *Scharnhorst*s 31.5 knots. The fastest were America's *Iowa* (or *Missouri*) Class which developed thirty-three knots, even though they had a displacement of 56,432t (57,216 tonnes), with an incredible 212,000shp powerplant. The *Yamato*s, with a displacement of 71,748t (72,900 tonnes), had a power rating of 147,945hp (150,000CV).

Britain's two battleships, *Nelson* and *Rodney,* commissioned in 1927 and armed with nine 16in (406mm) guns, can still be regarded as dreadnoughts because they

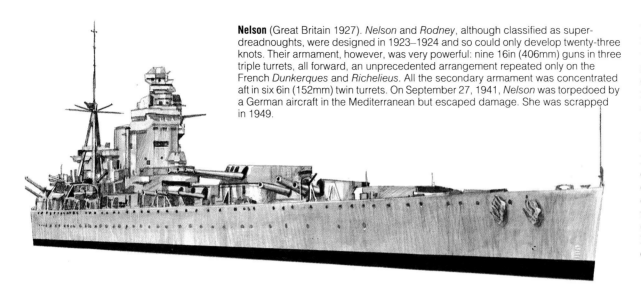

Nelson (Great Britain 1927). *Nelson* and *Rodney*, although classified as super-dreadnoughts, were designed in 1923–1924 and so could only develop twenty-three knots. Their armament, however, was very powerful: nine 16in (406mm) guns in three triple turrets, all forward, an unprecedented arrangement repeated only on the French *Dunkerques* and *Richelieus*. All the secondary armament was concentrated aft in six 6in (152mm) twin turrets. On September 27, 1941, *Nelson* was torpedoed by a German aircraft in the Mediterranean but escaped damage. She was scrapped in 1949.

were designed on the basis of concepts in force in 1920–1922. In fact, their speed was just twenty-three knots. Other capital ships of this period that cannot be considered as super-dreadnoughts are Germany's *Deutschland*, *Admiral Scheer*, and *Admiral Graf Spee*, built between 1929 and 1933. They had a nominal displacement of only 10,000t (actually about 11,700t), as stipulated by the Versailles Peace Treaty, and so, according to the displacements agreed at Washington, could be considered as cruisers. Moreover, they had only cruiser armor. But the caliber of their guns was 11in (280mm), well over the 8in (203mm) allowed for cruisers, and were therefore called ''pocket battleships.'' The

Admiral Scheer, Admiral Graf Spee and **Deutschland** (Germany). The three pocket battleships of this class were built by the German Navy when the displacement and armament limitations of the Versailles Treaty were still in force. This treaty stated that the German Navy could not include battleships with a displacement greater than 10,000 tons and armament with a caliber greater than 11in (280mm). These three units were built between 1929 and 1933 and were the only battleships in the world to be driven by eight diesel engines, four per shaft, linked to the latter by couplings, which, for their time, were an amazing technological achievement. The rating was 53,260hp (54,000CV) and speed twenty-six knots, reduced to 23–24 under full load, and displacement was 15,747t (16,000 tonnes). The main armament was six 11in (280mm) guns in two triple turrets. Secondary armament was eight 6in (150mm) guns in single mounts and there was one catapult and two aircraft. *Admiral Scheer* was used as a raiding cruiser and operated in the South Atlantic and Indian Ocean from the end of 1940 to the beginning of 1941. She was then used against convoys in the Arctic and sunk on April 9, 1945, at Kiel in an air raid. *Admiral Graf Spee,* also used as a raiding cruiser in the South Atlantic, was seriously damaged in an encounter with the British ships *Exeter, Ajax,* and *Achilles* on December 13, 1939, and took refuge in the neutral port of Montevideo, but came out into the open sea to scuttle on December 17, 1939. After November 5, 1939, *Deutschland* was renamed *Lützow* and used in operations against Norway and the Arctic convoys. She was sunk in an air raid on April 14, 1945, in the port of Gotenhaven. After being refloated by the Russians, she sank in September 1947 while being towed to Leningrad.

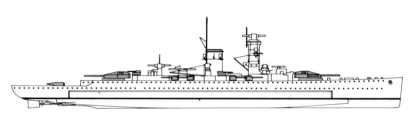

Dunkerque (France 1937). *Dunkerque* and *Strasbourg* were built between 1932 and 1937 and had all their armament forward, like Britain's *Nelson* and *Rodney* of 1927, but in two quadruple 13in (330mm) turrets, instead of three 16in (406mm) triples. They were the first super-dreadnoughts to have turrets of this type. *Dunkerque* took part in the hunt for the German battleships *Scharnhorst* and *Gneisenau* in November 1939. She was detached to the Mediterranean and was sunk at Mers-el-Kebir during attacks by the British fleet on July 4 and 6, 1940. After being refloated and taken to Toulon, she was scuttled on November 27, 1942.

Deutschlands were the only ships classified as battleships to have a diesel rather than a steam powerplant. This powerplant was made up of eight engines driving two propellers which in total developed 53,260 hp (54,000CV) and a speed of twenty-six knots, while all the battleships of this period had ratings of at least 138,082–147,945hp (140–150,000CV) up to the 212,000shp of the American battleships. Despite these limitations, the *Deutschlands* performed well in the Second World War, especially *Deutschland* which, after operating in Norwegian waters and attacking allied convoys in the Arctic, survived the war and was given to the Russians as part of the spoils of war, though she sank while being towed to the port of Leningrad.

Leaving aside the *Nelsons* and *Deutschlands*, the first real super-dreadnoughts, in chronological order, were France's *Dunkerque* and *Strasbourg* of 1935, armed with eight 13in (330mm) guns in two quadruple turrets, both forward. The side armor of the *Dunkerques*, like that of all the super-dreadnoughts except the British and German, sloped inwards from the top to the bottom. It had a maximum thickness of 9.5in (241mm). It was made of steel and had a hardened surface. Horizontal protection was very well developed, distributed between the 4.5–5in (115–130mm) thick gallery deck and the 1.5–2in (40–50mm) protective deck below it. The *Dunkerques* had a large armored tower mast, one funnel, and a catapult with a seaplane davit right aft.

Germany's two super-dreadnoughts *Scharnhorst* and *Gneisenau* were built in 1935–1939 after the signing of the Anglo-German naval agreement of 1935. With the restrictive clauses of the Versailles Treaty no longer in force, this agreement laid down that the Germany Navy could possess a war fleet with a displacement equal to 35 percent of the British one with battleships accounting for 181,093t (184,000 tonnes). These two units had an armament of nine 11in (280mm) guns in three triple turrets, two forward and one aft. Anti-aircraft armament was made up of fourteen 4.1in (105mm) guns, sixteen 1.4in (37mm) and ten 0.7in (20mm) machine guns. The fourteen 4.1in (105mm) guns were in seven twin turrets either side of the funnel and the machine guns on the superstructures. They were among the few examples of battleships with a triple-shaft powerplant, with a rating of 162,739hp (165,000CV), giving a speed of 31.5 knots. They had two catapults either side at the after end of the superstructure and four seaplanes.

The four Italian *Littorio* Class (the fourth, named *Impero*, was never completed) were armed with nine 15in (381mm) guns in three triple turrets, two forward and one aft. Anti-aircraft armament was made up of twelve 3.5in (90mm) guns in single turrets, six either side, abreast of the turret mast and funnels. There were also twenty 1.4in (20mm) machine guns plus four flare guns. The catapult and its plane davit were right aft. Underwater protection was particularly well-developed, based on the Pugliese system of shock absorption cylinders which was also installed on the modernized *Conte di Cavours*. The powerplant, with four turbine units powered by eight boilers, developed 138,082hp (140,000CV) and a speed of thirty knots. *Littorio* was torpedoed at Taranto in an attack on November 11, 1940, then again in a naval encounter on June 15, 1942. In both cases the underwater protection proved to be effective and stood up to the attacks fairly well.

Britain's five battleships of the *King George V* Class were the only ones to be built by the British Navy in the interwar years. During this period, however, the Royal Navy had begun building a considerable number of aircraft carriers, having already recognized the strategic superiority offered by this type of unit.

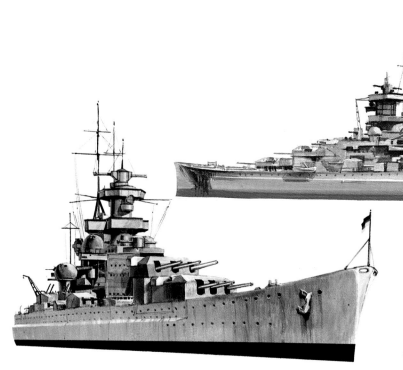

Scharnhorst and **Gneisenau** (Germany 1939). Like most super-dreadnoughts, these ships were armed with nine guns in three triple turrets, two forward and one aft. The caliber of the guns was 11in (280mm), like those on the pocket battleships, whereas other navies had used larger calibers: from the 13in (330mm) of the French *Dunkerques* to the 18in (460mm) guns of the Japanese *Yamatos*. *Scharnhorst* and *Gneisenau* were among the few super-dreadnoughts to be armed with six torpedo tubes. From November 1939 to February 1940, *Scharnhorst* operated in the Atlantic where she sunk the armed merchant cruiser *Rawalpindi*, the aircraft carrier *Glorious*, and two destroyers. She sank on December 26, 1943, in Norwegian waters after being hit by the *Duke of York* and torpedoed by aircraft. *Gneisenau* operated in the Atlantic as a convoy raider with *Scharnhorst*, sinking twenty-two steamships. She was bombed by aircraft at Brest in April 1941 and then at Kiel in February 1942 and put out of action. In March 1945 *Gneisenau* was run aground to prevent her sinking and she was broken up in 1947–1951.

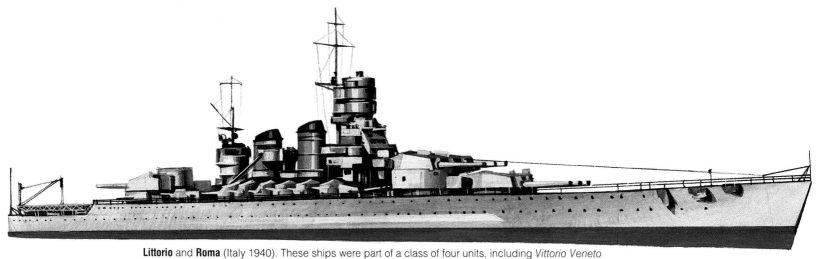

Littorio and **Roma** (Italy 1940). These ships were part of a class of four units, including *Vittorio Veneto* and *Impero,* although the latter was never completed. *Littorio* displaced 45,237t (45,963 tonnes) when fully-laden, and was armed with nine 15in (381mm) guns in three triple turrets, two forward and one aft. The caliber of 15in (381mm) was the same as that of France's *Richelieus* and Germany's *Bismarcks,* bigger than Britain's *King George V's* 14in (356mm), but smaller than the 16in (460mm) of the American *North Carolina, Alabama,*and *Missouri,* and the 18in (460mm) of Japan's *Yamatos.* Secondary armament was twelve 6in (152mm) guns in four triple turrets, and anti-aircraft armament comprised twelve 3.5in (90mm) guns and twenty 1.4in (37mm), and 20 0.7in (20mm) machine guns. Side armor was 13.7in (350mm) thick, the main deck 1.4–1.7in (36–45mm) and the protective deck 3.9–6.3in (100–162mm) thick. *Vittorio Veneto* and *Littorio* saw a fair amount of action during the war and escaped serious damage. The peace treaty stipulated that they be assigned to Great Britain and the United States who arranged for them to be broken up. While steaming from La Spezia to Malta with the Italian Squadron, *Roma* was sunk by German aircraft on September 9, 1943.

The *King George V*s had main armament of ten 14in (356mm) guns arranged, as usual, in three turrets, two quadruples at main-deck level, one forward and one aft, and one twin in a raised position abaft the single forward turret. The huge tower bridge was a distinctive feature. It will be observed that the belt armor was 15in (381mm) thick and that the horizontal armor, split between the 1in (25mm) thick main deck and the protective deck was 5–6in (127–152mm) and flat (not curved). These units had a full-load displacement of 43,757t (44,460 tonnes).

In 1935, France planned the construction of three super-dreadnoughts of which only one, *Richelieu,* was completed before the armistice of July 1940. These units had main armament of eight 15in (380mm) guns disposed as on the *Dunkerques* in two quadruple turrets, both forward. *Richelieu* was damaged at Dakar in the British bombardment of July 8, 1940. In 1943 she was refitted and modernized in the United States—the anti-aircraft armament in particular was strengthened with fifty-six 1.5in (40mm) machine guns. *Richelieu* had 12.8in (327mm) thick side armor which sloped at an angle of 15° inwards and downwards. The second unit, *Jean Bart,* was completed when the war was over and was commissioned in 1955. *Clemenceau,* the third unit, was never completed.

The *King George V*s, *Dunkerque*s, and *Richelieu*s were the only ones to have quadruple turrets. Almost all the super-dreadnoughts had three triple turrets: two forward and one aft, like Germany's *Scharnhorst*s; Italy's *Littorio*s; America's *North Carolina*s, *Alabama*s, and *Missouri*s and Japan's *Yamato*s.

The two German battleships, *Bismarck* and *Tirpitz,* with their displacement of 50,096t (50,900 tonnes), had eight 15in (380mm) guns in the conventional arrangement of two twin turrets forward and two twin turrets aft. The armor was not sloping, as on the majority of the other battleships of that period, but fitted vertically to the sides and was 12.5in (320mm) thick. The protective

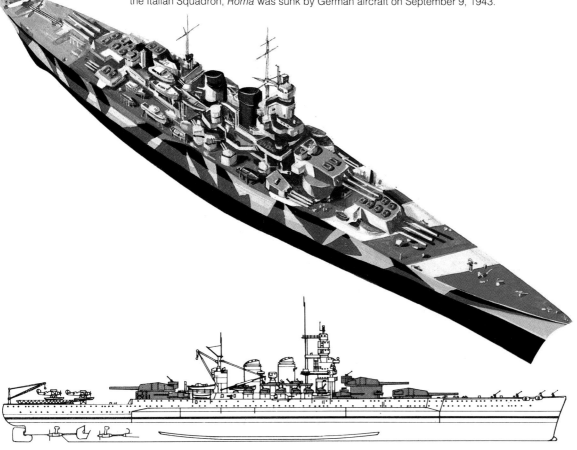

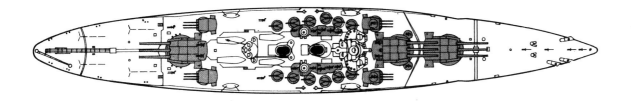

Bismarck and **Tirpitz** (Germany 1940). These were
the most powerful super-dreadnoughts of the
German Navy. They displaced 50,096t (50,900
tonnes) and were armed with eight 15in (380mm)
guns in four twin turrets, two forward and two aft,
not three triple turrets like the *Scharnhorsts*.
Secondary armament was twelve 5.9in (150mm)
guns in six twin turrets, three per side amidships,
and anti-aircraft armament was sixteen 4in
(105mm) guns in eight twin turrets, and sixteen
1.4in (37mm) and fifty-two 0.7in (20mm) machine
guns. These ships had triple-screws and could
develop twenty-nine knots. After a long chase
involving the entire Home Fleet, *Bismarck* was
sunk in the Atlantic on May 27, 1941. After having
seen a fair amount of action in the war, *Tirpitz*
suffered severe aerial and naval bombing from
February to October 1944 in Norwegian waters,
and was put out of service. She was used as a
floating battery at Tromsø and sunk on November
12, 1944.

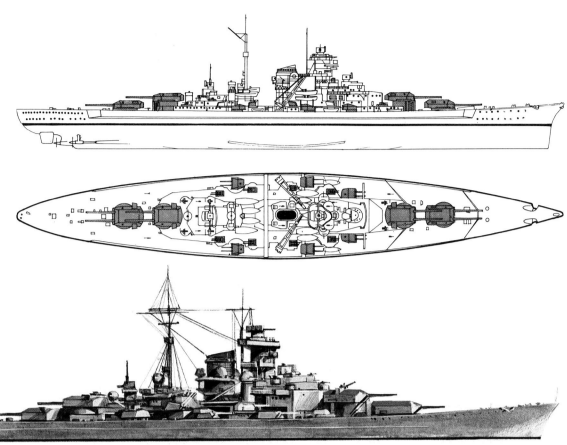

Richelieu (France 1940). One of a class of three
units: *Richelieu, Jean Bart,* and *Clemenceau,* and
the only one to be commissioned before the fall of
France. *Jean Bart* was moved to Casablanca
before the German occupation and completed in
1955. Never completed, the *Clemenceau* was
captured by the Germans and broken up. These
ships were a follow-up to the *Dunkerques,* except
that they had 15in (380mm) instead of 13in
(330mm) caliber guns. At the after end there were
nine 6in (152mm) guns in three triple turrets and
anti-aircraft armament was twelve 3.9in (100mm)
guns and sixteen 1.4in (37mm) machine guns.
While sheltering at Dakar, she was damaged by
the British fleet on July 8, 1940. In 1943, she
was taken to the United States and refitted.
In 1944, she was sent to the Far East and
then took part in the Indochina War.
Taken out of commission in 1956, she
was broken up in 1968.

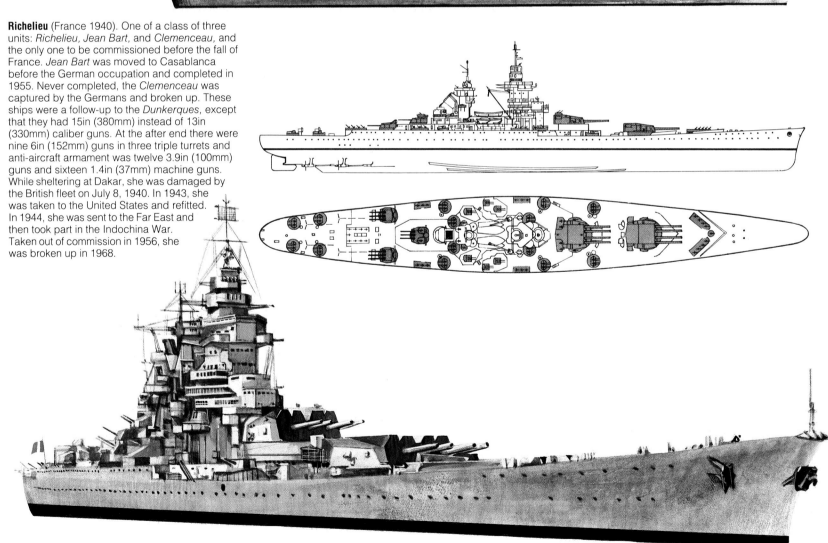

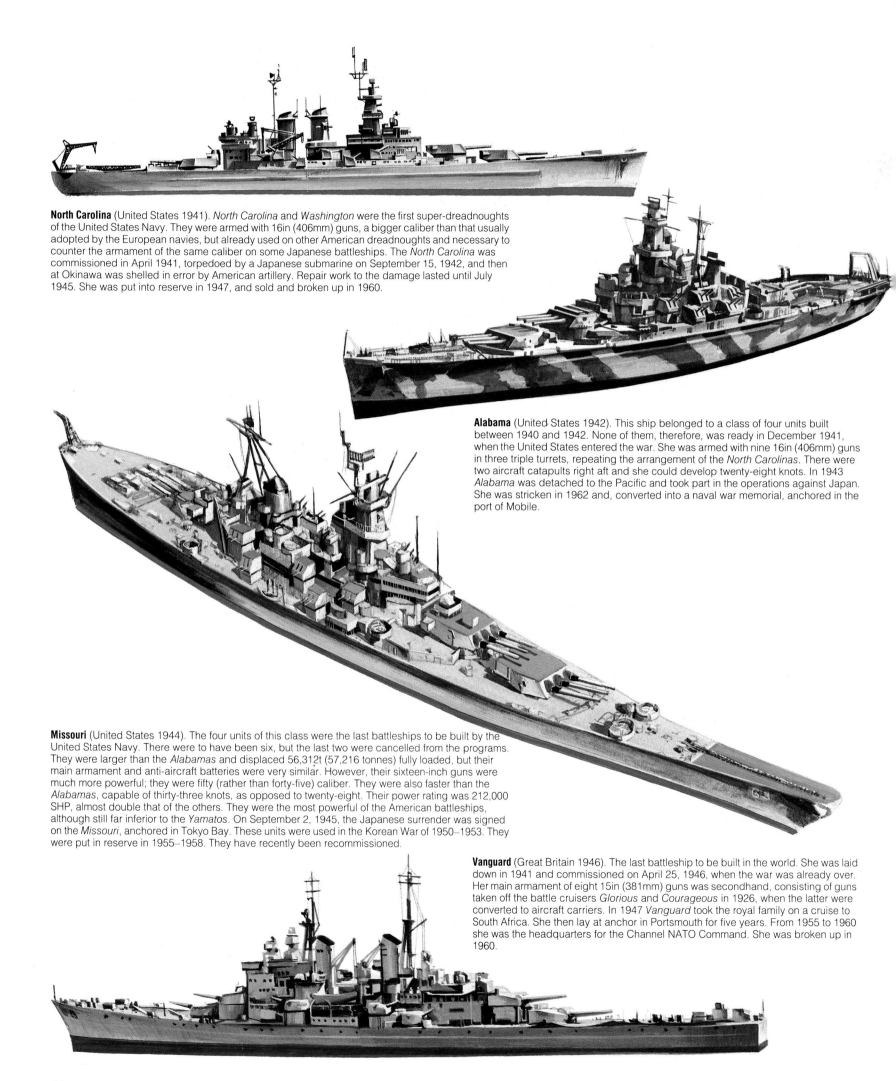

North Carolina (United States 1941). *North Carolina* and *Washington* were the first super-dreadnoughts of the United States Navy. They were armed with 16in (406mm) guns, a bigger caliber than that usually adopted by the European navies, but already used on other American dreadnoughts and necessary to counter the armament of the same caliber on some Japanese battleships. The *North Carolina* was commissioned in April 1941, torpedoed by a Japanese submarine on September 15, 1942, and then at Okinawa was shelled in error by American artillery. Repair work to the damage lasted until July 1945. She was put into reserve in 1947, and sold and broken up in 1960.

Alabama (United States 1942). This ship belonged to a class of four units built between 1940 and 1942. None of them, therefore, was ready in December 1941, when the United States entered the war. She was armed with nine 16in (406mm) guns in three triple turrets, repeating the arrangement of the *North Carolinas*. There were two aircraft catapults right aft and she could develop twenty-eight knots. In 1943 *Alabama* was detached to the Pacific and took part in the operations against Japan. She was stricken in 1962 and, converted into a naval war memorial, anchored in the port of Mobile.

Missouri (United States 1944). The four units of this class were the last battleships to be built by the United States Navy. There were to have been six, but the last two were cancelled from the programs. They were larger than the *Alabamas* and displaced 56,312t (57,216 tonnes) fully loaded, but their main armament and anti-aircraft batteries were very similar. However, their sixteen-inch guns were much more powerful; they were fifty (rather than forty-five) caliber. They were also faster than the *Alabamas*, capable of thirty-three knots, as opposed to twenty-eight. Their power rating was 212,000 SHP, almost double that of the others. They were the most powerful of the American battleships, although still far inferior to the *Yamatos*. On September 2, 1945, the Japanese surrender was signed on the *Missouri*, anchored in Tokyo Bay. These units were used in the Korean War of 1950–1953. They were put in reserve in 1955–1958. They have recently been recommissioned.

Vanguard (Great Britain 1946). The last battleship to be built in the world. She was laid down in 1941 and commissioned on April 25, 1946, when the war was already over. Her main armament of eight 15in (381mm) guns was secondhand, consisting of guns taken off the battle cruisers *Glorious* and *Courageous* in 1926, when the latter were converted to aircraft carriers. In 1947 *Vanguard* took the royal family on a cruise to South Africa. She then lay at anchor in Portsmouth for five years. From 1955 to 1960 she was the headquarters for the Channel NATO Command. She was broken up in 1960.

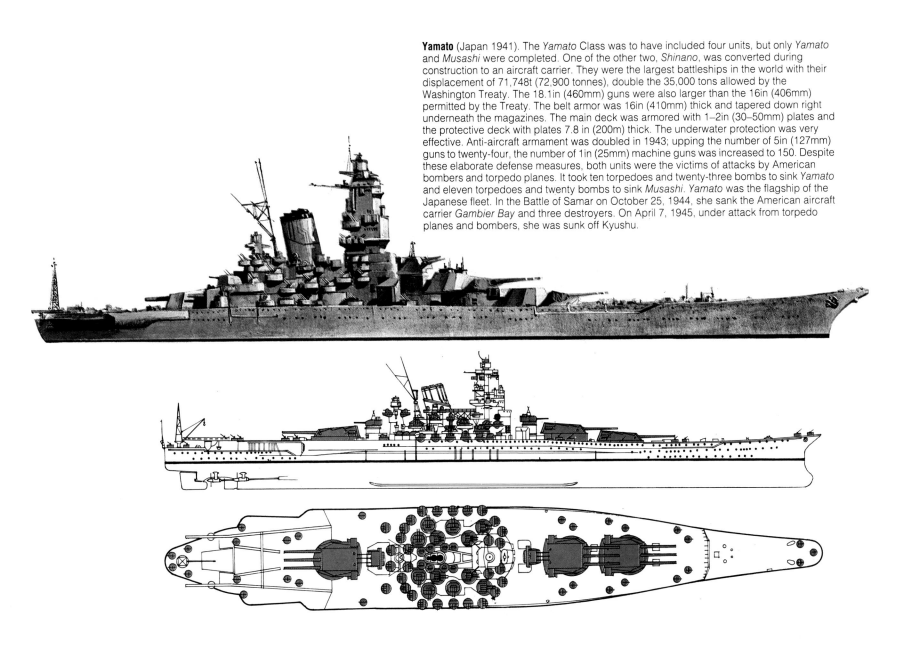

Yamato (Japan 1941). The *Yamato* Class was to have included four units, but only *Yamato* and *Musashi* were completed. One of the other two, *Shinano*, was converted during construction to an aircraft carrier. They were the largest battleships in the world with their displacement of 71,748t (72,900 tonnes), double the 35,000 tons allowed by the Washington Treaty. The 18.1in (460mm) guns were also larger than the 16in (406mm) permitted by the Treaty. The belt armor was 16in (410mm) thick and tapered down right underneath the magazines. The main deck was armored with 1–2in (30–50mm) plates and the protective deck with plates 7.8 in (200m) thick. The underwater protection was very effective. Anti-aircraft armament was doubled in 1943; upping the number of 5in (127mm) guns to twenty-four, the number of 1in (25mm) machine guns was increased to 150. Despite these elaborate defense measures, both units were the victims of attacks by American bombers and torpedo planes. It took ten torpedoes and twenty-three bombs to sink *Yamato* and eleven torpedoes and twenty bombs to sink *Musashi*. *Yamato* was the flagship of the Japanese fleet. In the Battle of Samar on October 25, 1944, she sank the American aircraft carrier *Gambier Bay* and three destroyers. On April 7, 1945, under attack from torpedo planes and bombers, she was sunk off Kyushu.

deck, with its conventional sloping sides, had a maximum thickness of 4.7in (120mm) above the magazines and 3in (80mm) above the powerplant. The *Bismarck*s, too, like the *Scharnhorst*s, had a triple-shaft powerplant driven by three geared turbine units. *Tirpitz* was also armed with eight torpedo tubes in two quadruple mountings in the middle of the main deck (not fitted on *Bismarck*).

The American battleships of the *North Carolina*, *Alabama*, and *Missouri* Classes had a main armament of nine 16in (406mm) guns in three triple turrets, two forward and two aft. The *Missouri*s, which were the most modern and were commissioned at the end of 1944, had a speed of thirty-three knots, five to six knots faster than the twenty-eight knots of the two other classes. The most notable structural difference was that, whereas on the two *North Carolina*s of 1940 underwater protection was in the form of bulges which protruded well out beyond the hull, on the *Alabama*s (1942) and *Missouri*s (1944) there were no bulges; the underwater protection was inside the hull, in the form of bulkheads running lengthwise either side. The 12in (305mm) thick sloping armor which made up the vertical protection on the *North Carolina*s, was 12.2in (310mm) thick on the *Alabama*s and *Missouri*s. Horizontal protection on the *North Carolina*s was 1.45in (37mm) on the main deck and 1 + 0.7in + 4.6in (27 + 19 + 117mm) on the protective deck. On the *Alabama*s and *Missouri*s it was 1.49in (38mm) on the main deck and 5 + 0.7 (127 + 19mm) on the protective deck because the war had shown just how vulnerable armor plating was to the huge bombs dropped from aircraft.

The battleships with the greatest displacement and heaviest armament were Japan's *Yamato*s and *Musashi*s which, fully laden, reached 71,748t (72,900 tonnes) and were armed with nine 18.1in (460mm) guns, an exceptional caliber, almost matched by the guns on board Britain's battle-cruiser *Furious* (1918) which had a single turret mounting one 18in (457mm) gun. Side armor sloped at an angle

of 20° and was 16in (410mm) thick. It ran along both sides of the magazines and from there continued underneath with a thickness of 3in (80mm). None of the other types of battleships had ever had armor on the bottom of their magazines before. Horizontal protection was split between two decks: 1.1–1.9in (30–50mm) thick on the main deck and 7.8in (200m) on the flat (not curved) protective deck, and even thicker where it joined the side armor. The bridge mast was armored with plates an incredible 19.6in (500mm) thick, in other words, with 1.6ft (0.5m) of steel.

The original anti-aircraft armament was increased after 1943 to twenty-four 5in (127mm) guns in twelve twin mounts, reducing the twelve 6in (155mm) original anti-aircraft guns to six, only the two triple turrets superfiring over the large-caliber fore and aft turrets being retained. The 1in (25mm) machine guns were increased from twenty-four to 150, positioned in triple or quadruple mountings grouped round the turret mast and funnel, forming a formidable concentration of fire-power.

This umbrella of shells from guns and machine guns was nevertheless insufficient to prevent America's bombers and torpedo planes from inflicting fatal blows on these giants which were so well-protected, but only against shells from guns. In order to sink *Yamato* ten torpedoes and twenty-three bombs with a high explosive charge were required, and eleven torpedoes and twenty bombs for *Musashi*.

The last battleship to be built in the world was Britain's *Vanguard*. This was a completely useless ship and obsolete even before she entered service because of her poor fighting capabilities. She was laid down on October 2, 1941, and commissioned when the war was over, on April 25, 1946. She was armed with eight 15in (381mm) guns in four twin turrets, two forward and two aft. These guns were made in 1916 for the battle cruisers *Glorious* and *Courageous*, and stored in 1926 when the latter were converted into aircraft carriers. She had a fairly short life since she was stricken and scrapped in 1960, after spending five years in Portsmouth harbor. She was built in an attempt to replace *Royal Oak*, but this was a final gesture of pride on the part of the British Navy since the battleships involved in the current war had already shown themselves vulnerable and of little use against air attack. In fact, all the world's navies soon took their battleships out of commission when the war was over.

Special types of armored ships: armored batteries, monitors, and Popoffkas

When discussing armored ships, the point was made that armored batteries had been built even before the ironclad frigates *Gloire* and *Warrior*. These were the forerunners of battleships proper, just as monitors were the forerunners of turret-battleships.

The idea of building floating batteries for use in naval blockades of cities or fortifications is quite an old one. History shows that during the war between France and England in 1782, in the attack on Gibraltar of September 13, 1782, the French fleet used ten floating batteries, the largest being armed with twenty-nine guns and the smaller ones with ten. These were, of course, made entirely of wood but armored, in a manner of speaking, with a few iron bars on the exterior of the ship's sides and a coffer dam inside full of wet sand. Unfortunately, all these batteries, designed by a certain Cavalier D'Arçon, were destroyed in the battle since the explosion of one of them set fire to all the others.

One well-known floating battery was *Fulton* (originally *Demologos*), built by Fulton for the U.S. Navy during the War of 1812. This battery had a hull in the form of a catamaran and was driven by one paddle wheel situated between the two floats. Protection was provided by several layers of crossed wooden beams reaching a thickness of 4.92ft (1.50m). Armament consisted of twenty thirty-two pounders, sixteen in a battery either side and two forward and two aft in a sturdy casemate supported by the two floats which were side by side. Apart from generating steam for the engine, the boiler was also used to "preheat" the gun shot. *Demologos* was commissioned in September 1815 when the war was already over, having been given the name *Fulton* on the death of her builder, on February 24, 1815. After fourteen years of peacetime service, *Fulton* sank in 1829.

Benton was another American catamaran-type armored battery, commis-

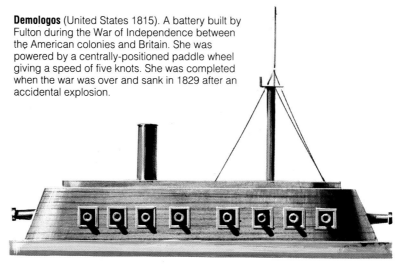

Demologos (United States 1815). A battery built by Fulton during the War of Independence between the American colonies and Britain. She was powered by a centrally-positioned paddle wheel giving a speed of five knots. She was completed when the war was over and sank in 1829 after an accidental explosion.

Benton (Confederate States 1862). A river armored battery used by the southern Confederate States in the American War of Secession. She was propelled by a paddle wheel at the after end, powered by two single-cylinder engines.

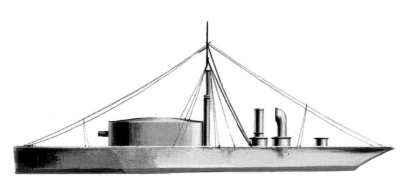

Dismountable Batteries (France 1859). These were small units that could be dismantled and transported to the places where they were to be used. They were laid down for use in the 1859 war against Austria but not completed in time. They were, however, used on the Seine to defend Paris in the Franco-Prussian War of 1870.

Dunderberg (United States 1867). An armored battery capable of undertaking long voyages and equipped with masts and sails as well as a single-shaft engine. She was sold to France under the name of *Rochambeau* and crossed the Atlantic to reach her new destination. In France the engine was modified and the speed increased from eleven to fifteen knots.

sioned in 1862 during the Civil War for the secession of the southern states from the northern states. The hull was made of iron, the gun casemate armored with 4.7in (120mm) thick iron plates and the armament consisted of sixteen guns, six 10in (258mm) (four forward and two aft) and ten 8in (203mm) (five per side). Propulsion was by means of paddle wheels with one wheel aft between the two hulls, as on the large American river boats.

The armored battery that the Stevens brothers began to build in 1854 in the United States, before the War Between the States, was of a very different type but was never completed. She had an iron hull with two steam engines and twin propellers and was intended to have a displacement of 5,905t (6,000 tonnes) and a speed of seventeen knots; but in 1874 she was sold still unfinished and broken up. The deck was armored with several superimposed iron sheets and was 6.6in (170mm) thick in the middle and 1.5in (40mm) at the bow and stern ends. The armament was exceptionally modern being made up of seven guns, not in casemates but on the main deck in trainable platforms, the two end guns with a caliber of 10in (254mm) and the five middle ones 15in (381mm). The seven gun platforms were placed one behind the other along the length of the ship, down the centerline and were moved by steam engines.

Although this American battery never took to the sea, in Europe, France and England built armored batteries that were used in the Crimean War waged against Russia by an alliance that included Turkey, France, England, and the Kingdom of Sardinia.

France's armored batteries were called *Dévastation*, *Lave*, *Tonnante*, *Foudroyant*, and *Congrève* and were armed with sixteen fifty-pounders and two twelve-pounders positioned along the sides on the gallery deck. Side armor was 4.3in (110mm) thick. They had masts and sails as well as a very low-power engine that developed a speed of just four knots, which meant that the three that were sent to the Black Sea, *Dévastation*, *Lave*, and *Tonnante*, were towed there by paddle-wheel frigates.

Britain's three batteries were called *Thunderbolt*, *Erebus*, and *Terror*, and were structurally similar to the French ones. They, too, were sent to Crimea but got there after the famous Kinburn bombardment of October 17, 1855, in which *Dévastation*, *Lave*, and *Tonnante* attacked and destroyed the Russian forts.

Voragine (Italy 1869). The Italian Navy built two ships, *Guerriera* and *Voragine*, classified as armored batteries. These were much more seaworthy than the French and English armored batteries of the Crimean War. They were stricken in 1875 after only a few years of service.

Kreml (Russia 1865). The Russian Navy had a class of three units classified as armored batteries and fitted with masts and sails. Under engine power they developed a speed of 8.5 knots, but they were quite fast under sail, too, because of the streamlined shape of the hull. They were never used in wartime.

In 1859 and 1864, a type of floating battery designed to operate in rivers, lakes, and canals was built in France. These units could be dismantled and transported by rail to the places where they were to be used. They had an iron hull and 3in (80mm) thick armor and carried two nontrainable 6in (160mm) guns, arranged in a semicircular casemate and firing ahead. They were used to defend Paris during the Franco-Prussian War of 1870.

As distinct from the above-mentioned armored batteries which were small self-propelled floats that were not very seaworthy, units with the characteristics of real ships were built in 1865–1866. These had more powerful engines and could steam at seven to fifteen knots. One of these vessels, *Dunderberg*, even crossed the Atlantic, having been built in the United States and sold to France where she was renamed *Rochambeau*. The hull was very low in the water and carried a central casemate armored with 3.5in (90mm) thick plates and containing the guns. There were two masts, the foremast setting square sails and the aftermast a spanker.

There were other batteries of this type, notably Russia's *Kreml*, *Perwenec*, and *Netrony-Menja*, the first being the only one to be built in a Russian dockyard, since *Perwenec* was built in England, and *Netrony-Menja* in Russia but by an English shipyard. These units had three masts, two square-rigged, and the aftermast with a spanker. Gallery-deck armor was 6in (152mm) thick, thicker than the belt, which was only 4.4in (114mm). The powerplant developed a speed of 8.5 knots.

Italy's two armored batteries *Guerriera* and *Voragine*, built in 1866, were similar in appearance to the *Dunderberg* (*Rochambeau*). They, too, had a low hull which accommodated a long central casemate armored with 6.2in (160mm) thick plates. The casemate had eight ports either side but there were only thirteen guns, three of which fired astern, so there were three ports per side that stayed empty. These units had three fore-and-aft rigged masts and their powerplant, one of the first of Italian construction, gave seven knots.

Monitors were so named after *Monitor*, built in 1861–1862 by a Swede named Ericsson for the U.S. Navy during the Civil War. It took part in the famous Battle of Hampton Roads on March 9, 1862, against the Southerners' armored battery *Virginia* (or *Merrimack*). *Monitor's* hull was very low in the water and covered by

a sort of upended wooden box that formed the support for the 3.9in (100mm) armor. There was a trainable, armored turret on the main deck, containing two 11in (280mm) guns. *Monitor* had no masts, sails, or superstructures and was powered by a single-screw steam engine. This prodigy of technology and artillery (*Monitor* was in fact the first to be armed with guns in a trainable turret) confronted an armored pontoon whose wooden hull was that of the frigate *Merrimack*, cut off at the waterline and surmounted by an armored casemate (also of wood) with walls sloping at an angle of 35°. Since there was no industry in the Southern states capable of manufacturing iron plating for the armor, the casemate was armored with two superimposed layers of railway track, giving a thickness of 3.9in (100mm). The armament consisted of four 11.3in (288mm), two 6in (152mm), and two 6.9in (177mm) guns, (which was what could be scraped together) all of the nontrainable type, six pieces firing on either side and two ahead. After this conversion, the ship was called *Virginia*.

In the Battle of Hampton Roads, these two ships shelled each other for a whole day without causing any damage. This event represented the first victory of armor over the gun and led to the introduction of guns of increasingly larger calibers. During the Civil War, the United States Navy built many more single-turret monitors. Other units had two turrets armed, in some cases, with one 15in (381mm) and one 11in (280mm) gun per turret; others had two 15in (381mm) guns in each turret.

Onondaga, which had seen service with the Northerners' Navy during the War of Secession, was sold to France in 1867 and served in the French Navy until 1902. Although she had a deck which lay very low in the water and two large turrets armored with plates 11in (280mm) thick, she crossed the Atlantic and reached Europe. *Miantonomoh* also crossed the Atlantic twice: outward, to carry Naval Secretary Knox, the bearer of a message from the President of the United States to the Czar of Russia, Alexander II (1866–1867), and then back home.

Miantonomoh (United States 1865). A monitor belonging to a class of four units having a hull armored with 5in (127mm) plates on the sides and 2in (5lmm) plates on the deck. *Miantonomoh* crossed the Atlantic in 1866–1867, was stricken in 1875, and gave her name to another monitor in commission from 1891 to 1915.

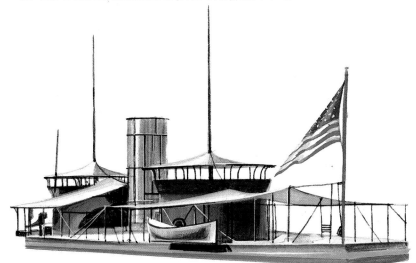

Onondaga (United States 1864). The first two-turret monitor to be built by the United States Navy. Her armor was made of 1in (25.4mm) thick superimposed plates, six layers on the sides and two layers on the deck. Armament was two 15in (381mm) guns, one in each turret. She was sold to France and served in that country's navy until 1902.

Scorpionen (Norway 1866). The Norwegian Navy had a class of four single-turret monitors with iron rather than wooden hulls, like the *Miantonomoh* and *Onondaga* types. The *Scorpionens* had a single-shaft engine that gave a speed of seven knots.

Glatton (Great Britain 1872). A breastwork monitor, in other words, one with a superstructure accommodating the guns that on other monitors were on the deck. *Glatton* was armed with two 12in (305mm) guns in a forward turret and had a two-shaft engine that gave a speed of twelve knots. Armor was 12in (305mm) round the belt and 1.4in (38mm) and 3in (76mm) on the two decks.

Cyclops (Great Britain 1872). A breastwork monitor, like *Glatton*, but with two turrets and four 10in (254mm) guns, belonging to a class of four iron-hulled units. The armor was 12in (305mm) thick on the sides, 9in (229mm) round the citadel and 1.4in (38mm) on the deck. *Cyclops* had a twin-shaft engine and did twelve knots.

Russia had ten monitors, the first of which, *Bronenosec*, was commissioned in 1864. These monitors had their hull covered with an upended wooden box to support the armor and just one central turret with two 9in (229mm) guns, like the early American monitors. Apart from the 4.9in (125mm)-thick side armor, they had 1in (26mm) thick armor on the deck and 11in (280mm) round the gun turret. They had single-shaft machinery that developed a speed of 7.5 knots.

In 1866, Norway built four single-turret monitors which made up the *Scorpionen* Class, armed with two 10.5in (267mm) guns, similar in appearance and structure to the American and Russian units. *Glatton* of 1871 and *Cyclops* of the same year were monitors of a rather special type, the so-called breastwork monitors. They were the prototypes from which the *Dévastation*-type ironclads derived. Whereas the monitors described above had no superstructures on the main deck and the turret, or turrets, were placed directly on the deck, *Glatton* and the *Cyclops* types had a proper superstructure with a bridge, masts, lifeboats, and deck rigging which gave them the appearance of ordinary ships. Furthermore, these monitors had a central citadel above the armored deck, to protect the turret bases. *Glatton's* citadel had 12in (305mm)-thick armor; on the *Cyclops* it was 9in (229mm) thick. *Glatton* had one twin turret with two 12in (305mm) guns, positioned ahead of the superstructure. An interesting feature was the flood

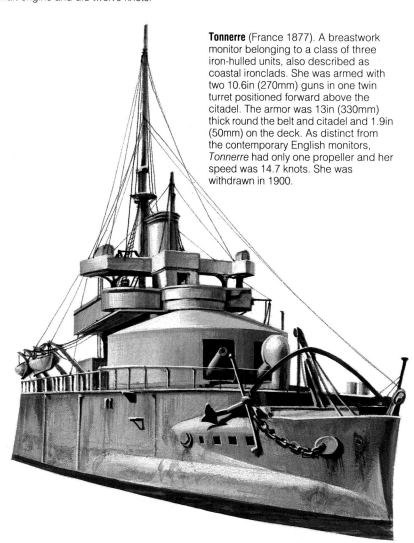

Tonnerre (France 1877). A breastwork monitor belonging to a class of three iron-hulled units, also described as coastal ironclads. She was armed with two 10.6in (270mm) guns in one twin turret positioned forward above the citadel. The armor was 13in (330mm) thick round the belt and citadel and 1.9in (50mm) on the deck. As distinct from the contemporary English monitors, *Tonnerre* had only one propeller and her speed was 14.7 knots. She was withdrawn in 1900.

chambers, which were filled with water before battle commenced so as to reduce the height of the ship's sides from 35.8in (91cm) to 24in (61cm) and thus offer less of a target to the enemy. Armor thicknesses were: 12in (305mm) round the belt and on the citadel; 1.4in (38mm) on the upper deck; 3in (76mm) on the main deck; and 14in (356mm) on the gun turret. *Glatton* was one of the first monitors to have two propellers.

The four *Cyclops* types had an armament of four 10in (254mm) guns in two twin turrets, one before and one abaft the superstructure. In their general lines they resembled *Glatton* and they too had a twin-propeller powerplant.

The French Navy also had breastwork monitors: the three *Tonnerre* Class and the four *Caiman* Class. The *Tonnerres* had a ram and were classified as ram monitors. Their main deck was just 15.7in (40cm) above the water but had a 6.5ft (2m) high superstructure which made the hull higher than on the English units.

There was only one gun turret which was positioned forward of the superstructure and contained two 10.6in (270mm) guns. These units had only one propeller. One of the last classes of monitors consisted of the four American *Arkansas* types. These were commissioned in 1902 and taken out of service after the 1914–1918 war. They had only one turret with two 12in (305mm) guns amidships, plus fairly heavy secondary armament made up of four 4in (102mm) guns at the four corners of the superstructure, three 2.2in (57mm) guns on the superstructure itself, four small 1.4in (37mm) guns in the mast top and two underwater torpedo tubes.

The line of the *Arkansas* types and their armament were very different from the early monitors; they also had twin propellers and could do 12.4 knots.

France's *Taureau* types of 1865 and Britain's *Hotspur* and *Rupert*, both built in 1870, and *Polyphemus* (1881) were armored rams and very different from the conventional monitors.

The main weapon of these units was the ram, not the gun, so they had to be very fast and maneuverable; they all therefore had two propellers and powerplants capable of providing a speed of 12–12.5 knots, and even seventeen knots of *Polyphemus*.

The five French *Taureaus* had wooden hulls surmounted by a superstructure covered in iron plates in the form of a turtleback; on this there was a barbette for the 9.4in (240mm) gun. The sides had belt armour 5.9in (150mm) thick and the flat area on top, forming the deck, was 2in (51mm) thick. The four units which were similar to *Taureau* were *Cerbère*, *Bélier*, *Tigre*, and *Bouledogue* and they had a heavier displacement and were armed with two 9.4in (240mm) guns arranged in a trainable turret.

Britain's *Hotspur* and *Rupert* were a sort of cross between ram and breastwork monitors: they had a 9ft (2.74m) ram, but no turtleback deck like the French

Taureaus. Originally they were armed with one 12in (305mm) gun in a barbette. This was later replaced by two 12in (305mm) guns in a trainable turret.

Polyphemus was armed with just a ram and torpedoes, and had no guns whatsoever. Her hull was totally different from that of the monitors and slightly resembled the *Taureaus*, being completely cylindrical like a submarine but with 2in (50.8mm)-thick armored sides. The bow ram could be removed and there were three torpedo tubes, all fixed and underwater. Speed was seventeen knots, achieved with two engines powered by twelve small boilers developing 5424.6hp (5500CV).

The Popoffkas, or circular armored ships, were two very strangely shaped ships built to a design by Admiral Popoff of the Russian Navy. Popoff's aim was to build very stable ships that would be unaffected by the rolling and pitching movements when the guns were being fired. He therefore widened the hull until its beam equalled its length, so that the deck was circular. The belt and barbette armor was an incredible 18in (457mm) thick and armament comprised two 12in (305mm) guns in a barbette, down the centerline of the circular hull. These vessels had six propellers, each driven by an alternating engine. They were an unsuccessful experiment, but one followed nonetheless with interest by all the world's main navies, although there was no follow-up.

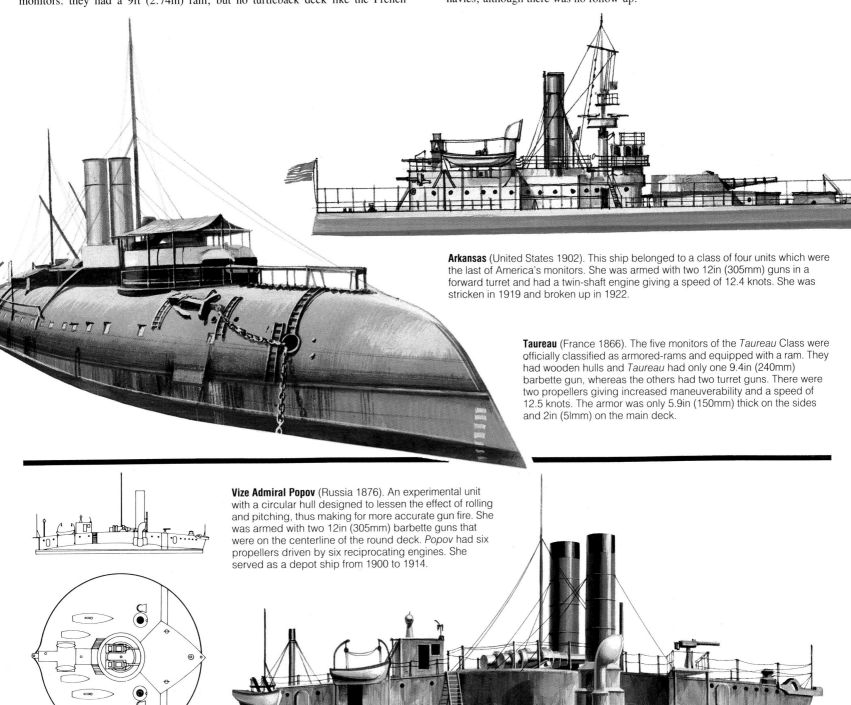

Arkansas (United States 1902). This ship belonged to a class of four units which were the last of America's monitors. She was armed with two 12in (305mm) guns in a forward turret and had a twin-shaft engine giving a speed of 12.4 knots. She was stricken in 1919 and broken up in 1922.

Taureau (France 1866). The five monitors of the *Taureau* Class were officially classified as armored-rams and equipped with a ram. They had wooden hulls and *Taureau* had only one 9.4in (240mm) barbette gun, whereas the others had two turret guns. There were two propellers giving increased maneuverability and a speed of 12.5 knots. The armor was only 5.9in (150mm) thick on the sides and 2in (51mm) on the main deck.

Vize Admiral Popov (Russia 1876). An experimental unit with a circular hull designed to lessen the effect of rolling and pitching, thus making for more accurate gun fire. She was armed with two 12in (305mm) barbette guns that were on the centerline of the round deck. *Popov* had six propellers driven by six reciprocating engines. She served as a depot ship from 1900 to 1914.

AIRCRAFT CARRIERS

The development of aircraft carriers from 1912 to the present day

The first ship from which an airplane took off was not an aircraft carrier but a United States Navy light cruiser named *Birmingham,* which had a temporary wooden platform at the bow. The plane took off at 3:16 P.M. on November 14, 1910, while the ship was cruising at a speed of about fourteen knots in Chesapeake Bay. The plane was a land Curtiss Golden Flyer fitted with conventional wheels and piloted by a civilian named Eugene B. Ely who worked for the Curtiss Aeroplane Factory.

Take-off experiments were also carried out in Great Britain with the battleship *Africa* which, like *Birmingham,* had a temporary platform at the bow. A plane took off at 2:20 P.M. on January 10, 1912, fourteen months after the American pioneer, but in this case the pilot was a naval officer, Commander Samson, and the aircraft a Short S27 biplane.

Samson also carried off the first takeoff from a ship under way, in May 1912, from the battleship *Hibernia.*

Although the first experiments were carried out by the American and British Navies, the French Navy was the first to have a seaplane carrier, in the form of *Foudre,* an old unit built in 1892–1895 and adapted for the purpose. In 1912, the Royal Navy also converted *Hermes* into a seaplane carrier. These seaplane carriers, which we can call the first generation, transported their aircraft like any other type of freight. The only special addition required was a superstructure above the main deck. The seaplanes took off and landed in the sea, the ship serving merely as a floating depot; the aircrafts were lowered into the sea for use and hoisted back on board by derricks.

Seaplane carriers of this type were said to be "without a takeoff deck" and some also had a special crane forward.

The need to lower the seaplanes into the sea before they could be used was a serious operational drawback and so the United States Navy decided to make them take off from a temporary platform, similar to the one used by Ely on *Birmingham.* As seaplanes have no wheels, they were made to run on a trolley, accelerated along its travel by weight-operated tackle. A trolley of this type was used to launch an AB 2 seaplane from the stern of the armored cruiser *North Carolina,* anchored in Pensacola Bay, on November 5, 1915.

Since 1914, the Royal Navy had also been carrying out experiments, but from the forward end, using aircraft launched from the seaplane carrier *Hermes* by a trolley. These experiments convinced the Admiralty to build seaplane carriers equipped with this rudimentary device. These were called "seaplane carriers with a takeoff deck." As it was already 1914, and Britain was at war, the navy was requisitioning ships. One of the first was Cunard's transatlantic liner *Campania,* bought by the navy on November 27, 1914. She was fitted with a 120.07ft (36.60m) long platform which ran from right forward to just in front of the bridge superstructure. This turned out to be too short, so in March–April 1916 modifications were made. The forward funnel was replaced by two set side by side and far enough apart to leave sufficient room for an aircraft to pass between them and the bridge superstructure was lowered so that the takeoff deck could be increased to 199.80ft (60.90m). Other merchant ships were also requisitioned and fitted with takeoff decks; these included *Manxman,* commissioned on April 7, 1916, *Nairana,* in August 1917, and *Pegasus,* three days later that same month.

After using the takeoff deck, pilots were convinced that seaplanes could well be replaced by landplanes with an undercarriage; they would take off in just 39–46ft (12–14m). The first takeoff by a Bristol Scout landplane was performed by Second Flight Lieutenant H. F. Towler on November 3, 1915, from the takeoff deck of *Vindex.* It should be stressed that this success was achieved two days before the launching of a seaplane using a trolley from the American cruiser *North Carolina.* Commander F. J. Rutland, chief of the air service on board the seaplane carriers *Campania* and *Manxman,* was an advocate of the use of landplanes. He took off from both ships in a Sopwith Pup. After installing a platform on the tall after-turret of various warships, he repeated his takeoff in June 1917 from the cruiser *Yarmouth* and on October 9, from the battle cruiser *Repulse.* As a result of these experiments all battle cruisers and a further twenty-two cruisers were fitted with platforms and landplanes.

The use of these aircraft during the early war years clearly showed the superiority of landplanes, which were faster, easier to handle, and better suited to engage the Zeppelin airships used by the German Navy for naval reconnaissance; so in May 1917, the Royal Navy decided to convert the battle cruiser *Furious,* launched on August 15, 1916, into a "fast seaplane carrier."

Although classified as a "seaplane carrier," *Furious* had a 228.01ft (69.50m) long, 40.02ft (12.20m) wide flight deck for landplanes, with a hangar below containing five Sopwith Pup fighter planes and three Short 184 reconnaissance seaplanes.

Birmingham (United States 1907). A United States Navy light cruiser from which the first successful aircraft takeoff was carried out on November 14, 1910. The wooden takeoff deck, purposely built for this experiment, is clearly visible forward. As can be seen, the short platform slopes slightly downwards to enable the aircraft to pick up sufficient speed to take off, assisted by the relative wind caused by the ship travelling at a speed of fourteen knots. The Curtiss Golden Flyer aircraft used in this experiment weighed only 828.7lb (376kg) and took off after a run of a few meters. When it no longer had the support of the platform, it lost height but then immediately regained altitude.

The problem of getting planes to take off from a ship's deck had been solved, but the problem of getting them to land on that same deck had not.

When their mission was over, seaplanes could land in the sea near the seaplane carrier and be hoisted on board by crane. Landplanes, however, had to fly off and land on a conventional airfield from where they were then transported to a port and reloaded on board. This was an unacceptable system which led the chief of the Air Service on board *Furious,* Commander Dunning, to try landing on the forward flying off deck. The first attempt, using a Sopwith Pup, was achieved successfully on August 2, 1917, but the second attempt, the following August, claimed both pilot and plane. The Admiralty thus put a stop to all further tests.

The first ship landing had been achieved six years before in the United States by Ely, the same pilot who carried out the first takeoff, on a platform positioned at the after end of the armored cruiser *Pennsylvania.* This platform was 119.75ft (36.50m) long, in other words, half that of *Furious,* but it had been fitted with equipment to slow down the airplane after its undercarriage had made contact with the deck. The braking system, designed by Lieutenant Theodore G. Ellison and used on *Pennsylvania,* consisted of twenty-two wires stretched across the platform at a height of about 1ft (30cm), and attached to 200lb (90kg) sand bags. The wires had to catch on pairs of hooks under the aircraft's tail. Ely landed on January 18, 1911, on a ship anchored to a buoy in San Francisco Bay.

After the Dunning tragedy, the Royal Navy decided to fit *Furious* with an after landing platform, equipped with wires attached to sand bags, as well as wires

Pennsylvania (United States 1903). A United States Navy armored cruiser on which the first successful aircraft landing was made on January 18, 1911. For this experiment the ship was fitted with a temporary wooden platform that was 119.75ft (36.50m) long and sloped downwards at the stern end. Note the slanting tarpaulin hanging from the mainmast, designed to act as a buffer in case the aircraft failed to stop. The twenty-two wires attached to sandbags and stretched across the platform to slow down the aircraft after it had landed are not visible. During the experiment the ship was not under way but moored to a buoy and therefore lying with the wind.

running lengthwise, to act both as arresters and guides. To prevent aircraft not caught by these arresters from crashing into the mast and funnel, netting was placed vertically at the end of the platform. In March 1918, landing experiments began again with the new platform. They revealed the difficulties caused by air pockets and turbulence generated by the superstructures and hot gases from the funnels.

Furious and, subsequently, *Vindictive* were the only two "aircraft carriers with takeoff and landing decks." While modifications to *Furious* were under way, the Admiralty decided to build a third unit with one deck having no superstructures and funnels, no longer to be classified as a takeoff and landing deck but as a "flight deck."

To speed things up, a merchant ship was bought. She was commissioned in September 1918, even before *Vindictive*, and was the first ever "flush deck carrier." This ship, named *Argus*, was the first to carry the Sopwith Cuckoo torpedo planes. The hangar had a large door aft which opened onto a platform with two cranes to lift the aircraft out of the sea or off the quay. The United States Navy's first aircraft carrier, *Langley*, commissioned in March 1922, also had a flight deck that was unencumbered by funnels and superstructures. The funnels, which could be lowered, were kept in a vertical position under normal conditions and lowered to a horizontal position (obviously below deck level) when flying operations were in progress.

The Japanese Navy's first aircraft carrier, *Hosho*, commissioned in December 1922, also had a flush flight deck. For the sake of accuracy, it should be mentioned that when she was commissioned she had a small turret superstructure and a tripod mast, both on the port side, although these were removed in 1923. There were three funnels, which could be lowered outwards, as on *Langley*. Many Japanese aircraft carriers had flush decks, such as *Akagi* and *Kaga* before modifications, *Ryujo*, *Shoho* and *Zuiho*, *Ryuho* and *Chiyoda*, and *Chitose*.

The first aircraft carrier to have an island right from the outset was *Eagle*, delivered to the Royal Navy on April 3, 1920, having been laid down as a battleship. On the starboard side of the flight deck were a bridge superstructure, a mast, and two large funnels. These superstructures became collectively known as an "island." Some subsequent British carriers had a "stepped flight deck," such as *Furious* after her 1921–1925 modifications, and the two former battleships converted into aircraft carriers in 1924–1930, *Glorious* and *Courageous*. These ships had two flight decks: a long one at hangar roof level and another, much shorter one, level with the hangar floor.

Japan's two aircraft carriers *Akagi* and *Kaga*, commissioned in 1926–1927, were also built using the hulls of a battle cruiser and a battleship and initially had three stepped flight decks. The longer flight deck was on the hangar roof and the other two were right aft, level with two of the hangar's three floors. *Akagi* and *Kaga* also had a large after platform below the flight deck.

The United States Navy did not have stepped flight deck carriers and its first two units built after *Langley*, *Lexington* and *Saratoga* of 1927, had only an upper deck, which was 770.01ft (234.70m) long and extended beyond both bow and stern.

Stepped flight decks remained unique to the British carriers *Glorious*, *Courageous*, and *Furious*, although after a certain time even they used only the upper deck. In 1935–1938, the two Japanese carriers *Akagi* and *Kaga* were modernized and their lower decks removed, thus becoming conventional carriers with a 907.48ft (276.60m) long flush flight deck.

From about 1928–1930 until 1952–1953, aircraft carriers retained a profile with a straight flight deck and an island on the starboard side, differing only in minor details. The position of the island on the starboard side was adopted by the Royal Navy from 1918 onwards, when *Hermes* was designed. This position was suggested by Captains W. S. Nicholson and Clark Hall, commander and aircraft commander of *Furious*, respectively. They had noticed that when an aircraft failed to land, the pilot preferred to regain height by turning to the port side. The only units with islands on the port side were Japan's *Akagi* and *Hiryu*.

Throughout the Second World War, aircraft carriers operated exclusively with propeller planes. The first experiments involving jet planes were carried out after the war. The first jet takeoff from an aircraft carrier was by a Vampire from the British *Ocean* on December 3, 1945. In the United States, a jet fighter took off from the *Franklin D. Roosevelt* on July 21, 1946.

Jet aircraft are larger and heavier than propeller planes. To accommodate them aircraft carriers had to undergo considerable structural modifications providing an "angled flight deck," plus new equipment for launching these heavier aircraft; this was the British-built steam catapult. The first angled-deck carriers were units built with a straight deck and later modified. Those completed after 1952, however, had an angled deck right from the start. Examples were America's *Forrestal*, *Saratoga*, *Ranger*, and *Independence*, and Britain's *Ark Royal*.

It should be pointed out that after the Second World War, only the United States Navy continued building aircraft carriers. Between 1951 and 1955 Great Britain completed just *Eagle*, *Ark Royal*, *Albion*, *Bulwark*, and *Centaur*, all of which had been laid down during World War II. The last conventional British carrier to be completed was HMS *Hermes* (1959), which had been laid down in 1944.

After the angled deck, the most important innovation for aircraft carriers was nuclear propulsion, used only on the American aircraft carriers, although the new Russian and French carriers under construction in 1983 were nuclear powered.

One special type of carrier, the use of which was limited to the war years, was the escort carrier, used by the American and British Navies to escort convoys in the Atlantic, and by the Japanese Navy in the Pacific. Many were merchant ships adapted by adding a flight deck, with a small contingent of aircraft. Examples are America's *Bogue* (eleven ships) and *Sangamon* (four ships) Classes. The *Casab-*

The steam catapult

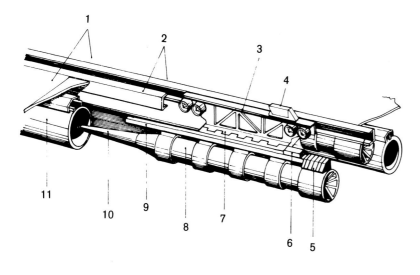

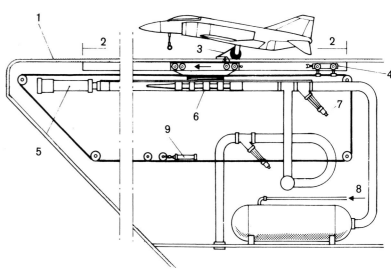

(1.) deck plates; (2.) guides; (3.) trolley; (4.) towing hook protruding above the deck; (5.) block; (6.) guide runner; (7.) coupling between trolley and piston; (8.) piston assembly; (9.) sealing strip; (10.) brake cylinder piston; (11.) cylinder.

(1.) flight deck; (2.) total run of about 197ft (60m); (3.) towing cable; (4.) trolley return mechanism; (5.) brake cylinder; (6.) trolley and piston unit; (7.) launching valve; (8.) high-pressure steam inlet; (9.) hydraulic cylinder of the cable return control.

Hibernia (Great Britain 1905). A battleship on which the Royal Navy carried out its first takeoff experiment from a moving ship, in May 1912. This ship also had a temporary wooden platform. The first takeoff from a stationary ship was on January 10, 1912, from a platform of the same type as that installed on the battleship *Africa*.

lanca (fifty ships) and *Commencement Bay* (nineteen ships) Classes were built as carriers, but on merchant-type hulls. Most of the British escort carriers were built in the United States, using U.S. standard-type (C-3) merchant hulls.

In the American Navy there was also a class of ''light'' carriers. These units, which had a smaller displacement than the large fleet carriers built during the war, were made by using the hulls of light cruisers, in the case of the nine *Independence* Class, and those of heavy cruisers, in the case of the two *Wright* Class. The Royal Navy also operated light fleet carriers, built from the beginning as such. Japanese light carriers (which were not designated as such) included both converted merchant and auxiliary naval hulls and specially built ships.

In the years following the Second World War, some navies built helicopter carriers, or amphibious assault ships. These had a flight deck running their entire length but they were designed to operate not with fixed-wing aircraft but with helicopters or rotary-wing aircraft. Examples are America's *Thetis Bay* of 1956, a converted escort-carrier, and Britain's *Bulwark* and *Albion* of 1960 and *Hermes* of 1973, converted from three light carriers. America's seven *Iwo Jima* Class (1961–1968) and five *Tarawa* Class (1976–1981) were, however, built specifically for this purpose. They all had straight, flush decks designed for helicopter operations. Russia's *Moskva* and *Kiev* types of 1967–1975, cruiser/helicopter carriers, represent a special type of flight-deck ship. They are hybrid ships, combining the forward half of a cruiser with the after half in the form of a large flight deck (angled on the *Kievs*). Japan's battleship *Ise* (after her 1943 refit) and the cruiser *Mogami* both resembled the current Russian cruisers.

More recently, both Britain and Italy have built small carriers, largely for anti-submarine operations. The British *Invincible* was initially described as a ''through-deck cruiser,'' presumably to avoid political conflict after the demise of conventional aircraft carriers in the Royal Navy. It is now officially described as a light V/STOL (vertical/short takeoff and landing) carrier. The only other current example of this type is the Italian *Garibaldi*. Both differ from more conventional aircraft carriers in having considerable anti-ship and anti-aircraft batteries; in a larger carrier (with more aircraft aboard) those functions would fall more completely to the embarked aircraft.

Aircraft carrier development, which began with a series of conversions carried out on *Furious* in 1917–1918, became standardized in 1982–1983 with just two types. One is the large carrier with a displacement of around 90,000 tonnes, nuclear powered and carrying ninety aircraft. The other is the light carrier with a displacement of between 12,000 and 20,000 tonnes, driven by gas turbines and capable of carrying fifteen to sixteen helicopters or vertical takeoff airplanes (V/STOL).

Until 1982, large 90,000-ton carriers were an exclusive feature of the United States Navy, which had four: CVAN 65, 68, 69, and 70. None of the minor navies had ships of this type; Russia alone had one under construction, but with a smaller displacement, and France had one on the drawing board. Until 1982, small 12–20,000-ton carriers were unique to the British and Italian Navies, but they seem likely to become the main units of the world's navies in years to come, because they are relatively cheap in relation to their fighting capabilities. The latest development of this type of ship is closely connected with the development of V/STOL aircraft, the best known being the British *Sea Harrier*.

Aircraft carrier armament

All ships are equipped with offensive armament which is, at the same time, defensive. When discussing battleships, we pointed out that the main-caliber guns were for attacking enemy ships at maximum range and so constituted both offensive and defensive weapons, whereas the anti-torpedo guns were chiefly defensive weapons. With the arrival of the airplane, anti-aircraft armament of a solely defensive type was added. Aircraft carrier armament can also be classified as offensive, consisting essentially of the aircraft on board (bombers and torpedo planes), with the fighter planes playing a defensive role. We shall not discuss this type of armament, but limit ourselves to the more conventional type: guns, machineguns, torpedoes, and, more recently, missiles. The older carriers had anti-ship armament made up of large- or medium-caliber guns and torpedo tubes. This armament was no longer fitted on more modern units built after 1930.

It will be remembered that the Washington Treaty limited the caliber of carrier guns to 8in (203mm). Old *Furious*, as she first appeared, with just a forward take-off deck, retained her anti-ship armament of one 18in (457mm) gun in a single turret aft, eleven 5.5in (140mm) guns symmetrically placed on the superstructure roof, and eighteen torpedo tubes, but had only five 3in (76mm) anti-aircraft guns.

Even the first flush-deck carriers, *Eagle* of 1920 and *Hermes* of 1923, had nine 6in (152mm) guns and six 5.5in (140mm) anti-ship guns respectively, with three to five 4in (102mm) guns and four 3in (76mm) anti-aircraft guns.

The heaviest anti-ship armament appeared on Japan's *Akagi* and *Kaga* of 1926–1927, and America's *Saratoga* and *Lexington*, armed with ten and eight 8in (203mm) guns in twin and single turrets, respectively. France's *Béarn* of 1927 was armed with eight 6.1in (155mm) anti-ship guns and four torpedo tubes. However, within a few years the major navies had become convinced that gun battles would never take place between aircraft carriers and battleships or cruisers, and that torpedoes would have to be launched only by torpedo planes. This resulted in the complete disappearance of anti-ship armament. (Note, however, that the German *Graf Zeppelin*, begun but not completed during World War II, had a powerful anti-ship battery, and that the U.S. Navy considered a carrier armed with 8in guns as late as 1941.)

Anti-aircraft armament for the largest carriers (the CV type) consisted of rapid-fire guns, usually with a caliber of 5in (127mm) on the American and Japanese ships, 4.7in and 4.5in (120mm and 114mm) on the British ones, and 3.9in (100mm) on the French *Clemenceau* Class, built in the postwar years.

Apart from these guns, there were machine guns, usually 1.5in (40mm) and 0.7in (20mm) in caliber, on the American and British ships, and 1in (25mm) on the Japanese. These machine guns were generally in groups of two, three, or four on a single mounting to give a greater concentration of firepower. The presence of the flight deck meant that the armament had to be positioned on both sides. The old ships with two stepped flight decks had a few anti-ship guns on the forward flight deck. *Akagi* and *Kaga* had two twin turrets containing 8in (203mm) guns on this deck and another six in single turrets, three per side, at the after end at main deck level. America's *Lexington* and *Saratoga*, however, had four twin 8in (203mm) turrets, two of which were before and two abaft the island. France's *Béarn* had her eight 6.1in (155mm) guns in single turrets, four (two per side) forward at main deck level and four right aft at gallery deck level.

Anti-aircraft weapons, both on carriers built after 1930 and on light- and escort-carriers, in other words, on those not equipped with anti-ship armament, were always positioned on small platforms extending beyond the sides of the flight deck, and at a lower level so as not to hinder aircraft maneuvers. For this reason, too, some machine guns on island carriers were mounted on the superstructure.

On light carriers commissioned after the war, anti-aircraft guns had disappeared and the armament consisted of just ten machine guns, or so.

On aircraft carriers built after the introduction of missiles, anti-aircraft armament was drastically changed. After modifications Britain's *Eagle* (commissioned in 1951) exchanged her sixteen 4.5in (114mm) guns and fifty-eight machine guns for eight 4.5in (114mm) guns and six Sea Cat missile launchers. Some American carriers, such as the *Kitty Hawk* Class of 1961, have only two Terrier missile launchers. The most recent nuclear-powered carriers, the three *Nimitz* Class (1975–1983) have only three launchers for Sea Sparrow Basic Point Defense Missiles (BPDMS) for short-range anti-anticraft defense. Since naval etiquette dictates that under certain circumstances ships should salute each other or let off ceremonial salvoes, some carriers armed only with machine guns—and especially those belonging to the traditionalist Royal Navy—have been supplied with four 3in (76mm) "saluting" guns for this purpose.

Seaplane carriers

Seaplane carriers pre-dated aircraft carriers but had no technical characteristics of any particular importance. The first ones, such as France's *Foudre* (1912), Japan's *Wakamiya* (1914), and Britain's *Hermes* merely had temporary shed-style hangars on the main deck. The first merchant ships converted by the Royal Navy (*Empress, Engadine, Riviera,* and *Ben My Chree*) also had this type of hangar. Britain's *Ark Royal* of 1914 did not even have a hangar, the planes being stowed in the holds, which had previously been oil tanks when the ship was a tanker. A similar conversion introducing simple hangars on the main deck was carried out on the German carriers *Answald, Santa Elena,* and *Oswald,* but the other two German Flugzeugmutterschiffe, *Glyndwr* and *Adeline Hugo Stinnes 3* did not even have a hangar; their two to four seaplanes were kept in the open on top of the hold hatchways.

The only First World War seaplane carrier to be built by converting a light cruiser was Germany's *Stuttgart,* which had a hangar for three seaplanes in a large superstructure abaft the third funnel.

After the torpedo plane carrier *Foudre,* the French Navy converted a Channel ferry (*Pas de Calais*) and a cargo ship (*Campinas*) into seaplane carriers with hangars on the main deck. They had two hangars, one before and one abaft the central superstructure. By contrast another Channel ferry, *Rouen,* carried her aircraft on deck.

The Italian Navy had a seaplane carrier called *Europa.* She was built by converting the cargo ship *Manila,* bought in February 1915; she had two hangars on the main deck and cranes for lowering and hoisting the planes in and out of the sea. She could carry up to eight aircraft and was stricken on September 10, 1920.

In the First World War, the Russian Imperial Navy also had seaplane carriers, the first being the armored yacht *Almaz,* stationed in the Black Sea, and capable of carrying three to four seaplanes on deck. In 1917, she was joined by six more ex-Rumanian units: *Romania, Dacia, Rege Carol,* and *Imperator Traian,* plus another

Foudre (France 1912). A torpedo boat carrier converted to carry aircraft but not fitted with a takeoff platform. The aircraft were kept in a temporary shelter abaft of the central superstructure. The seaplanes were lowered into the sea by a crane, from where they took off and landed.

Wakamiya (Japan 1914). Formerly a merchant cargo ship, converted in 1914 to a seaplane carrier. She had two temporary shelters, one before and one abaft the superstructure, each containing two aircraft. A derrick was used to lower the planes into the sea and recover them.

Empress (Great Britain 1914). Formerly a Channel ferry, converted in 1914. She had only one hangar aft and the aircraft were lowered and raised by two large cranes which can be seen on either side of the door. She was converted back to a merchantman in 1919.

Ben My Chree (Great Britain 1915). A Channel ferry converted in 1915. She had just one large hangar aft for four planes, inside a superstructure added on deck. Instead of a crane she had a derrick right aft. She sank on January 11, 1917.

Ark Royal (Great Britain 1915). A tanker converted in 1915. The aircraft were kept in the holds and hoisted on deck by two large cranes. In 1923, she was used as a mine sweeper tender and from 1934 as a depot ship and renamed *Pegasus.* She was sold in 1946 and converted to a cargo ship.

Oswald (Germany 1918). A British merchantman captured by the Germans, first converted in 1917 to a torpedo plane tender, then in 1918 given two hangars for four seaplanes in two large superstructures with side doors, one forward and one aft, served by derricks. Converted back to a merchantman in 1919.

Adeline Hugo Stinnes 3 (Germany 1915). A merchantman with no hangar but able to carry three seaplanes on deck, lifting them with derricks. She had no armament. At the end of the war she was handed over to Belgium as part of war reparations. In 1936 she came under the Finnish flag. Broken up in 1964.

Answald (Germany 1914). A merchantman converted in 1914 and fitted with two hangars with side doors, one forward and one aft, similar to those on *Oswald* but with room for two, as opposed to four, seaplanes. At the end of the war she was handed over to Great Britain as part of war reparations and served until 1933.

Glyndwr (Germany 1914). A British merchantman captured by the Germans and converted in 1914. She carried two seaplanes on deck and had no hangar. She was armed with two 2in (52mm) guns. At the end of the war she was returned to the shipowner Scarisbrick and in 1940 sold to a Greek shipowner. Broken up in 1954.

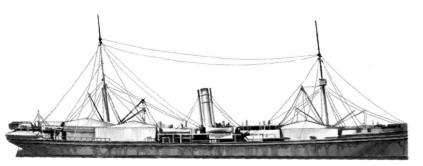

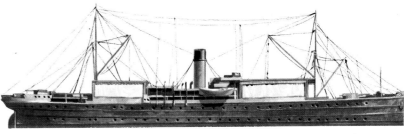

Pas de Calais (France 1914). A Channel ferry converted in 1914 by adding two hangars with side doors, one before and one abaft the central superstructure, served by derricks. At the end of the war she was handed back to the Northern Railway Company.

Santa Elena (Germany 1915). A German merchantman requisitioned in 1915 and given two three-to-four-plane hangars with side doors. At the end of the war she was handed over to the United States, then, in 1942, became an Italian ship named *Orvieto*. In 1943 she was captured by the Germans and sunk at Toulon in August 1944.

Campinas (France 1917). A merchantman bought by the navy and converted in 1917. She could carry from six to ten aircraft in two hangars, one before and one abaft the central superstructure, which had side doors and were served by derricks. At the end of the war, in 1920, she was returned to her owner.

Stuttgart (Germany 1918). The only warship to be converted into a seaplane carrier in 1918. She had only one after hangar with side doors, the aircraft being handled by the aftermast derrick. At the end of the war she was handed over to Britain and broken up.

Rouen (France 1914). A passenger steamer requisitioned and classified as a hangarless seaplane carrier in 1914. She was used as a troop transport ship, however, in the Mediterranean for the Gallipoli operation. She went back to being a merchantman from 1919 to 1939 and was again requisitioned as a transport ship in the 1939–1945 war, when she was renamed *Wullenwever*.

two whose names are not known. When the war was over, *Almaz* escaped to Bizerta along with other units of Russia's "White Fleet." She was interned there, and stricken in 1922.

In order to make better use of aircraft as weapons, the Royal Navy installed a forward takeoff deck on some of her seaplane carriers. The first unit to have such a deck was the former liner *Campania* which originally had a deck just 120.07ft (36.60m) long before the bridge. In 1916 the ship's superstructures were modified and the single funnel replaced with two abreast, so as to lengthen the takeoff deck to 199.80ft (60.90m). In 1917 she took on landplanes instead of seaplanes and became the first ever aircraft carrier, predating *Furious*, which only became operational in June 1917. *Campania* sank after a collision on November 5, 1918. The second British ship to have a takeoff deck was the Channel ferry *Manxman*, commissioned on April 17, 1916. Her deck was only 59ft (18m) long; at the after end there was a large lattice crane to lift the aircraft out of the sea. It was from *Manxman's* takeoff deck that Commander Rutland took off in March–April 1917, thus demonstrating the feasibility of operating with landplanes at sea, too.

Nairana and *Pegasus*, both originally cargo ships, also had a flight deck, hangars, and deck edge seaplane cranes. In 1921 *Nairana* returned to her career as a merchant ship, whereas *Pegasus* was converted into a seaplane tender and served from 1924 until August 1931.

Among the "historic" units of the First World War were *Vindex*, whose flight deck served as a runway for the first landplane, piloted by Second Flight Lieutenant Towler on November 3, 1915, and *Ben My Chree*, the first aircraft carrier to sink an enemy ship, a 5000t Turkish

Manxman (Great Britain 1916). A Channel ferry requisitioned and converted in 1916. She was fitted with a takeoff platform forward and two hangars, the after one with a crane to lift the seaplanes and the forward one below the takeoff platform. In early 1917, Commander Rutland took off from this platform on various occasions using landplanes. After returning to her role as a merchantman in 1920, she was again used as a transport ship in the Second World War.

Campania (Great Britain 1916). A liner bought in 1914 and converted in 1915. She had a takeoff deck forward but no hangar, the aircraft being parked on the deck below the flight deck. The ship is shown here after her forward funnel had been divided to extend the platform to 199.80ft (60.90m). She sank on November 5, 1918, after colliding with the battleship *Royal Oak*.

Nairana (Great Britain 1917). A merchant ship bought when still on the stocks and completed as a seaplane carrier with a takeoff deck forward and two hangars. Instead of a conventional crane to handle the aircraft, there was a bridge crane that ran on a guiderail supported by a lattice beam that extended beyond the stern. The foremast derrick was used to lift planes onto the platform. She was converted back to a merchant ship in 1921.

Pegasus (Great Britain 1917). A merchantman bought on the stocks and completed as a seaplane carrier with a takeoff platform forward and hangar aft, and equipped with two side cranes like *Empress*. She could carry nine aircraft and made over twenty-one knots. There were two symmetrically placed derricks forward to lift the seaplanes onto the takeoff deck. She was stricken in 1931.

Europa (Italy 1915). A British-built cargo ship that came under the Italian flag in 1898. She was bought by the navy in 1915 and fitted with two hangars with side doors. To lift the planes into and out of the sea there were four level-luffing cranes, one in front of each door. She was armed with two 3in (76mm) guns. In the First World War she was detached to Brindisi and Valona to assist the squadrons there, before being withdrawn in 1920.

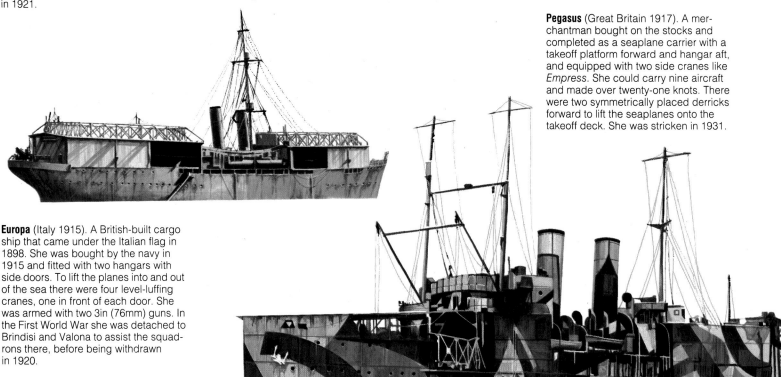

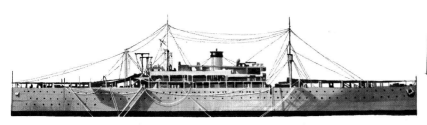

Kamoi (Japan 1932). Built in the United States for the Japanese Navy as an oil tanker, she was converted into a seaplane carrier in 1932. She had two wall-less shelters, that could house twelve seaplanes, and two derricks to handle the aircraft. In 1936–1937 a "Hein Carpet" was positioned aft to arrest the seaplanes after landing. She was converted back into a tanker in 1943.

Notoro (Japan 1924). *Notoro* and *Tsurumi* were oil tankers, converted into seaplane carriers in 1924. They could carry ten seaplanes. The aircraft were kept under two wall-less shelters on deck and lifted into the sea by two derricks. They were used during the war in 1941 and 1942, then reconverted to tankers. *Notoro* was then used as a floating depot and broken up in 1947.

Wright (United States 1921). The United States Navy's first seaplane carrier. She had neither flight deck nor catapults. She was stricken in 1948.

Giuseppe Miraglia (Italy 1927). The Italian Navy's one and only seaplane carrier, equipped with two catapults. She had two hangars, one forward for five aircraft and one aft for six, both with side doors and four jib cranes to lower the aircraft into the sea. There was also a hatchway with derricks to lift the planes onto the deck where the two catapults were, one forward and one aft. She was used as a troop ship at Taranto in 1940 and broken up in 1950.

merchantman hit off the Dardanelles on August 11, 1915, by a Short 184 piloted by C.M. Edmonds.

After the First World War, the various navies were using ships classified as seaplane carriers or seaplane tenders; such were Japan's *Notoro, Tsurumi,* and *Kamoi* (1924–1932), with their simple shelters on deck to house ten to twelve seaplanes.

Kamoi also had a "Hein Carpet," a roller apparatus used to lower a heavy tarpaulin in over the stern to act as a buffer for seaplanes as they approached the ship.

From 1921 to 1946, the United States Navy had a seaplane carrier called *Wright* (this name being given to *CVL 49* in 1945) with a clear deck aft fitted with rollers upon which the seaplanes' floats could slide.

Commandant Teste (France 1929). Seaplane carrier with four catapults and a large hangar with a door aft. Next to each of the catapults was a crane to lower the planes into the sea. There was a fifth crane at the stern to lift the aircraft on board or lower them into the sea from the platform situated in front of the hangar door. She was scuttled off Toulon on November 27, 1942, later refloated, but never restored to service; she was scrapped in 1950.

Albermarle (United States 1940). A seaplane tender with a spacious hangar aft and a door opening onto the deck, where the aircraft were kept. She was modernized in 1956–1957, taken out of commission in 1960, and stricken in 1962.

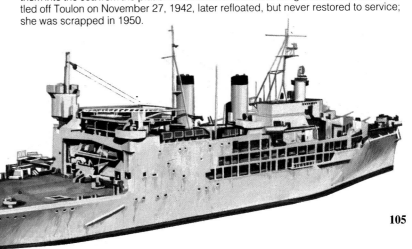

Dedalo (Spain 1922). A merchantman bought in 1922 and converted into a "mobile station for the naval airforce." She had a hangar for twenty-five seaplanes and, at the bow, an air-ship mooring mast. There was a spacious deck aft to park the planes in the open and one derrick on either side. She was stricken in 1931.

Ise (Japan 1943). The two battleships *Ise* and *Hyuga,* built in the war years (1914–1918), were converted into seaplane carriers in 1943. They were fitted with a twenty-two plane hangar aft, plus a crane and a lift to bring the aircraft on to the deck where there were two catapults. *Ise* was sunk in 1945.

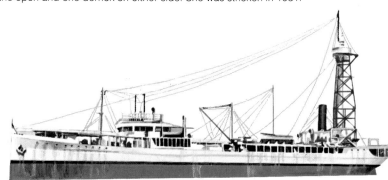

Patoka (United States 1924). An oil tanker converted into an airship and seaplane tender in 1924. There was an airship mooring tower aft plus workshops to repair the seaplanes, spare parts stores, and aviation fuel tanks. She could carry three aircraft on the open deck. She was stricken in 1946.

Italy's *Giuseppe Miraglia* (1927), Australia's *Albatross* (1928), and America's *Albermarle* and *Curtiss* (1940) were all custom-built seaplane carriers. *Giuseppe Miraglia* had a large superstructure amidships which contained the hangars, and two catapults at the bow and stern on the upper deck; she could carry eleven aircraft ready for action and six more requiring assembly. She was hardly used and in 1940 was converted into a troop ship at Taranto. She was stricken in 1950.

Australia's *Albatross* had her hangar below an extremely long forecastle, on either side of which were two lattice cranes to handle the aircraft. She had a catapult right forward and carried nine seaplanes. She was not a very satisfactory ship and served for only nine years: from 1928 to 1937. France's *Commandant Teste* had a large hangar in the midships to after area with a wide door opening on to the main deck aft. There were four trainable catapults on the upper deck and cranes for lifting the seaplanes. She served from 1931 to November 27, 1942, when she was scuttled in the port of Toulon to prevent her from falling into German hands.

The United States Navy had seventeen seaplane tenders, none of which had catapults. *Albermarle* and *Curtiss* had a large open deck aft where the seaplanes could be parked in the open, with access from a door in the large hangar within the central superstructure. In 1956–1957 these two units were modified and fitted with a stern slipway to haul on deck P6M Sea Master jet aircraft, which were heavier and impossible to lift by crane. In 1964, *Albermarle* was converted into a helicopter repair ship and renamed *Corpus Christi Bay*.

The Japanese Navy had five seaplane carriers, two of which, *Mizuho* and *Nisshin,* looked like merchant ships, with practically no superstructures; they were equipped with catapults and a large crane amidships to retrieve the seaplanes. The other three units were the two battleships *Ise* and *Hyuga* and the cruiser *Mogami,* built for the First World War. In 1943 they were converted to carry twenty-two seaplanes, retaining their forward armament and central superstructures. *Mogami* underwent a similar refit and became active again in November 1943. The seaplanes were positioned on a large platform that replaced the after big-gun turrets and there were two side catapults. *Ise* and *Hyuga* were never used as seaplane carriers; in 1944 their catapults were removed and they were used as battleships. Both were sunk in the air-raid on the port of Kure on the 24th and 28th of July, 1945. *Mogami* sank on October 29, 1944, in the Battle of Leyte Gulf.

Albatross (Australia 1928). Purposely built as a seaplane carrier, she had a nine-plane hangar below a long forecastle housing the aircraft service area, two big cranes, and a catapult. The planes were lifted from the hangar to the deck by the cranes through large hatchways, and there were no side doors in the ship's sides. She was transferred to Britain in 1938, converted to a repair ship in 1943, and then sold for conversion to a merchant ship in 1946.

Mizuho (Japan 1939). A seaplane carrier that could transport twenty-four aircraft in a hangar below the main deck. She had four catapults, two per side, two gantry cranes to lift the planes from the holds, and two jib cranes. She received the same modifications as *Nisshin,* becoming a submarine carrier. She was sunk on May 2, 1942.

Nisshin (Japan 1942). A fast seaplane carrier that made twenty-eight knots. She could carry twenty-five seaplanes in two hangars below the main deck, launched by two catapults on either side. She could also carry twelve minisubs, floated out through a hatch at the stern. In order to transfer the seaplanes from the holds to the deck there were two large gantry cranes, whose main structures can be seen, which also supported derricks and a jib crane. She was sunk by the Americans on July 22, 1943.

First-generation aircraft carriers

When discussing the development of aircraft carriers, we mentioned that they were preceded by seaplane carriers and that in May 1917 the Royal Navy decided to convert the cruiser *Furious* into a "fast seaplane carrier," even though it was foreseen that she would be used to operate with landplanes as well. *Furious* was a prototype on which further experiments were carried out. She was in fact designed as a cruiser armed with two 18in (457mm) guns; on June 26, 1917, she entered service with a narrow flight deck forward, measuring 228.01 × 40.02ft (69.50 × 12.20m) in place of the 18in (457mm) forward turret, followed by the normal cruiser superstructures, that is, conning tower, tripod mast, funnel, aftermast, and after 18in (457mm) turret.

Between November 1917 and March 1918, after the tragic end to Commander Dunning's landing test flights, the after turret was also removed and a deck added abaft the turret mast and funnel; it was much longer than the forward deck, measuring 300.19ft (91.50m) long and 50.03ft (15.25m) across, and was connected to the latter by two catwalks 169.94ft (51.80m) long and 11ft (3.35m) wide, either side of the central superstructures. Armament, reduced to ten 5.5in (140mm) guns, was arranged below the after flight deck (four pieces), and below the two catwalks (six pieces). Finally, in 1921–1925, *Furious* was again converted and given two stepped flight decks: the upper one being 582.51ft (177.55m) long and 65.61ft (20.00m) wide and the lower one 196.85ft (60m) long. During the refit, a large two-story hangar was also added below the flight deck. The removal of the funnel led to the installation of two flues inside the hull, with their outlets on either side over the stern. The removal of the turret mast meant that two pilot bridges had to be built below the two forward ends of the top flight deck. During the conversion, the eighteen torpedo tubes were removed and the longitudinal arrester and guide wires for aircraft landing removed, as well. Outriggers were installed on either side of the flight deck to support the horizontal safety nets.

Vindictive (Great Britain). First designed as a cruiser, completed as an aircraft carrier, then converted back to a cruiser. She had a takeoff deck forward and a landing platform aft, separated by the bridge, mast, and two funnels. The forward takeoff deck was very short, about 75ft (23m) long, the landing deck was about 164ft (50m). They were connected by a catwalk on the port side. From 1923 to 1925 she was converted back into a cruiser but retained one hangar before the bridge for four seaplanes and was fitted out with a catapult and crane to lift the aircraft. She became a training ship in 1936–1937, and a repair ship in 1939–1940. She was broken up in 1946.

Furious (Great Britain). Designed as a cruiser, in 1917 she was given a 229ft (69.50m) long forward takeoff deck. After an accident during a landing attempt, she was modified and given a 300.19ft (91.50m) after-landing platform. Between 1921 and 1925 she was again modified and given two flight decks: an upper one 582.51ft (177.55m) long and 65.61ft (20m) wide, and one forward, on a lower level, and 196.85ft (60m) long. The top deck was left completely clear with the removal of the bridge, mast, and funnel. Lastly, in 1939, a small island was added on the starboard side of the flight deck, but the funnels remained below the flight deck and discharged over the stern. She was taken out of operational service in 1944 and broken up in 1948.

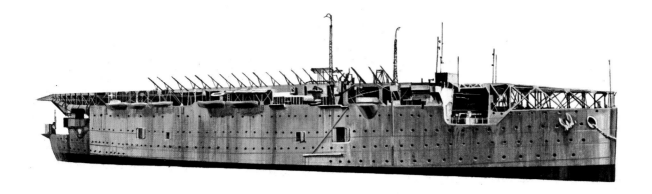

Argus (Great Britain 1918). The first British aircraft carrier to have a full-length flush deck incorporated into the design from the start. The hangar, below the deck, could accommodate twenty aircraft and communicated with the flight deck by means of two lifts. She was used in the Second World War and broken up in 1946.

Langley (United States 1922). America's first aircraft carrier, a conversion of the collier *Jupiter*. She had a full-length flush deck but no hangar and the aircraft were kept in four holds; they were hoisted by crane up to the main deck, wherefrom a lift took them to the flight deck. She became a seaplane tender in 1937, and was used as an aircraft transport ship in the Pacific, where she was sunk on February 27, 1942.

Hosho (Japan 1922). The Japanese Navy's first aircraft carrier built as such from the keel up, without converting other units. She had a full-length flight deck with a hangar below for twenty-one aircraft ready for flight and five requiring assembly. Originally there was a small island on the starboard side for the mast and bridge, but this was removed in 1923. The three funnels were on the starboard edge of the flight deck and could be directed downwards. She was used as a pilot training ship in 1943 and stricken in 1947.

Glorious (Great Britain 1930). *Glorious* and *Courageous* were both battlecruisers, armed with four 15in (381mm) guns; after serving in the First World War, they were converted to aircraft carriers between 1924 and 1930. They had one upper deck and one lower forward one, like *Furious*, but featured a large all-purpose island for the bridge, mast, and funnel. *Glorious* was sunk on June 8, 1940, by the German battleships *Scharnhorst* and *Gneisenau*.

The only other aircraft carrier to have a takeoff deck forward and a landing deck aft, with the conventional superstructures and funnels, was Britain's *Vindictive*, originally planned as a light cruiser and converted while still under construction between January and October 1918. Her flight decks were smaller than those of *Furious*, the forward one in particular being markedly shorter. They were joined by a single catwalk to port of the bridge and two funnels.

When *Furious* was converted into a flush-deck aircraft carrier, *Vindictive* was restored to her original specification as a light cruiser and recommissioned in 1925.

The first two units with a flush deck and no superstructures, Britain's *Argus* (1918) and America's *Langley* (1922), were not built as such, but resulted from converting hulls designed for other purposes. *Argus* came from the liner *Conte Rosso*, ordered from the Beardmore Yard in 1914 by the Italian shipping company Lloyd Sabaudo, and *Langley* from the collier *Jupiter*, built at the Mare Island Navy Yard between 1911 and 1913; she had therefore already served for several years as an auxiliary in the navy.

Argus had a flight deck that measured 550.32 × 67.94ft (167.74 × 20.71m). Her bridge was positioned in the middle of the forward area of the flight deck, but was retractable and could be lowered during aircraft maneuvers. The funnels were replaced by two horizontal flues below the flight deck carrying the smoke to the stern, where there were exhaust outlets in the ship's sides. Armament was fairly

Akagi (Japan). Built on the hull of an uncompleted battle cruiser, she had three flight decks with two half decks forward. She was built with two funnels instead of flues running to the stern. In 1935–1938 she was modernized and given a single full-length deck with two catapults forward and three lifts. *Akagi* also had a small island housing the bridge on the port side. During modifications the two twin 8in (203mm) turrets on the middle flight deck were removed, leaving only the six 8in (203mm) after single turrets. She was sunk on June 5, 1942.

Akagi **after modifications**

Kaga (Japan). Built on the hull of a battleship that was not completed because of the provisions of the Naval Disarmament Treaty. Originally there were three flight decks, two of which were half-decks set at a lower level forward. There was no island. Boiler smoke was discharged aft through two flues that ran under the flight deck. In 1935–1936 she underwent modifications: The two forward flight decks were removed, a single upper one fitted, and the hangar extended into the area left by the two decks that had been removed. An island was added on the starboard side, along with a funnel amidships that discharged downwards and replaced the stern flues. She was sunk on July 4, 1942.

Kaga after modifications

light, comprising four 4in (102mm) anti-aircraft guns: two forward on the main deck, which could fire upwards through two large openings in the sides of the flight deck, and the other two aft, also on the main deck, behind the end of the flight deck.

Langley (formerly *Jupiter*) had a flight deck measuring 533.95 × 31.16ft (162.75 × 9.50m). The bridge was forward below this deck, and the funnel, still in its original position, had a transverse flue that ended in two sections that could be lowered to discharge the smoke on the leeward side. Before long, however, this arrangement was changed: Two funnels were added, which could be lowered on the port side. The armament comprised four 5in (127mm) anti-ship guns and there were no anti-aircraft guns. Two of these four pieces were positioned forward on the forecastle deck and two aft on the main deck.

Langley had the first turbo-electric power plant to be tried out by the American Navy and was a twin screw ship. In 1937 she was down-graded to the status of seaplane tender. The forward part of the flight deck was removed and its length reduced to 328.08ft (100m); the bridge superstructure was reinstalled at the bow. She was sunk in the Pacific on February 27, 1942. The prototype of the Japanese aircraft carrier was *Hosho* (1922). She was, however, custom-built, as such. She had a flight deck measuring 509.02 × 74.80ft (155.15 × 22.80m) which initially had a small bridge superstructure and a mast, both removed in 1923. The eight boilers discharged into three funnels that could be lowered and were positioned on the edge of the flight deck. Anti-ship armament comprised four 5.5in (140mm) turrets on the main deck, two positioned symmetrically in front of the bridge and one per side amidships a little abaft the funnels. There were two 3in (76mm) anti-aircraft guns on the flight deck, one either side, abaft the funnels.

Although they do not belong to the first generation, the British stepped-deck aircraft carriers *Glorious* and *Courageous* and the Japanese *Akagi* and *Kaga* are included in this group.

Glorious and *Courageous* were cruisers belonging to the same class as *Furious*, and saw action in the First World War with their armament of four 15in (381mm) guns. After the signing of the 1922 Washington Treaty, the Royal Navy decided to convert them into aircraft carriers and gave them a stepped flight deck, like *Furious* after her 1925 refit. On the starboard side of the flight deck, however, an island was added which included the bridge and funnels, thus avoiding the horizontal flues below the flight deck on the prototype. The top flight deck measured 574.14 × 77.09ft (175 × 23.50m) and the forward one was 59ft (18m) long. Fighter planes could take off from the latter without interfering with the bombers and torpedo planes operating from the top deck. These ships had no anti-ship armament, just sixteen 4.7in (120mm) guns and fifty anti-aircraft machine guns, plus four 3in (76mm) saluting guns. The two forward 4.7in (120mm) guns were either side of the forward flight deck, the two after ones were on the main deck aft. The other twelve were six per side on platforms that extended beyond the edge at main deck level in individual rectangular openings in the bulwarks. The hull had retained its cruiser armor which was 3in (76mm) thick round the belt and 1.5in (38mm) on the central citadel, plus 1in (25mm) armor on the main deck and 1.4–1.9in (37–50mm) on the protective deck. There were bulges either side for underwater protection. *Glorious* was shelled and sunk by the German battleships *Scharnhorst* and *Gneisenau* on June 8, 1940, and *Courageous* was torpedoed by the submarine *U 29* on September 17, 1939.

The Japanese aircraft carrier *Kaga*, adapted from the hull of a battleship, was commissioned on March 31, 1926. She had three stepped flight decks and the boiler smoke discharged over the stern through two horizontal flues. Anti-ship armament comprised ten 8in (203mm) guns, four in twin turrets either side of the middle flight deck forward and six in three single turrets either side at main deck level aft: The anti-aircraft armament of twelve 4.7in (120mm) guns were in six twin mounts on individual side platforms amidships.

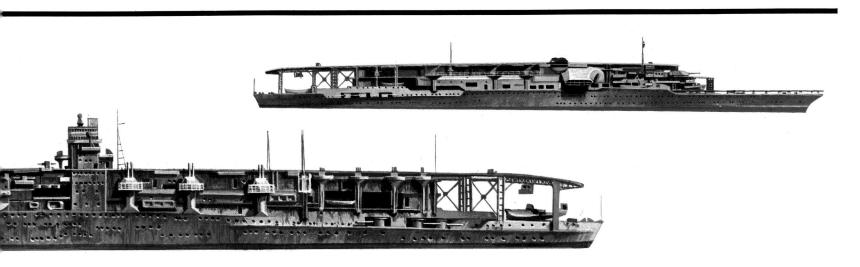

Béarn (France 1927). France's first aircraft carrier. She was built on the hull of an uncompleted battleship, and had a full-length flight deck supported fore and aft by pillars plus a large island to starboard, housing the bridge, mast, and funnel. This island was on the edge of the flight deck. She was not in French waters when her country surrendered and was refitted in 1944 as an aircraft transport for General de Gaulle's Free French Forces. She was broken up in 1967.

Hermes (Great Britain 1923). An aircraft carrier with a full-length flight deck and an island on the starboard side housing the bridge, mast, and funnel. The flight deck followed the lines of the hull and tapered to a point at the bow, where it was supported by hull structures. At the after end, however, it was supported by pillars and a large space was left in front of the after hangar door for aircraft maintenance. She was sunk on April 9, 1942, by Japanese aircraft off Ceylon.

Commissioned on March 25, 1927, *Akagi* had a battle cruiser hull and three stepped flight decks. She had two funnels on the starboard side of the flight deck which were at the same level as the deck itself. The forward funnel discharged outwards and downwards while the after one, attached to it, discharged upwards. There was no island as such, but a charthouse on the starboard side of the upper deck. The arrangement of the anti-ship and anti-aircraft armament was as on *Kaga*. Both ships were modernized (*Kaga* in 1935–1936 and *Akagi* in 1935–1938) resulting in the removal of the two forward flight decks and the addition of a single full-length deck 906.49 × 100ft (276.30 × 30.50m). *Kaga* had the two side flues removed and a single funnel to starboard slanting downwards added. *Akagi* also had her two funnels replaced by a single one of the same shape. Both units had a small island as their bridge: on the port side on *Akagi* and on the starboard side on *Kaga*. *Akagi's* anti-ship armament was reduced to six 8in (203mm) guns, removing the four in the two twin turrets forward. *Kaga* retained all ten of her guns, however, by increasing the six single after turrets to ten. Anti-aircraft armament was stepped up from twelve 5in (127mm) guns to sixteen on *Kaga*, these being positioned in eight twin mounts on individual platforms which extended well beyond the edges of the flight deck. *Akagi* retained her twelve 4.7in (120mm) guns, however. On both ships the lifts to bring the aircraft up from the hangar to the flight deck was increased from two to three.

Eagle (Great Britain 1924). Built on the hull of the battleship *Almirante Cochrane*, ordered by the Chilean Navy from the Armstrong Yard. She had a full-length flight deck, tapering at the bow and following the lines of the hull, which was supported aft by pillars, as on *Hermes*. The two elevators from the hangar to the flight deck are clearly visible. The forward one is shaped so that the aircraft wings can clear it. She was sunk in the Mediterranean on August 11, 1942.

France's *Béarn* was commissioned in May 1927. Whereas all the previously described aircraft carriers had rectangular or almost rectangular flight decks, *Béarn's* flight deck tapered sharply at both ends, roughly following the lines of the hull below it. *Béarn* was built on the hull of a battleship, a *Normandie* Class ship left incomplete after World War I. *Béarn* was the only aircraft carrier to have a four-screw power plant of two turbines and two reciprocating engines. The flight deck was clear, with the island extending beyond the hull on the starboard side, supported by a sort of bracket. In the side of the island there were large apertures to suck in cold air that was mixed with the combustion products to reduce the temperature and avoid the formation of swirls above the flight deck. Anti-ship armament comprised eight 6.1in (155mm) guns in eight armored casemates, two either side on the main deck in front of the island and four more, likewise two per side, right aft at gallery deck level. There were also four torpedo tubes. Anti-aircraft armament comprised six 4.7in (120mm) and eight 3in (76mm) guns plus twelve machine guns. The three aircraft lifts were covered by hatches with two flaps which were kept in an upright position when the lifts were in operation.

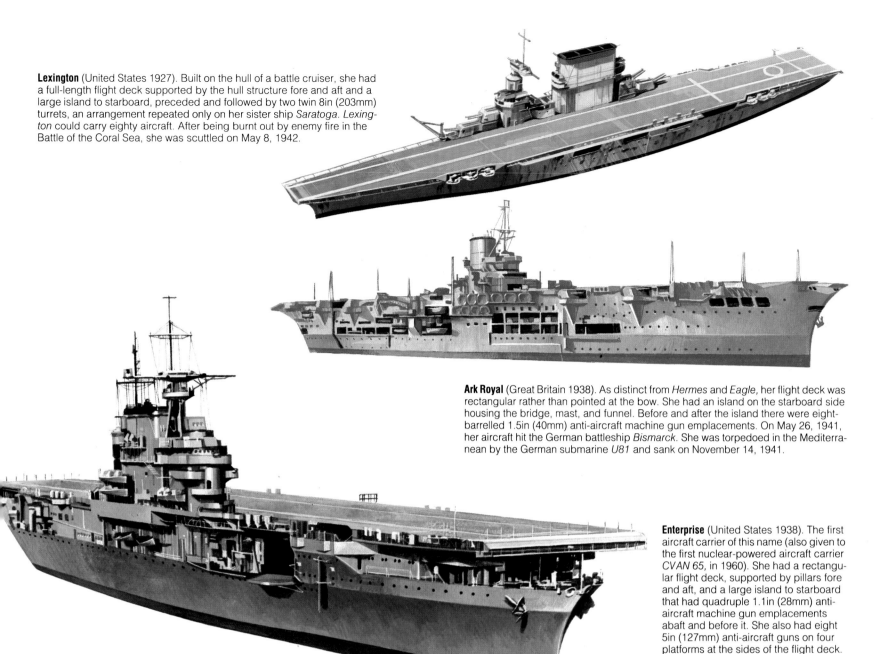

Lexington (United States 1927). Built on the hull of a battle cruiser, she had a full-length flight deck supported by the hull structure fore and aft and a large island to starboard, preceded and followed by two twin 8in (203mm) turrets, an arrangement repeated only on her sister ship *Saratoga*. *Lexington* could carry eighty aircraft. After being burnt out by enemy fire in the Battle of the Coral Sea, she was scuttled on May 8, 1942.

Ark Royal (Great Britain 1938). As distinct from *Hermes* and *Eagle*, her flight deck was rectangular rather than pointed at the bow. She had an island on the starboard side housing the bridge, mast, and funnel. Before and after the island there were eight-barrelled 1.5in (40mm) anti-aircraft machine gun emplacements. On May 26, 1941, her aircraft hit the German battleship *Bismarck*. She was torpedoed in the Mediterranean by the German submarine *U81* and sank on November 14, 1941.

Enterprise (United States 1938). The first aircraft carrier of this name (also given to the first nuclear-powered aircraft carrier *CVAN 65*, in 1960). She had a rectangular flight deck, supported by pillars fore and aft, and a large island to starboard that had quadruple 1.1in (28mm) anti-aircraft machine gun emplacements abaft and before it. She also had eight 5in (127mm) anti-aircraft guns on four platforms at the sides of the flight deck. She belonged to a class of three units which included *Yorktown* and *Hornet*, and was stricken in 1956.

Straight flightdeck aircraft carriers

Two of the oldest aircraft carriers to take part in the Second World War, Britain's *Eagle* and *Hermes*, were originally constructed with a straight full-length flight deck. Other later units, such as Britain's *Glorious* and *Courageous* and Japan's *Akagi* and *Kaga*, had stepped decks which were later changed (on the last two) to full-length decks.

Eagle used the hull of the battleship *Almirante Cochrane*, under construction at the Armstrong Yard for the Chilean Navy and requisitioned in 1916. She was delivered to the Royal Navy on April 13, 1920, completed above-decks at Portsmouth Navy Yard, and commissioned on February 26, 1924. The flight deck echoed the shape of the hull below; it was pointed at the forward end but extended across virtually the entire beam of the ship at the after end, making it almost rectangular in shape. Anti-ship armament consisted of nine 6in (152mm) guns below the flight deck, six on three platforms either side and three on the main deck right aft. The five 4in (102mm) guns and four 3in (76mm) anti-aircraft guns were positioned above the flight deck and on the superstructure. *Eagle* had a fairly sizeable island to starboard, whereas her predecessor, *Argus*, had had no island nor, incidentally, did *Furious* after her 1925 refit. The island was made up of a bridge superstructure, two tall masts (the forward one being a tripod mast), and two funnels. She was sunk in the Mediterranean on August 11, 1942, by the German submarine *U73*.

Hermes was the first British aircraft carrier to be designed and built without using the hull of another ship. She was very similar to *Eagle* both in her hull lines and the anti-ship and anti-aircraft armament arrangement. Her flight deck was pointed at the bow and a large crane was installed abaft the island, to lift the seaplanes in and out of the sea. *Eagle* and France's *Béarn* had a similar crane but it

was positioned differently on the more modern aircraft carriers. *Hermes* was sunk off Ceylon on April 9, 1942.

The first two American aircraft carriers to be built in accordance with the regulations laid down by the Washington Treaty were *Saratoga* and *Lexington*, commissioned in 1927. As distinct from their contemporary British *Glorious* types and Japanese *Akagis*, they did not have a stepped flight deck but a full length deck, which was virtually rectangular.

If we overlook their four twin 8in (203mm) anti-ship gun turrets, these 1927 units already had the lines of those built in 1940. Their 8in armament was removed at the beginning of the war in order to strengthen the anti-aircraft armament that had originally included twelve 5in (127mm) guns on four platforms either side of the flight deck. These ships had bulges for underwater protection, 6in (152mm) of armor in their belts, and a 3in (76mm) armored deck. They had a four-screw turbo-electric drive and could carry as many as eighty aircraft, whereas *Glorious* carried only forty-eight and *Akagi* sixty.

Lexington was sunk in the Battle of the Coral Sea on May 8, 1942, and *Saratoga* in the Bikini experiments of July 1946 to test the effects of the atomic bomb on ships. In the Royal Navy, the first unit to have a full-length flight deck was *Ark Royal*, commissioned on November 16, 1938. She had an island on the starboard side made up of a tripod mast and a big funnel. The deck had three aircraft lifts. America's *Langley*, *Saratoga*, and *Lexington* all had a catapult on the flight deck to launch their bombers, which were the heaviest planes, but this type of catapult was not fitted on contemporary British carriers. Japan's *Akagi* and *Kaga*, likewise, had no catapults. *Ark Royal* had no anti-ship armament, only anti-aircraft weapons, made up of sixteen 4.5in (114mm) guns and thirty-two 1.6in (40mm) machine guns. The 4.5in (114mm) guns were positioned in the conventional eight twin

Wasp (United States 1949). An aircraft carrier whose flight deck was separate from the hull and supported on pillars fore and aft. She also had a very large island on the starboard side. On this ship, too, there were quadruple 1.1in (28mm) anti-aircraft machine gun emplacements before and abaft the island. Apart from the two centrally positioned lifts on deck, there was also a deck-edge lift to port that could be folded away. She was sunk on September 15, 1942.

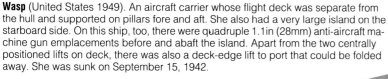

Victorious (Great Britain 1941). She belonged to a class of four units together with *Illustrious, Formidable,* and *Indomitable.* The flight deck and hull made up a single structure and sloped slightly downwards at either end. She had a large island on the starboard side. The sixteen 4.5in (114mm) anti-aircraft guns in twin turrets, two on each of the four platforms at either end of the flight deck, are an interesting feature. Between 1950 and 1957 she was modified to an angled-deck carrier.

Hiyo (Japan 1942). The passenger steamer *Izumo Maru,* bought on the stocks and completed as an aircraft carrier. She had an island on the starboard side with its funnel directed upwards rather than downwards, as was usually the case on Japanese aircraft carriers, and slanting outwards at an angle of 15°. She was sunk on June 19, 1944.

Zuikaku (Japan 1941). She formed a class with *Shokaku.* The flight deck was separate from the hull and supported by pillars at either end. There were two funnels, to starboard, which were angled outwards and below the flight deck. The island was small, housing just the bridge. *Zuikaku* was sunk on October 25, 1944, off Cape Engano.

Unryu (Japan 1944). Part of a class of sixteen units of which only six were laid down and only *Unryu, Amagi,* and *Katsuragi* completed. Her flight deck was separate from the hull and supported by pillars at either end. She had a small island to starboard housing the bridge and radar antennae. The two funnels were on the outside to starboard and directed downwards, a little abaft the island. She was sunk on December 19, 1944 after only five months' service.

Taiho (Japan 1944). One of the few Japanese aircraft carriers to have a funnel directed upwards and angled outwards at 15°. The island was therefore a large one, positioned outside the hull to starboard and supported by a bracket. The flight deck was connected to the structures below. She was commissioned on March 7, 1944, and sunk on June 19, 1944, just over three months later.

Shinano (Japan 1944). Laid down as the third battleship of the *Yamato* Class, she was converted and became Japan's aircraft carrier, displacing 71,890 tonnes, more than the American *Lexington* and *Essex* classes and Britain's *Victorious* types. Her funnel was directed upwards and she had a large island to starboard extending beyond the hull. The flight deck was supported by pillars at either end. She was sunk on November 29, before she was even commissioned.

Hancock (United States 1944). An *Essex* Class aircraft carrier shown here before her 1951–1952 refit, when her flight deck and lifts were reinforced and fuel tanks enlarged to operate with jet aircraft; she was later fitted with an angled deck and became part of the *Oriskany* Class. Note the four twin 5in (127mm) turrets, two before and two abaft the island which were removed in the course of modifications.

Implacable (Great Britain 1944). *Implacable* and *Indefatigable* were Britain's largest wartime aircraft carriers, displacing 32,110 tonnes, and exceeded only by those built after the war: *Eagle* 46,000t and *Ark Royal* 50,784t. The flight deck was an integral part of the hull, and the island, on the starboard side, occupied a strip of it. She saw service in the Pacific against Japan in 1945 and was stricken in 1955.

turrets, two either side at the four corners of the flight deck. There were four octuple machine gun mountings: two before and two abaft of the island above the flight deck.

Both *Ark Royal* and *Victorious*, and *Illustrious*, *Formidable*, and *Indomitable* that followed her, had a triple-screw power plant.

After *Saratoga* and *Lexington*, the United States Navy built units that were outwardly similar. The three largest were *Enterprise*, *Yorktown*, and *Hornet* of 1938, and a smaller one, *Wasp*, of 1940. The former were four-screw ships displacing 19,900t; *Wasp* had a twin screw with a standard displacement of 14,700t (full load 25,500 and 21,000t, respectively). They had rectangular flight decks (during the war years the *Enterprise*s were increased to 820.20 × 113.94ft [250.00 × 34.73m]) and all were equipped with three aircraft catapults, two on the flight deck and one in the hangar (two in the hangar in *Wasp*). The *Enterprise*s had three lifts, all on the flight deck; *Wasp* had two on the flight deck and a deck-edge one on the port side in the forward area, which was folded vertically against the ship's side when not in use. All had an anti-aircraft armament of eight 5in (127mm) guns grouped in pairs on four platforms at the ends of the flight deck, 1.1in (28mm) machine guns in quadruple mounts, some on the flight deck before and abaft the island, and 0.5in (12.7mm) machine guns in single mounts.

In Britain and Japan, in the years immediately preceding the war, work began on aircraft carriers which were commissioned after the war had begun, such as Britain's *Victorious*, *Illustrious*, *Formidable*, and *Indomitable* of 1941, and Japan's *Zuikaku* and *Shokaku* of 1941 and *Hiyo* and *Junyo*, commissioned in 1942. Britain's four *Victorious* types displaced 29,110 tonnes and had a flight deck with two lifts and no catapults. Anti-aircraft armament was sixteen 4.5in (114mm) guns in eight twin turrets at the four corners of the flight deck, plus 1.5in (40mm) machine guns in eight-gun mounts, four of which were on the flight deck (two in front of and two behind the island).

The two Japanese ships *Zuikaku* and *Shokaku* displaced 29,800t and had a 794.45 × 94.94ft (242.15 × 28.94m) flight deck with three lifts and two catapults. An interesting feature is the arrangement of the two funnels to starboard, angled outwards so as to be below the flight deck. This arrangement was typical of many of Japan's carriers. These four-screw ships could develop 34.2 knots.

Hiyo and *Junyo* had a very sizeable island which extended well beyond the starboard side of the hull. It was surmounted by a funnel which was raked slightly outwards. Their displacement of 26,949 tonnes was a little less than the *Zuikaku*s' 29,800t, since they had no side or deck protection. They were twin-screw ships and could do 25.5 knots.

Anti-aircraft armament consisted of just twelve 5in (127mm) guns in six twin mounts on three asymmetrically placed platforms either side of the flight deck. There were no catapults. Late in 1944, *Junyo* was equipped with six twenty-eight-tube rocket launchers (giving a total of 168 rockets) positioned before the end of the flight deck.

In the penultimate year of the war, 1944, the latest aircraft carriers *Taiho*, *Shinano*, and the three *Unryu* Class, saw service in the Japanese Navy. They were heavily armored on their sides and decks. *Shinano*, laid down as the third battleship of the *Yamato* Class, had 8in (203mm) sides and a 3.1in (80mm) flight deck. The other major Japanese carriers had thin belt armor, with extra protection over their magazines, for example, a 2.2in belt in *Taiho*, but 5.9in (150mm) over magazines. *Taiho* was the first Japanese carrier with an armored flight deck (3.1in). *Taiho* and *Shinano* had similar profiles, but the former displaced 34,600t, about half the 71,890t of the latter which was the largest aircraft carrier of the war. Both had a flight deck with two lifts and no catapults, and a large island which partially extended beyond the starboard side, surmounted by a large funnel angled outwards at 26°. *Shinano* was armed with sixteen 5in (127mm) guns and 145 anti-aircraft machine guns, the former being in eight twin turrets staggered down either side of the flight deck. *Shinano* never saw action because she was sunk by an American submarine, *Archerfish*, on November 29, 1944, while she was being taken to Kure Navy Yard for completion.

Unryo, *Amagi*, and *Katsuragi* were the only three of a class that was to have numbered sixteen when complete. *Aso*, *Kasagi*, and *Ikoma* were launched but never completed because of the end of the war. They had a displacement of 20,100t and features similar to those of the light aircraft carriers even though they were classified as heavy carriers. They had two side funnels that slanted downwards and a small island on the starboard side. The flight deck measured 711.45 × 88.58ft (216.85 × 27.00m) and had two lifts. Anti-aircraft armament consisted of twelve

Ranger (United States 1934). A small aircraft carrier built along the lines of *Langley*. She had a flight deck supported by pillars and surmounted by a small island to starboard with six funnels that could be lowered, three per side in the after area. She could carry eighty aircraft and the flight deck was served by two lifts but had no catapults. From 1941 to 1943 she saw service in the Atlantic and was also used as an aircraft transport ship. In 1944 she was used as a training ship before being posted to the Pacific in August 1944. She was stricken in 1947.

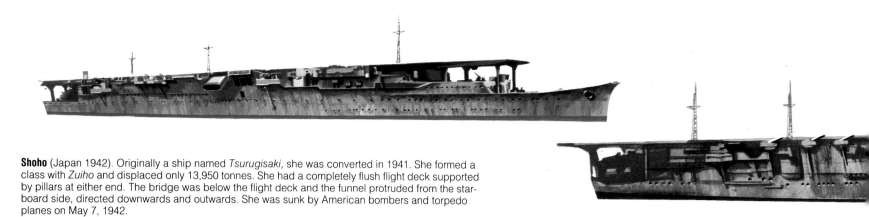

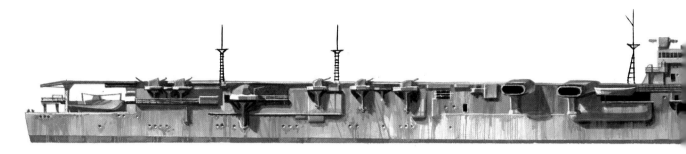

Shoho (Japan 1942). Originally a ship named *Tsurugisaki,* she was converted in 1941. She formed a class with *Zuiho* and displaced only 13,950 tonnes. She had a completely flush flight deck supported by pillars at either end. The bridge was below the flight deck and the funnel protruded from the starboard side, directed downwards and outwards. She was sunk by American bombers and torpedo planes on May 7, 1942.

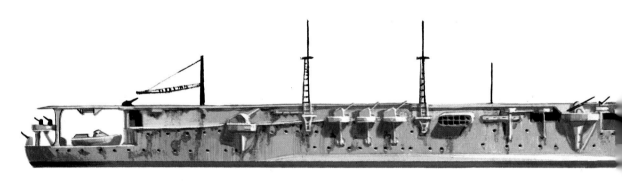

Chiyoda (Japan 1943). *Chiyoda* and *Chitose* were seaplane tenders that were fitted out in 1941 to carry an additional twelve minisubs. In 1942–1943 they were converted to aircraft carriers with an island-less flight deck that was 590.5ft (180m) long and 75.4ft (23m) wide. These ships had mixed propulsion: two turbines and two diesel engines; she had one funnel amidships for the boilers, and another much further aft, for the engines, both on the starboard side. *Chiyoda* caught fire on October 25, 1944, and was sunk by shelling.

5in (127mm) guns on six symmetrical side platforms, four forward and two aft. There were as many as ninety-nine anti-aircraft machine guns and in addition six twenty-eight-tube rocket launchers were installed. *Unryu* was sunk by the American submarine *Redfish* on December 19, 1944.

In mid-1944, *Implacable* and *Indefatigable* began service in the Royal Navy. They were fairly similar to *Victorious* but had two full hangars, as in the *Ark Royal*. These ships displaced 32,110t, had four-screw power plants, and could develop thirty-two knots.

In 1942–1945 the United States Navy commissioned twenty-three *Essex* Class units that displaced 36,680t, had a top speed of thirty-three knots, and could carry about a hundred aircraft.

One feature of this class was that the ships had a flight deck with two lifts amidships and one deck-edge lift on the port side, roughly opposite the island. A lift in this position had been tried out on *Wasp* in 1940, almost as a makeshift solution, but was then taken up because it enabled aircraft to be moved to and from the hangar without interfering with those in the process of taking off from the bow. On postwar carriers, it was in fact decided to place all the lifts on either side of the flight deck instead of in the middle, as can be seen in the *Midways* (after modifications), *Forrestals,* and subsequent types.

When the war was over, the development of jet aircraft, which were larger and heavier than propeller planes, brought about a decision by the United States Navy to modify *Essex* Class units by strengthening their flight deck and enlarging their lifts, so that they could operate with these new aircraft. These ships were converted in 1947–1955, and made up the SCB-27A/27C series.

The prototype for this conversion was the *Oriskany*, whose construction had been suspended in 1946. Work resumed on October 10, 1947. The hull was fitted

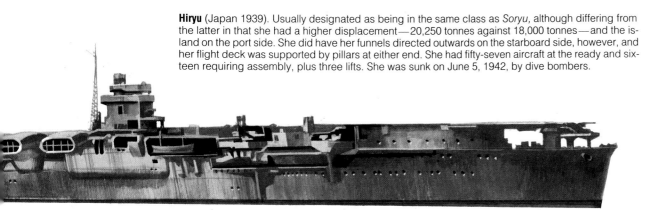

Hiryu (Japan 1939). Usually designated as being in the same class as *Soryu,* although differing from the latter in that she had a higher displacement—20,250 tonnes against 18,000 tonnes—and the island on the port side. She did have her funnels directed outwards on the starboard side, however, and her flight deck was supported by pillars at either end. She had fifty-seven aircraft at the ready and sixteen requiring assembly, plus three lifts. She was sunk on June 5, 1942, by dive bombers.

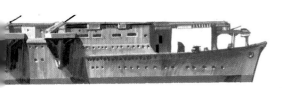

Soryu (Japan 1937). An aircraft carrier whose island housing the mast and bridge was on the starboard side of the flight deck which was supported by pillars fore and aft. The two funnels were on the starboard side and directed outwards. *Soryu* could carry fifty-seven planes at the ready with sixteen requiring assembly, and had three flight deck lifts. She was sunk on June 4, 1942, by aircraft from the American carrier *Yorktown.*

Ryuho (Japan 1942). A flush deck aircraft carrier whose flight deck was supported by pillars at either end. She was originally a submarine tender named *Taigei* but was converted in 1941–1942. The original two-screw, four-diesel engine power plant was replaced by steam turbines that made 26.5 knots. The funnel for the four boilers emerged from the hull amidships on the starboard side and was directed outwards. After being bombed in an air raid while lying at anchor on March 19, 1945, she was not repaired and was broken up in 1946.

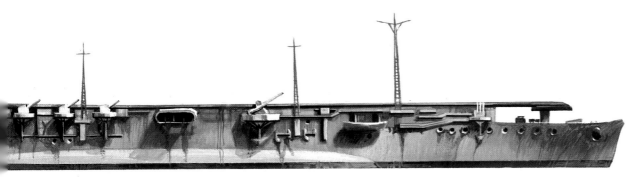

with bulges to increase the capacity of the tanks for the aircraft fuel, widening the beam from 93ft (28.34m) to 103ft (31.39m). The flight deck was reinforced, and the catapults replaced with more powerful ones (still hydraulic). The three lifts were enlarged and given more powerful machinery. The four twin 5in (127mm) gun turrets on the flight deck in front of and behind the island were removed and four single mounts were placed on starboard side platforms below the level of the flight deck. The machine guns were replaced with twenty-eight 3in (76mm) anti-aircraft guns of a new type, arranged on fourteen side platforms. In 1952, the angled-deck theory gained a firm footing, after being tried out by modifying another unit of the *Essex* Class: *Antietam*, and all but one of the modified ships were again modified (in 1954–1955) and given the new angled-flight deck. The two hydraulic catapults were also replaced by two steam-powered ones and the after centerline lift was removed and replaced by a deck-edge one to starboard.

Light aircraft carriers

On July 15, 1943, the United States Navy adopted a new term to identify its smaller aircraft carriers, which was given to the nine units in the *Independence* Class that became the CVLs twenty-two to thirty. These units had a displacement of 15,800t.

The first ship to have a displacement of around 15,000t (14,500t fully laden, to be precise) was *Ranger,* commissioned on June 4, 1934. Although built after *Saratoga* and *Lexington,* she represented a step backwards; she was in effect a replica of *Langley* except that instead of carrying her aircraft in four holds she had them in a hangar below the flight deck. The arrangement of the funnels was also similar to *Langley's* except that there were six (that could be lowered outwards),

Independence (United States 1943). A light carrier belonging to a class of nine units built on the hulls of nine cruisers of the *Cleveland* Class. A distinctive feature of these ships was their flight deck, which did not extend the full length of the hull but left an area uncovered at the bow; there were four funnels in all which were not incorporated in the island but protruded over the starboard edge alongside the flight deck. *Independence* was sunk on February 29, 1951, after service as a radiological laboratory, following damage in the Bikini nuclear test of 1946.

Wright (United States 1947). *Saipan* and *Wright* were two light carriers built on the hulls of the two *Baltimore* Class heavy cruisers. They shared the general lines of the *Independence* Class with their flight deck leaving part of the bow uncovered. *Wright* was commissioned in 1947, when the war was over. In 1963 she was converted into a command ship and telecommunications antennae were installed on the flight deck.

Bois Belleau (France 1953). Formerly United States Navy ship *Belleau Wood* of the *Independence* light carrier Class. She was handed over to France in September 1953 together with *Langley,* which was renamed *Lafayette. Bois Belleau* took part in French operations in Indochina, before being returned to the United States in 1960 and scrapped.

Unicorn (Great Britain 1943). Light carrier designed as an "aircraft maintenance carrier" to assist the aircraft of other units. She did have a normal flight deck, however, and a hangar on two decks for thirty-five aircraft as well as heavy anti-aircraft armament. She saw operational service, in particular during the Anglo-American Salerno landings, then later in the Korean War. She was down-graded to an aircraft transporter in June 1953 and stricken in 1959.

three on each side in the after part of the flight deck. Anti-aircraft armament comprised eight 5in (127mm) guns, two forward and two aft abreast on the main deck, and four on platforms either side of the flight deck. Within a short time all eight guns had been mounted on platforms alongside the flight deck. *Ranger* had a small island on the starboard side but no catapults. She was assigned to the Atlantic during the war, used as a training ship in 1944, then taken out of commission and broken up in 1947.

With her displacement of 12,732t, Japan's *Ryujo* (commissioned on May 9, 1933) was one of the many Japanese units to have no island. The flight deck, 513.45 × 75.45ft (156.50 × 23.00m), stopped 65.6ft (20m) short of the bow and the bridge was below the flight deck, in the forward part of the superstructure, overlooking the forward deck.

There were two funnels pointing downwards on the starboard side. Original armament comprised twelve 5in (127mm) anti-ship guns on six side platforms supported by large semicylindrical structures which protruded from the hull. In 1934, the four guns and two forwardmost platforms were removed. Anti-aircraft armament comprised twenty-four machine guns in six quadruple mounts on platforms either side of the flight deck. *Ryujo* was sunk on August 24, 1942, in the Battle of the Solomon Islands.

The next two Japanese carriers were *Soryu* and *Hiryu,* commissioned in 1937–1939, regarded as belonging to the same class even though they differed in size and displacement, and had their islands on different sides, starboard on *Soryo* and port on *Hiryu.* The reason for this arrangement was that the two units had to work in pairs in order to form a "central rectangle," with both flight decks abreast. Both units had a flight deck measuring 711.28 × 88.58ft (216.80 × 27.00m) which was slightly shorter than the hull and had three lifts. There were two side starboard funnels pointing downwards. The power plants were identical, with four screws and producing a speed of 34.3 knots.

Anti-aircraft armament of twelve 5in (127mm) guns was positioned on six side platforms which, on *Hiryu,* were arranged so that there were four in the forward area and two aft, whereas on *Soryu* they were staggered down each side. *Soryu* had twenty-eight machine guns in twin mounts; *Hiryu* had thirty-one in seven triple and five twin mounts.

Soryu and *Hiryu* were sunk on June 4 and 5, 1942, respectively during the Battle of Midway.

Shoho, Zuiho, and *Ryuho,* all commissioned in 1940–1942, were further examples of Japanese light carriers with no island. All three were built by modifying the hulls of ships previously built for other roles. *Shoho* and *Zuiho* were originally the submarine tenders *Tsurugisaki* and *Takasaki,* and *Ryuho* was a submarine tender named *Taigei.* Their flight decks measured 590.55 × 75.45ft (180 × 23m) and 606.95 × 75.45ft (185 × 23m) respectively. They were shorter than the hull, leaving a stretch of deck uncovered, with the bridge in the forward part below the flight deck but a short distance from its end. All had two lifts and a single funnel to starboard, pointing downwards. They had a displacement of 13,950 and 15,300t and a speed of twenty-eight and 26.5 knots. Anti-aircraft armament comprised eight 5in (127mm) guns of four platforms either side of the flight deck and 1in (25mm) machine guns usually in triple mounts. *Shoho* was sunk on May 7, 1942, in the Battle of the Coral Sea, and *Zuiho* sank in 1944; *Ryuho* survived the war and was broken up in 1946.

The last two Japanese light carriers, commissioned between the end of 1943 and March 1944 and named *Chiyoda* and *Chitose*, were converted seaplane tenders of the same name, which had been commissioned in 1938. They too had no island and a flight deck of 584.41 × 75.45ft (180 × 23m) with two lifts. From the outset, these ships had two steam turbine engines for the central propellers and two diesel engines for the side propellers; they thus had two funnels, both on the starboard side. The boilers discharged into the larger, halfway funnel, while the funnel that was set a quarter of the way from the stern and much smaller was for the diesel engines. Anti-aircraft armament comprised eight 5in (127mm) guns and thirty 1in (25mm) machine guns in the conventional arrangement of platforms on either side of the flight deck. Both ships were sunk in 1944.

The only units to be classified officially as CVLs were America's nine *Independence* Class and the two *Wright* Class ships. The former were built on the hulls of nine *Cleveland* Class light cruisers, the latter on two heavy cruisers of the *Baltimore* Class. The *Independence* Class saw service in the war, but *Wright* and *Saipan* were commissioned when it was over, in 1947.

The most remarkable feature of these units was that they had four funnels which emerged laterally amidships and ended up positioned vertically, one behind the other, on the edge of the flight deck to starboard, abaft the island. In 1953–1954, *Wright* and *Saipan* had their forward funnels removed, reducing the number to three. Another feature of these ships was the absence of anti-aircraft cannon; they only had machine guns numbering up to forty 1.5in (40mm) and forty 0.7in (20mm) (thirty-two 0.7in [20mm] on *Wright*), all the 40mm weapons in quadruple and twin mounts on platforms either side of the flight deck. The *Wrights* had eight machine guns forward and eight aft in two quadruple mounts on the main deck, in front of and behind the ends of the flight deck. The *Independence* types had one of these mounts forward and one aft.

Perseus (Great Britain 1945). A light carrier belonging to the *Colossus* Class. Together with *Pioneer*, she was completed as an aircraft maintenance carrier, like *Unicorn*, and therefore fitted with a light armament of thirty-two 1.5in (40mm) machine guns. She did not have an aircraft complement of her own. *Pioneer* was used to try out the first steam catapult in 1950–1951. In 1953 both units were downgraded to aircraft transport ships. *Pioneer* was stricken in 1954 and *Perseus* in 1958.

Warrior (Great Britain 1946). A light carrier belonging to the ten-unit *Colossus* Class. Originally she had a straight flight deck and could carry thirty-five aircraft. Immediately after being commissioned, she was handed over to the Canadian Navy in which she served from January 1946 to March 1948. From November 1948 to May 1949 she was fitted with a flexible flight deck for experiments in landing wheel-less planes. In 1955–1956 she was fitted with an angled flight deck, and in 1958 sold to Argentina where she was renamed *Independencia*.

Albion (Great Britain 1947). A light carrier of the eight-unit *Albion* Class of which only four were laid down. She displaced 18,300 tonnes standard and was the largest of the *Colossus* and *Majestic* types. This is how she would have looked with a straight deck; she was in fact modified on the stocks and commissioned with an angled deck on May 26, 1954. In 1961–1962 she was converted to an amphibious assault ship.

Hercules (Great Britain 1961). A light carrier of the six-unit *Majestic* Class. Construction of these ships was suspended because of the war, but resumed and they were completed between 1948 and 1961. All were handed over to Canada, Australia, and India, except for *Leviathan*, which was broken up in 1968. Fourteen years after being launched, *Hercules* was taken in hand for completion to a modified design and commissioned on March 4, 1961, with an angled deck as the Indian *Vikrant*.

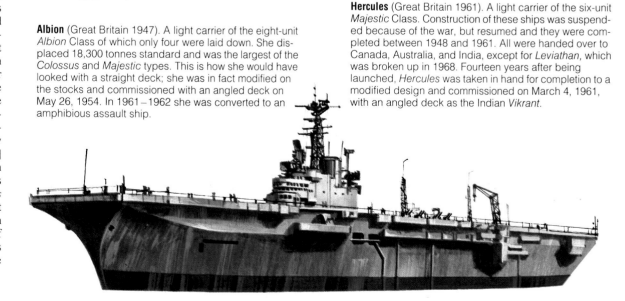

At the end of the war, two ships in the *Independence* Class were handed over to France: *Belleau Wood,* renamed *Bois Belleau,* and *Langley,* renamed *Lafayette.* Between 1962 and 1964, *Saipan* and *Wright* were converted to command ships.

The Royal Navy had many aircraft carriers with a fairly low displacement, later classified as light carriers, of which only one, *Unicorn* (commissioned on March 12, 1943), saw service in the war. Of the others, namely the six *Hercules* (or *Majestic*) Class, ten *Colossus* Class and four *Albion* Class, only the *Colossus* Class was completed in 1945–1946. The *Albion*s were completed, for the Royal Navy, only about a decade after the war was over. Five *Majestic*s were completed for other navies. The other was scrapped incomplete.

Unicorn had been designed as an "aircraft maintenance carrier," with the task of assisting and repairing the aircraft of other units, but she was also used as a light carrier. She had the customary flight deck with two lifts and an island on the starboard side. She was armed with eight 4in (102mm) anti-aircraft guns in four twin mounts on platforms supported by brackets on the outside of the hull and thirty-two machine guns in the usual position. She was classified as a transport carrier in June 1953 and scrapped in 1959.

Two units of the *Colossus* Class, *Pioneer* and *Perseus,* were completed in 1945 as aircraft tenders; their major features were the two large lattice cranes on the flight deck: one to port in the forward area and one to starboard behind the island. They were classified as transport carriers in 1953 and stricken in 1954–1958.

Another member of the *Colossus* Class, *Warrior,* was completed as a light carrier in 1946 and loaned to the Canadian Navy from 1946 to 1948. Her flight deck tapered slightly at the bow and had two lifts and a catapult. Behind the island was a large lattice crane to ship and off-load the aircraft. She was armed with forty-three 1.5in (40mm) anti-aircraft machine guns and four 3in (76mm) saluting guns. Back with the Royal Navy, *Warrior* was used in experiments to land wheelless aircraft; for this purpose, she was fitted with a flexible flight deck, covered with a rubber pad. In 1955–1956 she was given an angled deck and sold to Argentina in 1958 under the name of *Independencia.* All of the units of the *Hercules* (or *Majestic*) Class were handed over to other navies. Two of them retained their straight flight deck: *Magnificent,* loaned to Canada from 1948 to 1957, and *Terrible,* delivered to Australia in 1949, where she was renamed *Sydney.*

These units had roughly the same lines as the *Colossus* Class. Their flight deck narrowed at the bow and had two lifts and a catapult, with an island on the starboard side, followed by a large lattice crane. Armament was just thirty 1.5in (40mm) machine guns, and the twin screw power plant produced a speed of 24.5 knots. *Magnificent* was returned to Britain in 1957 and scrapped in 1962. *Sydney* (or *Terrible*) was withdrawn in 1973.

Of the eight planned units of the *Albion* Class, only four, *Hermes, Albion, Bulwark,* and *Centaur,* were built. *Hermes* was the last to be built; she was launched in February 1953 and completed in November 1959, already fitted with an angled deck. The other three, however, were completed with a straight flight deck and modified to take an angled deck when their fitting out was already at an advanced stage. The straight flight deck units had two lifts, two hydraulic catapults forward, a large island on the starboard side, armament consisting entirely of machine guns, and a large lattice crane to port. *Bulwark* (in 1959–1960) and *Albion* (in 1961–1962) were converted to amphibious assault ships, their installations for fixed wing aircraft being replaced by systems suitable for helicopters. *Hermes* was also similarly modified in 1971–1973. *Centaur* was stricken in 1972 without being modified.

Bogue (United States 1942). An escort carrier forming part of a class of eleven units, all converted single-screw, steam-powered cargo ships. The flight deck had a small island housing the bridge, but not the funnel, because the boiler smoke was discharged through a transverse flue below the flight deck. *Bogue* could carry thirty aircraft and had one hangar. In 1955 she was re-classified as an escort helicopter carrier. She was stricken in 1960.

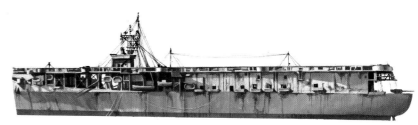

Charger (United States 1942). An escort aircraft carrier belonging to a class of four single-screw, diesel-engine ships. Only *Charger* stayed in the United States, the other three being handed over to Great Britain. The flight deck was supported by pillars forward and the hangar aft. *Charger* could carry fifteen aircraft. She was to train pilots, not to escort convoys. In 1949 she was converted back to a merchantman.

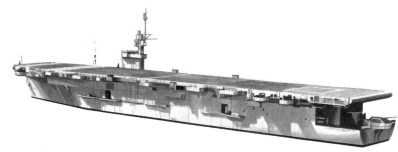

Anzio (United States 1943). An escort aircraft carrier belonging to a class of fifty units with two reciprocating engines and twin screws. She had a full-length flight deck with an island on the starboard side housing bridge. There were two very low funnels for the boilers, on the edge of the flight deck to starboard. Commissioned on August 27, 1943, *Anzio* was originally called *Coral* but renamed in September 1944 in memory of the landings in Italy. She was stricken in 1960.

Audacity (Great Britain 1941). A German merchantman named *Hannover,* captured in February 1941, and converted to a hangar-less escort carrier, the planes being lashed securely to the deck. She had a twin-screw diesel power plant and had to come out of formation and face into the wind in order to launch her aircraft. She was sunk on December 21, 1941.

Biter (Great Britain 1942). A merchantman converted to an aircraft carrier by the United States Navy and handed over to Great Britain in 1943. The flight deck did not run the full length of the ship but stopped 39ft (12m) short of the bow. She could carry fifteen aircraft. In January 1945 she was assigned to France where she was renamed *Dixmude.* She was later used as an aircraft transport ship and took part in the war in Indochina.

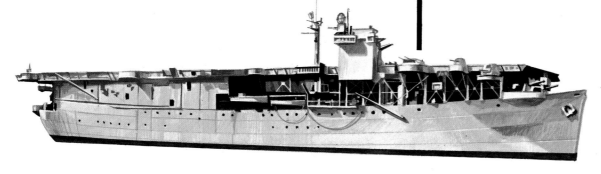

Archer (Great Britain 1941). Part of the same class as America's *Charger*, she was handed over to Great Britain in 1941–1942, together with *Avenger* and *Biter*. Her flight deck was supported by metal struts except in the hangar. She took part in the North Africa landings in November 1942, then from March 1943 escorted convoys in the Atlantic. She was converted back to a cargo ship in 1947.

Long Island (United States 1941). She was *Archer*'s sister ship and handed over to Great Britain. She had a single-screw diesel power plant. The flight deck left part of the bow exposed and had no island, the bridge being on a lower level; the hangar was below the flight deck. She was used as a pilot training ship and converted back to a merchantman in 1949.

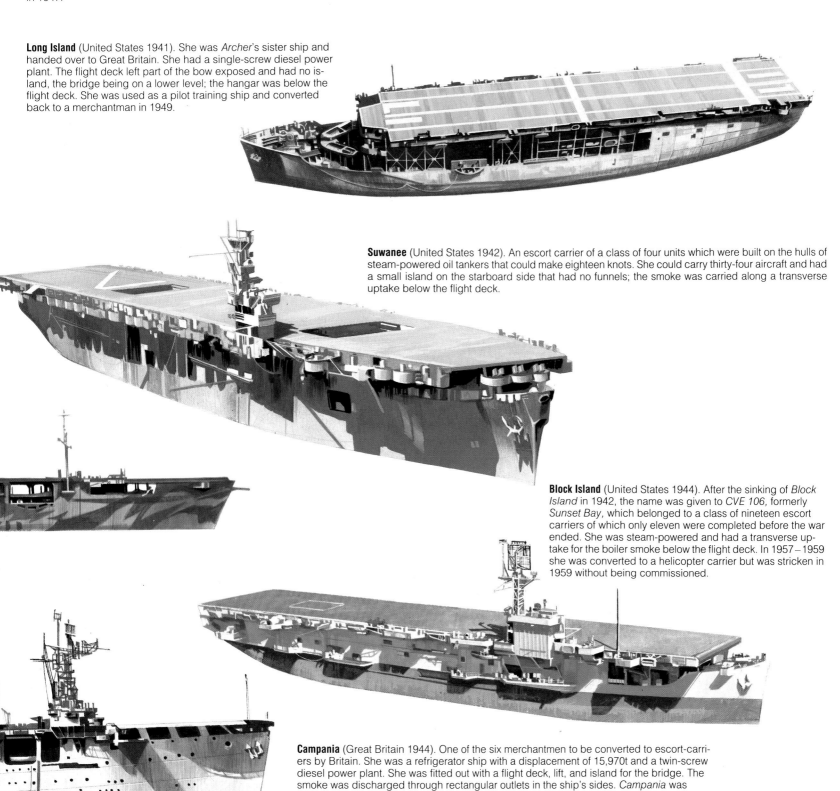

Suwanee (United States 1942). An escort carrier of a class of four units which were built on the hulls of steam-powered oil tankers that could make eighteen knots. She could carry thirty-four aircraft and had a small island on the starboard side that had no funnels; the smoke was carried along a transverse uptake below the flight deck.

Block Island (United States 1944). After the sinking of *Block Island* in 1942, the name was given to *CVE 106*, formerly *Sunset Bay*, which belonged to a class of nineteen escort carriers of which only eleven were completed before the war ended. She was steam-powered and had a transverse uptake for the boiler smoke below the flight deck. In 1957–1959 she was converted to a helicopter carrier but was stricken in 1959 without being commissioned.

Campania (Great Britain 1944). One of the six merchantmen to be converted to escort-carriers by Britain. She was a refrigerator ship with a displacement of 15,970t and a twin-screw diesel power plant. She was fitted out with a flight deck, lift, and island for the bridge. The smoke was discharged through rectangular outlets in the ship's sides. *Campania* was broken up in 1955, having served in 1951 as the "Festival of Britain" exhibit ship.

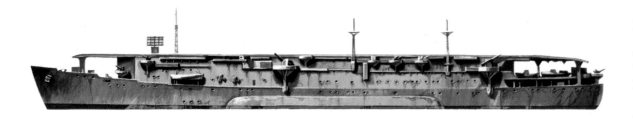

Shinyo (Japan 1943). A German liner by the name of *Scharnhorst* which sought refuge in Japan in 1939 and was converted in 1942–1943. She had no island, the funnel being on the starboard side and directed outwards. She carried twenty-seven planes at the ready and six requiring assembly. After serving as an aircraft transport ship, she was sunk on November 17, 1944.

Taiyo (Japan 1941). Together with *Chuyo* and *Unyo,* she formed the Japanese Navy's first class of escort carriers. These units were originally cargo steamers and were fitted with an island-less deck and an external funnel on the starboard side. They could carry twenty-seven aircraft and develop twenty-one knots. There were neither catapults nor arrester systems for the aircraft after landing. *Taiyo* was sunk on August 18, 1944.

Kaiyo (Japan 1943). Built as a passenger ship named *Argentina-Maru,* she was requisitioned in 1941 and used for troop transport. In 1942–1943 she was converted to an aircraft carrier, with no island, funnel to starboard, and a twenty-four-plane hangar with two lifts. She was turbo-driven and could make 23.5 knots. She was sunk in port on August 10, 1945.

Escort aircraft carriers

Heavy attacks on convoys and merchant ships by German submarines in the Atlantic, to prevent convoys from the United States reaching Britain, convinced the British and American Navies of the need for aircraft carriers of modest capabilities to be used purely to escort convoys. The Japanese Navy reacted likewise to ensure the safety of her vessels in the Pacific.

Escort carriers were usually converted merchant ships, incorporating a flight deck, a hangar, and a few anti-aircraft guns. In 1943, the United States was alone in building fifty purpose-built units of the *Anzio* Class and nineteen of the *Commencement Bay* (or *Block Island*) Class.

The first two escort carriers were the American *Long Island* and the British *Audacity,* both completed in June 1941. *Long Island*'s flight deck did not extend the full length of the ship and both units were without an island. They both had diesel engines, so the combustion products were discharged either side of the flight deck without using real funnels as such. They had a complement of twenty to twenty-one aircraft and one or two guns.

The United States Navy then converted five more units, four of which were delivered to the Royal Navy in the spring and summer of 1942. These units bore the designation BAVG and were numbered from one to five. They were named *Archer, Avenger, Biter,* and *Dasher. Charger* stayed in the United States as *CVE 30,* and *Tracker* was delivered to Great Britain in 1943 instead. These ships also had diesel engines and no funnel, with a small island on the starboard side. At the end of the war, *Biter* was assigned to France where she was renamed *Dixmude*.

Another twenty-five merchant ships were bought and converted in early 1942; of these units twenty-one had only one screw and eleven of them belonged to the *Bogue* Class. Another eight were delivered to Great Britain as the *Battler* Class, while four twin-screw ex-tankers, which were faster, made up the *Suwanee* Class.

The *Bogues* and *Battlers* had a 441.92 × 81.03ft (134.70 × 24.70m) flight deck with two lifts and a catapult, a small island to starboard, and no funnel because the smoke was discharged through a transverse flue beneath the flight deck. They carried thirty aircraft and were armed with one or two 5in (127mm)

guns and sixteen 1.5in (40mm) anti-aircraft machine guns. *Bogue* was stricken in 1960. The four *Suwanees* were similar to *Bogue* in appearance but carried thirty-four aircraft instead of thirty. When the war was over, *Sangamon* was converted back to an oil tanker.

The fifty units of the *Anzio* Class (*CVE 55* to *CVE 104*) were the first purpose-built escort carriers. They came from the Kaiser Company which delivered them in the remarkably short time of one year. Their flight deck was as long as the hull with two lifts, a catapult, and a small island on the starboard side. The boiler smoke was discharged through two very low funnels, set well apart on the starboard side of the flight deck. Their power plant was two reciprocating engines with two screws, giving a speed of 19.5 knots. They carried thirty aircraft and were armed with one 5in (127mm) gun and twenty-four machine guns. *Anzio* was stricken in 1960.

In 1955, a considerable number of these units were re-designated as escort helicopter carriers, but they were not modified, as all were out of service by that time.

The last class of United States Navy escort carriers was the nineteen *Block Island* types of which only eleven were completed; three were commissioned in late 1944–early 1945. They were twin-screw turbo-driven ships, similar to the *Suwanees.* In 1957–1959 *Block Island* was converted into an assault helicopter carrier (designation LPH 1), but she was not commissioned and was stricken in 1959.

The British escort carriers included *Campania,* a converted refrigerator ship, with a twin-screw diesel power plant. An interesting feature of this ship was that, instead of the usual exhaust ducts below the flight deck, she had two rectangular outlets in the ship's sides, half-way down and just above the waterline.

The Japanese Navy had five units classified as escort carriers. The first three, *Taiyo, Chuyo,* and *Unyo,* were cargo ships, commissioned in September 1941 and May and November 1942 respectively. Their flight deck measured 557.90 × 76.96ft (170.05 × 23.46m) and had two lifts. They had no island but a starboard-side funnel, directed downwards.

Taiyo's armament consisted of eight 5in (127mm) anti-aircraft guns. The machine guns were increased from the original eight, first to twenty-four, then to sixty-four. These ships carried twenty-seven aircraft and could develop twenty-one knots. All were sunk during the war.

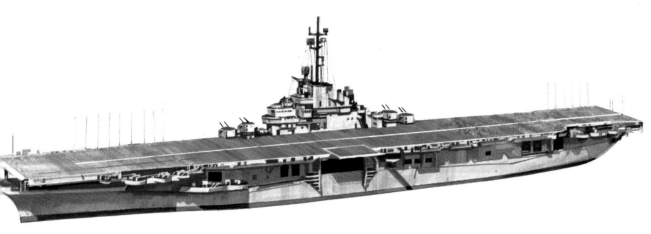

Antietam (United States). The first aircraft carrier in the world to have an angled flight deck. She belonged to the *Essex* Class, and, when built, had a straight flight deck with an island on the starboard side and three lifts, one of which could be folded down and was on the port edge opposite the island. She was not used in the Second World War, but saw service in Korea in 1951–1952. In September 1952 work began to fit her with an angled deck and she was back in commission in December that year. The deck was set at an angle of 8°, beginning right aft and ending at the port lift.

The fourth unit, *Shinyo,* was a conversion of the German liner *Scharnhorst* and commissioned in December 1943. She also had a completely flush deck with two lifts and a starboard-side funnel, discharging downwards. The armament consisted of eight 5in (127mm) guns in four twin mounts, and fifty machine guns. She carried thirty-three aircraft, only twenty-seven of which were ready for action, the other six with their wings requiring assembly. She was sunk in the China Sea on November 17, 1944.

The last ship, *Kaiyo,* was formerly the passenger ship *Argentina-Maru,* and was commissioned in November 1943. With her displacement of 16,748t she was the smallest of the Japanese escort carriers, but her general lines and armament were similar to the others. She was sunk on August 10, 1945.

Japan had another two units with flight decks. They were not escort carriers, as such, but Merchant Aircraft Carriers (or MACs), like Britain's *Ancylus.* The main difference as compared with escort carriers was that the MACs did not have a hangar and therefore had to keep their aircraft permanently on the flight deck. The two units were called *Otakisan-Maru* and *Shimane-Maru* and had a small hangar forward, containing twelve aircraft, and a lift. *Otakisan-Maru* was sunk before being commissioned, and *Shimane-Maru* was sent to the bottom on July 24, 1945, after only two months service. Japan had another two MACs on the stocks, *Chigusa-Maru* and *Yamashio-Maru,* which had neither hangar nor lifts.

One special-type served in the United States Navy: the Great Lakes ships which were paddle powered and had a flight deck for training pilots. These ships had no hangar and their aircraft were land based. For this reason they did not have the distinctive CV designation but bore the miscellaneous symbols, IX.

Angled flight deck aircraft carriers

When the Second World War was over, both the American Navy and the Royal Navy used jet as opposed to propeller planes. This change created problems for aircraft carriers, because these heavier planes required stronger flight decks, more powerful lifts and catapults, and taller hangars. For this reason the United States

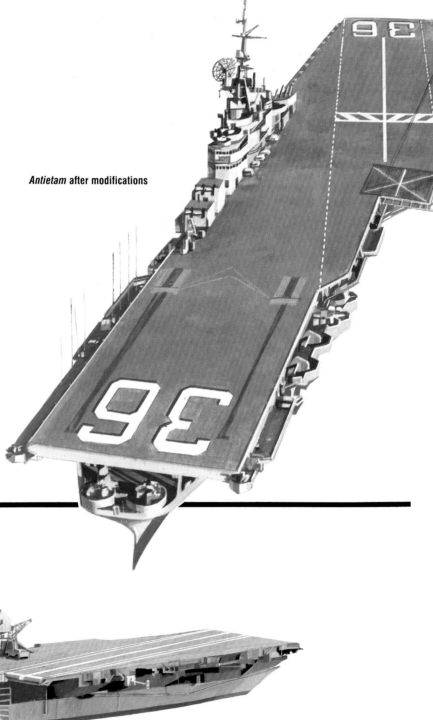

Antietam after modifications

Oriskany (United States 1959). One of the twenty-five units of the *Essex* Class, on the stocks at the end of the war but, whereas the others, such as *Antietam,* were finished, *Oriskany* was suspended in 1946. Work was resumed on October 1, 1947, and she was completed with a straight deck. She was used in the Korean War and in 1958–1959 converted to an angled-deck carrier with steam catapults. She was used in the Vietnam War.

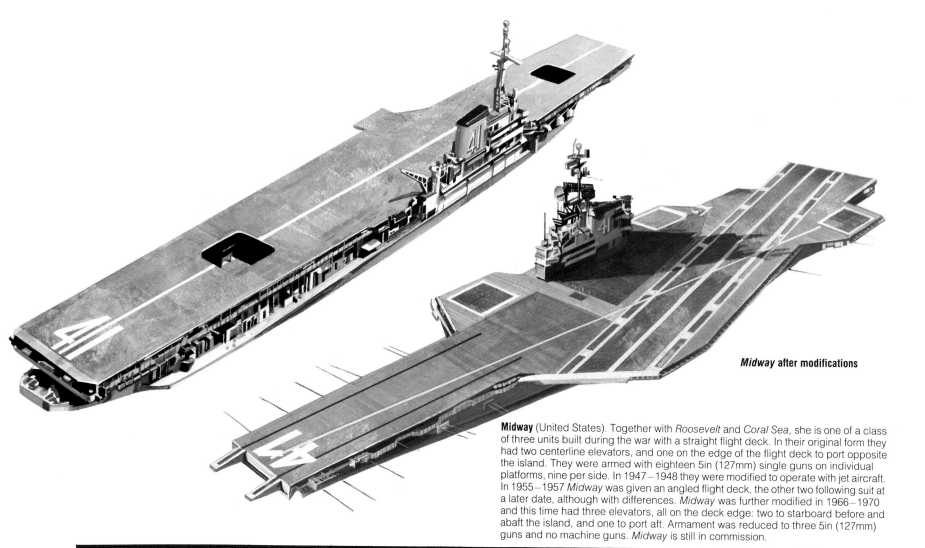

Midway after modifications

Midway (United States). Together with *Roosevelt* and *Coral Sea*, she is one of a class of three units built during the war with a straight flight deck. In their original form they had two centerline elevators, and one on the edge of the flight deck to port opposite the island. They were armed with eighteen 5in (127mm) single guns on individual platforms, nine per side. In 1947–1948 they were modified to operate with jet aircraft. In 1955–1957 *Midway* was given an angled flight deck, the other two following suit at a later date, although with differences. *Midway* was further modified in 1966–1970 and this time had three elevators, all on the deck edge: two to starboard before and abaft the island, and one to port aft. Armament was reduced to three 5in (127mm) guns and no machine guns. *Midway* is still in commission.

Navy converted seven *Essex* Class ships, which then became known as the *Hancock* Class. This modification was officially named SCB 27A.

In Great Britain, a special steam catapult was designed to launch jet aircraft. It was far more powerful than the catapults used in the past. Landing experiments were carried out with a rubber mattress, fitted on the aircraft carrier *Warrior*, and wheelless planes.

The most important modification brought about by the use of jet aircraft was the angled deck, in other words, a deck that followed a straight path in its forward section and then veered off at an angle of 5–8°, with the end extending beyond the side opposite the island. This deck enabled pilots who failed to land the first time round to climb again without interfering with the other aircraft parked at the bow.

Experiments began in Britain in February 1952 with an angled flight deck created by painting demarcation lines on the straight deck of the light carrier *Triumph*.

At more or less the same time, the United States Navy carried out similar experiments with an angled deck painted on *Midway*'s straight deck.

The first aircraft carrier to have a proper angled flight deck was the American ship *Antietam*, one of the *Essex* Class, modified between September and December 1952. The first British ships were *Ark Royal*, modified while she was being fitted out, in 1952, and her sister ship *Eagle*, which, after being commissioned in 1951 with a straight deck, was modified in the course of a refit that lasted from 1959 to 1964.

The new angled deck that appeared on *Antietam* and another twelve units of the *Essex* Class was set at an angle of 8° to the straight deck and ended opposite the island, by the deck edge lift for the old straight deck. As in SCB 27A ships, the gun battery was greatly reduced; within a few years, ships had only seven 5in (127mm) guns, all alongside the flight deck. The old hydraulic catapults were replaced by two steam catapults.

The United States crafted nine SCB 27A conversions, including *Oriskany*; all but one later underwent SCB 27C (angled deck) conversion, and six others were completed as SCB 27Cs with angled decks.

Oriskany was converted at the San Francisco Navy Yard in 1958–1959. The after section of the flight deck was modified by adding another deck set at an angle of 8°; the forward rectangular lift was tapered at one end to accommodate longer aircraft, and the after lift removed and replaced by another positioned on the edge of the flight deck to starboard abaft the island. The third external port lift remained

in the same position, now at the end of the angled deck. Two new steam catapults were installed at the forward end of the straight deck. In 1958, *Bennington*, *Bonhomme Richard*, *Hancock*, *Lexington*, *Randolph*, and *Shangri-La* were armed with Regulus missile launchers that could be stationed on the flight deck.

Other ships also built with a straight deck and then converted into angled-deck vessels were *Midway*, *Roosevelt*, and *Coral Sea*. These were commissioned in 1945–1946 and had the conventional straight deck with three lifts, one forward and one aft along the centerline, and one amidships, along the deck-edge to port. In 1952 *Midway* had an experimental angled deck painted on top of her straight one; then from November 1955 to September 1957 she was taken in for a refit at the Puget Sound Navy Yard, where *Roosevelt* had been modified between 1954 and 1956. The flight deck was set at an angle of 10° and the two centerline lifts were moved over to the starboard side, on the edge of the flight deck and in front of and behind the island. Two steam catapults were positioned forward and a third on the outer edge of the angled deck.

Coral Sea, which was modified in 1957–1960, had the deck-edge lift at the forward end of the angled deck removed. It was shifted to a wider area almost at the stern, although still on the port side. *Midway*'s lift was similarly re-sited during a 1966–1970 refit. The three catapults were also removed and two more powerful ones installed at the forward end of the straight deck. *Roosevelt* was not modified in this way, and retained her 1956 configuration. Armament which, with the straight deck, numbered eighteen 5in (127mm) guns, was reduced to three 5in (127mm) guns and the eighty-four 1.5in (40mm), and twenty-eight 0.7in (20mm) machine guns were removed. The aircraft complement of 137 propeller planes dropped to seventy-five jet aircraft. Ships of the Royal Navy that had their straight flight deck changed to an angled one included *Victorious* (1941) and *Eagle* (1951), while her sister ship *Ark Royal*, commissioned in 1955, was modified during construction.

Victorious belonged to the same class as *Illustrious*, *Formidable*, and *Indomitable*, but these were not modified and stricken between 1953 and 1956. These units had a straight flight deck with two lifts, one forward and one aft, anti-aircraft armament of sixteen 4.5in (114mm) guns in eight twin turrets and forty-eight 1.5in (40mm) machine guns, plus a triple-screw power plant producing a speed of thirty-one knots.

After her modifications, which lasted from 1950 to 1958, *Victorious'* displacement increased from 29,110t to 37,000t, and she had a flight deck set at an angle of 8°45′ plus two steam catapults. The lifts remained in the middle of the flight deck

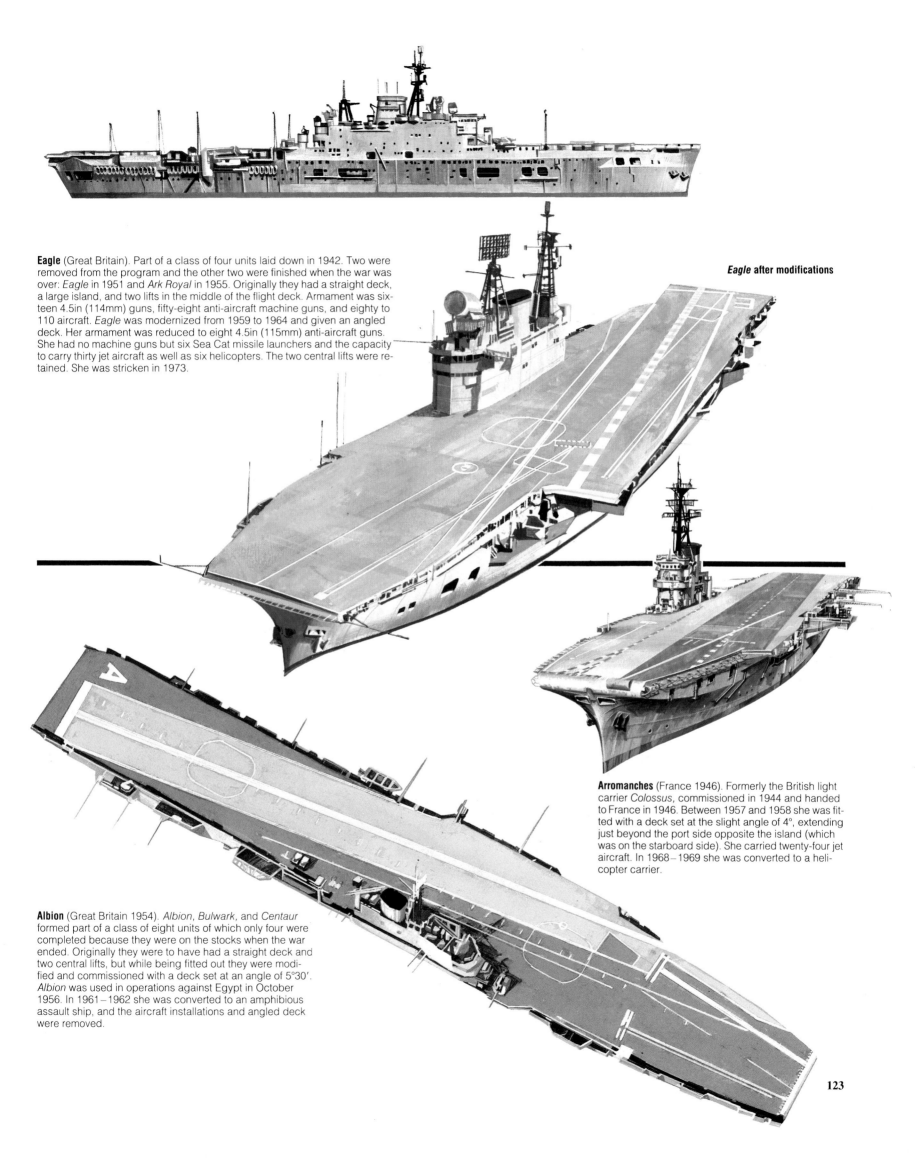

Eagle (Great Britain). Part of a class of four units laid down in 1942. Two were removed from the program and the other two were finished when the war was over: *Eagle* in 1951 and *Ark Royal* in 1955. Originally they had a straight deck, a large island, and two lifts in the middle of the flight deck. Armament was sixteen 4.5in (114mm) guns, fifty-eight anti-aircraft machine guns, and eighty to 110 aircraft. *Eagle* was modernized from 1959 to 1964 and given an angled deck. Her armament was reduced to eight 4.5in (115mm) anti-aircraft guns. She had no machine guns but six Sea Cat missile launchers and the capacity to carry thirty jet aircraft as well as six helicopters. The two central lifts were retained. She was stricken in 1973.

Eagle after modifications

Arromanches (France 1946). Formerly the British light carrier *Colossus,* commissioned in 1944 and handed to France in 1946. Between 1957 and 1958 she was fitted with a deck set at the slight angle of 4°, extending just beyond the port side opposite the island (which was on the starboard side). She carried twenty-four jet aircraft. In 1968–1969 she was converted to a helicopter carrier.

Albion (Great Britain 1954). *Albion, Bulwark,* and *Centaur* formed part of a class of eight units of which only four were completed because they were on the stocks when the war ended. Originally they were to have had a straight deck and two central lifts, but while being fitted out they were modified and commissioned with a deck set at an angle of 5°30'. *Albion* was used in operations against Egypt in October 1956. In 1961–1962 she was converted to an amphibious assault ship, and the aircraft installations and angled deck were removed.

Clemenceau (France 1961). Sister ship of *Foch*, although commissioned a little earlier. She had no bulges but these were added a few years later. The angled deck extended over the side amidships and had a steam-driven catapult on its outer edge, a second catapult being situated on the straight deck forward. These ships had no missiles, and just eight 3.9in (100mm) anti-aircraft guns; these originally numbered twenty-four but were reduced to twelve in 1956, and then to eight in 1958.

Foch (France 1963). *Clemenceau* and *Foch* were the first class of aircraft carriers to be built by the French Navy in the postwar period, and the first ones after *Béarn* (1927). As they were designed in 1955, they had a deck set at 8° right from the start plus two lifts, one centrally positioned forward and the other abaft the island on the deck edge but incorporated in the deck structure, not extending beyond it. Unlike *Clemenceau*, *Foch* was built with bulges. Both are steam-powered and make thirty-two knots.

but were enlarged and moved further aft. *Victorious* was equipped with radar, a new type of equipment for aircraft landing guidance, plus new and more powerful arresters. After these modifications, *Victorious* served until March 31, 1968.

After operating from 1951 to 1958 with a straight deck, *Eagle* was converted between October 1959 and May 1964 and fitted with an 8°30′ angle deck. The end of the angled deck on British ships did not extend sideways as far as it did on American ships, but it did extend further aft. *Eagle* was fitted with two steam catapults, one to port of the straight deck and one at the side of the angled deck. The original armament of sixteen 4.7in (120mm) guns and fifty-eight 1.5in (40mm) machine guns was replaced with eight 4.5in (115mm) anti-aircraft guns and six Sea Cat missile launchers. The number of aircraft fell from 80-110 propeller planes to thirty jet aircraft plus six helicopters. In 1966–1967, *Eagle* had further modifications made to her catapults and arrester mechanisms in order to operate with heavier aircraft. She was withdrawn at the end of 1973.

Other British ships that had a straight flight deck originally, later modified to an angled deck, were the light carriers completed in the postwar years and delivered to other navies: *Bonaventure* (ex-*Powerful)*, delivered to Canada and modified in

Hermes (Great Britain 1959). She belonged to the *Albion* Class but building work on her was suspended until 1953 and she was only finished in 1959 with a different layout. The flight deck was set at an angle of 6°30′ instead of 5°30′, the forward lift was on the deck edge at the end of the angled deck and armament consisted of just four 3in (76mm) guns and seventeen 1.5in (40mm) machine guns, replaced in 1964–1966 by two Sea Cat missile launchers. In 1971 *Hermes,* too, was converted to an amphibious assault ship like *Albion* and *Bulwark,* with a complement of twenty helicopters as opposed to the original forty-five aircraft.

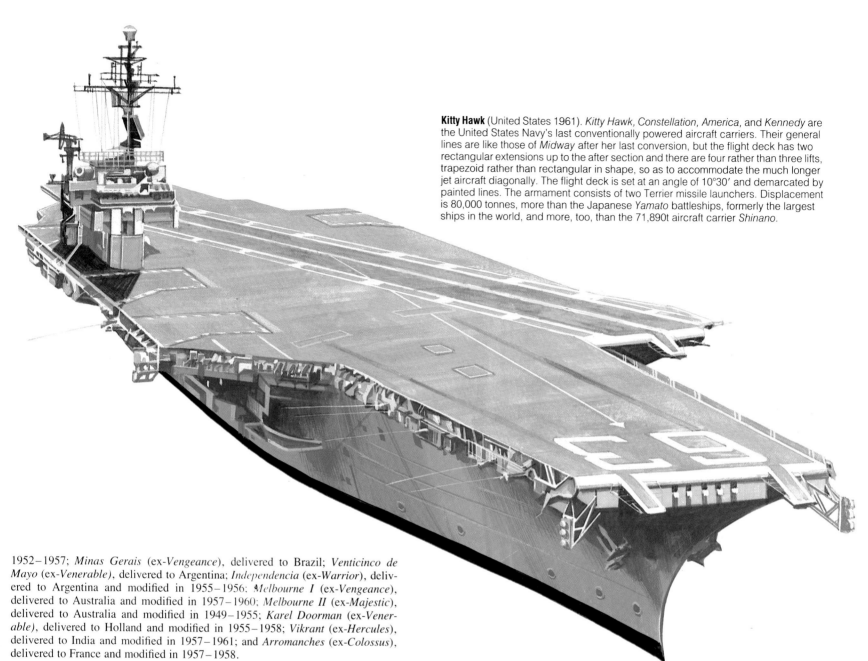

Kitty Hawk (United States 1961). *Kitty Hawk, Constellation, America,* and *Kennedy* are the United States Navy's last conventionally powered aircraft carriers. Their general lines are like those of *Midway* after her last conversion, but the flight deck has two rectangular extensions up to the after section and there are four rather than three lifts, trapezoid rather than rectangular in shape, so as to accommodate the much longer jet aircraft diagonally. The flight deck is set at an angle of 10°30′ and demarcated by painted lines. The armament consists of two Terrier missile launchers. Displacement is 80,000 tonnes, more than the Japanese *Yamato* battleships, formerly the largest ships in the world, and more, too, than the 71,890t aircraft carrier *Shinano*.

1952–1957; *Minas Gerais* (ex-*Vengeance*), delivered to Brazil; *Venticinco de Mayo* (ex-*Venerable*), delivered to Argentina; *Independencia* (ex-*Warrior*), delivered to Argentina and modified in 1955–1956; *Melbourne I* (ex-*Vengeance*), delivered to Australia and modified in 1957–1960; *Melbourne II* (ex-*Majestic*), delivered to Australia and modified in 1949–1955; *Karel Doorman* (ex-*Venerable*), delivered to Holland and modified in 1955–1958; *Vikrant* (ex-*Hercules*), delivered to India and modified in 1957–1961; and *Arromanches* (ex-*Colossus*), delivered to France and modified in 1957–1958.

As mentioned earlier, during the war the Royal Navy had programmed eight light carriers of the *Albion* Class, obviously enough, with straight flight decks, four of which were on the stocks when the war ended. Three of them were completed in 1954 and made up the *Albion* Class, and one, *Hermes*, in 1959. Modifications to the already-built hulls of the three *Albions* made it possible to add a flight deck, set at an angle of just 5°3′, while on *Hermes* this angle was 6°30′. They had a fairly large island, two lifts both in the center of the deck and two hydraulic catapults. Only *Centaur* had steam catapults. They had no anti-aircraft guns, and just twenty-six 1.5in (40mm) machine guns on side platforms, plus four 3in (76mm) saluting guns. They could carry forty-five aircraft.

In 1956, during the crisis resulting from the nationalization of the Suez Canal, *Albion* was in Egypt with a complement of helicopters and parachutists, although she had not yet become an amphibious assault ship. In 1959–1961, *Albion* and *Bulwark* were converted to helicopter carriers but *Centaur* did not receive the same treatment and she was withdrawn in 1971. *Hermes* was well behind schedule, but had more radical modifications made to her—as noted above, the flight deck was set at an angle of 6°30′. The forward lift was no longer in the center but on the port side at the end of the angled deck. *Hermes* had two steam catapults forward and a mirror system for landing guidance. Originally she was armed with seventeen 1.5in (40mm) machine guns but, in 1964–1966, these were replaced with two Sea Cat missile launchers. These ships also had the usual four 3in (76mm) guns for military salutes. In 1971–1973, *Hermes* was also converted to an amphibious assault ship.

The fifth British ship to have an angled deck from the outset was *Ark Royal*, which was modified while being fitted out, and commissioned on February 25, 1955. *Ark Royal* had three lifts, two in the center and one on the port side at the end of the angled deck. This third lift was removed in 1959. She had two steam catapults and a mirror landing–guidance system. These catapults and guidance system were replaced in 1961 with more modern types. Work was carried out between 1967 and 1971 to replace the original flight deck with a stronger one, angled at 8°30′; one of the new catapults was positioned on the port side of the straight deck and the other on the port side of the angled deck. The anti-aircraft guns were replaced by four Sea Cat missile launchers and an eight-tube rocket launcher was installed for electronic countermeasures. After 35 years' service, *Ark Royal* was withdrawn on September 19, 1980, when the new light aircraft carrier *Invincible* was commissioned.

Before the Second World War, the French Navy had had just the one carrier *Béarn*, because *Joffre* and *Painlève*, both laid down in 1938, had never been completed. When the war ended, the United States Navy handed over the escort carrier *Biter*, subsequently renamed *Dixmude*, to the French, and the two light carriers, *Belleau Wood*, which became *Bois Belleau*, and *Langley*, which became *Lafayette*. The Royal Navy, in turn, handed over *Colossus*, which became *Arromanches* and which was fitted with an angled flight deck in 1957–1958.

Clemenceau and *Foch* were laid down in 1955, and commissioned in 1961–1963. These two units had a flight deck measuring 904.19 × 87.27ft (275.60 × 29.60m) plus a deck set at an angle of 8° which was 543.3ft (165.60m) long. They had two lifts, one centrally positioned forward and another half way along on the deck edge abaft the island. There were two steam catapults, one on the port side of the straight deck and one on the outer edge of the angled deck. *Foch*, which was built later, had 6.5ft (2m) wide bulges incorporated in the design from the start and these were added to *Clemenceau* a few years later. Armament consisted of twenty-four anti-aircraft guns which were eventually reduced in number, first in 1956 and then in 1958 to eight 3.9in (100mm) guns in single mounts at either end of the straight deck. The 590.55 × 82.02ft (180 × 25m) hangar could contain forty intercepter, attack, and anti-submarine aircraft.

Super aircraft carriers

This section deals only with the following United States Navy aircraft carriers: *Forrestal, Saratoga, Ranger, Independence, Kitty Hawk, Constellation, America, John F. Kennedy, Enterprise, Nimitz, Eisenhower,* and *Vinson,* the last four being nuclear powered.

All these units had:

a) A high displacement: ranging from the four *Forrestals'* 75,900t and the four *Kitty Hawks'* 80,000t to the *Enterprises's* 89,600t and the three *Nimitzs'* 91,400t.

b) A large number of lifts, all positioned at the side of the flight deck. There were four lifts, as opposed to the usual three in the British and Japanese Navies.

c) A "rectangular" widening of the flight deck, not a single outer point just for the angled deck as on the early aircraft carriers. This widened area, which was rectangular on both sides, meant that both the island and the lifts could be positioned outside the lower hull structure. There were three lifts on the starboard edge and one on the port edge aft. They were all sited in areas of the deck that could not be used for flight operations, so they could carry planes to and from the hangars without interfering with aircraft maneuvers.

d) A large number of steam catapults, four in all, two on the straight deck and two on the angled one, whereas on the *Midways, Oriskanys,* and Britain's *Ark Royals* there were only two.

e) In all but the first four, the anti-aircraft armament made up entirely of missile launchers. The first four units were completed with eight 5in (127mm) guns, later reduced to four, and ultimately removed. *Enterprise* was unique in being completed entirely without guns or missiles.

f) A top speed of thirty-three to thirty-five knots.

g) A vast array of electronic equipment for seeking out and pinpointing targets, for missile fire control, and for conducting battle operations, including IFF radars to distinguish between friendly and enemy aircraft in flight.

h) A hangar height of about 25ft (7.60m as opposed to about 17.5ft (5.25m) on the previous classes.

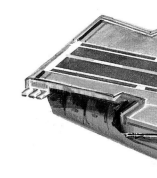

Forrestal (United States 1955). At the end of the war the United States Navy suspended their aircraft carrier program and completed just a certain number of those already on the stocks. *Forrestal, Saratoga, Ranger,* and *Independence* were the first in a new construction program designed after experience gained in the subsequent conversions of the three *Midways.* For the first time the flight deck had the two rectangular extensions and once again there were four elevators, three on the island side (one before and two abaft the island), and the fourth right forward on the angled deck, not aft as it was to be on subsequent types.

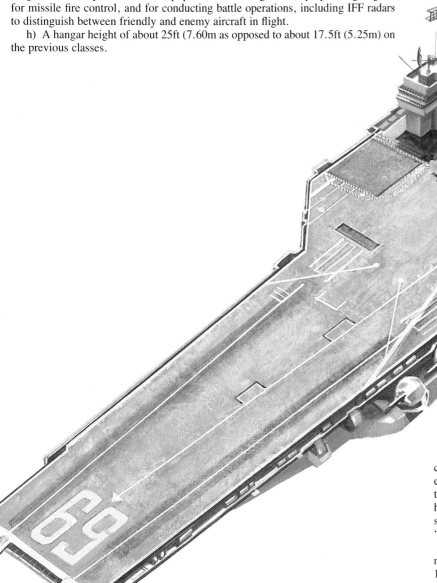

i) A flight deck set at an angle of 10°30′. With their four catapults, these units can launch eight aircraft per minute, that is, one aircraft every half a minute for each catapult. The *Forrestals* have their lifts on the starboard side, one before and two abaft the island. The *Kitty Hawks, Enterprises* and the *Nimitzes,* however, have two lifts before and one abaft the island, and they are not rectangular but in the shape of a trapezium with their forward end widened in order to accommodate the "nose" of the longer aircraft, which are transported with their wings folded.

These units represent the peak of perfection in aircraft carrier development. As a matter of interest, the costs of these giants of the sea were as follows: *Forrestal*—188.9 $US million in 1955; *Saratoga*—312.9 $US million in 1955; *Independence*—255.3 $US million in 1955; *Ranger*—173.3 $US million in 1955; *Enterprise*—451.3 $US million in 1961; *Nimitz*—683.9 $US million in 1975; and *Eisenhower*—784.5 $US million in 1977.

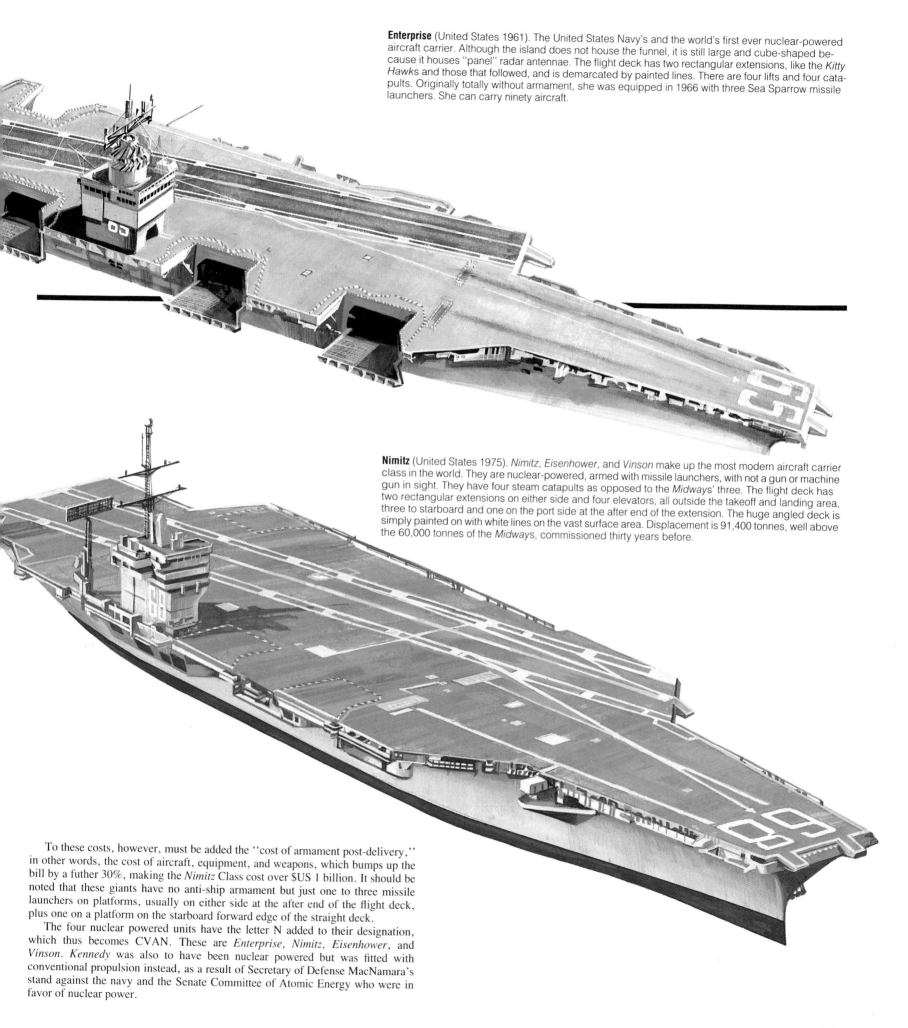

Enterprise (United States 1961). The United States Navy's and the world's first ever nuclear-powered aircraft carrier. Although the island does not house the funnel, it is still large and cube-shaped because it houses "panel" radar antennae. The flight deck has two rectangular extensions, like the *Kitty Hawk*s and those that followed, and is demarcated by painted lines. There are four lifts and four catapults. Originally totally without armament, she was equipped in 1966 with three Sea Sparrow missile launchers. She can carry ninety aircraft.

Nimitz (United States 1975). *Nimitz*, *Eisenhower*, and *Vinson* make up the most modern aircraft carrier class in the world. They are nuclear-powered, armed with missile launchers, with not a gun or machine gun in sight. They have four steam catapults as opposed to the *Midways*' three. The flight deck has two rectangular extensions on either side and four elevators, all outside the takeoff and landing area, three to starboard and one on the port side at the after end of the extension. The huge angled deck is simply painted on with white lines on the vast surface area. Displacement is 91,400 tonnes, well above the 60,000 tonnes of the *Midways*, commissioned thirty years before.

To these costs, however, must be added the "cost of armament post-delivery," in other words, the cost of aircraft, equipment, and weapons, which bumps up the bill by a further 30%, making the *Nimitz* Class cost over $US 1 billion. It should be noted that these giants have no anti-ship armament but just one to three missile launchers on platforms, usually on either side at the after end of the flight deck, plus one on a platform on the starboard forward edge of the straight deck.

The four nuclear powered units have the letter N added to their designation, which thus becomes CVAN. These are *Enterprise*, *Nimitz*, *Eisenhower*, and *Vinson*. *Kennedy* was also to have been nuclear powered but was fitted with conventional propulsion instead, as a result of Secretary of Defense MacNamara's stand against the navy and the Senate Committee of Atomic Energy who were in favor of nuclear power.

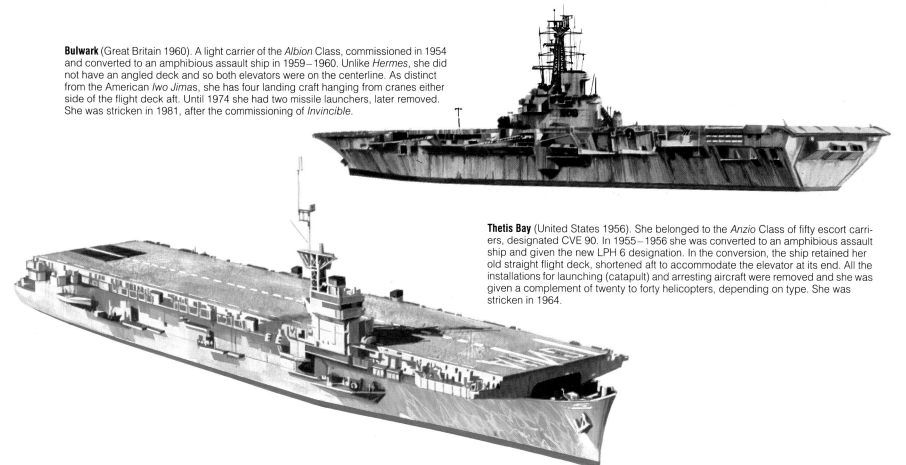

Bulwark (Great Britain 1960). A light carrier of the *Albion* Class, commissioned in 1954 and converted to an amphibious assault ship in 1959–1960. Unlike *Hermes,* she did not have an angled deck and so both elevators were on the centerline. As distinct from the American *Iwo Jima*s, she has four landing craft hanging from cranes either side of the flight deck aft. Until 1974 she had two missile launchers, later removed. She was stricken in 1981, after the commissioning of *Invincible.*

Thetis Bay (United States 1956). She belonged to the *Anzio* Class of fifty escort carriers, designated CVE 90. In 1955–1956 she was converted to an amphibious assault ship and given the new LPH 6 designation. In the conversion, the ship retained her old straight flight deck, shortened aft to accommodate the elevator at its end. All the installations for launching (catapult) and arresting aircraft were removed and she was given a complement of twenty to forty helicopters, depending on type. She was stricken in 1964.

Amphibious assault ships

The first helicopter amphibious assault ships were built very recently (around 1955–1956) and go hand in glove with the growing naval use of helicopters and helicopter development.

From the summer of 1948 onwards, helicopters began to be assigned in ones and twos to the various carriers, to rescue aircraft that crashed into the sea while taking off or landing.

Both the British and American Marine Corps experimented with helicopters in landing operations. In the United States, the escort carrier *Palau*, one of the three completed when the war was over, had a complement of five helicopters which were used in 1948 to carry out numerous air-borne troop landing exercises.

The British Navy performed the first real wartime landings with helicopters from the light carriers *Ocean* and *Theseus* (*Warrior* Class), on November 6, 1956, during the occupation of the area around the Suez Canal.

The first unit to have the CVHA designation was one of the escort carriers of the *Anzio* Class, *Thetis Bay,* which was later classified as an amphibious assault ship; from June 1955 to July 1956 she was converted to operate with helicopters. The modifications were fairly slight: The part of the flight deck abaft the after lift was removed, as were the two forward catapults and aircraft-arrester equipment, and the armament was reduced to sixteen 1.5in (40mm) machine guns. This unit could carry twenty to forty helicopters, depending on their type. *Thetis Bay* was stricken in 1964.

The same conversion work began on *Block Island,* but it was not completed and the unit was stricken in 1959.

In June 1955, without making any drastic structural modifications, the United States Navy assigned the CVHE designation to ten *Anzio* Class aircraft carriers, seven *Commencement Bay* Class, nine *Bogue* Class, and four others, making an overall total of thirty units.

Three *Essex* Class carriers, *Boxer, Princeton,* and *Valley Forge,* were also converted to helicopter carriers. In the meantime, *Block Island* had been reclassified LPH 1, and *Thetis Bay* LPH 6.

In the Royal Navy, the two light carriers *Albion* and *Bulwark* underwent a similar conversion and in 1959–1960 became "Amphibious Warfare Ships," followed in 1971–1973 by *Hermes. Albion* and *Bulwark* have retained their flight deck, with the wide area for the preexisting angled flight deck, and island superstructures practically intact. The two hydraulic catapults and the arrester and landing gear were removed. Armament was reduced to eight 1.5in (40mm) machine guns, but two Sea Cat missile launchers carrying four missiles each were added. These ships carried thirty helicopters and a unit of 900 marines with all their armament. *Hermes* retained her two lifts, but the catapults and other aircraft equipment were removed.

The armament, installed in 1964–1966, has remained the same: two quadruple Sea Cat missile launchers on side platforms aft. *Hermes* can carry twenty helicopters and a complement of 950 men. After having modified the four units, which had become *LPH 1, 4, 5,* and *8,* and withdrawn *LPH 6,* the United States Navy constructed purpose-built amphibious landing ships which formed the *Iwo Jima* and *Tarawa* Classes. The *Iwo Jima*s bear the LPH designation and the numbers 2, 3, 7, 9, 10, 11, and 12. The *Tarawa*s, with an inner docking well from which to launch landing craft, are designated LHA and numbered 1 to 5. The *Iwo Jima*s have a straight flight deck which follows the lines of the hull and from which seven twenty-man Sea Knight helicopters can take off at the same time. There are two deck-edge lifts, one on the port side opposite and slightly forward of the island, the other on the starboard side immediately abaft the island. The original armament was eight 3in (76mm) guns in twin mounts, two on the deck before the island and two aft. In 1970–1974 one mount before the island and the one to port aft were replaced with two Sea Sparrow missile launchers. These are single-screw ships with a top speed of twenty-three knots. They can carry twenty to twenty-four medium-sized helicopters and four large ones plus a contingent of 2,090 men with all their weapons and vehicles. The *Tarawa*s have a practically rectangular flight deck with a large island on the starboard side. The two lifts are both aft because the helicopter hangar takes up only the after area below the flight deck, the forward area being for the combat and troop transport vehicles. One of the two lifts is positioned centrally, the other on the port edge. Abaft the island is a large crane to lower the larger landing craft, which do not fit into the docking well, into the sea. The well measures 268.04 × 77.91ft (81.70 × 23.75m) and contains four medium-sized landing craft. Armament consists of two Sea Sparrow missile launchers, one before the island, and one on the after platform to port. There are three 5in (127mm) automatic anti-aircraft guns on the other three platforms. The *Tarawa*s are twin-screw ships with a top speed of twenty-two knots and can carry thirty helicopters and a contingent of 1,903 men.

The Japanese Navy, or rather Japanese Army, did have a few ships with a flight deck for amphibious operations, but, given their date of construction, they were equipped with aircraft rather than helicopters. *Akitsu-Maru* and *Nigitsu-Maru* of 1942, both converted passenger ships, had a flight deck measuring 398.06 × 73.81ft (121.33 × 22.50m) from which aircraft could take off but not land, because it was not long enough. They had only one lift, which was right aft, and they could carry twenty aircraft and twenty landing craft. *Akitsu-Maru* was sunk on November 15, 1944, by the American submarine *Queenfish.*

A third unit, *Kumanu-Maru,* was commissioned in March 1945. She had no island on her flight deck, and had her funnel on the starboard side; she likewise was too short for aircraft to land on her. She did not see active service, but at the end of the war was used to transport prisoners-of-war back home. In 1947, she was converted to a merchant ship.

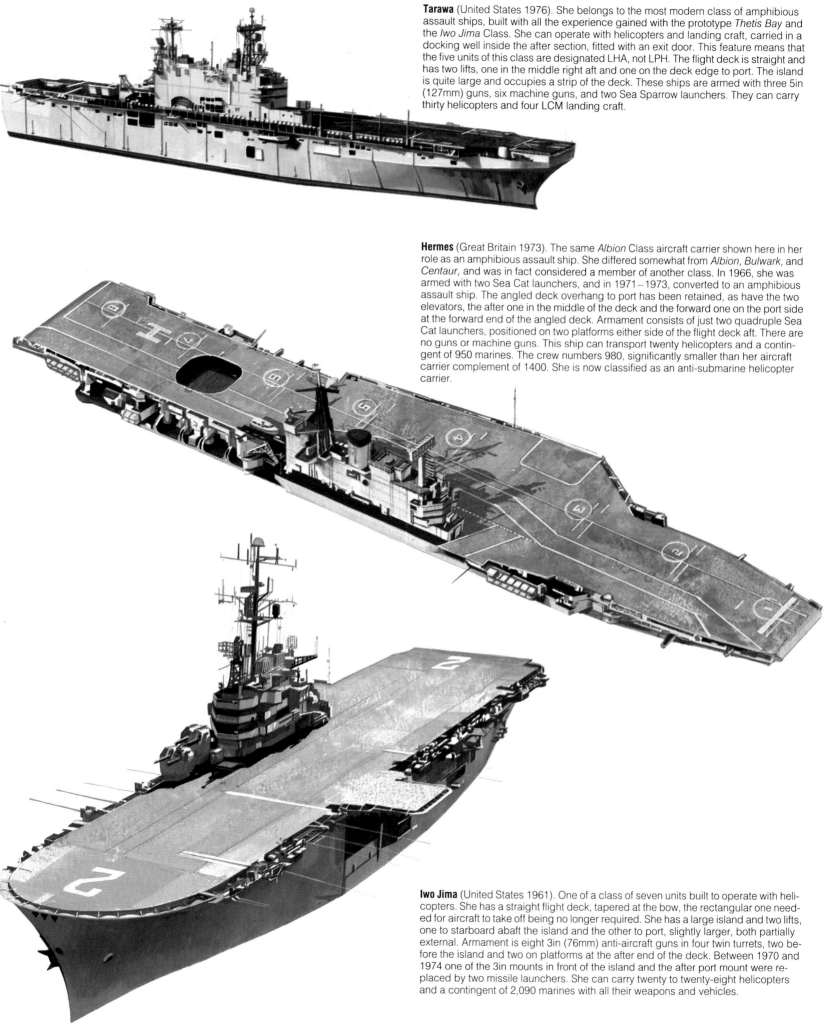

Tarawa (United States 1976). She belongs to the most modern class of amphibious assault ships, built with all the experience gained with the prototype *Thetis Bay* and the *Iwo Jima* Class. She can operate with helicopters and landing craft, carried in a docking well inside the after section, fitted with an exit door. This feature means that the five units of this class are designated LHA, not LPH. The flight deck is straight and has two lifts, one in the middle right aft and one on the deck edge to port. The island is quite large and occupies a strip of the deck. These ships are armed with three 5in (127mm) guns, six machine guns, and two Sea Sparrow launchers. They can carry thirty helicopters and four LCM landing craft.

Hermes (Great Britain 1973). The same *Albion* Class aircraft carrier shown here in her role as an amphibious assault ship. She differed somewhat from *Albion, Bulwark,* and *Centaur,* and was in fact considered a member of another class. In 1966, she was armed with two Sea Cat launchers, and in 1971–1973, converted to an amphibious assault ship. The angled deck overhang to port has been retained, as have the two elevators, the after one in the middle of the deck and the forward one on the port side at the forward end of the angled deck. Armament consists of just two quadruple Sea Cat launchers, positioned on two platforms either side of the flight deck aft. There are no guns or machine guns. This ship can transport twenty helicopters and a contingent of 950 marines. The crew numbers 980, significantly smaller than her aircraft carrier complement of 1400. She is now classified as an anti-submarine helicopter carrier.

Iwo Jima (United States 1961). One of a class of seven units built to operate with helicopters. She has a straight flight deck, tapered at the bow, the rectangular one needed for aircraft to take off being no longer required. She has a large island and two lifts, one to starboard abaft the island and the other to port, slightly larger, both partially external. Armament is eight 3in (76mm) anti-aircraft guns in four twin turrets, two before the island and two on platforms at the after end of the deck. Between 1970 and 1974 one of the 3in mounts in front of the island and the after port mount were replaced by two missile launchers. She can carry twenty to twenty-eight helicopters and a contingent of 2,090 marines with all their weapons and vehicles.

SUBMARINES

The development of submarines from their origins to the present day

So far we have discussed battleships, up to the Second World War, the most powerfully armed ships in the battle fleets, and aircraft carriers, which took over the battleship's role during the Second World War as the unit with the greatest offensive capacity. In this chapter we shall deal with submarines, at the present time equipped with an even deadlier offensive capability than battleships had in their heyday and aircraft carriers have even today.

Today's submarines, or, to be more precise, just the larger submarines armed with missiles with nuclear warheads, have the most powerful armament of all naval units. These are not anti-ship or anti-aircraft weapons, but atomic bombs designed to strike targets on land. So these submarines will never use their missiles in a ship-to-ship engagement, nor can they target them at aircraft, because these missiles are not suitable for such use. Battleships were used exclusively to engage other battleships, and only in exceptional cases to bombard targets on land; and aircraft carriers were and are equipped with aircraft designed for naval combat, in other words, to drop bombs or torpedoes on ships on passage or in port. But the arrival of the missile has ushered in a new role for the submarine; to act as an invisible mobile launching pad for long-range missiles with multiple nuclear warheads. This means that they carry not just one atomic bomb, but up to ten, each intended for a different target.

There has, therefore, been a fundamental change in the use of these underwater units. Born at the beginning of the century to destroy warships, and used in the First and Second World Wars by the Germans in their relentless attack on merchant convoys, they have today become a terrible weapon of destruction of land-based targets. Russian and American missiles are thought to have a range of five to six thousand nautical miles (about 10,000km), so a submarine in the north of the Tyrrhenian Sea, for example, could bomb targets in Switzerland, Austria, and Southern Germany; just as targets in the middle of the United States could be reached from the Atlantic or Pacific Oceans.

The serious threat posed by missile-launching submarines has led to the construction of numerous vessels specially equipped to detect and destroy them. These vessels are either surface ships, such as cruisers, frigates, and anti-submarine destroyers, or underwater units, such as anti-submarine submarines. The development of the submarine has therefore given rise to both large units armed with twelve to twenty-four multiple nuclear warhead missiles with displacements of up to 18–20,000 tonnes, and conventional submarines displacing as little as about 1000t.

When discussing the development of submarines, it is usual to start with historic prototypes such as *American Turtle,* built by Bushnell, which was used unsuccessfully in 1776 during the American War of Independence against the British frigate *Eagle,* or *David* in the service of the Confederate States of America (Southerners), which managed to sink the federal corvette *Housatonic* on February 17, 1864.

We shall not deal with these early prototypes. They were not submarines, because they could only operate near the surface. Nor shall we discuss purely electrically powered submarines, like France's *Gymnote* of 1888, Spain's *Peral* of 1887, and Nordenfelt's steam-accumulator units of 1885–1888; we shall start instead with the first real submarines, those that can operate both on the surface and underwater.

The birth of the submarine, a unit with one powerplant for use on the surface and another for use underwater, with a good range and adequate armament can be credited to the French Navy. On February 18, 1896, it held a competition to design a "submersible torpedo boat" with the following characteristics: surface speed—twelve knots; surface range—one hundred miles at eight knots; underwater range—ten miles at eight knots; armament—two torpedoes; displacement—no more than 200t. The competition was won by an officer of the French Navy, Engineer Laubeuf, with *Narval,* which was built and commissioned in 1900. *Narval* had twelve external torpedo tubes, a displacement of 117/202t (the displacements, engine ratings, speeds, and ranges will be expressed in fractions, the numerator being the surface value and the denominator the submerged one) and a crew of thirteen. Given the state of contemporary technology she had a steam engine for use on the surface.

The French continued to build steam-powered submarines although they undertook research into other types of propulsion. By contrast, the first submarine to be commissioned into the United States Navy had a gasoline engine and was built by J. Holland. In 1898–1899, after building a series of experimental units, he developed *Holland 7,* which was bought by the navy and commissioned on October 12, 1900, as *SS 1*. Nineteen hundred, thus, saw the commissioning of the world's first two submarines, one steam-powered and the other with a gasoline engine.

The gasoline engine was more compact and practical than the steam engine; it was used for surface power on submarines for about ten years, then was replaced by the diesel engine which did away with the risk of keeping highly flammable gasoline on board. Germany's *U 1*s, America's *Adder*s, Austria's *U 3*s, France's *Circé*s, Italy's *Foca*s, and all others had gasoline engines.

After 1907–1908, the various navies commissioned the first diesel-powered submarines, such as Britain's *D* Class (the *C* Class that came before having had "petroleum" engines with twelve–sixteen horizontal opposed cylinders), the French *Brumaire*s of 1910–1911, and others.

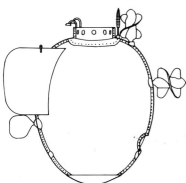

American Turtle (United States 1775). So called because of its shape which resembled two turtle shells stuck together. It was propelled by a hand-cranked propeller and carried an explosive charge that was attached to the hull of the enemy ship. In 1776, with Sergeant Lee at the controls, an unsuccessful attempt was made to sink the British frigate *Eagle*. This vessel cannot be properly regarded as a submarine because it could only operate just awash.

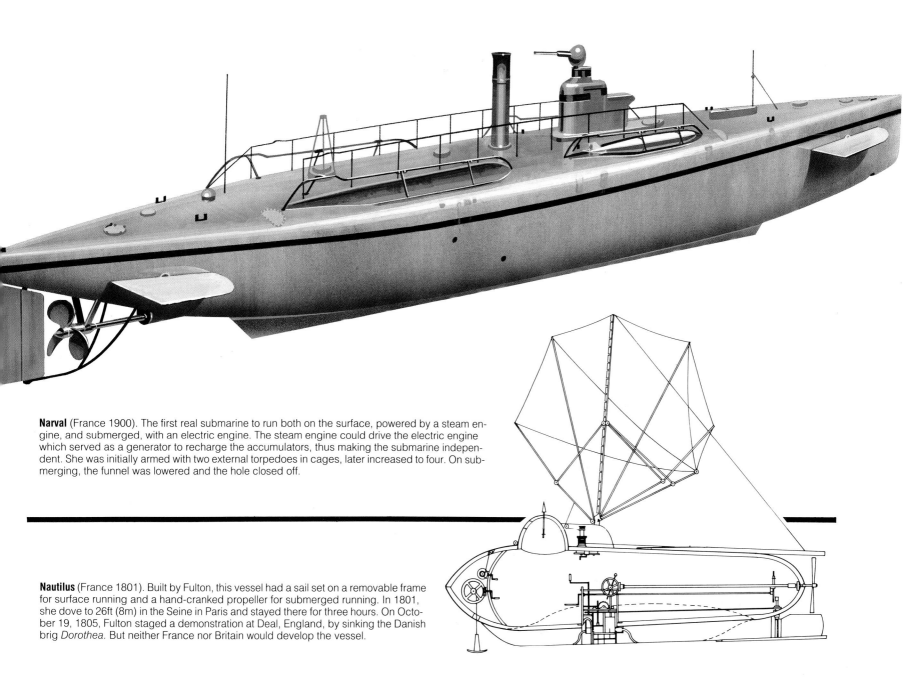

Narval (France 1900). The first real submarine to run both on the surface, powered by a steam engine, and submerged, with an electric engine. The steam engine could drive the electric engine which served as a generator to recharge the accumulators, thus making the submarine independent. She was initially armed with two external torpedoes in cages, later increased to four. On submerging, the funnel was lowered and the hole closed off.

Nautilus (France 1801). Built by Fulton, this vessel had a sail set on a removable frame for surface running and a hand-cranked propeller for submerged running. In 1801, she dove to 26ft (8m) in the Seine in Paris and stayed there for three hours. On October 19, 1805, Fulton staged a demonstration at Deal, England, by sinking the Danish brig *Dorothea*. But neither France nor Britain would develop the vessel.

Fulton (United States 1901). One of the first boats to have a gasoline engine for surface running. She was armed with one internal bow torpedo tube and had an embryonic conning tower that had glass ports for lookout purposes. There was no periscope. In 1904 she was bought by Russia and renamed *Som*. She was sunk on May 23, 1916.

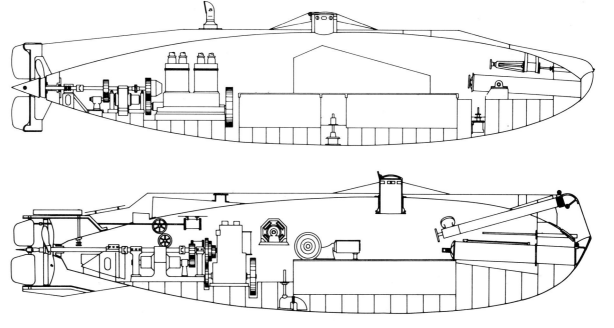

Holland (United States 1900). She was built privately by the Holland Torpedo Boat Company and fitted with a gasoline engine. Propulsion was by means of a large stern propeller, protected by a sort of tail unit that supported the rudder, made in two parts, one above and one below the propeller shaft. She had a pneumatic gun set at an angle of 45° forward and one bow torpedo tube. *Holland* was purchased by the United States Navy and designated *SS1*.

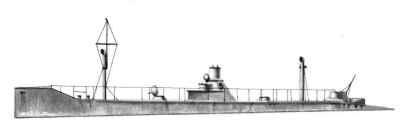

U 1 (Germany 1906). While other navies named their submarines, the German Navy classified them with the letter U, for *Unterseeboote* (submarine), abbreviated to *U Boot*. This was the German Navy's first submarine and she was powered by two 394.5hp (400CV) gasoline engines. The long vertical tube which can be seen aft was the exhaust for the engines. She had a conning tower, even at this early stage, and was armed with one internal bow torpedo tube.

U 3 (Austria 1908). Like the German Navy, the Austrians identified their submarines by the letter U followed by a number rather than giving them a proper name. The first Austrian boats also had twin-screw gasoline engines. Note the large conning tower on which the raised tubes of two periscopes can be seen forward, plus a very tall pole mast that was lowered on submerging. She was armed with two internal bow torpedo tubes.

The problem of the underwater weapon had concerned various governments and been a subject of international discussion even before the beginning of this century. At the Hague Conference of May 3, 1899, Russia had proposed banning its construction, with backing from Germany, Japan, Italy, and Denmark. France, the United States, and Austria, along with four lesser powers, had declared themselves opposed to the ban. Britain was in favor, providing there was unanimous approval. At a second Hague Conference in 1907, the problem was not discussed and the First World War broke out before international agreements about this type of warship had been reached.

The First World War was the most exacting test for the submarine and, from the outset, it revealed its formidable offensive capabilities. On September 5, 1914, the German submarine *U 21* sank the British cruiser *Pathfinder* and a few days later, on September 22, *U 9* took just a few minutes to sink the three cruisers *Hogue, Aboukir,* and *Cressy* on patrol in the English Channel. After this success Germany stepped up its submarine-building program, and between 1914 and 1918 commissioned no less than 338, which were also used against merchant shipping in the war.

The only weapon used in these early submarines was the torpedo; it was only shortly before the First World War that they began to be armed with a gun as well. Then, in 1912 the Russian Navy commissioned the submarine *Krab,* fitted out to carry sixty mines on the outside of her hull. It was the German Navy that built the greatest number of mine-laying submarines during the First World War. Some 118 were commissioned. The other navies showed much less interest; the Royal Navy had only about twelve, the French four, and the Italian three. By the Second World War, however, several navies had developed mines that could be laid from conventional torpedo tubes, so that specialized mine layers were relatively rare.

By the end of the First World War, submarines had much heavier displacements and armament than five years earlier. There were some exceptional ones worthy of mention: Britain's *K* Class displacing 1,880/2,650t, steam powered and armed with eight torpedo tubes; the *M,* or monitor submarine Class, displacing 1,600/1,950t and armed with one 12in (305mm) gun; and the two German ocean-going submarines *U 140* and *U 141,* 1,930/2,483t, built in 1918. The conventional types, like Britain's *L* Class of 1918–1920, had a displacement of 890/1,070t, representing an increase of 25 percent as compared to the *E* Class of 1915–1917, which displaced 662/807t. America's *L* types (classified as coastal) were smaller and displaced 490/720t whereas the ocean-going *AAs* displaced 1,100/1,490t. Germany's *UB* coastal submarines, from *UB 48* to *UB 249,* displaced 516/651t. Between the wars, submarines were discussed at the 1922 Washington Conference. Britain proposed that they be abolished, but the proposal was rejected. At the 1930 London Conference, displacement limits were set at 2000t and gun caliber at 5.1in (130mm). Submarines were classified as ocean going, if their displacement was

over 600t, and coastal, if it was less than that. The United States, Britain, and Japan were entitled to 52,700t standard of ocean-going submarines, but limits for the other powers and for coastal submarines were not decided upon. Between the wars there were no great structural or armament changes made to submarines. The great ocean-going navies of the United States and Japan built long range submarines with displacements of up to 2,500–3,000t (therefore over the London Treaty limits), that were armed with large numbers of torpedo tubes. In 1925–1930 the United States Navy began building the Class *V* cruiser-type fleet submarines, displacing 3,000t surfaced, 4,000t submerged, and armed with two 6in (152mm) guns and six torpedo tubes. Britain, France, and Italy built small submarines such as the British *Perseus* types of 1928 (1,475/2,040t), the French *Redoutables* of 1924–1930 (1,384/2,080t), and the Italian *Balillas* of 1930 (1,450/1,904t). Submarines built immediately before the war had similar displacements.

One exception was the French submarine *Surcouf* with a displacement of 2,880/4,300t and armed with two 8in (203mm) guns, but she was the only one.[*]

Germany was not entitled to have submarines under the Peace Treaty drawn up after the First World War; she began again to build them in 1935, when the restrictive clauses no longer applied. In fact, at the 1935 Naval Convention with Britain, she managed to get a submarine tonnage equivalent to 45 percent of Britain's. Germany's first program entailed the construction of thirty-two coastal, twenty-five sea-going, and fifteen ocean-going submarines, making a total of seventy-two, of which only fifty-seven were operational by September 1939, at the start of the war. During the war she built about a thousand submarines. They included supply submarines, which were underwater tankers carrying 600t of fuel oil to other submarines lying in ambush far from base, thus increasing their range. Torpedo-supply submarines were also planned, although never built. During the war, the Italian Navy planned to build twelve transport submarines, only two of which were commissioned: *Romolo* and *Remo.* They were to travel as far afield as Japan to obtain raw materials of strategic importance that were unavailable in Europe.

The most important submarine development that occurred towards the end of the war was the *snorkel.* This enabled the diesel engines to keep running, even when the submarine was submerged, and thus recharge its batteries without having to surface.

The German Navy had also built a few prototypes powered by closed-cycle steam turbines (the Walter engine) although these could not be developed in time for operational use.

When the war was over, the use of atomic power for the propulsion of submarines was looked into by the United States. This would provide the "single engine," for both surface and underwater use, a problem that the Germans had tried in vain to solve with the Walter engine. Submerged speeds, which were

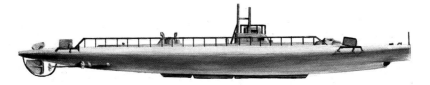

Foca (Italy 1908). A slightly modified *Glauco* type used to test out triple-screw propulsion. When submerged, however, only the side propellers operated, since the middle one had no electric motor. The middle propeller and its engine were removed in 1909. She was armed with two bow torpedo tubes abreast. During the First World War she was fairly active and was stricken in 1918.

Adder (United States 1903). Together with another seven units (from *SS2* to *SS8*) she formed the first class to be built after the prototype *Holland* (*SS 1*). She had one gasoline and one electric engine and a single propeller. There was no conning tower or periscope, but on the deck were two upright air inlet tubes in the forward to midships area and a large vertical tube, for the boiler smoke aft. The central walkway and access hatch cover are clearly visible.

Circé (France 1908). *Circé* and *Calypso* were the first two French submarines to have their surface power steam engine replaced by a gasoline engine. The conning tower was much smaller than that of the Austrian *U 3*. The externally carried torpedoes can be seen, two on either side of the conning tower amidships and two on deck aft. Between these two torpedoes and the conning tower was a small 1.8in (47mm) gun.

usually slower than surface speeds with the conventional power plant, were stepped up, the range became limitless, and the installed horsepower considerably higher.

The submarine had also changed its external shape and the number of propellers. The original cigar-like shape, tapering at both ends, developed a bulbous forward end. This shape had been proven more hydrodynamically suitable for high speeds. The conning tower, which was originally squat and wide, had become taller and thinner, like a fin; the forward diving rudders were often positioned either side of the tower, and the propellers (which around 1905 were increased to two beneath the hull) had been reduced to one right aft, coaxial with the hull. As a result of the propeller being moved, the rudder, too, moved from its position abaft the propellers to before them, with one blade above and the other below the hull, forming a sort of four-winged tail unit with the two after diving rudders. The hull structure had been immensely strengthened, enabling submarines to dive to a depth of at least 1000ft (300m). If we remember that in 1905–1915 submarines could dive just to around 100ft (30–35m) and in 1920–1945 to no more than 350–400ft (100–120m), it is easy to see the progress that had been made by this time in this field.

Today's submarines can be divided into two basic types: missile launching and attack submarines. Missile-launching submarines are practically all nuclear powered, whereas the attack submarines of the American, British, Russian, and French Navies can be either nuclear- or conventionally powered. Those in the world's other navies, however, still have diesel engines for surface cruising and for snorkeling, and electric motors for underwater operation. To sum up then, the development of the submarine from its origins to the present day has resulted in displacements of 14–16,000 tonnes, diving depths of 1,000ft (300m), and single power plant producing underwater speeds that would have been inconceivable during the Second World War. As regards hull shape, we now have a more bulbous shape, with a taller, narrower conning tower, and diving rudders on the tower instead of right forward.

Submarine armament

Until the Second World War the weapons of the submarine had been guns, anti-ship torpedoes, and mines. These have now been replaced by ballistic missiles and anti-submarine torpedoes.

In 1905–1910, submarines were armed with just torpedo tubes fore and aft. Then, at the beginning of the First World War, they were also fitted with one or two guns on deck and, on some types, on the conning tower. Britain's *L* types (numbered one to thirty-three), for instance, had one 3in (76mm) or 4in (102mm) gun in the forward part of the tower, and those numbered from fifty-one to seventy-one had two 4in (102mm) guns both on the tower, one forward and one aft. German submarines only had deck guns: two 3.5in (88mm), as on the *U55s*, and one 3.9in (100mm), before the tower, as on the *U43* to *U50* types and on the minelayers *U117* to *U126*. Some submarines, like the French *Lagrange* types of 1917–1919, had their guns abaft the tower.

The British *M* Class monitor submarines were unique in having a single 12in (305mm) gun, later replaced by a hangar on the *M2* for a seaplane and its crane. Another unusual form of armament was the four 5.2in (132mm) guns in two twin turrets on Britain's *XI* built in 1924, and the two 8in (203mm) guns in a twin turret before the tower on France's *Surcouf* built in 1934. But submarine guns usually had calibers of 3.9–5.1in (100–130mm), within the limits of the Washington Treaty, the pieces usually being unshielded. In the Italian Navy, submarine cruisers and sea-going submarines had only one gun, whereas the fleet submarines had two. In the Second World War, Italy's *Brin* types (1938) and Germany's *VII G 2s*, as well

as many American submarines, had their gun abaft the tower. During the Second World War, the gun proved to be a relatively ineffectual weapon and so was removed on submarines built after the war.

Narval was armed with four torpedoes carried in external slings; the *Holland* had a single internal torpedo tube. Subsequent boats usually had their tubes (internal) at the bow and stern, fitted with closable ports at both ends so that they could be opened from inside and reloaded.

The older boats (1904–1905) had from up to three tubes: America's *Adders* of 1903 and Germany's *U1* of 1906, for instance, had only one tube at the bow. Britain's *Ds* (1907) had three. In First World War submarines, there were as many as four to six torpedo tubes. They were usually housed at both ends, with more at the bow than the stern because of the propellers: For example, with a total of six tubes, four would be at the bow and two at the stern.

Some units of this period had an unusual arrangement, with the tubes being positioned athwartships in the middle of the hull. This was especially popular on the British types, such as the *Ls* (from one to eight) of 1916, which had four tubes at the bow and two athwartships in the middle; the *K* types of 1914 with four at the bow and four athwartships; and the *Es* and *Gs* of 1915–1916 with two tubes athwartships. The Dutch *Ks* (1917) and the German *UC* minelayers (from ninety to 118) of 1917–1918 also had two amidships tubes athwartships. On the German *UCs*, the tubes were above water when the submarine surfaced.

Other First World War submarines had conventional tubes at either end, such as the American *L* types of 1916, the German *U* and *UB* types of 1915–1916, the Japanese *Vickers* types (like the *No. 13*), the Spanish *Monturiöl* of 1917, and the Italian *Pacinotti* and *Barbarigo* of 1916–1918. Only French submarines carried torpedoes externally, like *Fulton* and *Lagrange* (1917), the *Dupuy de Lômes*, the *Zedés* (1913), and others that had eight to ten torpedoes in cages on either side of the deck.

External torpedo tubes were then replaced by a mixed arrangement of tubes at the bow and stern and trainable torpedo tubes on deck. Submarines with this arrangement included France's *Redoutable* (1928) with eleven tubes, two of which were in twin mountings—one at the bow and the other at the stern; the *Requins* (1924) with six tubes and two twin torpedo tubes, one before and one after the tower; the two minelayers *Pierre Chailley* and *Maurice Challot* (1922–1923) which had a twin tube on deck abaft the tower as well as the forward tubes; and *Surcouf* with four internal torpedo tubes, two before and two abaft the tower. Other navies that had submarines with external trainable torpedo tubes were: the Japanese *Kaiguns* (*RO 11–15* and *RO 16–24*); the Dutch *K III* and *K IV* of 1919; the United States *T1* of 1919; and the Danish *Flora* and *Bellona* of 1915–1920. The Russian Navy's *Bolshevik* Class (1915) had four bow tubes and eight in external cages, like those on the French submarines. Some units built from 1944–1945 onwards also had external torpedo tubes, such as Britain's *S* and *T* Classes (1944–1945) and *A* Class (1948) and France's *Creole* (1938) and *Narval* (1950–1953) types. Some of these units later had their external tubes removed.

With the introduction of the missile as a submarine weapon, torpedo tubes have lost some of their importance, although they have been retained even on the most modern missile-launching submarines, like the American *Ohio* Class of 1982–1983 and the Russian *Delta* Class. They still make up the armament of attack submarines, for firing both anti-surface torpedoes and anti-submarine torpedoes, and for launching anti-submarine missiles, as on America's *Threshers* and Russia's *Victors*.

Torpedo tubes are once again being positioned amidships rather than at either end. So, for example, Japan's *Uzusho* (1971–1974) and *Yuushio* (1981–1984) Classes have six central torpedo tubes and America's *Threshers*, *Sturgeons*, *Narwhals*, and *Lipscombs* all have four tubes amidships.

Missile-launching submarines keep their weapons in vertical tubes, usually in pairs abaft the tower. The number of tubes varies from submarine to submarine. America's *Ethan Allen* has sixteen for Polaris missiles, as do the *Washingtons*. There have been Russian submarines with three tubes but the more modern *Delta 2* and *Delta 3* Classes have sixteen. France's *Le Foudroyant* types also have sixteen.

Submarine power plants

When man began to venture underwater, the only motive power that existed was that produced by his arms and legs; thus we find Sergeant Lee of America manually turning the rudimentary propeller of *American Turtle* in his attempt to sink the British frigate *Eagle* in 1776. The same applied to *David,* which sunk *Housatonic* on February 17, 1864, and had her propeller powered by the arms of eight men. The first engine to replace human strength was the steam engine, fitted on other *David*s, including the one commanded by Lieutenant Glassell, who, on October 5, 1863, hit the Union battleship *Ironsides* with a spar torpedo.

But *Turtle* and *David* were neither submarines nor submersibles because they had to remain just awash to obtain the necessary air for combustion and for the crew to breathe. By 1860, however, technology had already produced the electric motor that worked without requiring air for combustion and did not produce exhaust gases. This motor was used to propel many of the early prototypes both on the surface and when submerged, and is still used today to provide power on the surface and underwater, even on some nuclear submarines.

Steam accumulators were also tried out, the steam being stored on the surface to be used later when submerged, as on the *Nordenfelt* submarines, but these experiments were not followed up.

When Laubeuf designed *Narval,* he equipped her with two types of power plant: a reciprocating steam engine for surface work and an electric motor powered by storage batteries for submerged runs.

During submerged runs, both in the days of *Narval* and today in the case of conventional submarines, the electric motors are powered by direct current from storage batteries. Although made up of a large number of huge elements, these batteries have a limited capacity and must be recharged very frequently. This frequency varies according to submarine use, and in wartime could be on a daily basis. The batteries are recharged by the same motors used for propulsion, which, when driven by the surface-running engine, operate as generators and produce electric current. In this way the submarine becomes an independent unit and can stay far away from base for a long period of time, determined by the amount of fuel it can carry. A submarine's power plant, therefore, comprises a thermal engine, either steam or diesel; a coupling; a motor and electric generator; a coupling; and the propeller shaft.

During normal surface runs, the two couplings are both engaged and the electric motors idle. When submerged, the thermal engine disconnects and the electric motor turns the propeller shaft. To recharge the batteries, the propeller coupling disconnects and they are recharged while the submarine is stationary.

In addition to the main engines (which are quite powerful), some submarines also have a low-power "cruising" motor for quiet running at slow speed. This "cruising" motor was installed, for instance, on the Italian *Balilla* (1928) and *Saint Bon* (1941) Class submarines and also on a certain number of units belonging to other navies.

The early submarine boats, built in 1900–1905, had only one thermal engine, one electric motor, and one propeller. The latter was positioned right aft and its centerline coincided with that of the hull. Around 1905, designers began to install two thermal engines, two electric motors, and two propellers, the latter being symmetrically positioned below the hull aft. As a result of this change of propeller position, the rudder was also moved to below the hull and abaft the propellers, as on surface ships.

After the Second World War, hydrodynamic research led to the use of just one propeller both for the very large nuclear-powered submarines armed with ballistic missiles, such as the American *Ohio*s (1982–1983), and for the conventional diesel-powered boats, such as the German *U*-boats (from *U1* to *U30*) of 1966–1975, and a great many more conventionally powered submarines belonging to other nations.

There have been very few submarines with three propellers. Examples are Italy's *Foca* of 1909 and the much more modern Russian *Golf, Tango, Foxtrot,* and *Zulu* Classes, all equipped with three diesel and three electric engines and built between 1955 and 1972. The only submarine to have had four propellers was Japan's *No. 44,* commissioned in 1924, a 1,390/2,430t experimental unit. In 1932, however, two of the propellers and their engines were removed and she became a conventional twin-screw unit.

Modern single-screw conventional submarines have a different power plant than that described above, with the propeller being driven by an electric engine both on the surface and when submerged. On the surface, current is supplied by electric generators driven by thermal engines; when submerged this current is supplied by conventional batteries. This arrangement has meant that the couplings, which are delicate, expensive, and heavy, have been completely done away with. This type of power plant, known as diesel-electric, has been in use since as early as 1941–1942 in twin-screw United States Navy submarines, with the aim of increasing the power by installing four engines instead of two, as on the *Gato* and *Balao* types of 1942–1943. These submarines had four thermal engines driving four generators that supplied current to the engines driving the two propellers. The most recent submarine power plant development has resulted in nuclear propulsion.

The "nuclear" power plant is a totally conventional steam-powered system of turbines that drive the propeller shaft by means of reduction and coupling gears.

The difference lies in the steam generator, which, instead of being a boiler, is a nuclear reactor whose cooling fluid circulates between heat exchangers where the steam is generated.

Paradoxically, progress has meant that history has turned full circle because the ultra-modern submarines of the *Ohio* Class of 1982–1983 have a steam power plant just like Laubeuf's *Narval* of 1900 or Nordenfelt's submarines of 1885–1888.

When discussing the development of the submarine, *Narval* was described as the first submarine because she could navigate both on the surface and when submerged, whereas previous types were actually "submersibles" because they were not really suited to navigation underwater.

The ultra-modern nuclear-powered boats cannot be regarded as "submersibles" because they are not designed for use on the surface, in either war or peacetime. Today's submarines can stay submerged for as long as ninety days and travel at high speeds, without being detected by standard radar scanners, which proved so fatal for the conventional German submarines in the Second World War.

The only existing system for the detection of nuclear-powered submarines is sonar, which has a limited range, and is both complex and costly.

Steam-powered submarines from 1900 to 1920

It has already been said that the first real submarine was the French *Narval*, built at the Cherbourg Naval Yard between 1898 and 1900. She had a 246.5hp (250CV) reciprocating steam engine, powered by a Seigle oil-fired water-tube boiler with five burners. Obviously there had to be a funnel to discharge the combustion gases when on the surface and its flue had to be closed off when the submarine submerged. It took twenty-five minutes to shut down the boilers, close off the funnel and combustion air inlets, and fill the ballast tank. This was reduced to twelve minutes on subsequent units of the *Triton, Sirène, Silure,* and *Espadon* Classes, which had four external torpedoes instead of two.

This series of single-screw boats was followed by the twin-screw units: the eight *Pluviôse* Class, the five *Papin*s, and the two *Ampère*s, built between 1907 and 1910. The latter were larger than the *Sirène*s and displaced 398/550t as opposed to 157/213t. They had two 690hp (700CV) triple-expansion engines, almost double the power of the previous types (246.5hp [250CV]), and they could make 12.5 knots. When submerged, the two 453.7hp (460CV) electric engines could develop a speed of eight knots. The time required for preparing for diving trim had dropped to about five to six minutes. These submarines were armed with six external torpedo tubes and some of them had one internal bow tube.

As with surface ships of that period, turbines replaced reciprocating engines. The first unit to have a turbine power plant was *Gustave Zedé,* built in 1911–1914, with a displacement of 740/1,000t and two reduction gear turbine units giving an overall power of 2,367hp (2,400CV) and driving two propellers. Steam was generated in four oil-fired boilers and the top speed was nineteen knots. Armament consisted of two internal torpedo tubes, six external torpedoes, and two guns, one before and one abaft the tower.

After the successful *Zedé* experiment, it was decided to build a class of eight turbo-driven units, laid down in 1914–1917. During construction, however, six of them were modified and fitted with diesel engines instead. These units were completed in 1919–1920, and so, only *Dupuy de Lôme* and *Sané* (1915–1916) were steam powered.

They had a displacement of 833/1,100t, two geared turbine sets developing 3,945hp (4,000CV), powered by four oil-fired boilers, and could make eighteen knots. Armament consisted of bow tubes and six external ones plus two guns, one before and one abaft the tower. But these two units also had to be converted into conventional diesel-powered boats. In 1922, the turbines were replaced by two 2,860hp (2,900CV) engines and so the speed dropped to sixteen knots. They remained in service until 1934–1935.

The Royal Navy also had a class of steam-powered submarines. These were built because of an operational need for units that could make twenty-four knots. They were larger than the French units, displacing 1,880/2,650t, and were 336.08ft (102.44m) long. The power plant used for surface running comprised two

Dupuy de Lôme (France 1915). One of the few French submarines to be designed and built with a turbine surface power plant, similar to the one installed in the British *K* Class. Power developed was only 3,945hp (4,000CV), however, less than half that of the *K*s' 9,863hp (10,000CV), and the top speed was twenty-four knots. She was armed with two small guns and eight torpedoes. In 1922 the steam turbines were re-placed with two diesel engines.

U 55 (Germany 1916). One of Germany's first ocean-going submarines, built for attacking merchant shipping and therefore armed with two 3.4in (88mm) guns, one before and one abaft the conning tower. She also had two bow and two stern torpedo tubes. She could make an impressive seventeen knots and had a remarkable range of 9,500 miles. When the war was over, she was assigned to Japan where she was redesignated *03*.

Romazzotti (France 1917). An ocean-going submarine with a surface and submerged displacement of 836t and 1,317t respectively. Unlike her contemporary German counterparts, armed with 4.1–3.4in (105–88mm) guns, she had two small 2.2in (57mm) guns, one before and one abaft the conning tower, which were far less effective in terms of range, weight, and penetration. This armament, intended mainly to attack merchant shipping, was completed by eight torpedo tubes.

UB 125 (Germany 1916). Part of a large class of ocean-going submarines built during the First World War for attacking merchant shipping. She had two diesel engines and could make 13.5 knots; her range was quite long because she was designed for long missions in the Atlantic. On the large conning tower there are two raised periscopes and a small mast. There were another two masts, one forward and one aft, all of which could be lowered.

D 1 (Great Britain 1907). She belonged to the first class of British submarines to have diesel rather than gasoline engines. Note the large non-water-tight free-flooding structure which gave the taper-ing hull a ship's profile with its torpedo boat bow and deck. She had a conning tower, periscopes, and no guns, only three torpedo tubes.

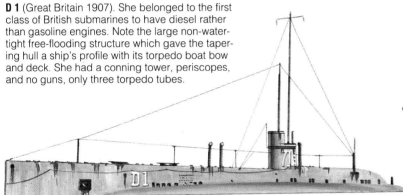

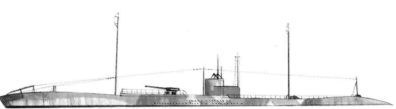

U 125 (Germany 1918). One of a class of large displacement mine-laying submarines called Minen Kreuzer. She carried forty-two mines in special tubes inside the hull that floated out through ports at the bottom of the tubes (which were usually in the after part). There were four bow torpedo tubes and one 3.4in (88mm) unshielded gun on the deck before the conning tower.

---

reduction geared turbine sets 10,000shp supplied by two boilers, each with its own funnel. The power plant for submerged running comprised two electric motors, one for each shaft, developing an overall power of 1,600hp and speed of 9.5 knots.

These units were probably the first to have an auxiliary engine designed both for cruising and to enable the submarine to run immediately after surfacing while the boilers were raising steam. It was an eight-cylinder 800bhp diesel engine that drove a generator to power the electric motors. Armament was made up of three 4in (102mm) or 3in (76mm) guns, originally one before, one abaft, and one on the superstructure. These were later all arranged on the superstructure, one before and two abaft the tower. There were ten torpedo tubes: four at the bow and four athwartships in the middle, plus two external ones on the central superstructure. The class was made up of seventeen units, plus an eighteenth modified one, designated *K26*. All the units were stricken between 1921 and 1926, except for *K26* which was stricken in 1931.

Submarines from 1900 to 1920

While *Narval* was being built in France with a reciprocating steam engine, a private individual in the United States named Holland had built and was testing six prototype submarines with a power plant for surface running made up of gasoline engines.

The first submarine to be commissioned into the United States Navy was the seventh of the prototypes, *Holland 7,* built by the Holland Torpedo Boat Company, which became *SS1 Holland* in the battle fleet. She was built in 1898–1899 and

No. 13 (Japan 1911). One of the first submarines to be built in Japan in the Kawasaki shipyard to a Brit-ish Vickers design. This single-screw boat had a petroleum engine for surface running and an elec-tric engine for submerged running; she was armed with one bow and one stern torpedo tube. Note the almost cylindrical shape of the conning tower on which the two periscopes can be seen. In 1923 the designation was changed to *Ha 6*. She was strick-en and broken up in 1928.

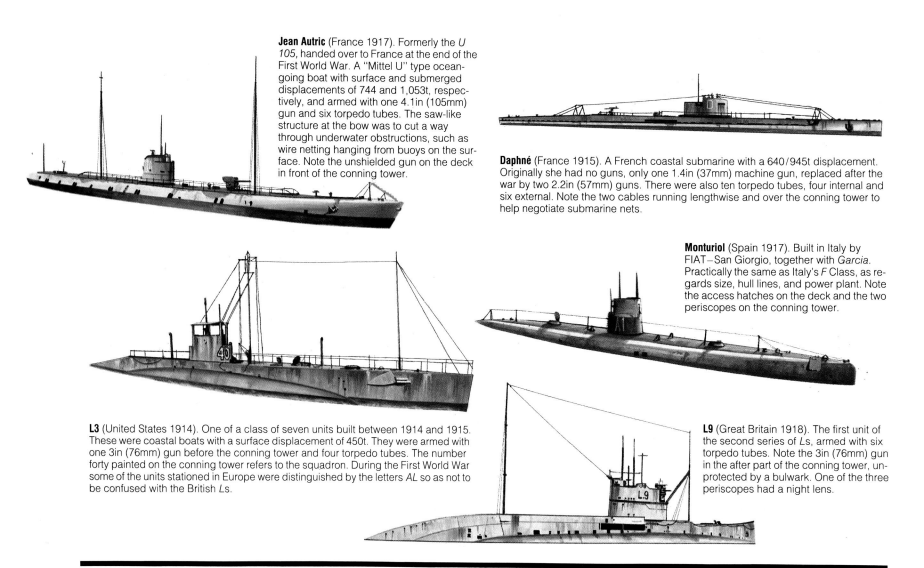

Jean Autric (France 1917). Formerly the *U 105*, handed over to France at the end of the First World War. A "Mittel U" type ocean-going boat with surface and submerged displacements of 744 and 1,053t, respectively, and armed with one 4.1in (105mm) gun and six torpedo tubes. The saw-like structure at the bow was to cut a way through underwater obstructions, such as wire netting hanging from buoys on the surface. Note the unshielded gun on the deck in front of the conning tower.

Daphné (France 1915). A French coastal submarine with a 640/945t displacement. Originally she had no guns, only one 1.4in (37mm) machine gun, replaced after the war by two 2.2in (57mm) guns. There were also ten torpedo tubes, four internal and six external. Note the two cables running lengthwise and over the conning tower to help negotiate submarine nets.

Monturiol (Spain 1917). Built in Italy by FIAT–San Giorgio, together with *Garcia*. Practically the same as Italy's *F* Class, as regards size, hull lines, and power plant. Note the access hatches on the deck and the two periscopes on the conning tower.

L3 (United States 1914). One of a class of seven units built between 1914 and 1915. These were coastal boats with a surface displacement of 450t. They were armed with one 3in (76mm) gun before the conning tower and four torpedo tubes. The number forty painted on the conning tower refers to the squadron. During the First World War some of the units stationed in Europe were distinguished by the letters *AL* so as not to be confused with the British *L*s.

L9 (Great Britain 1918). The first unit of the second series of *L*s, armed with six torpedo tubes. Note the 3in (76mm) gun in the after part of the conning tower, unprotected by a bulwark. One of the three periscopes had a night lens.

commissioned on October 12, 1900. She had a displacement of 64/75t, a 50hp gasoline engine that enabled a speed of six knots and an electric motor (also 50hp) powered by sixty storage batteries that provided a speed of five knots. She was armed with one internal bow torpedo tube and a "pneumatic gun" for use when submerged, which fired underwater charges of 110lb (50kg); but this was immediately abandoned. After *SS1*, the United States Navy ordered a class of seven units, from *SS2* to *SS8*, which included *SS3 Adder*. They displaced 135/175t and had a 160hp gasoline engine and a 70hp electric motor.

Apart from the Holland Torpedo Boat Company, there was another American firm called the Lake Torpedo Boat Company, which built a submarine named *Protector* in 1901–1902, but it was not accepted by the navy. In 1904, while at war with Japan, Russia bought two boats from Holland and one, *Protector,* from Lake. She was named *Ossetyr* and followed by a further five boats of the same type. The Lake boats had twin screws and were powered by gasoline engines on the surface and electric motors for submerged running. They could make 10/7 knots and were armed with three torpedo tubes, two forward and one aft.

In 1901–1902 the Royal Navy commissioned the Vickers Yard to build five boats similar to the American *Adder*s, named *Holland* and numbered one to five. These were followed in 1903–1904 by the A types, all of which had a single screw and gasoline engine. The German Navy, at that time the Royal Mary's great rival, commissioned its first submarine, *U1*, in 1906. She displaced 238/283t, had two 394.5hp (400CV) four-cylinder gasoline engines and was armed with one torpedo tube.

Since 1900 the French Navy had used steam-powered submarines and in 1905–1906 had begun building the *Pluviôse* Class, also steam powered. As early as 1904–1908, it tried out gasoline engines on *Circé* and *Calypso*, 351/450t submarines that could make eleven knots with their 453.5hp (460CV) engines.

In 1904, when the war with Russia broke out, the Japanese Navy had no submarines, and so, bought five *Holland*s from the United States, similar to the American *Adder*s, with a displacement of 103/124t, a single-screw, and one torpedo tube. These were followed by two similar Japanese-built units and then two more built by Vickers, identical to the British *C* types. They were all single-screw boats with gasoline engines.

In 1903–1905, the Italian Navy built five *Glauco* Class submarines, designed by Laurenti, a major in the Engineer Corps. They displaced 160/243t, had twin-screws, two gasoline engines for surface running, and were armed with two to three torpedo tubes. *Foca* was also in this class but initially had three gasoline engines driving three propellers.

As a result of diesel engine improvement, submarines built after 1907 no longer had gasoline engines. The first to have diesel engines in the Italian Navy was the *Medusa* Class, built between 1907 and 1910. In the United States Navy, the *Holland D* and *E* types of 1909–1911 had diesel engines and, during the war, *F2* and *F3* of the *Carp* Class also had their gasoline engines replaced by diesel ones. The Royal Navy first used diesel engines on the *D* Class units, built between 1907 and 1910. In the Japanese Navy, diesel engines were installed on the Vickers 8 and 9 of 1907–1908 and on subsequent units, and in the French Navy, all the *Pluviôse* types completed in 1910–1911 and not steam powered received the same treatment. In Germany, the birthplace of the diesel engine, all the submarines had diesel engines apart from four gasoline-engine prototypes. After the introduction of the heavy-oil engine there were no more important submarine innovations. The external appearance, internal compartmenting, and armament arrangement remained the same, except for an increase in displacement and the number of torpedo tubes.

Britain's *M* Class of submarines stood out among others of the same period because of their armament. They had a displacement of 1,600/1,950t, about double that of conventional units such as the *L* Class (from 1 to 33) which displaced 890/1,070t. The *M*s were armed with one 12in (305mm) and one 3in (76mm) gun, the 12in (305mm) one being in a sort of turret on deck before the tower. The gun was loaded on the surface and set at its maximum elevation. The submarine then submerged to a depth at which the muzzle remained out of the water so that the gun could be aimed with the help of the periscope, by moving the entire boat, and fired without surfacing. The gun could only be reloaded by returning to the surface. They were commissioned in 1920, when the war was over, and were immediately modified. *M2* became a seaplane carrier with a watertight hangar in place of the gun turret and a crane above it for the plane. *M3* was converted into a minelayer and fitted with a long tall superstructure to carry her mines. By contrast, the submarines of other classes were totally conventional, especially the *L* Class of

1916–1920. It was made up of three subclasses: *L1* to *L8, L9* to *L33,* and *L51* to *L71.* The first two subclasses were armed with one raised gun on the forward part of the tower and the third with two guns, one on the forward part and one on the after part of the tower. They had six torpedo tubes which on the second and third subclasses were all at the bow, whereas on the first there were four bow tubes and two athwartships in the middle.

The submarines belonging to the seventy-unit *E* Class (of which only sixteen survived the war) had two bow tubes, two athwartships and one aft. There were some units in this large class with only one tube athwartships and some without any tubes in this position.

During the First World War, the United States did not have any large ocean-going submarines, but only units with a surface displacement of 600t or less. The *AA* Class fleet submarines were not commissioned until the war was over. They had a displacement of about 1,000t. The most outstanding American submarines of this period were the *L* types, built between 1914 and 1915. They displaced 450/570t, had two 641hp (650CV) engines and a range of 4,500 miles. They were the first U.S. craft to have a 3in (76mm) gun on deck as well as four torpedo tubes. In wartime, when some were detached to Europe, they were designated *AL* to distinguish them from the British *L* Class.

During the war, the German Navy built about 300 submarines, including the "Mittel U" types, large ocean-going units with a displacement of 712/940t, the *UB*s, small ocean-going boats of 516/651t, and two types of minelayers. The larger of the two was known as the *Minen Kreuzer* (from *U 116* to *U 126*), displacing 1,164/1,512t, which carried forty-two mines and had four bow torpedo tubes. The smaller one, *UC80* to *UC152*, displaced 491/571t, carried seven mines and had one torpedo tube at the bow and two athwartships in the middle.

Like the American Navy, the Japanese only commissioned ocean-going submarines when the war was over. During the war, the only units it had were foreign-designed ones, like Nos. *18-21* by Ansaldo-Laurenti, No. *15* by Schneider-Laubeuf, Nos. *8* and *9* by Vickers of Britain, and the very old *Holland*s from *1* to *5,* bought in 1904–1905. Those numbered from 10 to 14 and 16 to 17, designed by Vickers but modified by the Japanese, were small 300/330t coastal boats with two torpedo tubes.

The French Navy had a small number of ocean-going boats, such as the 900/1,250t *Joessel* Class and the 833/1,100t steam-powered *Dupuy de Lôme* Class which, as already mentioned, had no torpedo tubes but carried eight to ten torpedoes in external cages. The most outstanding of the coastal submarines were the *Daphné* types, a name which frequently recurs in the French Navy and is still used today for a submarine class. They displaced 640/945t and were armed with ten torpedo tubes, four internal and six external.

In 1910–1915 the Italian shipbuilding industry had made an international name for itself in submarine construction and had built units for some of the minor navies, such as *Monturiol* and *Garcia* for the Spanish Navy, *Foca, Golginho, Hidra,* and *Espadarte* for the Portuguese Navy, and *F13* and *5* for the Brazilian Navy, which also ordered the famous submarine rescue boat *Ceará* from Italian shipyards. Submarines were also designed for Japan.

In the years leading up to the First World War, the Venice Dock Yards built the five *Glauco* Class boats, designed by Laurenti, while Fiat–San Giorgio was busy building *Foca* which was practically the same as the *Glauco*s except that, by way of experiment, it had three screws. On the surface, the propellers were driven by three 266hp (270CV) gasoline engines. When submerged, however, there were just two electric engines for the two side propellers while the middle one remained stationary. In 1909, the third propeller and its engine were removed.

During the war a great many coastal submarines were built, such as the twenty-one-unit *F* Class, built partly by Fiat–San Giorgio of La Spezia and partly by the Orlando Shipyard in Leghorn. They displaced 262/319t and were armed with one 3in (76mm) anti-aircraft gun and two bow torpedo tubes. Apart from coastal vessels, the Italian Navy also had six *Pietro Micca* Class ocean-going submarines, built by the La Spezia Naval Yard and commissioned in 1918–1919. They displaced 842/1,244t and were armed with two 3in (76mm) guns and six torpedo tubes, four forward and two aft. They had a range of 2,100 miles.

Submarines from 1920 to 1945

Between the wars and during the war there were no substantial changes in the structure, armament, and power plants of submarines. The most startling innovation, which appeared only on German submarines and only in the last two years of the war, was the snorkel, a long tube which enabled the engines to continue operating even when the hull was completely submerged. The invention of the snorkel is generally attributed to the Dutch Navy, but a similar device, designed by Major Ferretti of the Italian Engineer Corps, was tried out in Italy in 1925 on a submarine designated *H3*. It was to have been installed on units of the *Sirena* Class,

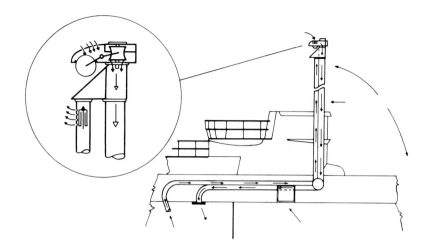

Snorkel. This diagram shows one of the early types of snorkel, made up of a folding tube that could rotate on a horizontal shaft, now replaced by a telescopic system. The inset shows the float valve which closes off the air inlet tube should the latter be covered by a wave, so as to prevent water from getting into the engine cylinders.

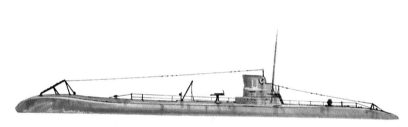

Uttern (Sweden 1921). One of a class of three units built in the Karlskrona Naval Yard and the Kokums Shipyard at Malmö between 1921 and 1922. They were armed with a small 1.8in (47mm) gun and four bow torpedo tubes. Note the saw forward to cut through submarine nets and the protective cable over the conning tower.

S 45 (United States 1923). One of a class of fifty units built between 1919 and 1923, divided into three series which differed in size and armament. In fact, some units had only four bow torpedo tubes and others had a fifth tube at the stern. Armament was completed by a 4.1in (105mm) gun. Note the canopy structure covering the forward part of the conning tower.

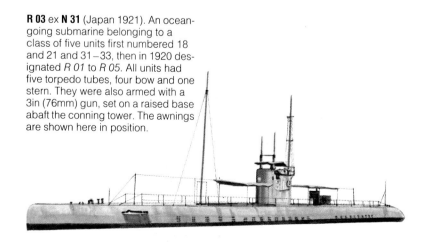

R 03 ex **N 31** (Japan 1921). An ocean-going submarine belonging to a class of five units first numbered 18 and 21 and 31–33, then in 1920 designated *R 01* to *R 05*. All units had five torpedo tubes, four bow and one stern. They were also armed with a 3in (76mm) gun, set on a raised base abaft the conning tower. The awnings are shown here in position.

but in 1937, even before they were commissioned, it was decided to abandon the idea; as a result, no Italian submarines were fitted with snorkels during the war.

In the Dutch Navy, a device similar to the snorkel was built to a design by Lieutenant Wickers and installed on the *O19* and *O20* submarines built in 1938–1939. When the Germans invaded Holland in May 1940, four submarines, designated *O21* to *O24*, took refuge in British ports. All four had snorkels. After a series of tests, however, the Royal Navy removed the devices, considering them to be of little use, and dangerous.

In 1940, the Germans also appropriated three Dutch submarines, *O25* to *O27*, which were still on the stocks and equipped with snorkels. These submarines were completed and incorporated into the navy of the Reich, which formed an unfavorable opinion of the device after putting it to the test; this resulted in the ''ventilation masts'' being abandoned. But three years later, in 1943, the British were using airborne radar to detect German submarines when they surfaced at night to recharge their batteries. Once detected, the submarines were hunted down and very often sunk. Due to these heavy losses, the German Navy decided, in the spring of 1943, to set to work on what later became the snorkel, and in August 1943 a prototype fitted to *U57* underwent sea trials. Another prototype with a folding tube was tried out on *U235* and *U237* in September 1943. At the end of September 1943, work gradually began on fitting the device on all operational units as they returned from their missions, as well as on new submarines. In 1944, the advantages of not having to surface to recharge the batteries began to be felt and, in fact, fewer submarines were lost.

In the period from 1920 to 1945, British submarines, like others of the previous period (1900–1920), were armed with one gun on the superstructure in front of the tower, or even in the forward part of the tower itself. On the *Triton (Triumph)* Class of fifteen units, classified as ocean-going submarines and commissioned in 1937–1940, the 4in (102mm) gun was positioned in the forward part of the tower and there were ten torpedo tubes, six bow and four stern. Displacement was 1,090/1,575t. The *Porpoise* minelayer class had their gun on a superstructure in front of the tower. By contrast, the *Odin* and *Oberon* types had their guns on the forward part of the tower. Lastly, the smaller units with a displacement of 600t had their guns on deck.

In 1934, the French Navy commissioned *Surcouf* (2,880/4,300t), the only submarine in the world to be armed with two 8in (203mm) guns and to be fitted with a hangar for a small seaplane. Apart from the 8in (203mm) gun, she also had two 1.4in (37mm) anti-aircraft machine guns plus a further four machine guns. There were twelve torpedo tubes, four internal bow tubes, and four external trainable tubes, two before and two abaft the tower. The experiment was a failure and not repeated on other units. French ocean-going boats had only one gun before the conning tower, as evidenced by the five *Morillot* Class, the thirty *Redoutable* Class, the fifteen *Aurore* Class, and the ten *Saphir* Class, which were minelayers. All these submarines had a very long conning tower. In addition to the two main 2,959hp (3,000CV) engines, the *Redoutable*s had a 740hp (750CV) auxiliary engine. They had eleven torpedo tubes, four of which were in two pairs (one forward and one aft), and seven external, four in a quadruple mount before the tower and three in a triple mount abaft it. All the external torpedo tubes were at a lower level than the upper deck and therefore were not clearly visible at a distance.

Before the war began, the German Navy had fifteen ocean-going submarines in service: *U25*, *U26*, *U37*–*U44*, and *U64*–*U68* with a surface displacement of 700t. Then there were twenty-four sea-going submarines: *U44* to *U55* and *U69* to *U71*, displacing 500t, plus thirty-two 500t coastals. Both ocean- and sea-going types were armed with one gun before the tower on deck and six torpedo tubes, four forward and two aft. They had a very small conning tower which made them almost impossible to see when surfacing. During the war, other types were designed, such as the ocean-going *Type XXI*, the first underwater vessel to achieve seventeen knots submerged; the *Type XXIII*, a single-screw coastal boat with an electric motor for silent running when lying in wait; and the *Type XVII* which had a hydrogen peroxide engine for submerged running.

Requiring craft which could operate throughout the vast spaces of the Pacific Ocean, the Japanese Navy had developed long-range ocean-going boats such as the *Kaidai I 44* of 1924, which could cover 20,000 miles at ten knots; the *Junsen*s of 1929, which could cover 24,400; and the *A* types, numbers 12 to 14, of 1943–1944 which had a range of 22,000 miles. The *Kaidai 6 A* types, numbers *I 68* to *I 73*, commissioned in 1938, had a displacement of 1,400/2,400t, a range of 14,000 miles, one 3.9in (101mm) gun and six torpedo tubes. The *I M* type *Junsen*s had a hangar for one or two seaplanes. *I 6* and all the *B* types also had a catapult. During the war, some of these boats had their seaplanes removed and were used to carry *Kaiten* underwater assault craft.

The United States Navy, also concerned largely with Pacific operations, developed its own long-range ocean-going submarines. For example, the *Salmon* Class, commissioned in 1938, had a displacement of 1,450/2,198t and an endurance of 11,000nm at ten knots. The smaller *Cuttlefish* type of 1934, (1,120/1,650t), had a similar endurance. Both were armed with one gun abaft the tower. These submarines were developed into the wartime *Gato* Class (1,526/2,410t). The only U.S.

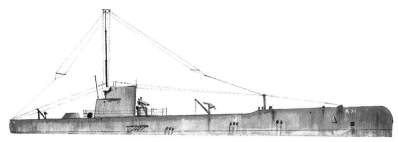

K XI (Holland 1924). Dutch-built submarines were identified by the letter O followed by an Arabic numeral, if they were to remain in Holland, and the letter K followed by a Roman numeral if they were going to the colonies. The colonial class from *K XI* to *K XIII* displaced 670/820t and was armed with four bow and two stern torpedo tubes, plus a 3.5in (90mm) gun in front of the conning tower. The radiotelegraphic aerial mast could be lowered.

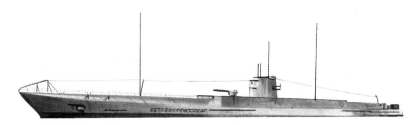

I 1 ex No. 74 (Japan 1929). This submarine belonged to a class of four units known as submarine cruisers, designated *Junsen* Type 1, derived from the German *U 142*. They had a range of 24,400 miles and were armed with two 5.1in (130mm) guns and six torpedo tubes. An interesting feature was that both the upper part of the hull and the conning tower were lightly armored. All saw service in the Second World War, and was sunk on January 29, 1943, by the New Zealand corvettes *Kiwi* and *Moa*.

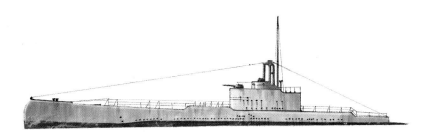

Oberon (Great Britain 1928). This ocean-going submarine belonged to a group of seven units that all had names beginning with the letter O. Note the shape and size of the conning tower which incorporated the gun emplacement. She was armed with one 4.1in (105mm) gun and eight torpedo tubes, six forward and two aft. She had a retractable telescopic mast and a protective cable running fore and aft.

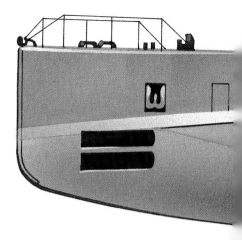

Surcouf (France 1934). The only submarine cruiser of her kind, she proved unsuccessful and the design was not repeated. She displaced 2,880/4,300t and was armed with two 8in (203mm) nontrainable guns positioned in a sort of armored casemate before the conning tower. There was a watertight hangar abaft the conning tower that could hold a small seaplane with its wings folded. *Surcouf*'s torpedo tubes were internal only at the bow and she also had four twin trainable units on the deck, two before and two abaft the conning tower.

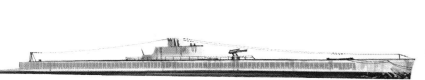

Tourquoise (France 1928). A mine-laying submarine which belonged to a class of six units built between 1927 and 1931. Note the large conning tower and the long structure over the hull to accommodate the thirty-two mines. Armament consisted of one 3in (76mm) gun before the conning tower and four torpedo tubes, all forward. The mines were stowed in cells outside the pressurized hull, using the so-called Normand-Fenaux system.

Vetehinen (Finland 1930). Belonged to a class of three coastal units and displaced 490/715 tonnes. She was armed with four bow torpedo tubes and one 3in (76mm) gun on deck before the conning tower. These units had a submarine net saw at the bow, protective cables running fore and aft, and could be fitted out as mine layers, carrying twenty mines. The retractable telescopic mast on the conning tower was lowered before submerging.

Perseus (Great Britain 1928). An ocean-going submarine displacing 1,475/2,040 tonnes, armed with eight torpedo tubes and one 3.9in (100mm) gun arranged in an emplacement within a superstructure in the forward part of the conning tower. The square structure running lengthwise on top of the conning tower houses the top part of the telescopic periscope tubes. The long mast could be lowered. Note the retracted port diving plane at the bow.

O'Brien (Chile 1928). Belonged to a class of three units built in Britain and so resembled the *Oberon*s, especially where the large conning tower was concerned. She had one 4.1in (105mm) gun in a shielded raised emplacement in the forward part of the conning tower and eight torpedo tubes, six forward and two aft. She had a submarine net saw and a protective cable running the length of the ship.

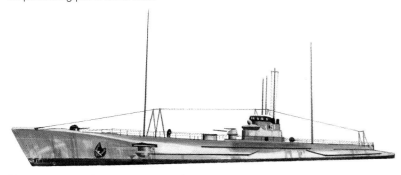

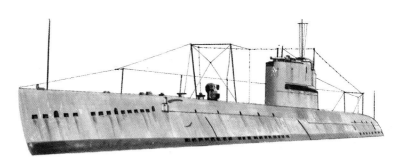

I 61 (Japan 1927). An ocean-going submarine of the *Kaidai* Type 4 Class, belonging to a class of three units. She was an improvement on the *Kaidai* 1, 2, and 3 types which belonged to a series of Japanese-designed submarine cruisers, initiated in 1924 with I44. She was armed with one 4.7in (120mm) gun on deck before the conning tower and six bow torpedo tubes. She was sunk on October 2, 1941, (before Japan entered the war) after colliding with the gunboat *Iki*.

Yakobinetz (Soviet Union 1935). Belonging to a class that was to have been made up of seventeen units, displacing 959/1,370t. Note the 4in (102mm) gun in a superstructure which had a very high bulwark and was incorporated into the conning tower. She was also armed with a 1.4in (37mm) anti-aircraft machine gun in the after part of the turret and eight torpedo tubes. She was assigned to the Black Sea Fleet.

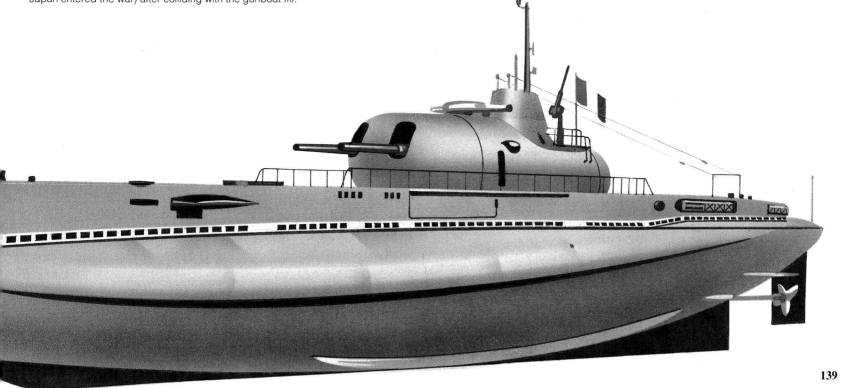

Severn (Great Britain 1935). This 1,850/2,723t submarine cruiser could make an impressive 22–25 knots with her 9,863hp (10,000CV) power plant. Armament consisted of one 4.1in (105mm) gun, in the forward part of the tower, and six bow torpedo tubes.

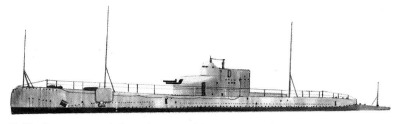

Delfim (Portugal 1934). One of a class of three ocean-going submarines built at Vickers-Armstrong in Britain. Her main feature was the casemate before the tower, containing one 4.1in (105mm) gun. Armament was completed by six torpedo tubes, four forward and two aft. Her range was 5,000 miles at the fuel-saving speed of ten knots.

Glavkos (Greece 1927). Belonged to a class of four French-built units. She displaced 730/930 tonnes but, unlike French submarines, had her 3.9in (100mm) gun in the forward part of the tower, in addition to a 3in (76mm) gun on deck behind the tower. She had eight torpedo tubes, six forward and two aft, and a range of 4,000 miles.

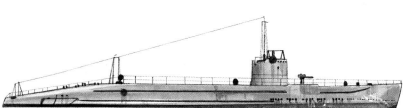

I 71 (Japan 1938). One of a class of six *Kaidai 6 A* type ocean-going submarines, designated from *I 68* to *I 73*, changed in 1942 to *I1 68* to *I1 73*. They had a special type of diesel engine, and developed a remarkable twenty-three knot surface speed. They were armed with one 3.9in (101mm) anti-aircraft gun and six torpedo tubes. In 1942 she was converted into a transport submarine before being sunk on February 1, 1944, by the American destroyers *Guest* and *Hudson*.

ocean-going submarines to have two guns, one before and one abaft the tower, were *Narwhal* and *Nautilus* of 1930 and the only minelaying submarine in the same category was *Argonaut* of 1928. Other noteworthy U.S. submarines were the four *Bonita* Class (2,000–2,506t) of 1924–1926, which, in addition to the main engines, had two auxiliary generating units to supply the electric engines. In December 1941, at the outbreak of the Pacific War, the U.S. Navy had a total of 111 submarines in service. Japan had seventy-four.

Between 1920 and 1940, the Italian Navy commissioned sixty-eight sea-going and forty-four fleet submarines and, during the war, eighteen coastal, four ocean-going, and two transport submarines. At the beginning of the Second World War, therefore, it was second only to the Russian Navy in its complement of submarines, followed by France with eighty-six, England with sixty-nine, Japan with sixty-five, and Germany with fifty-seven, figures which were to be practically reversed by the time the war ended. Italy's first fleet submarines were *Balilla*, *Millelire*, *Toti*, and *Sciesa*, commissioned in 1928. They displaced 1,450/1,904t and were armed with one 4.7in (120mm) gun and four 0.5in (13.2mm) machine guns, plus six bow and two stern torpedo tubes. They could make 17.5/8.9 knots and had a 419hp (425CV) auxiliary engine. By using this engine, their range increased to 12,000 miles at seven knots. They were too old to take part in the war and were broken up in 1946.

Italy's last fleet submarines were the four *Saint Bon* types, laid down in September–October 1939 and commissioned in mid-1941. They had a displacement of 1,703/2,164t, could make 16.9/8.5 knots amd had a 493hp (500CV) auxiliary engine which increased the range to 19,500 miles at seven knots. They were not armed with the conventional 21in (533mm) torpedoes, but with smaller 17.7in (450mm) ones, capable of sinking merchant ships. There were eight bow and six stern torpedo tubes with twenty reserve torpedoes forward and twelve aft.

The most active unit of this class was *Cagni* with its two runs to the South Atlantic: one lasting 137 days and the other eighty-four; the latter was cut short on September 8, 1943, because of the armistice. The other three units were sunk during the war.

Coastal boats that deserve a mention include the "Class 600," made up of *Perla* and *Adua* types (twenty-seven units commissioned between 1936 and 1938) and the *Platino* types (thirteen units commissioned in 1941–1942). They displaced about 700t on the surface and some 860t submerged and were armed with one 3.9in (100mm) gun and six torpedo tubes for conventional 21in (533mm) torpedoes. They were very active in the Mediterranean and suffered heavy losses: of the forty units of the class, twenty-nine were sunk during the war and four captured by the Germans on Armistice Day. Out of the seven that remained in Italy, six had to be handed over to the victorious navies in compliance with the Peace Treaty.

Apart from the above-mentioned major navies, minor navies also had submarines: One example is Brazil, with *Tamoio*, *Tupy*, and *Timbrya*, built by Cantiere Odero-Terni-Orlando of La Spezia in 1936–1938. Even Estonia, one of the three small Baltic States (Estonia, Latvia, and Lithuania) created after the break-up of the Russian Empire in 1919 and reabsorbed into Russia in 1940, had its own navy and is own submarines, such as *Kalev* and *Lembit*, built in Britain by Vickers-Armstrong in 1936. Latvia, another Baltic state, had, among others, *Ronis* and *Spidola*, built in France by the Loire shipyard in 1926–1928 which, like French submarines of that period, had two external twin torpedo tubes, one before and one abaft the conning tower. Finland had *Vetehinen*, *Vasihisi*, and *Iku Turso* (1930–1932), built in Finnish dockyards; Greece followed the French influence and bought the *Glaukos* types, built at the Loire shipyard in Nantes; Holland had the *019* and *020* (1939) and the units numbered *021* to *024*; and Portugal had *Delfim Espardarte* and *Golginho* (1934), built by Vickers-Armstrong in Britain.

Gato (United States 1936). The most numerous class of submarines to be built during the war, with 195 units. They displaced 1,825/2,424 tonnes and had a twin-screw unit driven by electric engines on surface runs, too. The *Gatos* were armed with one or two 3in (76mm) or 4in (102mm) guns, machine guns (usually at either end of the conning tower), and ten torpedo tubes, six forward and four aft.

Russia, which could not be regarded as a great naval power at the beginning of the Second World War, had about 150 units, about forty more than Italy. The specifications and names of these boats are not widely known. They included seventeen *Yakobinetz* types, commissioned in 1929–1935 and displacing 959/1,370t and twenty-two *Dekabrist* Class, built in 1929–1930, displacing 896/1,318t and armed with one 3.9in (100mm) gun and eight torpedo tubes, six forward and two aft. Other examples of Russian submarines are the sixteen (or more) *Chuka* types, the three *Bolsheviks*, already mentioned for having eight external torpedoes, and the four 375/467t *Metallists*, used as training vessels in the Black Sea.

Conventional submarines from 1945 to the present day

In the years that followed the Second World War, the submarine underwent many important structural and armament changes as a result of new ideas regarding its use. In this section we shall deal only with "conventional" submarines, in other words, those with a power plant made up of diesel engines and electric motors.

The main structural innovation has been the new shape of the hull and conning tower and, most recently and not on all submarines, the altered position of the diving rudders from the forward end to either side of the conning tower. Apart from changing shape, the hull has also become stronger, which has meant that greater diving depths can be reached.

The system of driving the surface-run propeller directly by the diesel engine has largely been abandoned; electric propulsion is generally used for this purpose, too, and the diesel engines serve only to power the generators. The number of propellers has dropped from two to one and the 1904–1905 position has been resumed, that is, right aft and coaxial with the hull. All submarines have been fitted with snorkels, and surface speeds have, on the whole, become slower than submerged speeds.

In terms of armament, the gun has been abandoned once and for all and all (strategic) non-missile launching units now only have tubes for firing anti-ship and anti-submarine torpedoes, and, in some cases, anti-submarine missiles. There are now also torpedo-tube–

U 33 (Germany 1936). A coastal submarine displacing 626/745t and one of a class of ten units designated from *U 27* to *U 36*, built in 1936–1937. They had quite a large prewar type conning tower that was later modified and reduced in size to make detection by radar less easy. Armed with one 3.4in (88mm) gun and five torpedo tubes, four forward and one aft.

Lembit (Estonia 1936). British-built by Vickers-Armstrong. She displaced 600/720 tonnes, had no guns, except for one 1.5in (40mm) anti-aircraft machine gun in the forward part of the tower, and four torpedo tubes. Range was 2,000 miles at ten knots.

Triumph (Great Britain 1939). One of a class of ocean-going submarines commissioned in the first year of the Second World War. Displacement was 1,090/1,575 tonnes and she still had a large tower that housed the 3.9in (100mm) gun emplacement in its forward part. They had six bow and four stern torpedo tubes and a distinctive hull shape with a stepped superstructure aft.

Tamoio (Brazil 1937). One of a class of three units laid down as *Ascianghi*, *Naghelli*, and *Gondar* for the Italian Navy, and so practically identical to the *Adua* Class. They were armed with one 3.9in (100mm) gun on deck before the conning tower, two 0.5in (13mm) anti-aircraft machine guns in the after part of the tower, and six torpedo tubes, four forward and two aft. They made a surface speed of fourteen knots.

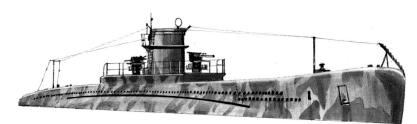

Saint Bon (Italy 1941). This submarine belonged to a class of four units, designed to operate against merchant ships as submarine cruisers. With extra fuel they could achieve a range of 19,500 miles, which, although less than the Japanese *Junsen* type's 24,400, was truly exceptional for Italian submarines. *Saint Bon* was armed with two 3.9in (100mm) guns, one before and one abaft the conning tower, and fourteen torpedo tubes, eight forward and six aft. She was sunk on January 5, 1943, by the British submarine *Upholder*.

CB1 to **CB22** (Italy 1941–1945). Pocket submarines with a displacement of 36/45 tonnes, a single-screw, and two external torpedoes positioned either side of the conning tower. Those numbered 1 to 6 operated in the Black Sea and on September 9, 1943, were seconded into the Rumanian Navy. Units *CB7* to *CB12* were delivered at the end of August 1943 but were not used and were eventually broken up in 1948. Units *CB13* to *CB22* were completed for the navy of the Italian Social Republic.

Type XXI C (Germany—not built). There were 150 *Type XXIs*, plus a further twenty-two that were never finished, built between 1943 and 1945. It was stipulated that the variant *XXI C*, projected in 1944, be armed with eighteen torpedo tubes, six in the conventional bow position and twelve, six per side, in two groups of three, angled astern. There was no provision for guns, except for four 1.1in (30mm) machine guns in two twin mounts.

launched anti-ship missiles, the U.S. submarine *Harpoon* and the French submarine *Exoceb (S.M. 39)*. Unlike their wartime predecessors, all have radar and electronic underwater detection equipment (sonar), for normal running and for torpedo fire control.

The Soviet Union, which has a very large fleet of nuclear-powered vessels, also retains many conventionally powered submarines, like the twenty *Tango* Class (completed from 1973 onwards). They have a displacement of 2,100/2,500t, three diesel engines and three propellers, and are armed with six torpedo tubes, all at the bow, some of which fire type SS-*N-15* anti-submarine missiles, the Russian equivalent of the American SUBROCs. In 1984, they were succeeded in production by a new *Kilo* Class. The seventy-six-unit *Foxtrot* Class also have three propellers and three diesels, making almost the same speed on the surface as submerged. The twenty-six *Zulu* types and the thirty *Quebec* coastals also have three propellers, whereas the twenty *Romeo* and 236 *Whiskey* types (many of which were later handed over to the navies of nations friendly to the Soviet Union) have only two propellers. Perhaps it should be explained why Russian submarines have

non-Russian names such as *Foxtrot* and *Zulu*. These are not their real names, which are difficult to discover, given the secrecy surrounding everything to do with Soviet defense systems, but names (actually the standard codes for letters of the alphabet) given to them by NATO; these names are now used in all the naval almanacs.

Britain currently has sixteen units of the *Oberon* Class in commission. This has been a very successful type and many are serving in other navies: Australia's *Oxley* Class, Chile's *O'Brien* types, Brazil's *Humanitas*, and Canada's *Ojibwas*. They displace 2,030/2,410t, have two diesel engines, giving a total horsepower of 2,629.5hp (3,680CV) and two 5,918hp (6,000CV) electric engines to drive the two propellers. As is evident, submerged power is greater than surface power, which means that the speed is 12/17 knots. Armament consists of eight torpedo tubes: six forward and two aft, and these boats are equipped with radar and sonar.

France has two very well-known classes of submarine in service: the four *Agosta* types of 1977–1978 and the nine *Daphné* types of 1964–1978. The *Agosta*s have also been built for the Spanish and Pakistan navies and the *Daphné*s for South Africa, Pakistan, Portugal, and Spain. The *Agosta*s displace 1,450/1,725t and have a diesel-electric power plant. This means that the two 3,551hp (3,600CV) diesel engines drive the two generators for the single 4,537hp (4,600CV) electric engine which drives the propeller both on the surface and when submerged. In addition to the main electric engine, there is a 296hp (300CV) auxiliary one for cruising speed. They make twelve knots on the surface and twenty knots submerged. Armament consists of four torpedo tubes with a reserve of twelve torpedoes. All are fitted with radar, sonar, and snorkel. The *Daphné*s displace 869/1,043t, have two propellers and two diesel engines driving two generating sets and two electric motors. Horsepower is 1,282/1,578hp (1,300/1,600CV) and speed is 13.5/16 knots. They can dive to a depth of 1,000ft (300m) and are equipped with sonar, radar, and snorkel.

Under the conditions of the Peace Treaty, the German Federal Republic was not permitted to have submarines. After she joined the Atlantic Alliance, however, she resumed construction in 1964 and commissioned the first *205* types in 1966–1967.

These units displace 419/450t, have two diesel-electric generating sets with a total horsepower of 1,184hp (1,200CV) and a 1,479hp (1,500CV) electric engine, driving a single propeller. The speed is 10/17 knots and the armament consists of eight torpedo tubes. The *206* types have a displacement of 450/498t, two 1,479hp (1,500CV) diesel-electric sets and a 1,775hp (1,800CV) electric engine for the single propeller. The speed is 10/17 knots and they have eight torpedo tubes. Although not in West German service, German builders have also developed a type *209* for export to Argentina (*Salta* Class); Brazil; Chile (*Simpson* Class); Colombia (*Pijao* Class); for Greece (*Glaukos* Class); Indonesia (*Cakra* Class); for Peru (*Islay* Class); Turkey (*Atilay* Class); for Venezuela (*Sabalo* Class); and Ecuador (*Shiry* Class). They displace 1,185/1,285t, have four diesel-electric generating units and one electric engine to drive the single propeller. The electric motor develops 4,931hp (5,000CV) and the speed is 10/22 knots.

In 1960, Japan (which was likewise not allowed to have submarines under the terms of the Peace Treaty), completed her first postwar submarine, *Oyashio*, followed by two *Hayashio* Class in 1962, two *Natsushio* in 1963–1964, and five *Oshio* in 1965–1969. They were followed in 1971–1978 by the seven *Uzushio* Class, and, in 1980–1983, by the four *Yushio* types. The *Oshio* types displace 1,650t standard on the surface, have two 2,860hp (2,900CV) diesel engines, two 6,214hp (6,300CV) electric engines and two propellers. Speeds are 14/18 knots. Armament consists of six bow torpedo tubes and two stern tubes to fire anti-submarine torpedoes. The *Uzushio*s and *Yushio*s are larger, with a different hull form, and with a large U.S.-style spherical bow sonar and U.S.-style amidships torpedo tubes (six in their case). The latter class is larger, displacing 2,200t standard on the surface. They have only one propeller and can make speeds of 12/20 knots. The forward diving planes are positioned on either side of the conning tower.

Golf II (Soviet Union 1967). The *Golfs* were one of the first classes of Soviet missile-launching submarines. The missiles were in tubes abaft the conning tower inside a large superstructure housing three missiles. They are conventionally powered, with a surface speed of seventeen knots, a submerged speed of fourteen knots, and a remarkable range of 22,700 miles. The *Golf II* Class is made up of thirteen units.

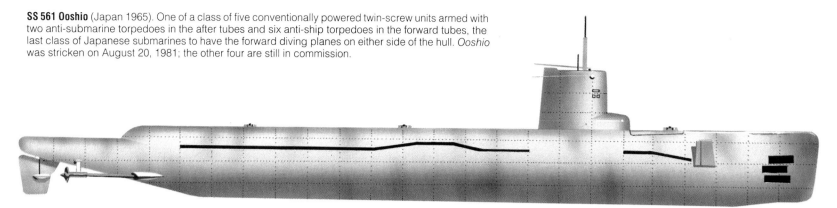

SS 561 Ooshio (Japan 1965). One of a class of five conventionally powered twin-screw units armed with two anti-submarine torpedoes in the after tubes and six anti-ship torpedoes in the forward tubes, the last class of Japanese submarines to have the forward diving planes on either side of the hull. *Ooshio* was stricken on August 20, 1981; the other four are still in commission.

Italy was also prohibited by peace treaty from having submarines. In February 1948, she was obliged to break up the few units that were left after those assigned to the victorious powers had been delivered. Construction was resumed in 1965 and in 1968–1969 she commissioned four *Toti* types, small coastal submarines, and, in 1980–1981, the four *Sauro* types. The *Toti*s, including *Mocenigo,* displace 524/582t, have two diesel engines and one 1,973hp (2,000CV) electric engine driving a single propeller, both on the surface and underwater. They have four torpedo tubes, radar, sonar, and snorkel. The *Sauro*s displace 1,456/1,631t, have three diesel-electric generating units, one 3,600hp (3,650CV) electric engine and one propeller. Speeds are 11/20 knots, range is 12,500 miles at four knots and there are six torpedo tubes. These were the first Italian submarines to have their diving rudders either side of the tower.

As far as other navies are concerned, it has already been mentioned that many have bought boats from France, Britain, and Germany. Furthermore, several navies of nations friendly to the United States received boats handed over to them by the United States Navy. Examples are the Italian Navy's *Piomarta, Romei, Longobardo,* and *Gazzana,* plus others received at an earlier stage. Navies within Soviet sphere, either past (like China), or present, have Russian-built boats of the *Romeo* and *Whiskey* types. China and North Korea have both built their own *Romeo*s and China was unique in building a *Golf* Class ballistic missile submarine from Soviet-supplied plans. China also built *Whiskey*s. The Dutch, Danish, and Swedish navies are among those that are ''independent'' as regards submarine construction.

At the Copenhagen Naval Yard, Denmark has built the four *Delfinen* Class of 1958–1964 and the two *Narhvalen* Class of 1970, twin-screw boats of a fairly conventional type.

Dutch shipyards have built the four *Potvis* triple-hulled types of 1960–1966, the two *Zwaardvis* types of 1972, and the two *Walrus* types of 1982. The *Potvis* types have twin screws and their diving rudders forward, but the others have a single propeller and their diving rudders are on the tower. The *Zwaardvis* types displace 2,350/2,640t, have three diesel generators and one electric engine, speeds of 13/20 knots, and six bow torpedo tubes.

Sweden's Kockums Shipyard at Malmo has built six *Sjöormen* Class and three *Näcken* Class for the navy. The former, commissioned in 1961–1962, displace 835/1,100t, have two diesel generators, one electric engine, and one propeller, and can make 17/20 knots. The *Sjöormen*s, commissioned in 1967–1969, are a little larger, displacing 1,130/1,400t, and with their diving rudders either side of the tower. The *Näcken*s have almost the same displacement as the *Delfinen*s, but their hull has a bulbous shape and they can also be used as minelayers.

The Norwegian Navy, on the other hand, commissioned fifteen small *207* type submarines in 1964–1967, built in Germany and forming the *U1a* Class. They displace 400/435t and have two diesel generators, one electric engine, and one propeller. They can make ten knots on the surface and seventeen submerged, and are armed with eight bow torpedo tubes.

Mocenigo (Italy 1968). One of the first four submarines to be built by the Italian Navy after the war. She has a modern-shaped hull and a single-screw aft driven by an electric engine, both on the surface and when submerged. Armament consists of four anti-ship torpedoes, all in bow tubes. The dome at the bow contains a sonar system. These units have a snorkel and their forward diving planes are positioned on either side of the hull.

Nuclear-powered submarines from the post-war period to the present day

There are only five navies with nuclear-powered submarines in commission: the American, Russian, British, French, and Chinese. The last has two types, the specifications of which are not yet known.

The first nuclear-powered submarine was USS *Nautilus*, commissioned on September 30, 1954, after many years of research and trials which included the construction of a full size section of a submarine with a complete nuclear-power unit in a tank of water. *Nautilus* has been taken out of commission (March 3, 1980) but she will be retained as a museum.

Nuclear-powered submarines are divided into two types: ballistic missile and attack. The former have a displacement of around 7,000 to 20,000 tonnes, such as the American *Ohio* Class of 16,600/18,700t. The latter displace about 2,500 to 6,000t, like the American 6,000/6,900t *Los Angeles* Class.

It should be remembered that the largest submarines in commission during the Second World War had surface displacements of around 3,000t and that the displacements agreed upon at the 1922 Washington Conference were 10,000t, not for submarines but for cruisers. It is thus apparent that the displacement of a 1982 missile-launching submarine is greater than that of a 1922–1940 cruiser and actually double that of Italy's *Montecuccoli* cruisers.

The first United States Navy submarines to be armed with ballistic missiles, the *George Washington* Class (designated *SSBN 598* to *SSBN 602*), were commissioned between December 1959 and March 1961. They displace 6,019/6,888t and have two turbine sets with an overall power of 14,794.5hp (15,000CV) driving a single propeller. The speeds are 20/31 knots and they are armed with sixteen Polaris missiles and six bow torpedo tubes.

They were followed by the five *Ethan Allens* of 1961–1963, the thirty-one *Benjamin Franklins* of 1963–1967, which have sixteen Poseidon as opposed to Polaris missiles, and finally the *Ohios*, of which only the first six of a planned twenty have been commissioned, armed with twenty-four Trident missiles. The *Ohios* displace 16,600/18,700t, have a 59,178hp (60,000CV) turbine power plant and an undisclosed speed, which must certainly be over thirty knots submerged. In addition to their missile complement they have four bow torpedo tubes.

American attack submarines include the early experimental units which were, apart from *Nautilus* (1954), *Seawolf* (1957), the four *Skates* (1957–1959), and *Triton* (1959), still all with a hull tapering at both ends, two propellers, and diving planes either side of the bow.

The first to have a bulbous hull, diving planes either side of the conning tower, and a single propeller were the five *Skipjack* Class of 1959–1961. They displaced 3,075/3,513t and were armed with four torpedo tubes which could also fire anti-submarine missiles. Their speeds were over sixteen/thirty knots.

The latest attack submarines, the forty-unit *Los Angeles* Class (about half of which have already been commissioned, with the remainder either under construction or programmed), displace 6,000/6,900t, about double the *Skipjacks*. They have a 34,520.5–39,452hp (35,000/40,000CV) S6G-type reactor and can reach a submerged speed of over thirty knots. They are armed with four amidships torpedo tubes that can fire conventional and anti-submarine torpedoes as well as anti-submarine SUBROC missiles.

The Russian Navy has more nuclear-powered missile-launching submarines

than the United States. The Russian Navy's first missile launching boats, the *Zulu V* Class, which first launched experimental missiles in September 1955, were conventional rather than nuclear-powered. These submarines were not built as missile launchers but adapted to the purpose by adding two external tubes. These boats are no longer operational.

The twenty *Golf* Class that followed were also conventionally powered by three diesel engines driving three propellers. The *Golfs* were built as missile launchers in 1958–1962, carrying three missile tubes rising through the hull and conning tower. Displacement is 2,300/2,800t, and the power plant develops 5,918–11,836hp (6,000–12,000CV) and speeds of seventeen/fourteen knots. The 22,700 mile range is impressive. Armament consists of three SS-N-4 or SS-N-5 missiles and six torpedo tubes. Eight nuclear-powered *Hotel* Class were similar missile launchers. These first-generation craft, with their weak missile batteries, were followed by the thirty-four *Yankee* Class of 1967–1976, armed with sixteen SS-N-6 missiles with a range of 1,600 nautical miles (about 3,000km). The tubes are positioned in eight pairs amidships, abaft the conning tower. They displace 7,800/9,300t, have a twin-screw 39,452hp (40,000CV) power plant and make thirty knots. In addition to missiles, they carry six torpedo tubes.

Subsequent classes of submarines armed with ballistic missiles and belonging to the *Delta I* and *Delta II* Classes (all built after 1972–1973) have been armed with SS-N-8s, which have a range of 4,200 miles, while the *Delta III*s SS-N-18s have a range of 4,000 miles and a multiple nuclear warhead.

There are twelve *Delta III* submarines, built between 1976 and 1982. They have a displacement of 11,000/13,250t, sixteen missile tubes in eight pairs abaft the conning tower, and six torpedo tubes. The power plant develops 59,178hp (60,000CV) and submerged speed is twenty-four knots.

The very latest units of the *Typhoon* Class have a submerged displacement of about 30,000 tonnes and are armed with twenty of the new multiple warhead SS-N-20s, in ten pairs of tubes before the conning tower. These units are thought to be powered by two nuclear reactors and have two propellers.

The Russian Navy also includes a "cruise-missile"-type of nuclear submarine. The United States Navy experimented with these missiles as early as 1948–1949 on the conventionally powered submarines *Cusk* and *Carbonero*, and later in 1960 on the nuclear-powered *Halibut*, but decided to abandon them in favor of ballistic missiles in 1960.

The cruise-missile series of submarines began with the conversion of at least twelve *Whiskeys* (1957–1962), then five *Echo I*s (1960–1962), twenty-nine *Echo II*s (1963–1967), and sixteen *Julietts* (1961–1969). The *Echo II*s have a displacement of 4,800/5,800t, eight SS-N-3 or SS-N-12 missile tubes and eight torpedo tubes. The nuclear power plant is twin-screw and develops 22,192hp (22,500CV) with a top speed of twenty-five knots. The nuclear-powered *Charlie* and *Papa* Classes are also cruise-missile submarines, firing the shorter-range SS-N-7 or SS-N-9. The *Echo I*s were later converted to attack submarines, their missile tubes being removed.

Russian nuclear-powered attack submarines belong to classes designated *November* (1958-1963), *Victor* (1967-1984), *Alfa* (1967-1982), *Mike* (1984-   ), *Sierra* (1984-   ), and *Akula* (1985-   ).

The six *Victor II* Class, commissioned in 1972, have a displacement of 4,600/5,680t and are armed with eight bow torpedo tubes, which can also fire anti-submarine missiles. These single-screw boats make sixteen/thirty-one knots.

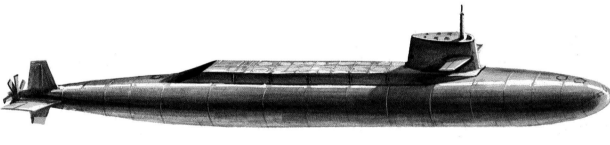

SSBN 598 Washington (United States 1959). One of the first five United States Navy nuclear-powered missile-launching submarines, armed with sixteen Polaris missiles in eight pairs of tubes housed within the hull abaft the conning tower. Apart from the missiles, they are armed with six bow torpedo tubes. The submerged speed is thirty-one knots, eleven knots faster than the twenty knots surface speed.

SSN 586 Triton (United States 1959). A nuclear-powered submarine designed as a "radar picket." In March 1961 she was reclassified as an attack submarine and on May 3, 1969, placed in reserve. She was fitted with six torpedo tubes, four forward and two aft; her surface speed was twenty-seven knots and her submerged speed twenty knots.

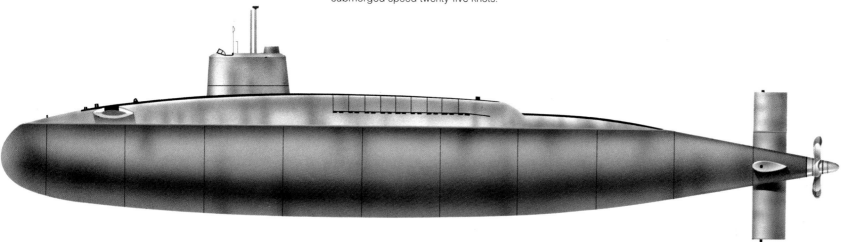

Revenge (Great Britain 1969). A nuclear-powered missile-launching submarine belonging to the first four-unit class of this type. She is armed with sixteen Polaris A3 missiles contained in sixteen tubes inside the hull abaft the conning tower, and six anti-ship bow torpedo tubes. Like other British submarines, the forward diving rudders are on either side of the hull. Surface speed is twenty knots and the submerged speed twenty-five knots.

All Russian nuclear-powered attack and cruise missile submarines still have their diving planes on either side of the hull forward.

The Royal Navy began its nuclear submarine-building program with *Dreadnought*, commissioned in April 1963. She has been followed by five *Valiant* Class, six *Swiftsure*, and four *Resolution (Revenge)* Class (1967–1969). The British boats have also retained their diving planes on either side of the hull forward.

Only the *Resolution* Class is made up of missile-launching submarines: They displace 7,500/8,400t and are armed with sixteen Polaris missiles and six bow torpedo tubes. These single-screw nuclear-powered boats make twenty/twenty-five knots. Britain is expected to build four *Trident* ballistic missile submarines during the next decade, to replace the *Resolutions*.

The two classes of attack submarines, *Swiftsure* and *Valiant*, are similar in that they both have a surface displacement of 4,000t, five or six torpedo tubes, a single-screw nuclear power plant, and a submerged speed of twenty-eight to thirty knots. The *Swiftsures* also have a 3,945hp (4,000CV) auxiliary diesel engine.

The French Navy has built five nuclear-powered ballistic-missile submarines of the *Le Redoutable* Class, commissioned between 1971 and 1980 and all built at the

Cherbourg Naval Yard. A sixth, of modified design, was completed in 1985, and a new class is planned for the 1990s.

These units displace 8,045/8,940t, have sixteen tubes for French-made missiles, positioned in pairs abaft the tower. They also have four torpedo tubes. They have a turbo-electric drive: Instead of driving the propeller, the steam turbines drive generators which power the electric engine which in turn drives the propeller. The main electric engine develops 15,781hp (16,000CV) and gives speeds of twenty/twenty-five knots. The diving rudders are positioned either side of the tower.

France has two nuclear-powered attack submarines in commission under the *Rubis* (formerly *Provence*) Class (1982–1984); three more are under construction. They are armed with anti-ship Exocet missiles, designated SM 39, which are fired from the torpedo tubes and have a range of twenty-seven nautical miles (50km). Displacement is 2,385/2,670t and these units have a single-screw turbo-electric drive like the *Le Redoutable* Class.

The Chinese Navy is thought to have two *Han*-type attack submarines in service, built in 1974–1977, and a few missile-launching units. We have neither technical data nor descriptions of these units.

Rubis (France 1982). A nuclear-powered "fleet" submarine armed not with ballistic missiles, but with torpedoes and Exocet anti-ship missiles. The turbo-electric power plant consists of two turbo-generators and one alternating current motor; it drives a single screw that is coaxial with the hull. These units can make twenty-five knots.

CRUISERS

The development of cruisers from 1860 to the present day

In the section dealing with battleships, we mentioned that the first battleships were the French batteries of the *Dévastation* type, even though this distinction is usually reserved for the two frigates *Gloire* and *Warrior* or 1860. Similarly, we claimed that the first aircraft carrier was Britain's *Furious* of 1917 and that the first real fighting submarine was *Narval* of 1900.

It is more difficult, however, to establish which were the earliest cruisers. Although there is, in fact, no doubt that the first warships to be classified as such were the five *Wampanoag* Class frigates of the U.S. Navy, three of which were completed in 1867–1868, it is not so easy to establish which were the first ships to have carried out the duties of cruisers, even though they were not actually defined as such.

In fact, it is worth noting that many sailing and steam ships of the 1860–1880 period that are treated as cruisers in this chapter were, in their day, classified as screw brigs, screw frigates, and even second-rate battleships or battle cruisers.

The peacetime task of the cruiser in the seventeenth and eighteenth centuries was to voyage to seas far from home, to escort convoys laden with plundered riches and precious goods from the colonies back to their own ports, and to plunder the merchant shipping of other countries. In time of war, cruisers formed reconnaissance squadrons to seek out the enemy and signal his position and strength to the main body of fighting ships following some distance behind.

In 1650 or thereabouts, various navies appointed ships specifically to reconnoitre, protect shipping, and cruise in distant seas, and they were called frigates. These frigates were not necessarily military ships. Some belonged to the British, French, and Dutch India Companies and were used to defend their convoys from privateers and pirates.

The first ships to be classified as cruisers—the six *Wampanoag* Class screw frigates—were specially built to hunt confederate commerce raiders. They would also have been formidable commerce raiders in their own right. The birth of the cruiser is, therefore, not only closely linked to a political event, the American Civil War, but also with a technological factor, the introduction of steam power. In fact, these early cruisers would have had, in the minds of their designers at least, a power plant so powerful that it could raise a speed of eighteen knots.

All the cruisers of the Confederate Navy were very fast, because they had to break the blockade imposed by the Northerners, and were equipped with both sails and steam power. The first cruisers of the French, British, Italian, and other navies also had sails and steam power.

The sails enabled these ships to make long passages, or else stay for long periods at sea in search of the enemy. Steam provided the speed required to reach the ships once sighted and also enabled the ships to make headway when otherwise becalmed, thus making them independent of the elements.

Even before the French, the Royal Navy divided its cruisers into classes based on displacement. For instance, there were first-rate cruisers such as the 5,782t *Inconstant* (1869) and the 6,075t *Shah* (1876), while the 3,078t *Active* and *Volage* (1870) were second-rate ships. A decree promulgated in 1871 classified ships of the French Navy as follows: first-rate cruisers were those with a displacement of over 4,000t, second-rate those between 2,000 and 4,000t and third-rate those below 2,000t. Another yardstick was to classify first-rate cruisers as being two-deckers, in other words, frigates and decked corvettes, second-rate as the larger single-deckers, and third-rate as the smaller ones.

On the basis of the 1871 decree, the first-rate cruisers of the French Navy were the two 5,522t screw frigates *Duquesne* and *Tourville* (1878); the 3,189t corvette

Duguay-Trouin (1879) was second-rate and the 1,643t Corvettes *Eclaireur* and *Rigault de Genouilly* (1879) were third-rate. There were no such distinctions in the Italian Navy and *Colombo* (1876), *Vespucci*, and *Flavio Gioia* (1884) were all classified as scout cruisers.

When cruisers were first being built, iron armor plating began to be fitted to the sides of frigates, ships, and corvettes, thus turning them into armored vessels. This protective concept extended to cruisers and so their sides were also armored, although usually over a smaller area than the armored ships, that is, a belt around the waterline. The resulting "belted" cruisers included the *Shannon* (Great Britain 1877), *Rurik* (Russia 1895), and *Admiral Nakimoff* (Russia 1888). *Shannon* was also classified as a second-rater because she had an armored citadel as well as a belt, whereas the British ships *Northampton* and *Nelson* (1879), classified as "cruiser ironclads," had only their belt and beams armored. The French *Duguesclin*, *Vauban*, *Bayard*, and *Turenne* (1886), with armored belt and deck, received the same classification.

Around 1890, the classification settled at "protected cruisers" and "armored cruisers." These definitions depended on the type of armor: "Protected" cruisers were those with no side armor and just an armored deck, usually in the form of a turtleback, also called a protective deck and "armored" cruisers were those with armor on the sides, or else only around the belt or also in the citadel, as well as on the deck.

The first country to have armored cruisers is usually considered to be Russia with her *General Admiral* and *Duke of Edinburgh* of 1875, which had an armored belt and citadel but no armored deck, whereas the next ship, *Rurik*, also had a protective deck. After the *General Admirals*, it appears that the first cruisers to have vertical and horizontal armor were the four French *Duguesclin* Class of 1886. They had an armored belt and deck. In their day, however, they were designated "cruiser ironclads." These ships might well be considered small or second-rate battleships for overseas service. Only later did a ship combine side and deck armor with high (cruiser) speed and long endurance: the French *Dupuy de Lôme*, commissioned in 1893, which had both an armored belt and a protective deck. A few later armored cruisers also had protection on a second deck, such as Germany's *Fürst Bismarcks* of 1900, France's *Jeanne d'Arc* of 1903, Italy's *Giuseppe Garibaldi* of 1901 and others.

Britain was the first power to build protected cruisers. The prototype was *Esmeralda*, built by Armstrong for the Chilean Navy and commissioned on July 15, 1884. But as early as 1879 the British Navy had commissioned the nine third-rate cruisers of the *Comus* Class, with a 1.4in (38mm) partially armored deck which, although not a true protective deck, fulfilled the same function for the part of the hull over the engine and boiler rooms.

Esmeralda was followed in the United States Navy by the two protected cruisers *Atlanta* and *Boston*, commissioned on July 19, 1886, and provided with a 1.2in (33mm) = thick protective deck. In April 1887, the Italian Navy got her first protected cruiser, *Dogali*, and in August 1889 her second, *Piemonte*, both built by the Armstrong Yard in Britain. The first protected cruiser of the French Navy was *Tage*, originally fitted out with masts and sails, commissioned in December 1890; the first to grace the German Navy was *Gefion* (1894), and both were followed by many others.

Progress in power plant construction led to reciprocating engines being replaced by turbines, first tried out in Britain on the cruiser *Amethyst*, commissioned on March 17, 1905. Regardless of the type of armor, turbine cruisers built between 1905 and 1922 were classified as light cruisers. On the basis of the armor concept, *Amethyst* types would have been protected cruisers since they had only an armored deck, whereas Britain's *Cambrians* of 1916 would have been armored cruisers

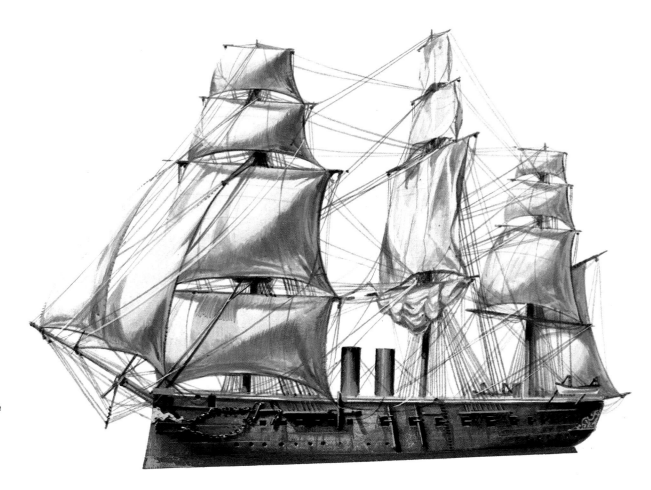

Inconstant (Great Britain 1869). A large frigate, shown here under sail. The jibs, fore- and mizzenmast sails, including the spanker, are "drawing." Those on the mainmast are counterbraced with the course brailed up, as if the ship has just gone about and not yet flattened in all her sails for the new tack.

because they had protection around the belt and on one deck. But by the first two decades of this century, this distinction was no longer drawn and these ships were classified as light cruisers to provide a contrast with battle cruisers.

As the years went by, armored cruisers became increasingly larger, better armed, and faster until eventually they became battle cruisers. The method used to distinguish between armored cruisers and battle cruisers, however, depended solely upon the composition of the armament, just as with dreadnoughts and pre-dreadnoughts.

An armored cruiser like *Léon Gambetta* (1905), for instance, was armed with four 7.6in (194mm) guns in two twin turrets, one forward and one aft, sixteen 6.4in (164mm) guns in six twin turrets and four casemates, and twenty-two small 1.8in (47mm) guns; whereas the battle cruiser *Invincible* (1908) had eight 12in (305mm) and sixteen 4in (102mm) guns, doubling the number and considerably increasing the caliber of the main guns and reducing the number of smaller caliber guns.

In the years between 1905 and 1922, only the German, British, and Japanese navies had battle cruisers. In the American and Russian navies, those on the stocks were not completed.

The Washington Treaty on naval disarmament, signed on February 6, 1922, did away with further battle cruiser construction and set the maximum displacement for cruisers at 10,000t standard and gun caliber at 8in (203mm), much lower than the displacement and gun caliber of the First World War battle cruisers. The London Conference of February–April 1930 created a new category of cruiser: the light cruiser, which could be armed with guns of a maximum caliber of 6.1in (155mm). Heavy cruisers were those armed with up to 8in (203mm) guns and displacing 10,000t.

Some of the most outstanding 10,000t cruisers were Britain's *Kents* (1928), Italy's *Trentos* (1929), France's *Duquesnes* (1928) and *Algérie* (1934), Germany's *Admiral Hippers* (1939), Spain's *Canarias* types (1936), Japan's *Tones* (1938), and the U.S. *New Orleans* (1934 –1937).

Examples of light cruisers with a standard displacement of 7,000t and armed with eight 6in (152mm) guns were France's *La Galissonières* (1935), Britain's *Leanders* (1933), Spain's *Principe Alfonsos* (1927), Italy's *Montecuccolis* (1935), Australia's *Sydney* (1935), and the U.S. *Brooklyn* (1938–1939). This shows that, although the Washington Treaty applied only to the signatory powers, (the United States, Great Britain, Japan, France, and Italy) the navies of other countries, such as Spain, also abided by what was agreed upon at the Conference.

Before and during the Second World War, advances in naval aviation led to the building of a special type of cruiser carrying chiefly anti-aircraft armament, in the form of a large number of small caliber rapid firing guns. Examples of anti-aircraft cruisers were Britain's *Didos* (1940), armed with ten 5.25in (133mm) guns;

America's *Atlantas* (1941), armed with twelve to sixteen 5in (127mm) guns; and, had they been completed, Italy's *Etna* and *Vesuvio*, armed with six 5.3in (135mm) guns. Britain and Japan also converted earlier, obsolete, light cruisers into anti-aircraft ships. It was quite standard for cruisers built between 1922 and 1945 to have catapults and one or two reconnaissance seaplanes.

After the Second World War, cruisers had shed their role as scouts and fast attack ships (taken on by aircraft), and given up their job of attacking merchant shipping (taken on by submarines); it was now their lot to act just as an anti-aircraft and anti-submarine force, especially after the introduction of missiles as a replacement for guns.

The changeover from guns to missiles began in 1953–1954; initially launchers replaced some or all of the gun turrets on existing ships. The first units to have their after turrets replaced by missile launchers were the American heavy cruisers *Canberra* and *Boston*, but they still retained six 8in (203mm) guns in two triple turrets forward as well as their anti-aircraft armament of ten 5in (127mm) and eight 3in (76mm) guns. The six light cruisers of the *Galveston* Class, the Italian cruiser *Giuseppe Garibaldi*, and the Dutch *De Zeven Provincien* also received a similar modification. The American cruisers *Albany*, *Chicago*, and *Columbus*, however, had both their forward and after turrets replaced by missile launchers.

Ships built after 1958–1959 no longer had a main armament made up of guns, but primarily of missiles, plus a few small-caliber anti-ship and anti-aircraft pieces, like America's *Long Beach* (1961), the first nuclear-powered cruiser, and subsequent American units, and Russia's *Kynda* Class cruisers as well as those of more recent construction.

The latest development in cruiser armament has been the introduction of the helicopter as an anti-submarine weapon. This has given rise to the helicopter cruiser.

Just as the cruisers of 1922–1945 had catapults to launch their reconnaissance seaplanes, so those built after 1960 were fitted with small flight decks from which the helicopters could land and take off.

Some of the first cruisers to have helicopter flight decks were the United States Navy *Galvestons*—formerly *Cleveland* Class light cruisers commissioned in 1942–1943 and, between 1956 and 1960, converted into missile cruisers. During this conversion, units that had been fitted with a stern catapult had it removed to install a small helicopter deck, the helicopters being kept in a hangar below. The French cruiser *Colbert* (1959), converted to a missile cruiser in 1970 –1972, and the American *Albanys* (1946), converted in 1959–1962, were also equipped with a helicopter without any drastic alterations having to be made.

Two of Britain's three *Tigers* (1959–1961) were converted into helicopter carriers between 1965 and 1972 and had a large after superstructure used as a hangar and a flight deck right aft, like almost all the cruisers designed as helicopter carriers. A similar hangar and takeoff pad also appeared on Britain's *Devonshire* Class (1962–1964), Italy's *Andrea Doria* types (1964), America's *Belknaps* (1964) and *Truxtun* (1967), and Russia's *Kresta* Class (1967).

The original complement of one or two helicopters was then increased. Italy's *Vittorio Veneto*, for instance, has nine; her hangar is thus very large and the takeoff pad resembles a flight deck. Those units that currently have the largest flight deck are Russia's *Moskva* and *Leningrad* (1968–1969) and can be described as being divided in half: the forward part being a cruiser and the after part a helicopter carrier, completely taken up by a flight deck.

Russia's *Kiev* Class cruisers represent a halfway house between helicopter cruiser and aircraft carrier. They have an angled deck extending from the stern to opposite the island and naval armament at the forward end. These ships, displacing about 36,000 tons (std), are designed to operate with V/STOL aircraft as well as helicopters.

Cruiser power plants and armament

Cruiser power plants have developed in parallel with those of battleships. In the period of mixed sail and steam propulsion they were horizontal- or oscillating-cylinder engines fed by coal-fired box-shaped boilers. Protected and armored cruisers used vertical double or triple-expansion reciprocating engines until 1905–1910.

Examples of cruisers with reciprocating engines were Russia's *Rurik* (1895) and America's *Brooklyn* (1896) which had two engines for each of the two screws, that is, four engines for two screws, and made 18.8 and twenty-one knots respectively.

Protected cruisers usually had only two screws whereas a large number of larger and more heavily armed armored cruisers were powered by three reciprocating engines on three screws. Examples were Germany's *Fürst Bismarck* (1900), *Scharnhorst* and *Gneisenau* (1907), *Blücher* (1909), and France's *Dupuy de Lôme* (1893), *Jeanne d'Arc* (1903), and *Léon Gambetta* (1905), and Russia's *Gromovoi* and *Aurora* (both 1901), although the latter was a protected cruiser.

When reciprocating engines were replaced by turbines, Britain's first light cruiser, *Amethyst* (1905), had one full-speed turbine and one cruising-speed turbine for each shaft, in other words, four turbines for two screws. The *Frobishers* (1917) also had one full-speed and one cruising-speed turbine for each shaft, in other words, eight turbines for four screws. Other cruisers of this period also had four screws, such as Germany's *Kolbergs* (1909), America's *Omahas* (1923), China's *Chao-Hos* (1912), Australia's *Melbournes* (1913), and Russia's *Admiral Greigs* (1913). Brazil's *Bahia*-type light cruisers (1910), Greece's *Helli* (1913), and Holland's *Java* (1925), however, had three screws driven by three turbines. All battle cruisers had four screws.

The interwar treaty-type cruisers all had reduction geared turbines, supplied by oil-fired boilers. Heavy cruisers usually had four screws but there were some with two, such as Italy's *Zara* types (1931). Light cruisers with a small displacement had two screws but there were also quite a few with four, in particular the American and British with displacements of 8,000 –14,000 tonnes. Triple-screw power plants were not commonly used on cruisers between 1922 and 1945: Rare examples were Germany's *Admiral Hipper* types of 1939 and Japan's *Yubari* of 1923.

Some cruisers of this period had a mixed diesel and steam turbine power plant; the diesel would provide increased endurance, just as the sails had on the old sail–steam cruisers. The Germans were the first to try out this type of system, having already used diesel engines on their *Deutschland*-type battleships. The three *Koenigsberg*-type light cruisers of 1929 had twin screws that could be powered by two reduction-geared turbine units at full speed and two diesel engines at economic speed. This was not totally satisfactory, so on the next cruiser, *Nürnberg*, three screws were fitted, the side ones being powered by geared turbines and the middle one by two diesel engines via a reduction and coupling gear unit. Russia's *Kirov* (1939) and *Chapaev*-type (1948–1950) cruisers were fitted with two steam turbines and two diesel engines, to drive two screws.

After 1960–1961, cruiser power plants underwent an important change, with steam turbines with reduction and coupling gears being replaced on newly built ships by gas turbines.

In the Royal Navy there has been only one example of combined steam and gas turbines — on the eight *Devonshire* Class, commissioned in 1962–1964. They had two steam turbine units and four gas turbines to drive two screws.

Gas turbines are installed in Britain's three *Invincibles* (actually helicopter carriers), (1980), Italy's *Garibaldi* (1983), and Russia's eight *Nikolayev* types (1973).

From 1961 to the present day, the United States Navy has commissioned nine nuclear-powered cruisers, the first three being of an experimental type, with the latest six making up two classes of units designed to operate with aircraft carriers, with the same type of propulsion. The only other nuclear-powered cruisers are the Soviet *Kirovs*, which are unique in having a conventional booster plant for high speed.

Cruiser armament has also developed in parallel with that of battleships, but because the cruiser category has continued to exist in the post-war period, their armament has developed further in the direction of missile and electronic weaponry, both anti-ship and anti-submarine. Unlike battleships, cruisers armed with torpedo tubes date back to around 1870. Britain's first-rate cruisers *Inconstant, Shah,* and *Shannon* of 1870–1877, for instance, along with the second-raters *Boadicea, Bacchante,* and *Euryalus* of 1878, all had one torpedo tube, whereas their French contemporaries, like the two *Eclaireur* (1879) and four *Duguesclin* (1886) type cruisers had just towed torpedoes. By contrast, Russia's *Admiral Nakimoff* and *Rurik* (1895) had four and six torpedo tubes respectively. Torpedo tubes made up part of the armament of all armored and protected cruisers. On such ships the tubes were usually fixed, underwater, and positioned two either side amidships, or one forward and one aft. Only on light cruisers—in other words, from 1910–1912 onwards—were torpedo tubes positioned on the main deck, like Britain's *Cambrians* (1916) and *Frobishers* (1924), which had two twin torpedo tubes either side plus two more fixed underwater tubes, one forward and one aft.

Some ships had four torpedo tubes in two twin trainable groups on deck; these included the three Austrian *Saida*-type light cruisers of 1914 and the ten American *Omaha* types of 1923. Battle cruisers had fixed tubes, however, like Britain's 1916 *Repulse* types, later replaced by four trainable twin groups, two either side amidships.

The treaty-type cruisers were nearly all well endowed with torpedo tubes, usually six in two triple groups, like Britain's 1935 *Arethusa,* 1940 *Dido,* and 1940 *Fiji* types. Germany's *Koenigsberg* (1929), *Nürnberg* (1935), and *Admiral Hipper* (1939) types, however, had twelve torpedo tubes in two triple groups either side aft. Spain's *Principe Alfonso* and *Canarias* also had twelve torpedo tubes in four triple groups. By contrast, Italy's *Trentos* (1929), Japan's *Nachis* (1928), and *Mogamis* had eight and twelve torpedo tubes respectively. All were fixed, and athwartships with half firing from one side and half from the other. Quadruple trainable torpedo tubes were installed on Britain's *Leanders* of 1933 in two groups placed on either side and in a similar position on America's *Atlantas* of 1941. Japan's *Aganos* of 1942, on the other hand, had two quadruple groups on the centerline. Russia's *Sverdlovs* (1955–1959) had ten torpedo tubes in two twin sets on the centerline. Some cruisers were not fitted with torpedo tubes, like Italy's *Zaras* (1931) and America's *Portlands* (1933), *New Orleans* (1934), *Brooklyns* (1938), *Clevelands* (1941), *Baltimores* (1943), *Worcesters* (1948), and *Des Moines* (1948–1949).

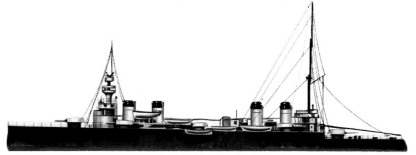

Léon Gambetta (France 1905). An early twentieth-century steam-powered armored cruiser. The four funnels are paired off and spaced well apart, indicating that the engine rooms are amidships between the boiler rooms. She was used in the southern Adriatic during the First World War and was sunk by a submarine on April 26, 1915.

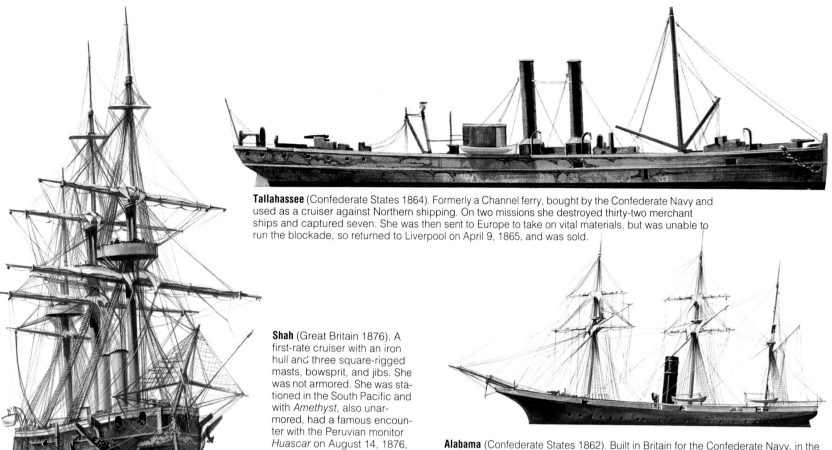

Tallahassee (Confederate States 1864). Formerly a Channel ferry, bought by the Confederate Navy and used as a cruiser against Northern shipping. On two missions she destroyed thirty-two merchant ships and captured seven. She was then sent to Europe to take on vital materials, but was unable to run the blockade, so returned to Liverpool on April 9, 1865, and was sold.

Shah (Great Britain 1876). A first-rate cruiser with an iron hull and three square-rigged masts, bowsprit, and jibs. She was not armored. She was stationed in the South Pacific and with *Amethyst,* also unarmored, had a famous encounter with the Peruvian monitor *Huascar* on August 14, 1876, putting the latter in a bad way even though she was armored and had two 300-pounders in a revolving turret.

Alabama (Confederate States 1862). Built in Britain for the Confederate Navy, in the space of two weeks cruising in the central Atlantic, she captured twenty ships either belonging to the Northerners or headed for the Northern States. She then operated in the Indian Ocean. She was sunk by the federal corvette *Kearsage* on July 19, 1864, as she left Cherbourg Harbor (France), where she had gone for a refit.

After the Second World War, the anti-ship torpedo disappeared from cruiser armament, but ships built after 1960 have been equipped with special anti-submarine torpedoes, such as Italy's *Dorias* (1964) and *Vittorio Venetos* (1969) with six torpedoes in two triple launchers and America's *Albanys*, after their 1962 refit, then *Long Beach*, the *Leahys*, *Belknaps*, *Bainbridge,* and the more recent ones. The Russian *Kynda* (1962), *Kresta I* (1967), *Kresta II* (1972–1977), *Nikolayev* (1973–1980), *Moskva* (1968), *Kiev* (1975), and *Kirov* (1978) Classes are equipped with ten anti-submarine torpedo tubes in two five-tube mountings.

Guns, which had been the major weapons of cruisers of all types up to 1962, were then replaced by missile launchers, usually for anti-aircraft (surface-to-air) missiles in reloadable single or twin launchers (with twenty to eighty missiles per launcher; the anti-ship launchers generally can be reloaded only in port. In some cases, anti-ship missiles can be fired from the anti-aircraft launchers), but also anti-ship (surface-to-surface) missiles, typically in two- or four-tube cannister launchers, and by anti-submarine missiles such as the American ASROC, the British Ikara, the French Malafon, and the Soviet SS-N-14.

Units built after 1960 have been equipped with the helicopter as an anti-submarine weapon as well as with sonar, an electronic device to detect submerged submarines by the emission of sound waves.

Mixed propulsion cruisers from 1860 to 1890

As already mentioned, the first cruisers to be so defined were ships belonging to the navies of the two opposing sides in the American Civil War. Some, like the Confederate ships *Alabama* and *Tallahassee,* were merchant ships armed with a few guns, designed primarily with speed in mind. Whereas *Alabama,* which was fitted with masts and sails, could make thirteen knots, *Tallahassee,* with no masts and sails, could make seventeen knots, but she had the then serious drawback of being able to stay at sea only for as long as her fuel supply lasted. The Federal *Wampanoag* screw frigates were required to make eighteen knots. Two of them, *Neshaminy,* and *Pompanoosuc,* were not completed. They generally failed to make

their designed speed. *Madawaska,* the first to be commissioned in 1867, could manage just 12.7 knots. *Wampanoag,* the fastest, made 17.5 on her trials.

British first-rate cruisers, such as *Inconstant* (1869) and *Shah* (1876), made 16.5 knots. Both were fully rigged in that they had three square-rigged masts, bowsprit and jibs, and they had an iron, as opposed to wooden, hull. *Inconstant* had ten 9in (229mm) and six 7in (178mm) guns, all muzzle-loading, positioned on the gallery deck in broadsides. She was the first cruiser to have a torpedo tube, which was Austrian-built and probably positioned underwater. *Shah* had two 9in (229mm), sixteen 7in (178mm) and eight sixty-four-pounders. She, too, had a torpedo tube.

Second-rate British cruisers, like *Volage* and *Active* of 1870, as well as the three *Boadiceas* of 1878, had iron hulls, made fourteen to fifteen knots, and were armed with six to fourteen 7in (178mm) guns plus two to four sixty-four-pounders. Only the *Boadiceas* had torpedo tubes.

The French Navy, which regarded itself as a rival to the Royal Navy even after the Napoleonic Wars, built two first-rate iron-hulled cruisers: *Duquesne* and *Tourville* (1878) that made seventeen knots, and the second-rate cruiser *Duguay-Trouin* (1879) that made sixteen. All three were single-screw ships but had two engines apiece. The two *Duquesnes* had seven 7.4in (19cm) guns, comparable to the British 7in (178mm) ones, and fourteen 5.5in (14cm) guns, comparable to the British sixty-four-pounders. *Duguay-Trouin* had ten guns, half of one caliber and half of the other. So the French ships were a little faster but less well-armed than the British ones and had no torpedo tubes.

It was common for iron-hulled cruisers, both British and French, but also those of other navies (such as Russia's *General Admiral* type, Holland's *Atjehs*, and others) to have their underbody (the part underwater) completely covered by one, or even two, layers of planking, that were then sheathed in copper. The reason for this is that iron hulls are more likely to foul up than wooden ones. This is quite a serious drawback for ships on long cruises, hence the copper sheathing which does not foul up so easily. This sheathing cannot be applied directly on to the iron, which would corrode as a result of electric phenomena. This is why the two metals must be separated by wooden planking.

The three *Villars* types and the two *Eclaireurs* were wooden-hulled French cruisers of 1881 and 1879 respectively, built after the above-mentioned iron-hulled ones. Both the second-rate *Villars* types and the third-rate *Eclaireurs* had a ram, made fifteen knots, and were armed with fifteen and eight 5.5in (140mm) guns respectively. These pieces were on the main deck since both ships were corvettes. Britain's *Inconstant* and *Shah* were frigates, like the French *Duquesnes*. The *Boadicea*s were decked corvettes so their guns were on a covered deck.

Ships of this period that were not officially classified as cruisers included Britain's *Shannon* (1877), a second-rate ironclad, the French *Victorieuse* types (1877), also classified as second-rate ironclads, and the *Duguesclin*s (1886), classified as cruiser ironclads.

The *Shannon* and *Duguesclin* types had iron hulls, covered in wood, and sheathed in copper. By contrast, *Victorieuse, Triomphante,* and *La Galissonière* had wooden hulls but were provided with a 5.9in (150mm) thick belt, 4.7in (120mm) armor on the citadel, and an iron main deck. *Shannon* had a 9in (229mm) belt, 10–8in (254–203mm) armor on the citadel, and 1.4in (38mm) on the main deck. The *Duguesclin*s had a 10in (254mm) belt and 1.9in (50mm) gallery deck. All had a ram. They were much slower than the cruisers described above because they could only make 12.6–14.0 knots. *Shannon* had a single screw powered by two engines. They were, however, more heavily armed: *Shannon* had fifteen guns, two of which were 10in (254mm); the *Victorieuse* types had thirteen, six of which were 9.4in (240mm), and the *Duguesclin*s had eleven, four of which were 9.4in (240mm) guns in individual barbettes on the main deck.

Italy's *Amerigo Vespucci* and *Flavio Gioia* scout cruisers of 1884 were built on the basis of experience gained from Italy's first cruiser, *Colombo* of 1876. They differed from the prototype in that they had an iron rather than a wooden hull and made fourteen knots as opposed to seventeen. These two-deckers had a modest armament of eight 5.9in (150mm) guns on the gallery deck and three 2.9in (75mm) guns on the main deck.

Japan's screw frigates *Yamato, Musashi,* and *Katsuragi* of 1887–1888 had just one deck and a composite hull, that is, iron framework and wooden planking. In 1900 they were modernized by removing their sails and changing their armament, after which they were classified as gunboats.

Russia's *Rurik,* built between 1890 and 1895, was a cruiser with masts and sails, as well as the features of a typical armored cruiser. She had an iron hull with a ram, a 10in (254mm) belt, and a 1.9–2.7in (50–70mm) protective deck. She was armed with four 8in (203mm) guns in single mounts, symmetrically placed either side of the main deck, and sixteen 6in (152mm) guns on the gallery deck, eight per side, plus six 1.8in (47mm) and twelve 1.4in (37mm) guns on the main deck. The armament was rounded off by six fixed above-water torpedo tubes, one forward, one aft, and two either side on the main deck. *Rurik* had four reciprocating engines on two screws and made 18.8 knots.

Other examples of twin-screw cruisers of this period were Russia's *Admiral Nakimoff* types of 1888 and Britain's *Northampton*s of 1879.

Armored cruisers from 1890 to 1910

The elimination of masts and sails as a means of propulsion affected not only the hull profile, but also, and above all, armament positions. As occurred on armored ships, there was no clear-cut move involving all guns in the broadsides position being moved to turrets or casemates. One of the most interesting examples of gun positioning during the transitional phase came in the shape of Germany's four *Sachsen* Class cruisers, officially classified as second-rate armored corvettes; because of their 7,400t displacement and fourteen-knot top speed, they can be legitimately included as armored cruisers. These ships had two 10.2in (260mm) guns in a barbette forward and four (also 10.2in [260mm]) on each wing of the armored citadel amidships. Armored cruisers, all built between 1890 and 1905, usually had armament similar to that of pre-dreadnought battleships, namely guns in turrets or casemates. The first ship to be regarded as a true armored cruiser, the French *Dupuy de Lôme* (built in 1888–1893), had two 7.6in (194mm) guns in two symmetrically placed barbettes amidships and six 6.4in (154mm) guns in turrets, three forward and three aft, one turret on the centerline right aft (or forward) and the other two farther in abreast.

Like battleships of the same period, armored cruisers also usually had a small number of main-caliber guns in single or twin turrets fore and aft and a large number of middle-caliber guns in casemates, both on the gallery deck and in the superstructure on deck.

Austria's *Kaiserin und Koenigin Maria Theresia* of 1895 had two 9.4in (240mm) guns in two barbettes fore and aft and eight 5.9in (150mm) guns in casemates, four in the superstructure and four on the gallery deck. Chile's armored cruiser *Esmeralda II* of 1897 had a similar layout with two 8in (203mm) guns in shielded emplacements, one forward and one aft, and sixteen 6in (152mm) guns, twelve of which were on either side of the main deck and four on the superstructure. The French *Jeanne d'Arc* was another ship with two large-caliber guns in single turrets fore and aft. She had two 7.6in (194mm) guns in two turrets at each

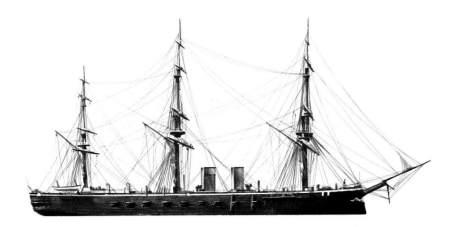

Inconstant (Great Britain 1869). A first-rate iron-hulled cruiser. She can also be classified as a frigate, as she had two decks and two gun batteries. One hundred eighty tonnes of ballast were taken on, since she was not very stable under sail.

Volage (Great Britain 1870). A second-rate cruiser with a displacement of 3,078 tonnes, less than *Inconstant* (5,782t) and *Shah* (6,075t). She was a single-decker, in other words a corvette, and her armament of eight 7in (178mm) and four 6.2in (160mm) guns were positioned on either side of the main deck. Under steam she made just over fifteen knots.

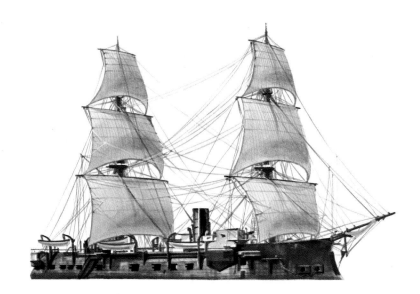

Duguesclin (France 1886). Classified as a cruiser ironclad, she had brig sails on two square-rigged masts. The iron hull had 10in (254mm) thick armor. She was armed with four 9.4in (240mm) guns in individual barbettes on the main deck.

Duguay-Trouin (France 1879). A second-rate cruiser with an iron hull covered in copper-sheathed planking. She was unarmored but had a sizeable ram. She was a single-decker, all ten guns being on the main deck, and an extremely sea-worthy ship. Under steam she made sixteen knots.

Eclaireur (France 1879). A third-rate cruiser, smaller than *Duguay-Trouin*, displacing 1,643t. She had a wooden rather than an iron hull with a pointed iron ram, one deck, and eight 5.5in (140mm) guns, all on the main deck on trainable mounts. Under steam she made fifteen knots.

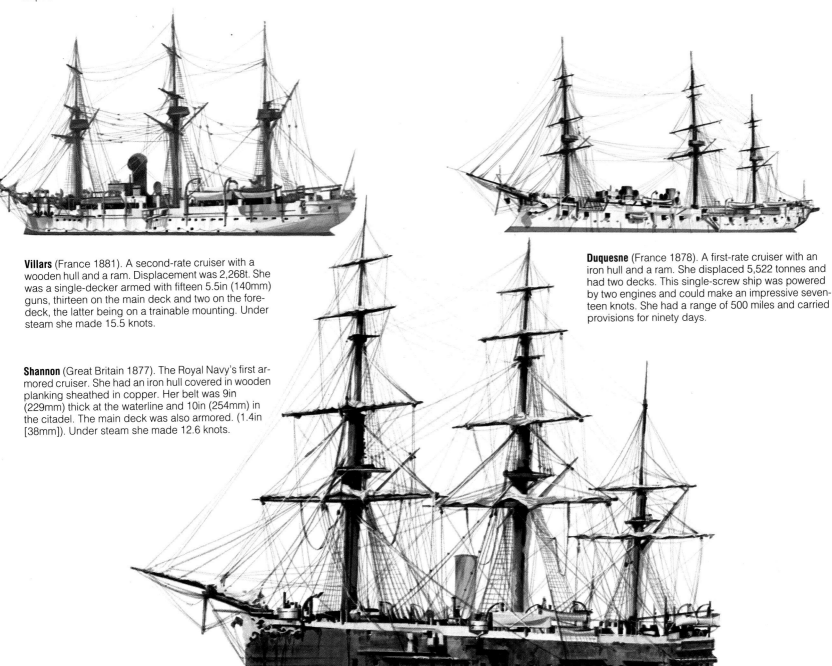

Villars (France 1881). A second-rate cruiser with a wooden hull and a ram. Displacement was 2,268t. She was a single-decker armed with fifteen 5.5in (140mm) guns, thirteen on the main deck and two on the fore-deck, the latter being on a trainable mounting. Under steam she made 15.5 knots.

Shannon (Great Britain 1877). The Royal Navy's first ar-mored cruiser. She had an iron hull covered in wooden planking sheathed in copper. Her belt was 9in (229mm) thick at the waterline and 10in (254mm) in the citadel. The main deck was also armored. (1.4in [38mm]). Under steam she made 12.6 knots.

Duquesne (France 1878). A first-rate cruiser with an iron hull and a ram. She displaced 5,522 tonnes and had two decks. This single-screw ship was powered by two engines and could make an impressive seven-teen knots. She had a range of 500 miles and carried provisions for ninety days.

151

Amerigo Vespucci (Italy 1884). An iron-hulled cruiser with an armored turtle back deck and cellular subdivision, thus warranting the classification of protected cruiser. Although she was a two-decker, the lower deck had no guns, these all being on the main deck. In 1893 she was converted into a training ship and served as such until 1927. She was stricken in 1928.

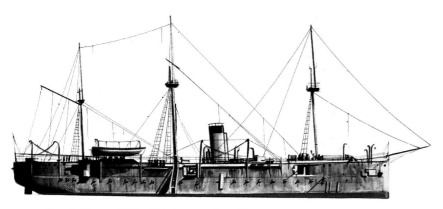

Yamato (Japan 1887). A third-rate cruiser with a composite hull and a displacement of 1,478t. She was also classified as a screw corvette. She had had square-rigged main and foremasts and a spanker on the mizzen, but is shown here after modifications made in 1900, when masts and sails were removed. She had one deck with a quarter- and foredeck. Speed was thirteen knots.

Rurik (Russia 1895). An armored cruiser with an iron hull, 10in (254mm) side armor and a 1.9–2.7in ((50–70mm) armored deck. She displaced 10,920t and was therefore very big and very well-armed. She had four 8in (203mm) guns on four side platforms on the main deck and sixteen 6in (152mm) pieces on the gun deck, as well as six 1.8in (47mm) and twelve 1.4in (37mm) guns on the main deck. She had six torpedo tubes. This twin-screw ship had four engines and made almost nineteen knots.

end and fourteen 5.4in (139mm) guns in casemates, eight in the citadel and six on the upper deck.

Italy's armored cruisers, *Garibaldi, Varese,* and *Ferruccio* of 1901, had a similar layout. They had one 10in (254mm) gun in a single turret forward and two 8in (203mm) guns in a twin turret aft, plus fourteen 6in (152mm) guns, ten of which were in casemates on the gallery deck and four on the main deck.

Germany's *Fürst Bismarck* of 1900 had her armament in two twin turrets, one forward and one aft. She had four 9.4in (240mm) guns in these turrets, plus twelve 5.9in (150mm) guns, six of which were in casemates and six in single turrets on the main deck. The fore and aft twin turret layout also appeared on Britain's *Minotaur, Defence,* and *Shannon* of 1908, with four 9in (230mm) guns and ten 7.4in (190mm) in single turrets on the main deck, and on the French *Léon Gambetta* types of 1905, with four 7.6in (194mm) guns and sixteen 6.4in (164mm) in six twin turrets and four casemates.

Main armament in four turrets was not a common layout on armored cruisers. It appeared on Chile's *Generale O'Higgins* of 1898, with four single 8in (203mm) guns in four single turrets, one forward and one aft on the centerline, and two on either side amidships, as well as ten 6in (152mm) guns, six of which were in casemates and four in turrets. Sweden's *Fylgia* (1906) and America's *Brooklyn* (1896) had four double turrets in a similar layout.

The Italian cruiser *Vettor Pisani* (1898), the Russian *Gromovoi* (1901), and the three American *Charleston* Class (1906) had a special gun layout. *Pisani* had twelve 6in (152mm) guns, six each side; *Gromovoi* had sixteen 6in (152mm) guns, seven each side in casemates, plus one forward and one aft, as well as four 8in (203mm) guns on the citadel wings; *Charleston* had fourteen 6in (152mm) guns, six each side in casemates, plus one forward and one aft.

Italy's *San Giorgio* and *San Marco* (1910) and Japan's *Ibuki* and *Kumara* (1909) had their main armament of 10in (254mm) and 12in (305mm) guns respectively in two twin turrets, one forward and one aft, and their secondary armament of 7.4in (190mm) and 8in (203mm) guns, respectively, in four twin turrets symmetrically placed amidships. As previously mentioned, due to the caliber of their guns, the two *Ibukis* were also classified as battle cruisers, but since they had only four large-caliber guns, it would be more correct to classify them as armored cruisers. Germany's *Blücher* (1909) was another cruiser that could have been classified as a battle cruiser because of the number of her large-caliber guns. She was armed with twelve 8.2in (210mm) guns in six twin turrets positioned like those of the *San Giorgios* and *Ibukis*. Since the caliber of these guns was only 8.2in (210mm), however, rather than the 12in (305mm), 13.5in (343mm), or 15in (381mm) of the battle cruisers, *Blücher* has been placed in the lower category.

All armored cruisers were usually equipped with fixed underwater torpedo tubes, varying in number from two to six. All armored cruisers were also well protected. Vertical protection covered the belt, sides, citadels, and beams, and was added round the gun turrets and the bridge turret masts. Horizontal protection, still in the form of a protective deck, could also extend to the main deck and citadel roof.

Germany's *Scharnhorst* and *Gneisenau* had 5.9in (150mm) on the belt, 5.9in (150mm) on the citadel, 2.3–1.5in (60–40mm) on the protective deck, 6.6in (170mm) on the turrets, and 7.8in (200mm) on the turret mast. Italy's *Vettor Pisani* had a 4.3–5.9in (110–150mm) belt, 5.9in (150mm) citadel, 1.4–0.8in (37–22mm) protective belt, and 5.9in (150mm) bridge. The two *San Giorgios* had almost the same protection as a battleship would have had and had horizontal protection on all three decks. The belt was 7.8in (200mm), citadel 7in (180mm), protective deck 1.5–1.1in (40fs1–30mm), gallery deck 0.3–1.3in (10–35mm), main deck 1.7–0.3in (45–10mm), turrets 7in (180mm), and conning tower 9.8in (250mm). This was considerably more than the armor on the *Ibukis*, which had a 7in (178mm) belt and 8in (203mm) conning tower. Germany's *Blücher* was also quite well protected. She had a 7.3–9in (180–100mm) belt, 5.5in (140mm) citadel, 1.9–2.7in (50–70mm) protective deck, 7in (180mm) turrets, and a 9.8in (250mm) conning tower. Other cruisers usually had side armor consisting of just a belt, and horizontal armor only on the protective deck.

On all ships using coal as fuel, the side bunkers served partly for protection, both against gun shells and underwater weapons. In fact, when full, the bunkers above the waterline and behind the side armor provided an extra buffer against shells and reduced the damage caused by fragmentation bombs. The bunkers below the waterline could help to reduce flooding caused by torpedoes.

The underwater protection of cruisers was proved to be almost useless from the very beginning of the First World War in a famous incident involving the sinking of the three British armored cruisers *Hogue, Aboukir,* and *Cressy* by torpedoes from the German submarine *U 9* in just thirty minutes on the night of September 22, 1914.

Almost all armored cruisers had coal-fired boilers and reciprocating engines. One exception was *San Marco*, which, although the sister ship of *San Giorgio*, had a power plant of four turbines driving four screws, as opposed to two reciprocating engines for two screws. Japan's *Ibuki* and *Kurama*, which were crosses between armored cruisers and battle cruisers, had two turbines for two screws.

Sachsen (Germany 1878). Officially classified as a second-rate armored corvette, she can be regarded as an armored cruiser. Although built before *Rurik,* she had no rigged masts, only a pole aft. The power plant was two reciprocating engines driving two screws, and the top speed was fourteen knots.

Garibaldi (Italy 1901). An armored cruiser belonging to a class of three units. She had 5.9in (150mm) armor on her belt and in the citadel, and 1.4in (38mm) on the protective deck. She was a twin-screw ship and made 19.7 knots. At the beginning of the First World War she was torpedoed by the German submarine *U 4* and sank on July 18, 1915.

Kaiserin und Koenigin Maria Theresia (Austria 1895). An armored cruiser with a steel hull and a ram. She had two funnels amidships and an armored bridge. Protection was limited to the middle of the belt and a protective deck. She is one of the few cruisers to have a cellular raft. She had twin screws and made 19.4 knots.

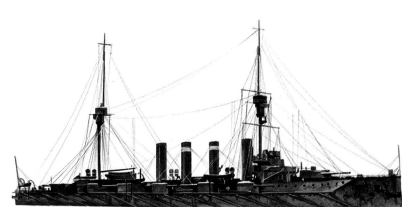

Minotaur (Great Britain 1908). Together with *Defence* and *Shannon, Minotaur* formed the first class of Royal Navy cruisers with twin gun turrets. Note the four funnels for the twenty-four boilers, some coal-fired and some oil-fired. She had twin screws and made twenty-three knots. She was assigned to the Far East Squadron, then, on returning to Britain, saw service in the First World War. She was stricken in 1920.

Dupuy de Lôme (France 1893). Regarded as the first modern armored cruiser. Belt armor was 3.6in (92mm) and the protective deck 2.1in (55mm). The two 7.6in (194mm) guns were in two turrets on either beam between the two funnels and almost hidden from view. There were six 6.1in (155mm) turrets in two groups of three at the bow and stern. The first French three-screw ship, she made 20.5 knots.

Fürst Bismarck (Germany 1900). An armored cruiser with a belt and two armored decks: the main deck 1.1–1.9in (30–50mm) and the protective deck 0.7–1.9in (20–50mm). She had two funnels and two masts and, like many German ships, three screws, one central and one on either side.

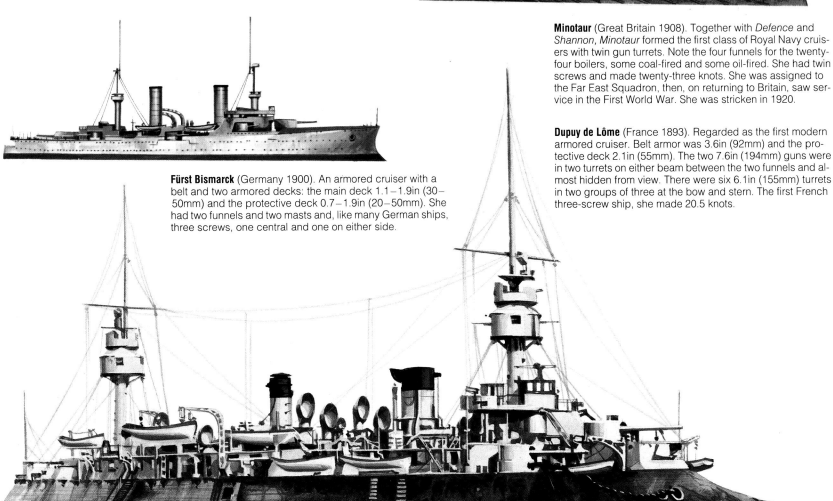

Esmeralda (Chile 1897). An armored cruiser built in Britain for the Chilean Navy, not to be confused with an earlier *Esmeralda*, a protected cruiser. Side armor was an amidships strip incorporated into a cellular structure. She was less well-armed than *O'Higgins*, had twin-screws, and made 22.25 knots.

Generale O'Higgins (Chile 1898). An armored cruiser built in Britain for the Chilean Navy. She had a steel hull covered in wooden planking sheathed in copper and fitted with a ram at the bow. This twin-screw ship made 21.2 knots.

Charleston (United States 1906). A cruiser with 4in (102mm)-thick belt armor and 3–4in (76–102mm) on the protective deck. She had two screws and made 21.5 knots.

Coal-fired boilers required at least two funnels and they had to be very tall to improve the draught and, thus, the combustion in the furnaces. There were four funnels on Britain's *Cressy* types (1901), Russia's *Gromovoi* (1901), and America's *Charleston*s (1906). Sweden's *Fylgia* (1906), America's *Brooklyn*, Chile's *O'Higgins* (1898), and Japan's two *Ibuki*s (1909) had three funnels. The prize for the highest number of funnels went to France's *Jeanne d'Arc* (1903), which had six. The reason for all these funnels was because of the large number of boilers: as many as thirty on the British *Cressy*s, twenty-four on the *Minotaur*s, forty-eight on the French *Jeanne d'Arc*, twenty-four on the Italian *Garibaldi* types, thirty on the Russian *Gromovoi* and Chilean *O'Higgins*, and twenty-eight on the American *Brooklyn* types. Although the *Ibuki*s developed 24,657.5hp (25,000CV), they had only eighteen boilers that, however, could burn both coal and oil.

Cressy (Great Britain 1901). One of a class of six armored cruisers displacing 12,000 tonnes, almost as much as contemporary battleships. This twin-screw ship had thirty boilers. Together with *Hogue* and *Aboukir* of the same class, she was sunk by the German submarine *U 9* on the night of September 22, 1914, while patrolling at slow speed in the English Channel.

Protected cruisers from 1877 to 1912

One of the distinctive features of protected cruisers lay in their protection, which was restricted to one turtle deck and also, in some cases, a "cellular raft." This raft had to be on top of and on each of the sloping sides of the protective deck and consisted of numerous small cells made by the close division of lengthwise and transverse bulkheads. These cells had to be filled with light bulky material, such as cork, or used as coal bunkers. They thus formed a protective structure that could be hit by enemy fire without being seriously damaged, and prevented the shells from reaching the magazines situated farther inboard. The cellular raft was invented by an Italian named Benedetto Brin, who installed it on the battleships *Italia* and *Lepanto*, built between 1875 and 1885; but it was not adopted on the vast majority of protected cruisers, which had only a protective deck and side bunkers.

Esmeralda I is regarded as the prototype of the protected cruiser. She was built in Britain's Armstrong Yard for the Chilean Navy between 1881 and 1884 and is not to be confused with the armored cruiser of the same name, also built by Armstrong between 1893 and 1897, and commissioned after the first *Esmeralda* had been sold to Japan and renamed *Izumi*. The first *Esmeralda* had a steel hull with a rounded bow, a flush deck and a central superstructure that contained six 6in (152mm) guns in side casemates, and there were two 10in (254mm) shielded guns fore and aft. The armament was rounded off by seven machine guns and three torpedo tubes. As far as armament and armor were concerned, protected cruisers were decidedly inferior to armored cruisers. The Royal Navy, however, was obliged to station ships at her many colonies overseas, so built large numbers of protected cruisers because they were less expensive; a large armored cruiser might cost more than a battleship. The United States Navy, on the other hand, was not in favor of cruisers with no armor, even though she did later build a few such classes. Protected cruisers had their supporters in other navies as well as the Royal Navy: these included the Italian, French, Austrian, German, and Argentinian Navies.

Vettor Pisani (Italy 1898). *Pisani* and *Carlo Alberto* were, like the American *Charlestons*, examples of cruisers with no heavy-caliber guns, but twelve 6in (152mm), six 4.7in (120mm), two 2.9in (75mm), ten 2.2in (57mm), and ten 1.4in (37mm) guns, plus many lesser weapons. She had twin screws and managed only 18.6 knots.

Fylgia (Sweden 1906). A small armored cruiser displacing only 4,100t, much less than Italy's 7,200t *Pisani* and 11,300t *San Giorgio*. Armament comprised eight 6in (152mm) and fourteen 2.2in (157mm) guns. She had twelve boilers and three funnels. The twin-screw power plant developed 21.5 knots.

San Giorgio (Italy 1910). A large heavily armored cruiser: 7.8in (200mm) round the belt, 7in (180mm) in the citadel, and with three armored decks. After having seen action in the 1911 war between Italy and Turkey and the First World War, she was modernized in 1937–1938 and had her fourteen coal-fired boilers replaced by eight oil-fired ones, resulting in the number of funnels dropping from four to two. She was sunk at Tobruk on January 22, 1941, before the city was abandoned.

Brooklyn (United States 1896). A large armored cruiser, armed with eight 8in (203mm) guns in four twin turrets, one forward, one aft, and two symmetrically placed either side amidships between the second and third funnels. There were also twelve 5in (127mm) guns in casemates either side of the gun deck and five torpedo tubes. In 1909 the boilers were changed and the torpedo tubes removed. In the First World War she was stationed in the Far East and did not see action. She was stricken in 1921.

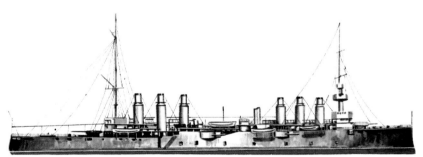

Jeanne d'Arc (France 1903). An armored cruiser protected round the belt, on the sides, and on two decks. She had two 7.6in (194mm) guns in turrets, one forward and one aft, and fourteen 5.5in (140mm) guns, some in casemates on the main deck, and some shielded on the superstructures. Like *Dupuy de Lôme,* she had three screws and made a good twenty-three knots. She had forty-eight boilers and six funnels in two groups of three. She was stricken in 1927.

Gromovoi (Russia 1901). An armored cruiser protected only by a central strip 6in (152mm) thick and 328ft (100m) long. There were no centerline turrets fore and aft and all the guns were positioned along the sides. She was a triple-screw ship and made twenty knots. She took part in the battle of Tsushima and was stricken in 1922.

Scharnhorst (Germany 1907). *Scharnhorst* and *Gneisenau* were cruisers that had a central citadel. They displaced almost 13,000 tonnes, and had 5.9in (150mm)-thick side armor, and a 2.3–1.5in (60–40mm) deck. They had three screws and made 22.5 knots. Both were sunk by a British squadron in the Battle of the Falklands on December 8, 1914.

Esmeralda (Chile 1884). Regarded as the first protected cruiser in the world and built in Britain for the Chilean Navy. She had armor only on the protective deck, 1–3in (25–76mm) thick, had two screws, and made eighteen knots. In 1894 she was sold to Japan and there had her armament and power plant modified. She was stricken in 1912 after serving for ten years in the Chilean Navy and eighteen years in the Japanese.

Pelorus (Great Britain 1897). One of a class of eleven small cruisers displacing 2,167 tonnes and classified as third-rate cruisers. Their two reciprocating engines drove two screws and they could make twenty knots.

Tage (France 1890). The largest sailing cruiser of her day, displacing 7,590 tonnes. In 1897–1898 she was modified and masts and sails removed. She had twin screws and made nineteen knots. There was a protective cellular structure over the gallery deck.

In 1879, the Royal Navy commissioned the first unit of the *Comus* Class. These ships, classified as third-rate cruisers (although they had the characteristics of protected cruisers), were still fitted with masts and sails and had a 1.4in (28mm) thick partially armored deck, two 7in (178mm) guns and twelve sixty-four-pounders, all on the main deck, and a single-screw power plant that produced almost fourteen knots.

The eleven *Pelorus* types formed another class of protected cruisers. They were commissioned in 1897–1898 and armed with eight 4in (102mm) guns in single mounts on the main deck, eight 1.8in (47mm) guns, and two above-water torpedo tubes on the main deck amidships. The protective deck was 1–2in (25–51mm) thick.

The *Hermes* Class cruisers, the first of which was commissioned in 1899, had a displacement of 5,600t, and armament of eleven 6in (152mm) and nine 3.5in (90mm) guns, in shielded emplacements either side of the main deck, and a 3in (76mm) thick protective deck. They were twin-screw ships making eighteen knots with a range of 9,000 miles at ten knots.

Many protected cruisers of the French Navy had the characteristic hull shape of the armored cruiser *Dupuy de Lôme* and a few other French ironclads of the same period.

Tage, commissioned in 1890, had a bulbous hull and concave sides. Apart from the 1.9in (50mm) protective deck, she had two 3.9in (100mm) armored beams delimiting a central citadel that had no side armor and contained ten 5.4in (138mm) trainable guns. There were a further eight 6.4in (164mm) guns on individual platforms either side of the main deck. The remainder of the armament consisted of seven fixed above-water torpedo tubes, three on either side and one at the bow. *Algier, Jean Bart,* and *Isly* (1891–1892), classified as second-rate cruisers, displaced 4,300t against *Tage's* 7,590t and were among the few cruisers to have a cellular raft on their 3.5in (90mm) protective deck. They were armed with four 6.4in (164mm) and four 5.4in (138mm) guns on side platforms, plus two 5.4in (138mm) guns, one forward and one aft. They also had twenty small 1.8in (47mm) and 1.4in (37mm) guns on the superstructures and in the tops, plus four torpedo tubes, two either side.

The eight second-rate *Chasseloup-Laubat*-type cruisers commissioned four years later had two platforms extending beyond the deck edge on either side on sturdy cylindrical supports. Armament comprised six 6.4in (164mm) guns, one forward, one aft, and four on the above-mentioned platforms. These ships also had four 3.9in (100mm) and fifteen 1.8in (47mm) and 1.4in (37mm) guns, plus four torpedo tubes.

The Russian cruiser *Svietlana,* built in France between 1895 and 1897, had the same shape hull as well as a cellular raft. She was armed with six 6in (152mm) guns laid out as on the *Chasseloup-Laubats.* She was one of the first ships to have an electrical generator and electric motors for the ammunition hoists.

The Italian Navy bought her first protected cruisers from Armstrong's in Britain. These were *Dogali, Bausan,* and *Piemonte.* The three *Etna* Class and those of the *Liguria* Class (modeled on *Bausan* and *Piemonte,* respectively) were built later in Italy.

Piemonte was armed with six 6in (152mm) guns, one forward, one aft, and two either side. *Liguria* also had four 6in (152mm) guns, but they were in three symmetrical pairs. Other units of the class, however, had two 6in (152mm) guns on either side interspersed with six 4.7in (120mm) guns, three per side amidships. Both *Piemonte* and the seven *Ligurias* saw action in the First World War, after which they were stricken. From August 29, 1903, to April 18, 1905, *Liguria* sailed around the world under the command of the Duke of Abruzzi. The United States Navy had relatively few protected cruisers. Exceptions were the partially protected *Atlanta* and *Boston* (1886); and the larger *Chicago* (1889); *Newark* (1891); *Charleston* (1889); *Baltimore* (1890); *Philadelphia* (1890); *San Francisco* (1890); *Columbia* and *Minneapolis* (1894); *New Orleans* (1898); *Albany* (1900); *Olympia* (1895); and the six *Chattanooga* Class (1904–1905).

The *Atlantas* were armed with two 8in (203mm) guns, this large caliber also being used on *Olympia.* One interesting feature of *Atlanta's* arrangement was that the 8in guns were not on the centerline, the forward one being set to port and the after one to starboard. The two 6in (152mm) fore and aft guns of the citadel were similarly positioned although the opposite way round, while the other four were symmetrically placed. All these guns were shielded and the 8in (203mm) ones were also protected by 1.9in (50mm) thick barbettes. The protective deck was 1.2in (33mm) thick. *Olympia* had four 8in (203mm) guns in two twin turrets on the centerline, protected by 4in (102mm) armor both on the revolving part and on the fixed barbettes. In addition to these, she had ten 5in (127mm) guns in a casemate in the citadel on the main deck, ten 2.2in (57mm) guns on the gallery deck, and four on the superstructure. She was a twin-screw ship that made twenty-one knots and had a range of 12,000 miles. She had a cellular raft either side of the protective deck. The *Chattanooga* Class cruisers displaced 3,100t. They had ten 5in (127mm) guns, one forward and one aft, in shielded emplacements, and eight inside casemates on the gallery deck. They had no torpedo tubes. An outstanding feature of

Comus (Great Britain 1879). One of a class of nine units classified as armored corvettes and still carrying masts and sails. They can be regarded as Britain's first protected cruisers because their decks were armored, over the magazines and engine rooms only, with plates 1.5in (38mm) thick. The hull was iron covered with planking sheathed in copper. These single-screw ships could make 13.8 knots.

Algier (France 1891). The three cruisers of this class had a very protruding bow, the main deck being shorter and narrower than the hull at the waterline and the sides curved inwards. These were twin-screw ships, powered by two reciprocating engines, and made 19.5 knots.

Chasseloup-Laubat (France 1895). One of a class of eight cruisers displacing 3,740 tonnes. They, too, had their bow and stern extending beyond the ends of the main deck and sides that curved inwards. Armor comprised a 1.1–3.1in (30–80mm)-thick protective deck. They were twin-screw ships and made eighteen knots.

Hermes (Great Britain 1898). One of a class of three protected cruisers displacing 5,600t. She had no main-caliber guns, all her armament being made up of medium-caliber pieces. Like other ships built at the turn of the century, she had two reciprocating engines for two screws and eighteen coal-fired boilers.

Piemonte (Italy 1889). Classified as a catcher, she was built in Britain and displaced 2,780t. She had a bow ram and three torpedo tubes, and was armed with six 6in (152mm) and six 4.7in (120mm) guns. She had two screws and made twenty-two knots. In 1898–1900 she sailed round the world. She was stricken in 1920.

Liguria (Italy 1894). Similar to *Piemonte* and one of the 'Regions' Class, which differed somewhat in terms of displacement and armament. She was a twin-screw ship, made seventeen knots, and had a 1.9in (50mm) protective turtle deck. She sailed round the world under the command of the Duke of Abruzzi in 1903–1905 and was stricken in 1921.

the *Atlanta*s and *Chattanooga*s was their very tall funnels and masts that were originally designed to set a spanker.

The smaller navies also had protected cruisers, such as Austria's *Franz Josef* and *Kaiserin Elizabeth*, built in Trieste, and Germany's *Gefion*, built in Danzig. By contrast, Argentina's *25 de Mayo*, China's *Hai-Chi* and *Hai-Tien*, Brazil's *Almirante Barrozo*, and Uruguay's *Montevideo* were all built by Armstrong's, in Britain, the international supplier of this type of protected cruiser. As a point of interest, the Brazilian protected cruiser *Tamandaré* was built in the Rio de Janeiro Naval Yard with British assistance, but her engines and guns were all brought from Britain. Many protected cruisers had their hulls covered with wooden planking sheathed in copper. Examples were Britain's *Pelorus* and *Comus*, America's *Chattanooga*s, Argentina's *Buenos Aires*, and Brazil's *Almirante Barrozo*.

Battle cruisers from 1908 to 1945

The increase in displacement and armament turned armored cruisers into battle cruisers. It is not easy to define the concepts adopted when drawing a distinction between battle cruisers and battleships. In fact, both types were heavily armed with large-caliber guns and had extremely thick armor on their sides, decks, gun turrets, and conning tower.

The major factors in assigning a ship to one class or the other were speed and protection. Battle cruisers were usually faster than the battleships (dreadnoughts) of their day: the British battle cruisers making from twenty-eight to thirty-one knots and the German ones about twenty-six to twenty-four. Their armor, however, was not as thick as on battleships, like the British *Queen Mary* and *Tiger* with 9in (229mm) side armor, and the German *Von der Tann*s with 9.8in (250mm), the *Goeben*s with 10.6in (270mm), and the *Derfflinger*s with 11.8in (300mm). Some

Atlanta (United States 1886). *Atlanta* and *Boston* were protected cruisers with a displacement of 3,189t, an unusual gun layout, a flush deck, central superstructure, two pole masts, and two tall funnels. They had two screws and did 15.6 knots. In 1905, *Atlanta* was used as a training ship for the Annapolis Naval Academy and then as a troop ship at Norfolk. She was stricken in 1912.

Olympia (United States 1895). She displaced 5,870t, almost twice as much as *Atlanta*, and had a steel hull with a bow ram and a rounded stern that curved inwards. She was the flagship of the Far East Squadron (1895–1898), sailed round the world, and saw action in the First World War. Taken out of commission in 1922, she was stricken in 1931, then converted to a depot ship, and finally restored and opened as a museum ship in Philadelphia.

Chattanooga (United States 1904). One of a class of six units classified as third-rate protected cruisers. She made 15.5 knots with her twin-screw power plant. She was taken out of commission in 1921 and stricken in 1930.

had very thin belt armor, such as Britain's *Invincible* and *Repulse* with 6in (152mm) and *Courageous* with just 3in (76mm). On the other hand, *Hood's* armor was 12in (305mm) thick. She was, therefore, sometimes described as a fast battleship rather than as a battle cruiser. As far as caliber and number of guns was concerned, battle cruisers were on a par with battleships: eight 12in (305mm) guns on Britain's older 1908 *Invincible* and 1911 *Indefatigable* types; eight 13.5in (343mm) on the 1913 *Queen Mary* and 1914 *Tiger* types: four 15in (381mm) on the 1917 *Courageous* types; six 15in (381mm) on the 1916 *Repulse*s; and eight 15in (381mm) on the 1920 *Hood*. German battle cruisers had guns of a slightly smaller caliber: eight 11in (280mm) on the 1910 *Von der Tann*: ten 11in (280mm) on the *Goeben*s; and eight 12in (305mm) on the 1914 *Derfflinger*s.

Japan built four *Kongo* Class battle cruisers, completed in 1913–1915, armed with eight 14in (356mm) caliber guns. However, later Japanese and U.S. battle cruisers that were cancelled due to the Washington Treaty were to have had 16in (406mm) caliber guns, eight on the American *Lexington*s and ten on the Japanese *Akagi*s.

Except for Britain's *Courageous* types, armed with four 15in (381mm) guns (although these ships were officially classified as ''large light cruisers''), all the others in practice had eight guns in four twin turrets, which justifies *Ibuki* and *Kurama* being classified as protected cruisers, since they were armed with four 12in (305mm) guns.

In the Royal Navy, between 1908 and 1911, *Invincible*, *Inflexible*, and *Indomitable* were classified as armored cruisers, then in 1912 they became ''dreadnought cruisers,'' and finally in 1915, when the new classification had been introduced, they became battle cruisers. They were armed with eight 12in (305mm) guns in four twin turrets and sixteen 4in (102mm) guns. The belt armor was 6in (152mm) thick, the main deck 0.7in (19mm), and the protective deck 1.4–2.5in (38–64mm) thick. Gun layout was similar to that followed on the dreadnoughts: one turret forward and one turret aft on the centerline and two diagonal turrets amidships. It will be remembered that *Dreadnought* had two, as opposed to one turret aft. The power plant was made up of four turbines driving four screws and developed 26.5 knots.

Gefion (Germany 1894). A protected cruiser with a cellular area over the protective deck. The power plant of two reciprocating engines had two screws that were protected by a 1in (25mm)-thick cylindrical skirt and produced nineteen knots.

25 de Mayo (Argentina 1890). A British-built protected cruiser with armament and profile similar to *Esmeralda*, built in the same yard seven years before. Armament was two 8in (203mm) guns in shielded emplacements, one forward and one aft, and eight 4.7in (120mm) guns, four either side amidships on platforms slightly overhanging the hull. This was a twin-screw ship that made twenty-two knots.

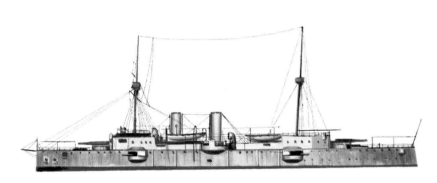

Kaiser Franz Josef (Austria 1890). A protected cruiser with a displacement of 4,000t. Armament was two 9.4in (240mm) guns in barbettes, one forward and one aft, and six 5.9in (150mm) guns, two on side platforms extending beyond the hull on either side of the second funnel and four in casemates overhanging the gallery deck, plus fifteen smaller pieces. She had twin screws and made nineteen knots.

Hai-Chi (China 1898). The Chinese Navy, like those of the South American countries, some European states, and the Japanese, was also a customer of the Armstrong shipyard from which she ordered protected cruisers. The Chinese Navy's *Hai-Chi* and *Hai-Tien* were similar to *25 de Mayo*, *Esmeralda*, and *Piemonte*. They had twin screws and made twenty-four knots. *Hai-Chi* ran aground on September 25, 1937, and was not salvaged.

Tamandaré (Brazil 1893). She was similar to the protected cruisers built at Armstrong's, but did not have the two 8in (203mm) guns. She had a ram, foredeck, and quarterdeck, two masts and two funnels and, with twin screws, made seventeen knots.

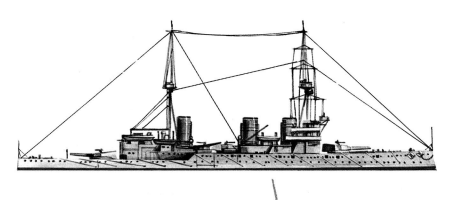

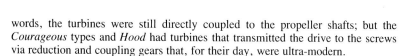
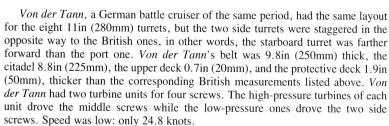

Invincible (Great Britain 1908). Together with another two units, she formed the Royal Navy's first class of battle cruisers. She had a hull with an extended bow, but no real ram as such. The forecastle extended to the after turret. There were two tripod masts and three funnels, two of which were close together abaft the forward mast. *Invincible* was sunk in the Battle of Jutland on May 31, 1916.

Von der Tann (Germany 1910). Built by the German Navy in answer to Britain's three *Invincibles*, which she closely resembled. The main difference lay in the caliber of the main guns: 11in (280mm), as opposed to the British 12in (305mm). She took part in the Battle of Jutland, in which she sank *Indefatigable*. In 1918, at the end of the war, she steamed to Scapa Flow where she was scuttled together with the rest of the German Fleet on June 21, 1919.

Von der Tann, a German battle cruiser of the same period, had the same layout for the eight 11in (280mm) turrets, but the two side turrets were staggered in the opposite way to the British ones, in other words, the starboard turret was farther forward than the port one. *Von der Tann's* belt was 9.8in (250mm) thick, the citadel 8.8in (225mm), the upper deck 0.7in (20mm), and the protective deck 1.9in (50mm), thicker than the corresponding British measurements listed above. *Von der Tann* had two turbine units for four screws. The high-pressure turbines of each unit drove the middle screws while the low-pressure ones drove the two side screws. Speed was low: only 24.8 knots.

Subsequent British battle cruisers, *Queen Mary, Lion,* and *Princess Royal,* were commissioned in 1913–1914 and were also classified as dreadnought cruisers until 1915. They were armed with eight 13.5in (343mm) guns in four turrets, all on the centerline, two forward, one amidships between the funnels, and one aft, an abnormal arrangement that restricted the field of fire of the middle turret. As regards armor, they were better protected than the *Invincibles,* their belt being 9in (229mm), upper deck 1in (25mm), and protective deck 1–2.5in (25–64mm). This extra protection was inadequate, because in the Battle of Jutland, on May 31, 1916, both *Queen Mary* and *Invincible* were sunk by shells from German battle cruisers.

Germany's reply to Britain's *Queen Mary* Class was *Moltke, Goeben,* and *Seydlitz,* armed with ten as opposed to eight guns, although of the smaller caliber of 11in (280mm), in five turrets. Three of the turrets were on the centerline and two diagonally placed amidships. Armor was thicker than on their British counterparts: 10.6in (270mm) on the belt, 7.8in (200mm) on the citadel, 1in (25mm) on the upper deck, and 1.9in (50mm) on the protective deck. Their secondary armament of twelve 5.9in (150mm) guns, in casemates either side of the citadel, was quite heavy. *Goeben* and *Moltke* had two turbine units driving four screws, like *Von der Tann,* whereas *Seydlitz* had three turbines for three screws.

The most outstanding German battle cruisers were *Derfflinger, Lützov,* and *Hindenburg,* commissioned at the end of 1914. Armament had been increased to eight 12in (305mm) guns in four twin turrets, all on the centerline, two forward and two aft; and secondary armament was twelve 5.9in (150mm) guns in casemates either side of the citadel. Armor thicknesses had also been increased and the belt measured 11.8in (300mm), the citadel 9in (230mm), and the armored decks now numbered three measuring 1.9in (50mm), 0.7–1in (20–25mm), and 1.1in (30mm). These thicknesses were exceeded only by Britain's *Hood,* six years later. The *Derfflingers* also had two turbine units for four screws and they could make a modest 26.5 knots.

Britain's *Repulse* (1916), *Courageous* (1917), and *Hood* (1920) battle cruisers had discarded the old coal-fired boiler idea and were powered only by oil-fired ones. The two *Repulses* had two turbine units for each of four screws, in other words, the turbines were still directly coupled to the propeller shafts; but the *Courageous* types and *Hood* had turbines that transmitted the drive to the screws via reduction and coupling gears that, for their day, were ultra-modern.

The *Repulse* types had six 15in (381mm) guns in three twin turrets, two forward and one aft. Their protection was fairly light: 6in (152mm) round the belt, 1.4in (37mm) in the citadel, and horizontal protection on three decks: 1.4in (37mm), 0.4–1.4in (12–37mm) and 0.4–2in (12–51mm). Her speed of thirty-two knots was decidedly faster than that of the German battle cruisers.

Courageous, Glorious, and *Furious* were all converted into aircraft carriers: *Furious* in 1917–1918 during construction, and *Courageous* and *Glorious* after the signing of the Treaty of Washington in 1924–1928.

Hood was the world's most powerful battle cruiser. She was laid down in 1916 but not commissioned until March 5, 1920, when the war was over. She was armed with eight 15in (381mm) guns in four twin turrets, two forward and two aft. Secondary armament was twelve 5.5in (140mm) guns in casemates, and four 4in (102mm) anti-aircraft guns as well as six torpedo tubes. Her armor was the same thickness as that on battleships: the belt was 12in (305mm), citadel 7–5in (178–127mm), forecastle deck 2–1in (51–25mm), main deck 3–1.4in (76–37mm), and protective deck 1.4–2in (37–52mm). There was also a fourth 1–3in (26–76mm) lower armored deck. Underwater protection was provided by a series of internal bulkheads. All in all, she was, at least on paper and by 1920 standards, an unsinkable ship. On May 24, 1941, however, a well placed shell from the 15in (381mm) guns of the German battleship *Bismarck* sent her to the bottom in a matter of minutes, down into the icy waters off Iceland. Only three out of a crew of 1,341 survived.

The last examples of such "large cruisers," not, however, classified officially as battle cruisers, were America's *Alaska* and *Guam,* plus a third (*Hawaii*) which was unfinished; three more were planned but not built. These ships were built not during the First World War period but in the Second World War; they were, thus, designed on the basis of completely different operational concepts. They were armed with nine 12in (305mm) anti-ship guns in three triple turrets, two forward and one aft. They had neither secondary armament nor torpedo tubes but heavy anti-aircraft armament of twelve 5in (127mm) guns and fifty-six 1.5in (40mm) and thirty-four 0.7in (20mm) machine guns. They also had aircraft-warning and fire-control radar. For the 1939–1945 period, armor was very light indeed: in fact it was simply a 9in (229mm) thick strip that ran about half the length of the ship and extended along the waterline. There was no other vertical protection. There were two armored decks: the upper one that was 1.4in (37mm) thick and the protective deck 3.8–4in (95–102mm). The gun turrets were protected by 13in (330mm) thick armor and the control tower by armor 10.5in (269mm) thick. Underwater protection was a series of longitudinal bulkheads. These two ships were used in the War in the Pacific, but after just three years service (from 1944 to 1947) were taken out of commission and stricken and broken up in 1960–1961, several projects for reconstruction with missile armament having failed.

Light cruisers from 1903 to 1922

This section deals with cruisers built between 1903 and 1922, powered by turbines as opposed to reciprocating engines (the name light cruiser also refers to another category of cruisers built between 1922 and 1945).

Steam turbines were first tried out in 1900–1901 on ships that at the time were classified as torpedo-boat destroyers but displaced less than the torpedo-boats of the First World War.

In 1903, the Royal Navy decided to try out turbines on cruisers too, choosing *Amethyst* for this purpose. She was one of a class of four units, the other three of which (*Topaze*, *Diamond*, and *Sapphire*), were powered by conventional reciprocating engines so as to be able to assess the turbines' performance against that of reciprocating engines installed on identical ships.

The German Navy had a similar idea when they fitted turbines to the cruiser *Lübeck*, commissioned in June 1905, three months after *Amethyst*. *Lübeck* had four shafts with two screws per shaft, however, making a total of eight screws, whereas the other six units of the same class, fitted with reciprocating engines, had only two screws. In the *Koenigsberg* Class that followed, there was one unit, *Stettin*, with turbines and four screws, whereas the others had reciprocating engines and two screws.

The first Italian Navy turbine ship was *San Marco*, an armored cruiser of 1910, with four screws, while her sister ship, *San Giorgio*, had reciprocating engines and two screws.

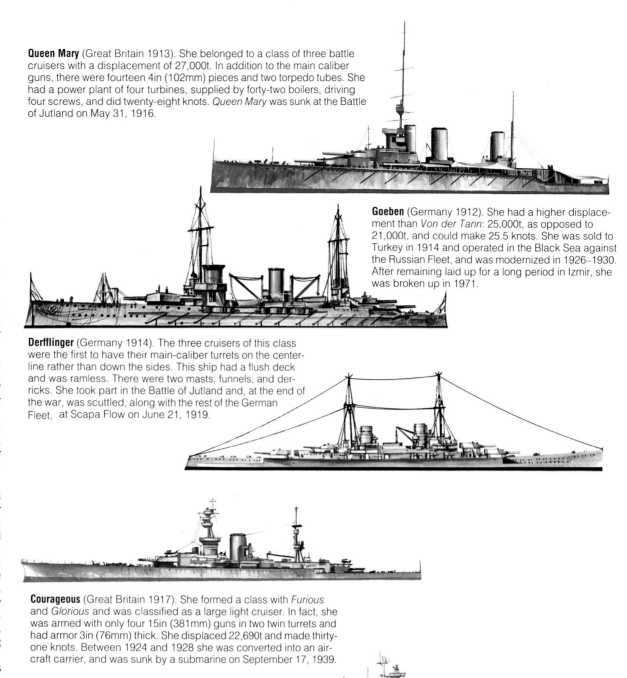

Queen Mary (Great Britain 1913). She belonged to a class of three battle cruisers with a displacement of 27,000t. In addition to the main caliber guns, there were fourteen 4in (102mm) pieces and two torpedo tubes. She had a power plant of four turbines, supplied by forty-two boilers, driving four screws, and did twenty-eight knots. *Queen Mary* was sunk at the Battle of Jutland on May 31, 1916.

Goeben (Germany 1912). She had a higher displacement than *Von der Tann*: 25,000t, as opposed to 21,000t, and could make 25.5 knots. She was sold to Turkey in 1914 and operated in the Black Sea against the Russian Fleet, and was modernized in 1926–1930. After remaining laid up for a long period in Izmir, she was broken up in 1971.

Derfflinger (Germany 1914). The three cruisers of this class were the first to have their main-caliber turrets on the centerline rather than down the sides. This ship had a flush deck and was ramless. There were two masts, funnels, and derricks. She took part in the Battle of Jutland and, at the end of the war, was scuttled, along with the rest of the German Fleet, at Scapa Flow on June 21, 1919.

Courageous (Great Britain 1917). She formed a class with *Furious* and *Glorious* and was classified as a large light cruiser. In fact, she was armed with only four 15in (381mm) guns in two twin turrets and had armor 3in (76mm) thick. She displaced 22,690t and made thirty-one knots. Between 1924 and 1928 she was converted into an aircraft carrier, and was sunk by a submarine on September 17, 1939.

Alaska (United States 1944). This battle cruiser was built later than the others on this page and is very different. The class was to have numbered six but only *Alaska* and *Guam* were completed. *Alaska* displaced 34,250t and was armed with nine 12in (305mm) guns in three triple turrets, two forward and one aft, like many battleships of the same period. She made thirty-three knots and had two catapults and four planes. She was used in the Pacific during the war and was stricken in 1960.

Repulse (Great Britain 1916). *Renown* and *Repulse* are the only two battle cruisers to have taken part in both the First and Second World Wars. In 1934–1936 they were modernized by being fitted with a hangar and catapult for seaplanes and armed with anti-aircraft guns. During the Second World War, *Repulse* took part in the hunt for *Bismarck*, and then was sent to the Indian Ocean in October 1941, where she was sunk by Japanese aircraft on December 10, 1941.

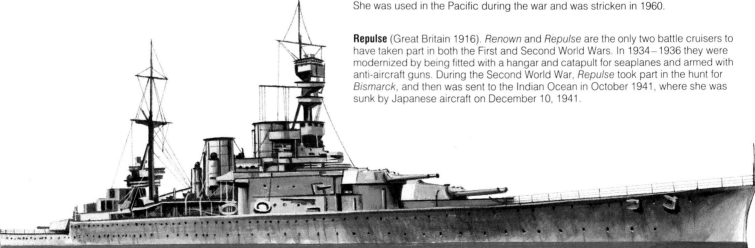

Amethyst (Great Britain 1905). A 3,000t cruiser with a turbine power plant and a 2in (51mm)-thick protective deck. She had eighteen boilers in three groups and three funnels. The other three units of the class had reciprocating engines, so it was possible to compare the performance of the turbines and reciprocating engines installed on units of the same class.

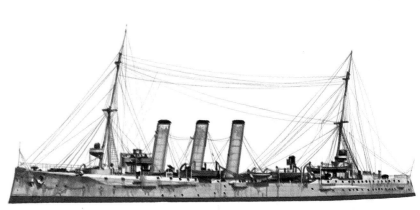

Lübeck (Germany 1905). A light 3,815t cruiser, with a four-shaft turbine power plant, with two screws on each shaft. The other six units of the class had reciprocating engines and twin screws. After a brief experimental period, the twin screws on each shaft were removed and replaced by a single one with a wider diameter. At the end of the First World War, *Lübeck* was assigned to Britain, where she was broken up in 1922–1923.

In the United States Navy, experiments involved not only the comparison between reciprocating engines and turbines, but also between different types of turbines and varying numbers of screws, so that in the three-unit *Salem* Class, one, *Salem,* had two Curtis turbines and two screws; the second, *Chester,* four Parsons turbines and four screws and the third, *Birmingham,* two reciprocating engines and two screws.

The Japanese Navy did not make comparisons among ships with reciprocating engines and turbines, experimenting only with varying numbers of turbines and screws; in the *Hirato* Class, for example, two units, *Hirato* and *Chikuma,* had two Curtis turbines and two screws, whereas the third, *Yahagi,* had four Parsons turbines and four screws.

As far as the makeup of the early turbine engines was concerned, it should be noted that the screws were directly driven by the turbines, as on Britain's *Amethyst* (1905), Austria's *Saidas* (1914), America's *Salem* and *Chester* (1908), Japan's *Hirato* Class (1912), China's *Chao-Ho* (1912), and Russia's *Admiral Greig* Class and others. Britain's *Amethyst* and *Frobisher* had two turbines for each screw, one abaft the other. One turbine was for cruising speed while the other was driven and for full speed. This turbine arrangement was not repeated on other classes of cruisers. Several classes had two turbine units for four screws, the high-pressure turbine in each driving one screw and the low pressure one the other. But technological progress soon led to the use of turbine units coupled to the screw by means of reduction gears.

In a turbine unit the steam, as a rule, first acts in a high-pressure Curtis "impulse" turbine and then in a low-pressure Parsons "reaction" turbine.

Light cruisers had oil-fired boilers, even if they were combined with coal-fired ones, several years before the British battle cruisers *Repulse, Courageous,* and *Hood,* commissioned from mid-1916 onwards.

The guns of light cruisers rarely exceeded 6in (152mm) in caliber, although there were exceptions, such as Britain's *Frobishers* with their seven 7.5in (190mm) guns in single turrets; but these units had a displacement of nearly 10,000t, well above that of other ships of the period. The *Cambrian* types (Great Britain 1916), displacing 3,750t, had four 6in (152mm) guns in four shielded mounts, one forward, one abaft the funnels, and two aft, all on the centerline. Britain's 4,800t *Bristols* had two 6in (152mm) guns in shielded emplacements, one forward and one

aft. China's 2,600t *Chao-Ho*s had two 6in (152mm) guns. Japan's 5,040t *Hirato*s and Australia's 5,400t *Melbourne*s had eight 6in (152mm) guns. The Dutch 7,050t *Java*s had ten and the American 9,190t *Omaha*s had twelve guns, four in twin turrets, one forward and one aft. German light cruisers, and those under German influence, had 4.1in (105mm) as opposed to 6in (152mm) guns, such as the 3,815t *Lübeck*s with ten guns and the 4,350t *Kolberg*s with twelve.

Virtually all light cruisers were armed with torpedo tubes, which began to be above-water and trainable, like four of the six installed on the *Cambrian*s, in two side twin mountings, whereas the *Frobisher*s, commissioned in 1924 (eight years later), still had their six torpedo tubes fixed, four being positioned in pairs on either side of the main deck. Austria's *Saida*s (1914) and America's *Omaha*s (1923) had four trainable torpedo tubes in two twin mounts either side of the main deck. (The *Omaha*s also had two triple trainable tubes on their upper decks; the four tubes lower down were removed, and their posts plated in, because they were too wet.) By contrast, Brazil's *Bahia*s (1910) had two single torpedo tubes on the main deck aft. The older ships had two fixed underwater tubes, one forward and one aft, such as Britain's *Bristol*s and *Amethyst*s, Germany's *Lübeck*s and *Kolberg*s, America's *Salem*s, and others.

Given the great diversity of displacement and armament, these cruisers had very varied types of protection. Some were similar to armored cruisers and others to protected cruisers. The ones resembling armored cruisers, with side and deck armor, always had very thin plating. Examples were Britain's *Cambrian*s, with 3in (76mm) round the belt and 1in (25mm) on the deck; Britain's *Frobisher*s, with a 3in (76mm) belt, 2in (51mm) citadel, and 1in (25mm) deck; Austria's *Saida*s, with a 2.4in (63mm) belt and 0.7in (20mm) deck; America's *Omaha*s, with a 3in (76mm) belt and 1.4in (37mm) deck; Australia's *Melbourne*s, with a 3in (76mm) belt and 2in (51mm) deck; and Holland's *Java*s, with a 3in (76mm) belt and 1.4–2in (37–51mm) deck. Consequently, the belt was usually 3in (76mm) thick and did not always extend the entire length of the ship. Only in a few cases was the deck (not always a turtleback) 2in (51mm) thick, being 1in (25mm) thick in most others.

Examples of cruisers with just one armored deck, and therefore similar to protected cruisers, were Britain's *Amethyst*s (2in [51mm]), Germany's *Lübeck*s (1.9–3.1in [50–80 mm]), Brazil's *Bahia*s (1.4in [37 mm]), Japan's *Hirato*s (3–2in [76–51 mm]), and China's *Chao-Ho*s (3–1.4in [76–37 mm]). As regards

Cambrian (Great Britain 1916). One of a class of six units with a displacement of 3,750t, 3in (76mm) armor on the sides, and 1in (25mm) on the deck. Although built in 1916, their power plant comprised four sets of reduction geared turbines turning four screws. This was the first class of cruisers to have oil-fired boilers. *Cambrian* was stricken and broken up in 1934.

Hirato (Japan 1912). *Hirato, Yahagi,* and *Chikuma* were three light cruisers used to try out two different types of power plants. *Hirato* and *Chikuma* had Curtiss turbines and two screws, whereas *Yahagi* had Parsons turbines and four screws. In 1924 all three units were modified, their sixteen coal-fired boilers being replaced with six oil-fired ones. *Hirato* was stricken in1939 and broken up in 1947, after being used as a harbor ship.

Salem (United States 1908). She was one of a class of three units, each having different power plants: Curtiss turbines and twin screws on *Salem*; Parsons turbines and four screws on *Chester,* and reciprocating engines and twin screws on *Birmingham.* In 1916–1917, those turbines directly coupled to the shafts were replaced by others with reduction gears. *Salem* was stricken in 1921.

Frobisher (Great Britain 1924). One of a class of five 10,000t units with 3in (76mm) side armor, 2in (51mm) citadel, and 1in (25mm) main deck. The power plant was on four screws, each driven by a turbine coupled directly to the shaft for high speed and by a reduction geared turbine for cruising speed. She was used as a convoy escort from 1942 to 1944 in the Indian Ocean and the Red Sea and then took part in the Normandy landings. She was broken up in 1949.

Omaha (United States 1923). She belonged to a class of ten units, with a displacement of 9,190t, 3in (76mm) side armor, and 1.4in (37mm) main deck armor. The power plant comprised four sets of reduction geared turbines turning four screws. In 1941, *Omaha* captured the German merchantman *Odenwald.* During the war she was on patrol in the Atlantic and in 1944 took part in the landings in Southern France. She was stricken in 1945.

Kolberg (Germany 1909). One of a class of four units with a displacement of 4,350t, 2–0.4in (51–12mm)-thick deck and a 3in (76mm) beam at either end of the midships rooms. She had two turbine sets directly coupled to the propeller shafts. At the end of the war she was assigned to France where she was renamed *Colmar.* She was stricken in 1927.

general appearance, the hull usually had a low freeboard, with or without a forecastle, and small superstructures with simple pole masts, although some even had tripod masts, like the *Cambrian*s, *Frobisher*s, and *Omaha*s, which had a tripod foremast for the top containing the fire-control.

The number of funnels varied from two to four: The oil-fired *Cambrian*s and *Frobisher*s had two funnels whereas the coal-fired *Amethyst*s (British), *Lübeck*s and *Kolberg*s (both German) had three. The coal-fired *Saida*s (Austrian), *Salem*s (American), and *Hirato*s (Japanese) had four funnels and so, too, did America's *Omaha*s, with their twelve oil-fired boilers.

Light cruisers should be regarded as part of a transitional period during which reciprocating engines were replaced by steam turbines, coal-fired boilers by oil-fired ones, and fixed torpedo tubes by trainable tubes. The early directors were another novelty. Those ships belonging to the navies involved in the First World War and used operationally revealed the inherent weakness of this hybrid ship to the extent that, during the years of peace that followed and within the limits of the naval disarmament treaties, agreements were made that led to the birth of two new types of cruisers, later to play leading roles in the Second World War.

Washington-type cruisers from 1925 to 1947

During the meetings between the representatives of the United States, Great Britain, Japan, France, and Italy that led to the formulation of the Washington Treaty, agreements were reached regarding the maximum displacement and armament of battleships and aircraft carriers, as well as the tonnage "quota" of each type of ship to which each country was entitled. No agreement was reached about the total number of cruisers, but warships that were neither battleships nor aircraft carriers could not have a displacement of more than 10,000t standard or guns larger than 8in (203mm) in caliber.

At a later conference, held in London in 1930, it was agreed that the United States would be allotted 180,000t, in other words, eighteen 10,000t cruisers, Britain 146,800t (fifteen cruisers), and Japan 108,400t (11–12 cruisers). No agreement or tonnage "quota" was reached for France and Italy, the quota being fixed by the money available to each of the two navies, which meant that France and Italy each built a total of seven 10,000t cruisers. The French cruisers were *Duquesne* and *Tourville* of 1925, *Suffren*, *Colbert*, *Foch*, and *Dupleix* of 1929, and *Algérie* of 1934. The Italian ones were *Trento* and *Trieste* of 1929, *Zara*, *Fiume*, *Gorizia*, and *Pola* of 1931, and *Bolzano* of 1933.

The main armament of these cruisers was virtually the same in all cases, comprising eight 8in (203mm) guns in four twin turrets, two forward and two aft. Exceptions to this rule were America's cruisers, all (except for the two *Pensacola*s of 1929–1930, with their ten guns) *Portland*s of 1933, with nine 8in (203mm) guns in three triple turrets, two forward and one aft; and Japan's *Nachi*s of 1928 and *Takao*s of 1932, with ten 7.8in (200mm) guns in five twin turrets. The Japanese *Mogami* Class, built in 1935, had fifteen 6.1in (155mm) guns in five triple turrets. They were modified in 1939 by replacing the five triple 6.1in turrets with five 8in (203mm) twin turrets. Only the Russian *Kirov* types of 1939 were armed with nine 7.1in (180mm) guns.

Anti-aircraft armament was more developed than on the battle- and light cruisers of the First World War. Only those cruisers built after 1930 were armed with anti-aircraft guns, like America's *Pensacola*s of 1930, armed with four 5in (127mm) guns; *Portland*s of 1933 with eight; Japan's *Nachi*s of 1928 with six; and *Mogami*s and *Tone*s with eight, all 5in (127mm). The French *Duquesne* types had eight 3in (76mm) guns, and *Algérie* twelve 3.9in (100mm). Russia's *Kirov* types had eight 3.9in (100mm) and six 1.7in (45mm) guns. After the war, the United States Navy introduced a rapid-fire 3in (76mm) radar-trained anti-aircraft gun. The cruisers *Des Moines*, *Newport News*, and *Salem*, commissioned in 1948–1949, had an anti-aircraft armament of twelve 5in (127mm) guns in six twin turrets and twenty-four 3in (76mm) guns of this type, in twelve mounts, as well as twelve 0.7in (20mm) machine guns.

All heavy cruisers also had an anti-aircraft armament of 1.5in (40mm), 1.4in (37mm), 0.7in (20mm), and 0.5in (13.5mm) machine guns, initially varying in number from twenty to thirty but later increased during the war to close on one hundred.

All Washington-type cruisers were armed with torpedo tubes varying from six to twelve in number, usually in triple and quadruple mountings on the main deck. Italy's *Zara*s, America's *Portland* and *Des Moines* types, and a few others had no torpedo tubes.

The sides and decks were protected, the most notable exception being Britain's seven *Kent* Class of 1928 that had no side armor and only one deck, the gun deck, protected by armor 1.4–3in (38–76mm) thick. The American *Des Moines* types had the heaviest belt armor, 6in–4in (152mm–102mm). Other ships also had very thick belt armor: Italy's four *Zara*s, 5.9in (150mm) and 2.7in (70mm) deck; Japan's *Nachi*s, 3.9in (100mm) and 1.4in (38mm) deck and *Mogami*s, 5in (127mm) and 2.3in (60mm) deck; and France's *Algérie*, 4.3in (110mm) and 3in (76mm) deck. Practically all cruisers of this type had two to four reconnaissance

Saida (Austria 1914). With *Helgoland* and *Novara*, she formed a class of three cruisers with a displacement of 4,417t and outdated lines, like the 1910 cruisers. *Saida* had no large superstructures but a small pilothouse for the bridge and four funnels for the sixteen coal-fired boilers. Vertical armor was on the midships section of the sides and was 2.4in (63mm) thick. The protective deck was 0.7in (20mm) thick. After the war *Saida* and *Helgoland* were assigned to Italy and renamed *Venezia* and *Brindisi*. *Saida* was stricken in March 1937.

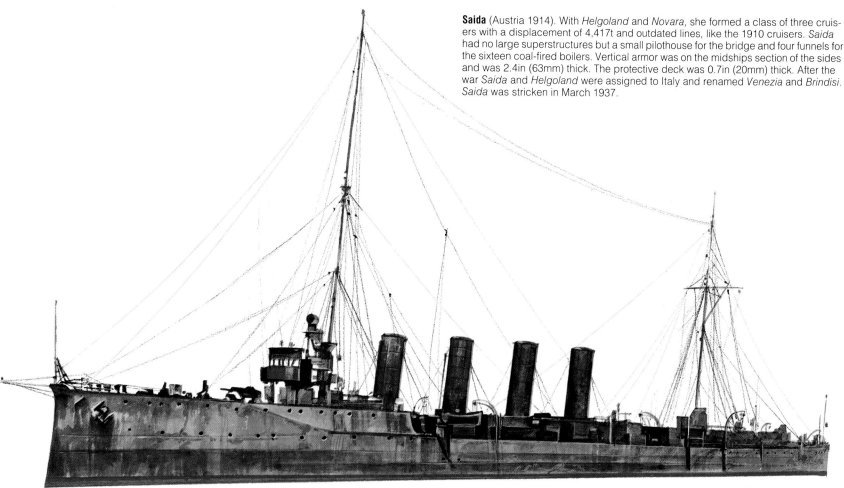

Algérie (France 1934). One of the first 10,000t cruisers to be armed in compliance with the Washington Treaty. She had turbine units with reduction gears and four screws. In 1940 she carried the Bank of France's assets to Halifax. She was sunk in November 1942 when the Germans occupied Toulon.

seaplanes and one to two catapults to launch them. Italy's *Trento* and *Trieste* types of 1929 and the four *Zara*s of 1931 had fixed bow catapults. Britain's *Kent*s (1928), Germany's *Hipper*s (1939), Spain's *Canarias* (1936), and France's *Dunkerque*s (1928) had one trainable catapult on the amidships superstructure. The French *Algérie* (1934), American *Pensacola*s (1930) and *Portland*s (1933), Japanese *Nachi*s (1928), *Mogami*s (1935), *Tone*s (1938) and others had two trainable catapults amidships.

All had turbine units powered by oil-fired boilers, with four as a rule. The only twin-screw heavy cruisers were the Italian *Zara* types and Russian *Kirov*s and *Chapaev*s. The three German *Hipper*s were triple-screw ships, two screws being driven by steam turbines and one by two diesel engines.

There were far fewer boilers than there had been on the old coal-fired ships. There were usually eight but the *Hipper*s, *Trento*s, and *Nachi*s had twelve and the *Mogami*s ten. Consequently, there were also fewer funnels and, except for the British *Kent*s, which had three, and the German *Hipper*s, Japanese *Mogami*s and

American *Oregon City* and *Des Moines* types, which had one very large one, all the others had two funnels.

Most of these ships had a tripod foremast for the director, often incorporated into the bridge superstructure. The Japanese *Nachi*s, *Mogami*s, and others, however, had a large "pagoda" bridge, like a battleship's, that also incorporated the fire control tower; the masts were therefore simple tripods or poles.

All could make quite high speeds: *Algérie* thirty-one knots, *Kent* 31.5, *Hipper*s and *Zara* thirty-two, *Canarias, Pensacola, Portland, Des Moines,* and *Duquesne* thirty-three, and Japan's *Nachi, Mogami,* and *Tone* thirty-five knots. During the Second World War, British, American, and Japanese units were fitted with search and fire-control radar, also used to a lesser extent on German ships and on a handful of Italian vessels in 1943. In many cases, the seaplane catapults were removed, although both the cranes and hangars were retained and still used on some cruisers; they were converted after the war to accommodate helicopters, as occurred on the American *Galveston* and *Albany* types.

Trento (Italy 1929). *Trento* and *Trieste* were Italy's first two 10,000t cruisers. They had four screws and made thirty-five knots. This speed was achieved by having only light protection (belt 2.7in [70mm], deck 1.9in [50mm]). *Trento* was armed with eight 8in (203mm) guns and eighteen 3.9in (100mm) anti-aircraft guns, as well as machine guns and eight torpedo tubes. She was sunk on June 15, 1942.

Pensacola (United States 1930). *Pensacola* and *Salt Lake City* were the United States Navy's first ever 10,000t cruisers. During the Second World War they served as escorts for the aircraft carriers *Lexington* and *Enterprise* and saw a lot of action in the Pacific. At the end of the war, *Pensacola* was used in the Bikini nuclear experiments. She was sunk on November 10, 1948.

Admiral Hipper (Germany 1939). *Hipper* and *Blücher* were the German Navy's first two Washington-type cruisers. They displaced about 4,000t more than the prescribed 10,000, and had the standard eight 8in (203mm) guns. *Admiral Hipper* operated in Norwegian waters, in the Atlantic and the Arctic, and was scuttled on April 4, 1945, to prevent her from falling into Russian hands.

Canarias (Spain 1936). *Canarias* and *Baleares* were the only 10,000t cruisers in the Spanish Navy. They had the standard eight 8in (203mm) guns, fairly light belt armor, and a four-screw power plant. During a 1953 refit, a second funnel was added. *Canarias* was the last Washington-type cruiser to be stricken, and was, in fact, taken out of commission in 1975.

Kent (Great Britain 1928). Eight of these Washington-type cruisers were built, five for Great Britain and three for Australia. They were distinguished by their three funnels, the middle one being bigger. Their eight 8in (203mm) guns were in four twin turrets and they had a catapult behind the funnels and also four aircraft. They had four screws and made 31.5 knots. *Kent* was stricken in 1948.

Mogami (Japan 1935). The four cruisers of this class were built with a light cruiser armament of fifteen 6.1in (155mm) guns in five triple turrets, but in 1939, four years after they were commissioned, these were replaced with ten 8in (203mm) guns in five twin turrets and they became heavy cruisers. They had a displacement of 11,169t. *Mogami* was sunk on October 25, 1944.

Zara (Italy 1931). *Zara, Fiume, Gorizia,* and *Pola* formed the second group of 10,000t cruisers to be built by the Italian Navy after the prototypes *Trento* and *Trieste.* They were armed with eight 8in (203mm) guns and had armor on the sides and on the deck. *Zara* was sunk on March 29, 1941, at the end of the naval battle of Gaudo and Matapan.

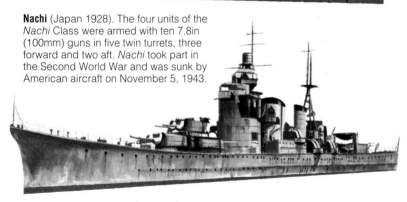

Nachi (Japan 1928). The four units of the *Nachi* Class were armed with ten 7.8in (100mm) guns in five twin turrets, three forward and two aft. *Nachi* took part in the Second World War and was sunk by American aircraft on November 5, 1943.

Kirov (Soviet Union 1939). With another five units, *Kirov* formed a class of Italian-designed cruisers. She was a light 9,000t cruiser but her armament of nine 7.1in (180mm) guns in three triple turrets exceeded the 6.1in (155mm) limit, which, how-ever, was not binding for the Soviet Union, who was not a signatory to the Treaty of London. *Kirov* had six torpedo tubes in two triple mounts either side, one catapult, and two aircraft. She is thought to have been stricken in 1977.

London-type cruisers and anti-aircraft cruisers from 1925 to 1947

When discussing heavy cruisers, we mentioned the London Naval Conference, held from February 6, to April 22, 1930, in which regulations were made concern-ing a second type of cruiser, armed with guns of a maximum caliber of 6.1in (155mm), called a light cruiser, in contrast to heavy cruisers which were armed with 8in (203mm) guns.

As the term *light cruiser* had already been used to indicate the turbo-cruisers of the 1903–1922 period, these ships are more correctly referred to as "London-type" cruisers. The term *light* will also be used, however, in the text.

At the Conference it was agreed that Britain could have 192,200t of light cruisers, the United States 143,500 and Japan 100,400. No accord was reached for France and Italy, who were in disagreement with each other over the question of "naval parity." It will be noted that Britain had a higher "quota" than the United States; but the latter had a greater heavy cruiser "quota," given that operational needs had created different requirements in the two countries. In fact, Britain needed large numbers of small, not very heavily armed cruisers, whereas the United States wanted only large well-armed cruisers, as had already been the case in 1890–1900, when she showed a preference for armored rather than protected cruisers. While the displacement limit for 10,000t cruisers set by the Washington Treaty was regarded as valid, it was considered unnecessary to set any limit for light cruisers. This gave rise to the paradoxical situation of there being heavy cruisers with a displacement of 9,850t, like the British *Kent*s of 1928, and light cruisers with a displacement of 14.500t, like the American *Worcester*s of 1948.

All the above-mentioned classes were armed with 5.9in (150mm), or 6.1in (155mm) anti-ship guns; the smaller caliber was used in German-built units, such as *Koenigsberg* and *Nürnberg*, or in units built using German models, such as the Dutch *De Ruyter*s of 1936. For some unknown reason Japan's *Agano* types of 1942 also had 5.9in (150mm) guns. The number of these guns ranged from a minimum of six to a maximum of fifteen, invariably in twin or triple turrets. Britain's *Arethusa*s of 1935 had six guns in three twin turrets, two forward and one aft. Britain's *Leander*s of 1933, Italy's *Colleoni*s of 1932 and *Eugenio di Savoia*s of 1936, and Australia's *Sydney*s of 1936 had eight guns in four twin turrets, two forward and two aft. Spain's *Principe Alfonso*s of 1925–1928 were also armed with eight 6in (152mm) guns, in an unusual layout of two in single turrets, one forward and one aft, and six in three twin turrets, one forward and one aft, before the single ones, and one on the amidships superstructure abaft the funnels. The French *La Galissonière* types of 1935 had nine guns in three triple turrets, two forward and one aft. Germany's *Nürnberg* and *Koenigsberg*s had two triple turrets aft and one forward, all on the centerline on *Nürnberg* and with one of the after turrets on *Karlsrühe, Koenigsberg,* and *Köln* being offset to starboard and the other to port. On ten-gun ships, the pieces were in two triple and two twin turrets, like the Italian *Duca degli Abruzzi* types of 1937. There were two layouts for twelve guns: either four triple turrets, like Britain's *Fiji*s (1940), America's *Galveston*s (1942), and Britain's *Southampton*s (1937), or six twin turrets like America's *Worcester*s (1948). On fifteen-gun units, the only layout was five triple turrets, like America's *Brooklyn*s (1938) and Japan's *Mogami*s before their conversion in 1939.

The Japanese *Katori* types of 1940 had only four 5.5in (140mm) guns in two twin turrets, one forward and one aft. The three *Agano*s had six 5.9in (150mm) guns in three twin turrets, two forward and one aft, and the two Dutch *De Ruyter*s seven 5.9in (150mm) guns in four turrets, two twins aft and a single and a twin forward.

Anti-aircraft armament on the older units was usually made up of a fairly small number of guns and machine guns. Britain's *Leander*s and *Arethusa*s (1933–1935), in fact, had four 4in (102mm) guns and fourteen to eighteen machine guns. This complement was later increased to eight to twelve 5in (127mm) guns on the *Mogami*s (1939), *Brooklyn*s (1938), and *Cleveland*s (1942), and reached twenty 3in (76mm) guns on *Worcester*s.

Almost all these cruisers had torpedo tubes, the most noteworthy being on the German *Koenigsberg*s (1929) and *Nürnberg*s (1935) and the Japanese *Mogami*s (1939), the Germans having twelve trainable tubes in four triple mountings and the Japanese having the same, only fixed and set athwartships. Spain's *Principe Alfonso*s also had twelve torpedo tubes in four trainable mounts. Other units had fewer torpedo tubes: eight on the British *Leander*s and Australian *Sydney*s and four on the Italian *Colleoni*s and *Montecuccoli*s. The American *Brooklyn, Cleveland,* and *Worcester* types had no torpedo tubes.

Armor was quite thick in comparison to that of the heavy cruisers which, as stated, usually had belts of around 3in (76mm), running to 3.9in (100mm) on Japan's *Tone*s and 5.9–3.9in (150mm–100mm) on Italy's *Zara*s. In fact, the American *Worcester* types of 1948 had a 6in (152mm) belt, equivalent to the caliber of their guns, as well as heavy horizontal armor on two decks: 3in (76mm) on the main deck and 2in (51mm) on the upper deck. Most cruisers had only one armored deck. Italy's *Duca degli Abruzzi* and Japan's *Mogami*s had belt armor of

Leander (Great Britain 1933). A light 7,000t cruiser with 3in (76mm) armor round the belt and 2in (51mm) on the deck. She had eight quadruple trainable torpedo tubes down the sides, four screws, and made 32.5 knots. She was stricken in December 1949.

CL40 Brooklyn (United States 1938). A light 11,000t cruiser with no torpedo tubes but two catapults right aft and four aircraft. She had four screws, made 32.5 knots, and in 1951 was handed over to Chile, where she was renamed *O'Higgins*.

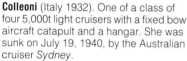

Arethusa (Great Britain 1935). One of a class of four 5,000t light cruisers with 2.7in (70mm) armor on the sides and 1.9in (50mm) on the deck. She had four screws and made thirty-two knots. During the war she operated in Norwegian waters and was then stationed at Gibraltar to escort convoys. She was stricken in 1950.

Colleoni (Italy 1932). One of a class of four 5,000t light cruisers with a fixed bow aircraft catapult and a hangar. She was sunk on July 19, 1940, by the Australian cruiser *Sydney*.

La Galissonière (France 1935). One of a class of six 7,000t light cruisers. She had four torpedo tubes, one trainable catapult amidships, 4.1–3in (105mm–76mm) armor round the belt and 1.4in (37mm) on the deck. The twin-screw power plant gave thirty-one knots. She was scuttled in November 1942 when the Germans occupied Toulon, then recovered and assigned to Italy, and retaken by the Germans on September 8. She was destroyed by bombing on April 18, 1944.

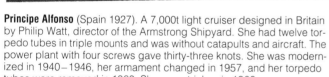

Principe Alfonso (Spain 1927). A 7,000t light cruiser designed in Britain by Philip Watt, director of the Armstrong Shipyard. She had twelve torpedo tubes in triple mounts and was without catapults and aircraft. The power plant with four screws gave thirty-three knots. She was modernized in 1940–1946, her armament changed in 1957, and her torpedo tubes were removed in 1960. She was stricken in 1966.

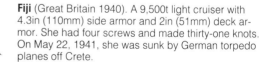

Koenigsberg (Germany 1929). A 7,000t light cruiser with twelve torpedo tubes, one catapult, and a plane. She made thirty-two knots and, on April 10, 1940, was sunk by British planes off Bergen during the Norway landings.

Katori (Japan 1940). A 5,000t light cruiser that, apart from the main armament, had two 5in (127mm) anti-aircraft guns, four torpedo tubes, one catapult, and an aeroplane. The power plant consisted of two turbines and two diesel engines and she could just manage eighteen knots. She and another two units of the same class were used for training purposes; *Katori*, herself, was stricken in 1948.

Fiji (Great Britain 1940). A 9,500t light cruiser with 4.3in (110mm) side armor and 2in (51mm) deck armor. She had four screws and made thirty-one knots. On May 22, 1941, she was sunk by German torpedo planes off Crete.

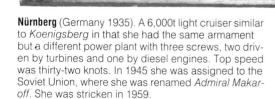

Nürnberg (Germany 1935). A 6,000t light cruiser similar to *Koenigsberg* in that she had the same armament but a different power plant with three screws, two driven by turbines and one by diesel engines. Top speed was thirty-two knots. In 1945 she was assigned to the Soviet Union, where she was renamed *Admiral Makaroff*. She was stricken in 1959.

CL55 Cleveland (United States 1942). One of a class of twenty-nine 11,000t cruisers, armed with twelve 6in (152mm) guns in four triple turrets, which, with the *Brooklyn*s and *Worcester*s, were the largest and best armed of that type. *Cleveland* was a four-screw ship that made thirty-three knots; she was stricken in 1959.

Agano (Japan 1942). A 7,000t light cruiser armed with six 5.9in (150mm) guns in three twin turrets, four 3.1in (80mm) anti-aircraft guns, eight torpedo tubes, and one catapult. Belt armor was 2.3in (60mm) thick, and on the deck 0.7in (20mm). She was a four-screw ship that made thirty-five knots and belonged to a class of four units, three of which (including *Agano*) were sunk during the war and the fourth in the Bikini experiments.

De Ruyter (Holland 1936). A 6,000t light cruiser armed with seven 5.9in (150mm) guns, four of which were in two twin turrets aft and three in one twin and one single forward. She had a catapult amidships and no torpedo tubes. The power plant had two screws and produced thirty-two knots. She was sunk on February 27, 1942, when the Japanese took Java.

Eugenio di Savoia (Italy 1936). With *Duca d'Aosta* she formed a class of 9,000t light cruisers armed with eight 6in (152mm) guns. Belt armor was 2.7in (70mm) and deck armor 1.3in (35mm) thick. In compliance with the peace treaty, she was handed over to Greece in 1951 and renamed *Helli*. She was stricken in 1964.

considerable thickness: 3.9 + 1.1in (100 + 30mm) on the former and 3.9in (100mm) on the latter. Italy's *Colleoni* types, with their 0.9in (24mm) belt and 0.7in (20mm) deck, had almost nonexistent protection. Over the years, the general trend was to increase the protection, which resulted in increased displacements.

On the whole, the power plants were usually quite powerful so as to enable high speeds to be reached. The fastest light cruisers were the Italian ones, although all twin-screw ships could make thirty-seven knots, such as the *Colleoni*s and *Monte-cuccoli*s. Japan's *Mogami*s developed the same speed although they were four-screw ships. Virtually all the other light cruisers were four-screw ships and made thirty-two to thirty-three knots.

The mixed power plants (steam turbines and diesel engines) of the German *Koenigsberg* type cruisers, with two turbine units and two diesel engines, and the *Nürnberg*, with two turbine units and four diesel engines, deserve a special mention. On the *Koenigsberg*s both the two turbine units and the two engines drove reduction gears that turned the two screws. *Nürnberg* had three screws, the two side ones being driven by the steam turbines and the middle one by the four diesel engines. The top speed attainable with the steam turbines was thirty-two knots.

Like the Washington-type, the light (or London-type) cruisers also had catapults and reconnaissance seaplanes. The American *Brooklyn*, *Cleveland*, and *Worcester* types had two catapults, both right aft with the hangars. The Japanese *Mogami*s had two catapults abaft the funnels.

It will be remembered that during her June 1942–April 1943 refit, *Mogami* was converted to a seaplane carrier by removing the two after 8in (203mm) turrets and fitting a platform with an aircraft hangar underneath that took up the entire after section.

The Russian *Sverdlov* and *Chapaev* Classes represented a special type of light cruiser. In the ten years or so after the Second World War, the Russian Navy was still a long way behind the Western navies.

The six *Chapaev* cruisers, laid down in 1939–1940, were commissioned in 1948–1950. They displaced 15,500t and were armed with twelve 6in (152mm) guns in four triple turrets.

The *Chapaev*s were fitted to carry and launch two hundred sea mines. They might therefore be considered minelaying cruisers. They had a fairly heavy anti-aircraft armament of eight 3.9in (101mm) guns and twenty-eight 1.4in (37mm) machine guns. They could make thirty-five knots and had a mixed power plant of two turbine units and two diesel engines, driving two screws.

The *Sverdlov*s, commissioned in 1953–1958, were already out-of-date when they began service. Originally, they were to have numbered twenty-four, but of twenty laid down only fourteen were completed, three being broken up on the slips and three immediately after being launched. They were then reduced to twelve after one was transferred to Indonesia and another was converted into a missile test ship. They were armed with twelve 6in (152mm) guns, twelve 3.9in (100mm) anti-

aircraft guns, and thirty-two 1.4in (37mm) machine guns, and also ten torpedo tubes and equipment to carry 125 mines.

Both the *Chapaev*s and *Sverdlov*s had 3.5–4.9in (90–125mm) belt armor. The *Chapaev*s had only their main decks armored (2in [51mm] thick), whereas the *Sverdlov*s had both this and the upper deck armored (3in [76mm] thick).

One of the *Sverdlov* Class was converted to missile-launching cruiser by fitting a launcher aft and keeping the conventional armament in the forward area: *Dzerzhinsky* in 1962, *Admiral Senyavin* in 1972, and (in 1974) *Zhdanov* were converted to command cruisers, a large deckhouse (with a short-range missile launcher) replacing the No. 3 6in turret. *Admiral Senyavin* had both after turrets removed.

During the war, the use of torpedo planes and bombers against naval formations had shown that all units had inadequate anti-aircraft armament, so many more anti-aircraft machine guns were added to the existing ones on battleships, cruisers, destroyers, and even aircraft carriers. These guns were usually in double, triple, and quadruple mounts and were positioned on the superstructures or, following American practice, at either end fore and aft of the main deck. The need for greater anti-aircraft protection, however, had already been felt as early as 1938–1939 and cruisers armed with small-caliber rapid-fire guns had already been designed and were in the process of being built. These guns were dual-purpose, anti-ship and anti-aircraft, and those manufactured toward the end of the war were radar-trained. These ships were called "anti-aircraft cruisers."

Outstanding examples of pre-war anti-aircraft units included Britain's eleven *Dido* Class, commissioned in 1940–1941, armed with ten 5.2in (133mm) guns in five twin turrets and sixteen 1.5in (40mm) and 0.4in (12mm) machine guns, and America's eleven *Atlanta* Class, commissioned in 1941–1942, armed with twelve to sixteen 5in (127mm) guns in twin turrets and forty-eight 1.5in (40mm) and 0.7in (20mm) machine guns. The armament of these units, however, turned out to be lighter than those not classified as anti-aircraft cruisers, built a few years later, and incorporating new features based on lessons learned during the war. America's *Cleveland* cruisers of 1942–1943, thus, had, apart from their anti-ship armament, an anti-aircraft armament of twelve 5in (127mm) guns and fifty-two 1.5in (40mm) and 0.7in (20mm) machine guns. The *Worcester* types that followed (1948–1949) had twelve 5in (127mm) anti-ship and anti-aircraft guns and twenty 3in (76mm) anti-aircraft guns of the new automatic type, as well as twenty-four machine guns. Moreover, their 6-inch main-battery guns were designed for anti-aircraft fire. The French *De Grasse* and *Colbert* types were examples of post-war design anti-aircraft cruisers. They were commissioned in 1956–1959 and were armed with sixteen 5in (127mm) anti-aircraft and anti-ship guns and twenty 2.2in (57mm) anti-aircraft guns. Holland's *De Ruyter* and *De Zeven Provincien* types (1953–1954) were further examples of post-war anti-aircraft cruisers.

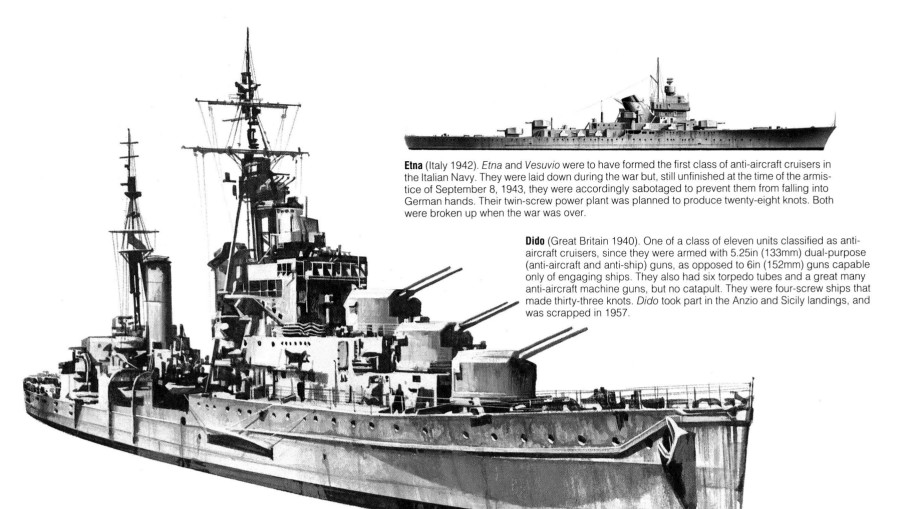

Etna (Italy 1942). *Etna* and *Vesuvio* were to have formed the first class of anti-aircraft cruisers in the Italian Navy. They were laid down during the war but, still unfinished at the time of the armistice of September 8, 1943, they were accordingly sabotaged to prevent them from falling into German hands. Their twin-screw power plant was planned to produce twenty-eight knots. Both were broken up when the war was over.

Dido (Great Britain 1940). One of a class of eleven units classified as anti-aircraft cruisers, since they were armed with 5.25in (133mm) dual-purpose (anti-aircraft and anti-ship) guns, as opposed to 6in (152mm) guns capable only of engaging ships. They also had six torpedo tubes and a great many anti-aircraft machine guns, but no catapult. They were four-screw ships that made thirty-three knots. *Dido* took part in the Anzio and Sicily landings, and was scrapped in 1957.

This armament was superseded when ships began to be fitted with missiles as anti-aircraft weapons. *De Zeven Provincien* was converted into a missile cruiser and six American *Cleveland* Class cruisers received the same treatment. When the latter were commissioned, they were heavily armed with the conventional type of anti-aircraft guns.

Britain's *Dido*s of 1940–1941 had five 5.2in (133mm) twin turrets, three before the central superstructure on three successive levels, and two abaft on two levels. There were eight machine guns in quadruple mounts on platforms either side of the after funnel. Armament also included six torpedo tubes in two trainable triple mountings on the main deck either side of the after funnel.

America's *Atlanta* Class of 1941–1942 had heavier anti-aircraft armament that was more concentrated amidships. Those with sixteen 5in (127mm) guns, namely *Atlanta*, *San Diego*, *Juneau*, and *San Juan*, had eight twin turrets: three before and three abaft the superstructure on two levels and two symmetrically placed on platforms on either side of the bridge. The ten 1.5in (40mm) machine guns were in three twin and one quadruple mounts, the latter right aft. The 0.7in (20mm) machine guns were in single mounts, two of which were right aft. The next four units of the class had their two 5in (127mm) side turrets replaced by two twin 1.5in (40mm) machine guns; they were completed with a total of eight twin mounts. The first eight *Atlanta*s had eight torpedo tubes in quadruple mountings; the last three units had no torpedo tubes.

The Italian Navy sought to equip itself with anti-aircraft cruisers and began building *Etna* and *Vesuvio*, which, however, were not completed by the time of the armistice on September 8, 1943; they were, in fact, scuttled to prevent them from falling into German hands. They were to have been armed with six 5.3in (135mm) guns in three twin turrets and ten small 2.5in (65mm) guns in single turrets, five per side amidships alongside the superstructure, and twelve 0.7in (20mm) machine guns in six twin mounts, also positioned alongside the superstructure.

Worcester (United States 1948). A post-war cruiser belonging to a class of two units. She can also be classified as an anti-aircraft cruiser since she had dual-purpose (anti-ship and anti-aircraft) main-caliber guns. She had no torpedo tubes, and, with her four-screw power plant, she made thirty-two knots. She was decommissioned in 1958 and scrapped in 1970.

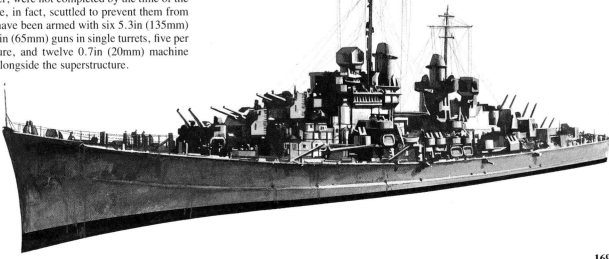

Atlanta (United States 1941). An anti-aircraft cruiser belonging to a class of eleven units built between 1941 and 1946, armed exclusively with anti-aircraft weapons. They had a twin-screw power plant and made thirty-three knots. *Atlanta* was sunk in the Battle of Guadalcanal on November 13, 1942, and her name was given to CL104 of the *Cleveland* Class.

Sverdlov (Soviet Union 1955). A post-war cruiser armed with twelve 6in (152mm) guns in four triple turrets. She belonged to a class of fourteen units that displaced 19,200t and with her twin-screw power plant made thirty-four knots. Her armament of ten torpedo tubes is worth noting. Three units of this class have been modified and have been equipped with missile launchers in place of the after turrets.

De Ruyter (Holland 1953). An anti-aircraft cruiser not to be confused with the 1935 light cruiser of the same name. She was commissioned in 1953 with exclusively anti-aircraft armament, and in 1973 was sold to Peru.

De Grasse (France 1956). An anti-aircraft cruiser laid down in 1938. Building work was suspended in 1940 and resumed in 1946, after important changes had been made to the original design. She was the French Navy's first large post-war surface ship and was stricken in 1973.

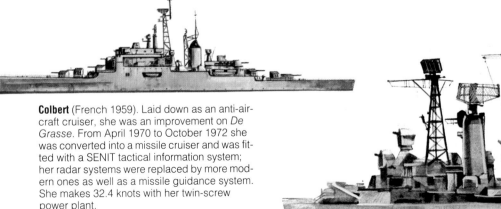

Colbert (French 1959). Laid down as an anti-aircraft cruiser, she was an improvement on *De Grasse*. From April 1970 to October 1972 she was converted into a missile cruiser and was fitted with a SENIT tactical information system; her radar systems were replaced by more modern ones as well as a missile guidance system. She makes 32.4 knots with her twin-screw power plant.

Chapaev (Soviet Union 1948). A post-war cruiser that was part of a class of six laid down in 1939–1940, although they later had their original design changed. *Chapaev* was armed with twelve 6in (152mm) guns and had no torpedo tubes. With twin screws, her top speed was thirty-five knots. She was scrapped in 1961.

The French anti-aircraft cruisers *De Grasse* and *Colbert* were armed with sixteen 5in (127mm) guns in eight twin turrets, two forward and two aft on the main deck, and four symmetrically placed either side of the superstructure. There were twenty 2.2in (57mm) guns in ten twin shielded mounts, eight either side and one before and one abaft the central superstructure. In April 1970, *Colbert* was converted into a missile cruiser, recommissioned in October 1972. During the conversion, her sixteen 5in (127mm) guns were removed and the twenty 2.2in (57mm) guns reduced to twelve. Two 3.9in (100mm) guns in two single turrets were positioned forward and a twin anti-aircraft Masurca missile launcher added aft along with its loading gear. The helicopter and landing pad right aft were retained.

The Dutch anti-aircraft cruisers *De Ruyter* and *De Zeven Provincien* were armed with eight 6in (152mm) anti-ship and anti-aircraft guns in four twin turrets, two forward and two aft, eight 2.2in (57mm) guns in four twin mounts, two of which (one forward and one aft) were behind the 6in (152mm) turrets and two either side, and eight 1.5in (40mm) machine guns. In 1961–1962, *De Zeven Provincien* was converted to a missile cruiser by replacing the two after turrets with a launcher. *De Ruyter* was not converted but was sold to Peru in March 1973 and renamed *Almirante Grau*. *De Zeven Provincien* was also sold to Peru (in August 1974) where she was renamed *Aguirre;* her missiles were removed and she was converted to a helicopter carrier.

Missile cruisers from 1945 to the present day

In the decade following the Second World War, warship construction slowed very greatly. This virtual standstill was not imposed by treaties, unlike the ten-year ''naval holiday'' agreed at Washington, but by circumstances. There were even cases where ships in an advanced stage of construction stayed in the yards for years and were finished at a later date completely different from their original design, as occurred with many Royal Navy aircraft carriers. For cruisers, this lull meant that no new units were laid down until about 1955–1958. The only exceptions were the Russian *Sverdlov*s, laid down in 1948–1950, almost exclusively for reasons of prestige. From 1945 to 1955, only those cruisers laid down before or during the war were commissioned. Examples were America's *Worcester* and *Des Moines* types, France's *De Grasse*, Holland's two *De Ruyter*s, and Russia's *Chapaev*s. All had features generally similar to those of the pre-war and wartime cruisers.

De Zeven Provincien (Holland 1953). Sister ship of *De Ruyter*, she was laid down in 1939 and, after suspension of work due to the war, completed in 1950. In 1961–1962 she was converted to a missile cruiser, retaining the two 6in (152mm) turrets and the forward 2.2in (57mm) turret and installing a twin Terrier missile launcher aft. In 1974 she was sold to Peru and renamed *Aguirre*.

In 1953–1955, a new type of weapon, the missile, had gained a firm footing and was being used both on land and at sea. A missile has much greater destructive power than the shells of even the largest-caliber guns and is far more accurate than artillery. The major navies were immediately keen to equip their ships with this new weapon but they were not prepared to build special ships for the purpose. So, just as in the period between 1932 and 1945 there was a trend to modernize battleships, between 1955 and 1965 the tendency was to convert cruisers, armed originally only with guns, to missile cruisers. The first to convert its cruisers was the United States Navy which, in 1955–1956, installed two twin Terrier missile launchers in place of the after turrets of the cruisers *Boston* and *Canberra*, leaving the armament in the forward area and in the midships superstructures as they were. A similar modification involving only the after part was carried out between 1956 and 1960 on six light cruisers of the *Cleveland* Class, commissioned in 1942–1943. Three of them, namely *Galveston*, *Little Rock*, and *Oklahoma City*, were given one twin Talos launcher. The other three, *Providence*, *Springfield*, and *Topeka*, had a twin Terrier launcher.

A decision was finally made to install missile launchers at both ends. The first three "double-ended" missile cruisers were *Albany*, *Chicago*, and *Columbus*, converted between 1958 and 1962. Other navies also converted some of their cruisers already in service to missile cruisers. In 1962, the Russian Navy installed a twin launcher at the after end of the *Sverdlov* Class cruiser *Dzerzhinsky*. France modified *Colbert* in 1970–1972, Holland *De Zeven Provincien* in 1961–1962, and Italy *Garibaldi* in 1957–1962.

These modified units usually had missile launchers only at their after end and retained the existing guns forward.

By 1963, eighteen years after the war, many of the ideas held in 1945 had changed, and the alliance between the United States, Great Britain, and the Soviet Union had turned into bitter antagonism between the latter and her two ex-allies. Furthermore, both defeated Germany, or rather that part of Germany which had not been occupied by the Soviet Union in 1945, and Italy and Japan, had switched from being former enemies to allies in the Western Bloc, with Italy and Germany even being admitted to the North Atlantic Treaty Organisation (NATO).

The various navies began building ships again. The days of armament modification were over. The new cruisers were no longer armed with guns, just missiles.

It is important to stress that whereas Washington-type cruisers had been armed with eight to ten 8in (203mm) guns and the London- and anti-aircraft types with eight to fifteen 5in (127mm) to 6in (152mm) guns, missile cruisers are armed with only two or four launchers, so, compared to the ships of the past, bristling with guns and machine guns, they give the impression of being virtually unarmed.

But if good artillery fire could be counted on to hit its target 20–25 percent of the time, missiles are more or less guaranteed to reach their target and, moreover, cause much greater damage.

The first newly built missile cruisers were the American *Long Beach* types,

Tiger (Great Britain 1959). *Tiger, Blake,* and *Lion* were to have been conventional cruisers but building work was suspended at the end of the war. They were completed between 1959 and 1961, with twin dual-purpose (6-inch) turrets fore and aft. In 1965–1972, *Tiger* and *Blake* were converted to helicopter carriers and fitted with a flight deck and hangar aft.

Boston (United States 1955). *Boston* and *Canberra* were two heavy cruisers of the *Baltimore* Class, converted to missile cruisers in 1955–1956, and designated *CAG 1* and *CAG 2*. They retained their original armament of two triple 8in (203mm) turrets and five twin 5in (127mm) anti-aircraft turrets forward, whereas at the after end the 8in (203mm) turret was removed and two Terrier missile launchers put in its place. Decommissioned and stricken in 1970.

Albany (United States 1962). With *Chicago* and *Columbus*, she formed the only class of cruisers to be converted to missile ships by removing both the forward and after gun turrets. Missile armament consists of two twin Tartar missile launchers, either side of the bridge, and two twin Talos missile launchers, one forward and one aft. In 1967–1969 *Albany* received improved electronic systems in a major modernization. She was decommissioned in 1980.

Garibaldi (Italy 1937). The only Italian missile cruiser obtained by converting a light cruiser originally armed with ten 6in (152mm) guns. During modifications the after turrets were replaced by a twin Terrier missile launcher and the after turrets replaced by two twin 5.3in (135mm) anti-aircraft turrets. She was discarded in 1972.

commissioned on September 9, 1961, *Bainbridge* on October 6, 1962, and the nine *Leahy* Class in 1962–1964; Italy's *Andrea Dorias* of 1964, Russia's *Kyndas* of 1962, and Britain's *Devonshires* of late-1962. Note that by this time the distinction between cruiser and destroyer was no longer very meaningful; the cruiser was, in effect, a larger destroyer. Of the ships listed above, for example, the *Bainbridges* and *Leahys* were officially described as large destroyers, and the *Devonshires* as missile destroyers. The *Kyndas* were no larger.

As far as power plants were concerned, the post-war years saw the practical application of an engine that in 1935–1936 had been regarded as a mechanical curiosity and, in 1944–1945, had been used on aircraft: the gas turbine. This engine, used in aircraft to generate a very strong jet of high-temperature gas, can, with the appropriate modifications, be used in a ship's engine to drive the screws. This has led to the various navies commissioning ships powered exclusively by gas turbines (COGOG and COGAG), or gas turbines combined with diesel engines to be used at high and low speeds (CODOG and CODAG). There have also been cases of steam and gas turbines combined (COSAG).

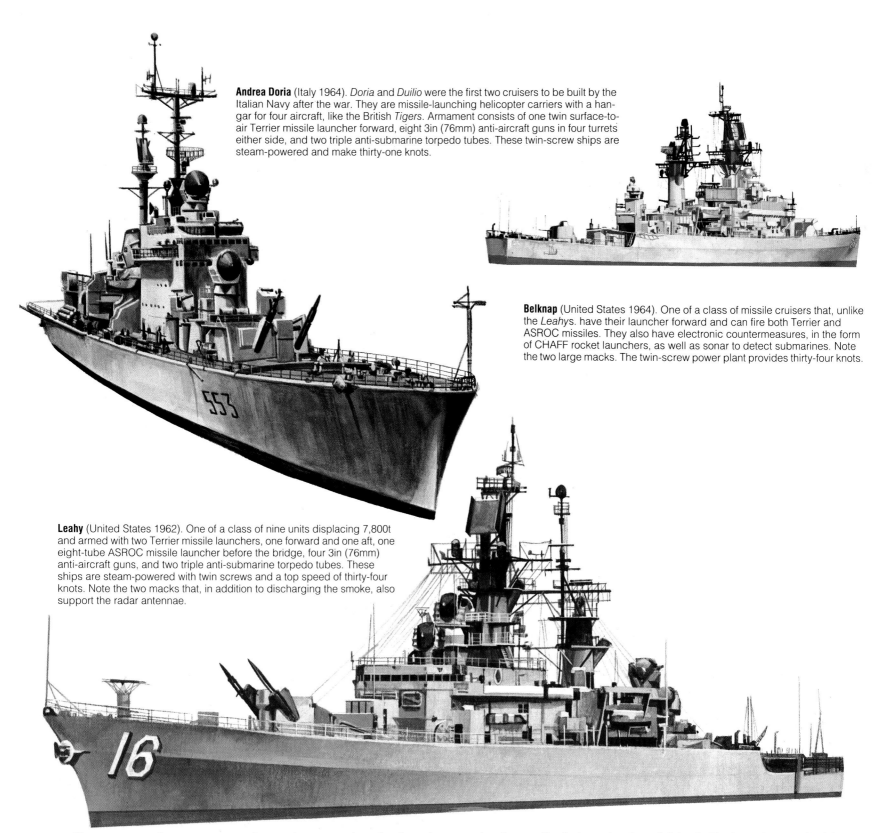

Andrea Doria (Italy 1964). *Doria* and *Duilio* were the first two cruisers to be built by the Italian Navy after the war. They are missile-launching helicopter carriers with a hangar for four aircraft, like the British *Tigers*. Armament consists of one twin surface-to-air Terrier missile launcher forward, eight 3in (76mm) anti-aircraft guns in four turrets either side, and two triple anti-submarine torpedo tubes. These twin-screw ships are steam-powered and make thirty-one knots.

Belknap (United States 1964). One of a class of missile cruisers that, unlike the *Leahys*. have their launcher forward and can fire both Terrier and ASROC missiles. They also have electronic countermeasures, in the form of CHAFF rocket launchers, as well as sonar to detect submarines. Note the two large macks. The twin-screw power plant provides thirty-four knots.

Leahy (United States 1962). One of a class of nine units displacing 7,800t and armed with two Terrier missile launchers, one forward and one aft, one eight-tube ASROC missile launcher before the bridge, four 3in (76mm) anti-aircraft guns, and two triple anti-submarine torpedo tubes. These ships are steam-powered with twin screws and a top speed of thirty-four knots. Note the two macks that, in addition to discharging the smoke, also support the radar antennae.

The most recent improvement regarding marine power plants has been the application of nuclear energy. Only the following United States Navy cruisers have nuclear steam-generator power plants: *Long Beach, Bainbridge, Truxtun, California, South Carolina, Virginia, Texas, Mississippi,* and *Arkansas.*

In the Soviet Navy, the three *Kirov* Class cruisers of 1978–1984 are powered by nuclear reactors, apparently boosted by conventional steam plants.

Missile cruisers have had their launchers positioned in various places. Some have quite a large helicopter complement, whereas others have just one helicopter or else just a pad with no aircraft complement or hangar on board.

Some ships with extensive helicopter installations can be classified as missile or helicopter cruisers. Examples are Britain's *Tiger* and *Blake* of 1969–1972, Italy's *Doria* and *Duilio* of 1964, and *Vittorio Veneto* of 1969 and Russia's *Moskwa* and *Leningrad* of 1968. All these units have a helicopter pad aft.

The British cruisers *Tiger, Blake,* and *Lion* were completed as anti-aircraft gun cruisers in 1959–1961, with two twin automatic 6in guns and three twin 3in guns. From 1965 to 1972, first *Blake* and then *Tiger* were converted to helicopter carriers. *Lion* was not modified and was stricken in 1974.

During the conversion they were fitted with a large box-like superstructure abaft

the aftermast (for the hangar) and a pad right aft. The forward part retained the two 6in (152mm) anti-ship and anti-aircraft guns in a twin turret, and the two 3in (76mm) anti-aircraft guns in a second twin turret. Two quadruple Sea Cat short-range missile launchers were installed on two raised platforms either side of the after funnel.

By this time, some missiles were so small, and had so little impact on ship structure, that they could be fitted without much structural alteration. Ships so fitted could hardly be called missile cruisers. Sea Cat is the main example; it was designed to replace 40mm guns. Others in this category include the U.S. Sea Sparrow and the Soviet SA-N-4. Terrier and Talos were a very different proposition.

The Italian *Andrea Doria* and *Vittorio Veneto* types have a decidedly better profile, both with an after flight pad (131.2 × 55.7ft [40 × 17m] on the *Dorias* and 213 × 65.6ft on *Veneto*). The hangar for the four helicopters on the *Dorias* is in the superstructure abaft the second funnel. The hangar for the nine helicopters on *Veneto* is below the flight deck aft. Their armament is practically the same, comprising one twin anti-aircraft Terrier launcher on the *Dorias* that, on *Veneto*, can also launch ASROC anti-submarine missiles. There are also eight 3in (76mm) anti-aircraft guns of a new type, built by the Italian firm OTO-Melara of La Spezia, in eight single turrets along the sides of the main deck, and two triple torpedo tubes for anti-submarine torpedoes.

The two Russian cruisers, *Moskva* and *Leningrad,* of 1968, have one 295.2 × 114.8ft (90 × 35m) flight deck that occupies the entire after section and has a hangar below for eighteen helicopters. These ships can therefore be regarded as being split into two separate parts: the forward part of a missile cruiser, and the after part a helicopter carrier. In the area before the bridge superstructure there are: 1) two twelve-tube anti-submarine rocket launchers; 2) one twin anti-submarine missile launcher; 3) one twin SA-N-3 anti-aircraft missile launcher on a raised platform; 4) a second twin launcher for the same missiles on the roof of the superstructure. Armament is completed by four 2.2in (57mm) anti-aircraft guns in two twin mounts either side of the bridge superstructure and two quintuple sets of anti-submarine torpedo tubes below the main deck amidships that fire through openings in the sides.

Missile cruisers with more limited helicopter installations can be divided into three groups: those with launchers only at the after end, those with launchers only at the forward end, and those with launchers at both ends.

Britain's eight *Devonshire* or *County* Class (1962–1970) and America's *Truxtun* (1967) belong to the first group. They have a forecastle that extends beyond amidships and almost up to the stern. There is a helicopter pad at the after end of the forecastle: *Truxtun* has no hangar, but on the *Devonshires* there is one abaft the second funnel. Missile armament is on the lowest area of the main deck aft and comprises one twin Sea Slug launcher on the British ships and one twin Terrier and ASROC launcher on *Truxtun.* The *Devonshires* have another two quadruple launchers for Sea Cat short-range anti-aircraft missiles either side of the hangar. Gun armament consists of four 4.5in (115mm) anti-aircraft pieces in two twin turrets forward on the British ships and one single 5in (127mm) dual-purpose and two 3in (76mm) anti-aircraft guns on *Truxtun.* The 5in (127mm) is at the bow and the two 3in (76mm) on side platforms. There are also two triple anti-submarine torpedo tubes. Four of the *County* Class, *Norfolk, Antrim, Glamorgan,* and *Fife* were later modified with a quadruple Exocet launcher in place of the second twin 4.5in (115mm) turret.

The only class to have launchers only at the forward end is America's nine-unit *Belknap* Class, built between 1962 and 1967. They have a forecastle that extends almost to the stern with a pad right aft and a hangar for one helicopter abaft the second mack. The twin terrier and ASROC launcher is on the forecastle forward and the 5in (127mm) anti-aircraft gun is aft on the lowest part of the main deck. The two 3in (76mm) pieces are on two platforms alongside the after funnel.

All the other cruisers have missiles at both the forward and after ends and, in the case of many Russian units, amidships, too. America's *Long Beach* and *Virginia* types have a helicopter pad right aft instead of on the superstructure, with a hangar below. Russia's *Kresta I, Kresta II,* and *Kara* types, however, have their hangar forward in the superstructure at the same level as the pad.

Long Beach was the United States Navy's and the world's first nuclear-powered surface ship. She was ordered on October 15, 1956, and commissioned on September 9, 1961. She is armed with three twin launchers, two forward and one aft. The two forward launchers, one on the main deck and one raised, are for Terrier missiles and the after one, before the helicopter pad, for Talos missiles. Armament is rounded off by two 5in (127mm) anti-aircraft and anti-ship guns, side by side on the deckhouse abaft the bridge, where there is also an octuple ASROC launcher.

The *Virginias* are the United States Navy's most recent nuclear-powered missile cruisers. They are flush-decked and their armament is evenly distributed before and abaft the central superstructure. In both the forward and after areas of the main deck

there are two twin launchers for standard anti-aircraft and ASROC anti-submarine missiles. There are two single 5in (127mm) anti-ship mounts either side of the forward section of the superstructure. There are also two triple anti-submarine torpedo launchers. The *Virginias* have two helicopters, whereas the *Belknaps* had only one.

The Russian missile cruisers usually have ship-to-ship missiles and anti-submarine rockets as well as anti-aircraft missiles. The earliest are the four *Admiral Fokins* (NATO name: *Kynda* Class), commissioned in 1962–1963, with a helicopter pad right aft but no hangar or helicopter complement. Starting at the forward end, the *Admiral Fokins* have the following weapons: two twelve-tube anti-submarine rocket launchers side by side; one anti-aircraft twin launcher (SA-N-1) on a slightly raised platform on the main deck; one quadruple anti-ship launcher (SS-N-3) comprising a bank of four large housings on a single base; six anti-submarine torpedo tubes in two triple mounts amidships either side of the superstructure; another quadruple anti-ship launcher aft, identical to the forward one, on the main deck behind the superstructure step, and four dual-purpose 3in (76mm) guns in two centerline twin turrets, one behind the other.

The four *Kresta I* types, represented by *Vize Admiral Drodz,* were commissioned in 1967–1968 and have a more compact armament system laid out as follows: two twelve-tube anti-submarine rocket launchers abreast right forward; one twin anti-aircraft launcher on the superstructure top before the bridge (for SA-N-1); four anti-ship launchers (SS-N-3) in two twin tubes on the main deck either side of the bridge; two quintuple anti-submarine torpedo tubes symmetrically placed on the main deck abaft the funnel; two twin turrets for the four 2.2in (57mm) anti-aircraft guns abreast on the superstructure top further abaft the funnel; a second twin anti-aircraft launcher yet further abaft and two six-tube anti-submarine rocket launchers. The ten *Kresta II* types are designed for anti-submarine operations, with eight SS-N-14 anti-submarine missiles, replacing the four SS-N-3 of *Kresta I.* They also have a newer anti-aircraft missile, SA-N-3, reportedly with increased anti-ship capability.

The eight *Kara* Class cruisers, represented by *Nikolayev,* are a step up in terms of quality. They displace 10,000t, a 25 percent increase as compared to the *Krestas'* 7,500t, and are powered by gas turbines, making thirty-four knots, one knot less than the 35 knots of the steam-powered *Krestas.* It should be stressed that data relating to the dimensions, displacement, power rating, and speed of Russian ships are not taken from official documents, but estimated from findings and comparisons by NATO experts, because unlike the Western powers, the Soviet Union does not publish any of these data. The *Karas,* with a gas-turbine power plant, have just one large box-shaped funnel and a single large pyramidal radar tower, but the general armament layout is identical to the *Krestas* and so too are the two quadruple launchers (for SS-N-14) either side of the bridge. There are, however, an extra two "pop up" anti-aircraft launchers (SA-N-4) concealed in cylindrical containers either side of the radar tower. The four anti-aircraft guns are 3in (76mm) as opposed to 2.2in (57mm) and there are also eight 1.1in (30mm) machine guns in four twin mounts either side of the funnel. The latter are also installed on the *Kresta IIs.*

The latest development of Russian cruisers is represented by the three *Kirov* types, the prototype having been commissioned in late 1978, with more undoubtedly on the way. They have a mixed power plant combining steam from nuclear generators and steam superheaters. The rating is estimated at 152,876.5hp (155,000CV), 83,835.5hp (85,000CV) from the nuclear power plant and 69,041hp (70,000CV) from the gas turbines. The missiles are in tubes forward of the superstructure. There are twenty tubes for anti-ship (SS-N-19), plus twelve vertical launchers for anti-aircraft and two for anti-submarine missiles. The armament is

Devonshire (Great Britain 1962). One of a class of eight units designed and built as missile cruisers. Their most interesting feature is the mixed propulsion system of two steam turbines linked to four COSAG turbines, driving two screws and giving thirty knots. They have no torpedo tubes but one helicopter with its hangar at flight deck level aft.

Long Beach (United States 1961). The first nuclear-powered cruiser in the world, armed with missile launchers both fore and aft. The twin-screw power plant gives twenty-five knots. Note the large box-like bridge superstructure that supports the fixed radar panels.

Truxtun (United States 1967). The United States Navy's fourth nuclear-powered ship. Initially she was classified as a nuclear-powered missile frigate bearing the designation *DLGN 35*, but since June 1975 has been reclassified as a nuclear-powered missile cruiser, changing her designation to *CGN 35*. Unlike *Long Beach*, which has fixed radar panels, *Truxtun* has a normal revolving radar aerial on a lattice mast. There is another lattice mast to support the antennae of other electronic equipment.

California (United States 1974). *South Carolina* and *California* form the first class of nuclear-powered cruisers. They have no funnel but large truncated conical masts that are virtually the same as those on the *Leahy* and *Belknap* types. They are armed with two single Tartar launchers, one ASROC launcher, two 5in (127mm) anti-aircraft guns, and two triple anti-submarine torpedo tubes. The nuclear power plant has two screws with a top speed of over thirty knots.

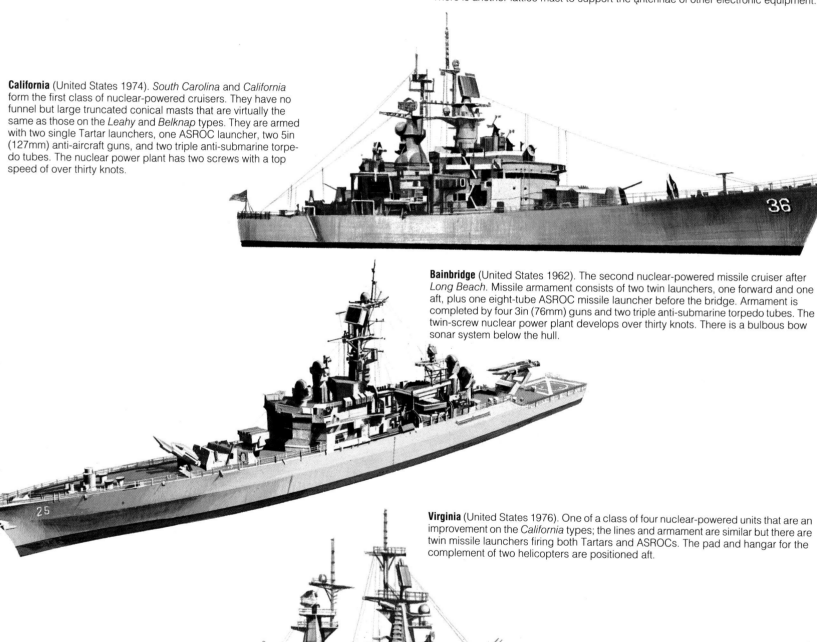

Bainbridge (United States 1962). The second nuclear-powered missile cruiser after *Long Beach*. Missile armament consists of two twin launchers, one forward and one aft, plus one eight-tube ASROC missile launcher before the bridge. Armament is completed by four 3in (76mm) guns and two triple anti-submarine torpedo tubes. The twin-screw nuclear power plant develops over thirty knots. There is a bulbous bow sonar system below the hull.

Virginia (United States 1976). One of a class of four nuclear-powered units that are an improvement on the *California* types; the lines and armament are similar but there are twin missile launchers firing both Tartars and ASROCs. The pad and hangar for the complement of two helicopters are positioned aft.

Admiral Fokin (Soviet Union 1962). One of a class of missile cruisers designated by NATO as the *Kynda* Class. These twin-screw ships are steam-powered and make thirty-five knots. Their distinguishing features are the two large pyramidal structures with pointed ends that replace the masts and macks to support the numerous heavy radar antennae. They are a considerable improvement in Soviet naval armament.

Kirov (Soviet Union 1978). The *Kirov* Class comprises at least three units and is the most modern of the Russian Fleet. Due to her displacement of 23,000t, her anti-ship and anti-aircraft armament in tubes, and the two twin anti-aircraft missile launchers, *Kirov* has been classified by some as a battle cruiser. She is powered by a nuclear reactor with fossil-fuel boost, developing a total power of over 152,876.5hp (155,000CV) and can make thirty-four knots.

Vize Admiral Drodz (Soviet Union 1967). One of a class of missile cruisers designated by NATO as the *Kresta I* Class. She has a formidable anti-submarine and missile armament, and, unlike *Admiral Fokin,* has a hangar aft and a pad for her single helicopter. She has a twin-screw steam power plant of two turbine sets and makes thirty-five knots. Note the large pyramidal mast and the two macks.

rounded off by two 3.9in (100mm) anti-aircraft guns and eight six-barrelled 1.1in (30mm) machine guns. There are a pad and hangar for three to four helicopters right aft.

Helicopter and V/STOL aircraft carrier cruisers

Since 1980, large aircraft carriers have only been retained by the United States and French Navies, because other navies, including the British Navy, regard them as too expensive.

Apart from those of the United States Navy, a large nuclear-powered aircraft carrier is also under construction for the Soviet Navy, and another, smaller one, also nuclear-powered, is programmed for the French Navy.

The current trend in other navies is toward units that are much smaller and more economical than aircraft carriers, and designed to operate with the new V/STOL aircraft.

The first examples of such units were the four Russian cruisers *Kiev, Minsk, Karkov,* and *Novorossik,* commissioned in 1975–1985. These units, classified as "anti-submarine cruisers," are a considerable improvement on the 1968 *Moskva* Class. Their displacement is 42,000 tonnes, over double that of the *Moskva*s, and they have a flight deck set at an angle of 4°, 292ft (89m) long and 68.8ft (21m)

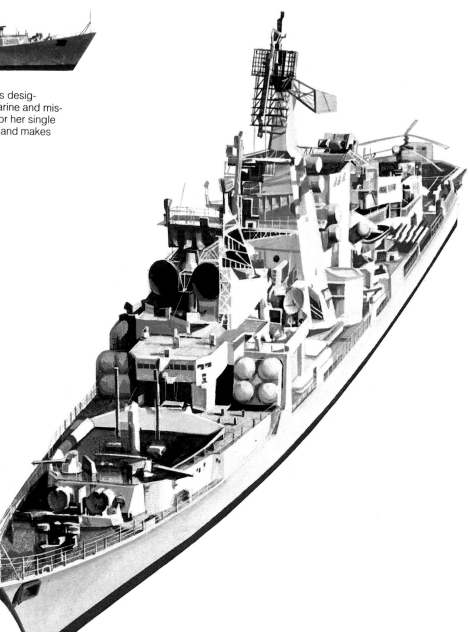

Nikolayev (Soviet Union 1971). The *Nikolayev* Class is thought to be made up of eight units with a displacement of about 10,000t, gas turbines, and a top speed of thirty-four knots. They have the typical Russian pyramidal mast, followed by a large box-like uptake for the gas turbines. *Nikolayev* has two quadruple anti-submarine missile launchers, and two twin anti-aircraft, one forward and one aft, and two "pop up" amidships. She has a helicopter pad aft and a hangar for one aircraft.

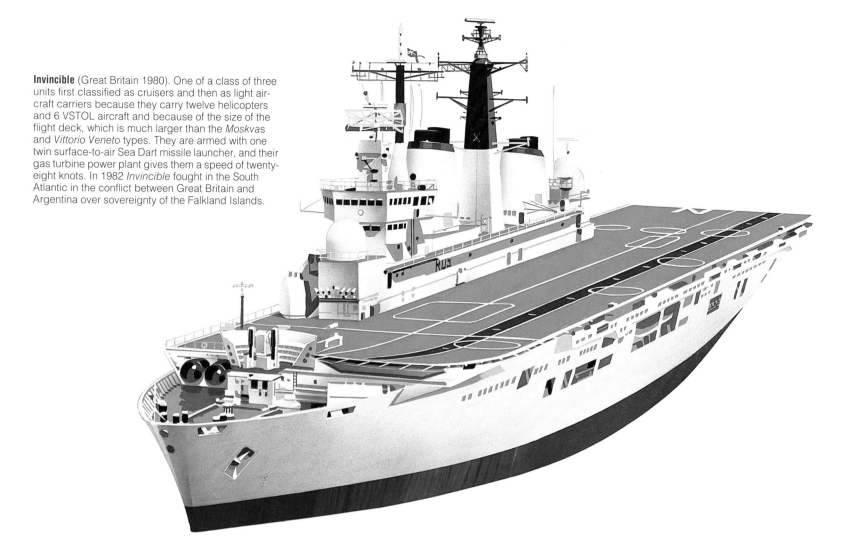

Invincible (Great Britain 1980). One of a class of three units first classified as cruisers and then as light aircraft carriers because they carry twelve helicopters and 6 VSTOL aircraft and because of the size of the flight deck, which is much larger than the *Moskva*s and *Vittorio Veneto* types. They are armed with one twin surface-to-air Sea Dart missile launcher, and their gas turbine power plant gives them a speed of twenty-eight knots. In 1982 *Invincible* fought in the South Atlantic in the conflict between Great Britain and Argentina over sovereignty of the Falkland Islands.

wide, which does not have a straight deck alongside, like a normal aircraft carrier, and conventional cruiser armament in the bows. Starting forward on the main deck there are two twelve-tube anti-submarine rocket launchers abreast; one twin SUW anti-submarine missile launcher; four twin SS-N-12 anti-submarine missile launchers; one twin SS-N-3 anti-aircraft missile launchers; and a twin 3in (76mm) anti-aircraft turret.

There is another SS-N-3 anti-aircraft missile launcher abaft the island with a second 3in (76mm) anti-aircraft turret next to it. There are another two SA-N-4 launchers in a housing on the starboard side of the island from which they are fired, and lastly ten anti-submarine torpedo tubes in two quintuple launchers. The hangar houses thirty to thirty-five helicopters or V/STOL aircraft and is served by two lifts. These four-screw steam-powered cruisers can make thirty-two knots.

Britain's *Invincible, Illustrious,* and *Ark Royal* are of a very different design. The first was commissioned on June 11, 1980. They have a displacement of only 19,500t, less than half that of the *Kiev*s, and transport only eighteen helicopters or V/STOL aircraft against the *Kiev*s' thirty to thirty-five.

The flight deck is straight as opposed to angled and runs the entire port side of the ship stopping a few feet from the bow. There is a large island to starboard with two funnels, two masts, and tall radar aerials. Armament comprises one twin Sea Dart anti-aircraft missile launcher forward at the side of the starboard end of the flight deck. These twin-screw ships have four gas turbines and make twenty-eight knots. *Invincible* was stationed in the South Atlantic during the conflict between Great Britain and Argentina over the Falkland Islands question. It should be stressed that these units are officially classified as light aircraft carriers.

After the four Russian *Kiev* types and the three British *Invincible*s, the eighth through deck ship is Italy's *Garibaldi*. This unit displaces about half as much as the British and a quarter of the Russian ships. She, too, has a straight full-length flight deck and can carry a combination of sixteen helicopters and V/STOL aircraft. Armament is four anti-ship missile launchers, on platforms either side aft, and three twin anti-aircraft missile launchers on the starboard side of the flight deck, two before and one abaft the island. Lastly, there are six anti-submarine torpedo tubes in two triple launchers and six 1.5in (40mm) machine guns in three twin mounts. These twin-screw units have four gas turbines and make twenty-nine knots.

Experience gained with these prototypes will be decisive in the formation of future battle fleets and for the survival of the large 90,000-tonne aircraft carriers.

Vittorio Veneto (Italy 1969). One of the first helicopter carriers to have a large flight deck and a complement of nine aircraft. She was to have had a sister ship named *Trieste* but she was never built. In the forward section, *Vittorio Veneto* has a twin surface-to-air Terrier or ASROC anti-submarine missile launcher and eight 3in (76mm) anti-aircraft guns in single turrets (four either side), and two triple anti-submarine torpedo tubes. The twin-screw power plant enables thirty-two knots.

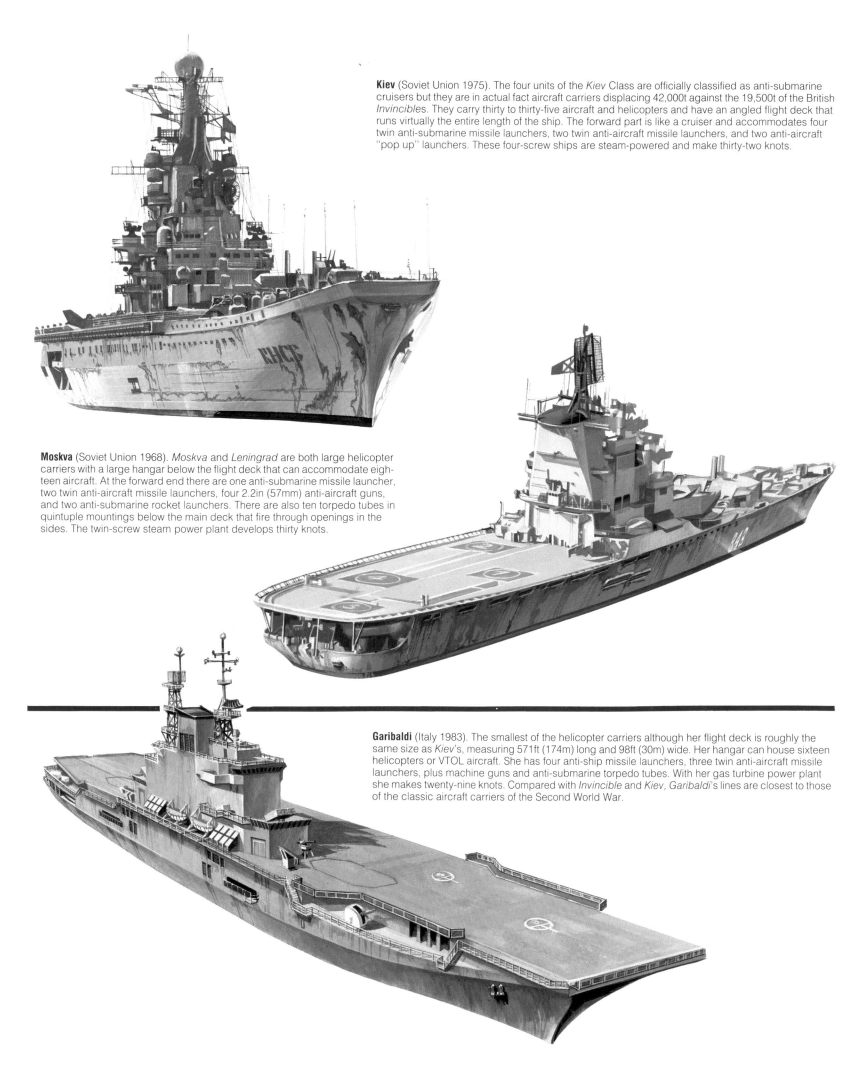

Kiev (Soviet Union 1975). The four units of the *Kiev* Class are officially classified as anti-submarine cruisers but they are in actual fact aircraft carriers displacing 42,000t against the 19,500t of the British *Invincible*s. They carry thirty to thirty-five aircraft and helicopters and have an angled flight deck that runs virtually the entire length of the ship. The forward part is like a cruiser and accommodates four twin anti-submarine missile launchers, two twin anti-aircraft missile launchers, and two anti-aircraft "pop up" launchers. These four-screw ships are steam-powered and make thirty-two knots.

Moskva (Soviet Union 1968). *Moskva* and *Leningrad* are both large helicopter carriers with a large hangar below the flight deck that can accommodate eighteen aircraft. At the forward end there are one anti-submarine missile launcher, two twin anti-aircraft missile launchers, four 2.2in (57mm) anti-aircraft guns, and two anti-submarine rocket launchers. There are also ten torpedo tubes in quintuple mountings below the main deck that fire through openings in the sides. The twin-screw steam power plant develops thirty knots.

Garibaldi (Italy 1983). The smallest of the helicopter carriers although her flight deck is roughly the same size as *Kiev*'s, measuring 571ft (174m) long and 98ft (30m) wide. Her hangar can house sixteen helicopters or VTOL aircraft. She has four anti-ship missile launchers, three twin anti-aircraft missile launchers, plus machine guns and anti-submarine torpedo tubes. With her gas turbine power plant she makes twenty-nine knots. Compared with *Invincible* and *Kiev*, *Garibaldi*'s lines are closest to those of the classic aircraft carriers of the Second World War.

TORPEDO BOATS

The Development of torpedo boats from 1877 to 1945

The torpedo boat came into being as a result of the introduction of the torpedo as a naval weapon. In fact, in the early years the torpedo was the main or, more precisely, the only weapon on this boat.

The torpedo, or self-propelled mine, was invented by an Englishman named Robert Whitehead, who lived in Austria and was the manager of the Fiume Technical Works. In 1866, he demonstrated the prototype to the Austrian government: it could travel about 218yd (200m) at a speed of six knots. A few years later, in 1871, an improved version was moving as far as 656yd (600m) at twenty-four to twenty-eight knots, carrying a 66lb (30kg) explosive charge. It was quickly seized upon by the major European navies: British, French, Italian, German, and Russian, alike. Not until 1891, some 20 years later, did the United States Navy adopt it.

Between 1880 and 1890 the torpedo had been a secondary weapon for large ironclads and cruisers, but it was later used as an excellent means of coastal and harbor entrance defense. Because it could travel only 437 to 656yd (400–600m), it was allocated to small fast ships which could get close to larger ones by dodging their gun fire, and position themselves at the correct range from which to fire their torpedoes. As they were small craft with a very poor range, they could be used only for coastal defense. A way was also found, however, to use them as an offensive weapon by moving them close to the enemy coastline on board special ships called torpedo boat carriers that then lowered them into the sea from whence they could attack enemy ships at their harbor moorings.

The Royal Navy was the first to build a fast boat armed solely with torpedoes in 1887. *Lightning* was only about 84ft (25.62m) long, but capable of a then incredible 18.75 knots. Torpedo boats soon split into two types: long-range first-rate or seagoing boats that could operate at a considerable distance from the coast, and second-rate or coastal boats that could be towed or transported by larger ships, suitable for coastal defense or attacking inside enemy naval bases. Second-rate torpedo boats could also be transferred by rail from one site to the next.

Around 1882, the British shipyard, Thornycroft, specialized in building two types of units: the second-raters, with a displacement of about 12.5 tonnes, 59ft (18m) long, a top speed of 17.5 knots and armed with two torpedo tubes, and the first-raters, with a displacement of thirty-five tonnes, armed with one torpedo tube, and having a top speed of twenty-one knots. In 1883, the Schichau shipyard in Germany designed and built much larger boats with a displacement of eighty tonnes, 128ft (39m) long and a top speed of twenty knots. Britain followed the German example by building increasingly larger boats. In fact, in 1887, torpedo boat *N 80* displaced 105 tonnes and in 1894, *N91-97* 130 tonnes. Similar displacements were adopted by other navies, most of which bought their boats from British and German shipyards.

In 1887, in addition to the seagoing and coastal torpedo boats, the German Navy built a third type, to be used as the command ship of a torpedo boat division. For this reason, it was larger, had a higher displacement, and could accommodate the General Staff of the Flotilla. This type of torpedo boat was known in German as a *"Torpedo-Division-Boote,"* and in English as a "Division boat."

In 1886–1888, two units named *Folgore* and *Saetta* were built in Italy. They were classified as scout torpedo boats and displaced 370 tonnes. They differed from the German Division-Boote. However, the five *Aquila* Class, built by Schichau in 1888, were typically German, however, and displaced 139 tonnes. The Austrian Navy also acquired seven German Torpedo-Division-Boote.

In short, by the end of the century, three types of torpedo boats were in commission: coastal boats with a displacement of between 40 and 100t, seagoing vessels, and Division-boats with a displacement of around 200 to 300 tonnes.

The small coastal torpedo boats soon came to be regarded as having no importance in warfare and so disappeared from the navies, but the importance of the seagoing torpedo boat grew and the division boat types came to be included in this category too. Their capabilities were such that they could be used in combination with larger ships.

Between 1880 and 1900, there were no naval battles to serve as a test-bed for the use and offensive capabilities of torpedo boats. The first naval conflict to provide this opportunity was the Russo–Japanese War of 1904, during which the Japanese seagoing torpedo boats carried out numerous offensive actions against Russian ships, both at anchor in port and at sea. The torpedo boat fared badly in this war. In fact, it became clear that the offensive duties of seagoing torpedo boats could be performed much more efficiently by torpedo boat destroyers which were faster, better-armed ships with greater range and better seagoing qualities. For this reason, from 1905 onwards all the major navies stopped building torpedo boats, except for Italy and Austria, which still considered that the vessel could be put to good use in coastal or sheltered waters. Between 1905 and the end of the First World War, practically the only type to be built was the seagoing torpedo boat.

The experience gained in the First World War confirmed that of the 1904 Russo-Japanese War and highlighted the extremely poor fighting capabilities of torpedo boats, demonstrating on the other hand that the torpedo boat destroyer was the real seagoing torpedo boat, fit for both action against bigger ships and escorting battleship and cruiser convoys.

This did not mark the end of torpedo boats, however. They survived amd were also used in the Second World War although their duties and specifications were no longer anything like those of the forty-tonne coastal torpedo boats of 1882.

From 1918–1920 to 1933–1935, there was a lull in torpedo boat construction, but in this period many navies reclassified some of their older smaller torpedo boat destroyers as torpedo boats. The Japanese Navy was the only one to continue building torpedo boats and commissioned twenty-three 770-tonne boats (that had been laid down as second-class destroyers) in 1923.

The experience gained in the Second World War confirmed that torpedo boats were of little use in warfare, even if they had considerable displacements and were well-armed. The result was that such units finally ceased to exist. In the post-war years, existing torpedo boats remained in service until they were run into the ground, but no navy ordered the construction of new units.

Torpedo boat power plants

The early torpedo boats were small vessels, but they were powered by steam because in 1880 neither the diesel nor the gasoline engine had yet been invented.

The small coastal vessels of the 1880–1890 period had one screw, one reciprocating engine, and one coal-fired boiler. Some of the seagoing torpedo boats built in the same period, however, had two engines and twin screws.

In 1904–1905, the first turbine torpedo boats were commissioned. The first experimental unit was *Caroline*, built privately at the Yarrow shipyard. She displaced 130 tonnes, had three screws and a power plant of one turbine unit and a reciprocating engine. The high-pressure turbine turned the port screw, the low-

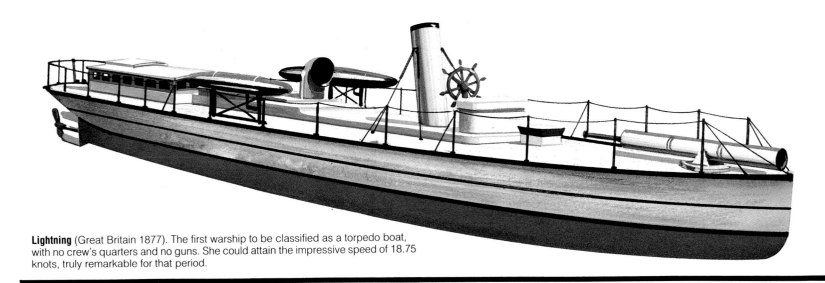

Lightning (Great Britain 1877). The first warship to be classified as a torpedo boat, with no crew's quarters and no guns. She could attain the impressive speed of 18.75 knots, truly remarkable for that period.

pressure one the starboard screw, and the reciprocating engine the middle screw. This unit was later purchased by the Brazilian Navy and was renamed *Goyaz*. A reciprocating engine was required on at least one of the screws because the early turbines only turned in one direction, so the two side screws served only for going forward, the reciprocating engine being used for reversing as well as going forward. A mixed propulsion system of this type was tried out by the Italian Navy about ten years later on the *39 RM*, although in this case the two side screws were driven by reciprocating engines and the middle one by a low-pressure turbine into which the two reciprocating engines discharged their exhaust.

The Royal Navy was first to use turbine engines on boats (later redesignated coastal destroyers) numbered from *1* to *36*, commissioned between 1906 and 1909. All these units had triple-screws powered by one set of four Parsons turbines directly coupled to the shafts. The high-pressure turbine drove the starboard shaft, the medium-pressure one the port shaft, and the low-pressure, plus a fourth turbine for reversing, the middle shaft. In the French Navy, the first experimental turbine torpedo boat was *No. 293*, built at the Normand shipyard in 1903–1904, powered by five 2,173hp (2,000CV) Parsons turbines and making a speed of twenty-six knots. There were three screws, the starboard screw driven by a high-pressure turbine, the port by a medium-pressure turbine, and the middle by a low-pressure turbine plus one cruising-speed turbine and one for reversing.

In the Italian Navy too, the large numbers of torpedo boats built before 1918 were powered by two reciprocating engines except for a few experimental units such as *39 RM* with two reciprocating engines and one turbine on three screws; *31 AS* with four Parsons turbines on three screws; *32 AS* with two Ansaldo turbines on two screws and *74* and *75 OLT* with two turbines and two screws.

In the German Navy, the first turbine torpedo boats were the seagoing vessels numbered *S 125* to *G 137* of 1904–1907 that had three screws with seven or eight Parsons turbines arranged in more or less the same way as on their British counterparts. Those numbered from *V 161* to *G 197* had two turbines and two screws. Only after 1914–1915 were the coastal torpedo boats fitted with turbines, such as the four numbered *V 105* to *V 108* that had two turbines and two screws, followed by the *A 26*–*A 55*s with one turbine and one screw and the *A 56*–*A 113*s with two turbines and two screws.

In the Dutch Navy, the six boats numbered *Z1* to *Z6*, built in 1915–1919, had two turbines and two screws. Four of these, built at the German Vulcan yard, were later incorporated into the German Navy and designated *V 105* to *V 108*.

In the Spanish Navy, the first turbine torpedo boats were those numbered *1* to *22*, built in the Cartagena Shipyard between 1910 and 1919. They were similar to the *Cyclone* types because they were of the French Normand design. The first seven units had three screws with the above turbine arrangement; the last fifteen, numbered *8* to *22*, had two screws driven by two turbines, one high- and one low-pressure.

All torpedo boats built after 1930 had twin screws driven by turbine units that transmitted the drive to the shafts via gears that reduced the speed of rotation.

It was usual for all torpedo boats built from 1880 to 1945 to have steam power plants, but there were a few experimental units with diesel or gasoline power plants such as Russia's *Dzerzhinsky* and *Kirov* of 1938 with three diesel engines, and Britain's *Mercury* of 1911 with five sets of six-cylinder gasoline Napier engines.

The boilers of the older torpedo boats were coal fired. The first to have oil-fired boilers was Russia's *Vyborg, No. 102*, built in Britain in 1886 with coal-fired boilers and modified in 1896 to operate with oil-fired ones. After this experiment,

all Russian torpedo boats with locomotive-style coal-fired boilers were modified to burn oil.

In the British Navy, the first oil-fired torpedo boats were the *Cricket* Class, later numbered *1* to *12*, commissioned in 1906–1907.

In the Italian Navy, oil-fired boilers were first used in 1890 on torpedo boat *104 S*. Then, as from 1896, thirty-seven *S* types were modified for oil burning, some of them even having their original locomotive-type coal-fired boilers replaced by water-tube oil-fired boilers. Examples of torpedo boats converted to oil-combustion were *Condore* (1900), the four *Pegaso* series, and the three *Alcione* (1906) series belonging to the *Pegaso* Class. The modifications were done between 1909 and 1913. The first Italian torpedo boats to have oil-fired boilers from the very beginning were *Calypso* and *Climene* of the *Pegaso* Class, commissioned in 1907–1909, *Gabbiano* of 1907, and all those of the numerous *PN* Class.

In the Austrian Navy, units *TB 1* to *TB 6*, built in the Trieste Technical Works, and *TB 7* to *TB 12*, built in the Danubius shipyard in Fiume between 1909 and 1914 all had oil-fired boilers. In the Dutch Navy, so, too, did *Hydra* and *Scylla* of 1899–1900.

All torpedo boats built after 1930 had oil-fired boilers. The screw-rudder experiment carried out on the torpedo boat *Fatum* deserves special mention. She was built privately in the Orlando shipyard of Leghorn in 1892 and had a single adjustable screw that made it possible to steer without a rudder.

Torpedo boat armament

The armament of the early torpedo boats was made up exclusively of torpedoes: *Lightning* had one above-water torpedo tube in the bows and two more on stands either side of the deck.

The torpedo tubes soon became fixed underwater ones in the conventional bow position, the position they usually occupied on battleships and cruisers. All Thornycroft and Yarrow torpedo boats of 1887–1895 had a tube, or tubes, fixed at the bow and inclined slightly downwards.

In addition to fixed bow tubes, some units were also fitted with trainable deck torpedo tubes, such as Yarrow *No. 24* with one aft; the French *Forban*s with two on the centerline, one forward between the two funnels and one aft; and the Japanese *No. 15*s with just one stern tube.

Single torpedo tubes were replaced by twins, early examples being those installed on the British Thornycrofts Nos. *25* to *29*, and *41* to *60* of 1885, and, in particular, on the French Normands Nos. *130* to *144* of 1891, later modified by turning one of the tubes round 180°, enabling torpedoes to be fired in both directions at the same time.

Twin tubes were replaced by triples, as on the Danish torpedo boats *Dragen*, *Hvalen*, and *Laxen* of 1930, with two centerline mounts abaft the funnels; the German *Möwe* and *Wolf* types (formerly torpedo boat destroyers) of 1926–1928, with two centerline mounts amidships; and the Japanese *Tidori* Class of 1933–1934 that had a single mount.

As for the gun and machine gun armament, first- and second-class torpedo boats had only one or two machine guns, as did, for example, the British-type Yarrows Nos. *39* to *49* of 1887–1890, (one machine gun); the French Nos. *126* through *369*, constructed between 1887 and 1908, were armed with two 1.4in (37mm) machine guns; and the Germans, bearing Roman numerals and numbered from *S7* to *S57*, were built between 1886 and 1890, and armed with two 1.4in (37mm) machine guns. However, those built by Schichau and numbered *S 58* to *S 89* had a 2in (50mm) light gun. In the Italian Navy, the coastal torpedo boats built up until 1887 were armed with one or two 1in (25mm) machine guns; those built thereafter, from the *76–77 YA* of 1887 on, had, instead, two 1.4in (37mm) machine guns, while those of Pegasus Class and subsequent craft built from 1904 to 1906 had two 1.8in (47mm) machine guns. Torpedo boats of the PN Class, first series, had one 2.2in (57mm) light gun abaft. By contrast, those of the second series had two 3in (76mm) guns on the foredeck.

In the Japanese Navy, as well, torpedo boats were armed with 1.4in (37mm) and 1.8in (47mm) machine guns. In the Austro-Hungarian Navy, units built in 1913 and 1916 were armed with two 2.5in (66mm) guns. In the Russian, American, and minor navies, machine guns were usually 1in (25mm), 1.4in (37mm), or 1.8in (47mm), except for the Dutch *G 15* and *16* and *Z 1-8* which had two 3in (76mm) guns.

The armament of torpedo boats built after 1930—and, thus, operating during the Second World War—was different. These boats had large numbers of guns, anti-aircraft machine guns, and anti-submarine depth charges.

In conclusion then, up until the 1914–1918 war the main weapon of the torpedo boat was the torpedo, together with a few machine guns or small guns as secondary armament, but by the Second World War, guns and anti-aircraft machine guns had become just as important as torpedoes.

Coastal defense torpedo boats from 1878 to 1898

The first real torpedo boat, as such, armed with torpedo tubes, was the already mentioned British *Lightning*, built by Thornycrofts and commissioned in May 1877. Even before this, however, various navies had been building torpedo boats armed with "spar torpedoes," as opposed to Whitehead torpedoes. These spar torpedoes comprised an explosive charge attached to the end of a long spar at the torpedo boat's bow that exploded on contact with the side of the enemy ship. This weapon was used in the American Civil War (1861–1865) on the *David*s which moved underwater or awash. Another example was the experimental torpedo boat designed during the Crimean War (1853–1856) by a Russian, General Tiesenhauser, that was built at Nikolayev but sunk during trials and the second, *Opyt* by name, which succeeded in sinking the sailing ship *Meteor* in September 1862. Spar torpedo boats were built by the navy of the North German Confederation during the Franco-Prussian War of 1870–1871, and others by Thornycroft in 1874 and Yarrow in 1871–1874.

Lightning was a small vessel, 84ft (25.62m) long, 11ft (3.30m) in the beam, and with a draft of 4ft (1.15m). She had a displacement of twenty-seven tonnes, a locomotive type boiler, and a two-cylinder reciprocating engine to drive one screw. The position of the propeller was unusual in that it was abaft the rudder which (although single and on the centerline) was in two separate sections, one above and one below the propeller shaft. *Lightning* was armed with one bow torpedo tube on the deck and two torpedo tubes on stands either side amidships.

Italy's *Nibbio* was very similar. She, too, was built by Thornycroft and was 79.65ft (24.28m) long, 10ft (3.05m) in the beam, with a draft of 3ft (0.90m), and a displacement of 26t. The power plant was the same as *Lightning*'s but the rudder was in the normal position abaft the screw. *Nibbio* was armed with two bow torpedo tubes abreast and inside the hull.

As a rule, all these early torpedo boats had underwater bow torpedo tubes positioned inside the hull and inclined slightly downwards. All the British Thornycroft, Yarrow, and White torpedo boats built between 1878 and 1904 numbered twenty upwards for instance, had one tube in this position, whereas the first twenty had an external bow tube on deck like *Lightning*.

The following units had two twin tubes: Britain's second-rate torpedo boats numbered *51* to *100*, built between 1878 and 1887; France's Yarrow, Claparède, and Normand types numbered *33* to *130* (1879–1889); Germany's Thornycroft, Yarrow, Schichau, and Germania-Werft designated *Th 1* and *2*, *G*, *S* and *Y* and those bearing Roman numerals from *XII* to *XXXIII* (1884–1887); and Italy's Thornycrofts, Yarrows, and Schichaus of 1881–1894.

The older coastal, or second-rate, torpedo boats were armed solely with torpedoes, and there were several different types of such vessels, especially the French and a few German ones, that did not even have Whitehead torpedoes, relying exclusively on spar-torpedoes. Then, after 1885, the Royal Navy (and a few years later the Italian and German Navies) began to put a few machine guns on board: the British Thornycrofts from *25* to *29* and Yarrows *30–33* had three 1.4in (37mm) machine guns (1886); the French numbered *126* upwards, commissioned from 1887 onwards, were armed with two 1.4in (37mm) machine guns; and the Italian *Falco* and *Aquila* of 1881 had two 1in (25mm) machine guns.

Large numbers of coastal torpedo boats were built: the French Navy had 369, the British sixty-two, the Italian 105, the Austrian about fifty, and the Russian about a hundred. As mentioned, the French Navy had many more torpedo boats than any of the other navies. This was because the "Jeune École," headed by Admiral Aube (navy minister from January 1886 to May 1887), considered that the age of the large battleships was over and entrusted coastal defense entirely to small coastal torpedo boats that were to constitute a "mobile defense" that could be moved to where it was required either by rail or along inland waterways. In this way it should have been possible to move entire flotillas of torpedo boats by rail from the Mediterranean to the Atlantic, and vice versa, or send these torpedo boats along the inland waterways that criss-cross France and provide a communication route between the two seas. As a point of interest, inland waterways were used to bring the Papal Navy's first three steam tugs from Britain to the Tiber in 1842. The French Navy, therefore, built about sixty experimental units between 1878 and 1883 with displacements varying between the 11.8 tonnes of *No. 30*, built by Thornycroft in 1878, to the 103t of *No. 1*, built by Claparède in 1878. For the most part, however, they had displacements of 30 to 40 tonnes and almost all were armed simply with spar torpedoes or one or two bow torpedo tubes. As they were experimental units, they were built both in French shipyards, like Claparède, Normand, Chantiers de la Méditerranée, and in naval yards, such as the ones in Rochefort and Brest, as well as in the British yards of Yarrow and Thornycroft, so that each one would be of a different type and offer different features.

From 1883 onwards, the units were standardized, the first type being the 115ft (35m) long Normand design numbered *65* to *125*. These were followed by type *126*, again designed by Normand, numbered *126* to *129*, *145* to *149*, and *152* to *200*. They were 120.89ft (36.85m) long and displaced 79.4 tonnes. Then there were the type *130*s numbered *130* to *144*, the extremely numerous 121.39ft (37m) type with two boilers and numbered *201* to *294*, displacing around ninety tonnes, and finally the 124.67ft (38m) type numbered *295* to *369* and displacing about one hundred tonnes, built between 1903 and 1908. The French doctrine of mobile defense was also espoused by the Italian Navy which, on a smaller scale, followed in French footsteps in 1878–1888 by ordering, first from the British Thornycroft and Yarrow yards and then from Italian yards, fifty-nine torpedo boats, three of which were Yarrow types (bearing the letter Y) and fifty-six Thornycrofts (distinguished by the letter T). Displacements varied from thirteen to forty-four tonnes and all were armed with two bow torpedo tubes. After this experiment, like the French Navy, it was decided to plump for displacements of eighty to 110 tonnes. The first were the *Schichau*s, distinguished by the letter *S* and numbered from *57* to *75* and *84* to *154*, and the 110t boats were the *Yarrow*s, marked *YA* and numbered *76* to *79*.

Between 1878 and 1890, the British built sixty-three second-rate torpedo boats with displacements of between eleven and sixteen tonnes, practically all of which were armed with two fixed bow torpedo tubes. Then between 1877 and 1895 they built eighty-nine first-raters displacing twenty-seven to 100t, almost all armed with one fixed bow torpedo tube and many with two to four deck torpedo tubes. The early torpedo boats of the German Navy were also built by Thornycroft and Yarrow, such as *Th 1*, *Th 2*, and *Y*. *Th 1* and *Y* displaced 81t and 83t, respectively, and *Th 2* was a small 14.5t boat. A third type displacing 86t was built by Germania-Werft and bore the letter *G*.

In 1884, the six *W*s were built, from *W 1* to *W 6*, at the Weser shipyard in Bremen; then came the ten *V*s, from *V 1* to *V 10*, at the Vulkan shipyard in Stettin; and the six *S*s from *S 1* to *S 6*, at the Schichau shipyard in Elbing. These boats were 108–121ft (33–37m) long with displacements of 60 to 100t and armed with two bow torpedo tubes. Subsequently, Schichau was given the task of building fifty boats displacing 103 tonnes, numbered *S 7* to *S 57*, and armed with one bow and two side torpedo tubes.

The Japanese Navy tried out various types of torpedo boats, numbered one to thirty, built by Yarrow in Britain, Schneider and Normand in France, and Schichau and Vulkan in Germany, all commissioned between 1880 and 1898, the smallest displacing around 53–54t and the largest and last, around 75–88t.

In 1898–1899, the Japanese shipyards Kawasaki and Mitsubishi built their first eight torpedo boats, to Schichau design, which displaced 89t and had one bow and two side torpedo tubes. These units were numbered *31* to *38*. More units followed, displacing 89–102t, armed with three deck torpedo tubes and numbered *39* to *75*, built in 1899-1903.

The Austro-Hungarian Navy followed the same procedure by purchasing Thornycroft, Yarrow, and Schichau types, plus a few built at the Pola Naval Yard. They displaced from fifteen to ninety-five tonnes and in general were armed with two bow torpedo tubes.

The Russian Navy purchased torpedo boats in Germany from Schichau and Vulkan; in Britain from Thornycroft and Yarrow; in France from Normand, Claparède, and Chantiers de la Méditerranée and also from the Finnish shipyards Abo and Kolpino. Units based on foreign models were then built in the St. Petersburg, Sevastopol, Odessa, and Nikolayev Naval Yards. Most of these units displaced 70–80t and were armed with two bow or deck torpedo tubes.

The minor navies followed the same route, purchasing most of their boats from Yarrow, Thornycroft, Schichau, and Vulkan.

Italy's Ansaldo shipyard in Sestri Ponente supplied Greece with two torpedo boats and Turkey with ten.

Coastal torpedo boats soon proved to be of little use as a weapon, the smaller ones, in particular, were soon taken out of commission, thus putting an end to the mobile defense doctrine.

Seagoing torpedo boats from 1884 to 1919

Together with coastal torpedo boats, the major European navies began building other larger units with better seagoing qualities. These seagoing torpedo boats were not to be used for coastal defense nor carried on board larger ships, but for operations with large warships far away from base.

The criterion adopted in assigning a torpedo boat to one class or another is not clearly defined. The Italian Navy classified all those units commissioned between 1881 and 1900 as coastal boats, including the Schichaus that displaced 80t, *Condore, Pelican,* and all the *PN* types, built in 1911–1918 and displacing 140–150t. The French Navy classified even their 124.67ft (38m) types, numbered *295* to *369,* commissioned in 1903–1908 and displacing 102t as coastal torpedo boats. *Coureur* and *Avant Garde,* displacing around 130t, and the 120t *Aquilon* were, however, classified as ''seagoing'' boats. The Royal Navy classified both *Lightning,* which displaced 27t, and those units numbered *21* to *36,* built in 1908–1909, and displacing 263t, as first-raters. Other navies, such as the Japanese, Russian, and Austrian did not make this official distinction.

In this book, seagoing torpedo boats are regarded as those with a displacement of around 150t or more.

The major distinguishing feature of torpedo boat hulls, whether coastal or seagoing, was that, instead of being covered by a conventional flat deck, the bow had curved edges that joined up with the sides. This was to allow water, which washed over the deck even when these small boats were in relatively calm seas, to run off again. The early seagoing torpedo boats had no real bridge superstructure, but a conning tower with small side ports like the coastal boats. Examples were the British first-rate 67t torpedo boat *No. 24 Yarrow* and her contemporaries: the French 152t *Forban* of 1895; the Japanese 53t *No. 15* of 1891, and the Italian 140t *PN* Class of 1906–1912.

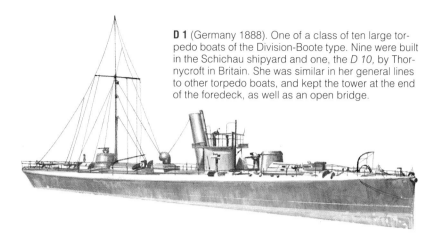

D 1 (Germany 1888). One of a class of ten large torpedo boats of the Division-Boote type. Nine were built in the Schichau shipyard and one, the *D 10,* by Thornycroft in Britain. She was similar in her general lines to other torpedo boats, and kept the tower at the end of the foredeck, as well as an open bridge.

As far as funnels were concerned, coastal torpedo boats usually had only one because they were powered by only one boiler, but the seagoing boats, with their two boilers, had two funnels, like the British ones numbered *82* upwards, built between 1899 and 1909; the French 121.39ft (37m) and 124.67ft (38m) types; and the Italian *Pegaso*s of 1906–1907 and *PN* Class of 1911–1918. Some even had three funnels, like America's *Stringham No. 19,* and *Porters Nos. 6* and *7,* and the French *Lansquenet* of 1894. Some single-boilered coastal and seagoing torpedo boats had two funnels, not one behind the other down the centerline, but two abreast, both for the one boiler. Examples were the French *No. 1* (1878) built by Claparède, the Normand's Nos. *64* and *65* (1885), and Nos. *130–144* (1891); Britain's Yarrows No. *80* (1887); Italy's *Euterpe* (1883); and Russia's *Batum* (1880).

Another peculiarity of some of the early torpedo boats was that they had masts and sails, which were rigged for long deep water passages. Britain's first-raters Nos. *21* and *22,* for instance, had three masts setting one square sail and a spanker each, plus a jib, although they were built in 1884–1885. Other examples of rigged three-masters were Britain's colonial *Childer* types (1883); the French *Ouragans* (1887); the German *Th 1* and *Th 2* (1884); the Russian *Suchum No. 257* (1883) and *Vyborg No. 102* (1886); the Danish *Delfinen*s (1883); the Spanish *Habana* (1887); and others.

Sails were only used when under way, never in attacking exercises, let alone in actual battle, and so they were soon eliminated.

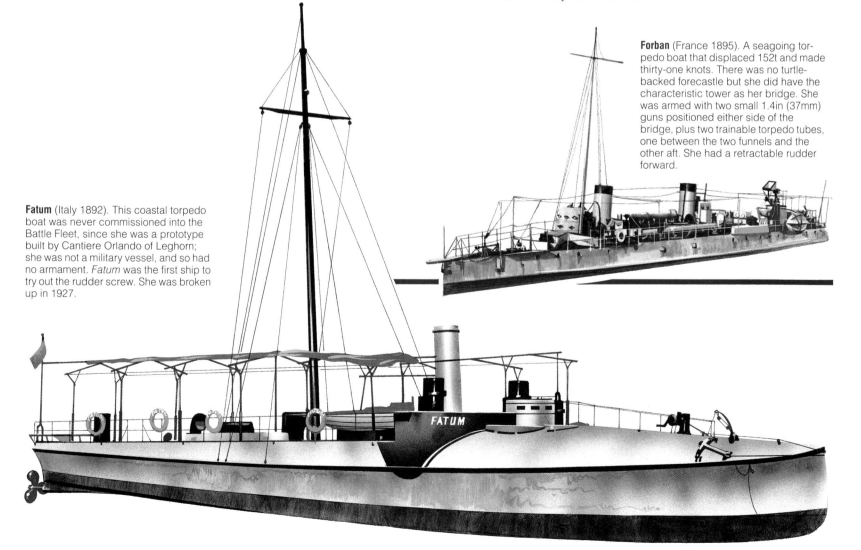

Fatum (Italy 1892). This coastal torpedo boat was never commissioned into the Battle Fleet, since she was a prototype built by Cantiere Orlando of Leghorn; she was not a military vessel, and so had no armament. *Fatum* was the first ship to try out the rudder screw. She was broken up in 1927.

Forban (France 1895). A seagoing torpedo boat that displaced 152t and made thirty-one knots. There was no turtle-backed forecastle but she did have the characteristic tower as her bridge. She was armed with two small 1.4in (37mm) guns positioned either side of the bridge, plus two trainable torpedo tubes, one between the two funnels and the other aft. She had a retractable rudder forward.

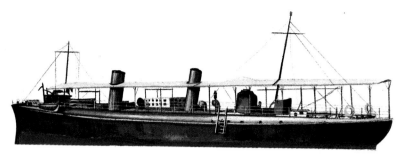

Condore (Italy 1900). Classified as a coastal torpedo boat even though she had a displacement of 140t. She was armed with two 1.4in (37mm) machine guns and two single centerline torpedo tubes, one forward and one aft, not visible in the illustration because it is based on a photograph taken in 1899, while Condore was being fitted out. She had an impressive range of 2,000 miles but could only make 25.7 knots.

Shirataka (Japan 1900). A first rate, or seagoing, torpedo boat built in the German Schichau yard. Her profile was similar to that of the numerous S Class Schichaus (1885–1895) of the Italian Navy, but being a little larger, she was better armed.

Some of the most interesting examples of seagoing torpedo boats were Britain's Yarrow built first-raters Nos. *23* and *24*, commissioned in 1886, displacing only 67t and armed with one fixed bow and one trainable stern torpedo tube, as well as 2 1.4in (37mm) machine guns. The French 152t *Forban,* designed by Normand and commissioned in 1895, was armed with two single centerline torpedo tubes, one between the two funnels and one aft; she made thirty-one knots with her power plant of almost 3,945hp (4,000CV). She also had one rudder before the screw aft and a second retractable rudder forward; other Normand-design torpedo boats, like *Mistral* and *Scirocco* (1901), and some units belonging to other navies, also had this arrangement.

Austria's *Viper No. 17*, built by Yarrow and commissioned in 1896, displaced 126 tonnes and was armed with three torpedo tubes, all on the deck, abaft the tower, plus two 1.8in (47mm) guns before the side torpedo tubes. She was powered by one 1,973hp (2,000CV) reciprocating engine on a single screw, supplied by two water-tube boilers discharging into two funnels, and made twenty-six knots.

The United States Navy had no coastal boats, only units displacing around 150–200 tonnes. Of course, even in this navy there were exceptions like *No. 23*, built by Yarrow in 1898, displacing only 16t and never actually commissioned, and *No. 15* and *No. 16*, also built in 1898, displacing 46.5t. But all the others were much larger, like *Foote (No. 3), Rodgers (No. 4)*, and *Winslow (No. 5)*, displacing 165t and commissioned in 1897. These had a small forecastle, as well as three 1.4in (37mm) machine guns, one on top of the conning tower, and two staggered amidships on deck. The power plant arrangement was interesting. There were two water-tube boilers and two reciprocating engines for two screws. The two boilers were in separate rooms, one before and one abaft the engine room, which resulted in the funnels being very far apart. The rudder was before the screws. Another interesting feature was that the crew's quarters were aft and the officers' and petty officers' quarters forward, in other words, in the reverse position when compared to the torpedo boats of European navies. *Porter (No. 6)* and *Dupont (No. 7)* which followed (commissioned in 1898) also had a turtle deck, a conning tower, and armament positioned in a similar manner. There were three funnels, however, since they had three boilers. Two of the boiler rooms were before and one abaft the engine rooms, so the fore-funnels were very close together, whereas the after one was some distance away. The officers' quarters were forward and the crew's aft. Neither the *Winslow* nor the *Porter* types had fixed bow tubes, but trainable torpedo tubes instead, one on the centerline aft and two staggered at the sides, plus three 1.4in (37mm) machine guns, one forward and two between the funnels on the *Winslow* type and two staggered beside the funnels on the *Porters*.

Examples of units belonging to the minor navies were the Dutch *Hydra* and *Scylla* (1900), built by Yarrow. They displaced 103 tonnes and were armed with three torpedo tubes, one aft and two at the sides. They had one reciprocating engine driving one screw, fed by two oil-fired boilers, and attained a speed of 24.3 knots. The two funnels were quite far apart because the boilers were set opposite each other, leaving a single central space for stoking the fires.

The first torpedo boats to be classified as seagoing in the Italian Navy were the six *Sirio* Class of 1905, that displaced 215 tonnes and were armed with three single centerline torpedo tubes and three 1.8in (47mm) machine guns, one either side of the funnel and one aft. During the First World War, these machine guns were replaced by two 3in (76mm) guns. Although these units had two coal-fired boilers, there was only one large funnel amidships. They were twin-screw ships powered by two reciprocating engines. These six units were built in Germany in the Schichau yard, whereas the eighteen *Pegaso* Class that followed were built in Italian yards and commissioned between 1905 and 1909. They displaced 210 tonnes and were armed with three torpedo tubes, one on the centerline aft and two on opposite sides of the deck at the break of the forecastle. There were also three 1.8in (47mm) machine guns, two in front of the side tubes and one behind the after one. They had two funnels for their two coal-fired boilers, but in 1908 seven of the class were fitted with oil-fired boilers. In the course of the First World War, armament was also modified, the after torpedo tube being removed and the three machine guns replaced by two 3in (76mm) guns.

As mentioned previously, the Russo-Japanese War, was fought from February 1904 to May 1905, and was the first major naval conflict in which torpedo boats were used. (Torpedo boats had been used earlier in Latin America, in several minor wars.) The Russians had seventeen boats and the Japanese sixty-eight and both also had large numbers of torpedo boat destroyers. Only the Japanese mounted torpedo boat attacks against ships at anchor and under way, and the results were disappointing. Take, for example, the attack by forty-four Japanese torpedo boats against six battleships and four cruisers, on the night of June 23–24, 1904. Thirty-five torpedoes were fired and all missed their targets. In a subsequent attack by forty-eight torpedo boat destroyers and torpedo boats against Russian ships on the run,

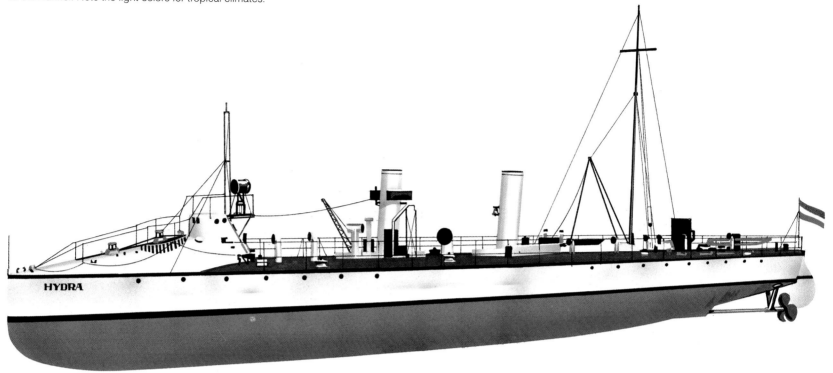

Hydra (Holland 1900). *Hydra* and *Scylla* were two torpedo boats built for colonial service. They had a fairly small displacement and were powered by one reciprocating engine and two boilers, each with its own funnel. Note the light colors for tropical climates.

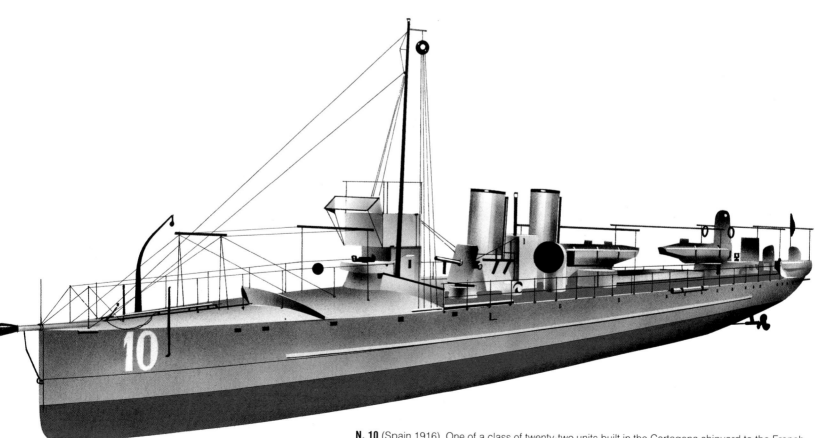

N. 10 (Spain 1916). One of a class of twenty-two units built in the Cartagena shipyard to the French Normand design. They displaced 190t; seven were triple-screw ships, and fifteen twin-screws, all with turbine power plants. They were armed with one twin torpedo tube amidships and one single aft. The two boilers were before the engines and so the two funnels were set close together.

after the Battle of Shantung on the night of August 10–11, 1904, forty-four torpedoes were fired without one enemy ship being hit. On the night of May 27–28, 1905, however, twenty torpedo boats attacked five large Russian ships after the Battle of Tsushima, firing fourteen torpedoes, six of which found their mark on three ships. The consequence of this disappointing performance was that many navies put a stop to torpedo boat construction. After 1905, only the British, Italian, and Austrian Navies continued to build these units, but only the seagoing types.

Between 1906 and 1909, thirty-six torpedo boats were commissioned into the British Navy. They were originally classified as torpedo boat destroyers, numbered *1* to *36*, with displacements ranging from 225 to 278 tonnes, all powered by turbines on three screws and two oil-fired boilers. They had a small forward superstructure above the conventional conning tower and were armed with three torpedo tubes, which on some units were one forward, one between the two funnels and one aft, while others had one between the two funnels and two on the centerline aft. There were two 3in (76mm) guns, one on the conning tower and one on the after superstructure.

The Austrian Navy built two types of seagoing torpedo boats: one with a displacement of 200 tonnes, comprising twenty-three units numbered *51* to *63T* and *64* to *73 F*, and another of twenty-seven units displacing 250 tonnes and numbered *74–81, 82–97 F*, and *98–100 M*. The letters stood for the shipyard where they were built: T stood for Trieste, F for Fiume (present-day Rijeka), and M for Monfalcone. The first twenty-three had reciprocating engines and a single screw, two coal-fired boilers, rating of 2,959hp (3,000CV) and top speed of twenty-seven knots. The second batch of twenty-seven were powered by turbines, had two boilers (one coal-fired and the other oil-fired), had a rating of 4,931hp (5,000CV) and top speed of 28.5 knots. Armament was also different since the first group had three torpedo tubes, one forward and one either side, plus four 1.8in (47mm) side machine guns, while the second group had four torpedo tubes in two twin series, one forward and one aft, and two 2.5in (66mm) guns, one on the foredeck and one on the deck aft. They had two funnels and a proper superstructure for the bridge in place of the old conning tower.

After 1905, the Italian Navy commissioned the *Pegaso*-type seagoing torpedo boats, designed before the Russo-Japanese War, followed by the seventy-two *PN Class*, officially classified as coastal torpedo boats, but regarded here as seagoing vessels because they displaced 140–156 tonnes.

These units were divided into two types: the first series, comprising forty units numbered *1* to *39* and the second series of thirty units numbered *40* to *69*, plus two special units numbered *74* to *75*. Apart from a number, they also bore two distinguishing letters indicating the shipyard and town where they were built: PN stood for Pattison-Naples; OS Odero-Sestri; AS Ansaldo-Sestri; OL Orlando-Livorno; and RM, Regia Marina, for *39 RM*, built at the La Spezia Naval Yard; and *74* and *75 OLT*, the letters standing not only for the yard and town of construction, but also indicating that these boats had turbine power plants: Orlando-Livorno-Turbina. They had the characteristic bow with a low foredeck, with its upper surface connected to the sides: those of the first series had the old tower whereas the second series had a bridge superstructure. The first series was armed with two centerline single torpedo tubes abaft the funnels, the second series had one twin torpedo tube aft. The first series had only one 2.2in (57mm) gun aft, the second series had two 3in (76mm) guns, one forward and one aft. They all had two reciprocating engines and twin screws, two oil-fired boilers, and a top speed of twenty-seven knots. The *PN*s performed extremely well in the First World War, especially in the Southern Adriatic, and many remained in service until 1932–1933.

The German Navy built seagoing torpedo boats with much higher displacements than those of other navies. The most outstanding examples were the *S 125–139* (1903–1904), displacing 454–693 tonnes; the *V 105–108* (1914–1915), displacing 421 tonnes; and the *V 150–190* (1907–1910) displacing 690–810 tonnes, officially classified as "*Grosse Torpedo Boote.*" The *V 105–108* were formerly Dutch, captured on the stocks at the Vulkan shipyard. They had two oil-fired boilers, two turbines, and twin screws. The *V*s, from *150* to *190*, plus others bearing the letters G, T, and S, depending on which shipyard built them, also had oil-fired boilers and turbines. The *S 125–149*, however, had reciprocating engines on twin screws, except for *S 125* and *G 137* which had turbines and triple screws. All had a short foredeck and a bridge superstructure. They were armed with one 3.4in (88mm) and two 1.9in (50mm) guns, plus three to four torpedo tubes, enough to put them in the torpedo boat destroyer bracket.

Torpedo boats from 1930 to 1935

In the years following the First World War, torpedo boat construction ceased until after the London Conference of 1930, when some navies began to commission units that were classified as torpedo boats and displaced about 600 tonnes standard, much more than the First World War seagoing torpedo boats, the German ones

excepted. This new tonnage limit was a consequence of the terms of the London Treaty, which attempted to limit destroyer construction. The boats built after 1930 had duties that were very different from those of the early torpedo boats, whether coastal or seagoing. They were no longer used for defending coastlines or attacking enemy shipping at anchor or in the open sea, but for escorting naval formations and merchant convoys, which resulted in the armament of conventional torpedoes being stepped up with anti-ship guns, anti-aircraft machine guns, and even depth charges for anti-submarine operations. In effect they were small destroyers.

The French Navy divided torpedo craft into three types: "*contre torpilleurs,*" "*torpilleurs,*" and "*torpilleurs légers.*" The first were large or "super" destroyers; The second, what other navies considered destroyers. We shall consider only the third as torpedo boats and include the other two types in the section on destroyers. In 1936–1938, the French Navy commissioned twelve light torpedo boats of the *La Pomone* Class. They displaced 700 tonnes full load and were armed with two 3.9in (100mm) guns, one forward on the foredeck and one aft on the superstructure, and only two torpedo tubes in a twin mount abaft the funnels. There were, however, four anti-aircraft machine guns. These twin-screw boats had two sets of reduction-geared turbines and made 34.5 knots. In 1938–1939, another fourteen torpedo boats of the *L'Agile* Class were laid down. They were slightly larger, displacing 994 tonnes, and had double the armament: four 3.9in (100mm) guns and four torpedo tubes, as well as four anti-aircraft machine guns. None of the units was ready by the armistice of 1940 and even the six captured by the Germans were never completed. However, the design was adopted later by the Spanish Navy as the *Audaz* Class (1953–1956, 1961–1965).

In 1927–1928, the German Navy commissioned twelve *Wolf* and *Möwe*-type torpedo boat destroyers, later down-graded to torpedo boats, even though they displaced over a thousand tonnes. They had a long foredeck, a bridge superstructure, and two funnels, the forward one being twice the size of the other one. Armament comprised three 4.1in (105mm) guns, one forward on the foredeck and two aft (one on the superstructure and one on deck). There were six torpedo tubes in two groups of three, one between the two funnels and one between the after funnel and gun deckhouse. The original pair of anti-aircraft machine guns was later increased to four during the war. These boats had two geared turbine units, fed by three boilers, and attained thirty-two to thirty-four knots.

In 1939–1940, seventy-two units designated from *T 1* to *T 72* were programmed and laid down. The first thirty-six were commissioned but the others were never completed. These units were split into five groups: from *T 1* to *T 21*, displacing 1,088 tonnes; *T 22* to *T 36*, displacing 1,754 tonnes; the uncompleted ones from *T 37* to *T 51*, 2,155 tonnes; *T 52* to *T 60*, 1,794 tonnes, and lastly *T 61* to *T 72*, 2,166 tonnes.

Those in the first group were armed with one 4.1in (105mm) gun, eight 0.7in (20mm) anti-aircraft machine guns and six torpedo tubes in two groups of three. More or less the same armament was planned for the other series. *T 1–T 21* had four boilers, the other series had two and speed varied from thirty-one to 35.5 knots.

Italy built two classes of torpedo boats: *Spica* of 1935–1938 and *Ariete*. In addition to these, two classes of escort scout torpedo boats were built: the four *Pegaso* types of 1938 and the sixteen *Ciclone* types of 1942. They were designed mainly for escort duty, not for attack. The *Spicas* formed a very numerous class, divided into three series, varying slightly in armament and displacement. The two *Spica* series, in fact, displaced 901 tonnes, had four torpedo tubes in two single side mounts and one twin centerline mount, four 1.5in (40mm) machine guns and four 0.5in (13.2mm) anti-aircraft machine guns. The six *Climene* and eight *Perseo* series of 1936–1937 displaced 1,010 tonnes and had all their torpedo tubes in single side mounts, and eight 0.5in (13.2mm) anti-aircraft machine guns in twin mounts. Lastly, the sixteen *Alcione* series of 1938 displaced 1,050 tonnes and had four torpedo tubes in two twin centerline mountings.

All were armed with three 3.9in (100mm) guns, one on the forecastle and two aft, (one on deck and one raised). They also had two depth-charge launchers and mine-laying equipment. The *Ariete* Class torpedo boats displaced 1,127 tonnes and were armed with six torpedo tubes in two triple centerline mounts and only two 3.9in (100mm) guns, one forward on the foredeck and one raised aft. Anti-aircraft armament was ten 0.7in (20mm) machine guns and there were also two depth charge launchers. Thirteen of these were completed and used in fighting operations in which all were sunk. The other two were captured by the Yugoslavs in 1945. The *Pegaso* Class escort scouts displaced 1,600 tonnes and were designed to carry out long escort missions; they carried 510 tonnes of fuel, giving them a range of 5,100 miles at fourteen knots. The *Spicas* had only 185–220 tonnes of oil fuel and a range of 1,800–1,900 miles. Both types were armed with four torpedo tubes in two twin side mounts, two 3.9in (100mm) guns, one forward on the foredeck and the other raised aft, four 0.5in (13.2mm) anti-aircraft machine guns, four depth charge launchers, and mine-laying equipment. The sixteen *Ciclone* Class escort torpedo boats were a replica of the *Pegasos*. According to the design, they were to have had three 3.9in (100mm) guns, two in the same arrangement as on the other class, and the third on a platform behind the funnel, but this piece was never installed, being replaced by a twin 0.7in (20mm) anti-aircraft machine gun mounting, thus bringing

Möwe (Germany 1927). The five *Möwe* Class, like the six *Wolfe*s, were immediately downgraded to torpedo boats because of their full load displacement of about 1,000t. They were the first torpedo boats in the rebuilt German Navy after the First World War. They were armed with three 4.1in (305mm) guns, one forward and two aft, and six torpedo tubes in two triple sets amidships. Her speed was thirty-two knots.

the number of these machine guns to ten (eight in twin mounts and two in singles). Out of the sixteen units of the class, seven were sunk during the war, four were captured by the Germans and lost in combat, and the remaining five were assigned to the Soviet Union and Yugoslavia after the war, in compliance with the conditions of the Peace Treaty.

In 1931–1937, the Japanese Navy commissioned two classes of torpedo boats: the four-unit *Tidori* Class and the eight-unit *Otori* Class. Another eight *Otori* Class were programmed although never built. The four *Tidoris* displaced 737 tonnes full load and were armed with four torpedo tubes in two twin centerline mountings, abaft the funnel, reduced by half in 1935, leaving just one twin torpedo tube. They had three 5in (127mm) guns, one forward on the foredeck and two aft, originally in a twin turret and then in single centerline mounts. The eight *Otoris* displaced 1,040 tonnes, had one triple torpedo tube mounting behind the funnel and three 1.8in (47mm) guns, one forward and two on deck aft. During the war years, the aftermost gun was replaced by a 1.5in (40mm) anti-aircraft machine gun.

Between 1932 and 1942, the Soviet Navy built three classes of torpedo boats, officially classified as "escort ships" but, because of their armament of three torpedo tubes in one triple mount, they can be regarded as torpedo boats, like the Italian escort scouts.

The fifteen units of the *Shtorm* Class, commissioned between 1932 and 1936, displaced 740 tonnes and were armed with two 3.9in (100mm) guns, six machine guns, and three torpedo tubes. The eight *Yastreb* Class that followed, commis-

sioned in 1941–1942 displaced 1,059 tonnes, had three 3.9 in (100mm) guns and twelve anti-aircraft machine guns, four of which were 1.4in (37mm), as well as three torpedo tubes. The last twelve of the *Albatros* Class, commissioned in 1944–1945, displaced 1,300 tonnes and had the same armament.

After 1900, the United States Navy no longer built torpedo boats, while the Royal Navy ceased building them in 1909–1910.

The Danish Navy was one of the minor navies to build torpedo boats after 1930. Examples were *Glenten, Högen,* and *Örnen,* then *Dragen, Hvalen,* and *Laxen,* small 290 tonne boats, and lastly *Huitfeld* (ex *Nymfen*) and *Willemoes* (ex *Najaden*), commissioned in 1943, displacing 890 tonnes fully loaded and armed with two 4.1in (105mm) guns, six torpedo tubes, two depth-charge launchers, and anti-aircraft machine guns.

In 1937–1940, Norway commissioned six *Sleipner* types, 708 tonnes full load, armed with three 4in (102mm) guns and two torpedo tubes.

Even the Thai Navy followed European trends and in 1935–1938 had nine *Puket* (or *Adriatico*) types built in the Cantieri Riuniti dell 'Adriatico in Monfalcone. They displaced 470 tonnes standard and were armed with three 3in (76mm) guns and six torpedo tubes in two triple mounts. After the Second World War, the classic type of steam-powered torpedo boat, armed with torpedoes and guns, was no longer built. Their role of attacking enemy shipping and protecting merchant convoys was allocated to units with diesel, gasoline, or gas turbine power plants, broadly defined as motor patrol boats, motor gunboats, and motor torpedo boats.

Glenten (Denmark 1933). A small 290t standard torpedo boat belonging to a class of three built in the Copenhagen Naval Yard, named "Class *T4*." They were armed with six torpedo tubes, two fixed bow tubes, and four in two twin mounts abaft the funnels. The turbine power plant produced 27.5 knots. They had a low forecastle, and a small bridge superstructure, followed by two funnels.

Shtorm (USSR 1932). One of a class of fifteen with a displacement of 740t, 13,019hp (13,200CV) turbine power plant and top speed of twenty-five knots. Their profile was similar to the Italian *Spica*s and they were armed with two 3.9in (100mm) guns and six machine guns, plus a triple torpedo tube set. *Shtorm* and *Shkval* were stationed in the Black Sea.

Spica (Italy 1935–1938). She belonged to a very large class, divided into three series that differed in displacement and armament. *Spica* displaced 901t and was armed with four torpedo tubes in two side mountings and one on the centerline, four 1.5in (40mm) machine guns and four 0.5in (13.2mm) anti-aircraft machine guns. She had a turbine power plant and made thirty-four knots.

Kantan (Thailand 1937). One of a class of three coastal torpedo boats built at the Ishikawashima shipyard in Japan. She displaced 135t full load, had a turbine power plant, and made nineteen knots. Armament was one 1.4in (37mm) gun, two 0.7in (20mm) machine guns, and two single centerline torpedo tubes.

DESTROYERS

The development of destroyers from 1892 to the present day

Around 1892–1894, some seagoing torpedo boats had reached displacements of 120–180 tonnes and speeds of twenty-two to twenty-five knots. The German and French seagoing torpedo boats represented a serious threat to the Royal Navy so the Admiralty decided to build units with better fighting and seagoing capabilities than these torpedo boats. This special ship was called a torpedo boat *catcher*.

The catcher's great advocate was Rear Admiral John A. Fisher who was appointed Third Sea Lord in February 1892. He commissioned the Yarrow Shipyard to draw up the specifications for a ship with the above-mentioned capabilities which would, in particular, outclass the French torpedo boats. Fisher stipulated that the major role of these ships would be to fight torpedo boats, their secondary role being to attack enemy ships with torpedoes. They therefore had to be faster than the ships they were to fight, have larger caliber guns than torpedo boats, and, thirdly, carry a certain number of torpedoes.

In short, the main weapon on the torpedo boat was the torpedo, backed up by a few machine guns, that were later replaced by larger guns; but the main armament of the torpedo boat destroyer, right from the start, was the gun, with torpedo tubes acting as secondary armament. The specifications drawn up by the Yarrow Shipyard for Admiral Fisher were for a ship with a displacement of about 250t and a top speed of twenty-seven knots; but the Royal Navy decided to invite tenders from three yards: Yarrow, Thornycroft, and Laird, giving them a free rein to come up with the best solution.

The 1892–1883 building program included six destroyers: *Havock* and *Hornet* from Yarrow, *Daring* and *Decoy* from Thornycroft, and *Ferret* and *Lynx* from Laird.

The first to be commissioned was *Havock,* in October 1893. She displaced 240 tonnes and was armed with one 2.5in (66mm) and three 2.2in (57mm) guns as well as one torpedo tube forward and one on deck. In trials she attained a speed of 26.18 knots. The two built by Thornycroft displaced 260 tonnes, had one 2.5in (66mm) gun, five 2.2in (57mm) guns and two torpedo tubes, and they attained twenty-nine knots. The two from Laird displaced 280 tonnes, made twenty-eight knots, and had the same armament. After these six prototypes, the Royal Navy built thirty-six more destroyers known as the "twenty-seven knotters" and classified as "torpedo boat destroyers." These were ordered from various yards and so had different profiles.

Other navies followed the Royal Navy's lead and equipped themselves with destroyers. The French appointed various yards to build the prototypes. In 1896, *Durandal (M 0), Hallebarde (M 1), Fauconneau (M 2),* and *Espingole (M 3)* were ordered from Normand; *Pique (M 6)* and *Epée (M 7)* from Forges et Chantiers de la Méditerranée; and *Framé (M 4)* and *Yatagan (M 5)* from Chantiers de la Loire. These eight prototypes were followed by a further twenty-six similar units, designated from *M 8* to *M 31,* built between 1890 and 1903.

In the German Navy, after the Torpedo Division-Boote, there was a move between 1886 and 1894 to build boats with a higher displacement and speed; although they shared the characteristics of the "Torpedo-Boote Zerstörer," they were officially classified as torpedo boats. In 1898–1901, the twelve *S 82–S 101* Torpedo-Boote were built. They were double the displacement of the *S 82–87* and *G 88–89* series torpedo boats and even more than the ships classified as destroyers

by the other navies, although these German units were not destroyers because their main weapon was the torpedo and not the gun.

In 1897, the Italian Navy laid down *Fulmine,* commissioned in 1900. *Fulmine* was followed by the six *Lampo* Class ordered from Germany's Schichau yard and similar to the German *S 90-101* and *G 108-113* type Grosse Torpedo-Boote.

The Japanese Navy had its first destroyers built in Britain in the Yarrow and Thornycroft yards. The Austro-Hungarian Navy also turned to British yards for the design of a destroyer that was built at the Triete Technical Works and commissioned as *Huszar* in 1905.

In 1894, the Russian Navy ordered *Sokol,* a destroyer prototype commissioned in 1896, from Yarrows. Ten more Russian-built *Krecet,* or *Pylkji,* Class followed along with four *Kit,* or *Bditelny,* Class ordered from Schichaus and commissioned in 1900–1902.

In the United States Navy, the construction of the first sixteen destroyers was authorized by Congress in 1898. They were built in various yards and commissioned in 1902–1903.

The minor navies also had their own destroyers. In South America, in 1896, Argentina commissioned *Santa Fé, Corrientes, Entre Rios,* and *Misiones*; Brazil had her first destroyers in 1909–1910, the *Amazonas* Class built by Yarrow; and Chile bought four *Capitan Orella* types in 1897 from Laird.

China purchased the four *Hai-Lung* types from Schichaus. In Europe, Greece ordered the four *Aspis* types in 1907–1908 from Yarrow; in 1911 Holland commissioned the Dutch-built *Wolf* and *Fret*; in 1908–1909 Norway commissioned *Drang* and *Troll*; Portugal *Douro* and *Gaudiana* in 1914; Sweden *Mode,* built in Britain by Yarrow, in 1901; Spain *Terror* and *Furor,* ordered from the British yard Thomson, in 1896–1897; and Turkey the four *Samsun* types, ordered from the French Schneider yard in 1906.

Between 1893 and 1909, practically every navy had destroyers. These units had a higher displacement, were faster, and were armed with more guns than the torpedo boats.

As with torpedo boats, the first "test bed" for destroyers was the Russo-Japanese War of 1904–1905. The experience gained led to an increase in the displacement and speed of these units, which were widely used in the First World War. Several factors contributed to these improvements: the use of turbine engines, which had a higher power:weight ratio than reciprocating engines; the use of oil fuel, which enabled higher power ratings than coal; progress in torpedo manufacture, giving the weapons a range of 6,500yd (6,000m), and the increase in gun calibers from the early 2.5in (66mm) to up to 4.7–5in (120–152mm).

By 1914, then, destroyers were larger, better-armed, and faster than some cruisers of 1890, the difference being that they were not armored.

In the First World War, after the famous sinking of the three British cruisers *Hogue, Aboukir,* and *Cressy,* on September 22, 1914, in the English Channel, the French cruiser *Léon Gambetta* in the Adriatic on April 26, 1915, and the torpedoing of the French battleship *Jean Bart* in the Adriatic on December 21, 1914, destroyers were used as anti-submarine escorts for convoys of larger ships. They were also used to defend merchant convoys, provide anti-aircraft cover, and as minesweepers ahead of naval squadrons. Lastly, they were used for reconnaissance and seeking out the enemy, in combination with light cruisers. None of these duties was in any way connected with their original role of destroying small torpedo boats.

In the Battle of Jutland of May 31, 1916, destroyers were used for both day and

SAM Kotlin (USSR 1967). The *Kotlin*s were armed with guns and torpedo tubes and built in 1954–1957. A group of them have been converted to missile destroyers by replacing the after gun turrets with a superstructure accommodating the surface-to-air missile launcher (hence the SAM designation). During the refit, a pyramid-shaped structure was placed before the second funnel to support the radar antennae, in place of the original quadripod lattice mast.

nighttime attacks. The Royal Navy had forty-five destroyers in the battleship unit and twenty-nine in the scouting unit. The Germans had thirty-two in the main body and thirty for reconnaissance. During the many attacks mounted by both sides, firing torpedoes at a distance of 6,500–10,000yd (6,000–9,000m), five British and two German destroyers were sunk. This battle showed the effectiveness of daytime attacks, provided they were carried out by large numbers of ships, as well as nighttime attacks, during which Germany's *Pommern* and *Rostock* were sunk.

One destroyer development in this period was the "Flotilla Leader," comparable to the Torpedo Division-Boote. As early as 1906, the Royal Navy laid down *Swift,* which was larger than the others so that it could accommodate the general staff of a flotilla. She was called a "destroyer leader." Between 1914 and 1922, twenty more were commissioned. In the Italian Navy, the larger destroyers were called "esploratori" (scouts).

As a result of the subsequent increase in destroyer displacements, the distinction between leaders and ordinary destroyers gradually disappeared, whereas the term "super destroyer" was used for some of the larger units. In the Italian Navy, the *Leone* type scouts of 1924 were reclassified in 1938 as destroyers, as were the *Navigatori* types of 1929–1930.

The Washington Treaty of February 6, 1922, on Naval Disarmament made no restrictive provisions for destroyers. The London Treaty of April 22, 1930, however, did impose some limitations. After establishing that destroyers were surface vessels with a standard displacement of no more than 1,880 tonnes, armed with guns of a caliber no larger than 5.1in (130mm), it established a quota of 152,400 tonnes for the United States and Great Britain and 107,188t for Japan. No limit was established for France and Italy, who were bound by no more than a vague commitment.

The 1,880 tonne standard limit corresponded to about 2,500t full load. This limit had already been exceeded by the French Navy's *Vauban*s of 1930 (3,100t) and *Guépard*s of 1929 (2,900t), armed, moreover, with 5.5in (138mm) guns, also over the 5.1in (130mm) limit.

The next London Treaty of March 25, 1936, which was not signed by Japan and Italy, established a new subdivision of warships, defining light surface ships as those displacing less than 10,160 tonnes and armed with guns of a caliber no bigger than 8in (203mm). Light surface ships were, in turn, divided into three subcategories: those displacing more than 3,048 tonnes, armed with guns of between 6.1 and 8in (155 and 203mm), commonly known as "heavy cruisers"; and those displacing less than 3,048 tonnes and armed with guns no larger than 6.1in (155mm), including those ships classified in the 1930 Treaty as torpedo boat destroyers. The term torpedo boat destroyer had therefore disappeared from naval treaties and in practice it no longer corresponded to the new role these units had to assume, either.

In English, the new term *destroyer* came into use, *Zerstörer* was the German term, while in the Russian Navy the official term was *Eskadernyi Minonosetz,* meaning seagoing torpedo boat. The Spanish simply used *destructores,* but the French and Italians kept the terms *contre-torpilleur* and *cacciatorpediniere* (torpedo boat destroyer).

Between the two World Wars, destroyers followed the same development as all the other ships, increasing in size, displacement, speed, and armament. They were armed with considerably more torpedo tubes, because destroyers had taken on the role, once filled by torpedo boats, of attacking enemy shipping.

During the Second World War, the destroyer duties of scouting, attacking, and providing anti-submarine and anti-aircraft cover for naval formations included escorting merchant convoys. In the Royal Navy and the United States Navy, special destroyers, called destroyer escorts, were built for this purpose; these units were slower than the normal squadron destroyers. In the Mediterranean, for instance, the Italian Navy and the Royal Navy used them in both Battles of Gabès (1941–1942). In the Atlantic, British destroyers took part in the attack against the German battleship *Bismarck* (May 27, 1941) and in the Pacific, the Japanese used them as attack craft, particularly in the Battle of the Java Sea of February 27, 1942, and the Battle of Tassafaronga of November 29, 1942, among others. Japanese destroyers were also used as troop transporters with such regularity that their efforts to reinforce island garrisons became known as the "Tokyo Express."

After the war, guns were replaced by missiles on destroyers as they were on cruisers.

As with cruisers, the first destroyer to be armed with missiles was not a newly built ship but an existing American destroyer, *Gyatt DDG-1,* commissioned in July 1945 and modified in 1955–1956. Only later were U.S. missile destroyers completed as such from the first. Similarly, in the French Navy, four *Surcouf* Class, or *T 47* types, commissioned in 1956–1957, were converted in 1962–1965; and in the Soviet Navy eight *Kotlin* Class converted to *SAM Kotlin*s after 1961. In the Italian and German Navies, however, only newly built units were armed with missiles: *Impavido* and *Intrepido* of 1963–1964 in Italy, and the three *Lütjen*s types of 1969 in Germany. Several navies fitted small Sea Cat missiles to existing destroyers. Since these weapons involved little structural change, the ships cannot really be classed with full missile destroyers.

The introduction of the helicopter as an anti-submarine weapon led to the construction of destroyer helicopter carriers, with a flight deck and hangar.

The French Navy *Geroges Leygues* type destroyers of 1979–1982 had a flight deck and helicopters; so, too, did Italy's *Ardito* and *Audace* of 1972–1973, Japan's four *Takatsuki* types of 1967–1970, Britain's *Sheffield*s of 1975–1980, and America's *Spruance* types of 1975–1983. By contrast, the Russian *Kanin* types of 1968 and *Svetly* (one of the *Kotlin*s) had a flight deck but typically carried no helicopters.

Progress in engine construction led to the introduction of gas turbines in place of the traditional steam turbines.

The modern destroyer, then, has become a much larger ship than many of the light cruisers used in the Second World War. She is armed with missiles, carries helicopters, and is powered by gas turbines. Destroyer development has totally changed both use and armament. What is more, the introduction of the new types of frigates and corvettes has meant that the old torpedo boat destroyer, now known as a destroyer, has had to take on all the duties once applied to the light cruiser, including the latter's armament and displacement.

Proof of this difficulty in distinguishing between today's destroyers and cruisers are the Royal Navy's seven *County* Class that were laid down in 1959 as guided missile destroyers but are often described unofficially as light cruisers.

187

Destroyer power plants

These faster destroyers have had twin screws virtually from the outset; post-dating torpedo boats by some twenty years as they do.

The early destroyers had reciprocating triple expansion engines, locomotive-type boilers being installed only on a few of the older units.

Boilers were coal-fired until about 1907, when they began to be oil-fired. The first British destroyers to have oil-fired boilers were the *Afridi* types of 1905, but there was a return to coal with the *Beagle*s of 1909. In the French, Italian, and German navies too, 1907–1911 heralded the change to oil-fired boilers with the French *Bouclier* types, the Italian *Alpino*, and the German *V 162–164*. In the Russian, American, and Japanese navies, oil came in a bit later with Russia's *Bespokojnyj*, United States' *DD 22–DD 31*, and Japan's *Umikaze* and *Shiratsuyu* types.

Around the turn of the century, the reciprocating engine was overshadowed by the steam turbine. Steam turbines were tried out by the Royal Navy on two ships named *Viper* and *Cobra,* on the suggestion of the Parsons Marine Steam Turbine Company. The power plants were supplied by this company and trials began in November 1899. On July 13, 1900, *Viper* attained 37.113 knots, which was a real world record.

The most interesting aspect of these ships was that they had more than one screw on the same shaft, this being to counteract the turbines' high revolution count. *Viper* had two screws on each of her four shafts, making a total of eight; *Cobra* had three per shaft, making a total of twelve. There were two turbine units, each with one high-pressure and one low-pressure turbine. The two high-pressure turbines drove the outer shafts while the low-pressure ones drove the two middle shafts. The middle shafts also had reversing turbines and so the turbines numbered six in all. Both ships were lost at sea in August and September 1901, so the Parsons Marine Steam Turbine Company had a third experimental unit built (*Velox*), which had only one larger-diameter screw on each shaft. This was a four-shaft power plant, like the ones on the two previous ships, the difference being that instead of a reversing turbine, there was one reciprocating engine on each of the two middle shafts, for reversing and cruising speeds. Three years later, however, in 1905, the two reciprocating engines were replaced by two cruising speed turbines. These were followed by thirty-four destroyers of the *River* (later *E*) Class, all with reciprocating engines and coal-fired boilers, commissioned in 1902–1903. But in 1904, Admiral Fisher, by now the First Sea Lord, ordered fourteen destroyers with turbine power plants and oil-fired boilers, that formed the *Afridi*, or *Tribal* Class. They had triple-shaft engines like those installed on the torpedo boats, the turbines being arranged as follows: high-pressure turbine on the starboard shaft, medium-pressure turbine on the port shaft, low-pressure turbine and reversing turbine on the middle shaft.

Triple-shaft turbine engines were greatly improved by the introduction of cruising turbines. These were installed on twenty *Acorn* Class destroyers, commissioned in 1912. These ships had seven turbines, that is, one high-pressure turbine on the middle shaft, for moving forward and one low-pressure, one cruising, and one reversing turbine on each of the two side shafts.

Triple-shafts were followed by twin-shafts on the experimental destroyer *Brisk* (also *Acorn* Class), and *Ferret* and *Foster* of a subsequent *Acorn* Class. The performance of these last two was unexpected because they turned out to be faster than their three-screw sister ships. This resulted in all subsequent classes having twin-screw engines. Two outstanding examples in the development of destroyer engines were Britain's *Badger* and *Beaver* of 1912, the first to have reduction gears on the two high-pressure turbines only while the low-pressure ones were directly coupled to the shafts.

The first French Navy destroyer to have a three-shaft turbine engine was *Chasseur,* belonging to the *Spahi* Class, which were numbered *M 55* to *M 60* and commissioned in 1909; two others, *Voltigeur* and *Tirailleur,* had a combined system of turbines on the side shafts and reciprocating engine on the middle shaft. Two units in the next class, *Lansquenet* and *Mameluck,* had two reciprocating engines, whereas *Janissaire, Fantassin,* and *Cavalier* had turbines on two shafts. Units *M 66* to *M 72* of the *Bouclier* Class varied, some had turbines on three shafts, like *Bouclier* and *Casque,* whereas others had them on two, like *Boutefeu, Cimet-terre, Dague, Faux,* and *Forque.* The ones that followed all had twin-screw engines.

The first German Navy destroyer to have a turbine power plant was *S 125,* commissioned in 1905, with three screws and cruising and reversing turbines on the two side shafts only. She was followed by *G 137* in 1907, also a triple-screw ship, and then by more units with reciprocating engines and numbered *V 150* to *V 161* of 1907–1908 (one of which, however, *V 161,* had turbines on two shafts). Those that followed all had turbine power plants, some with twin screws, such as *V 162* to *V 168* and *G 173,* and others with three, such as *G 169* to *G 172.* In the Italian Navy, the first destroyers to have a turbine power plant, namely the *Indomito* Class of 1913–1914, had twin screws.

In the Japanese Navy, the ten *Kaba* Class of 1915 had three screws and were still powered by reciprocating engines. *Umikaze* and *Yamakaze* (1911) and the *Amatsukaze* Class (1917) had three-screw turbine units.

The first (and only) Austrian Navy Class of turbine destroyers, the *Tatra* Class, had twin screws. In the Russian Navy, the prototypes *Nowick* (1913) had three screws, but the next nine of the same class had only two and the same went for those built later. In the United States Navy, the first turbo-destroyers were commissioned in 1908–1910. These were the three-screw *Smith*s. Six of the ten *Paulding* Class that followed had three screws and four had two. Two more classes followed: *Monaghan* and *Fanning.* The former was made up of four triple-screw ships and one twin screw, *Walke*; the latter, three triple-screws and one twin.

This situation was repeated for the *Cassin* Class too and the *O'Brien* Class that followed, with twin- and triple-screws, the majority being twin-screw ships. The three-screw units of the last two classes had a reciprocating engine on the side shafts, as well as turbines, and the twin-screws had a reciprocating engine on the port or on both shafts.

The early destroyers of the minor navies also had twin or triple screws, depending on which shipyard built them.

As with other types of ships between 1917 and 1920, destroyers also had turbines coupled directly to the propeller shaft replaced by reduction-geared turbines.

In the Royal Navy, many ships were therefore fitted with reduction geared turbines: the destroyer leaders *Bruce, Keppel,* and *Valentine* (1917–1920), then the "*S*" Class (1918) and the "*V and W*" Class built in 1917–1918.

The American Navy "Flush Deckers," commissioned from 1917 onwards, had reduction geared turbines. In the Italian Navy, destroyers with reduction geared turbines were not built until several years after the war. The first to have them were the *Sauro* destroyers (1926–1927) and the *Leone* scouts (1924). Geared turbines are still used: the two most recent Italian destroyers, *Ardito* and *Audace,* commissioned in 1973, still have their steam power plant made up of reduction geared turbines, although they are double reduction and not single reduction as they were in 1924. However, great advances have been made in boiler design.

Other navies have fitted their most recent destroyers with gas turbines. The first were the Soviet *Kashin*s, with four gas turbines developing a total of 96,000 SHP (1963–1972). Three were built for the Indian Navy. In the Canadian Navy, the four destroyers of the *Iroquois* Class, commissioned in 1972–1973, have a twin-screw power plant driven by two Pratt and Whitney GTs developing 7,298.6hp (7,400CV) for cruising speed (twenty knots).

France has the three *Georges Leygues* types of 1979–1982, powered by two Rolls Royce GTs developing 41,424.6hp (42,000CV) overall enabling thirty knots, and two 9,863hp (10,000CV) diesel engines for cruising speed (eighteen knots).

The two Dutch Navy *Tromp*s of 1976 have two 49,315hp (50,000CV) Olympus GTs for full speed and two 7,890.4hp (8,000CV) Tyne GTs for cruising speed.

The Russian, American, and Royal Navies have the greatest number of destroyers with GT power plants.

The Soviet Union built twenty *Kashin* Class destroyers (1963) with GT power plants. In the United States Navy, the four *Kidd* type missile destroyers of 1983 and the thirty-one *Spruance* Class all have four LM 2500 GTs that drive two shafts.

In the Royal Navy, both the *Broadsword*s and *Sheffield*s have two 55,233hp (56,000CV) GTs for full speed and two 8,383.5hp (8,500CV) for cruising speed.

No nuclear-powered destroyers have yet been built, although the American *Spruance*s have a full load displacement of 7,810 tonnes and the *Kidd*s 8,300t, almost the same as the 8,592t *Bainbridge,* which is classified by the United States Navy as a cruiser and has a nuclear power plant.

Destroyer armament

Until the advent of missiles, destroyer armament always consisted of guns and torpedo tubes. The guns on destroyers built between 1890 and 1910 were fairly small in caliber, mostly 3in (76mm) in the Royal Navy, and Russian and Japanese navies: 2.5in (65mm) in the French and American Navies; 1.9in (50mm) in the German Navy and 2.2in (57mm) in the Italian Navy. During the First World War, the caliber was increased to about 3.9–4in (100–102mm) for the British, French, Italian, Russian, and American Navies; 3.4in (88mm) for the German and 4.7in (120mm) for the Japanese. Between the wars, the calibers were further increased to 4.7–5.1in (120–130mm) and the number of guns reached as many as eight. In most cases, however, there were only four in single mountings, either two at each end or one forward and one aft, and two amidships between the funnels on raised platforms. The Japanese Navy adopted the twin mount, one forward and two aft. The Italian Navy adopted the two twin mount arrangement, one forward and one aft. Twin mounts were also popular with other navies, especially on ships armed with more than four guns. In the 1930s, anti-aircraft weapons were also installed on destroyers. These generally took the form of 0.5in (13.8mm) or 0.7in (20mm) machine guns in single and multiple mounts; but also larger guns, like the 5in

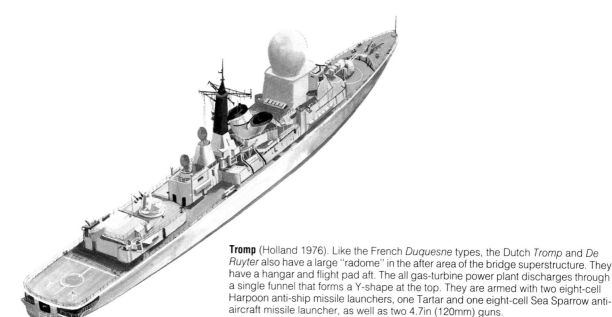

Tromp (Holland 1976). Like the French *Duquesne* types, the Dutch *Tromp* and *De Ruyter* also have a large "radome" in the after area of the bridge superstructure. They have a hangar and flight pad aft. The all gas-turbine power plant discharges through a single funnel that forms a Y-shape at the top. They are armed with two eight-cell Harpoon anti-ship missile launchers, one Tartar and one eight-cell Sea Sparrow anti-aircraft missile launcher, as well as two 4.7in (120mm) guns.

(127mm) ones on the American and Japanese ships that were dual-purpose, anti-ship and anti-aircraft guns. Single torpedo tubes were replaced by twin mountings about 1910, positioned either at the sides or on the centerline, and later by triple mountings on the centerline. Between the wars, torpedo tubes became quadruples and even quintuples, bringing the number of torpedoes to eight or ten in two mounts. The American Navy even had ships with sixteen torpedo tubes in four quadruple side mountings.

The anti-submarine weapons of Second World War destroyers included acoustic detection equipment, called sonar, and weapons for submarine destruction, initially towed explosive "sweeps" that were detonated when they struck an underwater object. From about 1916 on, they were largely supplanted by depth charges fused to explode when they sank to a set depth. They could, therefore, damage submarines, even when they did not strike directly. Depth charges were from stern tracks, or else launched from the side or the bows. Later, depth charges were supplemented by devices such as the hedgehog, which fired twenty-four depth charges in a submarine-shaped pattern. Post-World War II depth charge launchers included the British Limbo, the U.S. weapon Alfa, the Soviet RBU, and the Bofors mortar.

After the Second World War, destroyer armament changed radically, first with the introduction of missiles to replace guns, and second, with the introduction of anti-submarine torpedoes and the disappearance of anti-ship torpedoes.

Helicopter installations are now commonplace on all destroyers built after 1968–1970. Many have a hangar and a flight deck aft: Canada's *Iroquois* types, France's *Georges Leygues* types, Italy's *Audace* types, Japan's *Shirane*s and *Haruna*s, Holland's *Tromp*s, Britain's *Broadsword*s and *Sheffield*s, America's *Spruance* Class, and many others. Russia's *Kanin*s have an after flight pad, but no hangar or helicopters.

Destroyers from their origins to 1918

The first destroyers were designed and built by the same shipyards that had been building torpedo boats for the past ten years or more, so in their hull shape, internal layout, and power plant they resembled their smaller sisters. In fact, their bow had a short turtleback foredeck that curved downwards as it joined the ship's sides, a low main deck with no superstructures like the torpedo boat, and the early British and French units even had a slanted torpedo tube within the bow structure, although this was soon removed. The major and most obvious difference between destroyers and torpedo boats lay in the funnels that always numbered at least two, like the British *Daring*s, but in most cases numbered three, four, or even five.

For instance, *Viper* and *Cobra,* the first ships to have turbines, had four funnels and so too did the majority of four-boilered units built for the Royal Navy between 1900 and 1915. The Greek *Aetos*-type destroyers of 1912, built in Britain and fitted with five boilers, had five funnels.

There were some, however, with four boilers and only three funnels, the fore and aft funnels serving just one boiler and the one in the middle, which was larger, serving two.

In the Royal Navy, after the six prototypes *Daring* and *Decoy* (three boilers), built by Thornycroft; *Havock* and *Hornet* (eight boilers), built by Yarrow; *Ferret* and *Lynx* (four boilers), built by Laird, the Admiralty ordered thirty-six destroyers. These formed the "twenty-seven knotter" Class, built between 1893 and 1895, displacing 270–290 tonnes and all armed with one 3in (76mm) gun, five 2.2in (57mm) guns, and two torpedo tubes. These ships, which were built in various yards, had different numbers of boilers and funnels: two boilers and two funnels on five units; four boilers and two funnels on six units; four boilers and three funnels on thirteen units; four boilers and four funnels on three units; eight boilers and three funnels on six units; and eight boilers and four funnels on three units. *Surly,* which belonged to this class, had the classic round-sided foredeck, no superstructures on the main deck and three funnels, the middle one serving two boilers. There was no bridge superstructure, but a tower at the break of the forecastle, as on the old torpedo boats. The 3in (76mm) gun emplacement was on the roof of this tower. The other five 2.2in (57mm) guns were on deck, two symmetrically placed behind the bridge, two staggered next to the second and third funnel, and one aft. The two torpedo tubes were on the centerline, one between the gun and after funnel and one between the second and third funnel. The next class, comprising forty-five units and known as the "thirty-knotter" class, was built between 1895 and 1900; it, too, had a round-edged foredeck and a tower with the 3in (76mm) gun on top, plus the five 2.2in (57mm) guns and two torpedo tubes in the usual position. One of the most interesting ships was *Virago,* built by Laird in 1895–1896. She had a flat rather than a curved foredeck. For this reason, the two 2.2in (57mm) guns that on the other ships were in the forwardmost part of the deck, were, on *Virago,* on the foredeck, a little abaft the 3in (76mm) gun. Another interesting feature was that her four funnels were grouped together in pairs.

All the "thirty-knotters" had a small open bridge abaft the forward 3in (76mm) gun emplacement, clearly visible in the drawing of *Quail* which, although a *Virago* type, had a foredeck that joined up with the sides and four funnels set at equal distance apart.

The first two units to have turbine power plants, *Viper* and *Cobra* (1901), had the same profile as the reciprocating-engine "thirty-knotters." *Cobra* had the conventional foredeck, joined at the edges and the tower surmounted by the open bridge. There were four equidistant funnels and the usual gun and torpedo tube layout. She had four turbines and made thirty knots. *Viper* had three funnels, the same number of turbines, but a higher top speed—33.5 knots. Both ships sank under mysterious circumstances in 1901, after just one year of service. As from the *Afridi* (or *Tribal*) Class of 1905–1909, the curved edges disappeared and there was a proper flat foredeck and a proper bridge superstructure rather than a conning tower. The elimination of the tower meant that the 3in (76mm) forward gun was replaced by two symmetrically placed guns either side of the foredeck, plus a third

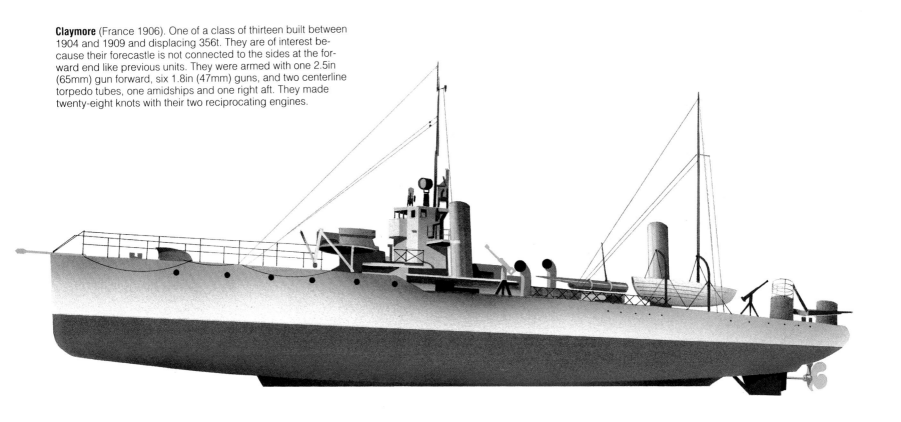

Claymore (France 1906). One of a class of thirteen built between 1904 and 1909 and displacing 356t. They are of interest because their forecastle is not connected to the sides at the forward end like previous units. They were armed with one 2.5in (65mm) gun forward, six 1.8in (47mm) guns, and two centerline torpedo tubes, one amidships and one right aft. They made twenty-eight knots with their two reciprocating engines.

gun on deck aft. Units built after 1908 were armed with two 4in (102mm) guns, one forward and one aft.

The Class *L* and *M* destroyers, built at the beginning of the First World War, were armed with three 4in (102mm) guns, one 1.4in (37mm) machine gun, and four torpedo tubes in two twin mounts. The gun layout of the *Beagle* or (*Basilisk*) Class (1908–1909) was interesting: one 4in (102mm) gun on the foredeck and three 3in (76mm) guns, one aft and two offset either side of the funnels, plus two torpedo tubes.

In the French Navy, after the prototypes of the *Durandal* (1895–1903), *Yatagan* (1897–1901), and *Carabine* (1901–1904) Classes, came the thirteen-unit *Claymore* Class, commissioned between 1906 and 1909. The prototype, *Claymore M 37*, built in the Rochefort shipyard, displaced 356 tonnes and was armed with one 2.5in (65mm) and six 1.8in (47mm) guns, plus two torpedo tubes.

Like their British contemporaries, the early French destroyers had their control station in a tower below the forward gun emplacement; but the *Claymore* Class, even at this stage, had a superstructure on the foredeck, abaft the gun. There were two funnels spaced well apart because one of the boilers was before and the other abaft the engine room, that housed two 7,101hp (7,200CV) triple expansion reciprocating engines producing a speed of twenty-eight knots. Gun layout was conventional, the 2.5in (65mm) gun forward on the foredeck and the six 1.8in (47mm) guns symmetrically placed, two before and two abaft the bridge and two on deck abaft the second funnel. There were two single torpedo tubes, one on deck aft and one amidships between the two funnels.

The first French ships to have turbine power plants, commissioned in 1909–1910, namely *Voltigeur*, *Tirailleur*, and *Chasseur* of the *Spahi* Class (another three of which still had reciprocating engines), had a flat deck, that was not curved round the edge. The same applied to the three turbo-driven *Janissaire*, *Fantassin*, and *Cavalier*, from *M 63* to *M 65*, of the *Lansquesnet* Class that followed (1910). All these units still retained the archaic bow torpedo tube even though they had more modern lines, a foredeck that was not curved at the edges, a bridge superstructure, and all the boiler rooms before the two turbine rooms. All were triple-screw ships.

The next class, *Bouclier* from *M 66* to *M 73*, had a similar profile with a bridge superstructure and four funnels, but the bow torpedo tube had disappeared and the other tubes, instead of being centerline singles, were twins either side of the deck, still abaft the funnels.

Bouclier and *Casque* had triple screws whereas *Boutefeu*, *Cimetterre*, *Dague*, *Fourche*, and *Faux* had two.

In the German Navy, destroyers were designated by a letter and number combination, the letter standing for the shipyard of construction: S for Schichau; G for Germania-Werft of Kiel; V for Vulkan of Stettin, and W for Weser of Bremen.

The *S 90* to *S 131* series (built between 1898 and 1905), with ships with displacements of between 394 and 482 tonnes, armed with three 1.9in (50mm) guns and three torpedo tubes, was followed by the *G 132* to *V 160* series (built between 1905 and 1908), with a top speed of thirty knots, armed with one 3.4in (88 mm) gun and three torpedo tubes. Then came the *V 161* to *G 172* series, with a top speed of thirty-two knots, armament of two 3.4in (88mm) guns, and three to four torpedo tubes, and finally, in 1914–1915, the *V 25* to *S 36* types, making 35.5 knots and armed with three 3.4in (88mm) guns and six torpedo tubes.

S 125, *G 137*, from *S 138* to *S 149*, and from *V 161* onwards all had turbine power plants on two or three screws. *V 162* was a twin-screw ship and commissioned in 1909. She had a flat foredeck, a bridge superstructure, two funnels, and four boilers. The two turbine rooms were abaft the boiler rooms. One 3.4in (88mm) gun was on the foredeck and the other on deck aft. The three centerline torpedo tubes were positioned one between the two funnels and the other two, one behind the other, between the second funnel and after gun.

G 172 had triple screws and displaced slightly more: 777 tonnes, as opposed to *V 162*'s 739 tonnes; but she was the same in all other respects.

G 137 was an experimental unit with a turbine power plant and, like units *S 90* to *G 173*, was unusual in that her three torpedo tubes were all on the centerline, the forwardmost one being abaft the bridge so that after the foredeck break there was a well in which the torpedo tube was positioned, the other two being between the two funnels.

In the Italian Navy, the *Lampo* Class (built in the Schichau yard in Germany) was followed by the six *Nembos*, built by Pattisons in Naples and commissioned between 1902 and 1905. They had the usual bow with a round-edged foredeck, the tower crowned by a gun, plus a second open bridge. Originally they had two funnels and three coal-fired boilers, but in 1908, oil-fired boilers were installed and funnels increased to three. The original armament of five 2.2in (57mm) guns was also replaced with four 3in (76mm) guns, one forward on the foredeck and one aft on the main deck, two more being staggered amidships abreast of the funnels. The original torpedo tubes numbered four in all, two at the sides amidships and two on the centerline aft; but the side ones were later removed, leaving only the two on the centerline aft. These units had two reciprocating engines. The most modern First World War destroyers to be used by the Italian Navy were the six *Pilo* Class, commissioned between May and December 1915. They were twin-screw turbo-driven ships with four oil-fired boilers and three funnels. The foredeck was flat and

Surly (Great Britain 1895). One of the "twenty-seven-knotter" Class, comprising thirty-six ships, ordered in 1892 and differing from each other in the number of their boilers and funnels. The *Surlys* had four boilers and three funnels, the middle one being larger than the other two. They were armed with one 3in (76mm) gun forward and two single centerline torpedo tubes. They could make twenty-seven knots.

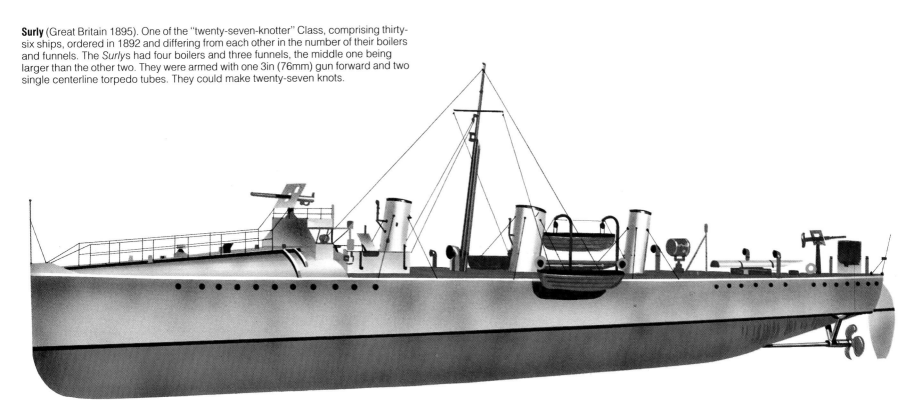

not curved where it joined the edges. There was a bridge superstructure and six 3in (76mm) guns, two abreast on the foredeck, two offset alongside the first funnel and two offset aft. During the war, the 3in (76mm) guns were replaced by five 4in (102mm) guns. The torpedo tubes, initially two singles either side, were replaced by two twins.

In the Russian Navy, the war with Japan resulted in an increase in the number of destroyers; these were laid down in 1904–1905, and orders were placed abroad too: ten *Iskusuyj* Class from France; four *Bditelny* Class and four *Vsadnik* types from Schichau and Germania-Werft in Germany; and the *Emir Bucharskij* and *Stereguszyj* types—some built in Sweden and the rest in Finland.

Emir Bucharskij, built at the Sandwik Weft Shipyard in Helsinki, together with *Finn* and *Moskvitjanin,* was designed by Schichau, displaced 650 tonnes, and had four coal-fired boilers and two reciprocating engines, making twenty-six knots. The bow structure did not have rounded connecting edges either side of the foredeck, but flat connecting pieces in which there were light ports for the rooms below the foredeck. Another interesting feature was the two spray shields: one in front of the anchor chain capstan and one in front of the gun on the foredeck. The bridge superstructure was quite large and surmounted by an open pilot bridge. One of the boiler rooms was before and the other abaft the engine room, which resulted in the two funnels being very far apart. Armament comprised two 2.9in (75mm)

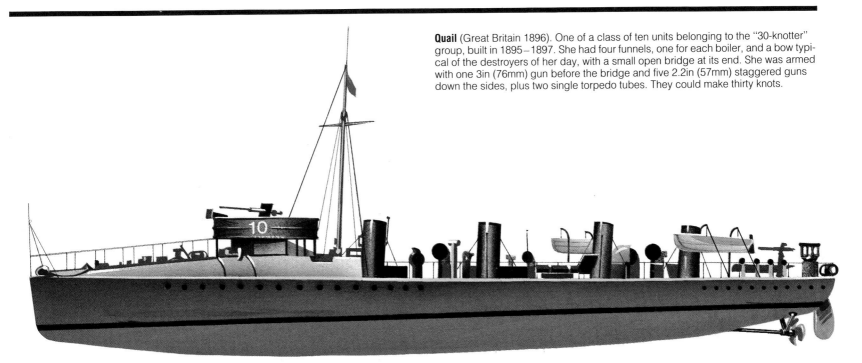

Quail (Great Britain 1896). One of a class of ten units belonging to the "30-knotter" group, built in 1895–1897. She had four funnels, one for each boiler, and a bow typical of the destroyers of her day, with a small open bridge at its end. She was armed with one 3in (76mm) gun before the bridge and five 2.2in (57mm) staggered guns down the sides, plus two single torpedo tubes. They could make thirty knots.

guns, one forward and one aft, plus six small 2.2in (57mm) guns, three per side on the main deck, and three centerline torpedo tubes, two between the funnels and one aft.

The United States Navy began to build its first destroyers in 1899–1900 and could therefore take advantage of the experience gained by the British, French, and Germans over the past ten years. Her first destroyers displaced 420 tonnes from the word go, unlike the 240t British prototype *Havock*, the French 343t *Durandal* or the Russian 220–240t *Sokol* and *Yastreb*. Only the very early destroyers had curved connecting edges either side of their foredecks. All had their guns raised above the main and foredecks.

Bainbridge had a small flat foredeck, surmounted by a superstructure for the 2.5in (65mm) forward gun, followed by the bridge. There was also a small superstructure aft for the after gun. The six 2.2in (57mm) guns were on main deck level, three per side amidships. There were two boiler rooms before and two abaft the engine rooms, which meant that the funnels were far enough apart for there to be room for one of the two torpedo tubes between the second and third funnels, the other one being right aft.

Hopkins and *Hull* of 1903, however, had a foredeck with curved side connections and a similar gun layout. Moreover, out of the six 2.2in (57mm) side guns, the two forward ones were below the forecastle and fired through openings in the sides. Most of the units with turbine power plants, from *Smith* onwards, had three screws whereas *DD 26, 27, 30, 31, 34, 39,* and from *DD 41* onwards had two screws. As regards armament, *DD 17–DD 42* had five 3in (76mm) guns and six torpedo tubes: the fore and aft guns were no longer in a raised position but level with the main deck, and the six torpedo tubes were in three twin mounts, one either side and one on the centerline.

In the Japanese Navy, as with the Russians, the 1904–1905 war led to a great many destroyers being built, notably the thirty-two unit *Asakaze* Class. In addition, three Russian destroyers were captured: *Resitelnyi*, renamed *Akatusuki*, *Silnyj*, renamed *Fumizuki*, and *Bedovyj*, renamed *Setsuki*, all belonging to the *Sokol* and *Pritkyj* Classes.

The *Harusame* Class, built in Japan to a Thornycroft design in 1903–1905, had a foredeck with rounded edges, a superstructure for the bridge and forward funnel, and four funnels. Armament was two 3in (76mm) guns, one forward and one aft, and four small 2.2in (57mm) guns on the main deck, plus one centerline torpedo tubes aft. The power plant consisted of two reciprocating engines and four boilers.

Turbo-driven units were not commissioned into the Japanese Navy until 1916–1917 with the arrival of the four *Momo* Class; these displaced about 1,100 tonnes, and were armed with three 4.7in (120mm) guns (one forward on the foredeck, one amidships between the two funnels, and one aft) and six torpedo tubes in two triple mountings. They were twin-screw ships powered by two turbines and four oil-fired boilers that discharged into two funnels.

Some of the most outstanding destroyers of the minor navies were the Greek *Thyella* Class with reciprocating engines and four funnels, built at Yarrow in 1907, and the four *Aetos* types, built by Laird in 1912. The latter had five boilers and five funnels plus two turbines and they displaced 1,175 tonnes. These destroyers had been ordered by Argentina but were later bought by Greece at the start of the Balkan War in 1912.

In the Austrian Navy, the first destroyers of the *Huszar* Class were commissioned in 1905. They had reciprocating engines, unlike the *Tatra* Class, commissioned in 1914, which had turbines, six boilers and four funnels.

Destroyers from 1918 to 1950

In the thirty year period between the end of the First World War and the resumption of shipbuilding after the Second World War, the destroyer considerably increased its displacement, armament, and speed.

Let us limit ourselves to just a few examples built in 1939–1940: the British *Jervis* and *Afridi* Classes of 1939 displaced 1,870 tonnes whereas those built at the end of the First World War, such as the *Wishart* (1919) and *Venturous* (1917) types, displaced 1,325–1,339 tonnes, 300–400 tonnes less. (Note, however, that most British destroyers of the interwar period were more nearly like the *Wishart*.) As far as armament was concerned, the *Jervis* type had six 4.7in (120mm) guns rather than four 4in (102mm) guns and ten rather than six torpedo tubes. Speed had increased from thirty-four to 36–36.5 knots.

There was no great change in the external appearance: The hull still had a forecastle that ran roughly half the length of the ship, and there were a lot of superstructures both on the main and fore decks. Funnels had dropped in number from three or four to two or even one, although the single one would be quite wide in diameter. In order to follow the development of the destroyer (now no longer the torpedo boat destroyer) over this thirty-year period, we shall describe four groups of units: destroyers commissioned in 1916–1920; units commissioned in 1929–1930; units of 1935–1939; and destroyers of the post-war years up to 1949–1950.

Of the destroyers in the first group, Britain's *Bruce* types of 1919 were larger than all the others since they were flotilla leaders. They displaced 1,801t, their forecastle extended along about a third of the hull and there was a superstructure on the forecastle and aft, plus two tall funnels. They were armed with five 4.7in (120mm) guns arranged as follows: two forward, one on the forecastle, and one on the superstructure; one between the two funnels and two aft, one on the deck, and one on the superstructure. There was a sixth gun (3in [76mm] anti-aircraft) behind the second funnel. There were six torpedo tubes in two triple mounts on the main deck amidships. The power plant was two reduction geared turbines on two screws and top speed was thirty-six knots.

The American *Brooks* types (*DD 232*), commissioned in 1920, were flush-deckers with a bridge superstructure, another superstructure amidships, and four funnels. They displaced 1,308 tonnes and were armed with four 4in or 5in (127mm) guns, one forward, two opposite each other at the sides on the roof of the amidships superstructure between the second and third funnel, and one aft on the superstructure. There were twelve torpedo tubes in four triple sets slightly offset, two per side aft. There was also one 3in (76mm) anti-aircraft gun right aft. The power plant comprised four boilers and two geared turbine sets developing 26,630hp (27,000CV), and producing a speed of thirty-five knots.

The Japanese *Amatsukaze* types, commissioned in 1917, displaced 1,570 tonnes, had a forecastle one third the length of the hull, three funnels, and a small bridge superstructure. They were armed with four 4.7in (120mm) guns, one forward on the forecastle, one between the first and second funnel, and two aft, and six torpedo tubes in three twin centerline mountings. These triple-screw ships had turbines coupled directly to the shafts and made thirty-four knots.

In 1917, the French Navy commissioned twelve "Tribal" Class ships, starting with names such as *Algérien* and *Annamite* and ending up with *Touareg*. They were built in Japan and then sent to Europe. They displaced about 700 tonnes, had a short foredeck, one bridge superstructure, and four funnels. Armament was one 4.7in (120mm) gun on the foredeck and four 3in (76mm) guns, one either side

Bruce (Great Britain 1919). A large flotilla leader destroyer belonging to a class of ten, two of which were not built because of the end of the war. She had a forecastle and was armed with five 4.7in (120mm) guns in single mountings, two forward, two aft, and one between the funnels, plus six torpedo tubes. The power plant comprised two sets of geared turbine units and in trials she attained a speed of 36.5 knots.

Amatsukaze (Japan 1917). A class of four units, all with three funnels and a forecastle that ran a third of the length of the hull. These triple-screw ships had three turbines and made thirty-four knots. *Amatsukaze* had six torpedo tubes in three twin centerline mountings, one behind the bridge and two behind the third funnel.

Goteborg (Sweden 1936). One of a class of six, commissioned between 1936 and 1941, all with a flush deck and a large bridge superstructure. *Goteborg* sank in September 1941, due to an accidental explosion, but was recovered and put back into service. She was armed with three 4.7in (120mm) guns and six torpedo tubes in two triple mountings abaft the funnels.

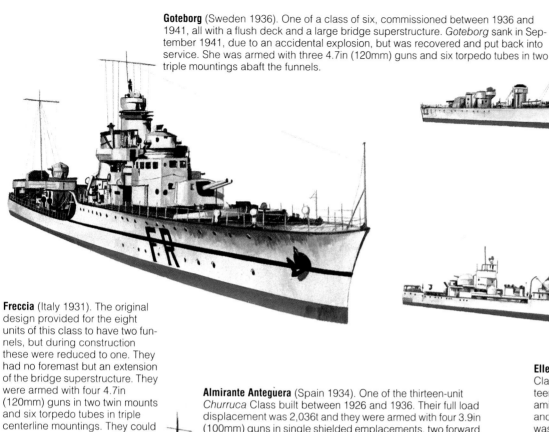

Freccia (Italy 1931). The original design provided for the eight units of this class to have two funnels, but during construction these were reduced to one. They had no foremast but an extension of the bridge superstructure. They were armed with four 4.7in (120mm) guns in two twin mounts and six torpedo tubes in triple centerline mountings. They could make thirty-two knots. All units were sunk during the war.

Almirante Anteguera (Spain 1934). One of the thirteen-unit *Churruca* Class built between 1926 and 1936. Their full load displacement was 2,036t and they were armed with four 3.9in (100mm) guns in single shielded emplacements, two forward and two aft, four anti-aircraft machine guns, and six torpedo tubes in two triple sets. Two of the class were sunk during the civil war but they were later recovered and put back into service. Note the tall tripod mast.

Ellet (United States 1938). One of the twenty-two unit *Gridley* Class, commissioned between 1938 and 1940, all with sixteen torpedo tubes in four quadruple mounts down the sides amidships. They were armed with four 5in (127mm) anti-ship and anti-aircraft guns in single turrets and their top speed was 36.5 knots. They were one of the very few American destroyer classes to have only one funnel.

Anderson (United States 1939). One of the *Sims* Class of just twelve units, commissioned in 1939–1940, before the United States entered the war. They were similar to the *Gridleys* but had five, as opposed to four, 5in (127mm) guns, three of which were aft, and twelve torpedo tubes in three quadruple sets, one on the centerline behind the funnel and one either side.

---

amidships and two on the centerline aft. The four torpedo tubes were in two twin centerline mountings, one between the forecastle and first funnel and one aft. The power plant still consisted of reciprocating engines and boilers (part coal- and part oil-fired) and top speed was twenty-nine knots.

In Italy, too, destroyers built at the end of the war had an old-fashioned appearance, such as the so-called ''*tre pipe*'' (three-stackers) of the *Pilo, Sirtori,* and *La Masa* Classes, which, however, did have turbines coupled directly to the propeller shafts.

The *Sirtori* types, built in the Odero Shipyard in Sestri, had a short forecastle, a small bridge superstructure, and three funnels. Armament comprised six 4in (102mm) guns, two abreast on the foredeck, two offset at the sides of the main deck, and two offset aft. There were four torpedo tubes in two twin side mountings. Anti-aircraft armament consisted of two 1.5in (40mm) machine guns and these ships could make thirty knots.

This overview of the destroyers of 1918–1920 can be rounded off by a mention of the Russian *Isyaslav* class, the last to be built by the Tsarist Navy, three of which (*Lenniuk, Stratilat,* and *Briatshislav*) were not completed. The *Isyaslav,* later renamed *Karl Marx,* displaced 1,350 tonnes, had a forecastle that extended up to the first funnel, and a superstructure that ran the full width of the ship, between the second and third funnel. She was armed with five 4in (102mm) guns, all on the centerline, two (one behind the other) on the foredeck, and three (one behind the

other) aft. She had nine torpedo tubes in three triple mountings, one between the first and second funnel, and two behind the third funnel. She was turbo-driven and made thirty-five knots.

Moving on now to the group of destroyers built in 1929–1930, the Royal Navy commissioned the eight ships of the *Acasta* Class in 1929. They displaced 1,330 tonnes and their hull had a foredeck, after superstructure, and two funnels. They were armed with four 4.7in (120mm) guns, two forward and two aft, the end piece being at deck level and the one nearest the middle level with the superstructure roof, plus seven anti-aircraft machine guns and eight torpedo tubes in two quadruple sets. These units had three boilers, two sets of 33,534hp (34,000CV) geared turbines, and made thirty-five knots.

In France, *Guépard, Bison,* and *Léon* were commissioned in 1928–1929, followed by *Vauban, Valmy,* and *Vardun.* They displaced 2,900–3,100 tonnes and their hull had a forecastle, a forward and after superstructure, and still retained the old four funnel arrangement. They were armed with five 5.5in (138mm) guns, two forward and two aft, the outermost ones on the deck and the innermost ones on the deckhouse roof, plus a fifth on the superstructure between the third and fourth funnel. There were also four 1.4in (37mm) anti-aircraft machine guns, six torpedo tubes in two triple mountings, plus four depth charge launchers. These ships had four boilers and two sets of geared turbines developing 63,123hp (64,000CV) and at trials they attained a speed of over thirty-six knots. In 1927–1928, Germany,

Artemiz (Iran 1967). Formerly the British destroyer *Sluys*, built between 1943 and 1946, she was delivered to Iran on January 26, 1967. She displaced 3,360t fully laden and was armed with one eight-cell Standard anti-ship missile launcher and one four-cell Sea Cat anti-aircraft missile launcher, as well as four 4.5in (115mm) guns in two twin turrets, both forward. She is steam-powered and makes thirty-one knots. There is only one funnel for the two boilers and two pyramid-shaped masts.

William C. Lawe (United States 1964). One of the numerous *Gearing* Class, commissioned in 1945–1946. In 1964–1966, 131 of the class were modernized and armed with ASROC anti-submarine missiles, DASH helicopters, and anti-submarine torpedo tubes to increase their anti-submarine capabilities. The ASROC launcher can be seen abaft the first funnel. They are armed with four 5in (127mm) guns in two twin mounts.

which was still bound by the Versailles Peace Treaty, commissioned the *Möwe* and *Wolf* types, displacing about 1,000 tonnes full load and 880 standard, as stipulated by the treaty. These units were later down-graded to torpedo boats. In 1930, the Italian Navy laid down the four *Dardo* Class destroyers and in 1928–1929 the numerous *"Navigatori"* Class was commissioned. At the time they were classified as "light scouts" and only became destroyers in 1938.

In the Japanese Navy, the twenty-unit *Fubuki* Class was commissioned in 1927–1930, displacing 2,090t full load. These ships had a forecastle, bridge superstructure, after deckhouse, and two funnels. Armament consisted of six 5in (127mm) guns in three twin mounts, one forward and two aft (one of these being on deck and one on the deck house); two 0.5in (13mm) anti-aircraft machine guns, and nine torpedo tubes in three triple mountings amidships. They had four boilers, two 49,315hp (50,000CV) sets of geared turbines, and could make thirty-eight knots.

Examples of destroyers in minor navies included *Regele Ferdinand I* and *Regina Maria*, built in Pattisons of Naples for the Rumanian Navy to a Thornycroft design and, therefore, similar to the British *Shakespeares*. They displaced 1,900t and were armed with five 4.7in (120mm) guns, two forward and two aft, the outermost ones on the deck and the others on the deckhouse, and one amidships abaft the second funnel. The power plant developed 73,972.5hp (75,000CV) and top speed was thirty-four knots.

The British *Jervis* types, commissioned in 1939–1940, displaced 1,690t–1,695t, had a long forecastle, big forward superstructures and deckhouses amidships and aft and, lastly, one funnel. The armament was six 4.7in (120mm) guns in three twin mounts. There were also six anti-aircraft machine guns and ten torpedo tubes in two quintuple sets amidships. These ships had just two boilers and two sets of 39,452hp (40,000CV) geared turbines and made thirty-six knots.

In the French Navy, the *Mogador* (1938–1939) and *Le Fantasque* (1934) superdestroyers had a full load displacement of about 3,500t. Both classes had a long forecastle, a sizeable forward bridge superstructure, a big deckhouse aft, and two funnels. They differed in armament and the number of boilers: the six *Le Fantasques* were armed with five 5.5in (138mm) guns, two forward and three aft with the outermost ones on the deck and the others raised (there were two pieces on the deckhouse roof aft). Anti-aircraft armament was four 1.4in (37mm) and four 0.5in (13mm) machine guns, and there were nine torpedo tubes in three triple mounts, as well as four depth charge throwers. There were four boilers, the power plant developed 72,986hp (74,000CV) and top speed was thirty-seven knots. By contast, the *Mogadors* had eight 5.5in (138mm) guns in four twin turrets, two forward and two aft, as on cruisers. Anti-aircraft armament was the same as on the *Le Fantasques*, although there were ten torpedo tubes in four mountings, two twins and two triples, all at the sides. The six-boiler power plant developed 88,767 (90,000CV) and top speed was thirty-eight knots.

Germany, with the fourteen *Von Roeder* types (1938–1940) and sixteen *Maas* (1935–1937), reached full load displacements of 3,415–3,190 tonnes, although officially the standard displacements were 1,811 and 1,625t. Both classes had the same hull profile with a foredeck, forward superstructure, after deckhouse, and two funnels. Armament was also the same, consisting of five 5in (127mm) guns, two forward and three aft. Anti-aircraft armament was four 1.4in (37mm) and eight 0.7in (20mm) machine guns and there were eight torpedo tubes in two quadruple sets, one between the two funnels and one between the second funnel and the deckhouse. These twin-screw ships had six boilers, a 69,041hp (70,000CV) power plant, and top speed of 38.2 knots.

The Italian Navy built units displacing 2,460t, such as the *Camicia Nera* types of 1938–1939, and 2,320t, the *Oriani* types of 1937. Both classes were armed with four 4.7in (120mm) guns in two twin mounts, one forward on the foredeck, and one aft on the deckhouse; one or two 4.7in (120mm) guns for firing illuminating rounds (flares) on a small deckhouse between the two torpedo tube sets, ten or

Le Fantasque (France 1934). The six destroyers in this class were the fastest of their time, reaching a speed of forty-five knots in trials. They were armed with five 5.5in (138mm) guns, two forward on the foredeck and three aft (one on the deck and two on the superstructure) and nine torpedo tubes in three triple-side mountings. All three surviving units were refitted in the United States in 1942–1944.

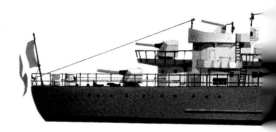

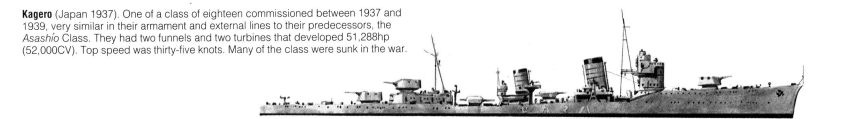

Kagero (Japan 1937). One of a class of eighteen commissioned between 1937 and 1939, very similar in their armament and external lines to their predecessors, the *Asashio* Class. They had two funnels and two turbines that developed 51,288hp (52,000CV). Top speed was thirty-five knots. Many of the class were sunk in the war.

twelve 1.4in (37mm) and 0.7in (20mm) anti-aircraft machine guns and six torpedo tubes in two triple centerline mounts. They had three boilers discharging through a single funnel and two turbine units. These developed 49,315hp (50,000CV) and top speed was thirty-eight knots.

Although an ocean-going navy, the Japanese Navy built destroyers with displacements of only 2,490–2,370 tonnes for the *Kagero* (1937–1941) and *Asashio* (1935–1939) types. In this navy too, destroyers had two funnels, even though they had three boilers. The power plant developed 49,315–51,288hp (50–52,000CV) and the top speed was thirty-five knots. These destroyers were quite well-armed: six 5in (127mm) guns in three twin mounts (one forward on the foredeck, one on the main deck, and one on the deckhouse aft), four 1in (25mm) anti-aircraft machine guns and eight torpedo tubes in two quadruple centerline mountings. They were well equipped with sixteen depth charge launchers in all.

The Japanese rival, the U.S. Navy, also had destroyers with full load displacements of around 2,300–2,500t. The *Sims* Class (from *DD 409* to *DD 420*) of 1939–1941 and the *Benson* Class (*DD 421–444, 453–464, 483–497, 598–628, 632–641, 645–648*) of 1938–1942 displaced 1,570t and 1,630t standard respectively. Like the Italian destroyers, the *Sims* Class had just one funnel, even though they had four boilers. They were originally armed with five 5in (127mm) guns in single mounts, two forward and three aft. In wartime, however, one of the after guns was removed, and anti-aircraft weapons added. The *Sims* type originally had twelve torpedo tubes in three quadruple mountings, one on the centerline and one either side; however, it was top-heavy, and the battery was soon reduced to eight tubes. The *Benson*s had ten in two quintuple mountings, later reduced to just five in the later units of the *Benson* Class by removing one of the two quintuple mountings. These ships could make thirty-six to thirty-seven knots and had an impressive range of 6,000 miles, which was essential for operations in the Pacific.

There was a dramatic turnaround in the Russian Navy in destroyer construction. This resulted from the success of the prototype *Tashkent*, built in the Cantiere Orlando of Leghorn in 1936–1937. In fact, the *Leningrad* types of 1935–1938, of French design, built in the Black Sea and displacing 3,500t full load, were superseded by the *Stremitelny* (or *Gromki*) types, designed by Odero Terni Orlando, of which twenty were built between 1936 and 1941 in the Leningrad shipyards. Out of the twenty units of the class, twelve were destroyed during the war.

Examples of ships commissioned in 1939–1940 by minor navies were the Greek *Vasileus Georgio I* destroyers, built by Yarrow in Britain and similar to the British *Intrepid* Class. They displaced 1,350 tonnes, had a forecastle, a forward superstructure and an after deckhouse, and two funnels. They were armed with four 5in (127mm) guns, two forward and two aft, four anti-aircraft machine guns, and eight torpedo tubes in two quadruple mountings. Top speed was thirty-six knots.

Moving on now to the destroyers of 1944–1950, it is worth noting that, because of the way the war went, France neither laid down nor commissioned destroyers after June 10, 1940; the same went for Italy after September 8, 1943, and Germany and Japan after May 1945.

Between 1944 and 1950, the British, American, and Russian Navies commissioned a few units of wartime design that represented the final stage of destroyer development before the advent of missile armament.

The Royal Navy commissioned eleven units in 1947–1948: four *Battleaxe*, or 'Weapon' Class, laid down in 1944, and seven *Agincourt*, or 'Battle' Class, laid down in 1943.

Both the *Battleaxe*s and *Agincourt*s had a hull with a forecastle, a large forward superstructure, and an after deckhouse. The *Battleaxe*s had two funnels and a big lattice mast for the radar antennae whereas the *Agincourt*s had just one funnel and no lattice mast. The *Battleaxe*s displaced 3,000t and were armed with four 4in (102mm) guns in two twin turrets, both forward (one on the foredeck and one on the superstructure). Anti-aircraft armament was six 1.5in (40mm) guns, four of which were in twin mountings abreast on the after superstructure and two in singles either side of the bridge. Anti-submarine armament was two three-tubed Squid depth-charge launchers, one on the foredeck and one on the after superstructure. The power plant developed 39,452hp (40,000CV) and the top speed was thirty-one knots.

The *Agincourt*s had five 4.5in (114mm) guns in two twin and one single emplacement. The twins were forward (one on the foredeck and the other on the superstructure) and the single was on a platform abaft the funnels. There were eight 1.5in (40mm) anti-aircraft machine guns in three twin mountings on the after deckhouse and one single either side of the bridge. Armament was rounded off by ten torpedo tubes in two quintuple mountings and one Squid triple depth charge thrower. The power plant developed 49,315hp (50,000CV) and the top speed was thirty-one knots.

During the war, the United States Navy built large numbers of destroyers in various classes, the most representative being the *Gearing* Class, made up of ships completed in 1945–1946, and the *Sumner* Class, completed in 1943–1945. Both

Halland (Sweden 1956). One of a class of two units, the first to be built by Sweden after the war. They were originally armed solely with four 4.7in (120mm) guns but, after 1973, were fitted with a missile launcher. They have two quadruple depth charge launchers forward and anti-submarine rocket launchers aft. Their power plant develops 57,205hp (58,000CV) with a top speed of thirty-five knots.

Södermanland (Sweden 1959). One of the four-unit *Östergötland* Class, a little smaller than the *Halland*s, with a flush deck surmounted by a large bridge superstructure. They have four 4.7in (120mm) guns and four 1.5in (40mm) anti-aircraft machine guns. They can also carry sixty mines. They were later converted to missile destroyers.

Siete de Agosto (Colombia 1958). The two destroyers *7 Agosto* and *20 Julio* were built in Sweden and are a modified version of the *Halland*s. The hull lines are similar to the *Halland*s but there are three twin 4.7in (120mm) turrets, one anti-submarine rocket launcher forward and four torpedo tubes. The power plant develops 54,246.5hp (55,000CV) with a top speed of thirty-five knots.

Casablanca (France 1956). One of the twelve-unit *Surcouf* Class built between 1951 and 1956. Originally they were anti-aircraft destroyers but four were later converted to missile launchers, three into destroyer leaders, and five, including *Casablanca*, into anti-submarine destroyers, by replacing the second forward gun with a multi-tube depth charge mortar. Those that were converted into missile destroyers had their superstructures and masts modified and the central and after guns removed.

Marques de la Ensenada (Spain 1960). One of a class of three units ordered in 1947–1948 as conventional destroyers, then modified and later modernized in 1962–1963. They are not armed with missiles, but with just three 5in (127mm) guns and anti-submarine weapons. The power plant develops 59,178hp (60,000CV) with a top speed of thirty-eight knots.

Akigumo (Japan 1978). One of the six-unit *Yamagumo* Class, commissioned between 1966 and 1978, all with six diesel engines driving two screws. They displace about 2,600t full load and are armed with four 3in (76mm) guns in two twin turrets and one eight-cell anti-submarine ASROC launcher, as well as four four-tube rocket launchers and six anti-submarine torpedo tubes in two triple mountings.

displaced about 3,400t and were flush-deckers, this hull form being adopted in the *Fletcher* Class, with its units that were commissioned between 1942 and 1945 and handed over to a variety of navies when the war was over. The external appearance of these three classes was roughly the same: there was a long superstructure on the deck that extended from before the bridge to the stern; there were two quite tall narrow funnels, a tripod mast, and a wide bridge superstructure. Between the bridge and second funnel amidships, there were two continuous bulwarks. In the Soviet Navy, the most representative class of destroyers of this period is the *Skory* Class, which were commissioned between 1950 and 1953. They have a full load displacement of 3,500 tonnes, a forecastle with a large superstructure for the bridge and fire control, one tall tripod mast, and two funnels. They are armed with four 5.1in guns (130mm) in two twin mounts, two 3.4in (85mm) guns and seven 1.4in (37mm) anti-aircraft machine guns in twin mounts on platforms either side of the second funnel and on the after deckhouse. There are also ten torpedo tubes in two quintuple mountings and four depth charge launchers. The power plant develops 59,178hp (60,000CV) and the top speed is thirty-six knots.

Missile and helicopter carrier destroyers from 1950 to the present day

Between 1950 and 1957, some navies commissioned destroyers armed with guns. In this section, however, only missile destroyers and missile and helicopter carrier destroyers will be discussed. They represent the most recent form of destroyer development and appear both in the major navies and in those called minor navies in this book.

The first navy to build missile destroyers was the U.S. Navy, with ten *Farragut* Class completed in 1959–1961 and twenty-three *Charles F. Adams* Class in 1960–1964.

One of the first minor navies to build new missile destroyers was the Italian Navy. In 1963–1964, *Impavido* and *Intrepido* were commissioned, They are armed with two 5in (127mm) guns in one twin turret forward, four 3in (76mm) anti-aircraft guns on four platforms either side of the funnels and one single Tartar missile launcher on the after superstructure. Like all post-war Italian destroyers, they are flush-deckers with a large superstructure extending the full width of the ship before the first funnel. There are two funnels and two masts, both lattice masts, the after one supporting the large radar antenna. These destroyers are powered by two sets of 69,041hp (70,000CV) double reduction geared turbine units with four boilers and the top speed is thirty-three knots.

DD 948 Morton (United States 1959). One of the *Forrest Sherman* Class of eighteen destroyers built between 1953 and 1959, that were converted from 1964 onwards by fitting Tartar launchers and anti-submarine DASH helicopters. This modification led to the removal of one of the three 5in (127mm) anti-aircraft turrets. They are armed with two hedgehogs forward and two triple anti-submarine torpedo launchers.

D 183 Bayern (Germany 1964). One of the four-unit *Hamburg* Class, originally armed with four 3.9in (100mm) guns. After 1975, the after superfiring mount was replaced by four anti-ship Exocet launchers. Anti-submarine armament consists of two four-tube depth charge launchers and four anti-submarine torpedo tubes. The power plant drives twin screws, for a top speed of thirty-four knots. During her refit the bridge was also modified.

Neulovimy 197 (USSR 1973). One of the four-unit *Kildin* Class built in 1957–1958 and modified in 1971–1976. The units are currently armed with four SS-N-2C anti-ship missiles housed in four large inclined launchers either side of the central superstructure, four 3in (76mm) guns in two after twin mounts and sixteen 2.2in (57mm) machine guns in four quadruple mountings. Anti-submarine armament consists of two sixteen-tube depth-charge launchers and the top speed from the steam power plant is thirty-five knots.

Zhguchy (USSR 1967). Part of the eight-unit *Kanin* Class built between 1957 and 1962 and modernized in 1968–1978. After modifications, armament consisted of one twin SA-N-1 anti-aircraft missile launcher aft, eight 2.2in (57mm) machine guns in two quadruple mountings before the bridge, and eight 1.1in (30mm) behind the funnels. Anti-submarine armament is three twelve-tube rocket launchers. The steam power plant gives thirty-four knots.

Obraztsovy (USSR 1963). One of the twenty-unit *Kashin* Class built between 1963 and 1972, six of which were modified between 1972 and 1978. They have two twin SA-N-1 anti-aircraft missile launchers and four single SS-N-2-C anti-ship missile launchers. Anti-submarine weapons are two twelve-tube and two six-tube rocket launchers. These were the first destroyers in the world to be powered exclusively by gas turbines.

D 571 Intrepido (Italy 1964). *Impavido* and *Intrepido* were the Italian Navy's first two missile destroyers. They have one single Tartar anti-aircraft missile launcher on the after superstructure, as well as two 5in (127mm) guns in a twin mounting forward and four 3in (76mm) guns in single turrets. These ships are steam powered, and have four boilers, and two turbine units giving a speed of thirty-three knots. They have rocket launchers for electronic counterattack.

Hampshire (Great Britain 1963). One of the eight-unit *County* Class missile destroyers, sometimes described as light cruisers. They have a mixed power plant of two steam and four gas turbines driving two screws. There is a twin Sea Slug anti-aircraft missile launcher right aft.

Hobart (Australia 1965). One of a group of three destroyers built in the United States and similar to the U.S. Navy *Adams* Class. Their full load displacement is 4,500t and they have one Tartar anti-aircraft missile launcher aft plus two automatic 5in (127mm) gun turrets and two Ikara anti-submarine missile launchers. They have a steam power plant and make thirty-five knots.

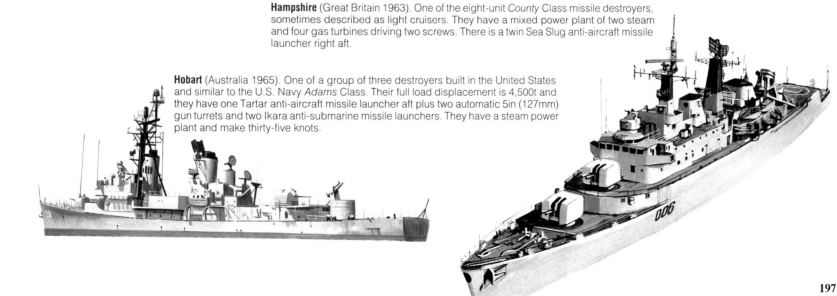

Buchanan (United States 1962). Part of the *Charles F. Adams* Class, made up of the United States' first twenty-three missile destroyers. She has a twin Tartar launcher aft, two single 5in (127mm) guns, and one ASROC anti-submarine launcher. She has a steam turbine power plant and makes thirty-five knots.

Preble (United States 1960). One of the ten-unit *Coontz* Class that, according to pre-1965 American classification regulations, were described as missile frigates. They have one 5in (127mm) gun forward and four 3in (76mm) guns in two twin mounts amidships, plus one twin Terrier launcher aft and one ASROC anti-submarine launcher before the bridge. They are steam powered and make thirty-four knots.

Luda Class (China 1971–1975). The *Luda* Class, which would appear to be made up of eight units commissioned between 1971 and 1980, is made up of the latest Chinese destroyers, which do not, however, have the same level of armament as Western destroyers. Missile armament consists of six anti-ship missiles in two cumbersome triple launchers, one behind each funnel. They are steam powered and have twin screws. They have no helicopter, multiple anti-submarine rocket launchers, and depth charge launchers.

Iroquois (Canada 1972). The four destroyers of the *Iroquois* Class were truly exceptional for their time. They had two helicopters with a hangar and pad, were powered exclusively by gas turbines, and had two quadruple Sea Sparrow anti-aircraft launchers. as well as a variable depth sonar, a Limbo, and six anti-submarine torpedo tubes that make them powerful anti-submarine units. Top speed is thirty knots.

Some minor navies chose instead to modernize existing destroyers and fit them with missile launchers in place of guns; one such was the Chilean Navy, which, in 1964, installed two quadruple Sea Cat short-range anti-aircraft launchers, and in 1971–1975, four Exocet missiles on the destroyers *Almirante Riveros* and *Almirante Williams*, built by Armstrongs in 1956–1960. The German Navy installed Exocet missile launchers on the 1964–1968 *Hamburg* destroyers.

The Swedish Navy's *Östergötland* (1958–1959) and *Halland* Class (1955–1956) destroyers received similar treatment in 1965–1969. The *Hallands* still have a forecastle whereas the *Östergötlands* have a flush deck. Both types have retained some of their guns. The *Östergötlands* have four 4.7in (120mm) guns in two twin turrets, one forward and one aft, and four 1.5in (40mm) single anti-aircraft machine guns as well as a sextuple anti-ship torpedo tube. The quadruple Sea Cat missile launcher is aft. The *Hallands* have four 4.7in (120mm) guns in two twin turrets forward, one twin 2.2in (57mm) anti-aircraft gun mounting aft and six 1.5in (40mm) single machine guns. An anti-ship missile launcher (for Rb 08A missiles) is on the superstructure top abaft the second funnel.

In the Soviet Navy, all destroyers built after 1963 have been modified and fitted with missile launchers. The first to be modified was the *Kotlin* Class of 1954–1956, nine of which were converted into *SAM Kotlins* in 1967–1972 by replacing the after gun turrets with a twin anti-aircraft missile launcher. Then came the *Kanin* (*Zhgucy*) Class of 1968–1975, followed by the *Kildins* (*Neulovimy*) of 1958 and *Kashins* (*Obraztsovy*) of 1963. (The first name is the conventional NATO name of the Class and the one in brackets is the actual name of the first ship of the class to be built). Missile launchers have been installed on the *SAM Kotlins* in place of one of the gun turrets, but on the *Kildins* the after anti-ship missile launcher was later removed and replaced by two twin 3in (76mm) turrets and missile armament is four single anti-ship missile launchers, two on either side of the after funnel.

Six out of twenty units of the *Kashin* Class of 1963–1972 were converted in 1974–1979. During the conversion the hull was made 9.8ft (3m) longer. To the original missile armament of two twin SA-N-1 anti-aircraft missile launchers, one forward and one aft, on the roof of the superstructure were added four single SS-N-2 anti-ship missile launchers either side of the after superstructure. Armament is completed by four 3in (76mm) guns in two single turrets, one forward and one aft, four Gatlings, rocket launchers, and four multiple depth charge launchers. These ships have five anti-ship torpedo tubes in a quintuple mounting between the two funnels. They were the first in the world to be powered by gas turbines.

Coming back to purpose-built missile destroyers, we should mention the Chinese *Luda* Class of 1971–1975, armed with four 5.1in (130mm) guns in two twin turrets, one forward and one aft, eight 1.4in (37mm) machine guns, and six anti-ship missiles in two triple centerline launchers, one behind the first and one behind the second funnel.

In the French Navy, *Suffren* and *Duquesne* of 1967–1970 are armed with two 3.9in (100mm) guns in two single turrets, both forward, four anti-ship Exocet missiles in individual launchers on the superstructure behind the funnel and one anti-aircraft missile launcher aft, plus one single anti-submarine "Malafon" missile launcher on deck amidships, behind the funnel. A distinctive feature of these destroyers is their large "radome," the large sphere containing radar antennae, abaft the bridge, as well as the big mack. The most modern missile launchers in the United States Navy are the *Ticonderoga* (Aegis) Class ships, with twin missile launchers forward and aft. They are distinguishable by their flat-faced electronically-scanned radars, that feed an advanced and highly automated missile control system. Their hulls are similar to those of *Spruance* Class destroyers. Next most modern are the four *Kidd* types of 1981–1983. They were originally ordered by the Iranian Navy but after the fall of the Shah the contract was broken and the ships were bought by the U.S. Navy. They are *Spruance*-type destroyers fitted with missile armament. Their full load displacement is 8,300 tonnes and they are flush-

Hercules (Argentina 1976). *Hercules* and *Santissima Trinidad* are British type 42s, and therefore practically identical to the British *Sheffields*. Both were built in Britain, and they were commissioned in 1976 and 1981 respectively. They are powered exclusively by gas turbines and have a hangar and helicopter pad. Armament is one 4.5in (114mm) gun, four Exocet anti-ship missiles, and a Sea Dart anti-aircraft missile launcher.

deckers with a huge superstructure and two big lattice masts. Being powered exclusively by gas turbines, they have two large funnels that are incorporated into the superstructure. They are armed with two twin anti-aircraft and anti-submarine missile launchers, one of which is on the bow and the other on the stern, plus two 5in (127mm) automatic guns in single turrets, also positioned one forward and one aft.

The twenty-three 4,500-tonne *Charles F. Adams* (*Buchanan*) Class, commissioned between 1961 and 1964 are also flush-deckers with a large superstructure before the first funnel and another abaft the second funnel. Missile armament consists of one single or a twin anti-aircraft Tartar missile launcher on the after deckhouse and one eight-tubed ASROC anti-submarine missile launcher on the superstructure between the two funnels. As regards anti-submarine weapons, there are also six torpedo tubes in two triple mountings. These ships are powered by two 69,041hp (70,000CV) turbine units with four boilers and make thirty-five knots.

The German Navy had the three *Lütjens* destroyers built in the United States; they are essentially duplicates of the *Adams* Class.

So far, we have only discussed missile destroyers, but there are many ships of this period that are armed with missiles, but also have a hangar and pad for helicopters used for anti-submarine operations.

Examples of such vessels are Argentina's *Almirante Browns*, or *Meko 360*s, ordered from Germany. They have four 55,233hp (56,000CV) and two 10,534hp (10,680CV) gas turbines. Another two Argentina Navy ships are *Hercules* and *Santissima Trinidad,* commissioned in 1976 and 1981. These too are powered exclusively by gas turbines and duplicate the British *Sheffield*, or Type *42*.

The Canadian Navy has missile and helicopter carrier destroyers with gas turbine power plants, the four *Iroquois* Class of 1972–1973. These ships have an unusual profile in that their flush deck has two large box-like superstructures amidships. The forward one is for the bridge and operational rooms and the after one for the hangar of the two helicopters on board. Another interesting feature is the funnel. It is positioned between the two superstructures and branches out at the top into two sections, one raked to starboard and the other to port. The stern is also unusual in that the transom is cut in two by a chute down which the variable depth sonar is lowered into the sea. Armament comprises two quadruple anti-aircraft Sea Sparrow missile launchers in the forward part of the superstructure that can be drawn back into recesses below the bridge. These destroyers have one 5in (127mm) Italian-built OTO Melara gun in a turret forward, one "Limbo" depth charge launcher and six anti-submarine torpedoes in two triple launchers.

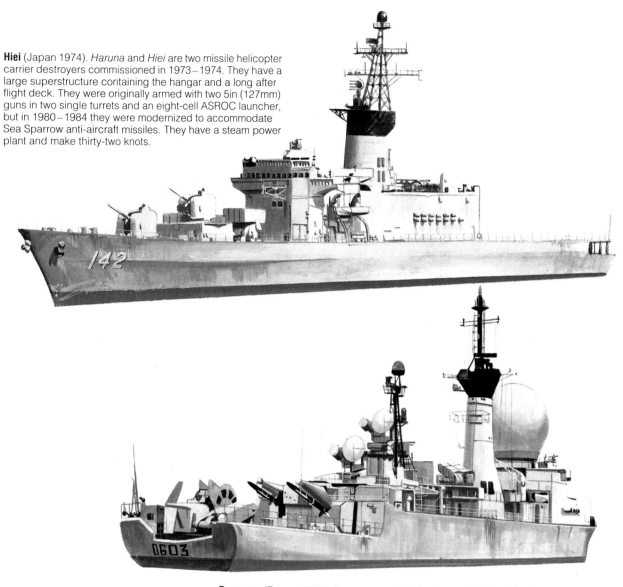

Hiei (Japan 1974). *Haruna* and *Hiei* are two missile helicopter carrier destroyers commissioned in 1973–1974. They have a large superstructure containing the hangar and a long after flight deck. They were originally armed with two 5in (127mm) guns in two single turrets and an eight-cell ASROC launcher, but in 1980–1984 they were modernized to accommodate Sea Sparrow anti-aircraft missiles. They have a steam power plant and make thirty-two knots.

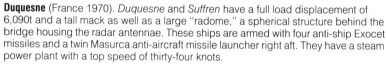

Duquesne (France 1970). *Duquesne* and *Suffren* have a full load displacement of 6,090t and a tall mack as well as a large "radome," a spherical structure behind the bridge housing the radar antennae. These ships are armed with four anti-ship Exocet missiles and a twin Masurca anti-aircraft missile launcher right aft. They have a steam power plant with a top speed of thirty-four knots.

Audace (Italy 1973). *Ardito* and *Audace* are missile helicopter carrier destroyers with a hangar and after flight pad. They are armed with two single 5in (127mm) guns, both forward, and a Tartar anti-aircraft missile launcher on the superstructure as well as two triple anti-submarine torpedo tubes. They have a steam power plant and make thirty-three knots.

Battleaxe (Great Britain 1980). One of a class of six units powered by gas turbines and commissioned between 1979 and 1983. They have two tall box-like masts and a large uptake for the GTs. They have a hangar and helicopter pad aft. Armament consists of four Exocet anti-ship missiles and two six-cell Sea Wolf anti-aircraft missile launchers, one forward and one aft. They are powered by a COGOG system and make thirty knots.

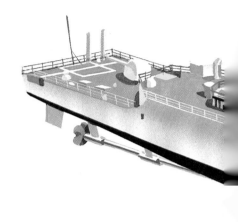

The three *Georges Leygues* types of 1979–1982 are French Navy missile and helicopter carrier destroyers powered by gas turbines, whereas the three *Tourville* types of 1974–1977, although missile and helicopter carrier destroyers, are steam-powered. The *Georges Leygues* types are flush-deckers with two large superstructures, one before and one abaft the big funnel. The after superstructure contains the hangar while the helicopter pad is on the main deck right aft. Armament comprises one 3.9in (100mm) gun in a turret forward and two 0.7in (20mm) machine guns. Then there are four single anti-ship Exocet missiles on the roof of the after superstructure, one Crotale anti-aircraft missile launcher slightly further abaft, and, lastly, two single anti-submarine torpedo tubes.

Whereas the Argentinian and Canadian destroyers have a purely gas turbine power plant (COGOG), both for full and cruising speed, the *Georges Leygues* types have two 9,863hp (10,000CV) diesel engines (CODOG) for cruising.

The two Italian Navy helicopter carrier missile destroyers, *Ardito* and *Audace* of 1972–1973, are steam-powered. These flush-deckers displace 4,400 tonnes and have two large superstructures, one forward and one aft, and a helicopter pad right aft. The two extremely tall macks are very distinctive: the forward one for a tripod mast and the after one for the large radar aerial. These units are armed with two 5in (127mm) guns in two single turrets forward and four 3in (76mm) anti-aircraft guns in single turrets, two either side amidships on the main deck. The single Tartar missile launcher is on the after superstructure. There are also six anti-submarine torpedoes in triple launchers.

The Japanese Navy missile and helicopter carrier destroyers of the *DD 145* Class are powered by gas turbines. The two *Shirane* types of 1980–1981 and the two *Haruna* types of 1973–1974 are steam-powered and similar in appearance and armament. The two *Shirane*s displaced 5,250 tonnes, the others 4,700t. They are flush decked and have a single large central superstructure with the bridge and operational rooms in its forward part and the hangar aft. This superstructure on the *Haruna*s has a large mack supporting a quadripod while the *Shirane*s have two macks. Armament consists of two 5in (127mm) guns in two turrets, one behind the

other forward, followed by an eight-tubed ASROC anti-submarine missile launcher. The single Sea Sparrow anti-aircraft missile launcher is on the after superstructure. There are also six anti-submarine torpedo tubes in two triple mountings. The power plant consists of two 69,041hp (70,000CV) of steam turbine units and the top speed is thirty-two knots.

The two Dutch *Tromp* types are a case apart because of their completely gas turbine power plant (COGOG). They were commissioned in 1975-1976 and have a large spherical "radome," like the French *Suffren*s, and a funnel with two raked sections, like the Canadian *Iroquois* types. They are flush deckers with a superstructure in the midships to forward area and another superstructure aft. Abaft the

Shirane (Japan 1980). *Shirane* and *Kurama* are the two most modern destroyers in the Japanese Navy. They have a large superstructure for the hangar of the three helicopters abaft the second funnel, and a large flight deck that stretches along one-third of the length from the stern. They are armed with two single 5in (127mm) guns forward, one ASROC launcher before the bridge, and one Sea Sparrow launcher on the superstructure. They have a steam power plant and make thirty-two knots.

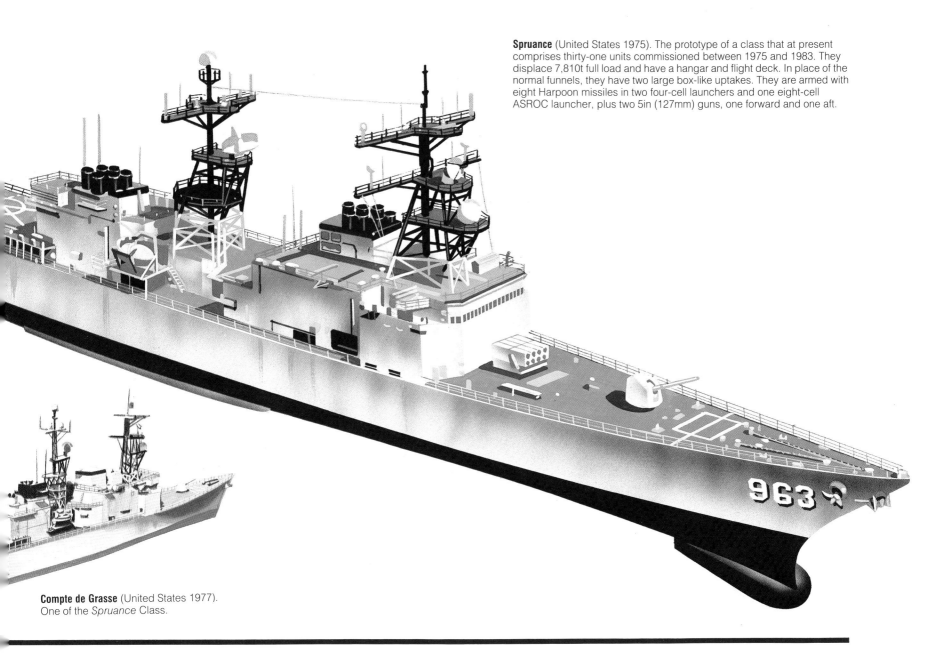

Spruance (United States 1975). The prototype of a class that at present comprises thirty-one units commissioned between 1975 and 1983. They displace 7,810t full load and have a hangar and flight deck. In place of the normal funnels, they have two large box-like uptakes. They are armed with eight Harpoon missiles in two four-cell launchers and one eight-cell ASROC launcher, plus two 5in (127mm) guns, one forward and one aft.

Compte de Grasse (United States 1977). One of the *Spruance* Class.

funnel there is a mast that is a pyramid-shaped turret at the bottom and cylindrical at the top.

The Royal Navy missile helicopter carrier destroyers make up two classes, both with gas turbine power plants: the 4,000-tonne *Broadsword*s and the 4,500-tonne *Sheffield*s. Both classes are flush decked but whereas the *Sheffield*s have their main midships to forward superstructure arranged so that there are two strips of deck left free for a passageway on either side, the superstructure on the *Broadsword*s spans the entire width of the ship, the passageway being level with the roof of the superstructure. The *Sheffield*s have two "radomes," one on the bridge and one on the after part of the superstructure, a large radar antenna supported by a low box-shaped structure, and two box-like masts between which is a huge funnel. These destroyers are armed with one 4.5in (115mm) gun in a turret forward, two 0.7in (20mm) anti-aircraft machine guns and two saluting guns. At the bow, abaft the gun turret, is a twin Sea Dart anti-ship missile launcher. They also have the usual anti-submarine armament of two triple torpedo tubes and a helicopter.

The *Broadsword*s also have two box-like masts and a large funnel. They have no ordinary guns, only one 1.5in (40mm) machine gun either side of the forefunnel. However, the last units of the class will have a 4.5-inch gun forward, and eight (rather than four) anti-ship missiles. The anti-ship missiles are Exocets in four single launchers positioned forward in a well in the main deck. The anti-aircraft missiles are Sea Wolfs housed in two six-canister launchers, one forward behind the Exocets and one aft on the hangar superstructure. Each unit carries two anti-submarine helicopters and there are also six anti-submarine torpedo tubes in two triple launchers. These ships can make about twenty-nine to thirty knots.

In the U.S. Navy, the most modern helicopter carrier destroyer class is the *Spruance* Class, currently numbering thirty-one units. They displace 7,810 tonnes

and were commissioned after 1976 (only the prototype *Spruance* was commissioned in 1975) but are not classified as missile destroyers. They are armed, however, with Harpoon anti-ship missile launchers, Sea Sparrow anti-aircraft missiles, and ASROC anti-submarine missiles. As far as external appearance and weapon layout are concerned, they are identical to the four *Kidd*s, although they have a hangar in the after superstructure and a flight deck. Armament comprises two 5in (127mm) guns in two single turrets, one forward and one aft. Before the bridge is the eight-cell launcher for ASROC missiles and on the superstructure behind the fore-funnel are the installations for launching the Harpoon anti-ship missiles. At the after end, on the hangar superstructure, one 'tween deck higher than the gun emplacement, is the Sea Sparrow launcher. The power plant consists of four General Electric gas turbines that drive two screws. The GTs and propeller shafts are coupled by means of reduction geared couplings that enable the GTs to be coupled and uncoupled so as to operate just one turbine per shaft at economic speeds. This power plant is exceptionally quiet, a very important feature for anti-submarine work.

In 1983, then, destroyers have reached displacements of around 8,000 tonnes, which is higher not only than the 7,000-tonne London-type cruisers such as the Italian *Montecuccoli*s and British *Leander*s, but is even greater than some battleships built in the last century.

The destroyer is no longer armed with guns and anti-ship torpedoes. Her armament is made up of highly sophisticated remote controlled weapons that require equally sophisticated electronic equipment to seek out the target, aim the weapon, and guide it to the target. She no longer has a power plant of boilers and steam turbines. And, lastly, the new destroyer now uses that indispensable accessory, the helicopter, so she must have a flight pad and hangar.

FRIGATES AND CORVETTES

The development of anti-submarine craft from the First World War to the present day

The names frigate and corvette were revived during the Second World War to describe ships that have nothing in common with the rigged ships of the same names, that were in service until the end of the last century. These names have been revamped to indicate two types of escort ships, used chiefly for anti-submarine work. The larger type with a greater displacement is called a frigate, and the smaller type displacing less (with a consequent drop in performance) is called a corvette. With the shifts in destroyer and cruiser role after World War II, the meaning of these terms has blurred, and the distinctions between frigate and destroyer are no longer very clear.

The need for ships specially equipped to fight submarines dates back to the First World War when the Royal Navy, in particular, had to combat widespread convoy attacks by German submarines. At that time there were no ships specially equipped to detect and hunt down submarines. The Royal Navy was first to build flotillas of submarine chasers, initially used only for coastal work. Some were purposely built, like the *ELCO* motor launches, others were adapted requisitioned merchant ships, such as fishing boats or trawlers. These were followed by units built for open sea and convoy escort work: patrol boats, or "*P* Class," soon followed by the "*PC* Class," which were much larger and had a longer range. The true prototypes of the Second World War frigates and corvettes, however, were the sloops, officially designated as squadron minesweepers, displacing 1,200t against the *PC*'s 700t and the *P*'s 600t.

The second major navy to equip itself with submarine chasers was the U.S. Navy which built 448 submarine chasers in 1917–1918, wooden-hulled ships for coastal work, displacing a mere 85t. These were followed by other, larger iron-hulled units, designated "escort ships," and making up the *Eagle* Class. Only twelve were completed before the war ended. They were much smaller than the British sloops and displaced 615t.

The French Navy built two types of submarine chasers: the *Agile* Class gunboats, displacing about 350t, and the *Arras* and similar sloops, displacing 550 to 700 tonnes. Only when the war was over did France acquire the *Le Normand*-type submarine chasers.

The Italian Navy, which did not have the problem of protecting convoys on the high seas, did not build oceangoing submarine chasers and just used requisitioned motor trawlers and the forty-seven ex-trawler minesweepers bought in Japan, as well as coastal torpedo boats, gunboats, and a considerable number of motor torpedo boats. By the end of the First World War, Britain's 1,200t sloops were the submarine chasers with the greatest operational capabilities. Between the wars, there was a lull in anti-submarine ship building and only in 1937–1939, on the brink of the Second World War, did the Royal Navy commission two types of sloops, belonging to the *Bittern* and *Egret* Classes, and a third smaller type, the *Kingfisher* Class. The United States built no such ships, but the French built the *Élan* Class minesweeper scouts that were similar to Britain's sloops. In 1934 the Italian Navy built an experimental submarine chaser named *Albatros* and, in 1938, the four *Pegaso* Class escort scouts. There was, however, a fundamental difference between the submarine chasers used in the First World War and those of 1937–1939. This difference did not lie in displacement or armament, but in ultrasonic equipment (known as Asdic) that could detect submerged submarines by the echoes bouncing off their hulls and determine where they were coming from and how far away they were. This equipment, which was much more sophisticated than that used in the First World War, was closely examined by all the navies.

As already mentioned, old names were revamped during the Second World War to describe submarine chasers: the name corvette was assigned for the first time to Britain's *Flower* Class, the first of which were ordered on July 27, 1939, and the term frigate was used for a new, larger type, the *River* Class. These ships were built in Canada and the United States, as well as Britain.

During the Second World War, large numbers of corvettes and frigates were built and made up the bulk of ships used by the Royal Navy to escort convoys. By contrast, the U.S. Navy built only a limited number of frigates, 102 in all, of the *River* and similar types. It chose another type of ship: the destroyer escort, or *DE* and ordered 1,005 of them, only 565 of which were completed before the end of the war. DEs had a displacement of about 1,350 tonnes, powerful anti-aircraft armament, fairly good anti-submarine armament, and, for the best part, a diesel-electric or turbo-electric drive.

The Japanese Navy also built DEs and escort ships but the German Navy did not have purposely built ships, and used destroyers to escort its convoys via Norway. The French Navy did not build ships of this type but the Free French Force Navy was given three British *River* Class anti-submarine corvettes and six U.S. destroyer escorts.

The Italian Navy built the *Gabbiano* Class anti-submarine corvettes and a few submarine vedette boats with a small displacement (also known as VAS—*vedetta antisommergibile*, or submarine vedette boat).

By the end of the war, frigates and corvettes had their own definite features that distinguished them from contemporary destroyers and the old sloops and scouts. They were armed mainly for anti-submarine work but also had anti-aircraft guns to defend themselves and the ships they were escorting. The British and American units also had search and fire-control radar. In the post-war years, far fewer new ships were built although some destroyers were converted for anti-submarine work. The Royal Navy converted some thirty destroyers into fast anti-submarine frigates and the U.S. Navy did likewise.

In 1950–1955, all navies resumed anti-submarine frigate construction but practically none built new corvettes, except for the Italian Navy and other minor navies.

Post-war frigates had more well-developed anti-aircraft and anti-submarine armament but no flight installations or helicopters. During this period, other frigates with special characteristics, apart from anti-submarine frigates, were also developed, such as anti-aircraft and general-purpose frigates. Examples of anti-aircraft frigates are the British *Leopard*s (1957–1959) and *Salisbury*s (1957–1960) and examples of the general-purpose types are the French *Commandant Rivière*s (1962–1965) and British *Tribal*s (1961–1964) and *Leander*s (1963–1973). Up until 1975, the U.S. Navy used the term 'frigate' for a very different type of ship, a destroyer leader larger than a destroyer.

In fact, the nuclear-powered *Bainbridge* and *Truxtun* (DLGN) and *Belknap*s and *Leahy*s (DLG) were initially classified as frigates. As from June 1975, the latter were reclassified as cruisers, whereas the DLGs of the *Coontz* Class have been classified as destroyers. The U.S. Navy then used the term frigate in the same sense as did its allies.

The most recent frigate development has been the introduction of the missile as an anti-aircraft weapon and the helicopter as an anti-submarine weapon. The first missile launchers were installed on newly built ships, not on modified units already in commission. In 1963, the British *Leander*s and American *Brooke*s were equipped with launchers. The first to have helicopters, pad, and hangar were the French *Commandant Rivière*s (1962–1965), the Italian *Bergamini*s (1961–1962) and *Alpino*s (1965), the Dutch *Van Speijk*s (1966–1969), the British *Tribal* (1961–1964) and *Leander* (1963–1973) Classes and, lastly, the Danish *Hvidbjornen* types (1962). Frigates and corvettes were the first fighting surface ships to be powered by diesel engines.

Subsequent developments led to frigates with gas turbine machinery although no nuclear-powered frigates have yet been designed.

Armament and power plants of anti-submarine units

When submerged, submarines are invisible to the surface ships that are supposed to destroy them. Submarines powered by conventional machinery must surface or snorkel about every twenty-four hours to recharge their electric batteries and it is then that they can be detected by radar. These radar search and detection operations are normally carried out by land-based stations or by aircraft rather than by equipment on board a ship.

Anti-submarine warfare ships have sonar equipment to detect submerged boats. Although this apparatus is not a weapon as such, its detection role can be likened to human sight in identifying and pinpointing surface ships before the introduction of radar.

Sonic equipment, or hydrophones, had been used since the First World War. These were called ''*tubo C*'' in the Italian Navy and they were installed on motor torpedo-boats and other anti-submarine units to detect the sounds made by submarines, especially the sound of their propellers churning up the water.

Between the wars, this equipment was improved, and ultrasonic, as opposed to plain sonic, waves were used. This meant that the position and distance of a submarine could be more accurately detected. Instead of picking up underwater noises originating from the submarine, a beam of ultrasonic waves bounces off the hull and is received by the search unit. Once the submarine's position was fixed either with this equipment, or by surface sighting, it was destroyed by depth charges, dropped into the sea from hoppers at the stern and set to detonate at a certain depth. Depth charges were used in the Second World War, the major improvement at that time being the fact that large numbers of depth charges could be dropped from the side of the ship all at once, using numerous launchers, thus covering a larger area, instead of dropping one after the other into the sea from the stern. Side launchers were superseded by a bow launcher that could dispatch twenty-four charges simultaneously over a distance of some 1,000ft (300m) in an oval pattern. This weapon was called a hedgehog.

After the war, depth-charge launchers were further developed and Britain produced the Squid mortars with three short barrels that fired three depth charges. These were followed by the Limbos (also British), which had three long barrels. Italy developed the single- and double-barreled Menon launchers and the United States the Weapon Alphas. All these weapons are fitted with automatic devices to vary the depth at which the charges detonate. The Soviet Navy introduced twelve-tube multiple rocket launchers.

Currently, the most widespread and effective anti-submarine weapons are anti-submarine torpedoes, either of the wire guided or homing type. These torpedoes,

Commandant Rivière (France 1962). The nine frigates of this class, commissioned between 1962 and 1965, started off with three 3.9in (100mm) guns in three turrets. One gun mount was later replaced by four Exocet missile launchers. All have diesel machinery except for *Balny*, which has a combined diesel and gas turbine power plant. They have an after helicopter pad but no helicopters of their own.

which are much shorter than conventional anti-ship torpedoes, are usually housed in triple trainable mountings with the centerline of the torpedoes on the vertices of an equilateral triangle and not coplanar, as with triple anti-ship torpedo tubes. One special type of torpedo is one that is combined with a missile and thus called an anti-submarine missile. These missiles can be fired from surface ships; the American ASROC is an example.

These special torpedoes are fired with a carrier missile; they thus have an aerial trajectory, and are released when they are near the target. Once they enter the water, they continue on their way underwater, guided in their search for the target by their homing nose.

Another way of using anti-submarine torpedoes from a distance is to carry them by helicopter, or by a special unmanned aircraft, such as the U.S. Navy Drone Anti-Submarine Helicopter (DASH).

All anti-submarine ships are also armed with anti-aircraft guns and machine guns, like all military craft, although these guns have recently been replaced by anti-aircraft missile launchers.

Power plant development has been similar to that of torpedo boat and destroyer power plants. It began, in other words, with reciprocating engines, went on to steam turbines, then, around the time of the Second World War, to diesel engines, and, after 1960, to gas turbines. Because these ships first came into being thirty to forty years after torpedo boats and destroyers, and because of the low displacement of some of the early units, there have been anti-submarine ships with gasoline or diesel engines right from the start. At the beginning of the Second World War, most power plants were still turbines, with reduction gears, driving twin screws, and oil fired boilers.

Then, during the war, the diesel engine gained more ground and was particularly widely used in the U.S. Navy for some classes of destroyer escorts such as the *Bostwick, Edsall,* and *Evarts* types (all 1943) with diesel-electric drive, as well as for *PC, PCE,* and *PCS* Class submarine chasers, powered solely by diesel engines. The Italian Navy also used diesel engines—on the *Gabbiano* Class corvettes, for instance. In the post-war years, there were still some frigates powered by steam turbines, but around 1960 almost all newly built units were diesel powered.

As from 1960, some new frigates were fitted with gas turbines, not as an entire power plant system, but to be used solely for full speed operations, diesel engines being used for normal running.

The only example of combined gas and steam turbines occurred on the seven British frigates of the *Tribal* Class, commissioned between 1961 and 1964. They had a single screw driven by one 12,329hp (12,500CV) turbine units with reduction gears; these gears could engage with the 19,726hp (20,000CV) gas turbine. All the other frigates had diesel engines for cruising speed and gas turbines for full speed.

Lastly, the most recent classes of frigates are powered exclusively by gas turbines. These include the Russian *Kirvak* Class of 1970 and the American *Perry* Class of 1976, the latter having two gas turbines driving a single screw.

Anti-submarine ships of the First World War

The Royal Navy was first to have ships specially equipped to chase submarines with its purpose-built motor launches and patrol boats.

Motor launches were small wooden-hulled twin-screw coastal boats powered by gasoline engines. Most of them were built in the United States and Canada between 1915 and 1918. They displaced thirty-four to thirty-seven tonnes, were armed with one 3in (76mm) gun forward, and had hydrophones and depth charge hoppers aft.

The patrol boats (P boats) were steel-hulled twin-screw vessels powered by turbines. They were built to replace destroyers in their role as escorts and submarine chasers. They were flush-deckers and had a superstructure in the midships to forward area, on which there was a 4in (102mm) gun, followed by the bridge and funnel. In the after area there were a machine gun and two fixed torpedo tubes, set at an angle of 45° to the ship's centerline, that fired astern. The two torpedo tubes were soon removed and replaced by tracks for thirty depth charges. They had a very large rudder for shallow water maneuvers.

A group of six of these units was modified during construction so as to give them the appearance of merchant men for use as "decoy" or "Q" ships. The task of these ships was to lure submarines close to them, wait for them to surface, and then hoist the war flag and open up with guns and depth charges. They displaced slightly more than the *P*s and had a merchant ship profile with a foredeck, central superstructure, and a tall funnel. They were armed with one 4in (102mm) gun on the deck aft which was usually hidden by a fake superstructure or a fake boat, or else a fake cargo of sacks of goods piled on deck. Originally they also had two torpedo tubes, which were soon removed, and could carry twenty-four to thirty depth charges on tracks aft.

The *Flower* Class sloops formed the most numerous anti-submarine class. Originally they were designed as minesweepers, the *Acacia* and *Arbis* Classes

being built as such; others were modified on the stocks and became convoy escort sloops, these being the *Aubrietia, Anchusa,* and *Sir Bevis* Classes.

The *Acacia* and *Arbis*-type minesweepers had two funnels, whereas the convoy escort sloops had only one for their two coal-fired boilers, one reciprocating engine and single screw. Displacements varied from the 1,250t of the 1916 *Aubrietia* types, and the 1,290t of the 1917 *Anchusa* types, to the 1,320t of the 1918 *Sir Bevis* types. They looked like merchant ships and could thus blend with the ships in the convoy so as not to arouse suspicions in any lurking submarines. Armament varied according to the type of ship. The *Aubrietia*s had three 2.2in (57mm) guns and two 3in (76mm) anti-aircraft guns, the *Anchusa*s had two 2.2in (57mm) guns and one 200lb depth charge mortar, and the *Sir Bevis* types had two 4in (102mm) guns. All were armed with depth charges, as well.

The United States Navy had just one type of patrol boat which was laid down in 1918, so only a small number could be commissioned before the end of hostilities. They formed the *Eagle* Class, which was to have numbered 112, but only the first sixty were actually completed. Units *61* to *112* were canceled when the war ended. They were interesting in that they were mass-produced, using the assembly-line technique, in a factory that was opened especially by the Ford Motor Company at River Rouge. They had a full load displacement of 615t, and, like their British counterparts, only one screw, but this was turned by a turbine unit, as opposed to reciprocating engines. Their two boilers were coal-fired. They had a flush deck with a squat central superstructure that extended the entire width of the ship, followed by a funnel. There was another superstructure in the midships-to-after area. Armament was two 3.9in (101mm) guns on the two superstructures, one before the bridge and one on the after superstructure, plus twelve depth charges.

French submarine chasers were classified neither as patrol boats, like the American ones, nor convoy escort sloops, like the British ones, but as anti-submarine gunboats. The most numerous was the twenty-unit *Agile* Class, which were also single screw ships powered by one reciprocating engine and two coal-fired boilers, making a top speed of just over seventeen knots. They were flush-deckers with a very sleek bow and a small central superstructure surmounted by two small-diameter cylindrical funnels. Armament consisted of two 3.5in (90mm) guns, one forward before the bridge and one aft on the deck. They also carried depth charges. During the war, other classes of anti-submarine gunboats with similar armament were built. The three *Diligente* types, for instance, were structurally similar to the *Agile*s but had a different power plant consisting of two diesel engines for two screws, and one funnel. The two *Conquérante*s of 1917, however, were also powered by two diesel engines driving two screws, but their hull shape was different. Lastly, the five *Dubourdieu* Class of 1918 had a turbine power plant on two screws and oil-fired boilers. As far as armament was concerned, the *Diligente*s and *Conquérante*s had two 3.9in (100mm) guns whereas the *Dubourdieu*s had one 5.1in (130mm) gun forward and one 3.5in (90mm) aft. All carried depth charges. Another type of French anti-submarine ship was the "scout," similar to the British sloops, and forming the *Aisne, Aldébaran, Ailette,* and *Arras* Classes, all commissioned between 1916 and 1918. They looked like merchant ships, with their short foredeck, and differed in their external appearance from class to class. The 1918 *Arras* types, of which twenty-nine were ordered and sixteen actually built, had a forecastle deck, a central superstructure, a quarterdeck, and one tall funnel. They were armed with two 5.5in (140mm) guns, one 2.2in (57mm) anti-aircraft gun and carried twenty depth charges. They were powered by steam turbines driving two screws and some had oil- and others coal-fired boilers. By contrast, the *Ailette*s (1918) and *Aisne*s (1916) had reciprocating engines driving two screws and oil-fired boilers, whereas the *Aldébaran*s (1916) had a single screw, reciprocating engine, and coal-fired boilers. All were armed with guns and depth charges.

Anti-submarine ships of the Second World War

During the Second World War, Germany again mounted an intense convoy attack program, as she had done in the First World War. The German Navy built huge numbers of submarines that she used in the Atlantic against convoys bringing vital supplies of raw materials, weapons, provisions, and war equipment from the United States to Britain, and later against convoys bringing the Expeditionary Forces of the United States Army to North Africa and the French Atlantic coast, and, lastly, the shores of Italy in the Mediterranean.

The need again arose for the British and Americans to have a sufficient number of vessels to withstand the threat of underwater attacks.

Between the wars, quite a few anti-submarine units had been built. These were fitted with very advanced search and detection equipment. Armament had also improved and ships were now armed with anti-aircraft guns.

In 1935–1938, the Royal Navy resumed construction of ships originally classi-

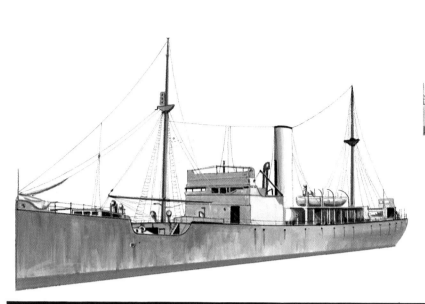

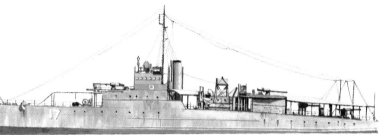

Eagle 17 (United States 1918). The sixty units of this type were numbered one to sixty. The name *Eagle* came from the shipyard where the units were built. They were flush-deckers armed with guns, a few machine guns, and depth charges. They had geared turbine machinery and a single screw, and could make eighteen knots.

Anchusa (Great Britain 1917). One of a class of thirty-nine units, belonging to the *Flower* type and officially classified as convoy escort sloops. They looked like merchant ships but were armed with two guns, one mortar, and four depth charge throwers. They had one reciprocating engine and two coal-fired boilers. Together with eight other units of the class, *Anchusa* was sunk during the war. All the others were taken out of commission when the war was over.

fied as ''patrol boats,'' but later as corvettes: the *Kingfisher* Class. These ships were purposely built as coastal convoy escorts and carried mainly anti-submarine armament, in the form of depth charges. They had a long forecastle, a bridge superstructure, and one funnel. They displaced 530t and had a turbine power plant driving twin screws. Armament consisted of one 3.9in (101mm) anti-aircraft gun and eight machine guns, as well as depth charges. At about the same time (1933–1938), a dozen *Egret, Bittern,* and *Leith* types were built. They displaced 1,000 to 1,200t, were turbo-driven with twin screws, and were heavily armed with guns.

The first to be classified as corvettes were the *Flower* Class, of which fifty-six were ordered in 1939, although this number increased to about 300 in the course of the war. The first of these units was commissioned at the end of 1940 and, after the war, many were delivered to the Danish, French, Greek, and Norwegian navies. Others were either sold or broken up. They displaced 925t and were single-screw ships powered by one reciprocating engine making just sixteen knots. They were fitted with Adsic and had depth charge tracks aft; later they were fitted with the more effective hedgehogs. Armament was rounded off by one dual-purpose 3in (76mm) or 4in (102mm) gun and a varying number of 0.7in (20mm) anti-aircraft machine guns.

During the war, corvettes of another type were built. They were larger and commissioned between late 1943 and late 1944 and formed the *Castle* Class. They had one reciprocating engine and one screw and made sixteen knots. Anti-submarine armament was in the form of Squids, these being three-barrelled mortars that could fire three depth charges at the same time. Anti-aircraft armament consisted of one 3.9in (101mm) gun and six to ten 0.7in (20mm) machine guns.

As already mentioned, these corvettes could make about sixteen knots, which soon proved to be too slow to catch the submarines of the day that could make twenty knots on the surface. In order to meet this need for greater speed and keep the cost and building time down, faster corvettes were ordered. These were also powered by reciprocating engines but had twin screws and were later classified as frigates.

The first class to bear this name was the 225-unit *River* Class. They were built mostly in the United States and Canada and, to a lesser extent, in British shipyards. They had a long forecastle, a midships-to-forward superstructure, and one funnel. They displaced 1,460t and were armed with one hedgehog and two 4in (102mm) dual-purpose guns plus ten 0.7in (20mm) anti-aircraft machine guns. The two engines developed 5,425hp (5,500CV) and the top speed was twenty knots. The successful performance of the *Rivers* led to two more classes of frigates being laid down, making a total of fifty-six, all built in Britain. They were the same as the *Rivers* externally and formed two classes: the *Loch* and the *Bay* Classes. They had two 5,425hp (5,500CV) reciprocating engines and made 19.5 knots. A very small number of *River* Class frigates (four) and *Lochs* (two) had turbine power plants and made twenty-one knots. For these two classes, anti-submarine armament was increased to two hedgehogs on the *Bays* and two Squids on the *Lochs*. Anti-aircraft armament was particularly well-developed on the *Bays*, classified as ''anti-aircraft frigates.'' They were, in fact, armed with four 3.9in (101mm) guns and eight 1.5in (40mm) and two 0.7in (20mm) machine guns. The *Lochs*, however, had only one 3.9in (101mm) gun and about ten 1.5in (40mm) and 0.7in (20mm) machine guns.

The U.S. Navy followed a different line of action and built large numbers of submarine chasers that bore the letters *PC, PCE, PCS,* and *SC* plus a number. They

all had small displacements, diesel power plants, and were armed with machine guns and depth charges. The forty-two *PCE*s, numbered 842 to 904 (a few numbers being skipped), and, built between 1942 and 1943, were exceptions because they were similar to the corvettes of other navies. They had a full load displacement of 903t, a twin screw diesel power plant, and were armed with one 3in (76mm) anti-aircraft gun, five 1.5in (40mm) machine guns, and four depth charge throwers. In 1943, ninety-six frigates (of the *Tacoma* Class) nearly identical to the British *Rivers* were built. Twenty of them were delivered to the Royal Navy and twenty-eight to the Soviet Navy. In addition to these ships, expressly designed as submarine chasers, the United States Navy also built large numbers of destroyer escorts, or DEs, to provide anti-aircraft and anti-submarine cover for convoys and other naval formations. These destroyer escorts were divided into six types: the 22 *Rudderow*s, 106 *John C. Butler*s, 102 *Buckley*s, 72 *Bostwick*s, 85 *Edsall*s, and 73 *Evart*s, making a total of 460. They were flush-deckers with a large superstructure surmounted by the bridge and one funnel and had a characteristic bulwark along the amidships part of their length. They can therefore be regarded as belonging to one and the same class and were fitted with a different type of power plant to meet the different demands of the war situation. The *J.C. Butler*s had geared steam turbines, the *Rudderow*s and *Buckley*s turbo-electric drive, the *Evart*s and *Bostwick*s diesel-electric drive, and, lastly, the *Edsall*s geared diesel engines. All had dual-purpose guns, a fair number of anti-aircraft machine guns, depth charge launchers, and, as distinct from the ships of other navies, triple anti-ship torpedo tubes.

At the end of the war, forty-six *Buckley*s and forty-six *Rudderow*s were converted to fast transporters (*APD*s) by having their hulls modified. The deckhouse was replaced by a superstructure that extended the entire width of the ship and accommodated two large davits to lower two landing craft into the sea. A lattice, or tripod mast was also added aft for a derrick. Another thirty (two *J.C. Butler*s and twenty-eight *Edsall*s) were later converted to radar pickets and were designated *DER*s. Their superstructure was widened and they had a large tripod mast to support the radar antennae. Before the war, the French Navy built twenty-five ships, officially designated ''minesweeper scouts,'' that formed the *Élan* Class. They displaced 630–700t, had a diesel power plant, twin screws, and a top speed of twenty knots. They had no special anti-submarine armament. During the war years, the Free French Forces Navy was loaned six British *Rivers*, which formed the *Aventure* Class, and six American DEs of the *Bostwick* type, which formed the *Sénégalais* Class, as well as thirty-two *PC*s with a full load displacement of 430t, which formed the *Carabinier* Class.

The Soviet Navy built no ships that could be described as frigates and corvettes, only patrol boats, or sloops, like the twenty *Cheka* types of 1935–1936, the first of which bore the letters *PS* and were numbered *1* to *6* (basically minelayers and minesweepers) or the *Dzerzhinsky* types of 1935 (ex *PS 8* and *PS 26*). The Russians also used twenty-eight *River* frigates, built in the United States, and about a hundred American sub-chasers (*SC*s). There were, however, various types of Russian-built anti-submarine motor launches that belonged to the *MO 2* (1935), *MO 4* (1936), *BO 2* (1938), and *BMO* (1939) types that displaced 50–70t, with the exception of the *BO 2*s which displaced 240t, and had a diesel power plant driving two or three screws.

Both before and during the war the Japanese Navy had no ships classified as frigates or corvettes, only small diesel-powered units. The first ones, built in 1933–

1934 and designated *Ch 1* and *Ch 2*, displaced 280t and were armed with four machine guns and thirty-six depth charges. Those that followed displaced around 300 to 310t and had similar armament. The types numbered *13* to *89* reached 460t and were armed with one 3.1in (80mm) gun and thirty-six depth charges. In 1939–1940, about 250 units of the *Cha* type were commissioned. They displaced 135t, had one diesel engine and a single screw, and were armed with twenty-two depth charges.

Some escorts, however, were more like frigates and corvettes. These were the *Etorofu*, *Mikura*, *Ukuru*, and *A*, *B*, *C*, and *D* types, all armed with depth charges varying in number from thirty-six to 120 and all powered by two-shaft diesel machinery, except for the *D*s, which had steam turbines and one screw. The *Mikura*s (eight units) displaced 1,020t, full load, and had a forecastle deck and a single funnel well aft. They were armed with three 4.7in (120mm) guns and four 1in (25mm) anti-aircraft machine guns, plus a 3in (76mm) depth charge mortar before the bridge and 120 depth charges. The power plant consisted of two 4,142hp (4,200CV) diesel engines and had a top speed of 19.5 knots.

The 102 *D* types, built between 1943 and 1945, had a full load displacement of 940t, two boilers, and a 2,466hp (2,500CV) geared turbine unit and made 17.5 knots. Due to the lack of diesel oil, these units had their boilers modified in 1945 to burn coal. They had a foredeck, and a tall narrow funnel, and were armed with two small 4.7in (120mm) guns, six 1in (25mm) anti-aircraft machine guns, a 3in (76mm) hedgehog mortar, twelve side launchers and 120 depth charges. The *A* and *B* types formed one class but differed in that the *A*s were steel-hulled (two units) and the *B*s were wooden-hulled (fifty-seven units). Construction of these units stopped when the war ended.

The German Navy, which did not require escorts and submarine chasers for its own purposes, built ten units in 1934–1935 classified as escorts and designated *F 1* to *F 10*. They displaced some 800t full load, had a big superstructure extending the full width of the ship, and two funnels, the forward one being the taller. They were armed with two 4.1in (105mm) guns, one on the foredeck and one on the after superstructure, six anti-aircraft machine guns, and depth-charge launchers. They had turbine machinery, twin screws, and made twenty-eight knots.

From the very beginning of the war, the Italian Navy, which had to use torpedo boats and destroyers to escort convoys bound for North Africa, felt the need to design ships expressly for this purpose that would be cheap to build and run. But a design for a unit with a standard displacement of 670t and a diesel power plant was not forthcoming until 1941. Toward the end of that year, sixty were ordered from various Italian shipyards; of these, only twenty-eight could be commissioned before the armistice of September 8, 1943.

The *Gabbiano* anti-submarine corvettes displaced 728t full load, had a forecastle that ran half their length and a bridge superstructure followed by a large diameter short funnel. Armament comprised one 3.9in (100mm) anti-aircraft gun on the foredeck, seven 0.7in (20mm) machine guns, two torpedo tubes and eight side launchers, plus two depth charge hoppers aft and two towed explosive sweeps. They were powered by two 3,452hp (3,500CV) diesels and made eighteen knots. Each shaft also had one 74hp (75CV) electric motor powered by sixty submarine-type accumulator batteries that could develop six to seven knots and was used for "lying in wait" when the hydrophones were being used or when the ship did not want submerged submarines to know she was there. This electric power plant proved to be of little use and was soon removed.

During their long period of service, these corvettes had considerable changes made to their superstructures and armament; some units, for instance, were given an after superstructure to increase crew's quarters when they were turned into command training ships.

Post-war frigates and corvettes

The terms frigate and corvette, used during the war, were carried over into the post-war period, and ships that had previously been described as destroyers, torpedo-boats, sloops, or scouts were reclassified as frigates.

What is more, the major navies, like the United States and Royal Navies, gave a considerable number of their old frigates to the navies of smaller countries. Lastly, the Royal Navy converted some destroyers to anti-submarine frigates and classified the entire *Hunt* Class of destroyer escorts, commissioned in 1940–1943, as anti-aircraft frigates.

The conversion was a "partial" one for the ten destroyers of the *O*, *P*, and *T* Classes, commissioned in 1941–1943, and involved modifying the bridge, installing two Squid or Limbo mortars, replacing four single 4in (102mm) mounts with one twin 4in (102mm) turret or two singles, and removing a set of quadruple torpedo tubes.

The conversion was "total" for the twenty-two destroyers of the *R*, *T*, *U*, *V*, *W*, and *Z* Classes, with a hull modification that involved lengthening the forecastle

almost to the stern, and installing a superstructure that spanned the whole width of the ship amidships. The four single mounts were replaced by a twin 4in (102mm) mount on the superstructure aft. Two twin 1.5in (40mm) anti-aircraft machine guns were installed before the bridge and, in a special well in the superstructure aft, there were two Limbos or two Squids.

As far as the *Hunt* destroyer escorts were concerned, it was a simple matter of changing classification without making any structural or armament modifications. Since these units were classified as "anti-aircraft frigates," they had no anti-submarine armament whatsoever, only a substantial anti-aircraft armament of four to six 4in (102mm) anti-aircraft guns and two to four 0.7in (20mm) and 1.5in (40mm) anti-aircraft machine guns.

In 1946–1950, the United States Navy converted seven *Gearings* and eighteen *Fletcher* Class into submarine chasers (ASW destroyers), designated *DDE*s (not to be confused with the *DE*s, or destroyer escorts). And in 1949–1950, eight *Gearing* Class destroyers (not completed in 1946) were completed as *DDE*s and formed the *Carpenter* Class. These eight units were armed with four to six 3in (76mm) anti-aircraft guns in two–three twin mounts, one forward and one or two aft. For anti-submarine armament they had two Weapon Alphas and two or three hedgehogs before the bridge, plus a few depth-charge launchers amidships.

The seven modified *Gearings*, forming the *Damato* Class, had four 5in (127mm) dual purpose guns in two twin mounts, one forward and one aft, four to six 3in (76mm) anti-aircraft guns, and one Weapon Alpha before the bridge. The eighteen *Fletchers* had two 5in (127mm) guns in two single mounts, one Weapon Alpha or hedgehog before the bridge, and side launchers.

Examples of newly built units are the British frigates of the *Leopard* (1955) and *Salisbury* (1953–1955) Classes, classified as anti-aircraft frigates and powered by diesel engines, whereas the *Blackwood* Class of 1956 had a turbine power plant driving a single screw. The *Leopard*s and *Salisbury*s can be regarded as flush-deckers, since they have only a short stretch of deck that is lower aft. They have a full-width superstructure, surmounted by the bridge, and two tall masts to support the radar aerials, replaced on some during a refit in 1963–1964 by one or two macks. The power plant of eight diesel engines, four for each of the two propeller shafts, has special hydraulic couplings that enable one or more engines to be coupled to or uncoupled from the set of reduction or reversing gears that drive the shafts. The *Leopard*s are armed with four 4.5in (115mm) guns in two twin turrets while the *Salisbury*s have two 4.5in (115mm) guns in one twin turret, plus two twin 1.5in (40mm) machine guns aft. Anti-submarine armament consists of one triple Squid.

The *Blackwood*s have a forecastle, full-width superstructure below the bridge, and a large funnel. Anti-submarine armament consists of two Limbos on the after superstructure and there are no guns, only two or three anti-aircraft machine guns. The four original torpedo tubes have been removed.

The United States Navy continued its construction of destroyer escorts (*DE*s) with the *Dealey* and *Evans* Classes of 1954–1957. These units have a full load displacement of 1,914t, a turbine power plant and single screw. They are armed with four 3in (76mm) dual purpose guns in two twin turrets, one Weapon Alpha and, for the first time, two triple torpedo tubes for ASW homing torpedoes instead of depth charges. In 1963, some units had their 3in (76mm) after mounts replaced by a hangar and pad for an unmanned DASH helicopter.

From 1955–1965 onwards, the Japanese Navy also built frigates. One of the first groups was the *Ikazuki* Class, with a full load displacement of 1,300t, armed with two single 3in (76mm) guns, one hedgehog, eight launchers and two depth charge tracks. These twin-screw ships are diesel powered.

A second group of four units, forming the *Isuzu* Class and commissioned in 1961–1964, displace 1,711 tonnes full load, are, too, are twin-screw diesel-powered ships. They are armed with four 3in (76mm) guns in two twin mounts, one four-tube launcher, two triple ASW homing torpedo tubes, and launchers and hoppers for depth charges.

Between 1955 and 1965, the French Navy commissioned two types of ships: one officially classified as "fast escorts" (fourteen units forming the *Le Normand* Class), and the other as "escort scouts" (nine units of the *Commandant Rivière* Class).

The *Le Normand*s, commissioned between 1956 and 1960, displace 1,700t and have a twin-screw steam turbine power plant. Their anti-aircraft armament consists of six small 2.2in (57mm) guns in three twin mountings, one forward and two aft, while anti-submarine armament is made up of twelve homing torpedoes in four triple sets, one six-barrelled and two single-barrelled mortars and one depth charge hopper.

The *Commandant Rivière*s, commissioned between 1962 and 1965, displace 2,250t full load and are armed with three 3.9in (100mm) anti-aircraft guns and two 0.7in (20mm) machine guns. They have only six anti-submarine torpedo tubes in two triple mountings and one four-barrelled depth charge mortar.

During this ten year period, the Soviet Navy built only two classes of frigates: *Riga*, around 1952–1958, and *Kola*, around 1950–1951. Both had a turbine power

De Cristofaro (Italy 1965). The four corvettes of the *De Cristofaro* Class were the last to be built by the Italian Navy. They are armed with two 3in (76mm) guns, one forward and one aft, and one depth charge mortar, as well as two triple anti-submarine torpedo tubes. These twin-screw diesel-powered ships can do 23.5 knots and are fitted with search and fire-control radar. They are an improved version of the *Albatros* types.

plant, the former with just one funnel, the latter with two. The *Riga*s were armed with three single 3.9in (100mm) guns, two forward and one aft, three 1.4in (37mm) machine guns and, for anti-submarine weapons, four depth charge launchers. The *Kola*s had four 3.9in (100mm) guns in four turrets, two forward and two aft, four 1.4in (37mm) machine guns and, depth charge launchers.

During its post-war rebuilding program, the Italian Navy equipped itself with anti-submarine frigates, the first being the four *Centauro* types with a full load displacement of 2,200t and a steam power plant. They had a modern appearance, a flush deck, curved bow, a full-width superstructure amidships, and two funnels. Their anti-aircraft armament was interesting in that the four 3in (76mm) guns in two twin turrets had their barrels superimposed one above the other rather than abreast. Anti-submarine armament was one three-barrelled mortar before the bridge, two side bomb launchers, and a hopper aft. The class that followed, the four *Bergamini*s commissioned in 1961–1962, was made up of twin-screw diesel-powered ships. They formed the first class of Italian frigates to have a helicopter, hangar, and flight pad. They displaced 1,650t full load and were armed with three 3in (76mm) guns in three turrets, two forward and one aft, one single-barrelled depth charge mortar, and six anti-submarine torpedo tubes in two triple sets.

Among the most outstanding ships of the minor navies are the Canadian *Annapolis* and *St. Laurent* Classes. They resemble each other and are now characterized by a box-like superstructure and two funnels placed symmetrically abreast. The *St. Laurent*s have a full load displacement of 2,800t and were commissioned between 1956 and 1957. Originally they had just one funnel and no hangar or helicopter pad. They were converted in 1961–1964 and given two funnels and a hangar. The stern was also modified by making a recess or step for the variable depth sonar. They are now armed with two 3in (76mm) guns in one twin mount forward, two Limbos aft and anti-submarine torpedoes. The *Annapolis* types have a full load displacement of 3,000t and were commissioned in 1964. Originally without a hangar and having just one funnel, they were later modified and fitted with two funnels, a hangar, flight deck, and stepped stern. They had the same armament as the *St. Laurent*s. Another eleven units forming the *Restigouche* and *Mackenzie* Classes, identical to the *Annapolis* Class, did not receive the above modification.

In 1946–1951, the Spanish Navy commissioned eight *Pizarro* Class frigates that displaced 2,246t and were steam-powered. After a refit their anti-submarine armament was one hedgehog, eight mortars, and one depth charge track, plus anti-submarine torpedo tubes.

In the 1955–1965 period, units classified as frigates were still being built, such

as the Italian *Albatros* and *De Cristofaro* types, the Danish *Triton*s, Argentinian *King*s, and Spanish *Atrevida*s.

Italy's *Albatros* types and Denmarks *Triton*s were built in Italy in the Cantiere Navalmeccanica di Castellammare di Stabia as part of the U.S. Mutual Defense Assistance Program. Originally, three units were supposed to be for Italy, four for Denmark, and one for Holland. After being commissioned in 1955–1956, the one assigned to Holland was handed over to Italy in 1961, where she was renamed *Aquila*. These twin-screw ships displace 960t fully laden and have a diesel power plant. They are flush-deckers with a superstructure for the bridge. Armament consisted of two 3in (76mm) guns, later replaced by four 1.5in (40mm) machine guns, two hedgehogs, and two anti-submarine torpedo tubes. The four *De Cristofaro* frigates were commissioned in 1965–1966 and have a full load displacement of 940t. They have a forecastle and a bridge superstructure and are armed with two single 3in (76mm) guns, one forward and one aft, one depth charge mortar behind the funnel, and six anti-submarine torpedo tubes in two triple mountings.

The Argentinian *King* Class corvettes, of older construction (1938–1946), have a twin-shaft diesel power plant, a full load displacement of 1,000t and four depth charge launchers as anti-submarine armament. Spain's six *Atrevida* Class are more modern, commissioned between 1954 and 1960. They have a full load displacement of 1,135t, a diesel power plant and were armed with four depth-charge launchers as anti-submarine armament, later replaced by two hedgehogs, three mortars, and two hoppers. *Descubierta*, one of the corvettes of the *Atrevida* Class, although commissioned on February 1, 1955, has already been withdrawn, whereas another four units of the class are still in commission. The name *Descubierta* has now been given to a newly built frigate commissioned in 1978.

Missile and gas turbine frigates and corvettes

From the 1960s onwards, the development of naval armament has led to the introduction of missiles as anti-aircraft weapons on frigates, too, which have thus been transformed, from units equipped mainly for anti-submarine warfare, into dual purpose (anti-aircraft and anti-submarine) escort ships.

The first frigate to be fitted with a missile launcher was probably Britain's *Zulu*, of the *Tribal* Class, commissioned in April 1964 and equipped with a quadruple Sea Cat launcher. The other units of the class were originally armed with two 4.5in

Leander (Great Britain 1963). The twenty-six frigates of the *Leander* Class were commissioned between 1963 and 1973 and are now split into three groups that have different armament. *Leander* herself belongs to the *Ikara* group, armed with Ikara anti-submarine launchers and two quadruple Sea Cat anti-aircraft launchers. They can carry one helicopter. The second and third groups have missile launchers in the forward area on the sloping part of the deck. These ships are steam powered and make thirty knots.

(115mm) dual-purpose guns, one Limbo and one helicopter. These frigates were withdrawn in 1981.

The first to have missile launchers from the very start was the British *Leander* Class frigate *Naiad*, commissioned on March 15, 1965, and equipped with Sea Cat missiles and launcher on the after superstructure, behind the radar aerial mast.

In the U.S. Navy, the first class of frigates to be armed with anti-aircraft missiles was the *Brooke* Class, made up of units commissioned between 1966 and 1968, which had a single Tartar launcher aft. They were otherwise identical to the *Garcia*s, commissioned between 1964 and 1968, which had two 5in (127mm) anti-aircraft guns.

In the Soviet Navy, the first frigates to be armed with anti-aircraft missiles were *Grisha I* and *Grisha III* of 1969–1970, with one twin SA-N-4 launcher on the after superstructure. They were followed by the *Krivak*s of 1970, with two twin pop-up launchers, one before the bridge and one abaft the funnel.

The French Navy *Commandant Rivière* frigates, commissioned in 1962–1965, had their 3.9in (100mm) gun on the after superstructure replaced in 1974–1975 by four single Exocet missile launchers.

The Italian Navy *Lupo* frigates have been armed with missiles right from the start.

There are some interesting frigates in the minor navies that are armed with missiles and powered by gas turbines. Here are a few examples:

Belgian Navy—four frigates of the *Wielingen* Class, commissioned in 1978. These are flush-deckers with a superstructure and full load displacement of 2,283t. Their power plant consists of one gas turbine for full speed and two diesel engines for normal running. They are armed with one 3.9in (100mm) gun forward, one anti-aircraft Sea Sparrow launcher and four single anti-ship Exocet launchers, plus one anti-submarine six-tubed rocket launcher and two torpedo tubes.

Brazilian Navy—six frigates of the *Niteroi* Class, designed by Britain's Vosper Thornycroft and commissioned between 1976 and 1980. They have a flush deck and a large superstructure that extends almost to the stern with a helicopter pad. They have a mixed power plant: gas turbine and diesel on two screws, producing thirty knots. They are armed with one or two 4.6in (117mm) guns, two twin Sea Cat anti-aircraft launchers, two twin Exocet anti-ship launchers, one Ikara anti-submarine launcher, one multiple anti-submarine rocket launcher and six anti-submarine torpedo tubes in two triple mountings.

Danish Navy—two frigates of the *Peder Skram* Class and three of the *Niels Juel* Class. The two *Peder Skram* frigates were commissioned in 1966–1967 and have a full load displacement of 2,720t, a flush deck, a big superstructure, and two large funnels. They have a mixed power plant: gas turbines and diesel, enabling thirty knots. Armament originally consisted of four 5in (127mm) guns in two twin mountings forward, four single 1.5in (40mm) machine guns, a triple 21in torpedo tube, and depth charges. Later, No. 2 5-inch mount and the torpedo tubes were replaced by two quadruple Harpoon anti-ship launchers, one octuple Sea Sparrow anti-aircraft launcher, and six lightweight ASW torpedo tubes. The three *Niels Juel* types were commissioned in 1980–1982 and displace 1,320t. They have a flush deck surmounted by a big full-width superstructure with a large box-shaped radar mast and a big funnel. They have a combined diesel and gas turbine power plant and make thirty knots. Armament comprises one 3in (76mm) anti-aircraft gun, two quadruple Harpoon anti-ship launchers, one eight-tube Sea Sparrow anti-aircraft launcher, and rocket launchers both for flares and for electronic countermeasures.

Indonesian Navy—three Dutch-built *Fatahillah*-type frigates, commissioned in 1979–1980, with a full load displacement of 1,450t. They are flush-deckers with a large full-width superstructure, a triangular mast, and large box-like uptake. They have a combined diesel and gas turbine power plant and make thirty knots. Armament consists of one 4.7in (120mm) gun forward, four Exocet anti-ship launchers, two anti-submarine multi-tube rocket launchers, and six anti-submarine torpedo tubes in two triple mountings.

Iranian Navy—Four British-built *Saam* Class frigates with a full load displacement of 1,400t, commissioned in 1971–1972. They have a flush deck and a combined diesel and gas turbine power plant, making thirty-nine knots. Armament consists of one 4.5in (114mm) gun, one quintuple Sea Killer anti-ship launcher and one triple Sea Cat anti-aircraft launcher, as well as one three-barrelled Limbo.

Libyan Navy—*Dat Assawari*, a British-built frigate commissioned in 1973. A Vosper Thornycroft design, like the four Iranian *Saam* Class, which they copy in both general lines and power plant. Armament consists of one 4.5in (114mm) gun, four machine guns, four Otomat anti-ship, and four Albatross anti-aircraft launchers, plus six anti-submarine torpedo tubes in two triple mountings.

Malaysian Navy—*Rahmat*, a British-built frigate with a displacement of 1,600t, commissioned in 1971. She was built in the Yarrow shipyard and closely resembles the Libyan and Iranian Vosper Thornycroft frigates. She is a flush-decker with a pyramid-shaped mast and a large funnel. The combined diesel and gas turbine power plant gives a top speed of twenty-six knots. Armament is one 4.4in (114mm) gun, two 1.5in (40mm) machine guns, one quadruple Sea Cat anti-aircraft launcher, and one Limbo. There is also a helicopter pad.

Nigerian Navy—*Aradu*, a 3,630t German-built frigate commissioned in 1981. She has a flush deck and an amidships superstructure followed by a hangar and flight pad aft. Her mixed diesel and gas turbine power plant give her a speed of 30.5 knots. Armament consists of one 5in (127mm) gun, eight 1.5in (40mm) machine guns, two quadruple Otomat anti-ship launchers, one eight-cell Aspide anti-aircraft launcher, and six anti-submarine torpedo tubes in two triple mountings, as well as one helicopter.

Peruvian Navy—Four 2,500t Italian-built *Meliton Carvajal* type frigates commissioned in 1979–1983. They are similar to the Italian *Lupo*s. Their combined diesel and gas turbine power plant gives a speed of thirty-five knots. Armament consists of one 5in (127mm) gun, four 1.5in (40mm) machine guns, eight Otomat anti-ship launchers, one eight-cell Aspide anti-aircraft launcher, two twenty-tube anti-submarine rocket launchers, and six anti-submarine torpedo tubes in two triple mountings.

Venezuelan Navy—Six 2,500t Italian-built *Mariscal Sucre*-type frigates commissioned in 1979–1982. They are similar to the Italian *Lupo*s and have the same specifications.

In addition to the above frigates, there are also a few missile corvettes, although they have a diesel as opposed to a gas turbine power plant. Examples of these are:

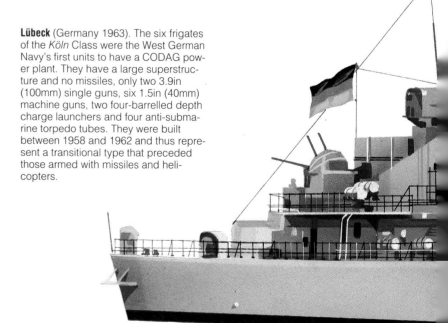

Amazon (Great Britain 1974). The eight *Amazon*-type frigates were commissioned between 1974 and 1978 and make up the first class to be powered exclusively by gas turbines: two more powerful ones for attaining thirty knots and two less powerful for cruising speed. They have a hangar and pad for one helicopter and are armed with Exocet and Sea Cat missiles, as well as one automatic 4.5in (114mm) gun in a turret forward.

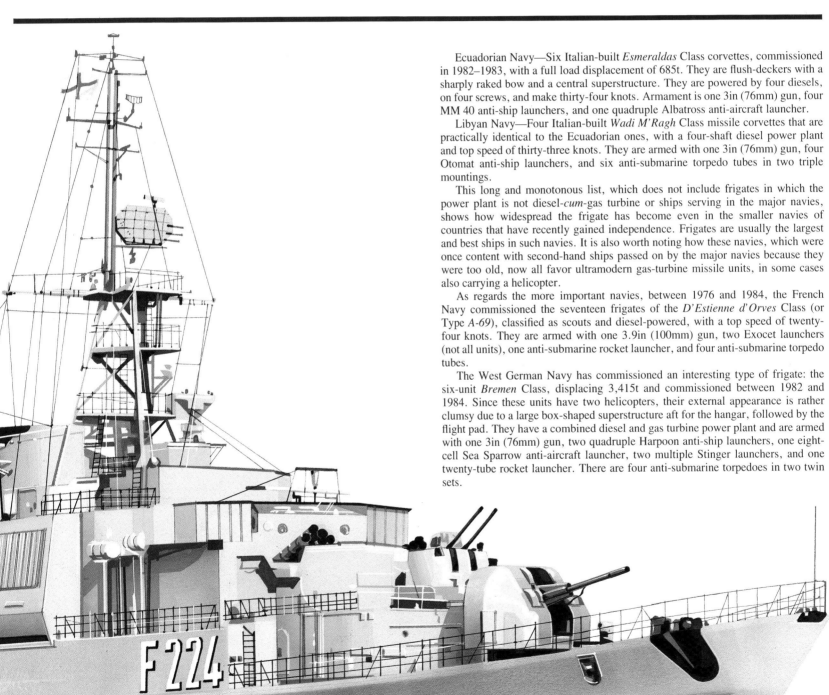

Ecuadorian Navy—Six Italian-built *Esmeraldas* Class corvettes, commissioned in 1982–1983, with a full load displacement of 685t. They are flush-deckers with a sharply raked bow and a central superstructure. They are powered by four diesels, on four screws, and make thirty-four knots. Armament is one 3in (76mm) gun, four MM 40 anti-ship launchers, and one quadruple Albatross anti-aircraft launcher.

Libyan Navy—Four Italian-built *Wadi M'Ragh* Class missile corvettes that are practically identical to the Ecuadorian ones, with a four-shaft diesel power plant and top speed of thirty-three knots. They are armed with one 3in (76mm) gun, four Otomat anti-ship launchers, and six anti-submarine torpedo tubes in two triple mountings.

This long and monotonous list, which does not include frigates in which the power plant is not diesel-*cum*-gas turbine or ships serving in the major navies, shows how widespread the frigate has become even in the smaller navies of countries that have recently gained independence. Frigates are usually the largest and best ships in such navies. It is also worth noting how these navies, which were once content with second-hand ships passed on by the major navies because they were too old, now all favor ultramodern gas-turbine missile units, in some cases also carrying a helicopter.

As regards the more important navies, between 1976 and 1984, the French Navy commissioned the seventeen frigates of the *D'Estienne d'Orves* Class (or Type *A-69*), classified as scouts and diesel-powered, with a top speed of twenty-four knots. They are armed with one 3.9in (100mm) gun, two Exocet launchers (not all units), one anti-submarine rocket launcher, and four anti-submarine torpedo tubes.

The West German Navy has commissioned an interesting type of frigate: the six-unit *Bremen* Class, displacing 3,415t and commissioned between 1982 and 1984. Since these units have two helicopters, their external appearance is rather clumsy due to a large box-shaped superstructure aft for the hangar, followed by the flight pad. They have a combined diesel and gas turbine power plant and are armed with one 3in (76mm) gun, two quadruple Harpoon anti-ship launchers, one eight-cell Sea Sparrow anti-aircraft launcher, two multiple Stinger launchers, and one twenty-tube rocket launcher. There are four anti-submarine torpedoes in two twin sets.

The Italian Navy has built one type of frigate, *Lupo*, several of which have been ordered by a few of the minor navies, such as the Peruvian and Venezuelan Navies. The improved version of this class is the *Maestrale* type, its successor. The four *Lupo*s, commissioned between 1977 and 1980, have a full load displacement of 2,500t and have the same characteristics as those built for other navies. They have a forecastle, a full-width superstructure, and a box-shaped radar mast followed by a large funnel, also box-shaped. This is followed by a superstructure that contains the hangar in its after part, made in separate telescopic sections so as to occupy less space when there are no helicopters inside. The entire after area is taken up by the flight pad. The eight *Maestrale*s, commissioned between 1981 and 1984, have a full load displacement of 3,040t and are enlarged versions of the *Lupo* type. The main difference lies in the fact that the hangar is below the flight deck, as opposed to being in the superstructure. They have a combined diesel and gas turbine power plant and make thirty-two knots. Armament comprises one 5in (127mm) gun forward, four Otomat anti-ship launchers on the after superstructure, one quadruple Aspide anti-aircraft launcher before the bridge, two helicopters, and six anti-submarine torpedo tubes in two triple mountings.

The Japanese Navy has turned its attention mainly toward destroyers, building them in large numbers and various types. In 1970–1977, however, the eleven *Chikugo* type frigates, with a diesel power plant and no missiles, came into service. It was not until 1981 that *Ishikari* (*DE 226*) was commissioned. She has a standard displacement of 1,250t, a combined diesel and gas turbine power plant, and is armed with two quadruple Harpoon anti-ship launchers, one 3in (76mm) gun, one four-barrelled depth charge mortar, and six anti-submarine torpedoes. This prototype has served as a model for the *DE 227* series.

In 1960–1961, the Soviet Navy commissioned some fifty *Petya* type frigates with a displacement of 1,100t and combined diesel and gas turbine propulsion, but no missiles. They were followed by the *Mirka* Class of 1964–1967, also without missiles, and finally by the 1970–1974 *Krivak* Class, displacing 3,800t. The *Krivak*s have a very long forecastle, raked bow, and a superstructure followed by a short box-like uptake. There are four large SS-N-14 anti-ship missile launchers on the superstructure plus two twin SA-N-4 anti-aircraft launchers. Unlike the frigates of Western navies, which usually have just one gun forward, these frigates have two or three aft. Anti-submarine armament comprises two twelve-tube rocket launchers and there are eight anti-ship torpedo tubes in two quadruple mountings. They are powered exclusively by gas turbines, two per screw, developing 71,014hp (72,000CV) overall, and make thirty-two knots.

In 1963–1973, the Royal Navy commissioned the twenty-six frigates of the *Leander* Class, which are steam powered, armed with missiles, and carry a helicopter. The Royal Navy has since adopted the all gas turbine power plant on its next frigates, the *Amazon* Class commissioned between 1974 and 1978. They displace 3,250t full load, have a superstructure that extends the entire width amidships, and is surmounted by a second superstructure for the bridge and operations rooms, surmounted by a box-like mast, followed by a large funnel, which, although serving gas turbines, is streamlined rather than box-shaped. The after part of the first superstructure contains the helicopter hangar and there is a flight pad aft, followed by a step with a well for the variable-depth sonar.

Armament consists of one 4.5in (115mm) gun at the bow, four Exocet anti-ship launchers on the superstructure before the bridge, and one quadruple Sea Cat anti-aircraft launcher aft. Anti-submarine armament is in the form of one helicopter that can fire anti-submarine torpedoes and the ships are also equipped with two triple anti-submarine torpedo tubes. The power plant comprises four gas turbines, two of which are more powerful (developing 55,233hp [56,000CV] overall and used for full speed) with the other two developing 8,384hp (8,500CV) for normal running.

The U.S. Navy has built a great many classes of frigates: the *Garcia*s, commissioned between 1964 and 1968, the *Knox* types, commissioned between 1969 and 1974, the *Brooke*s of 1966–1967 and, lastly, the *Oliver Hazard Perry* types of 1977–1984.

The *Garcia*, *Brooke*, and *Knox* types are powered by steam turbines driving a single propeller. They all have a helicopter but not all are armed with missiles. After commissioning, thirty-one *Knox* Class units were fitted with anti-aircraft missile launchers (Sea Sparrow), whereas they were equipped right from the start with ASROC anti-submarine missiles in eight-cell launchers, usually positioned forward before the bridge. The six *Brooke* Class had one Tartar anti-aircraft launcher aft and an eight-cell ASROC launcher forward from the outset.

The *O.H. Perry* Class embodies the lessons learned on these various types. The *Perry*s are officially classified as "missile frigates," designated *FFG* and numbered 7 to 56. The first six numbers were assigned to the *Brooke* Class. The *Perry* Class frigates have a full load displacement of 3,605t, a flush deck surmounted by a large superstructure that terminates in an ugly box-shaped structure that houses the hangar for the two helicopters. There is a quadripod lattice mast for the radar aerials. The power plant comprises two LM 2500 General Electric gas turbines working a single screw. Top speed is twenty-nine knots. Armament consists of one launcher forward that can fire both Standard anti-aircraft and Harpoon anti-ship missiles. In addition, there are one 3in (76mm) gun on the superstructure between the mast and funnel and two triple torpedo tubes.

As is evident, the major navies, like the Soviet and American Navies, and the Royal Navy, have reached a stage where their missile frigates are powered exclusively by gas turbines, whereas those of the other navies are, on the whole, powered by diesel and gas turbines combined. But some of the minor navies, too, like the Australian, Spanish, and Dutch, already have (or are acquiring) frigates powered exclusively by gas turbines.

The Australian Navy has had its four *Adelaide*-type frigates built in the United States. They were commissioned in 1980–1984 and are practically identical to the U.S. Navy's *Perry*s. The Spanish Navy, however, is building its three *Navarra* Class frigates, also *Perry*s, in its own yards. The Dutch Navy has commissioned ten frigates (two more were transferred to Greece, and two more, of a modified type, are being built) of the *Kortenaer* Class, powered by machinery similar to that of the British *Amazon*s, in other words, two GTs developing 49,315hp (50,000CV), overall, for full speed and two 7,890hp (8,000CV) GTs for normal running. The *Kortenaer*s have a full load displacement of 3,630t, a flush deck with a superstructure containing the hangar in its after section, a pyramid-shaped mast, and a short streamlined funnel. Missile armament consists of one eight-cell Harpoon anti-ship missile launcher and one Sea Sparrow anti-aircraft launcher.

Kortenaer (Holland 1978). Ten of these Dutch frigates were commissioned between 1978 and 1983; two more were transferred to Greece, and two more, with different armament, are replacing them. They are ultra-modern units, powered exclusively by gas turbines, and carry two helicopters. They are armed with Harpoon anti-ship missiles and Sea Sparrow anti-aircraft missiles. Anti-submarine armament consists of four anti-submarine torpedo tubes and two Lynx helicopters. These units have rather unharmonious lines but their performance is excellent.

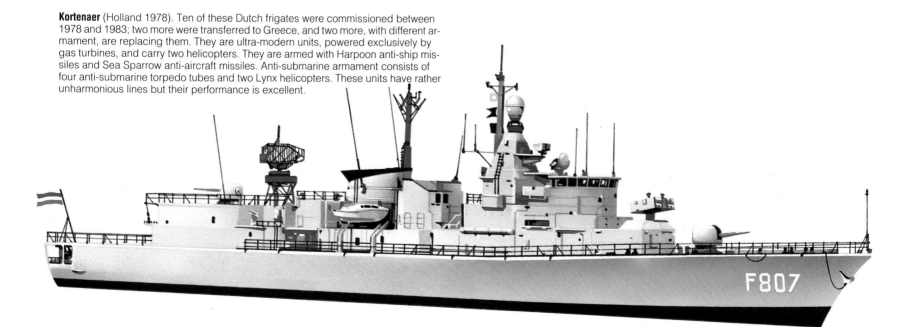

Yoshino (Japan 1975). One of the eleven-unit *Chikugo* Class commissioned between 1970 and 1977. They displace some 1,500t and have diesel engines driving twin screws, top speed being twenty-five knots. They have one eight-cell ASROC anti-submarine launcher and six anti-submarine torpedo tubes. Armament is completed by two 3in (76mm) guns and two 1.5in (40mm) machine guns.

To round off this overview of the modern frigates of the various navies, we shall include the meager information available about those in the navy of the People's Republic of China.

Immediately after the war, the Chinese Navy received frigates as spoils of war, formerly destroyer escorts and Japanese corvettes, in addition to one Canadian and two British corvettes. In the years when relations with the Soviet Union were friendly, until about 1960, materials supplied by the USSR were used in Chinese shipyards to build the four frigates of the *Cheng-Du* Class, commissioned in 1958–1969. They were steam-powered and had one SS-N-2 anti-ship missile launcher. They were followed by three diesel-powered frigate classes: the *Jiang-Nan* Class, commissioned in 1967–1968, the *Jiang-Dong* Class of 1977, and the *Jiang-Hu* Class of 1976–1978. These last two have two twin launchers for Russian SS-N-2 anti-ship missiles. Anti-submarine armament consists of two 12-tube Russian rocket launchers, two depth-charge launchers, and one hopper.

The future of the anti-submarine and anti-aircraft frigate probably lies in units like the American *Perry*s, with gas turbine engines and a single screw, carrying a helicopter and anti-ship, anti-aircraft, and anti-submarine missiles.

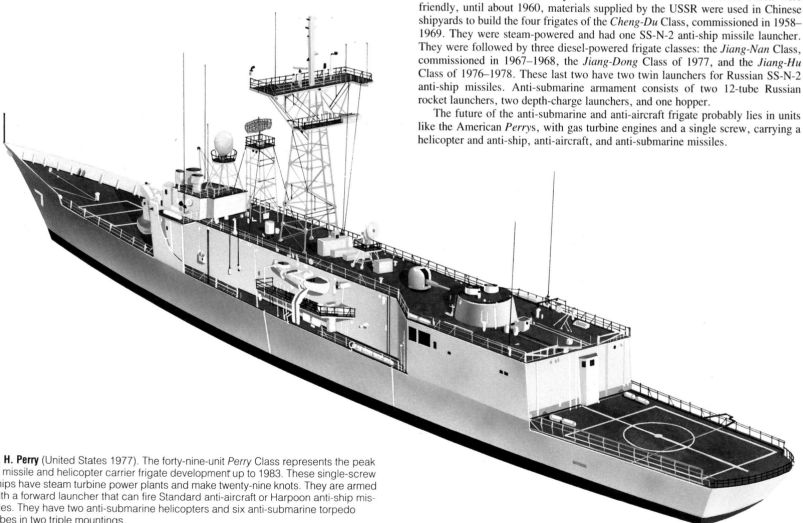

O. H. Perry (United States 1977). The forty-nine-unit *Perry* Class represents the peak of missile and helicopter carrier frigate development up to 1983. These single-screw ships have steam turbine power plants and make twenty-nine knots. They are armed with a forward launcher that can fire Standard anti-aircraft or Harpoon anti-ship missiles. They have two anti-submarine helicopters and six anti-submarine torpedo tubes in two triple mountings.

SUPPORT CRAFT

In addition to the fighting ships that have been discussed, battle fleets include many other types of vessels: patrol boats, motor torpedo boats, motor gunboats, hydrofoils, minelayers, ships for amphibious operations, minesweepers, mine hunters, gunboats and river gunboats, launches and small patrol boats, landing ships, landing craft, net defense ships and net layers, seaplane tenders, submarine tenders, destroyer tenders, repair ships, transport and supply ships, tankers, training ships, ammunition ships, rescue ships, ships for scientific experiments, hospital ships, icebreakers, and tugs.

Some of these ships are designed for offensive work, such as patrol boats, motor torpedo boats, minelayers, and, in particular, amphibious ships, landing ships, and landing craft; minesweepers and mine hunters, on the other hand, carry out defensive duties. All the others fall into the large category of auxiliary ships, in other words, those ships that any navy of any size must include in order to keep the fighting ships operational and effective.

To overcome problems posed by refueling, the United States Navy is turning towards nuclear-powered units. All the other navies, however, have opted for ships classified by the U.S. Navy as ''Fast Combat Support Ships'' (designated *AOE*), designed to supply ships on the high seas not only with fuel, but also ammunition, stores, and provisions, to avoid breaking off operational engagements in a wartime situation.

The list of descriptions makes it easy to understand what the task of each ship is. It would perhaps be helpful, however, to explain the difference between mine-sweeper and mine hunter. The former sweep mines anchored to or resting on the sea bed, without their exact position being known, covering vast areas of water thought to be mined, but which could just as well not be. Mine hunters, however, are fitted with equipment capable of detecting mines, or other metal objects, lying on the sea bed and then either identifying or destroying them. In short, minesweepers have mechanical or magnetic sweeping equipment, and mine hunters are fitted with electronic equipment that makes it possible to explore the sea bed.

One specific type of auxiliary ship is the icebreaker. These are part and parcel of navies that have bases in the Arctic and Antarctic, such as the Soviet, Canadian, United States, and Argentinian Navies.

The Soviet Navy is the only one to have used nuclear propulsion in an icebreaker. This is the *Lenin* (1959), the first surface ship in the world to have a nuclear power plant, followed in 1975 by *Arktika*, and then in 1977 by *Sibir*. Their unlimited range enables these ships to operate in icy waters without running the risk of being left without fuel: they thus have a much wider variety of uses than conventionally powered icebreakers.

Lastly, there are the tugs, which are divided into various types. They range from ocean-going tugs that can tow the heaviest ships in the world across the Atlantic or Pacific, working in pairs or in threes with two at the bow towing and one aft steering, to the medium- to small-powered harbor tugs that help ships in and out of port; they also assist in mooring, and cast off from the quay, and carry out rescue operations on ships in trouble at sea.

APPENDIX

Compendium of battleships drawn to scale

Palestro - 1871

Re d'Italia - 1863

Indomptable - 1883

Kaiser - 1874

Marengo - 1868

Temeraire - 1876

Tegetthoff - 1878

Bellerophon - 1865

Preussen - 1873

Dévastation - 1873

Amiral Duperré - 1879

Captain - 1869

Dreadnought - 1875

Inflexible - 1876

Hercules - 1868

Colossus - 1882

Collingwood - 1882

Alexandra - 1875

Andrea Doria - 1885

Monarch - 1868

Imperator Peter Velikey - 1872

Magenta - 1890

Duilio - 1876

Sinop - 1887

Amiral Baudin - 1897

Northumberland - 1866

Habsburg - 1900

Henry IV - 1899

Italia - 1880

Sardegna - 1890

Jaureguiberry - 1893

König Wilhelm - 1868

Petropavlovsk - 1894

Brandenburg - 1891

Kearsage - 1898

Potemkin - 1900

Royal Sovereign - 1891

Majestic - 1895

Cornwallis - 1901

Shikishima - 1898

Benedetto Brin - 1901

Kansas - 1905

South Carolina - 1908

España - 1912

Nassau - 1908

Dreadnought - 1906

Viribus Unitis - 1911

Minas Gerais - 1937

214

Jean Bart - 1911

Brétagne - 1913

Arkansas - 1942

Koenig - 1913

Bayern - 1915

Gangut - 1911

King George V - 1911

Pennsylvania - 1943

Deutschland - 1931

Giulio Cesare - 1932

Resolution - 1935

West Virginia - 1944

Tennessee - 1929

Queen Elizabeth - 1941

Agincourt - 1913

Fuso - 1914

Alabama - 1942

Dunkerque - 1935

Nelson - 1925

North Carolina - 1940

Kongo - 1937

Nagato - 1936

King George V - 1939

Scharnhorst - 1936

Littorio - 1937

Richelieu - 1939

Bismarck - 1939

Vanguard - 1944

Yamato - 1940

Missouri - 1944

0   1   2   3   4   5

2.54in (1cm) = 76.4ft (23.3m)

215

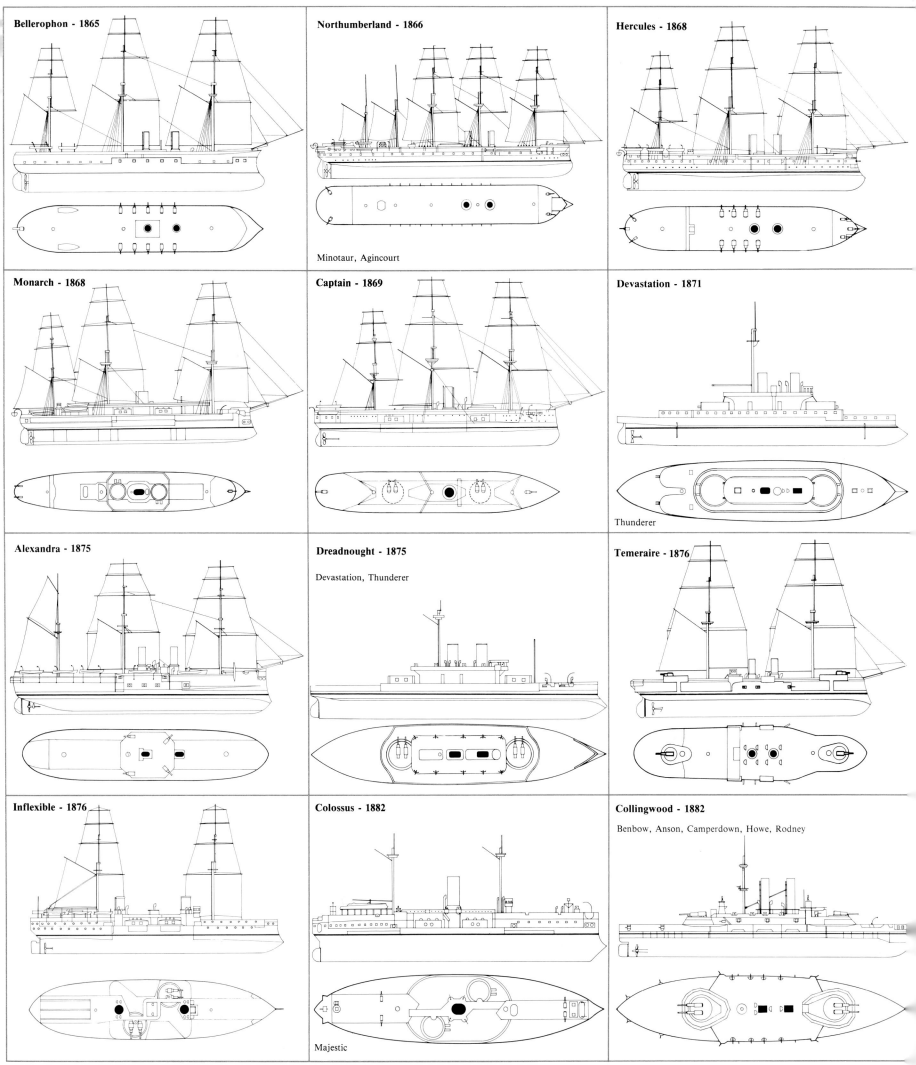

Bellerophon - 1865

Northumberland - 1866

Minotaur, Agincourt

Hercules - 1868

Monarch - 1868

Captain - 1869

Devastation - 1871

Thunderer

Alexandra - 1875

Dreadnought - 1875

Devastation, Thunderer

Temeraire - 1876

Inflexible - 1876

Colossus - 1882

Majestic

Collingwood - 1882

Benbow, Anson, Camperdown, Howe, Rodney

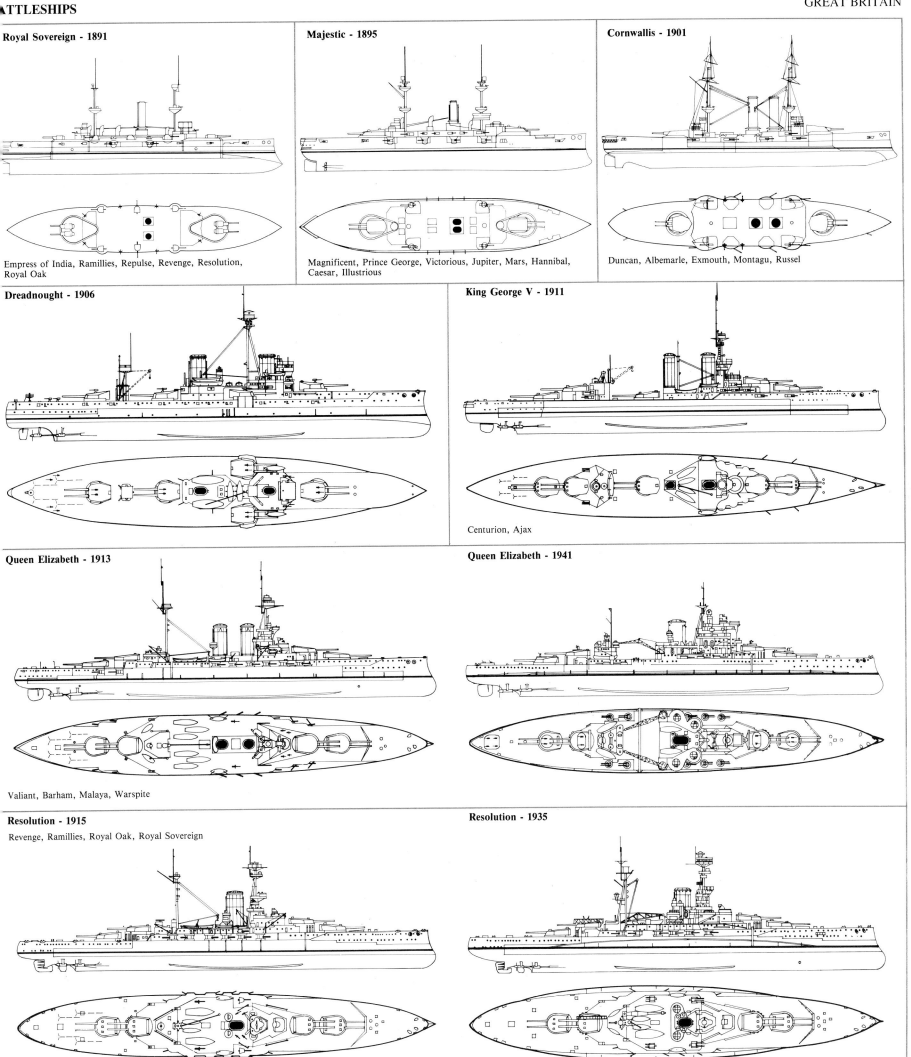

Royal Sovereign - 1891

Empress of India, Ramillies, Repulse, Revenge, Resolution, Royal Oak

Majestic - 1895

Magnificent, Prince George, Victorious, Jupiter, Mars, Hannibal, Caesar, Illustrious

Cornwallis - 1901

Duncan, Albemarle, Exmouth, Montagu, Russel

Dreadnought - 1906

King George V - 1911

Centurion, Ajax

Queen Elizabeth - 1913

Queen Elizabeth - 1941

Valiant, Barham, Malaya, Warspite

Resolution - 1915

Revenge, Ramillies, Royal Oak, Royal Sovereign

Resolution - 1935

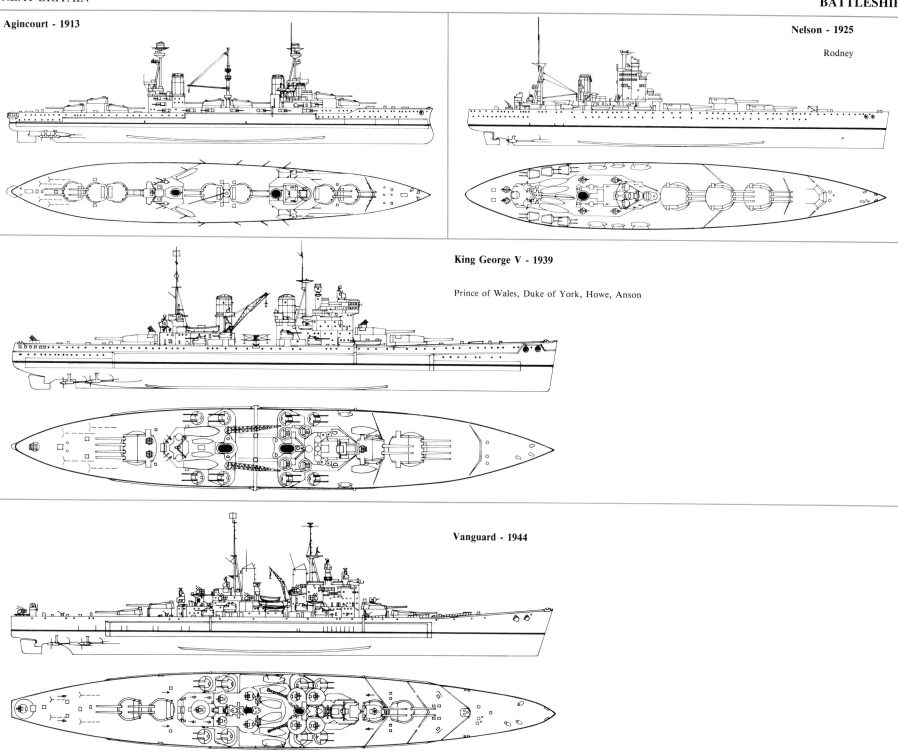

Agincourt - 1913

Nelson - 1925

Rodney

King George V - 1939

Prince of Wales, Duke of York, Howe, Anson

Vanguard - 1944

FRANCE

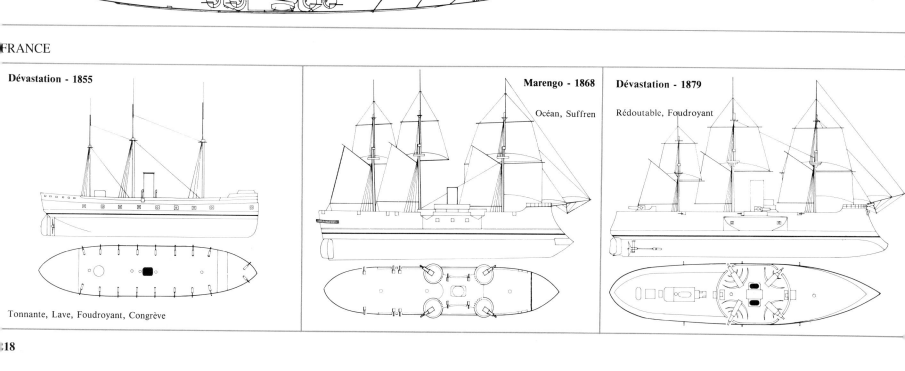

Dévastation - 1855

Marengo - 1868

Océan, Suffren

Dévastation - 1879

Rédoutable, Foudroyant

Tonnante, Lave, Foudroyant, Congrève

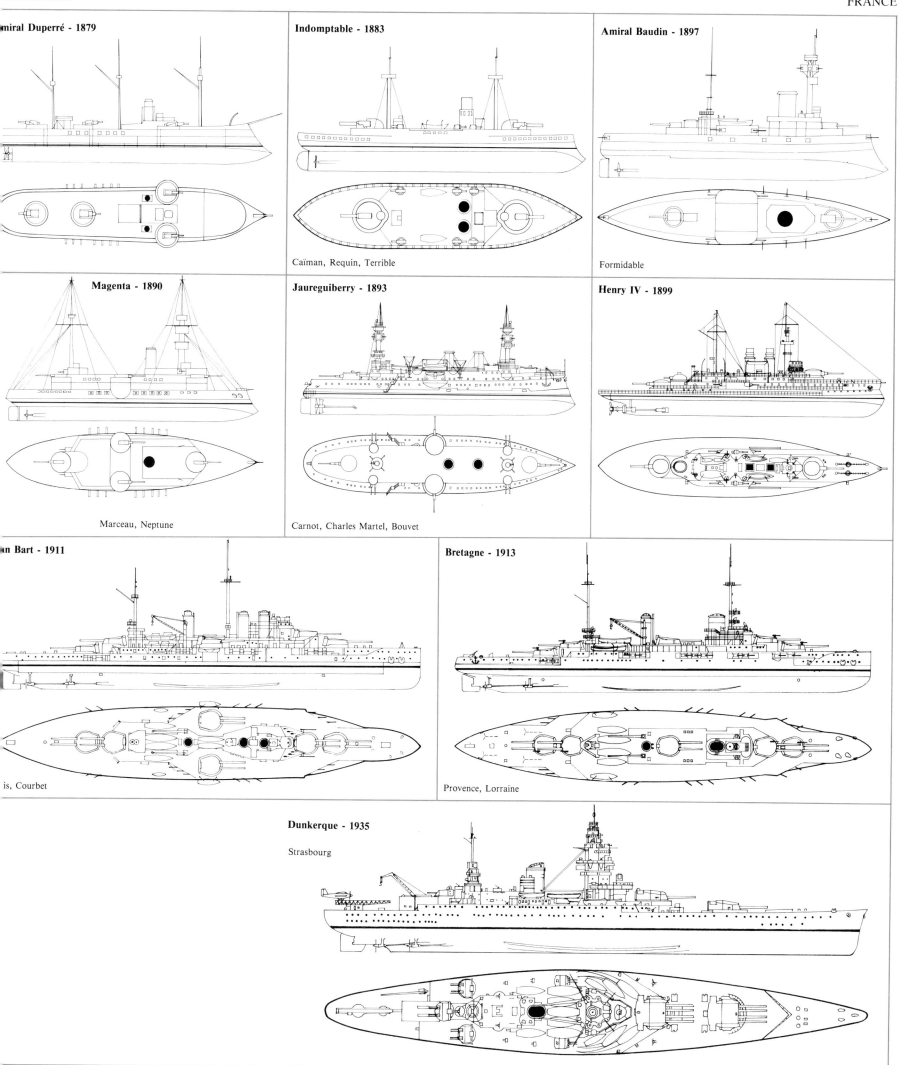

Amiral Duperré - 1879

Indomptable - 1883

Amiral Baudin - 1897

Caïman, Requin, Terrible

Formidable

Magenta - 1890

Jaureguiberry - 1893

Henry IV - 1899

Marceau, Neptune

Carnot, Charles Martel, Bouvet

n Bart - 1911

Bretagne - 1913

is, Courbet

Provence, Lorraine

Dunkerque - 1935

Strasbourg

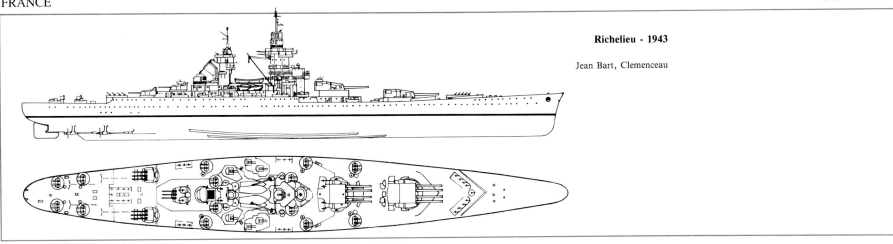

Richelieu - 1943

Jean Bart, Clemenceau

GERMANY

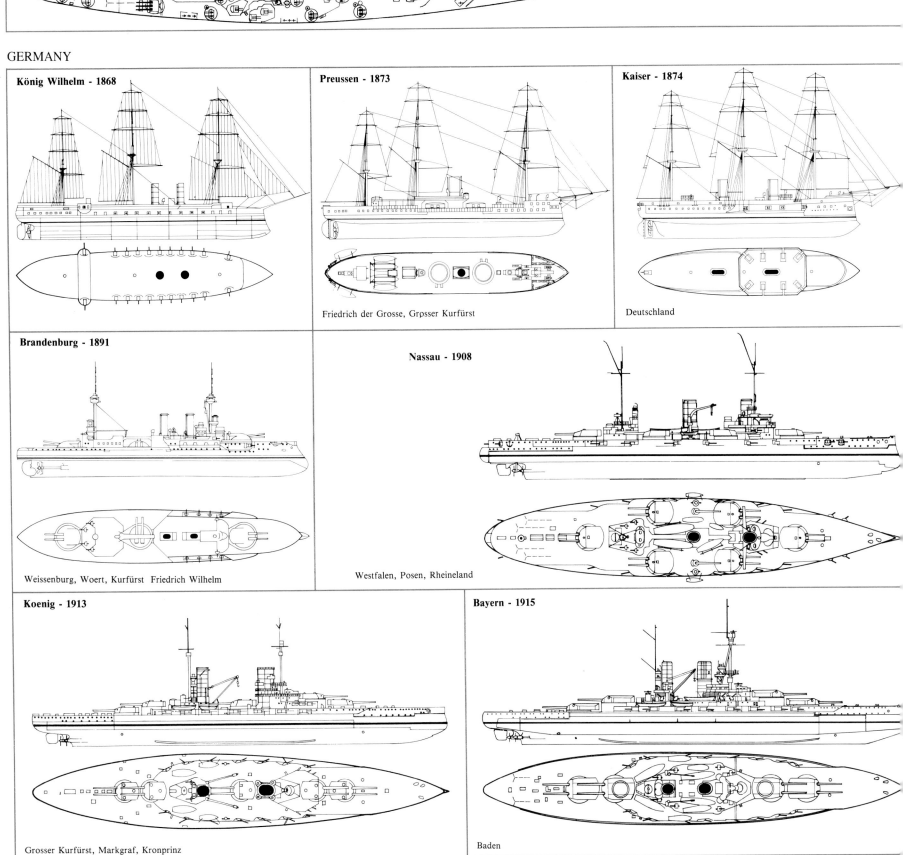

König Wilhelm - 1868

Preussen - 1873

Friedrich der Grosse, Grosser Kurfürst

Kaiser - 1874

Deutschland

Brandenburg - 1891

Weissenburg, Woert, Kurfürst Friedrich Wilhelm

Nassau - 1908

Westfalen, Posen, Rheineland

Koenig - 1913

Grosser Kurfürst, Markgraf, Kronprinz

Bayern - 1915

Baden

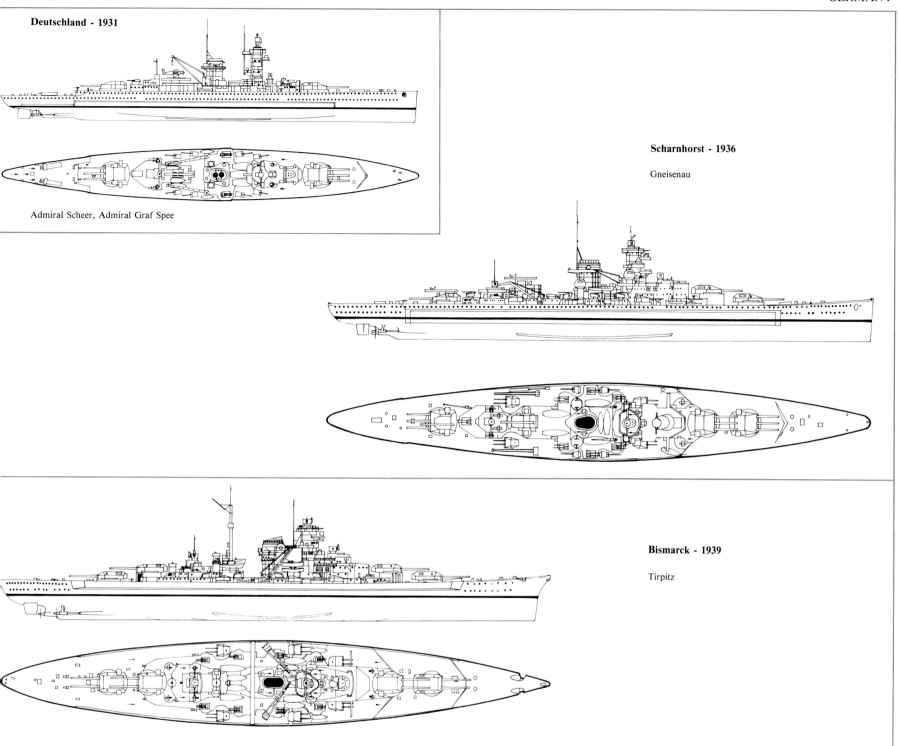

Deutschland - 1931

Admiral Scheer, Admiral Graf Spee

Scharnhorst - 1936

Gneisenau

Bismarck - 1939

Tirpitz

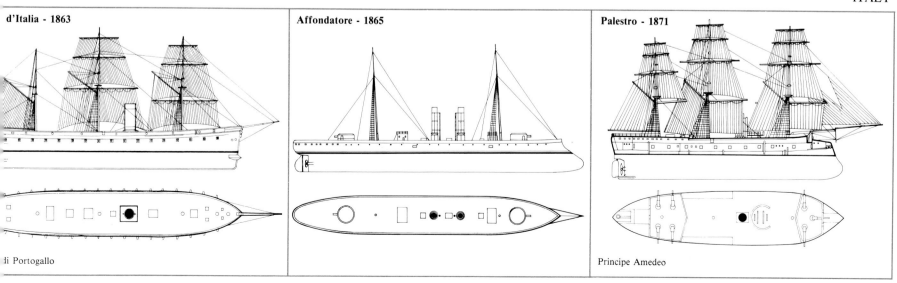

d'Italia - 1863

li Portogallo

Affondatore - 1865

Palestro - 1871

Principe Amedeo

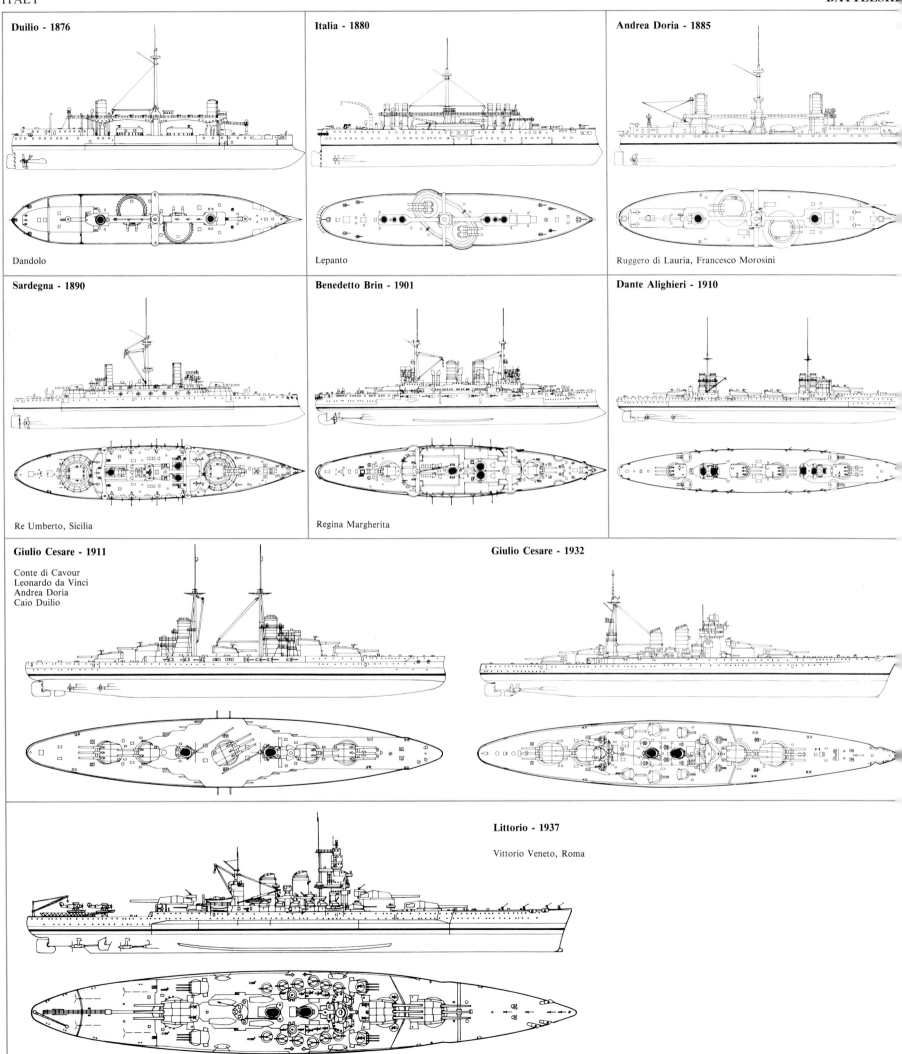

Duilio - 1876

Dandolo

Italia - 1880

Lepanto

Andrea Doria - 1885

Ruggero di Lauria, Francesco Morosini

Sardegna - 1890

Re Umberto, Sicilia

Benedetto Brin - 1901

Regina Margherita

Dante Alighieri - 1910

Giulio Cesare - 1911

Conte di Cavour
Leonardo da Vinci
Andrea Doria
Caio Duilio

Giulio Cesare - 1932

Littorio - 1937

Vittorio Veneto, Roma

getthoff - 1878

Habsburg - 1900

Viribus Unitis - 1911

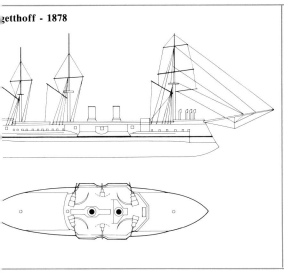

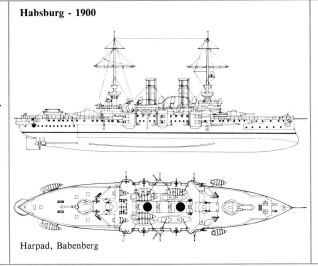

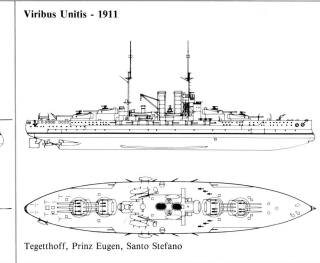

Harpad, Babenberg

Tegetthoff, Prinz Eugen, Santo Stefano

perator Peter Velikey - 1872

Sinop - 1887

Petropavlovsk - 1894

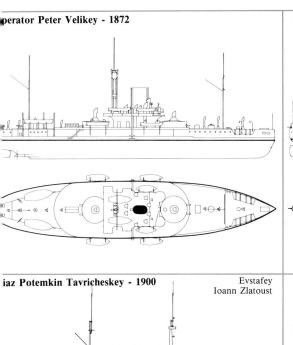

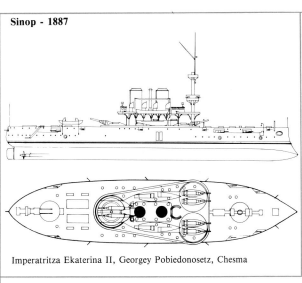

Imperatritza Ekaterina II, Georgey Pobiedonosetz, Chesma

Sevastopol, Poltava

iaz Potemkin Tavricheskey - 1900

Evstafey
Ioann Zlatoust

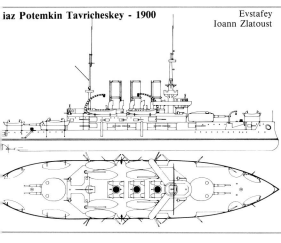

Imperator Alexander III - 1916

Imperatritza Maria,
Imperatritza Ekaterina II
Imperator Nicolaj I

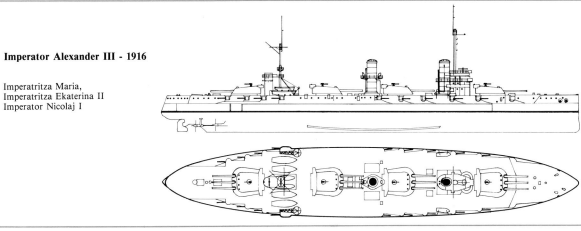

España - 1912

Alfonso XIII , Jaime I

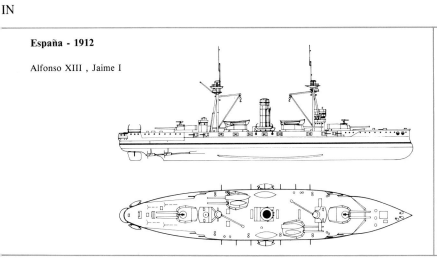

Minas Gerais - 1937

Saõ Paulo

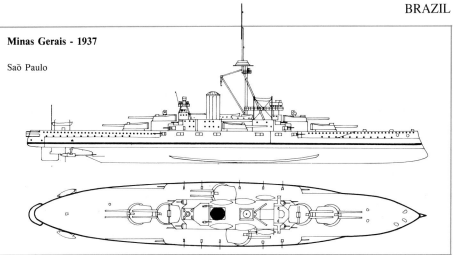

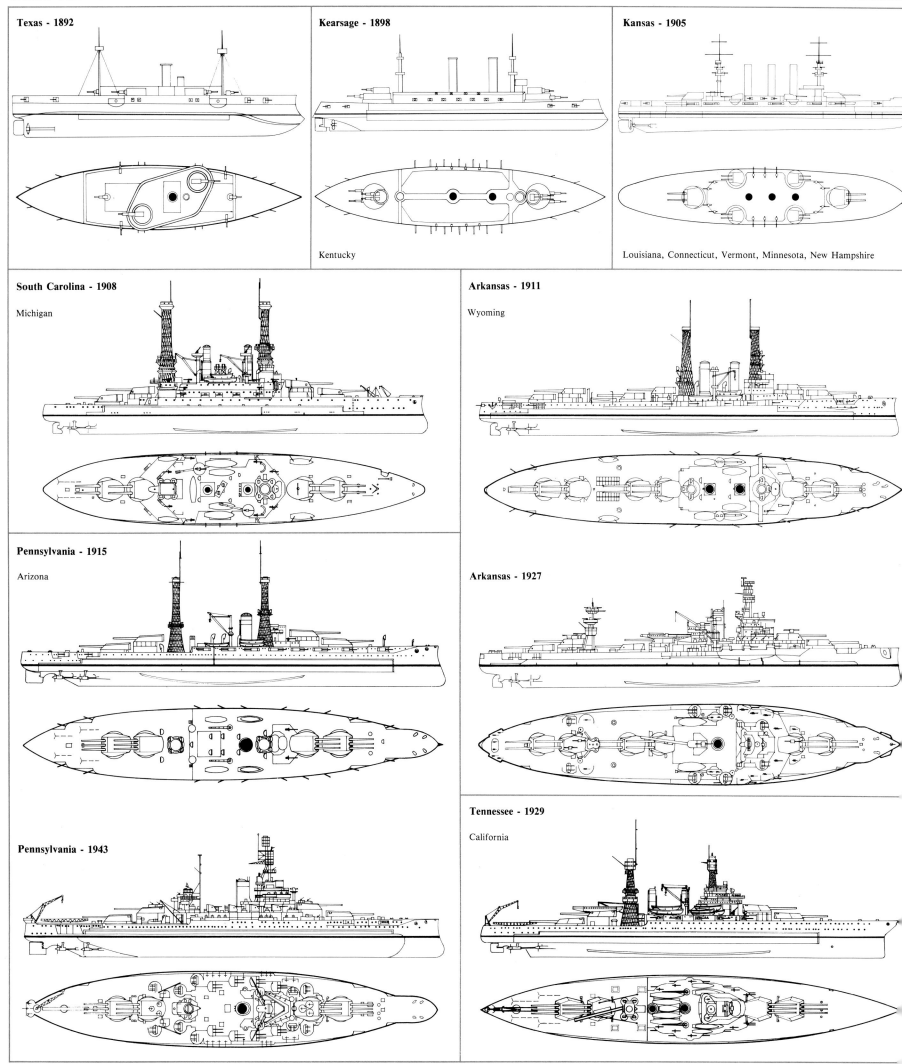

Texas - 1892

Kearsage - 1898

Kentucky

Kansas - 1905

Louisiana, Connecticut, Vermont, Minnesota, New Hampshire

South Carolina - 1908

Michigan

Arkansas - 1911

Wyoming

Pennsylvania - 1915

Arizona

Arkansas - 1927

Pennsylvania - 1943

Tennessee - 1929

California

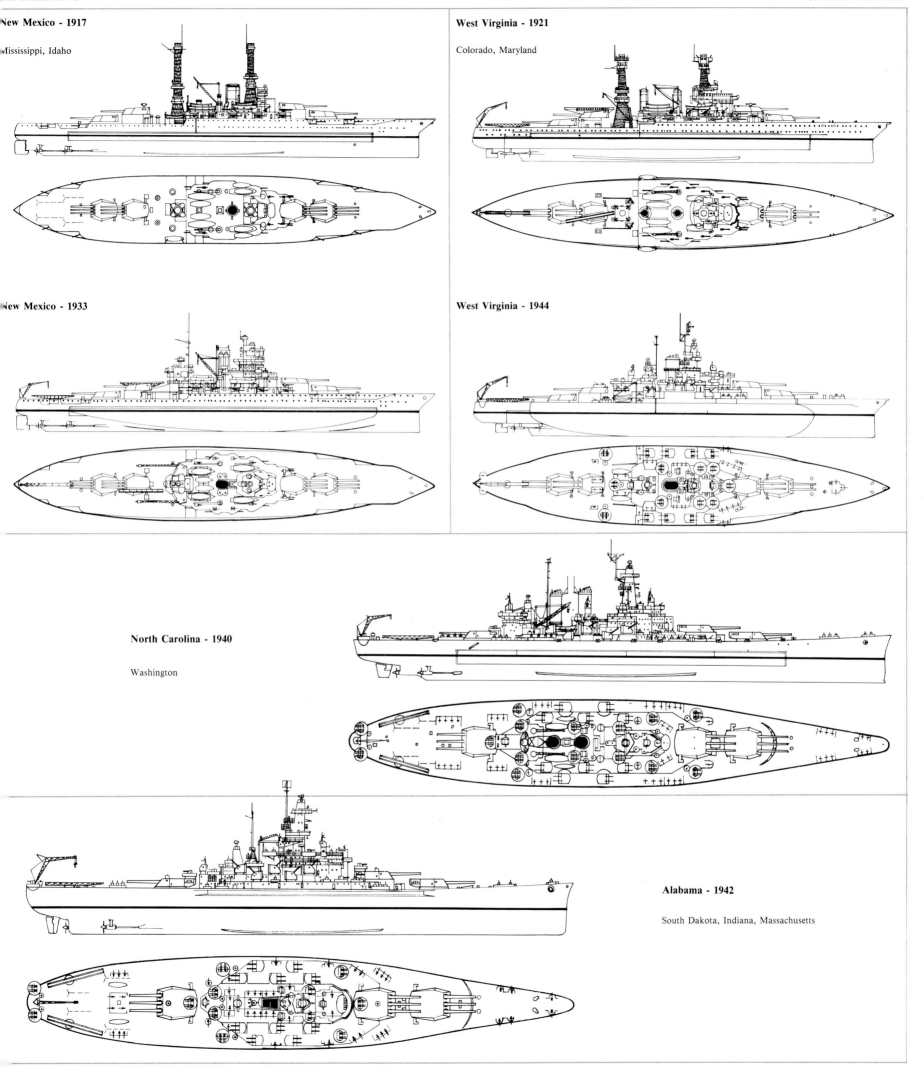

New Mexico - 1917

Mississippi, Idaho

West Virginia - 1921

Colorado, Maryland

New Mexico - 1933

West Virginia - 1944

North Carolina - 1940

Washington

Alabama - 1942

South Dakota, Indiana, Massachusetts

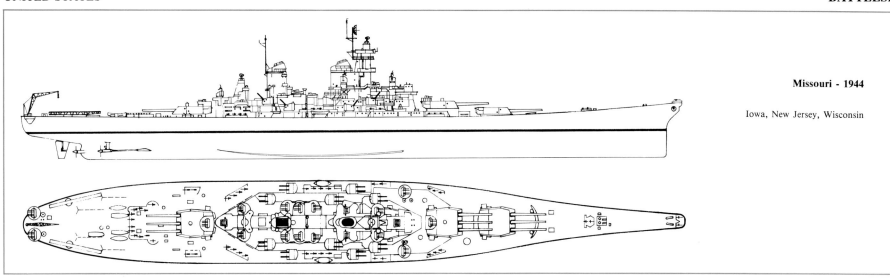

Missouri - 1944

Iowa, New Jersey, Wisconsin

JAPAN

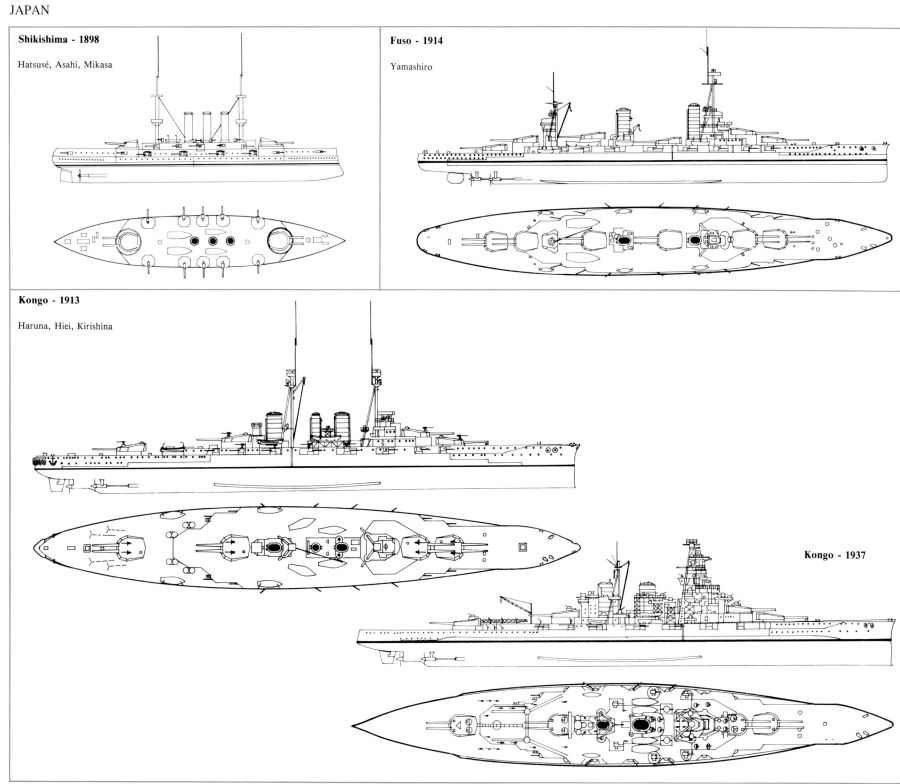

Shikishima - 1898

Hatsusé, Asahi, Mikasa

Fuso - 1914

Yamashiro

Kongo - 1913

Haruna, Hiei, Kirishina

Kongo - 1937

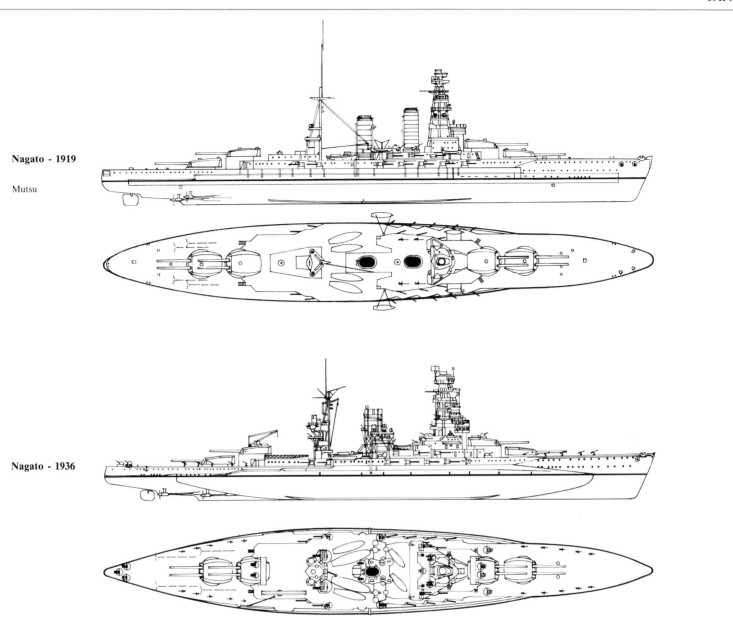

Nagato - 1919

Mutsu

Nagato - 1936

Yamato - 1943

Musashi

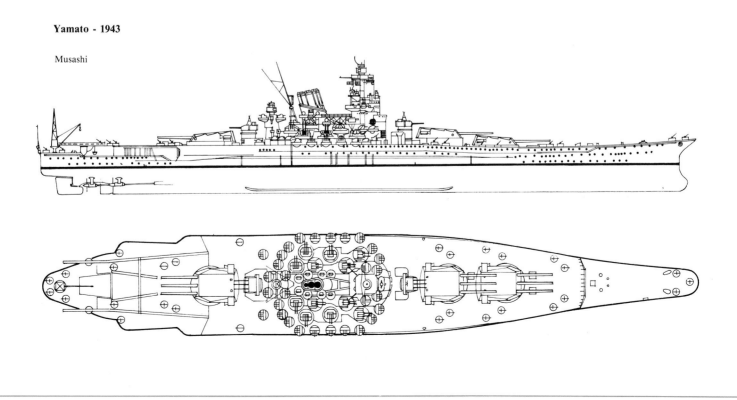

Compendium of aircraft carriers drawn to scale

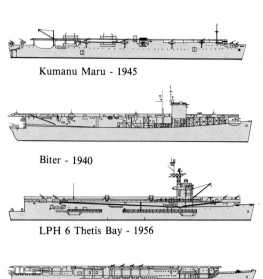

Kumanu Maru - 1945

LPH 2 Iwo Jima - 1960

CVL 49 Wright - 1945

Biter - 1940

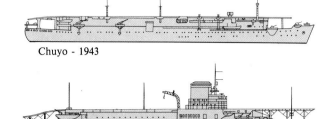

Chuyo - 1943

Venticinco de Mayo - 1969

LPH 6 Thetis Bay - 1956

Béarn - 1920

Perseus - 1944

Chigusa-Maru - 1945

Hermes - 1919

Minas Gerais - 1960

Otakisan-Maru - 1945

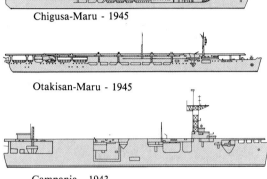

Campania - 1943

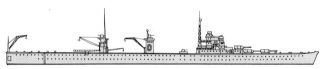

Shinyo - 1934

Karel Doorman - 1958

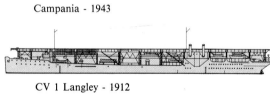

CV 1 Langley - 1912

CVL 22 Independence - 1942

Warrior - 1944

Kaiyo - 1938

Nisshin - 1939

Hercules - 1945

Hosho - 1921

Chiyoda - 1937

Indipendencia - 1959

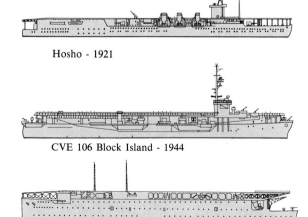

CVE 106 Block Island - 1944

Unicorn - 1941

Magnificent - 1944

Argus - 1917

Ibuki - 1943

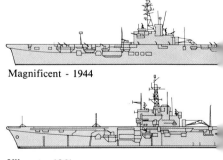

Vikrant - 1961

Ryujo - 1931

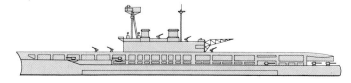

Eagle - 1918

Melbourne - 1955

Hiryu - 1937

Aquila - 1943

Hermes - 1953

Implacable - 1942

Unryu - 1943

CV 4 Ranger - 1933

CV 7 Wasp - 1939

Joffre - 1938

Bulwark - 1960

Victorious - 1958

Albion - 1947

Glorious - 1930

Bonaventure - 1957

Furious - 1939

Ise - 1943

Ark Royal - 1937

Hiyo - 1941

CV 6 Enterprise - 1936

Shoho - 1942

Kaga - 1936

Ryuho - 1942

Graf Zeppelin - 1938

0 1 2 3 4 5

2.54in (1cm) = 76.4ft (23.3m)

Compendium of aircraft carriers drawn to scale

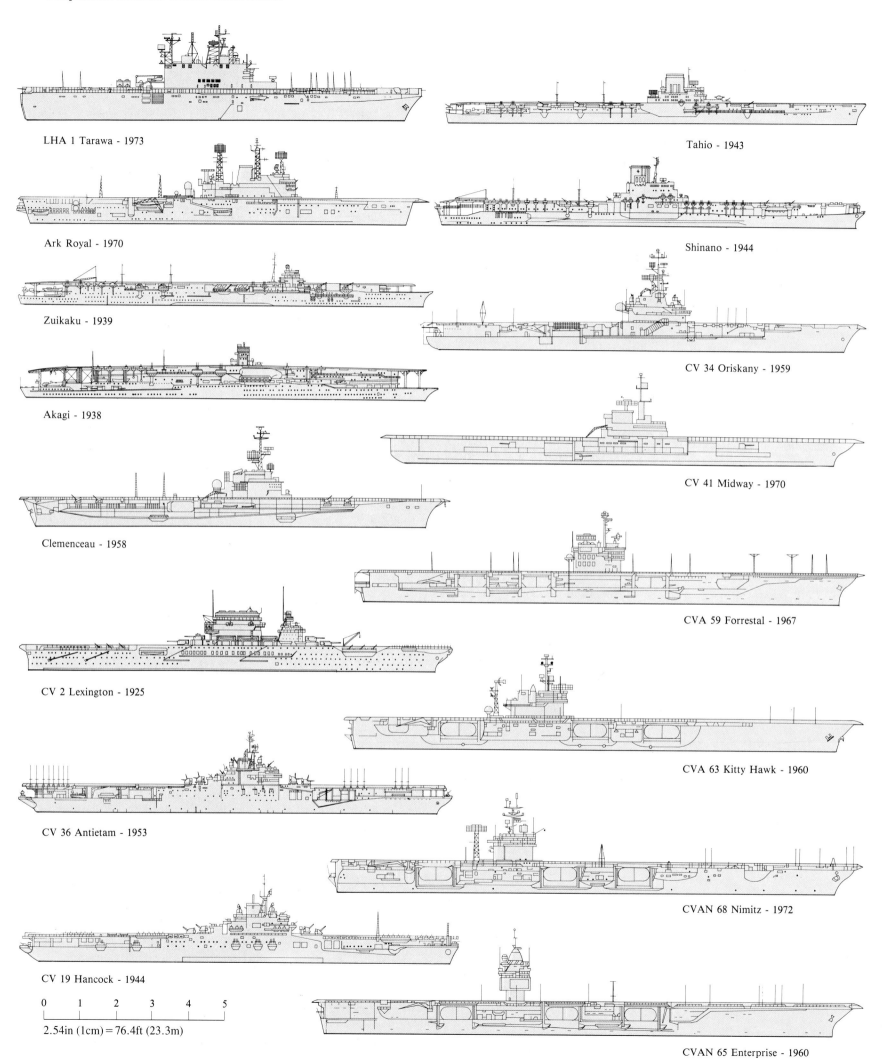

LHA 1 Tarawa - 1973

Tahio - 1943

Ark Royal - 1970

Shinano - 1944

Zuikaku - 1939

CV 34 Oriskany - 1959

Akagi - 1938

CV 41 Midway - 1970

Clemenceau - 1958

CVA 59 Forrestal - 1967

CV 2 Lexington - 1925

CVA 63 Kitty Hawk - 1960

CV 36 Antietam - 1953

CVAN 68 Nimitz - 1972

CV 19 Hancock - 1944

0   1   2   3   4   5

2.54in (1cm) = 76.4ft (23.3m)

CVAN 65 Enterprise - 1960

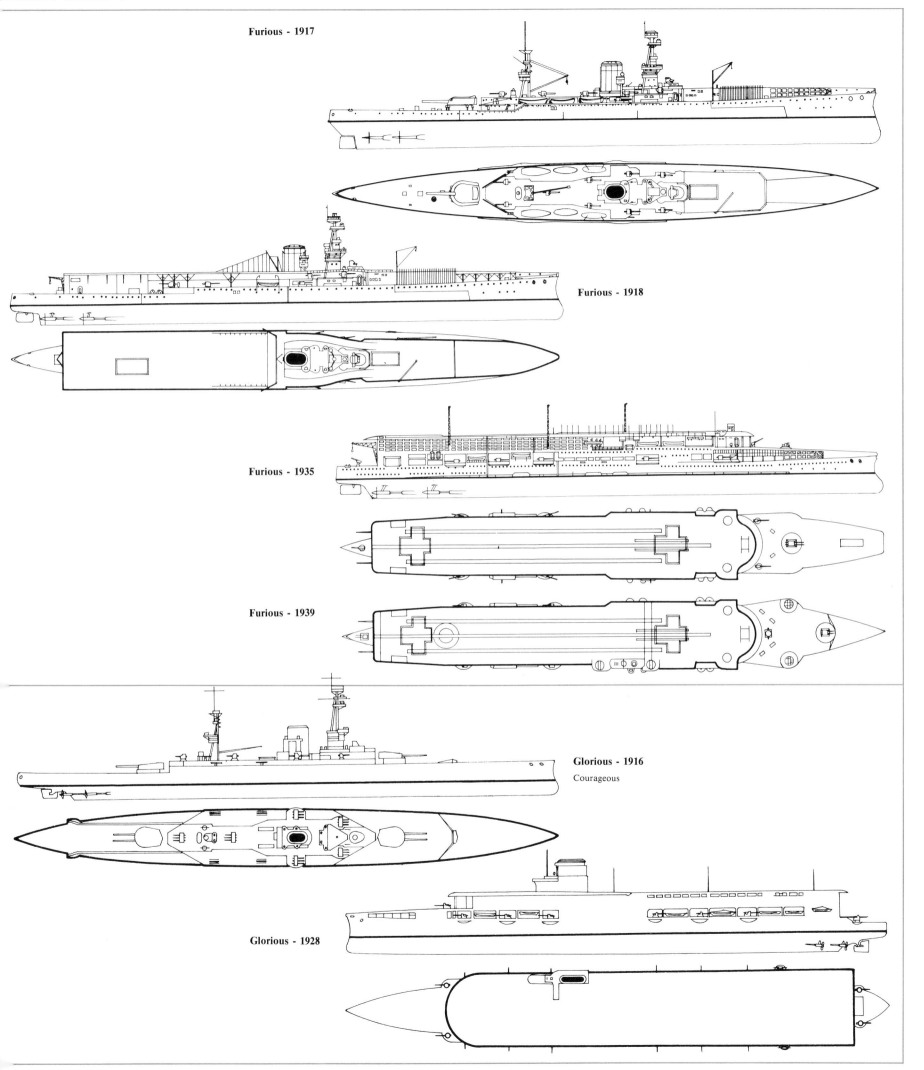

Furious - 1917

Furious - 1918

Furious - 1935

Furious - 1939

Glorious - 1916

Courageous

Glorious - 1928

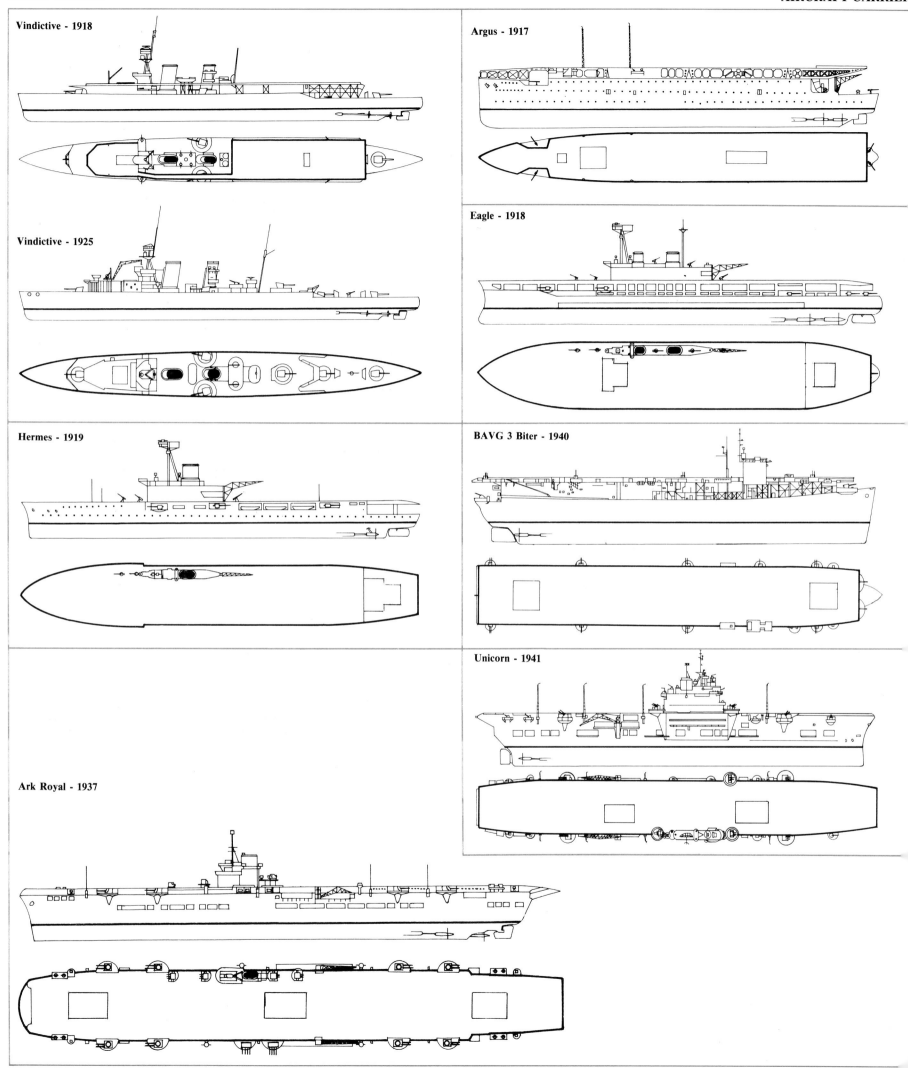

Vindictive - 1918

Argus - 1917

Vindictive - 1925

Eagle - 1918

Hermes - 1919

BAVG 3 Biter - 1940

Unicorn - 1941

Ark Royal - 1937

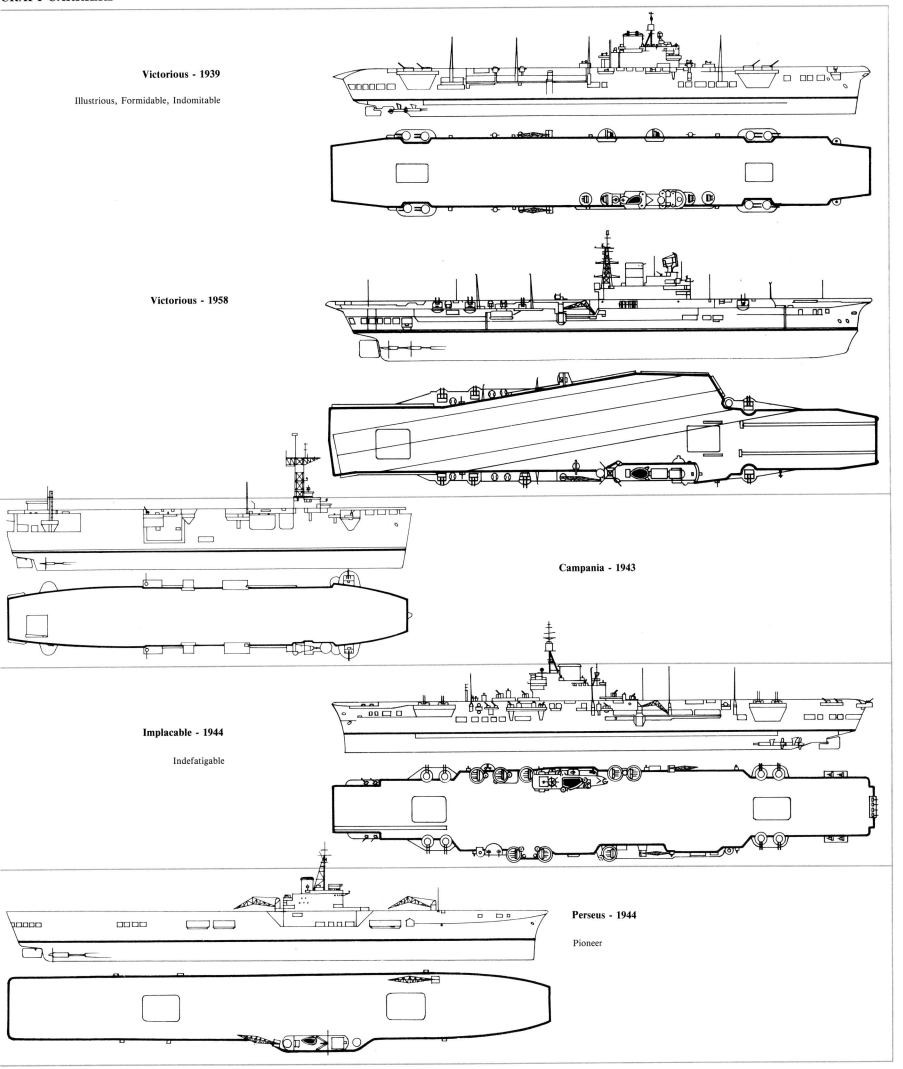

Victorious - 1939

Illustrious, Formidable, Indomitable

Victorious - 1958

Campania - 1943

Implacable - 1944

Indefatigable

Perseus - 1944

Pioneer

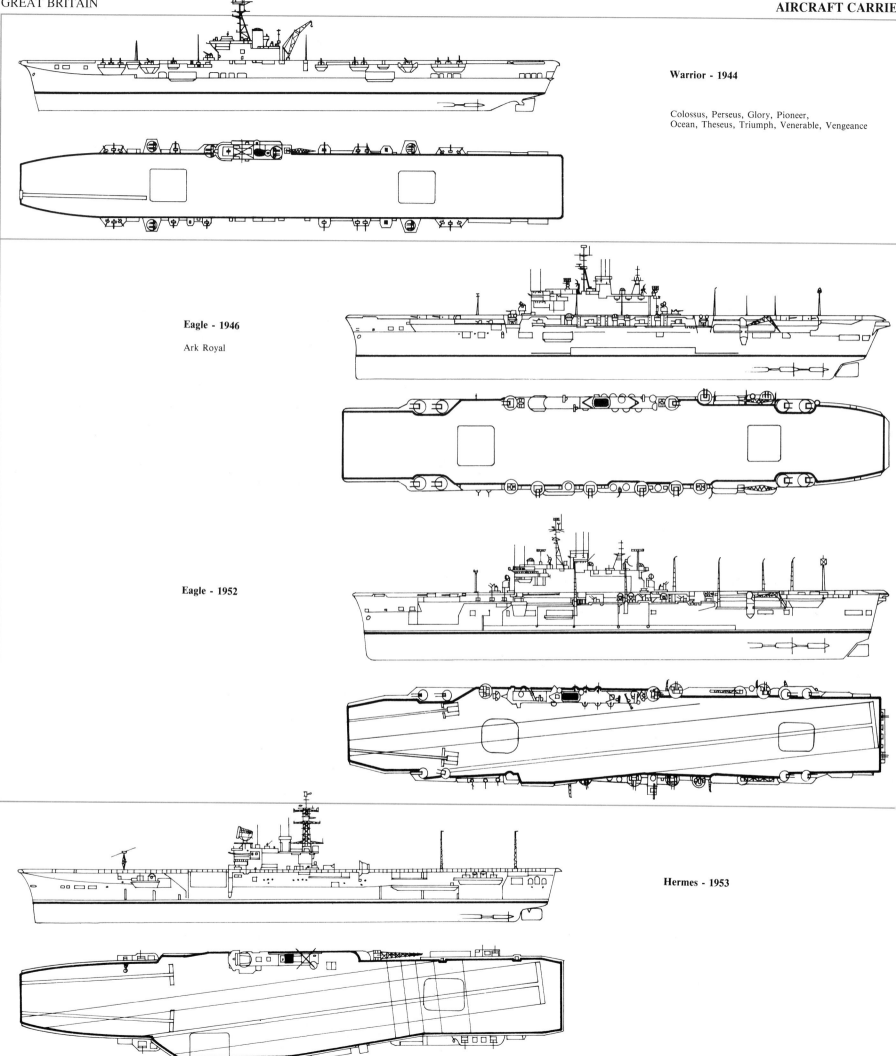

Warrior - 1944

Colossus, Perseus, Glory, Pioneer,
Ocean, Theseus, Triumph, Venerable, Vengeance

Eagle - 1946

Ark Royal

Eagle - 1952

Hermes - 1953

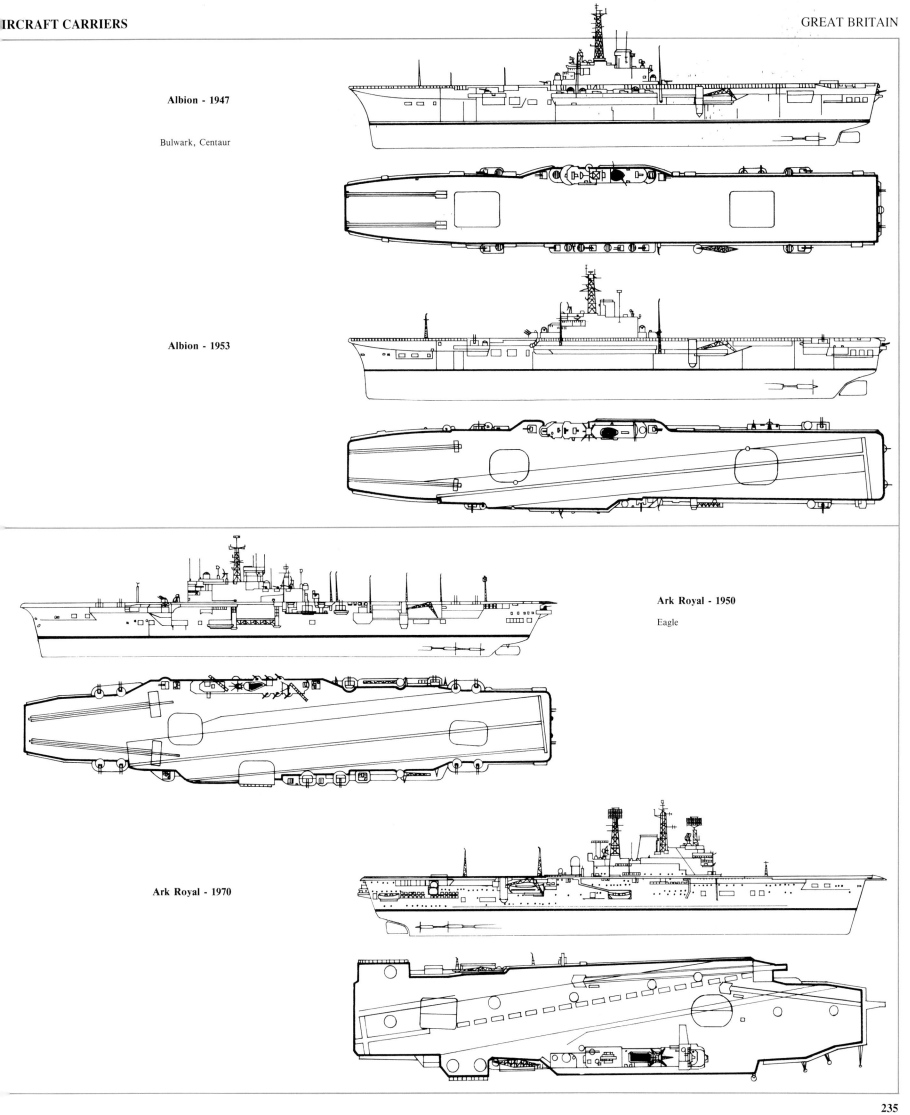

Albion - 1947

Bulwark, Centaur

Albion - 1953

Ark Royal - 1950

Eagle

Ark Royal - 1970

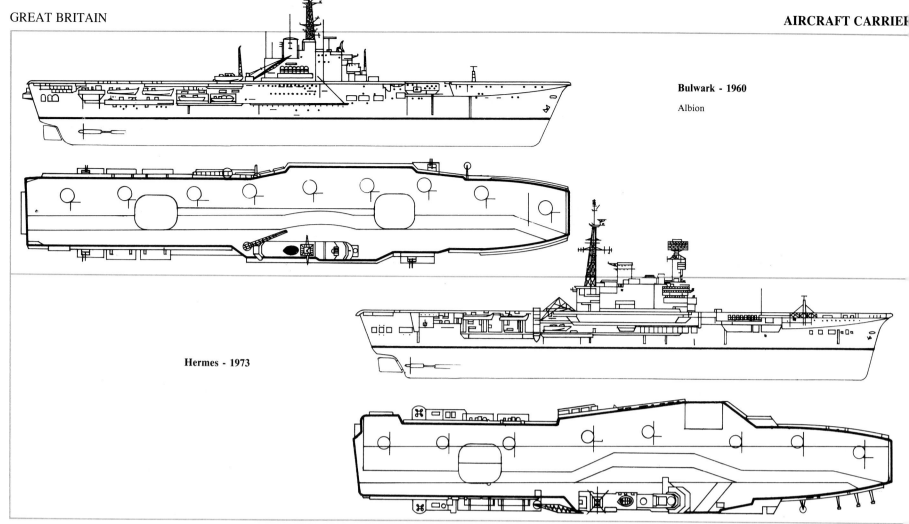

Bulwark - 1960

Albion

Hermes - 1973

FRANCE

Béarn - 1920

Commandant Teste - 1929

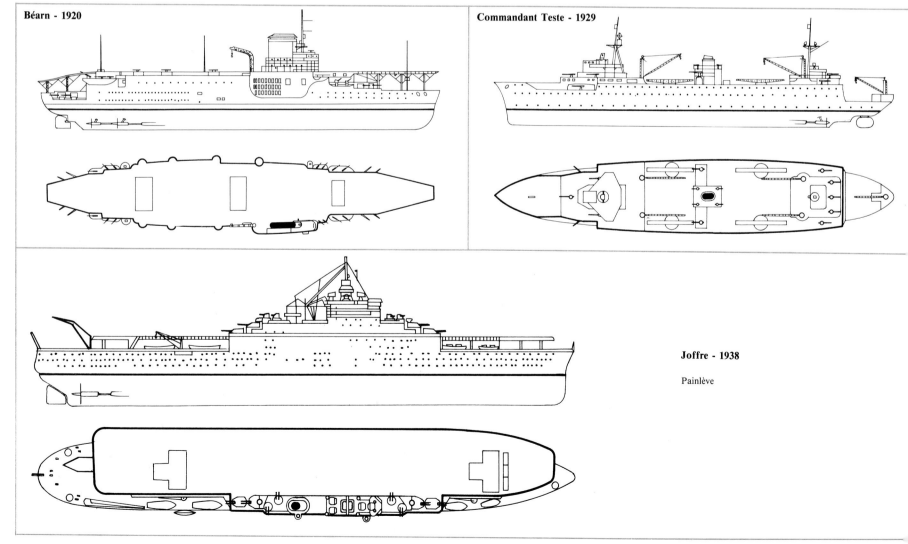

Joffre - 1938

Painlève

Clemenceau - 1957

Foch

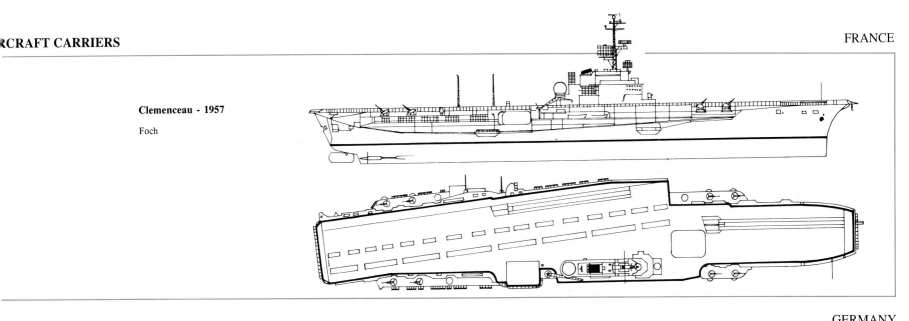

Graf Zeppelin - 1938

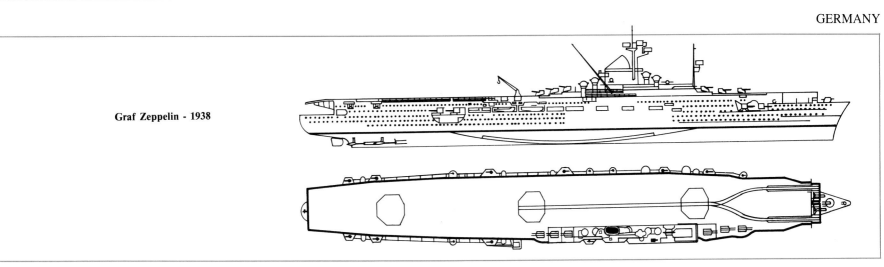

Aquila - 1943

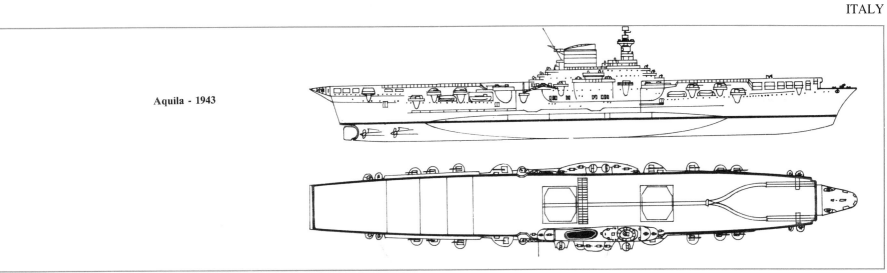

Karel Doorman - 1958

Bonaventure - 1957

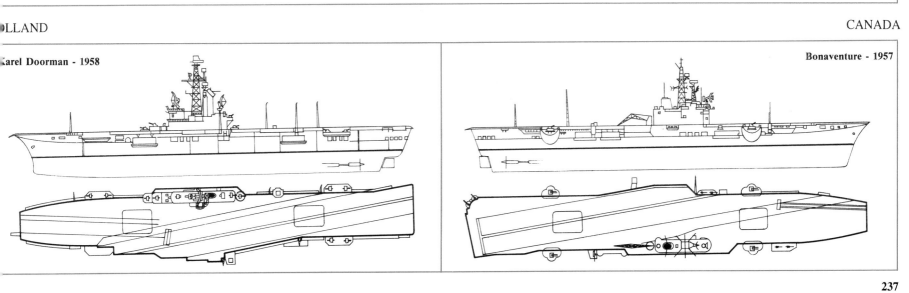

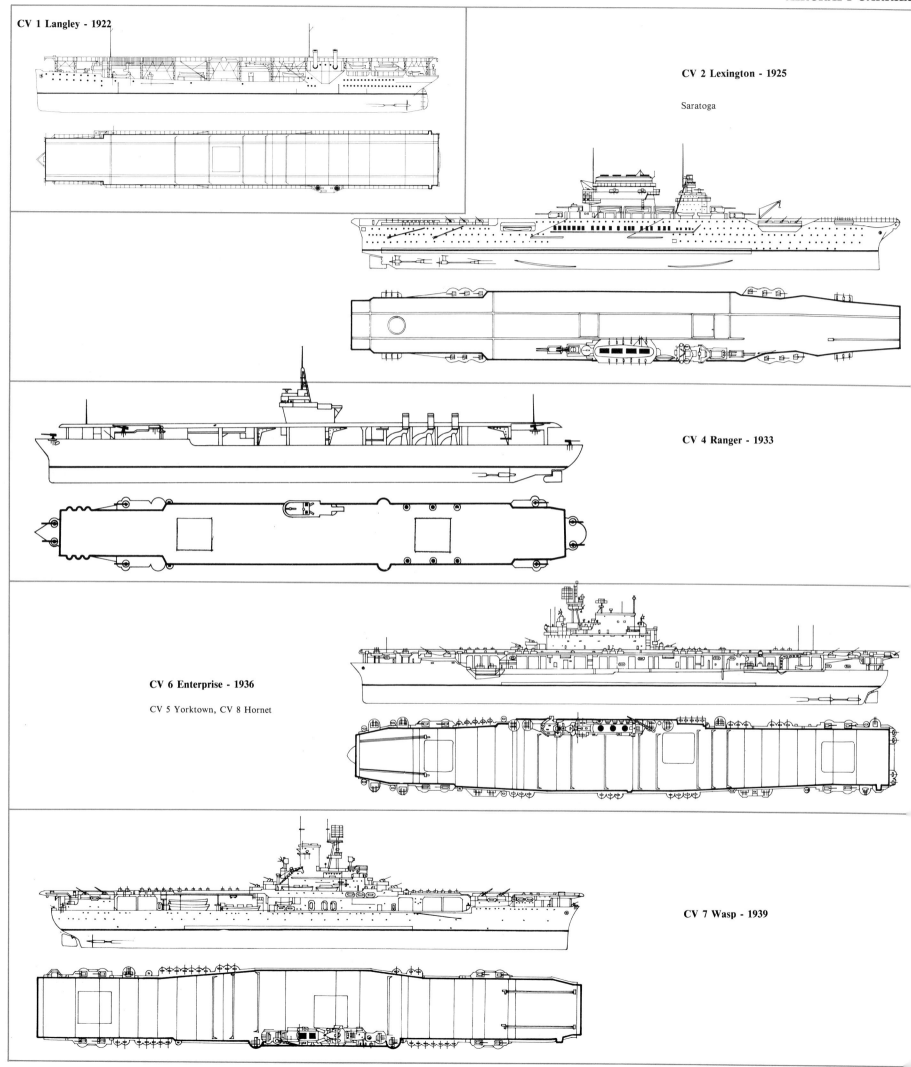

CV 1 Langley - 1922

CV 2 Lexington - 1925

Saratoga

CV 4 Ranger - 1933

CV 6 Enterprise - 1936

CV 5 Yorktown, CV 8 Hornet

CV 7 Wasp - 1939

CVL 22 Independence - 1942

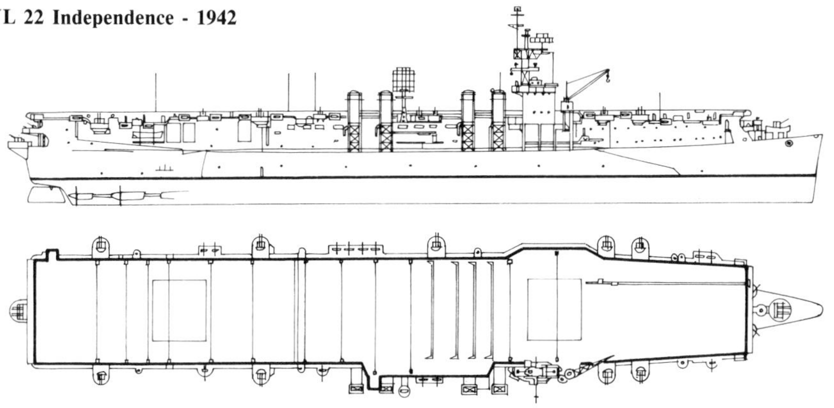

CVL 23 Princeton, CVL 24 Belleau Wood, CVL 25 Cowpens, CVL 26 Monterey, CVL 27 Langley II, CVL 28 Cabot, CVL 29 Bataan, CVL 30 San Jacinto

CVE 106 Block Island - 1944

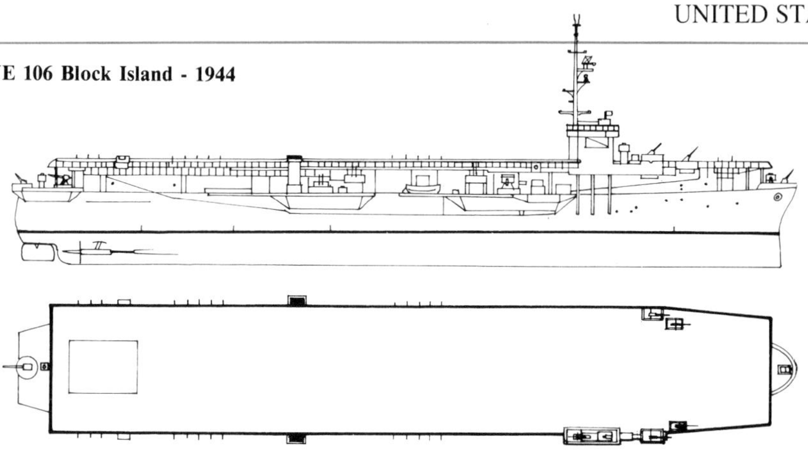

CVE 105 Commencement Bay, CVE 107 Gilbert Islands, CVE 108 Kula Gulf, CVE 109 Cape Gloucester, CVE 110 Salerno Bay, CVE 111 Vella Gulf, CVE 112 Siboney, CVE 113 Puget Sound, CVE 114 Rendove, CVE 115 Bairoko, CVE 116 Badoeng-Strait, CVE 117 Saidor, CVE 118 Sicily, CVE 119 Point Cruz, CVE 120 Mindoro, CVE 121 Rabaul, CVE 122 Palau, CVE 123 Tinian.

LPH 6 Thetis Bay - 1956

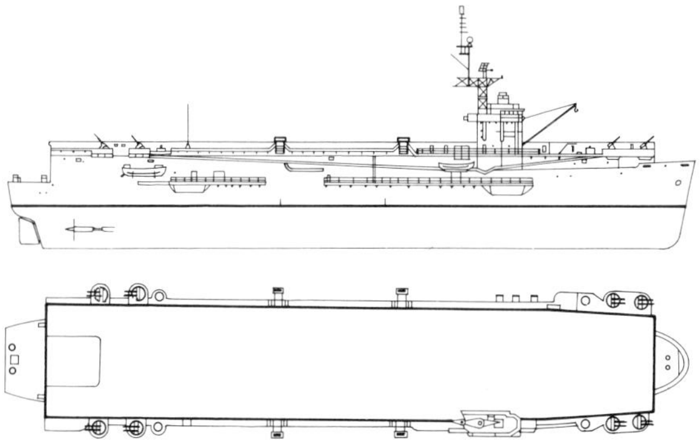

CV 19 Hancock - 1944

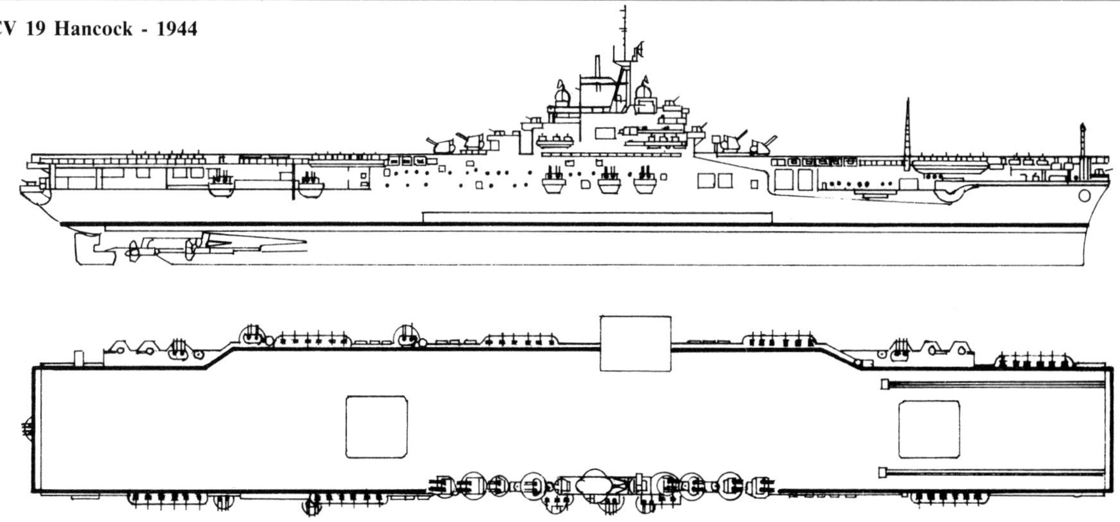

CV 11 Intrepid, CV 16 Lexington II, CV 14 Ticonderoga, CV 31 Bonhomme Richard, CV 34 Oriskany, CV 38 Shangri-La

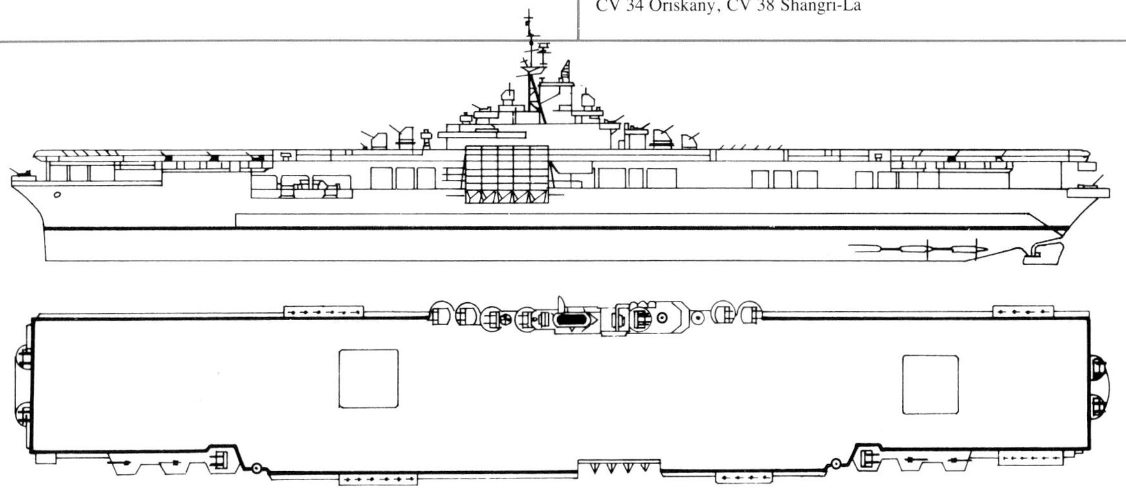

CV 36 Antietam - 1944

CV 10 Yorktown II, CV 12 Hornet II, CV 13 Franklin, CV 17 Bunker Hill, CV 18 Wasp II, CV 21 Boxer, CV 32 Leyte, CV 37 Princeton, CV 39 Lake Champlain, CV 40 Tarawa, CV 45 Valley Forge, CV 47 Philippine Sea

CV 36 Antietam - 1953

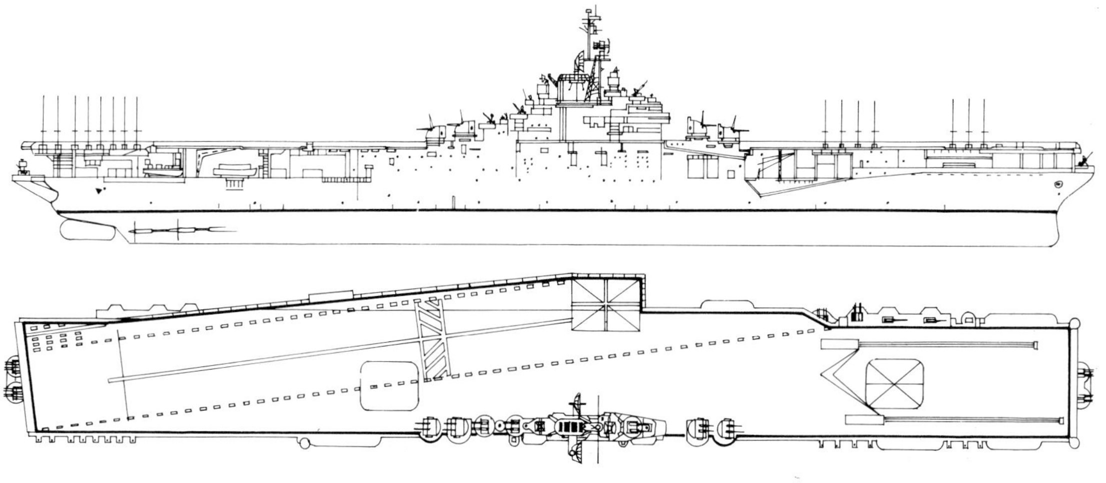

239

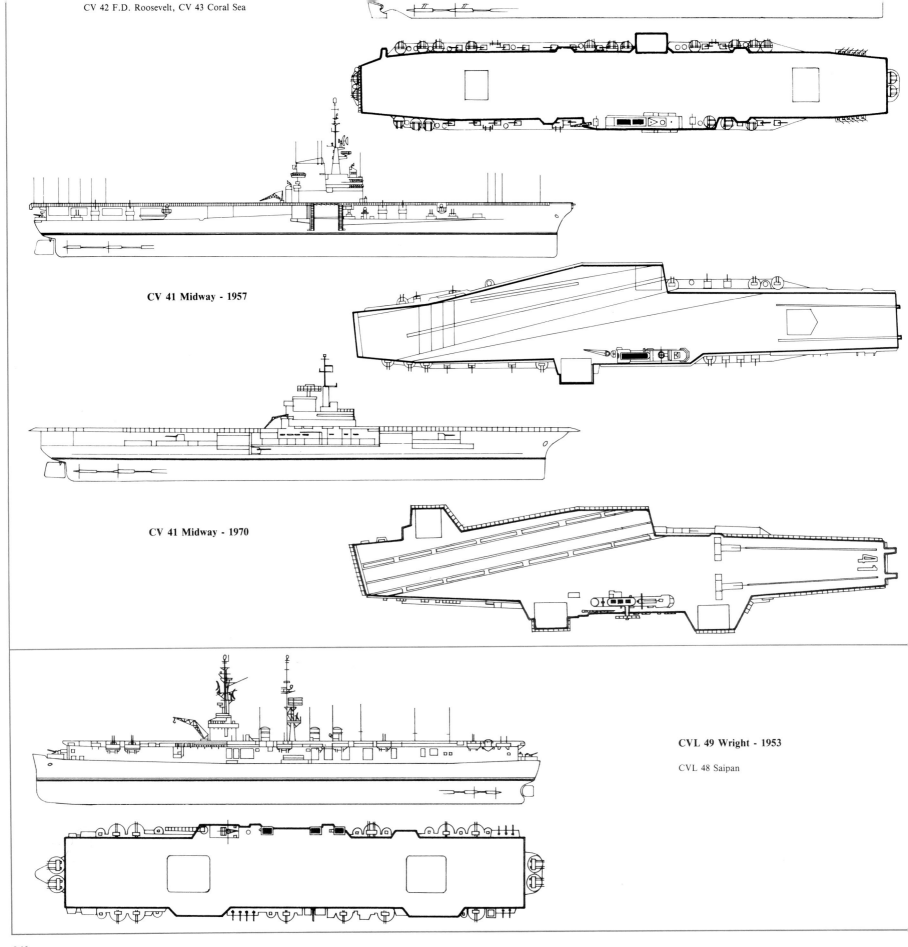

CV 42 F.D. Roosevelt, CV 43 Coral Sea

CV 41 Midway - 1957

CV 41 Midway - 1970

CVL 49 Wright - 1953

CVL 48 Saipan

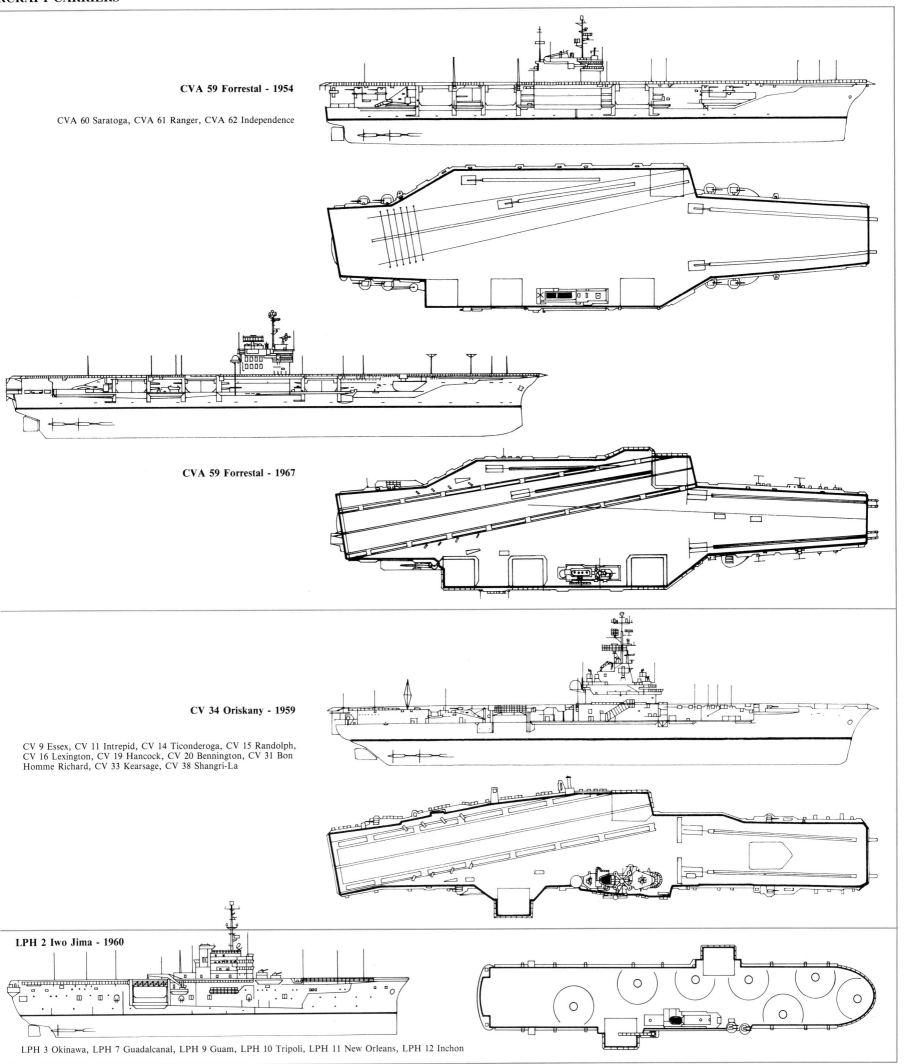

CVA 59 Forrestal - 1954

CVA 60 Saratoga, CVA 61 Ranger, CVA 62 Independence

CVA 59 Forrestal - 1967

CV 34 Oriskany - 1959

CV 9 Essex, CV 11 Intrepid, CV 14 Ticonderoga, CV 15 Randolph, CV 16 Lexington, CV 19 Hancock, CV 20 Bennington, CV 31 Bon Homme Richard, CV 33 Kearsage, CV 38 Shangri-La

LPH 2 Iwo Jima - 1960

LPH 3 Okinawa, LPH 7 Guadalcanal, LPH 9 Guam, LPH 10 Tripoli, LPH 11 New Orleans, LPH 12 Inchon

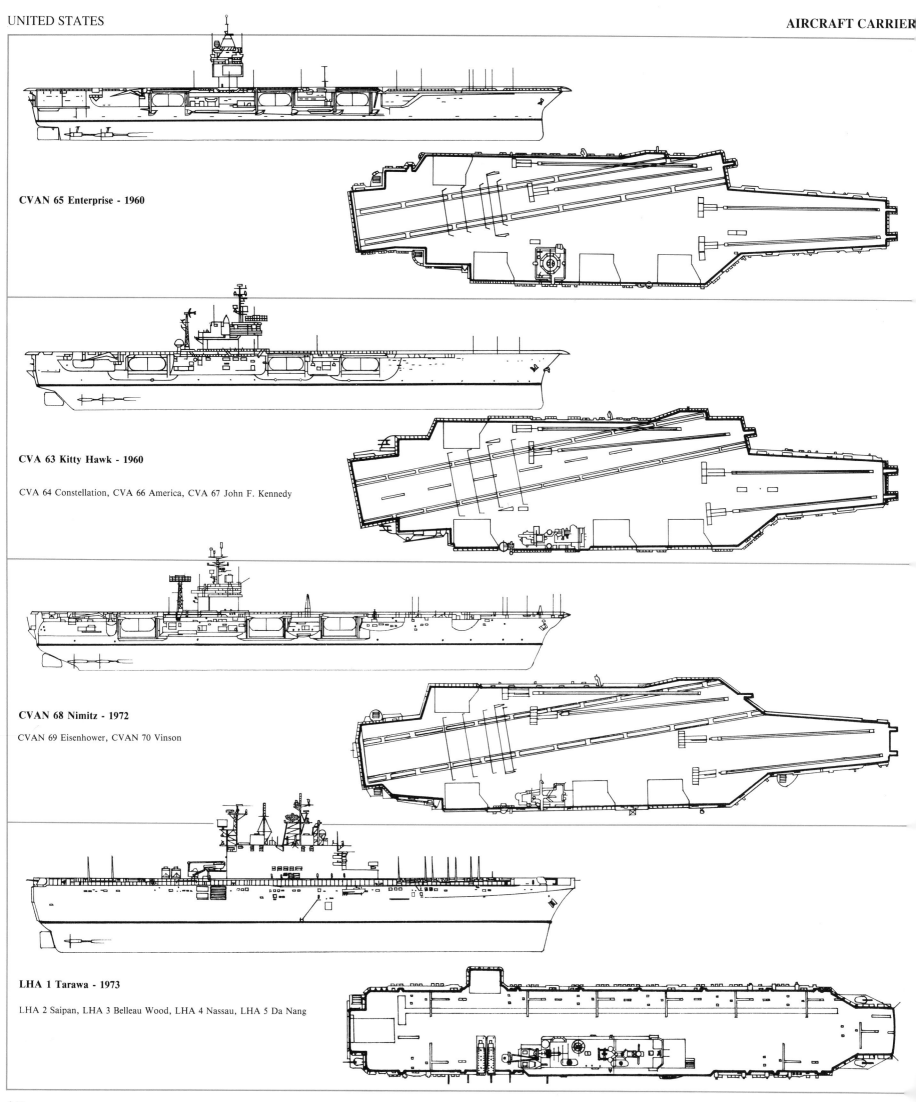

CVAN 65 Enterprise - 1960

CVA 63 Kitty Hawk - 1960

CVA 64 Constellation, CVA 66 America, CVA 67 John F. Kennedy

CVAN 68 Nimitz - 1972

CVAN 69 Eisenhower, CVAN 70 Vinson

LHA 1 Tarawa - 1973

LHA 2 Saipan, LHA 3 Belleau Wood, LHA 4 Nassau, LHA 5 Da Nang

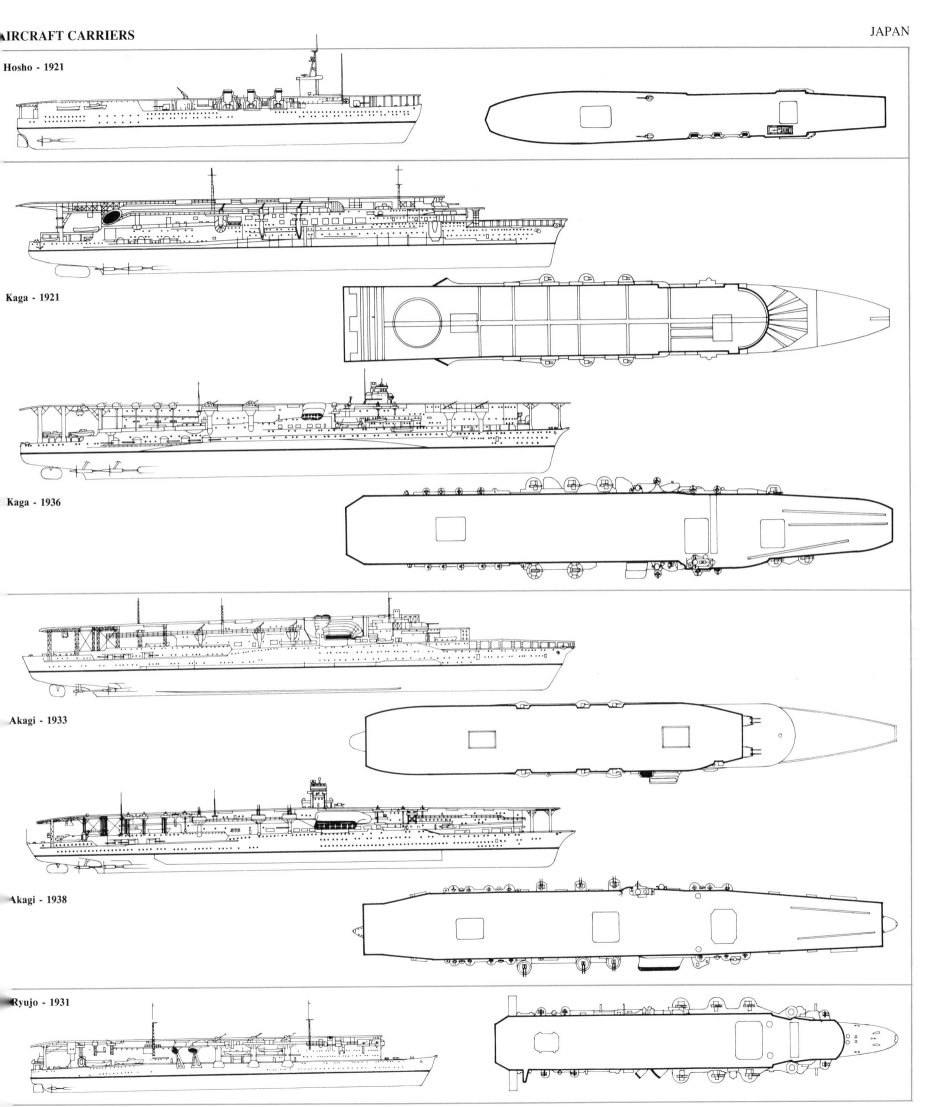

Hosho - 1921

Kaga - 1921

Kaga - 1936

Akagi - 1933

Akagi - 1938

Ryujo - 1931

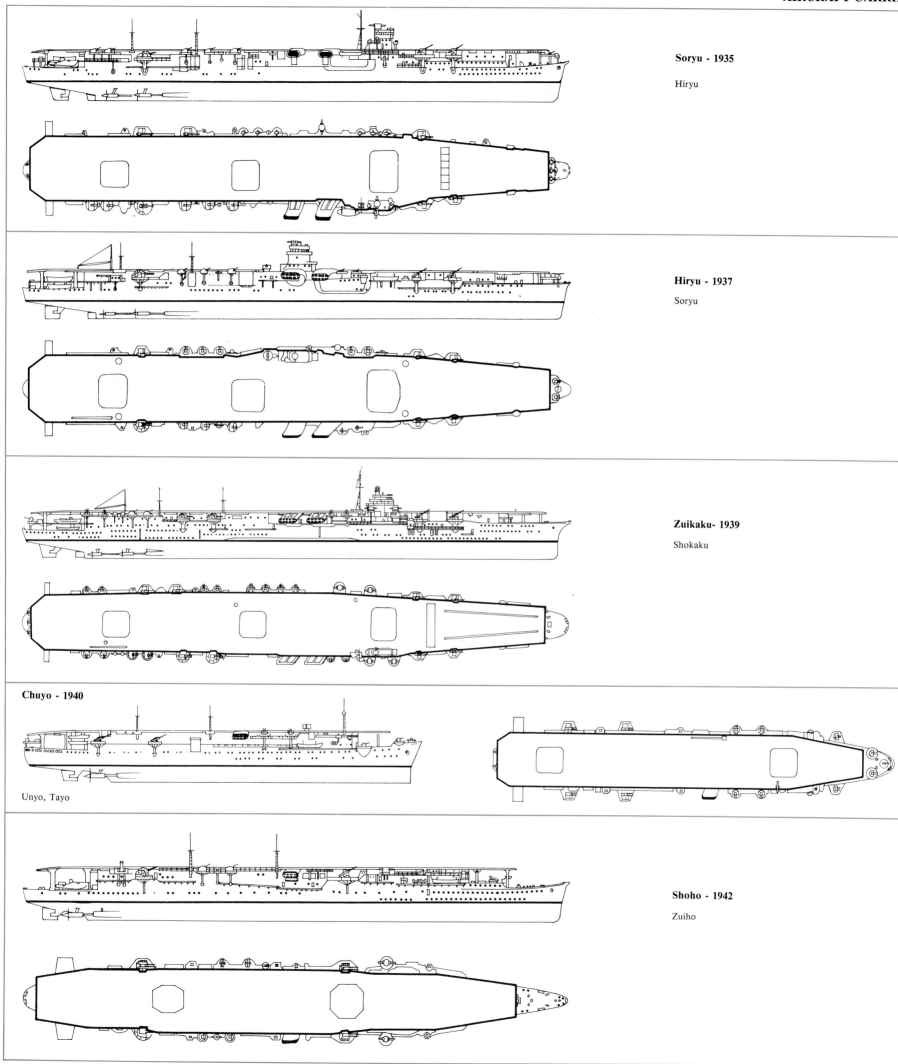

Soryu - 1935

Hiryu

Hiryu - 1937

Soryu

Zuikaku- 1939

Shokaku

Chuyo - 1940

Unyo, Tayo

Shoho - 1942

Zuiho

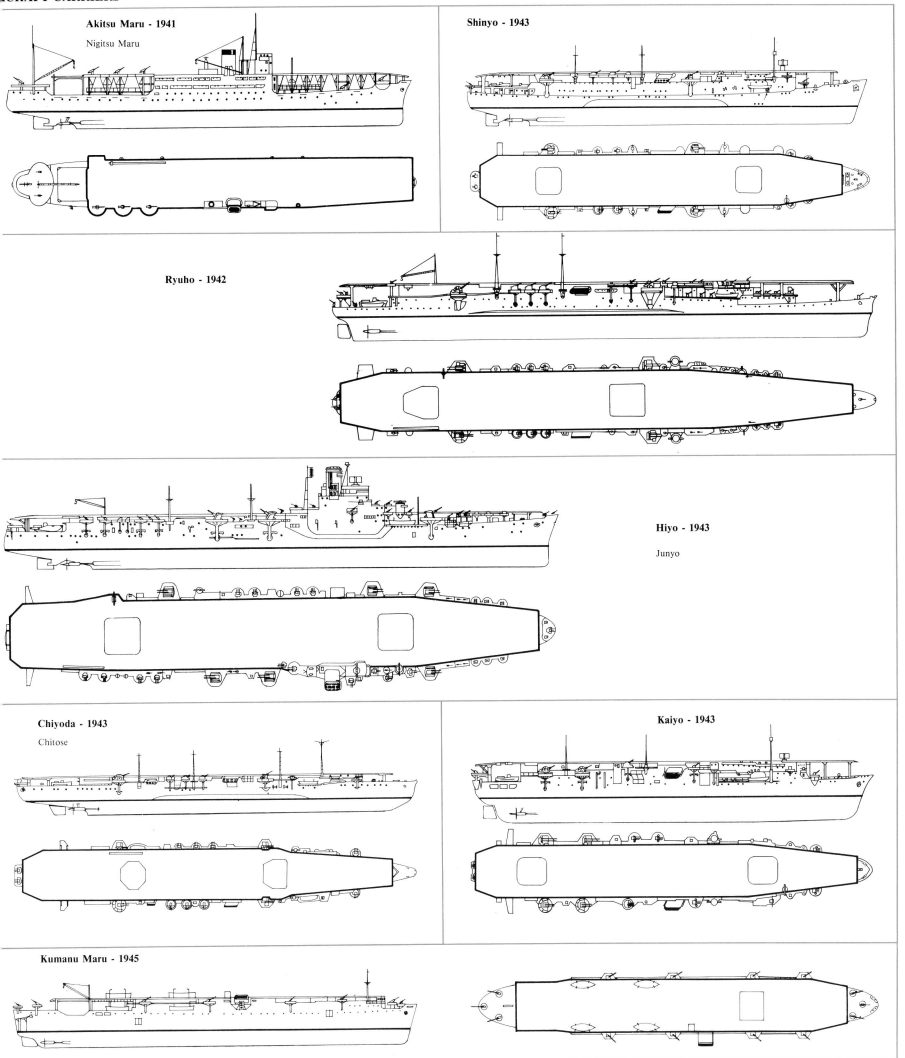

Akitsu Maru - 1941

Nigitsu Maru

Shinyo - 1943

Ryuho - 1942

Hiyo - 1943

Junyo

Chiyoda - 1943

Chitose

Kaiyo - 1943

Kumanu Maru - 1945

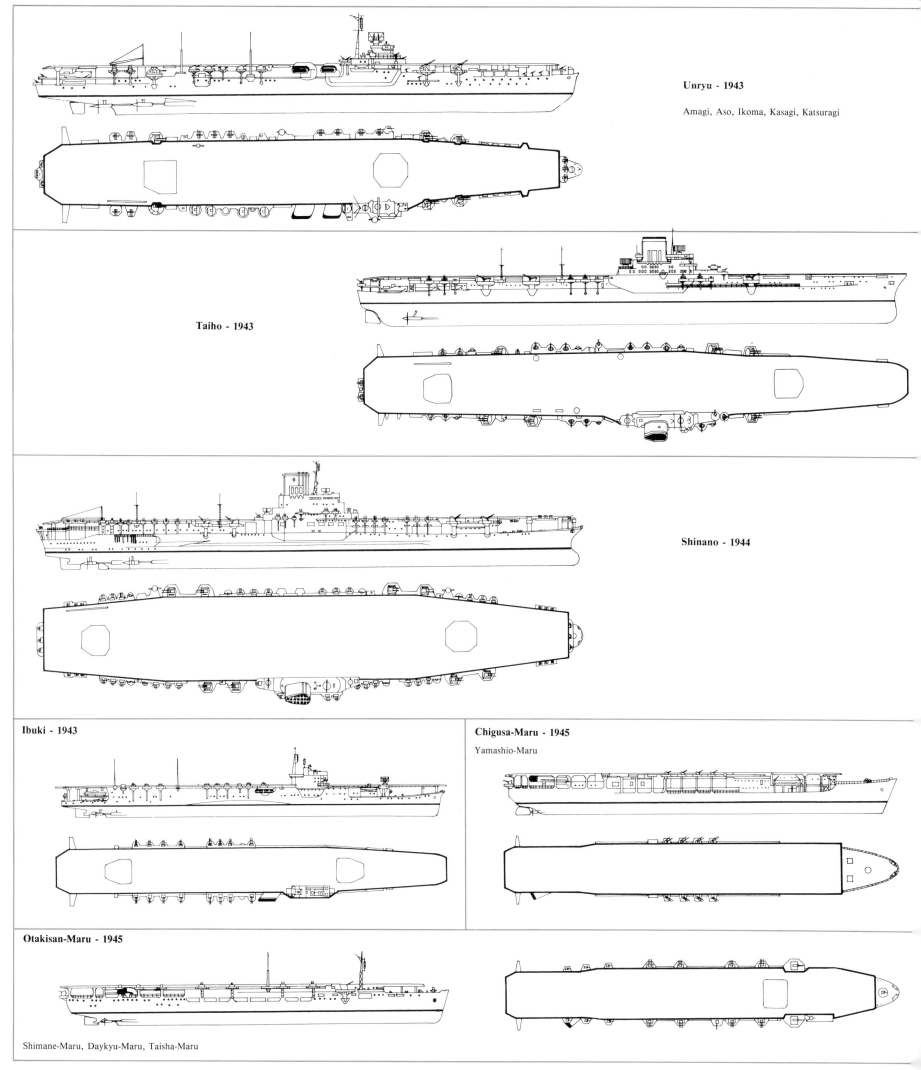

Unryu - 1943

Amagi, Aso, Ikoma, Kasagi, Katsuragi

Taiho - 1943

Shinano - 1944

Ibuki - 1943

Chigusa-Maru - 1945

Yamashio-Maru

Otakisan-Maru - 1945

Shimane-Maru, Daykyu-Maru, Taisha-Maru

Sydney - 1949

Melbourne - 1955

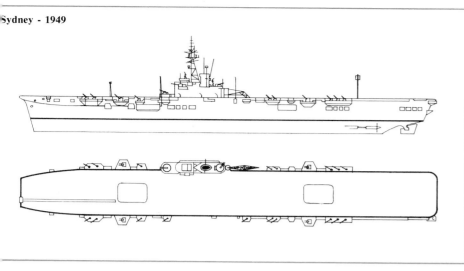

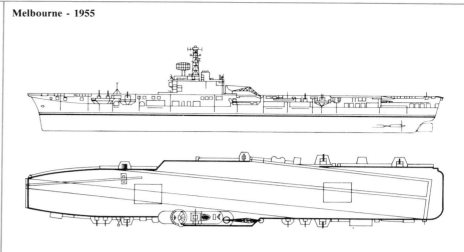

Indipendencia - 1959

Venticinco de Mayo - 1969

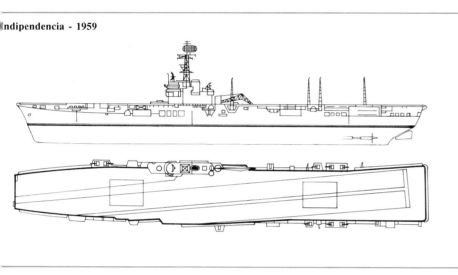

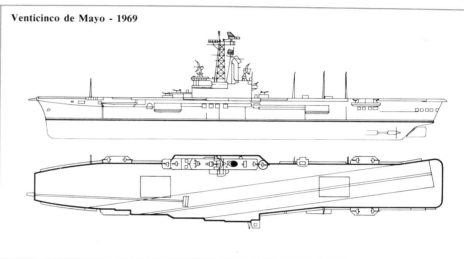

BRAZIL

Minas Gerais - 1960

Vikrant - 1961

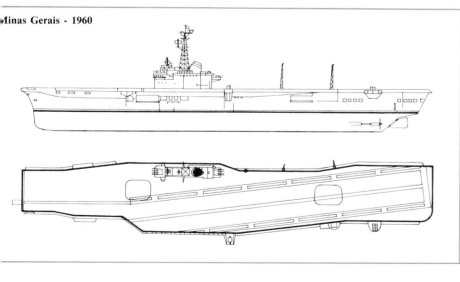

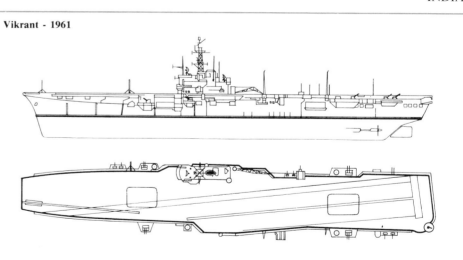

Compendium of submarines drawn to scale

Narval - 1900

Foca - 1908

Bonita - 1952

Saphir - 1928

Archimede 1° - 1934

Romolo - 1943

RO 33 - 1953

U 25 - 1936

Mocenigo - 1940

Brin - 1939

Aurore - 1938

XXI - 1944

Odin - 1928

Junsen 1 M - 1932

SSN 571 Nautilus - 1954

Gato - 1942

Redoutable - 1924

Salmon - 1937

Zulu - 1955

Cagni - 1942

Balilla - 1928

Triton - 1937

Whiskey - 1963

Porpoise - 1932

Perseus - 1928

Rainbow - 1930

Golf III - 1961

Severn - 1934

Seawolf - 1957

Kaidai I-68 - 1938

Halibut - 1960

Argonaut - 1928

Washington - 1960

Surcouf - 1934

I 400 - 1945

Yankee - 1967

Lafayette - 1962

Delta I - 1973

Triton - 1958

0   1   2   3   4   5

2.54in (1cm) = 45.9ft (14m)

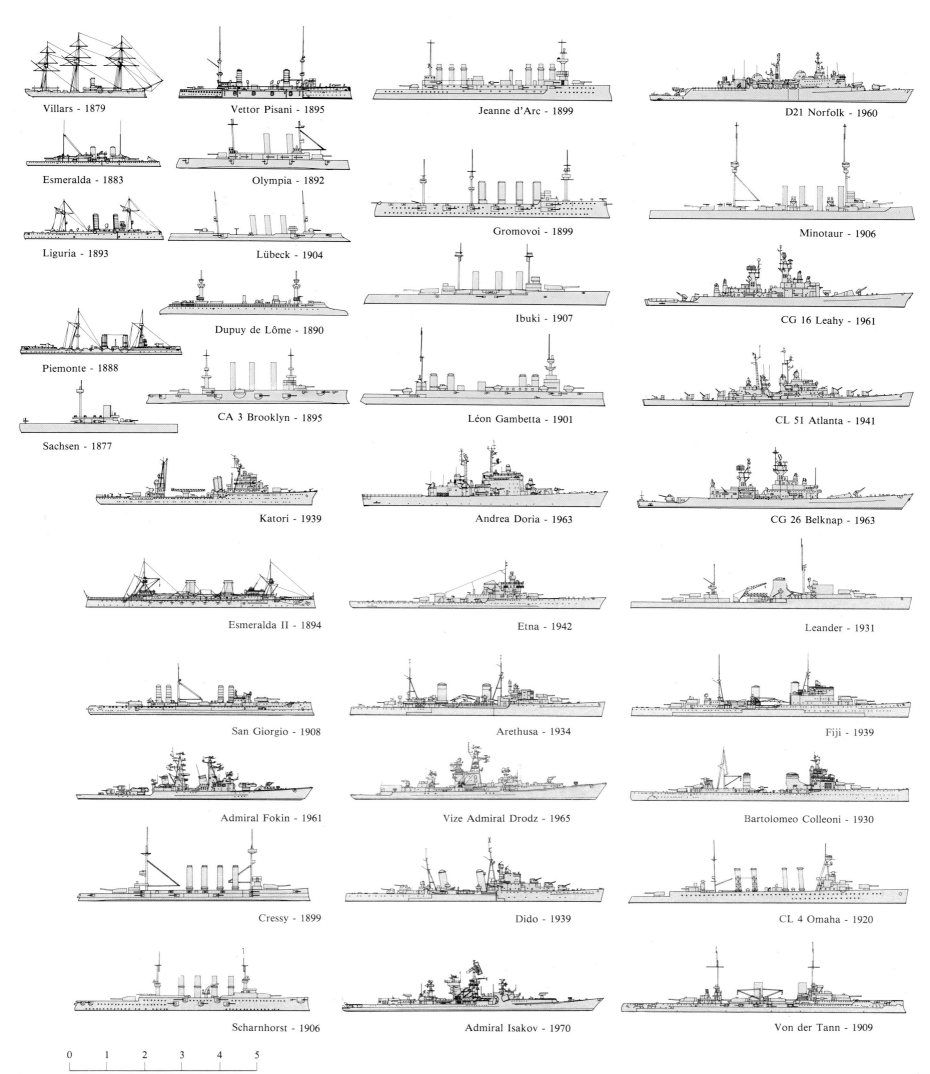

Villars - 1879

Vettor Pisani - 1895

Jeanne d'Arc - 1899

D21 Norfolk - 1960

Esmeralda - 1883

Olympia - 1892

Liguria - 1893

Lübeck - 1904

Gromovoi - 1899

Minotaur - 1906

Dupuy de Lôme - 1890

Ibuki - 1907

CG 16 Leahy - 1961

Piemonte - 1888

CA 3 Brooklyn - 1895

Léon Gambetta - 1901

CL 51 Atlanta - 1941

Sachsen - 1877

Katori - 1939

Andrea Doria - 1963

CG 26 Belknap - 1963

Esmeralda II - 1894

Etna - 1942

Leander - 1931

San Giorgio - 1908

Arethusa - 1934

Fiji - 1939

Admiral Fokin - 1961

Vize Admiral Drodz - 1965

Bartolomeo Colleoni - 1930

Cressy - 1899

Dido - 1939

CL 4 Omaha - 1920

Scharnhorst - 1906

Admiral Isakov - 1970

Von der Tann - 1909

0   1   2   3   4   5

2.54in (1cm) = 76.4ft (23.3m)

249

Compendium of cruisers drawn to scale

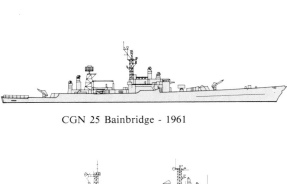

CGN 25 Bainbridge - 1961

CGN 38 Virginia - 1974

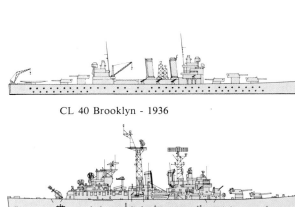

CL 40 Brooklyn - 1936

C 20 Tiger - 1945

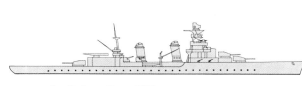

CA 24 Pensacola - 1929

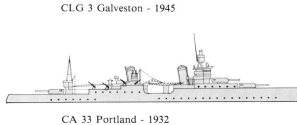

CLG 3 Galveston - 1945

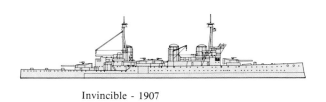

Invincible - 1907

La Galissonière - 1933

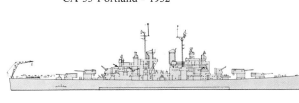

CA 33 Portland - 1932

De Ruyter - 1935

Giuseppe Garibaldi - 1983

CL 55 Cleveland - 1941

Nikolayev - 1971

Vittorio Veneto - 1967

Eugenio di Savoia - 1935

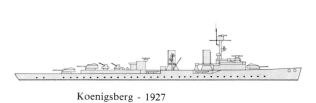

Koenigsberg - 1927

Colbert - 1956

Giuseppe Garibaldi - 1936

Agano - 1941

CGN 36 California - 1971

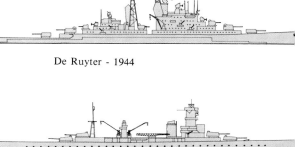

De Ruyter - 1944

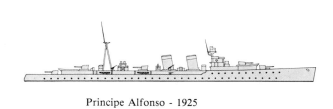

Principe Alfonso - 1925

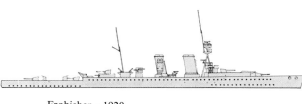

Zara - 1930

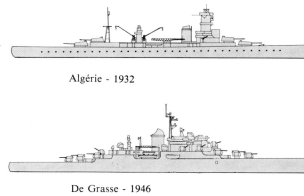

Algérie - 1932

Nürnberg - 1934

Frobisher - 1920

De Grasse - 1946

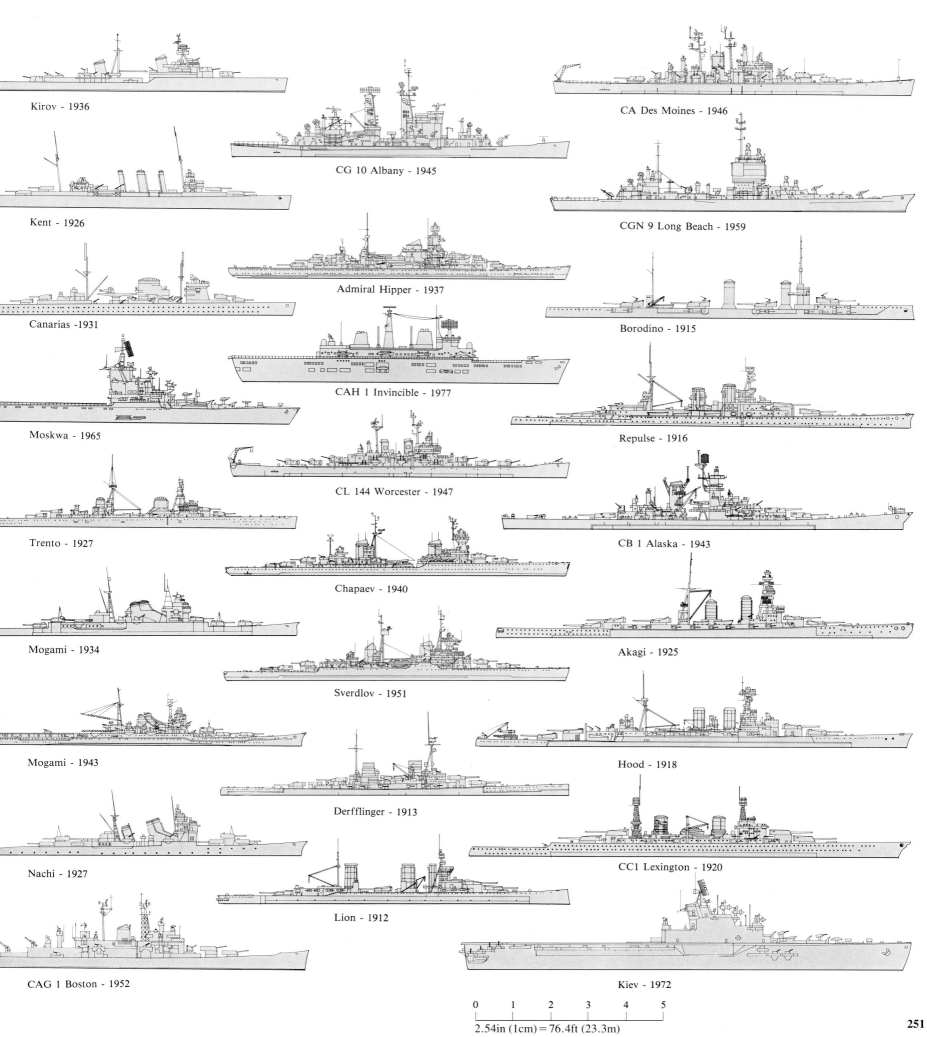

Kirov - 1936

Kent - 1926

Canarias -1931

Moskwa - 1965

Trento - 1927

Mogami - 1934

Mogami - 1943

Nachi - 1927

CAG 1 Boston - 1952

CG 10 Albany - 1945

Admiral Hipper - 1937

CAH 1 Invincible - 1977

CL 144 Worcester - 1947

Chapaev - 1940

Sverdlov - 1951

Derfflinger - 1913

Lion - 1912

CA Des Moines - 1946

CGN 9 Long Beach - 1959

Borodino - 1915

Repulse - 1916

CB 1 Alaska - 1943

Akagi - 1925

Hood - 1918

CC1 Lexington - 1920

Kiev - 1972

0   1   2   3   4   5

2.54in (1cm) = 76.4ft (23.3m)

Shannon - 1875

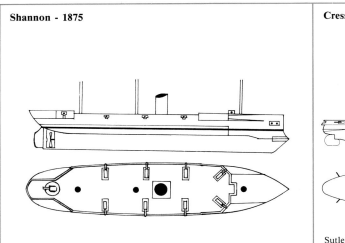

Cressy - 1899

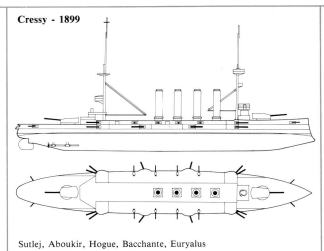

Sutlej, Aboukir, Hogue, Bacchante, Euryalus

Minotaur - 1906

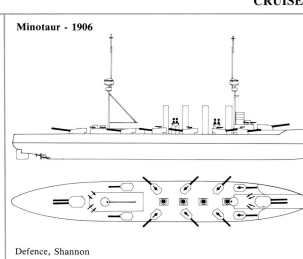

Defence, Shannon

Invincible - 1907

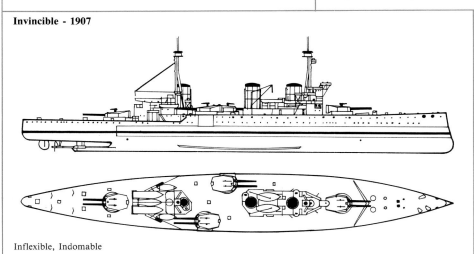

Inflexible, Indomable

Lion - 1912

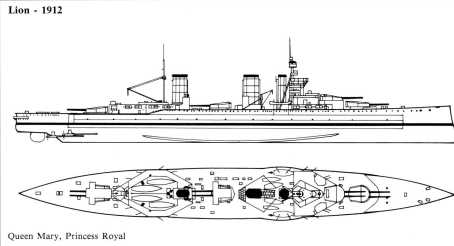

Queen Mary, Princess Royal

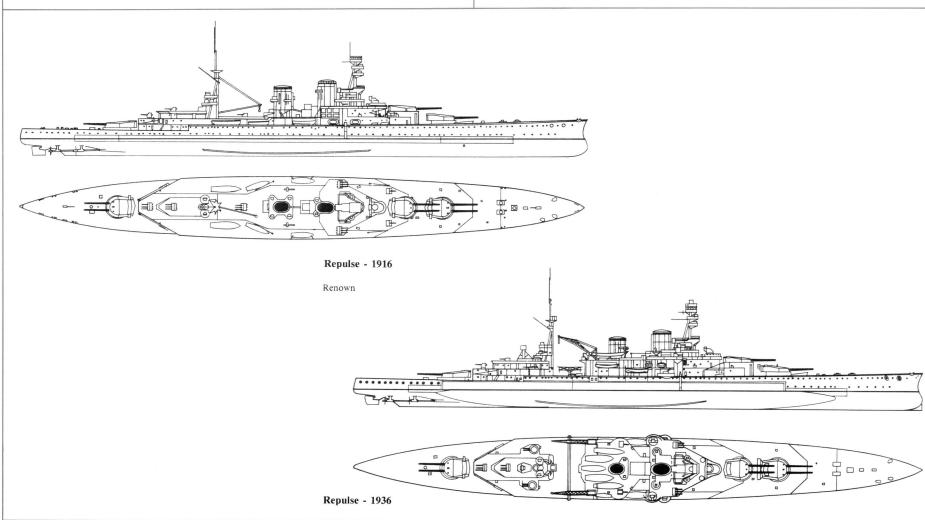

Repulse - 1916

Renown

Repulse - 1936

Hood - 1918

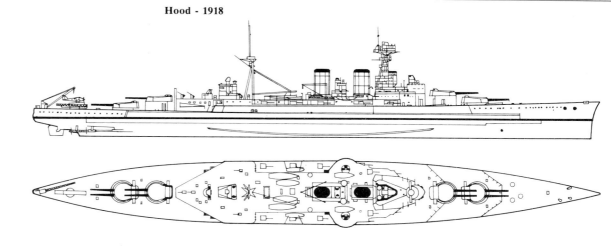

Frobisher - 1920

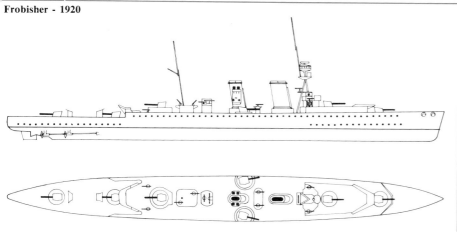

Effingham, Hawkins, Cavendish, Raleigh

Kent - 1926

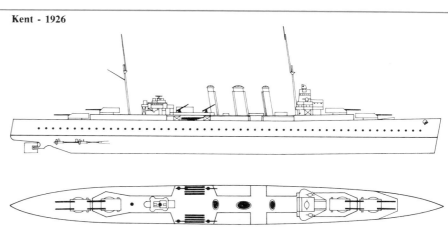

Berwick, Cornwall, Cumberland, Suffolk

Leander - 1931

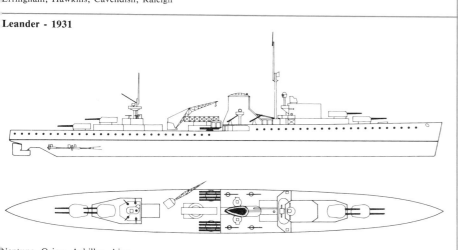

Neptune, Orion, Achilles, Ajax

Arethusa - 1934

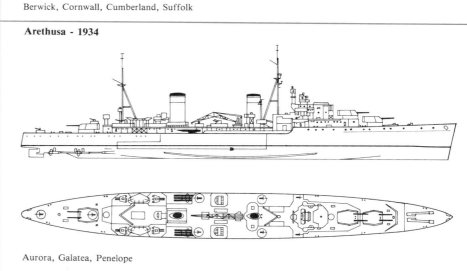

Aurora, Galatea, Penelope

Dido - 1939

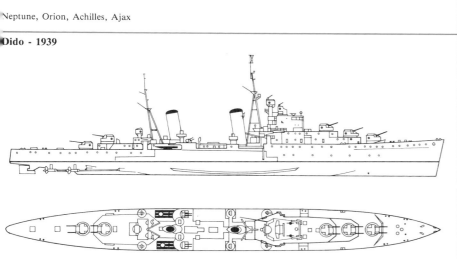

Argonaut, Bonaventure, Charybdis, Cleopatra, Euryalus, Hermione, Naiad, Phoebe, Scylla, Sirious

Fiji - 1939

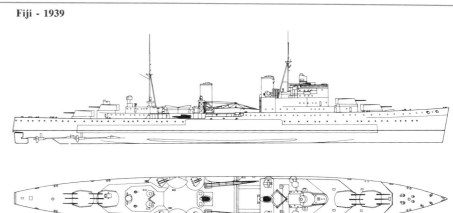

Bermuda, Ceylon, Gambia, Jamaica, Kenya, Mauritius, Newfoundland, Nigeria, Trinidad, Uganda

C 20 Tiger - 1945

C 99 Blake, C 34 Lion

D 21 Norfolk - 1960

D 02 Devonshire, D 06 Hampshire, D 12 Kent, D 16 London, D 18 Antrim, D 19 Glamorgan, D 20 Fife

CAH 1 Invincible - 1977

Illustrious, Ark Royal

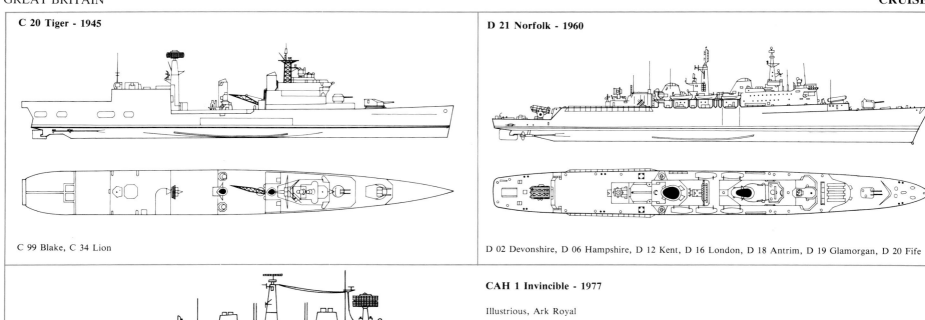
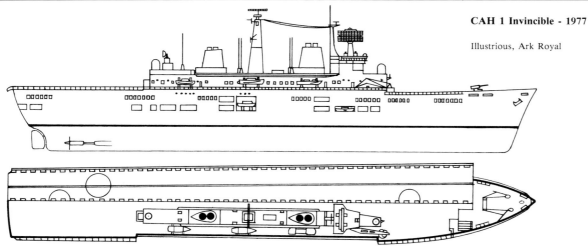

FRANCE

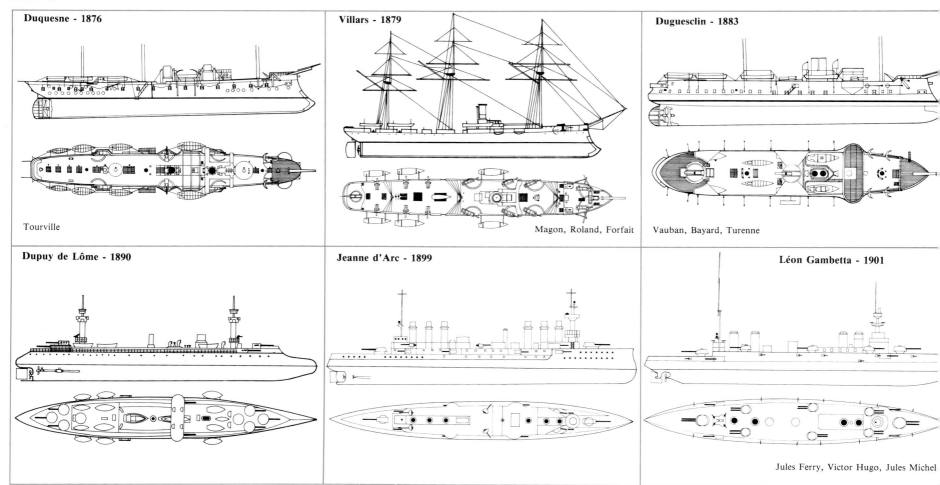

Duquesne - 1876

Tourville

Villars - 1879

Magon, Roland, Forfait

Duguesclin - 1883

Vauban, Bayard, Turenne

Dupuy de Lôme - 1890

Jeanne d'Arc - 1899

Léon Gambetta - 1901

Jules Ferry, Victor Hugo, Jules Michel

Algérie - 1932

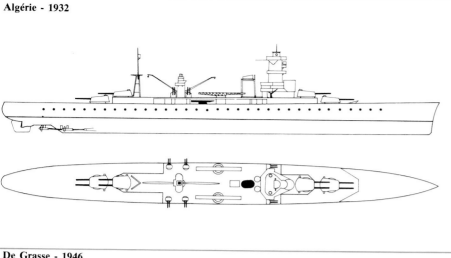

La Galissonière - 1933

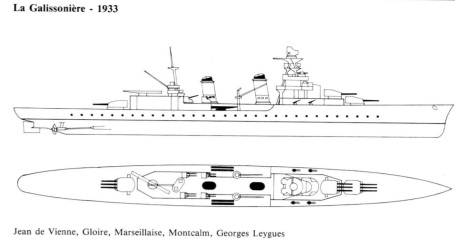

Jean de Vienne, Gloire, Marseillaise, Montcalm, Georges Leygues

De Grasse - 1946

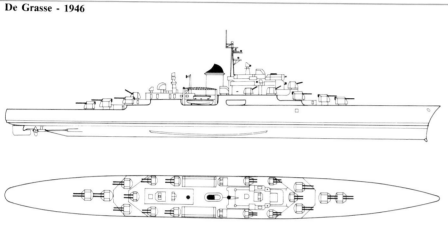

Colbert - 1956

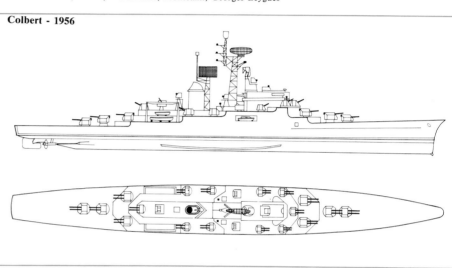

Jeanne d'Arc - 1964

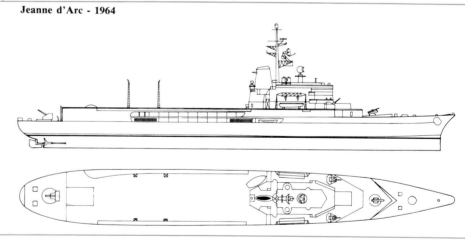

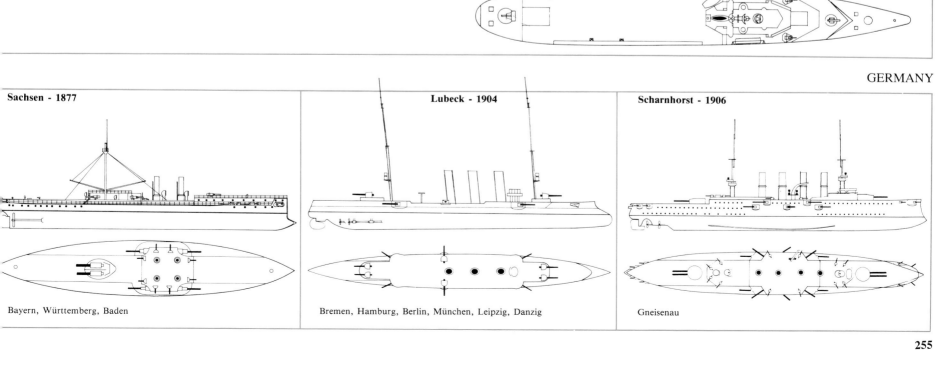

Sachsen - 1877

Bayern, Württemberg, Baden

Lubeck - 1904

Bremen, Hamburg, Berlin, München, Leipzig, Danzig

Scharnhorst - 1906

Gneisenau

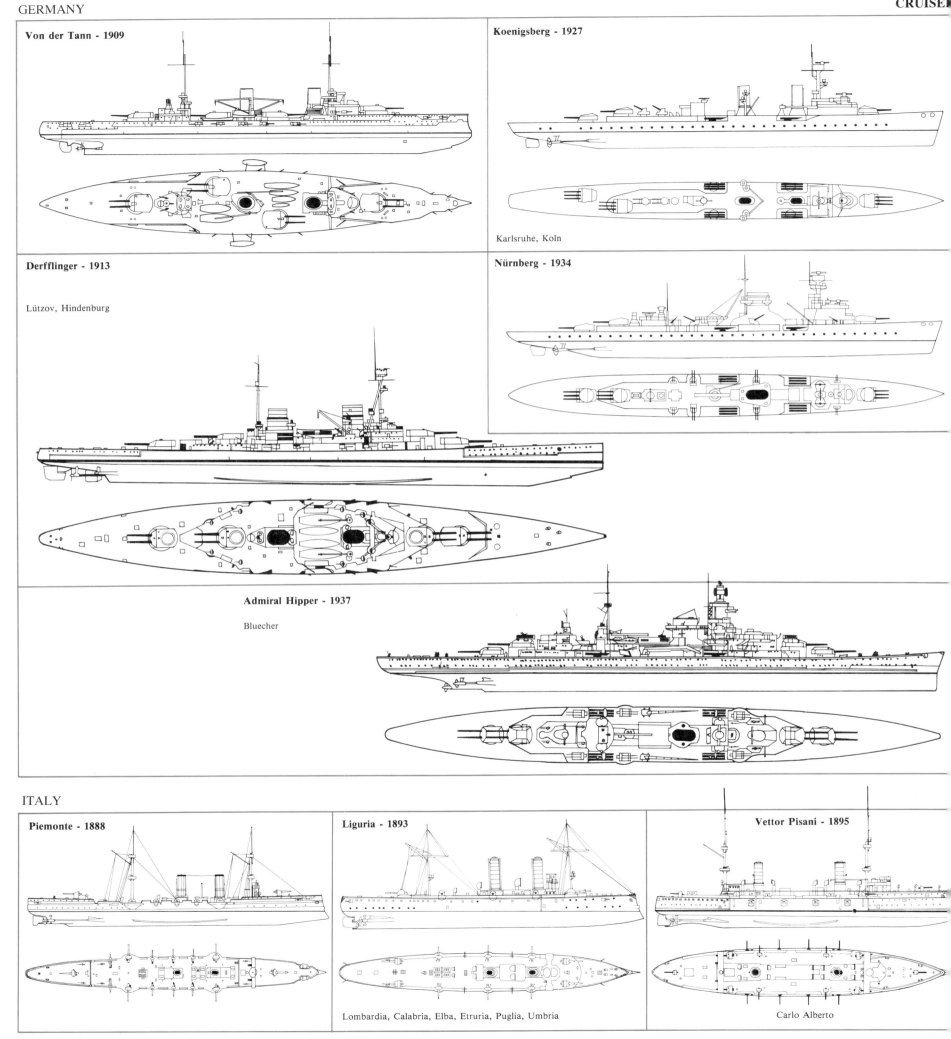

Von der Tann - 1909

Koenigsberg - 1927

Karlsruhe, Koln

Derfflinger - 1913

Lützov, Hindenburg

Nürnberg - 1934

Admiral Hipper - 1937

Bluecher

ITALY

Piemonte - 1888

Liguria - 1893

Vettor Pisani - 1895

Lombardia, Calabria, Elba, Etruria, Puglia, Umbria

Carlo Alberto

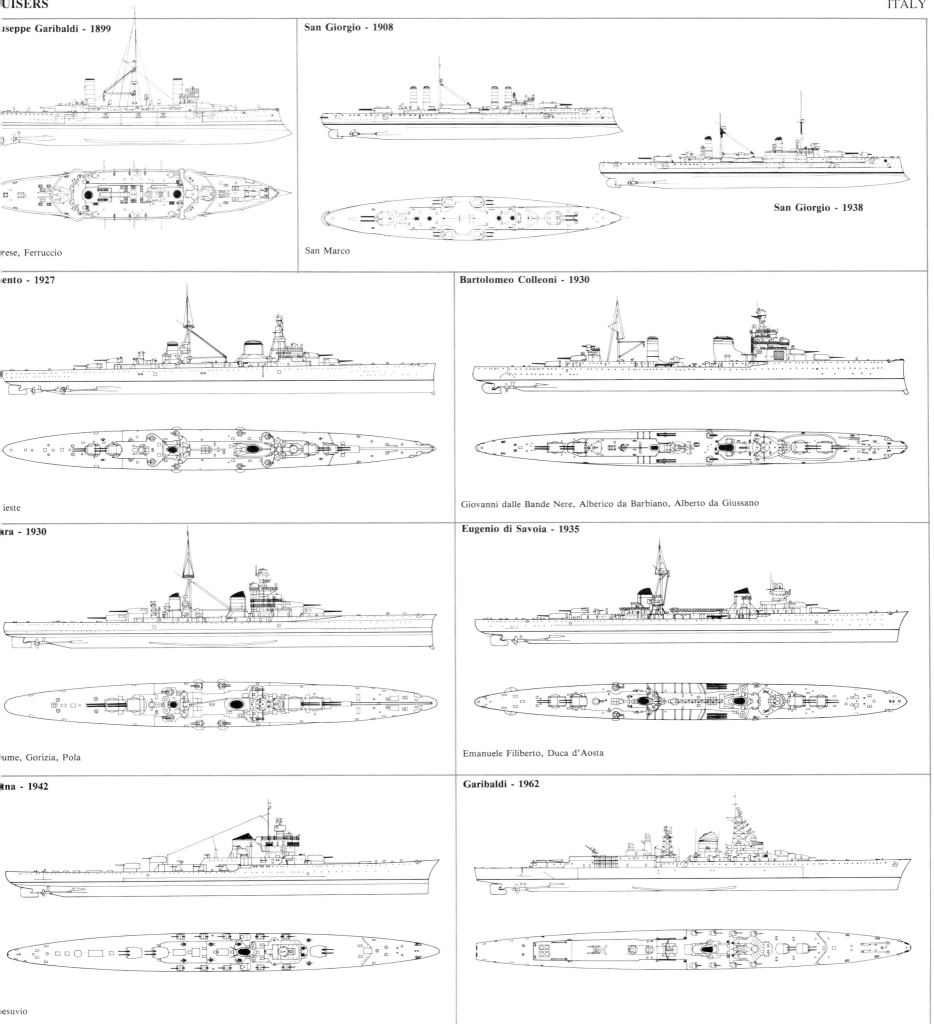

useppe Garibaldi - 1899

San Giorgio - 1908

San Giorgio - 1938

rese, Ferruccio

San Marco

ento - 1927

Bartolomeo Colleoni - 1930

ieste

Giovanni dalle Bande Nere, Alberico da Barbiano, Alberto da Giussano

ra - 1930

Eugenio di Savoia - 1935

ume, Gorizia, Pola

Emanuele Filiberto, Duca d'Aosta

na - 1942

Garibaldi - 1962

esuvio

Andrea Doria - 1963

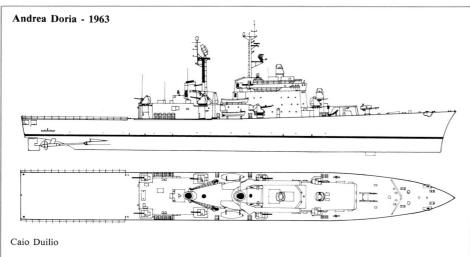

Caio Duilio

Vittorio Veneto - 1967

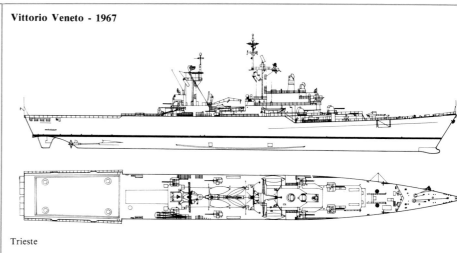

Trieste

Giuseppe Garibaldi - 1982

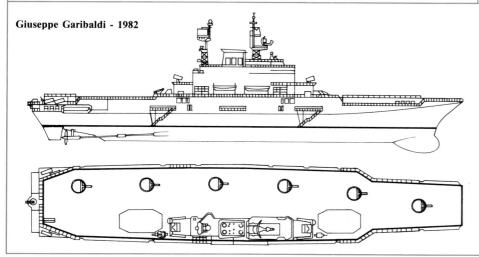

HOLLAND

De Ruyter - 1935

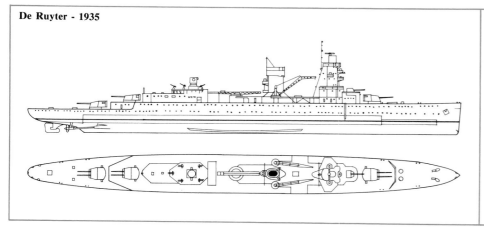

De Ruyter - 1944

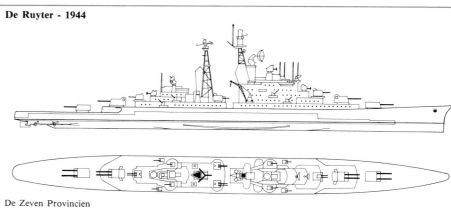

De Zeven Provincien

SPAIN

Principe Alfonso - 1925

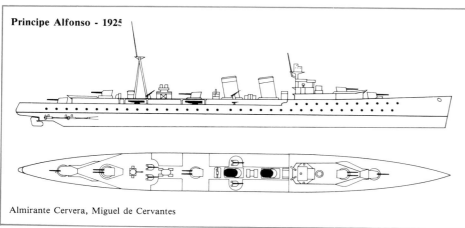

Almirante Cervera, Miguel de Cervantes

Canarias - 1931

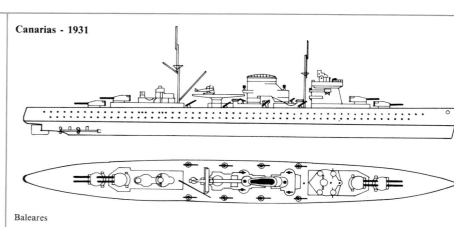

Baleares

Esmeralda II - 1894

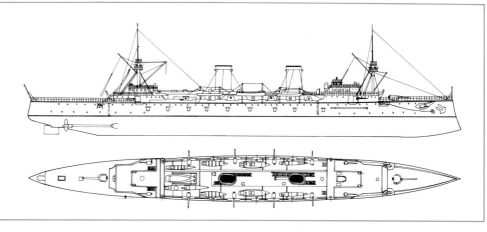

Olympia - 1892

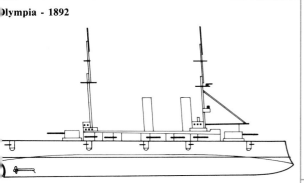

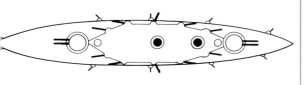

CA 3 Brooklyn - 1895

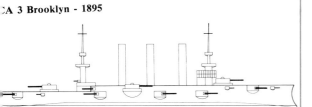

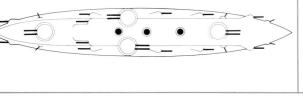

CL 4 Omaha - 1920

CL 5 Milwaukee, CL 6 Cincinnati, CL 7 Raleigh, CL 8 Detroit, CL 9 Richmond, CL 10 Concord, CL 11 Trenton, CL 12 Marblehead, CL 13 Memphis

CC 1 Lexington - 1916

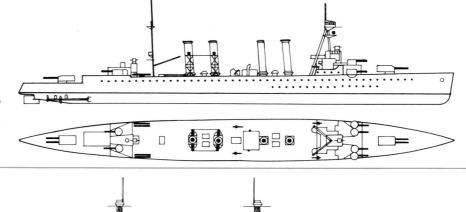

CC 2 Constellation, CC 3 Saratoga, CC 4 Ranger, CC 5 Constitution, CC 6 United States

CC 1 Lexington - 1920

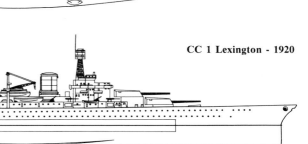

CA 24 Pensacola - 1929

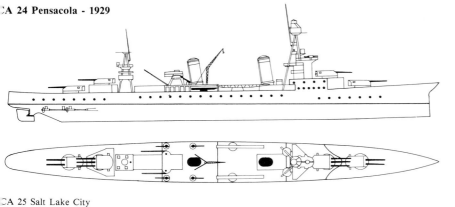

CA 25 Salt Lake City

CA 33 Portland - 1932

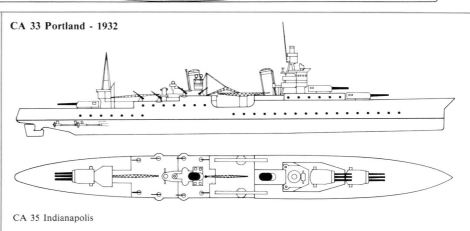

CA 35 Indianapolis

CL 40 Brooklyn - 1936

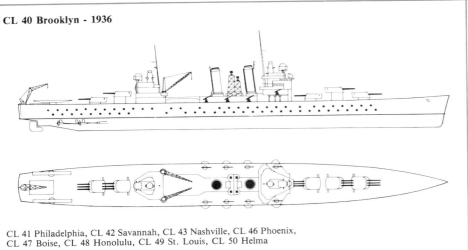

CL 41 Philadelphia, CL 42 Savannah, CL 43 Nashville, CL 46 Phoenix,
CL 47 Boise, CL 48 Honolulu, CL 49 St. Louis, CL 50 Helma

CL 51 Atlanta - 1941

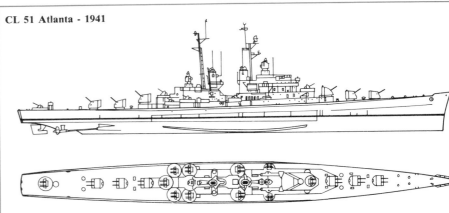
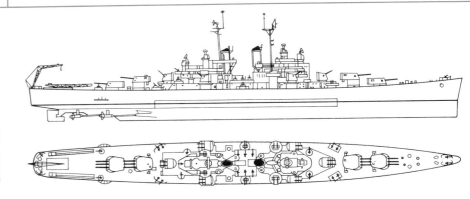

CL 52 Juneau I, CL 53 San Diego, CL 54 San Juan, CL 95 Oakland,
CL 96 Reno, CL 97 Flint, CL 98 Tucson, CL 119 Juneau II,
CL 120 Spokane, CL 121 Fresno

CL 55 Cleveland - 1941

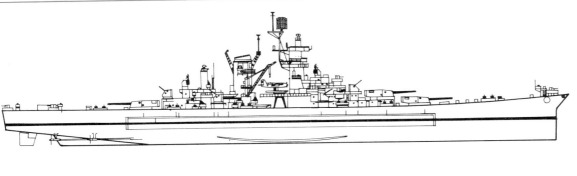

CL 56 Columbia, 57 Montpellier, 58 Denver, 59 Amsterdam I, 60 Santa Fé, 61 Tallahasse I, 62 Birmingham,
63 Mobile, 64 Vincennes, 65 Pasadena, 66 Springfield, 67 Topeka; CL 76 New Haven I, 77 Huntington I, 78
Dayton I, 79 Wilmington I, 80 Biloxi, 81 Houston, 82, Providence, 83 Manchester, 84 Buffalo I, 85 Fargo I,
86 Vicksburg, 87 Duluth I, 88, 89 Miami, 90 Astoria, 91 Oklahoma City, 92 Little Rock, 93 Galveston, 94 Youg-
stown, CL 99 Buffalo II, 100 Newark, 101 Amsterdam II, 102 Portsmouth, 103 Wilkes Barre, 104 Atlanta, 105
Dayton II, 106 Fargo II, 107 Huntington II, 108 Newark II, 109 New Haven II, 110 Buffalo III, 111 Wilmington
II, 112 Valleyo, 113 Helena, 114, 115 Roanoke, 116 Tallahasse II, 117 Cheyenne, 118 Chattanooga

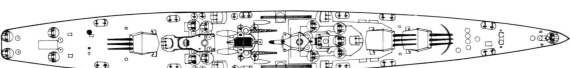

CB 1 Alaska - 1943

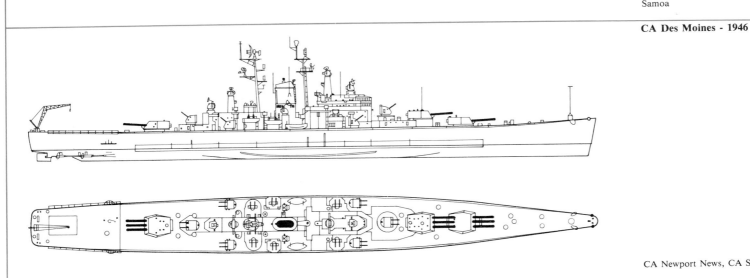

CB 2 Guam, CB 3 Hawai, CB 4 Philippines, CB 5 Puerto Rico, CB 6
Samoa

CA Des Moines - 1946

CA Newport News, CA Salem

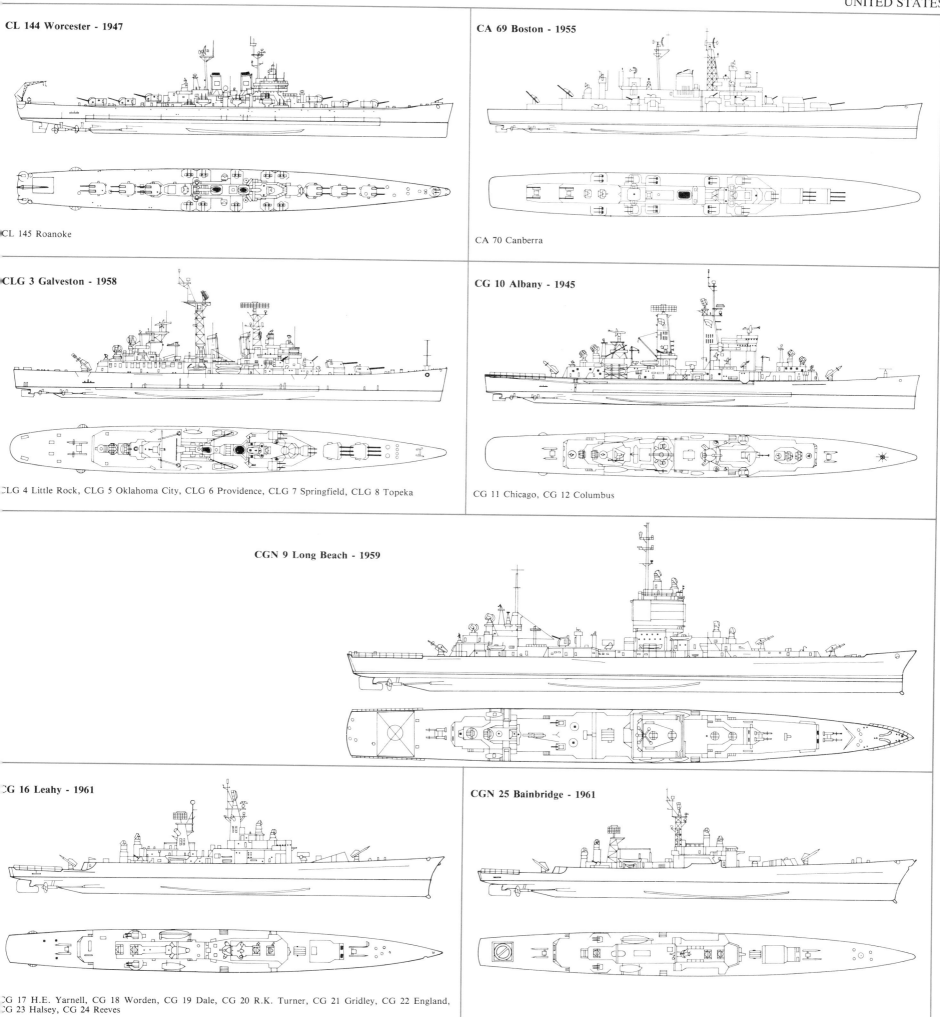

CL 144 Worcester - 1947

CL 145 Roanoke

CA 69 Boston - 1955

CA 70 Canberra

CLG 3 Galveston - 1958

CLG 4 Little Rock, CLG 5 Oklahoma City, CLG 6 Providence, CLG 7 Springfield, CLG 8 Topeka

CG 10 Albany - 1945

CG 11 Chicago, CG 12 Columbus

CGN 9 Long Beach - 1959

CG 16 Leahy - 1961

CG 17 H.E. Yarnell, CG 18 Worden, CG 19 Dale, CG 20 R.K. Turner, CG 21 Gridley, CG 22 England,
CG 23 Halsey, CG 24 Reeves

CGN 25 Bainbridge - 1961

CG 26 Belknap - 1963

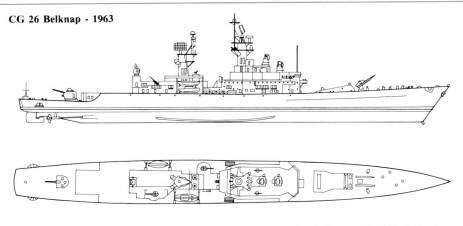

CG 27 J. Daniels, CG 28 Wainwright, CG 29 Jouett, CG 30 Horne, CG 31 Sterett, CG 32 W.H. Stanley, CG 33 Fox, CG 34 Biddle

CGN 35 Truxtun - 1964

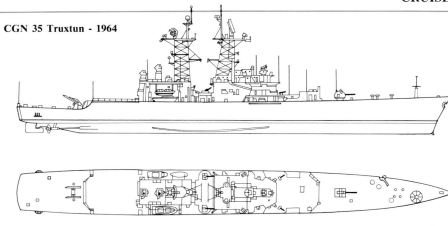

CGN 36 California - 1971

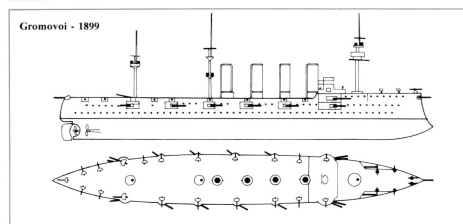

CGN 37 South Carolina

CGN 38 Virginia - 1974

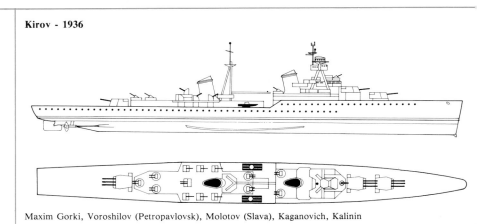

CGN 39 Texas, CGN 40 Mississippi, CGN 41 Arkansas

RUSSIA—USSR

Gromovoi - 1899

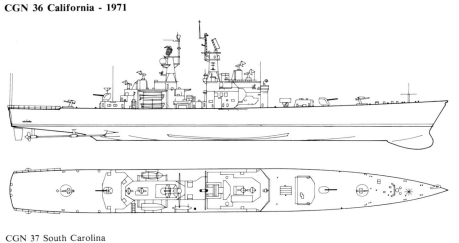

Kirov - 1936

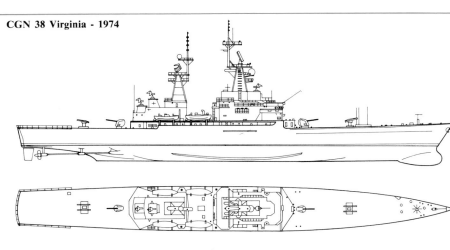

Maxim Gorki, Voroshilov (Petropavlovsk), Molotov (Slava), Kaganovich, Kalinin

Chapaev - 1940

Chkalov (Komsomolest), Frunze, Kuibishev, Ordzhonikidze, Zheleznyakov

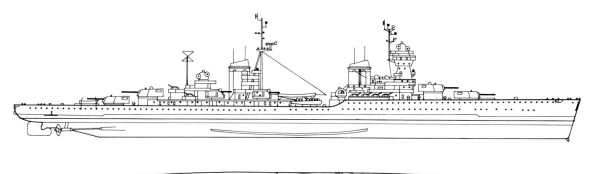

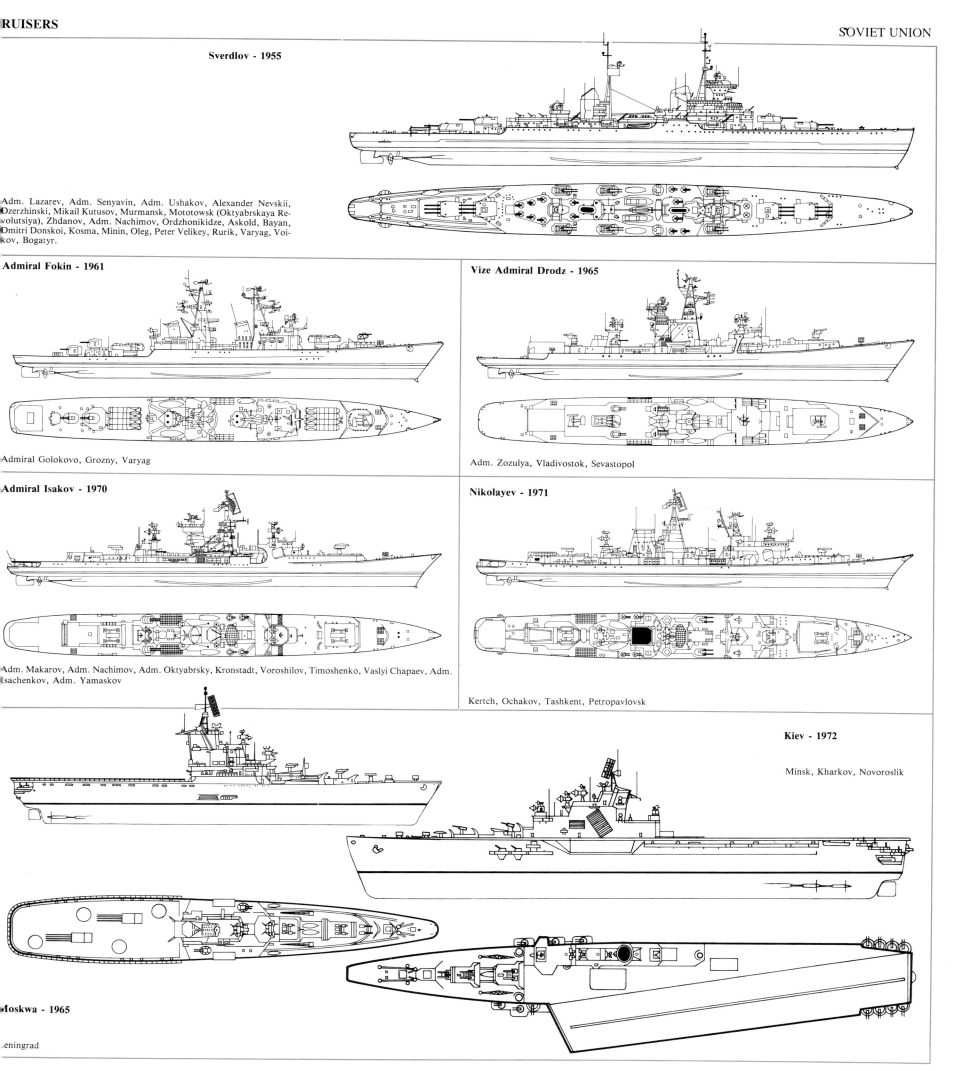

Sverdlov - 1955

Adm. Lazarev, Adm. Senyavin, Adm. Ushakov, Alexander Nevskii, Dzerzhinski, Mikail Kutusov, Murmansk, Mototowsk (Oktyabrskaya Revolutsiya), Zhdanov, Adm. Nachimov, Ordzhonikidze, Askold, Bayan, Dmitri Donskoi, Kosma, Minin, Oleg, Peter Velikey, Rurik, Varyag, Voikov, Bogatyr.

Admiral Fokin - 1961

Admiral Golokovo, Grozny, Varyag

Vize Admiral Drodz - 1965

Adm. Zozulya, Vladivostok, Sevastopol

Admiral Isakov - 1970

Adm. Makarov, Adm. Nachimov, Adm. Oktyabrsky, Kronstadt, Voroshilov, Timoshenko, Vaslyi Chapaev, Adm. Isachenkov, Adm. Yamaskov

Nikolayev - 1971

Kertch, Ochakov, Tashkent, Petropavlovsk

Kiev - 1972

Minsk, Kharkov, Novoroslik

Moskwa - 1965

Leningrad

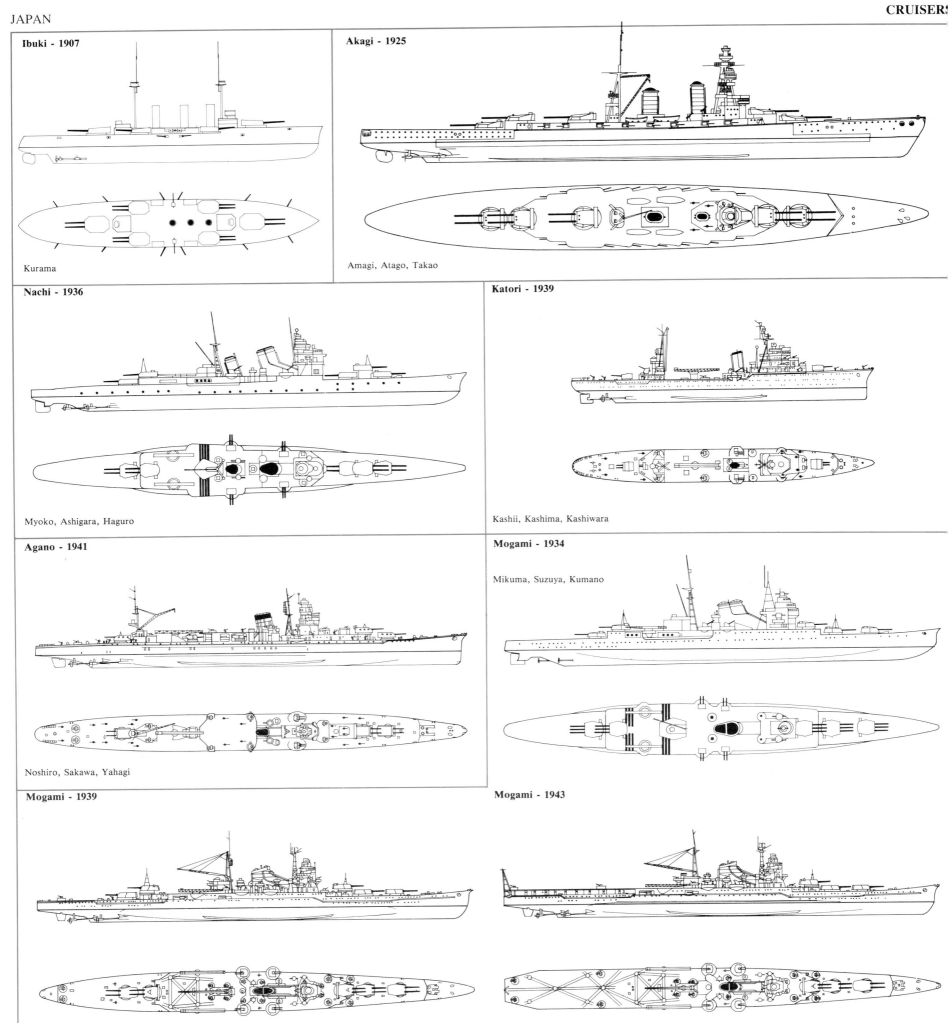

Ibuki - 1907

Kurama

Akagi - 1925

Amagi, Atago, Takao

Nachi - 1936

Myoko, Ashigara, Haguro

Katori - 1939

Kashii, Kashima, Kashiwara

Agano - 1941

Noshiro, Sakawa, Yahagi

Mogami - 1934

Mikuma, Suzuya, Kumano

Mogami - 1939

Mogami - 1943

Compendium of torpedo boats drawn to scale

Th 2 - 1884 (D)

Th 1 - 1884 (D)

Mistral - 1903 (F)

64 Th - 1880 (GB)

24 YA - 1886 (GB)

Aquila - 1888 (I)

Nibbio - 1878 (I)

Lightning - 1877 (GB)

Hydra - 1901 (NL)

Winslow N 5 - 1898 (USA)

2 Th - 1878 (GB)

80 YA - 1886 (GB)

98 Th - 1900 (GB)

10 Th - 1878 (GB)

TB 1-6 - 1910 (A)

Pellicano - 1900 (I)

Batum - 1880 (USSR)

Forban - 1895 (F)

1-22 - 1910-19 (E)

Aldebaran - 1883-84 (I)

91 Th - 1894 (GB)

Sirio - 1905 (I)

Fatum - 1888 (I)

Viper N 17 - 1896 (A)

Porter N 6 - 1895 (USA)

Svaerdfisken - 1881 (DK)

Coureur - 1888 (F)

14 - 1906 (GB)

130 - 1887 (F)

Ariete - 1885 (E)

Yastreb - 1939 (USSR)

22 Th - 1885 (GB)

Avant Garde - 1889 (F)

Ciclone - 1942 (I)

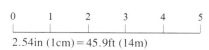

0 1 2 3 4 5

2.54in (1cm) = 45.9ft (14m)

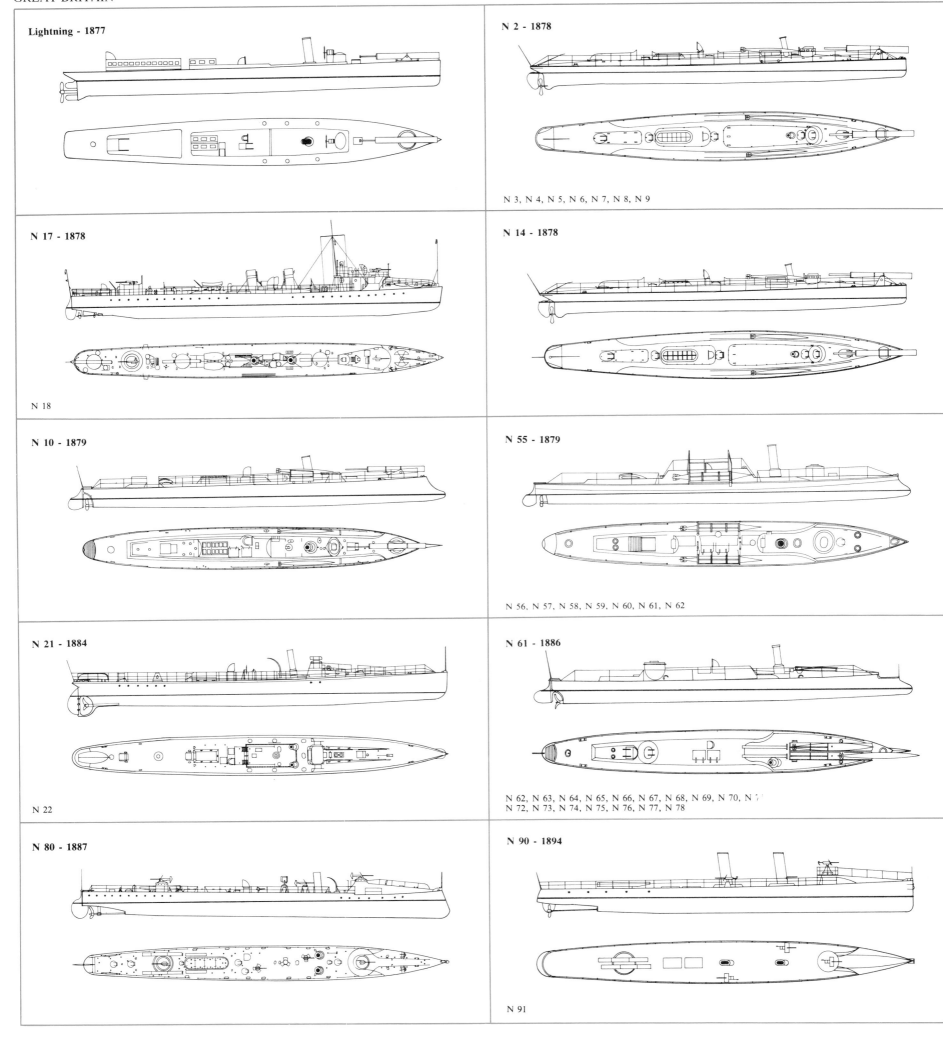

Lightning - 1877

N 2 - 1878

N 3, N 4, N 5, N 6, N 7, N 8, N 9

N 17 - 1878

N 18

N 14 - 1878

N 10 - 1879

N 55 - 1879

N 56, N 57, N 58, N 59, N 60, N 61, N 62

N 21 - 1884

N 22

N 61 - 1886

N 62, N 63, N 64, N 65, N 66, N 67, N 68, N 69, N 70, N 71,
N 72, N 73, N 74, N 75, N 76, N 77, N 78

N 80 - 1887

N 90 - 1894

N 91

N 98 - 1899

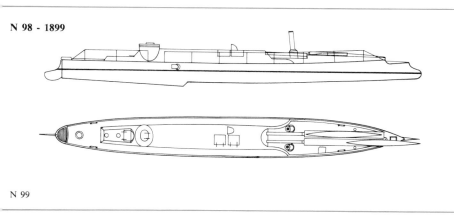

N 99

N 13 - 1907

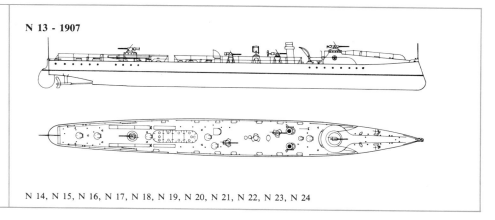

N 14, N 15, N 16, N 17, N 18, N 19, N 20, N 21, N 22, N 23, N 24

FRANCE

N 130 - 1887

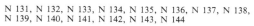

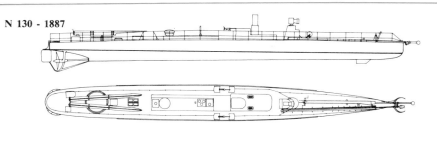

N 131, N 132, N 133, N 134, N 135, N 136, N 137, N 138,
N 139, N 140, N 141, N 142, N 143, N 144

Coureur - 1888

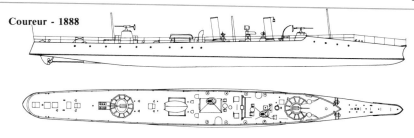

Avant Garde - 1889

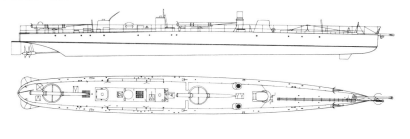
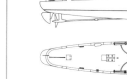

Alarme - 1888

Temeraire, Aventurier, Defi

Forban - 1895

Mistral - 1903

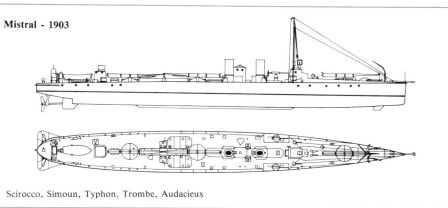

Scirocco, Simoun, Typhon, Trombe, Audacieux

GERMANY

Th 2 - 1884

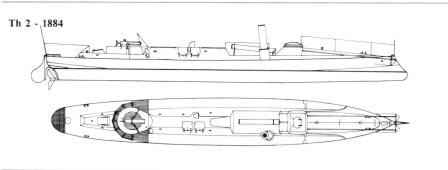

T 13 - 1944

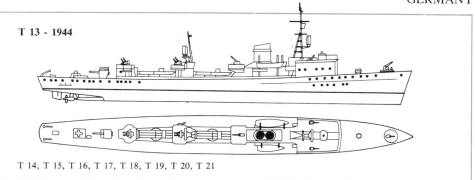

T 14, T 15, T 16, T 17, T 18, T 19, T 20, T 21

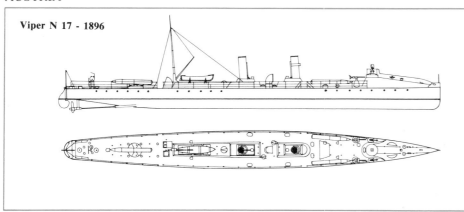

Viper N 17 - 1896

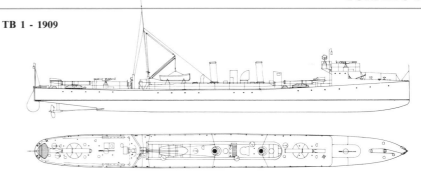

TB 1 - 1909

TB 2, TB 3, TB 4, TB 5, TB 6

HOLLAND

SWEDEN

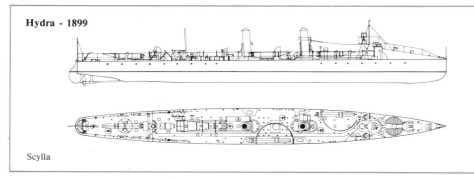

Hydra - 1899

Scylla

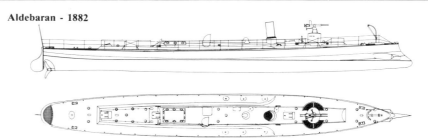

Agne - 1891

Agda

ITALY

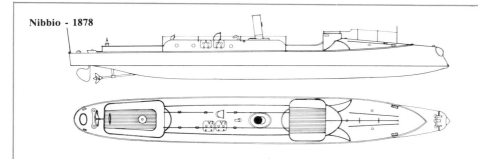

Nibbio - 1878

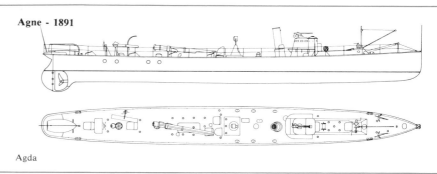

Aldebaran - 1882

Antares, Andromeda, Centauro, Dragone, Pegaso, Perseo, Sagittario
Sirio, Orione

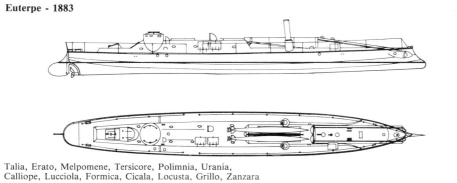

Euterpe - 1883

Talia, Erato, Melpomene, Tersicore, Polimnia, Urania,
Calliope, Lucciola, Formica, Cicala, Locusta, Grillo, Zanzara

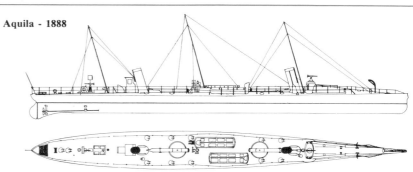

Aquila - 1888

Sparviero, Falco, Nibbio, Avvoltoio

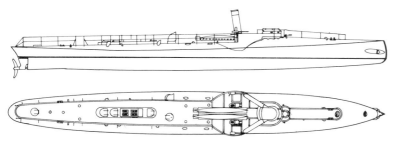

Fatum - 1892

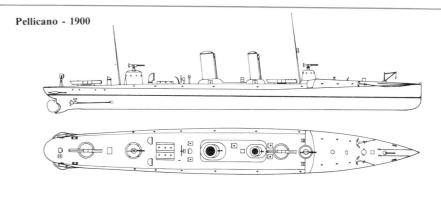

Pellicano - 1900

Sirio - 1905

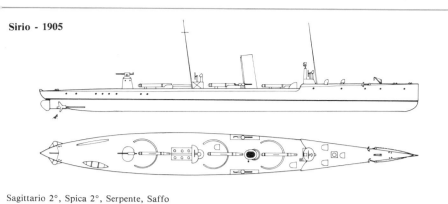

Sagittario 2°, Spica 2°, Serpente, Saffo

Ciclone - 1942

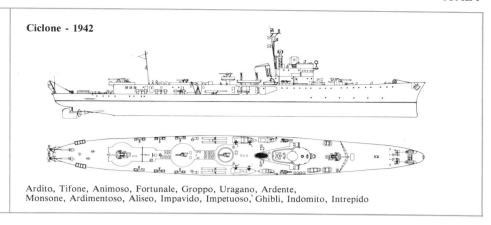

Ardito, Tifone, Animoso, Fortunale, Groppo, Uragano, Ardente,
Monsone, Ardimentoso, Aliseo, Impavido, Impetuoso,' Ghibli, Indomito, Intrepido

SPAIN

Ariete - 1885

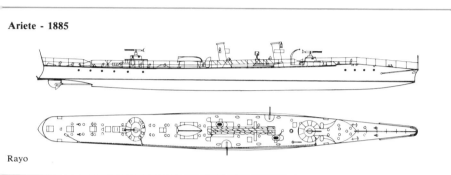

Rayo

N 1 - 1910

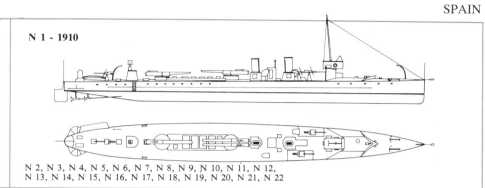

N 2, N 3, N 4, N 5, N 6, N 7, N 8, N 9, N 10, N 11, N 12,
N 13, N 14, N 15, N 16, N 17, N 18, N 19, N 20, N 21, N 22

DENMARK

Svaerdfisken - 1881

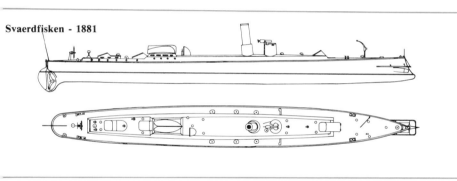

Havhesten - 1888

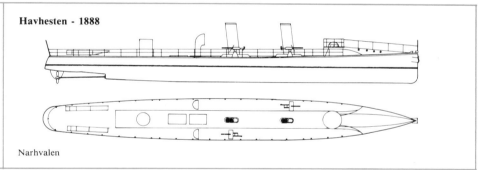

Narhvalen

RUSSIA

Batum - 1880

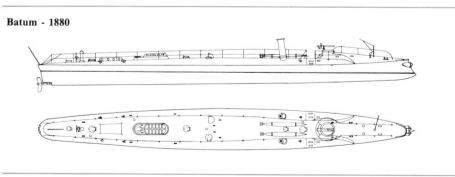

Normand - Pernov N 103 - 1891

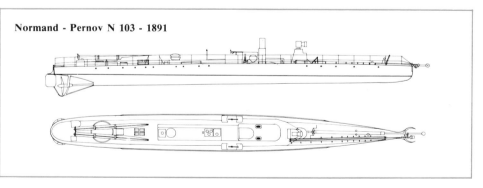

UNITED STATES

Porter N 6 - 1895

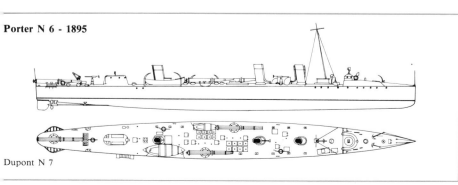

Dupont N 7

Foote N 3 - 1894

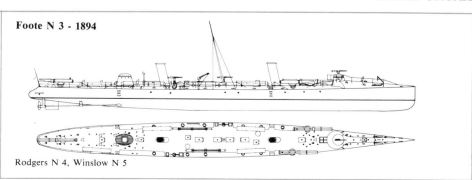

Rodgers N 4, Winslow N 5

Compendium of destroyers drawn to scale

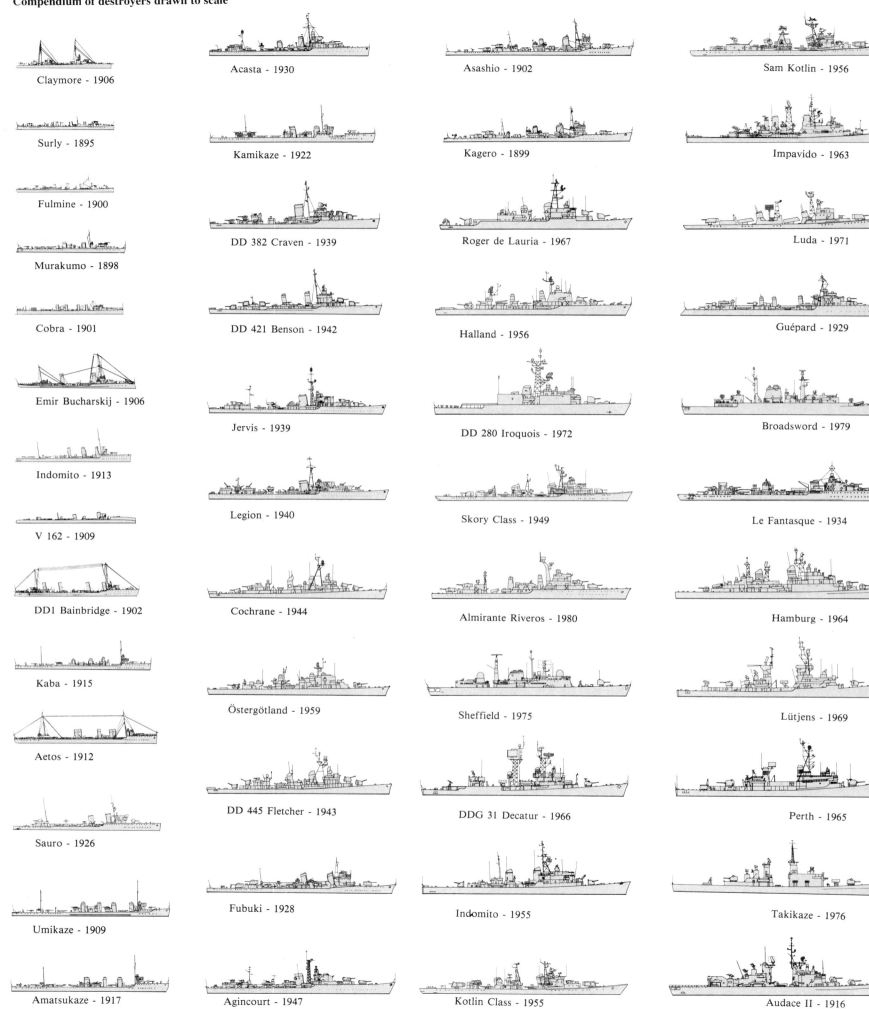

Claymore - 1906

Surly - 1895

Fulmine - 1900

Murakumo - 1898

Cobra - 1901

Emir Bucharskij - 1906

Indomito - 1913

V 162 - 1909

DD1 Bainbridge - 1902

Kaba - 1915

Aetos - 1912

Sauro - 1926

Umikaze - 1909

Amatsukaze - 1917

Acasta - 1930

Kamikaze - 1922

DD 382 Craven - 1939

DD 421 Benson - 1942

Jervis - 1939

Legion - 1940

Cochrane - 1944

Östergötland - 1959

DD 445 Fletcher - 1943

Fubuki - 1928

Agincourt - 1947

Asashio - 1902

Kagero - 1899

Roger de Lauria - 1967

Halland - 1956

DD 280 Iroquois - 1972

Skory Class - 1949

Almirante Riveros - 1980

Sheffield - 1975

DDG 31 Decatur - 1966

Indomito - 1955

Kotlin Class - 1955

Sam Kotlin - 1956

Impavido - 1963

Luda - 1971

Guépard - 1929

Broadsword - 1979

Le Fantasque - 1934

Hamburg - 1964

Lütjens - 1969

Perth - 1965

Takikaze - 1976

Audace II - 1916

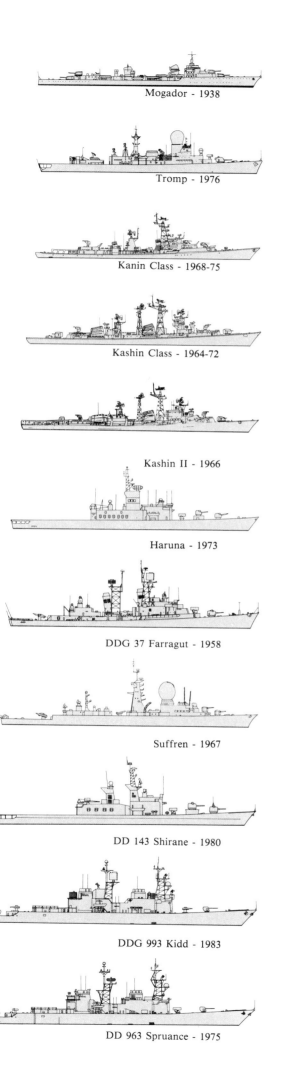

Mogador - 1938

Tromp - 1976

Kanin Class - 1968-75

Kashin Class - 1964-72

Kashin II - 1966

Haruna - 1973

DDG 37 Farragut - 1958

Suffren - 1967

DD 143 Shirane - 1980

DDG 993 Kidd - 1983

DD 963 Spruance - 1975

Compendium of frigates and corvettes drawn to scale

Flowers - 1940

Thetis Class - 1961

Hvidbjornen - 1961

Castle - 1943

D'Estienne D'Orves - 1973

Descubierta - 1975

Jiang-Nan - 1966

Riga Class - 1955

River - 1942

Loch More - 1944

Chikugo - 1970

Isuzu - 1961

Oliver Hazard Perry - 1976

Kortenaer - 1976

Niteroi - 1974

Brooke - 1966

Maestrale - 1981

Amazon - 1971

Leander - 1961

Lupo - 1976

Annapolis - 1963

Köln - 1958

Kola Class - 1960

E 52 Type - 1956

0   1   2   3   4   5

2.54in (1cm) = 76.4ft (23.3m)

Surly - 1893

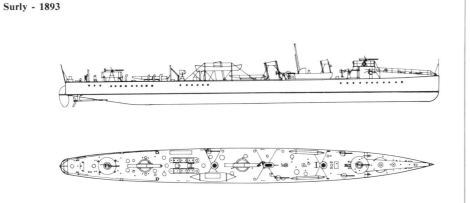

Rocket, Shark

Cobra - 1901

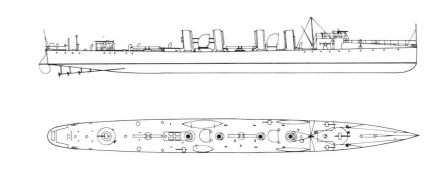

Quail - 1895

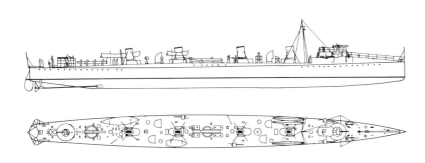

Sparrowhawk, Trasher, Virago, Earnest, Griffon, Locust, Panther, Seal, Wolf

Swift - 1908

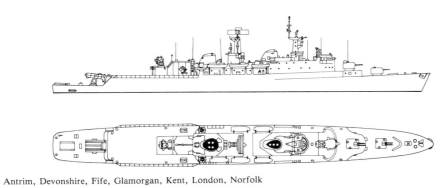

County - 1970

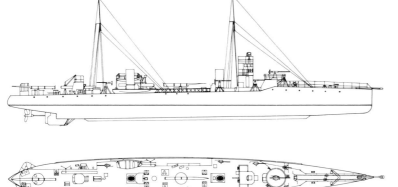

Antrim, Devonshire, Fife, Glamorgan, Kent, London, Norfolk

Sheffield - 1975

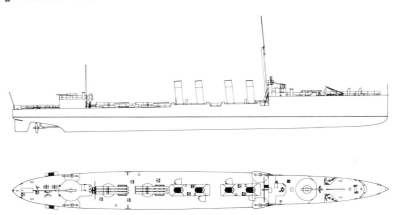

Birmingham, Coventry, Cardiff, Newcastle, Glasgow, Exeter, Southampton

FRANCE

Claymore - 1904

Stylet, Tromblon, Pierrier, Obusier, Mortier, Carquois,
Trident, Fleuret, Coutelas, Cognée, Hache, Massue

Enseigne Gabolde - 1913

Mecanicien Principal Letin, Enseigne Roux

ESTROYERS

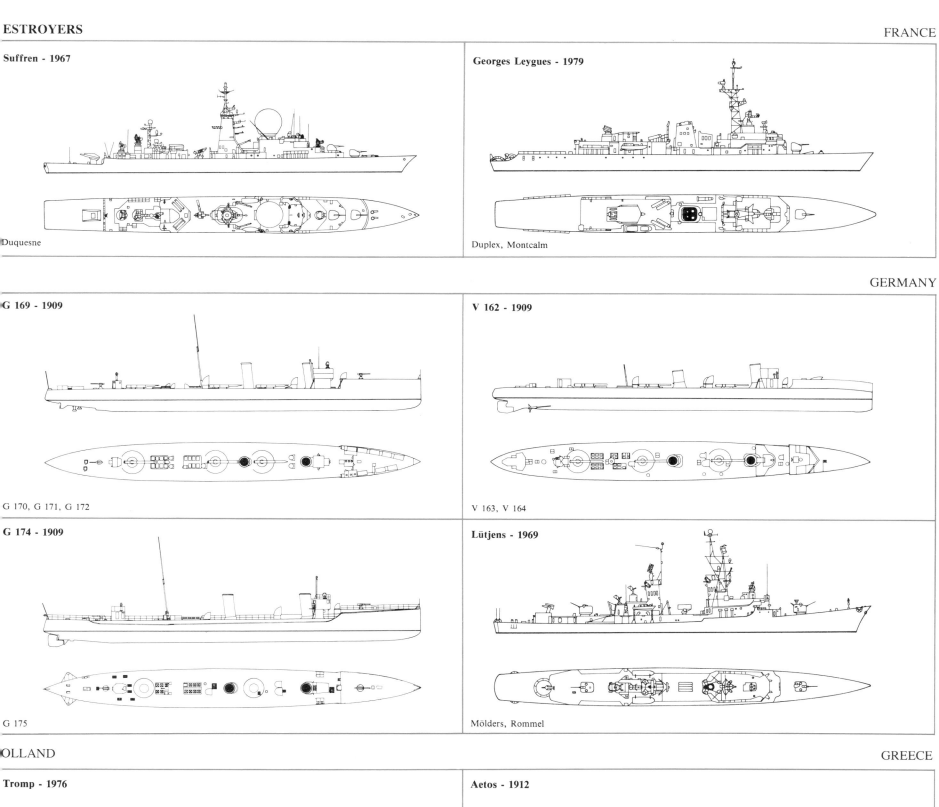

Suffren - 1967

Duquesne

Georges Leygues - 1979

Duplex, Montcalm

G 169 - 1909

G 170, G 171, G 172

V 162 - 1909

V 163, V 164

G 174 - 1909

G 175

Lütjens - 1969

Mölders, Rommel

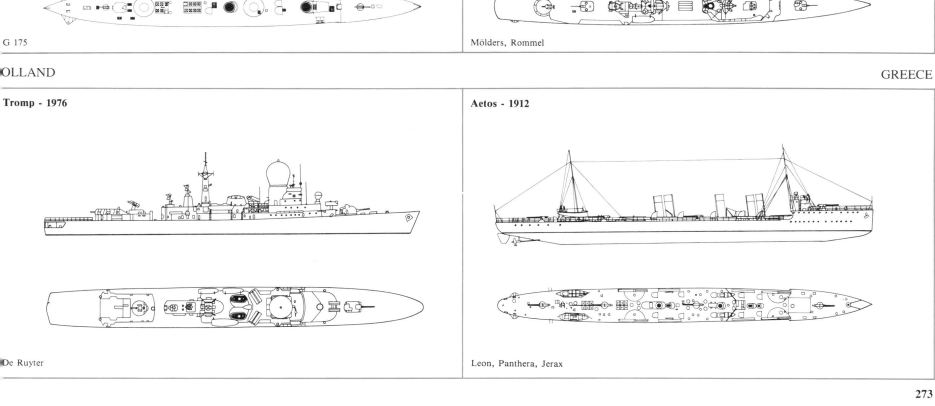

Tromp - 1976

De Ruyter

Aetos - 1912

Leon, Panthera, Jerax

Indomito - 1913

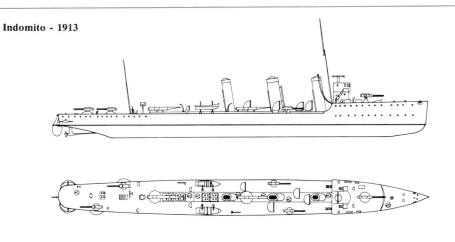

Intrepido, Irrequieto, Impavido, Impetuoso, Insidioso, Ardente, Ardito

Audace 2° - 1916

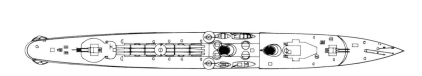

Sauro - 1926

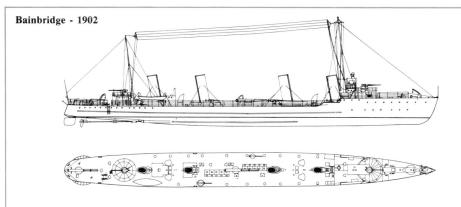

Battisti, Manin, Nullo

Impavido - 1963

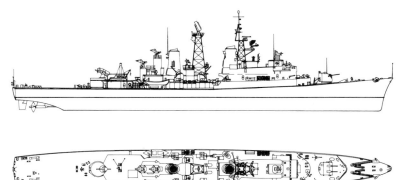

Intrepido

UNITED STATES

Bainbridge - 1902

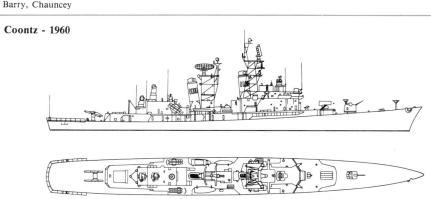

Barry, Chauncey

Hopkins - 1903

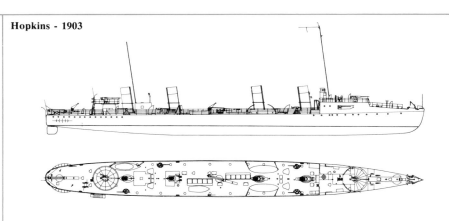

Hull

Coontz - 1960

Farragut, Luce, MacDonough, King, Mahan, Dahlgren, William V. Pratt, Dewey, Preble

Spruance - 1975

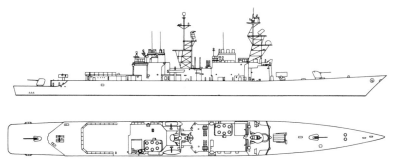

Paul F. Foster, Kinkaid, Hewitt, Elliott, Arthur W. Radford, Peterson, Caron, David R. Ray, Oldendorf, John Young, Comte de Grasse, O'Brien, Merrill, Briscoe, Stump, Conolly, Moosburgger, John Rodgers, John Hancock, Nicholson, Leftwich, Cushing, Harry W. Hill, O'Bannon, Thorn

Iroquois - 1972

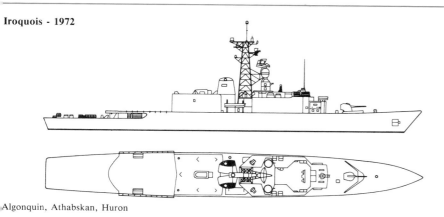

Algonquin, Athabaskan, Huron

Perth - 1965

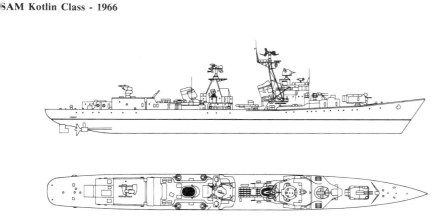

Brisbane, Hobart

Emir Bucharskij - 1904

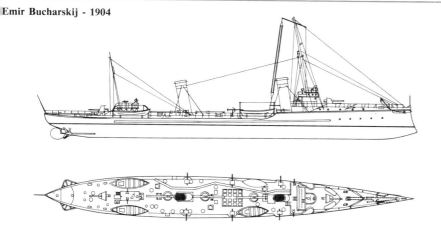

Finn, Moskvitjanin, Dobrovolec

Kanin Class - 1957

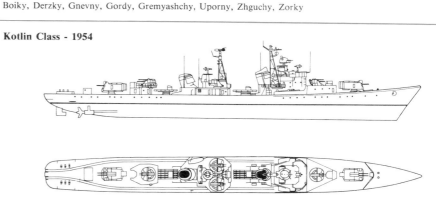

Boiky, Derzky, Gnevny, Gordy, Gremyashchy, Uporny, Zhguchy, Zorky

Skory Class - 1949

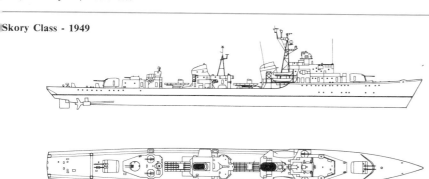

Bditelny, Bessnervny, Bessmenny, Bezupretchny, Bezukoriznenny, Ognenny, Ostervenely, Ostorozhny, Ostroglazny, Otchayanny, Otretovenny, Otvetstvenny, Ozhestochenny, Ozhivlenny, Serdity, Seriozny, Smely, Smotryashchy, Smyslenny, Sokrushitelny, Solidny, Sovershenny, Sposobny, Statny, Stepenny, Stojky, Stremitelny, Surovy, Svobodny, Vazhny, Vdumchivy, Verdushchy, Verny, Vidny, Vikhrevoy, Vnesapny, Vnimatelny, Volevoy, Vrazumitelny

Kotlin Class - 1954

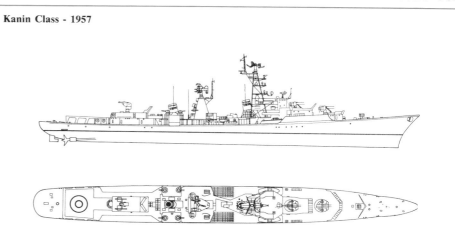

Bessledny, Blagorodny, Blestyashchy, Burlivy, Byvalvy, Dalnevostochny Komsomolets, Naporisty, Mostovsky Komsomolets, Plamenny, Speshny, Spokoiny, Svedushchy, Svetly, Vdokhnovenny, Vesky, Vliyatelny, Vozmushchenny, Vyderzhanny, Vyzyvayuschy

SAM Kotlin Class - 1966

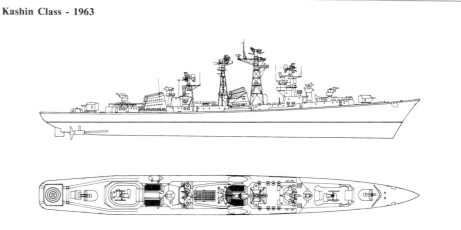

Bravy, Nakhodchvy, Nastoychivy, Nesokrushimy, Skromny, Skrytny, Soznatelny, Vozbuzhdenny

Kashin Class - 1963

Komsomolets Ukrainy, Krasny Kavkaz, Krasny Krim, Obraztsovy, Odarenny, Ognevoy, Provorny, Skory, Reshitelny, Sderzhanny, Slavny, Smely, Smetlivy, Smishlenny, Soobrazitelny, Sposobny, Steregushchy, Strogy, Stroyny

Murakumo - 1898

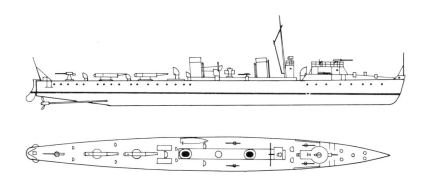

Shinonome, Yugure, Shiranui, Kagero, Usugumo

Umikaze - 1909

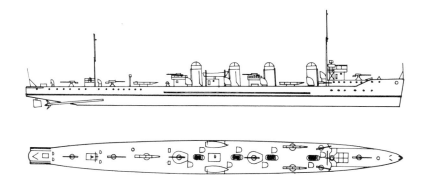

Yamakaze

Kaba - 1915

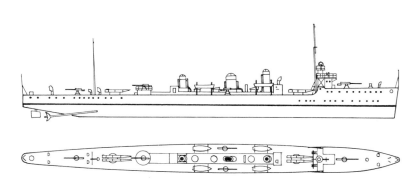

Maitsu, Kashiva, Katsura, Kaede, Kiri, Kusonoki, Ume, Sakaki, Sugi

Amatsukaze - 1917

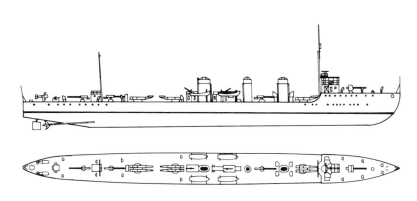

Isikaze, Takitsukaze, Hamakaze

Kamikaze - 1922

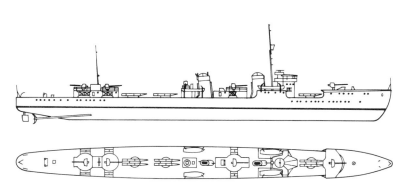

Asakaze, Harukaze, Matsukaze, Hatakaze, Oite, Hayate, Asamagi, Yumagi

Fubuki - 1928

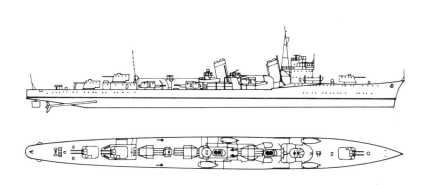

Shinonome, Usugumo, Shirakumo, Isonami, Shirayuchi, Hatsuyuki, Miyuki, Murakumo, Uranami, Shikinami, Ayanami, Asagiri, Sagiri, Yuguri, Amagiri, Oboro, Akebono, Sazanami, Ushio

Asashio - 1937

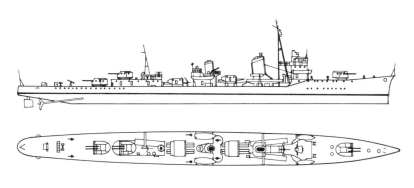

Oshio, Michshio, Arashio, Natsugumo, Yamagumo, Minegumo, Asagumo, Arare, Kasumi

Haruna - 1973

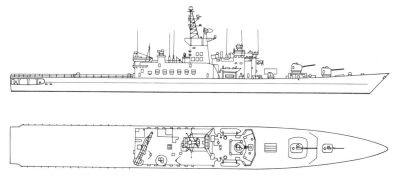

Hiei

TECHNICAL DATA

The following tables give the technical details of those ships either named or illustrated in the text. These ships represent only a part of those built and in service.

The dimensions refer to overall length, maximum beam, and mean draft under normal load. Displacement is usually full load.

For power plants consisting of reciprocating engines and turbines, the number indicates the number of propeller shafts; this does not necessarily correspond to the number of engines or turbines; in particular, ships with coupling and reduction gears usually had one three-turbine unit for each shaft.

A different criterion has been adopted for diesel engines and gas turbines, for which the number of engines has been indicated. For example, for *Deutschland*-type battleships, 8D does not mean that there were eight propellers (there were in fact only two) but eight engines, four per shaft. In most other ships the number of engines corresponds to the number of propellers. Similarly, four GT for cruisers and destroyers means four gas turbines to two propellers. Ships with two GT usually have two propellers, as well, except for the American *O.H. Perry*-type frigates which have two GT but only one propeller.

For armored ships, only the maximum thickness of the plates on the belt, decks, and gun turrets is given.

BATTLESHIPS – TECHNICAL DATA

Name	Launch Year	Length m	Length ft	Beam m	Beam ft	Draft m	Draft ft	Displacement t	Engine RE	Engine T	Horsepower	Speed in Knots	Range in Miles
GREAT BRITAIN													
Warrior	1860	127,8	419.2	17,6	58	8,07	26.4	9240	1		5470	14,3	727
Bellerophon	1865	91,94	301.6	17,0	56	7,5	24.8	7551	1		6520	14	602
Northumberland	1866	121,9	399.9	18,1	59.4	8,05	26.4	10627	1		7241	15,5	932
Hercules	1868	99,06	324.9	18,0	59	7,5	24.6	8677	1		7187	14,7	994
Monarch	1868	100,5	329.9	17,5	57.5	7,3	24.2	8322	1		7842	14,9	1242
Captain	1869	97,54	320	15,8	51.8	7,6	24.9	6950	2		5400	14,2	—
Devastation	1871	86,87	285	18,9	62.2	8,07	26.4	9387	4		6500	13,8	5716
Alexandra	1875	99,06	324.9	19,2	62.9	8,0	26.2	9492	2		8500	15	1242
Dreadnought	1875	97,54	320	19,4	63.8	8,1	26.7	10886	2		8200	15	3728
Inflexible	1876	97,54	320	22,8	75	7,5	24.6	11406	2		8407	14,7	
Temeraire	1876	86,87	285	18,9	62	8,1	26.7	8412	2		7500	14,6	
Colossus	1882	99,06	324.9	20,7	68	7,8	25.7	9150	2		5500	14	
Collingwood	1882	99,05	324.9	20,7	67.9	7,9	25.9	9640	2		7000	15	4350
Royal Sovereign	1891	115,8	379.9	22,8	75	8,3	27.4	14370	2		11500	17	1740
Majestic	1895	118,8	389.7	22,8	75	8,3	27.4	15000	2		12000	17,5	
Cornwallis	1901	120,7	428.8	23,0	75.4	8,0	26.2	14000	2		18000	19	
Dreadnought	1906	158,5	520	25,0	82	9,4	31	17900	2		23000	21	3604
King George V	1911	182,1	597.4	27,1	88.9	8,7	28.8	25700		4	27000	21	2522
Queen Elizabeth	1913	195,0	639.7	27,6	90.5	9,0	29.5	33000		4	75000	25	2734
Queen Elizabeth	*	195,0	639.7	31,7	104	9.7	31.8	36000		4	82000	24	3107
Agincourt	1913	204,5	670.9	27,1	88.9	8.2	26.9	30250		2	34000	22	
Resolution	1915	189,1	620.4	27,0	88.5	8,7	28.5	31200		4	40000	23	2610
Resolution	*	189,1	620.4	30,9	101.3	8,7	28.5	33000		4	42000	21	2610
Nelson	1925	216,4	710	32,3	106	9,1	29.8	38000		2	45000	23	3107
King George V	1939	227,1	745	31,4	103	9,7	31.8	44460		4	110000	27,5	9321
Vanguard	1944	248,3	814.6	32,9	107.9	10,9	35.7	51420		4	130000	29,5	5592
FRANCE													
Gloire	1859	80,39	263.7	17,0	55.7	7,7	25.4	5618	1		2537	12,8	1025
Marengo	1868	86,20	282.8	17,3	56.9	8,4	27.6	7749	1		3781	13,7	2050
Dévastation	1879	95,00	311.6	20,4	67	7,3	24	9639	2		8160	15	1740
Amiral Duperré	1879	97,50	319.8	20,4	66.9	7,8	25.7	10480	2		7396	14,5	
Amiral Baudin	1883	104,6	343.2	21,3	70.0	7,8	25.7	11900	2		8400	15,2	1864
Indomptable	1883	85,0	278.8	18,0	59	7,9	25.9	7600	2		6600	15	1553
Magenta	1890	103,0	337.9	24,2	79.5	8,0	26.2	10800	2		11000	17	2485
Jaureguiberry	1893	108,5	356	22,1	72.6	8,3	27.2	11820	2		13800	17,5	2485
Henry IV	1899	108	354.3	22,2	72.8	7,5	24.6	9000	3		14500	17	4722
Jean Bart	1911	164,5	539.6	26,8	87.9	8,8	28.8	25850		2	28000	20	3728
Bretagne	1913	166,0	544.6	26,9	88.2	9,8	32.1	28500		2	29000	20	2920
Dunkerque	1935	214,3	703	31,1	102	9,6	31.4	35500		4	112500	29,5	4660
Richelieu	1939	247,8	813	33,0	108.2	10,7	35.1	47458		4	150000	30	3417
GERMANY													
König Wilhelm	1868	108,4	355.8	17,8	58.4	7,7	25.4	9757	1		8000	14	
Preussen	1873	93,63	307.1	16,3	53.5	7,2	23.8	6770	1		5400	14	1553
Kaiser	1874	85,34	280	18,4	60.3	7,4	24.3	7676	1		8000	14,5	2112
Brandenburgh	1891	113,9	373.6	19,5	63.9	7,8	25.5	10033	2		9640	16,5	2796
Nassau	1908	143,5	470.7	27,1	88.9	8,3	27.4	18500	3		22000	19,5	3541
Koenig	1913	175,4	575.4	29,5	96.7	9,2	30.1	28148		3	31000	21	4971
Bayern	1915	180,0	590.5	30,0	98.4	9,4	30.8	31691		3	48000	22	3116
Deutschland	1931	186,0	610.2	20,6	67.5	7,2	23.6	15900		8D	54000	26	13360
Scharnhorst	1936	229,8	753.9	30,0	98.4	9,1	30	38900		3	165000	31,5	6214
Bismarck	1939	248,0	813.6	36,0	118.1	10,2	33.4	50900		3	138000	29	5766
AUSTRIA													
Herzherzog Ferdinand Max	1865	79,9	262.3	15,9	52.3	7,0	23.1	5140	1		3000	10,3	478
Tegetthoff	1878	87,4	286.9	19,0	62.4	7,8	25.6	7390	1		7200	14	1864
Habsburg	1900	107,6	353	19,8	64.9	7,1	23.2	8340	2		12000	19	1988
Viribus Unitis	1911	160,0	524.9	27,3	89.5	8,2	26.9	21370		4	25000	20	2610
ITALY													
Re d'Italia	1863	84,3	276.5	16,6	54.4	6,7	21.9	5700	1		800	12	

Number of Guns/mm	Number of Guns/in	Machine guns/mm	TT	C	Belt Protection mm	in	Deck Protection mm	in	Turret Protection mm	in
28/178; 4/203	28/7; 4/8			704	114	4.4				
10/229; 3/178	10/9; 3/7				152 + 39	5.9 + 1.5				
4/229; 22/203; 2/178	4/9; 22/8; 2/7			704	140	5.5				
8/254; 2/229; 4/178	8/10; 2/9; 4/7				229 + 37	9 + 1.4				
4/305; 2/229; 1/178	4/12; 2/9; 1/7			575	178	7			254	10
4/305; 2/178	4/12; 2/7			472	203	7.9			254	10
4/305	4/12		2	358	305	12			330	12.9
2/305; 10/254	2/12; 10/10			674	305	12				
4/317	4/12.5	7	2	453	356	14			178 + 178	7 + 7
4/406	4/16			350	305 + 305	12 + 12	76	3	229 + 178	9 + 7
4/305; 4/254	4/12; 4/10		1		280	11				
4/305; 4/152	4/12; 4/6		2	345	457	17.9	76	3	406	15.9
4/305; 6/152	4/12; 6/6		4	480	457	17.9	76	3		
4/343; 10/152	4/13.5; 10/6	8	7	730	457	17.9				
4/305; 12/152; 16/76	4/12; 12/6; 16/3	8	5	757	229	9	100	3.9		
4/305; 12/152; 12/76	4/12; 12/6; 12/3	8	4	750	178	7	63	2.4	279	10.9
10/305; 23/76	10/12; 23/3		5	800	280	11	70	2.7	203	7.9
10/343; 16/102; 2/76	10/13.5; 16/4; 2/3		3	812	305	12	102	4	279	10.9
8/381; 16/152; 2/76	8/15; 12/6; 2/3		4	1234	330	12.9	32	1.2	330	12.9
8/381; 20/114	8/15; 20/4.5	32/40; 52/20		950	330	12.9	63	2.4	330	12.9
14/305; 20/152; 10/76	14/12; 20/6; 10/3		3	1267	229	9	25	0.9	229	9
8/381; 14/152; 2/76	8/15; 14/6; 2/3		4	997	330	12.9	25	0.9	330	12.9
8/381; 12/152; 8/102	8/15; 12/6; 8/4	24/40; 8/20		1000	330	12.9	25	0.9	330	12.9
9/406; 12/152; 6/120	9/16; 12/6; 6/4.7	15	2	1361	356	14	76	3	406	15.9
10/356; 16/133	10/14; 16/5.2	48/40		1613	381	15	127	5	406	15.9
8/381; 16/133	8/15; 16/5.2	71/40		1600	356	14	127	5	330	12.9
36/160	36/6.3				120	4.7				
4/270; 4/240; 6/120	4/10.6; 4/9.5; 6/4.7				200	7.8				
4/340; 2/270; 6/140	4/13.4; 2/10.6; 6/5.5				380	14.9				
4/340; 14/140	4/13.4; 14/5.5				550	21.6	60	2.3		
2/370; 4/160; 8/138	2/14.5; 4/6.3; 8/5.4		4	630	550	21.6	100	3.9		
2/420; 6/100;	2/16.5; 6/3.9			360	500	19.6	80	3.1		
4/305; 17/140	4/12; 17/5.5		6	660	450	17.7	80	3.1		
2/305; 2/274; 8/140	2/12; 2/10.8; 8/5.5	8	6	630	450	17.7	70	2.7	370	14.5
2/274; 7/178	2/10.8; 7/7		2	460	280	11	90	3.5	300	11.8
12/305; 22/135	12/12; 22/5.3		4	1108						
10/340; 22/138; 4/76	10/13.4; 22/5.4; 4/3		4	1124	270	10.6	40	1.5	340	13.3
8/330; 16/130	8/13; 16/5.1	8/37; 32/20		1381	241	9.4	40	1.5	330	12.9
8/380; 9/152; 12/100	8/15; 9/6; 12/3.9	16/37		1550	327	12.8	40	1.5	430	16.9
18/240; 5/210	18/9.5; 5/8.3				203	8				
4/260; 2/170; 4/80	4/10.2; 2/6.7; 4/3.2			500	235	9.2	16	0.6	210	8.2
8/260; 1/210	8/10.2; 1/8.3			600	254	10				
6/280; 5/105; 8/88	6/11; 6/4; 8/3.5	20		570	400	15.7	60	2.3		
12/280; 12/152; 16/100	12/11; 12/6; 16/3.9		6	961	300	11.8	55	2.1	280	11
10/305; 14/150; 6/88	10/12; 14/6; 6/3.5		5	1136	350	13.7	60	2.3	300	11.8
8/380; 16/150; 4/88	8/15; 16/6; 4/3.5		5		350	13.7	120	4.7	350	13.7
6/280; 8/150; 3/88	6/11; 8/6; 3/3.5	8/37; 10/20	8	951	60	2.3	40	1.5	140	5.5
9/280; 12/150; 14/105	9/11; 12/6; 14/4.1	16/37; 10/20	6	1840	350	13.7	50	1.9	140	5.5
8/380; 12/150; 16/105	8/15; 12/6; 16/4.1	16/37; 52/20		2092	320	12.5	80	3.1	360	14.1
18/190; 4/90	18/7.5; 4/3.6			490	128	5				
6/280; 6/90	6/11; 6/3.6	6/25			369	14.5				
3/240; 12/152; 10/76	3/9.5; 12/6; 10/3		2	530	220	8.6	63	2.4	210	8.2
12/305; 12/147; 18/76	12/12; 12/5.8; 18/3		6	988	280	11	48	1.8	280	11
2/200; 30/160	2/7.9; 30/6.3			550	120	4.7				

BATTLESHIPS – TECHNICAL DATA

Name	Launch Year	Length m	Length ft	Beam m	Beam ft	Draft m	Draft ft	Displacement t	Engine RE	Engine T	Horsepower	Speed in Knots	Range in Miles
ITALY *(cont'd.)*													
Ancona	1864	81,2	266.4	14,6	47.8	6,3	20.6	4224	1		2500	13	1615
Affondatore	1865	89,5	293.8	12,2	40	5,8	19.1	4540	1		2700	13	1025
Palestro	1871	79,7	261.4	17,6	57.7	7,5	24.6	6274	1		3130		1106
Duilio	1876	103,5	229.5	19,7	64.6	8,8	28.8	12265	2		7710	15	2336
Italia	1880	122,0	400.2	22,4	73.7	9,6	31.4	15654	4		12000	17	10377
Andrea Doria	1885	100	328	19,8	64.9	8,7	28.5	11726	2		10300	16	2796
Sardegna	1890	125,1	410.5	23,4	76.7	9,0	29.5	15600	4		21000	20	3728
Benedetto Brin	1901	136,8	448.8	23,8	78	8,9	29.1	14574	2		20000	20	6214
Dante Alighieri	1910	168,1	551.5	26,6	87.2	9,4	30.8	21800		3	32200	23	3107
Giulio Cesare	1911	176,1	577.7	28,0	91.8	10,4	34.1	25086		3	31000	21,5	2982
Giulio Cesare	*	186,4	611.5	28,0	91.8	10,4	34.1	29100		2	93000	28	1926
Littorio	1937	237,8	780.1	32,9	107.9	10,5	34.4	45963		4	140000	30	2846
SPAIN													
Espana	1912	139,9	458.9	23,8	78	7,7	25.2	15840		4	15500	19,5	3728
RUSSIA													
Admiral Lazaref	1867	79,8	261.8	13,0	42.7	5,4	17.8	3900	1		2000	10,5	1056
Imperator Peter Velikey	1872	101,5	333.1	19,2	63.1	7,2	23.7	9820	2		8700	12,5	2299
Sinop	1887	103,4	339.4	21	68.8	7,6	24.9	10200	2		13000	16,8	1243
Petropavlovsk	1894	112,5	369	22,1	72.5	8,3	27.2	11400	2		14213	16	2330
Kniaz Potemkin Tavricheskey	1900	115,5	378.2	22,3	73.1	8,2	26.9	12600	2		10600	16	2113
Gangut	1911	182,9	600	26,9	88.2	8,3	27.2	25850		4	42000	23	2485
Imperator Alexander III	1914	167,8	550.5	27,3	89.5	8,3	27.2	24000		4	26500	21	621
UNITED STATES													
Texas	1892	91,75	301	19,5	64	6,9	22.7	6400	2		8600	17,8	1864
Kearsage	1898	114,6	375.9	22	72.1	7,1	23.2	11500	2		12000	16,8	3728
Kansas	1905	137,2	450.1	23,4	76.7	7,5	24.6	14348	2		20000	18	3231
South Carolina	1908	139,1	456.3	23,2	76.1	7,5	24.6	17617	2		16500	18,5	4350
Arkansas	1911	170,3	558.7	28,4	93.1	8,7	28.5	27700		4	28000	20,5	4971
Arkansas	*	170,3	558.7	32,3	105.9	9,7	31.8	31000		4	28000	20,5	4971
Pennsylvania	1915	185,3	607.9	29,6	97.1	8,8	28.8	33000		4	31500	21	
Pennsylvania	*	185,3	607.9	32,4	106,2	10,2	33.4	36500		4	31500	21	4971
New Mexico	1917	190,2	624	29,7	97.4	9,1	29.8	33500		2	27500	21	6214
New Mexico	*	190,2	624	32,4	106.2	10,4	34.1	36000		4	40000	21,5	5592
Tennessee	1919	190,4	624.6	29,7	97.4	9,2	30.1	34000		2	30000	21	5592
West Virginia	1921	190,4	624.6	29,7	97.4	9,3	30.5	33590		2	28900	21	6214
West Virginia	*	190.4	624.6	34,8	114.1	10,8	35.4	40350		2	28900	21	6214
North Carolina	1940	221,1	725.3	32,9	107.9	10,7	35.1	46670		4	121000	28	8070
Alabama	1942	207,5	680.7	32,9	107.9	11,0	36	44374		4	130000	28	9321
Missouri	1944	270,5	680.7	33,0	108.2	11,0	36	57216		4	200000	33	9321
BRAZIL													
Minas Gerais	1908	162,4	532.8	25,3	83	7,6	24.9	21200	2		23500	21	4971
JAPAN													
Shikishima	1898	133,5	437.9	23	75.4	8,3	27.2	15000	2		14600	19	3107
Kongo	1913	214,6	704	28	91.8	8,2	26.9	27500		2	6400	27,5	4971
Kongo	*	222	728.3	31	101.7	9,6	31.4	36300		4	136000	30	6214
Fuso	1914	205,1	672.8	28,7	94.1	8,7	28.5	30998		4	40000	23	4971
Nagato	1919	215,8	707.9	29	95.1	9,1	29.8	34116		4	80000	26,7	3107
Nagato	*	224,5	736.5	34,6	113.5	10	32.8	46350		4	82000	25	5344
Yamato	1940	263,0	862.9	38,9	121.1	10,4	34.1	72900		4	150000	27	6214

Number of Guns/mm	Number of Guns/in	Machine guns/mm	TT	C	Belt Protection mm	Belt Protection in	Deck Protection mm	Deck Protection in	Turret Protection mm	Turret Protection in
23/160	23/6.3			484	120	4.7				
2/220	2/8.7			309	127	5			127	5
1/280; 6/250	1/11; 6/9.9			548	220	8.6				
4/450; 3/120	4/17.7; 3/4.7	22/37	3	420	550	21.6			450	17.7
4/431; 8/152	4/17; 8/6	12		756			76	3		
4/431; 2/152; 4/120	4/17; 2/6; 4/4.7		5	506	450	17.7				
4/343; 8/152; 16/120; 2/76	4/13.5; 8/6; 16/4.7; 2/3		5	765	100	3.9				
4/305; 4/203; 12/152; 20/76	4/12; 4/8; 12/6; 20/3	6	4	797	150	5.9	80	3.1	200	7.8
12/305; 20/120; 16/76	12/12; 20/4.7; 16/3		3	970	203	8	50	1.9	250	9.8
13/305; 18/120; 19/76	13/12; 18/4.7; 19/3		3	1000	250	9.8			280	11
10/320; 12/120; 8/100	10/12.6; 12/4.7; 8/3.9	20		1236	250	9.8	80	3.1	280	11
9/381; 12/152; 12/90	9/15; 12/6; 12/3.6	20/37; 20/20		1872	350	13.7	100	3.9	290	11.4
8/305; 20/102	8/12; 20/4			854	229	9	38	1.4	203	8
6/229	6/9				114	4.4			152	6
4/305	4/12	2		274	355	13.9				
6/305; 7/152	6/12; 7/6	18/37	4	665	457	17.9			407	16
4/305; 12/152	4/12; 12/6	28/37	6	716	370	14.5	76	3	254	10
4/305; 16/152; 14/76	4/12; 16/6; 14/3	22	5	741	180	7	76	3	254	10
12/305; 16/178	2/12; 16/7		4	1125	225	8.8	37	1.4	203	8
12/305; 20/130; 8/76	12/12; 20/5.1; 8/3		4	1252	305	12			305	12
2/305; 6/152	2/12; 6/6		4	400	305	12				
4/330; 4/203; 4/125	4/13; 4/8; 4/4.9		4	520	410	16.1	127	5	375	14.6
4/305; 8/203; 12/178; 20/76	4/12; 8/8; 12/7; 20/3	22	4	880	229	9	78	3	305	12
8/305; 22/76	8/12; 22/3		2	889	228	8.9	76	3	305	12
12/305; 21/127; 2/76	12/12; 21/5; 2/3		2	1063	279	10.9			305	12
12/305; 6/127; 10/76	12/12; 6/5; 10/3	36/40; 26/20		1650	279	10.9			305	12
12/356; 22/127; 4/76	12/14; 22/5; 4/3		2	915	356	14			457	17.9
12/356; 16/127	12/14; 16/5	45/40; 50/20		2290	356	14			457	17.9
12/356; 22/127; 2/76	12/14; 22/5; 2/3		2	1084	356	14			457	17.9
12/356; 8/127	12/14; 8/5	16/40; 44/20		1930	356	14			457	17.9
12/356; 14/127	12/14; 14/5		2	1083	356	14			457	17.9
8/406; 14/127; 4/76	8/16; 14/5; 4/3		2	1084	406	15.9	89	3.5	457	17.9
8/406; 16/127	8/16; 16/5	40/40; 50/20		2100	406	15.9	102	4	457	17.9
9/406; 20/127	9/16; 20/5	40/40		2339	305	12			406	16
9/406; 20/127	9/16; 20/5	32/40; 56/20		2257	310	12.2			457	17.9
9/406; 20/127	9/16; 20/5	80/40; 49/20		2753	310	12.2			432	17
12/305; 22/120	12/12; 22/4.7			850	229	9	32	1.2	229	9
4/305; 14/152; 20/76	4/12; 14/6; 20/3		5	741	229	9			365	14.3
8/356; 16/152; 16/76	8/14; 16/6; 16/3		8	980	203	8	70	2.7	228	8.9
8/356; 14/152; 12/127	8/14; 14/6; 12/5	118/25		1437	203	8			228	8.9
12/356; 16/152; 6/80	12/14; 16/6; 6/3.2		6	1193	305	12			305	12
8/406; 20/140; 4/80	12/16; 20/5.5; 4/3.2	4	8	1333	300	11.8			356	14
8/406; 16/140; 8/127	12/16; 16/5.5; 8/5	98/25		1370	300	11.8			480	18.8
9/460; 12/155; 12/127	9/18; 12/6.1; 12/5	24/25		2500	410	16.1	200	7.8	650	25.5

RE = Reciprocating engines
T = Turbines
TT = Torpedo tubes
C = Complement

*after modifications

Under the heading ''Engine,'' the letter ''D,'' which sometimes appears after the number, stands for diesel.

Name	Launch Year	Length		Beam		Draft		Displacement	Engine		Horsepower	Speed in Knots	Range in Miles
		m	ft	m	ft	m	ft	t	RE	T			
GREAT BRITAIN													
Campania	1893	189,5	621.9	19,8	64.9	7,9	25.9		2		31050	23	
Ark Royal	1914	111,5	367	15,5	50.8	5,4	17.9		1		11000	10,5	
Empress	1914	96,3	316	12,4	40.9					2		21	
Ben My Chree	1915	114,3	374	14,01	45.9					2	14000	24,5	
Manxman	1916	103.9	341	13.1	42.9					2		21	
Nairana	1917	107,3	352	13,8	45.4	4,0	13.1			2	6700	19	
Pegasus	1917	101,1	332	13,1	42.9	4,5	14.9			2	9500	20,2	
Furious	1916	239,6	786	26,3	86.3	6,5	21.4	19513		4	90000	31	11000
Furious	*	240,1	787.7	27,3	89.6	6,6	21.6	22450		4	90000	31	11000
Argus	1917	172,2	564.9	20,7	67.9	7,01	22.9	15775		4	22000	20	
Vindictive	1918	184,4	605	19,8	64.9	5,3	17.4	9750		4	60.000	29,7	
Vindictive	*	184,4	605	19,8	64.9	6,2	20.5	10000		4	60000	30	
Eagle	1918	203,3	667	32	105	7,3	23.9	26200		4	50000	24	
Hermes	1919	183,2	601	21,3	69,9	5,7	18.7	10950		2	40000	25	
Glorious	1924	239,6	786	24,6	81	6,7	22.1	26500		4	90000	31	
Ark Royal	1937	243,8	800	28,6	93.9	6,9	22.8	27000		3	102000	30,7	
Victorious	1939	233,4	766	31,08	102	9,1	30	29110		3	110000	31	
Victorious	*	238,04	781	31,5	103.5	9,4	31	37000		3	110000	31	
Biter	1940	151,2	496	21,1	69,6	7,7	25.4	16000		2D	9000	16,5	30000
Audacity	1941	132,5	434.7	17,1	56.3	8,4	27.6			2D	4750	15	
Archer	1941	149,9	492	21,1	69.6	7,8	25.6	11300		1D	9000	17	
Unicorn	1941	196	640	27,4	90	5,7	19	20300		2	40.000	24	
Implacable	1942	233,6	766.4	29,1	95.7	9,03	29.6	32110		4	148000	32	
Ancylus	1943	141,7	464.8	18,1	59.3	10,3	33.7			1D		14	
Vindex	1943	159,7	524					13455		2D	11000	17	
Campania	1943	164,5	540	21,3	70	5,7	19	15970		2D	11000	17	
Perseus	1944	211,6	694.4	24,5	80.4	7,0	23	16475		2	42000	25	
Warrior	1944	211,8	695	24,3	80	6,5	21.9	18300		2	42000	25	
Hercules	1945	211,8	695	24,3	80	7,3	24	19000		2	42000	24,5	
Eagle	1946	245	803.9	34,3	112.6	10,2	33	46000		4	152000	31,5	
Eagle	*	247,4	811.6	34,4	112.8	11	36	50536		4	152000	31,5	
Albion	1947	224,7	737.4	27,4	90	8,2	27	27000		2	78000	28	
Ark Royal	1950	257,6	845.1	34,3	112.6	10,9	36	50786		4	152000	31,5	
Hermes	1953	226,8	744	27,4	90	8,5	28	27000		2	78000	28	
Bulwark	1960	224,9	737.8	27,4	90	8,5	28	27705		2	76000	28	
Engadine	1966	129,3	424.2	17,8	58.3	6,7	22	8000		1D	5500	16	
Hermes	1973	226,8	744	27,4	90	8,8	28.8	28700		2	76000	28	
FRANCE													
Foudre	1895	116	380.5	15,7	51.6	7,1	23.4	6100	2		11930	19,5	
Pas de Calais	1914	103	337.9	20,5	67.2	3,3	10.8	1540	1		7000	17,5	250
Rouen	1914	89,0	292	10,5	34.6	3,6	11.8	1656		3	10000	24	890
Campinas	1917	109	357.5	12,9	42.5	7,05	23.1	3319	1		1460	10	
Bapaume	1920	74,9	246	8,6	28.4	2,8	9.1	700		2	4000	20,5	1400
Béarn	1920	182,6	599	27,1	89	7,9	26	25000		2	39000	20	6000
Commandant Teste	1929	170,1	558	21,7	71.4	7,1	23.4	10000		2	21000	20	6000
Joffre	1938	236	774.2	34	111.5			18000		2	120000	33	
Dixmude	1940	151,1	496	21,1	69.4	7,7	25.4	16000		2D	9000	16	30000
Bois Belleau	1942	189,8	623	21,7	71.4	7,9	26	15800		4	100000	32	11000
Arromanches	1943	211,6	694.4	24,4	80	7,0	23	18040		2	42000	25	3200
Clemenceau	1957	265	869.4	31,7	104	8,6	28.2	32780		2	126000	32	7500
GERMANY													
Answald	1914	133,6	438.3	16,6	54.4	7,4	24.2	13200	2		3650	13,5	
Glyndwr	1914	100,7	330.3	13,4	43.9	5,8	19	6000	1		1600	10	
Santa Elena	1914	137,3	450.4	16,7	54.7	7,0	22.9	13900	1		2800	11	
Adeline Hugo Stinnes 3	1915	104,2	341.8	13,8	45.2	6,0	19.6		1		1700	11	
Oswald	1918	112,5	369	15,3	50.1	6,7	21.9	7640	1		2200	10	
Stuttgart	1918	117,4	385	13,3	43.6	5,4	17.7	4002	2		13898	24	4170
Graf Zeppelin	1938	249,9	829	26,9	88.4	5,6	18.4	23200		4	200000	32	8000

Number of Guns/mm	Number of Guns/in	Machine guns/mm	TT	ML	Airplanes	Helicopters	Catapults	Elevators	Complement min.	max.
/120; 1/76	6/4.7; 1/3				10					
/90	4/3.6	2			10				180	
/101; 1/90	2/4; 1/3.6				4-6					
/101; 1/90	2/4; 1/3.6				4					
/101; 1/76	2/4; 1/3				8					
/90	4/3.6				7				278	
/76	4/3				9				258	
/457; 11/140; 5/76	1/18; 11/5.5; 5/3		18		8	3			796	880
0/140; 6/101; 6/76	10/5.5; 6/4; 6/3	48			36				748	1100
/101	4/4				20			2	495	
/190; 8/76	4/7.5; 8/3	4	6		6					
/190; 3/101; 4/76	6/7.5; 3/4; 4/3	2/40	6		4		1		717	
/152; 5/101; 4/76	9/6; 5/4; 4/3				21			2	744	
/140; 3/101; 4/76	6/5.5; 3/4; 4/3				20			1	664	
6/120;	16/4.7	50			48			2	748	1100
6/120; 4/76	16/4.7; 4/3	48/40; 32/20			60			3	1575	
6/120	16/4.7	48/40; 8/20			72			2	1785	2200
2/76	12/3	6/40			72		2	2	2200	
/76	3/3	15/20			15			1	408	582
/100	1/4	6/20			6					
/101	3/4	15/20			15			1	950	
/100	8/4	16/40; 16/20			35			2		
6/120	16/4.7	68/40; 21/20			72		1	2	1785	2200
		6/20			4					
/100	2/4	16/40; 16/20			15			1		
/100	2/4	8/40; 16/20			20			1	700	
		32/40								
		43/40			35			2	1076	1300
		28/40			35		1	2	1343	
6/120	16/4.7	58/40			80-110		2	2		2750
/115	8/4.5			6	30	6	2	2	1745	
		26/40			45		2	2	1330	1390
6/120	16/4.7	34/40			50		2	3	2345	
/76	4/3	17/40			45		2	2	1400	
		8/40		2		20		2	1035	1935
						4			63	77
				2		20		2	980	1930
/100; 4/90; 2/76	8/3.9; 4/3.6; 2/3				2	2			328	
/95; 2/47	1/3.8; 2/1.8	1			2	2			105	
/50; 2/47	2/2; 2/1.8	1/10							179	
					6-10					
/138	1/5.4									
/155; 6/120; 8/76	8/6.1; 6/4.7; 8/3	12	4		40		1	3	875	
2/100; 8/76	12/3.9; 8/3	12					4		649	
/130	8/5.1	8/37; 28/13			40			2		
/76	3/3	19/20			20/30			2	408	582
		26/40; 6/20			26			2	1183	1400
		31/40			24		1	2	1620	
/100	8/3.9				40		2	2	1228	
/88	2/3.5				2-3				107	
/52	2/2.1	4/37			4					
/88	2/3.5				3-4				122	
					3				27	
/88	2/3.5				4				95	
/105; 2/88	4/4.1; 2/3.5		2		3				322	
6/147; 12/105	16/5.8; 12/4.1	22/37; 28/20			40		2	3	1760	

AIRCRAFT CARRIERS–TECHNICAL DATA

Name	Launch Year	Length		Beam		Draft		Displacement	Engine		Horsepower	Speed	Range
		m	ft	m	ft	m	ft	t	RE	T		in Knots	in Miles
ITALY													
Europa	1895	119,5	392	14,07	46.1	5,8	19	6400	1		2600	12	
Giuseppe Miraglia	1923	121,2	397.6	15	49.2	6,2	20.3	5914		2	16000	21	
Aquila	1943	232,5	762.7	30	98.5	7,3	23.9	27800		4	140000	30	5500
SPAIN													
Dedalo	1922	128,01	420	16,7	55	6,2	20.4	10800	1		3000	12,5	
HOLLAND													
Karel Doorman	1958	211,3	693.2	24,4	80	6,4	21.2	19896		2	42000	25	12000
RUSSIA													
Almaz	1916	110,6	363	13,2	43.4	5,3	17.5			2	7500	19	
UNITED STATES													
Wright	1921	136,5	448	17,6	58	8,4	27.7	11500		2	6000	15	
CV 1 Langley	1922	165,4	542.6	19,8	64.9	5,4	17.9	11050	2E	2	7150	15	
Patoka	1924	141,1	463.1	18,2	60	7,9	26.1	16800	2		2900	10,9	
CV 2 Lexington	1925	270,6	888	32,3	106	7,4	24.4	40000		4	180000	33,2	
CV 4 Ranger	1933	234,3	769	24,4	80	5,9	19.4	14500		2	53500	29,5	
CV 6 Enterprise	1936	246,7	809	25,3	83.2	6,6	21.6	19900		4	120000	34	
CV 7 Wasp	1939	225,2	739	24,4	80.1	6,09	19.9	14700		2	75000	29,5	8000
CVE 27 Suwanee	1939	168,5	553	22,8	74.9	9,3	30.5	24275		2	13500	18	
CVE 30 Charger	1941	149,9	492	21,1	69.4	7,8	25.6	11000		2D	8500	18	
CVE 1 Long Island	1941	149,9	492	21,1	69.4	7,8	25.6	11300		1D	8500	18	
CV 49 Bogue	1942	152,1	499.2	21,2	69.7	7,9	25.9	15700		1	8500	18	
CVL 22 Independence	1942	189,8	623	21,7	71.4	7,9	25.9	15800		4	100000	32	
CVE 57 Anzio	1943	156,04	511.9	19,8	64.9	6,1	20	10400	2		11200	19,5	
IX 81 Sable	1943	163,06	535	17,6	58	4,7	15.4	6564	1		12000	18	
CV 19 Hancock	1944	272,6	894	30,8	101	9,4	30.8	44700		4	150000	30	
CV 36 Antietam	1944	270,6	888	33,5	110	9,1	29.9	37500		4	150000	33	
CVE 106 Block Island	1944	169,7	557	22,8	75	9,3	30.6	24275		2	16000	19	
CV 41 Midway	1945	295,03	967.9	34,4	113	9,8	32.4	60000		4	212000	33	
CV 41 Midway	*	298,4	979	36,9	121	10,8	35.4	64000		4	212000	33	
CVL 49 Wright	1947	208,3	683	23,3	76.6	7,6	25	18760		4	120000	33	
CVA 59 Forrestal	1954	316,7	1039	38,5	126.3	11,3	37	75900		4	260000	33	
LPH 6 Tethis Bay	1956	152,7	500	19,8	64.9	6,1	20	11000		2	11200	19,5	11900
CV 34 Oriskany	1959	275,5	904	31,3	103	9,4	31	41900		4	150000	33	
CVA 63 Kitty Hawk	1960	323,9	1062	38,5	126.3	10,9	35.7	80000		4	280000	35	
CVAN 65 Enterprise	1960	341,3	1119	40,5	132.8	10,8	35.4	89600		4	280000	35	
LPH 2 Iwo Jima	1960	180	590	25,6	84	7,9	25.9	18000		1	22000	23	
CVAN 68 Nimitz	1972	332	1089	40,8	133.8	11,3	37	91400		4	280000	35	
LHA 1 Tarawa	1973	250	820	32,3	106	8,5	27.8	39300		2	140000	22	
JAPAN													
Wakamija	1901	111,24	364.9	14,7	48.4	5,7	19	7600	1		1600	9,5	
Notoro	1920	143,4	470.6	17,6	57.9	8,06	26.4	14050	2		5850	12	
Kamoi	1922	151,1	495.9	20,4	67	8,4	27.6	19550		2	9000	12	
Hosho	1921	168,2	551.8	18	59	6,1	20.2	9630		2	30000	25	8000
Kaga	1921	236	774.2	29,5	97	7,9	25.9	33693		4	91000	28,5	8000
Kaga	*	247,6	812.4	32,5	106.6	9,4	31	42541	4	4	127400	28,5	10000
Akagi	1925	248,8	816.4	28,9	95	8,06	26.4	34364		4	131000	31	8000
Akagi	*	260,7	855.3	31,3	102.6	8,7	28.7	41300		4	133000	31,2	8200
Ryujo	1931	179,9	590.3	20,8	68.2	4,6	15.2	12732		2	65200	29	1000
Soryu	1935	227,5	746.4	21,3	70	7,6	25	18000		4	153000	34,5	7750
Hiryu	1937	227,3	745.9	22,3	73.2	7,7	25.4	20250		4	153000	34,3	10300
Mizuho	1938	183,5	602.2	18,7	61.6	7,07	23.1	12150		4D	15200	22	8000
Nisshin	1939	192,4	631.4	19,6	64.4	7,0	23	125000		2D	47000	28	11000
Zuikaku	1939	257,4	844	26,05	85.4	8,8	28.9	29800		4	16000	34,2	9700
Hiyo	1941	219,2	719.4	26,7	87.6	8,2	26.9	26949		2	56250	25,5	
Taiyo	1941	180,2	591.2	22,4	73.6	8,06	26.4	20000		2	25200	21	6500
Akitsu Maru	1941	143,7	471.5	19,4	63.9	11,4	37.6	11800		2	7500	20	
Shoho	1942	217	711.9	18	59	6,6	21.6	13950		2	52000	28	7800

Number of Guns/mm	Number of Guns/in	Machine guns/mm	TT	ML	Airplanes	Helicopters	Catapults	Elevators	Complement min.	max.
/76	2/3									
/102	4/4				11		2		196	
/135; 12/65	8/5.3; 12/2.6	132/20			51		2	2	108	1312
/105	2/4.1				25				324	
/76	4/3	24/40; 10/20			39	1	1	2	1509	
/120	7/4.7	4/7,5			3-4				294	
,127; 2/76	2/5; 2/3								311	
/127	2/5				4				156	
/203; 12/127; 4/76	8/8; 12/5; 4/76				80		1	2	1899	
/127	4/5				34		1	1	341	
/127	8/5				80			2	1788	
/127	8/5	16/27; 16			100		2	3	2072	2919
/127	8/5	40			84			3	1800	2367
/127	2/5	8/40; 15/20			34		1	2	790	1000
/127; 4/76	1/5; 4/3	16/40			15			1	950	
/127; 2/76	1/5; 2/3				21			1	950	
/127	2/5	16/40; 20/20			30		1	2	800	
		16/40; 40/20			40		1	2	1183	1400
/127	4/5				80		2	3	3630	
2/127	12/5	72/40; 52/20			100			3	2100	2800
/127	1/5	24/20			30		1	2	643	800
									300	
/127	2/5	36/40; 30/20			34		1	2	924	1000
8/127	18/5	84/40; 28/20			137			3	2510	3300
/127	3/5				75		2	3	2615	4500
		40/40; 32/20			50			2	1763	1821
/127	8/5		1		100		4	4	2790	4940
		16/40				20-40		1	540	2140
/127; 28/76	8/5; 28/3				100		2	3	2970	3300
				2	90		4	4	2800	4950
				3	90		4	4	3100	5500
/76	8/3					32		2	528	2618
				3	90		4	4	3300	6100
/127	3/5	6/20		2		30		2	902	2805
/90	2/3.6				4					
/120; 2/80	2/4.7; 2/3.2				10				155	
/140; 2/80	2/5.5; 2/3.2				12					
/140; 2/76	4/5.5; 2/3				21			2	550	
0/203; 12/120	10/8; 12/4.7	22			60			2	1340	
0/203; 16/127	10/8; 16/5	22/25			91			3	2019	
0/203; 12/120	10/8; 12/4.7	22			60			2		
/203; 12/120	6/8; 12/4.7	28/25			91			3	2000	
2/127	12/5	24			48			2	924	
2/127	12/5	28/25			73			3	1101	
2/127	12/5	31/25			73			3	1101	
/127	6/5	18/25			24		4	1		
/127	6/5	18/25			25		2			
6/127	16/5	36/25			84			3	1660	
2/127	12/5	24/25			53			2	1224	
/120	6/4.7	8/25			27			2	747	
2/75	12/3				20			1		
/127	8/15	15/25			29			2	785	

AIRCRAFT CARRIERS–TECHNICAL DATA

Name	Launch Year	Length		Beam		Draft		Displacement	Engine		Horsepower	Speed in Knots	Range in Miles
		m	ft	m	ft	m	ft	t	RE	T			
JAPAN *(cont'd.)*													
Ryuho	1942	215,6	707	19,5	64.1	6,5	21.3	15300		2	52000	26,5	8000
Ise	1943	219,6	720.4	33,8	111	8,9	29.4	38676		4	80825	25,2	9449
Taiho	1943	259,6	835.5	27,6	90.7	9,6	31.6	34600		4	160000	33	8000
Unryu	1943	226	741.4	21,9	71.9	7,8	25.6	20100		4	152000	34	8000
Chiyoda	1943	192,5	631.5	20,7	68.1	7,4	24.4	13346	2D	2	44000	29	11000
Shinyo	1943	189,2	621	25,6	84	8,1	26.7	20916		2	26000	22	
Shinano	1944	265,8	872	36,2	118.7	10,2	33.6	71890		4	150000	27	10000
Kumanu Maru	1945	149,6	491	19,5	64.1	7	22.9	10500		2	10000	19	6000

Number of Guns/mm	Number of Guns/in	Machine guns/mm	TT	ML	Airplanes	Helicopters	Catapults	Elevators	Complement min.	max.
127	8/5	38/25			31			2	989	
355; 16/127	8/14; 16/5	57/25			22		2	1	1463	
/100	12/4	51/25			53			2	1751	
/127	12/5	51/25			65			2	1595	
127	8/5	30/25			30			2		
127	8/5	50/25			33			2	948	
/127	16/5	145/25			47			2	2400	
75	8/3	6/25			37			1		

RE = Reciprocating engines
T = Turbines
TT = Torpedo tubes
ML = Missile launchers

*after modifications

The year given is the year of launching except in the case of aircraft carriers that have undergone modifications, when the year of conversion is given, or aircraft carriers handed over to other navies, in which case the year of delivery is given.

Under the heading "Engine," the letter "D," which sometimes appears after the number, stands for diesel. "E" stands for electric.

SUBMARINES – TECHNICAL DATA

Name	Year	Length m	ft	Beam m	ft	Draft m	ft	Displacement t	Engine D	El	H P	Speed in Knots	N. Guns/mm	N. Guns/in	TT	ML	
GREAT BRITAIN																	
Holland 1-5	1901	19,5	63.9	3,6	11.8	3,6	11.8	104/122	1 G	1	160/70	8/7			1		
Tipo A 2-13	1903	30,4	99.7	3,8	12.6	3,4	11.1	180/207	1 G	1	450/150	11/7			2		
Classe C 19-38	1909	41,04	134.6	4,1	13.4	3,4	11.1	280/313	1 G	1	600/200	13/8			2		
Classe D 2-8	1911	55,02	180.5	6,8	22.3	3,7	12.2	550/600	2	2	1200/550	16/9			3		
Classe E	1915	55,02	180.5	6,8	22.3	3,7	12.2	662/807	2	2	1600/840	15/10			3-5		
Classe G	1916	56,8	186.4	6,8	22.3	4,02	13.1	700/995	2	2	1600/840	14/10			5		
Classe K	1916	102,4	336	7,9	25.9	4,8	15.7	1880/2650	2T	2	10000/1600	24/9,5	3/101	3/4	10		
Classe L	1917	70,2	230.3	7,1	23.2	4,1	13.4	890/1070	2	2	2400/1600	17,3/10,5	1/76	1/3	6		
Classe M	1917	92,1	302.1	7,4	24.2	4,7	15.4	1600/1950	2	2	2400/1600	15/9	1/305; 1/76	1/12; 1/3			
X1	1923	106,4	349	9,02	29.5	5,1	16.7	2780/3600	2	2	6000/2600	10,5/9	4/130	4/5.1	6		▮
Oberon	1926	82,08	269.2	8,5	27.8	4,02	13.1	1311/1831	2	2	2950/1350	15/9	1/105	1/4.1	8		
Perseus	1928	79,04	259.3	5,4	17.7	4,1	13.4	1475/2040	2	2	4400/1350	17,5/9	1/105	1/4.1	8		
Odin	1928	79,04	259.3	5,4	17.7	4,1	13.4	1475/2038	2	2	4400/1320	17,5/9	1/105	1/4.1	8		
Parthian	1929	79,04	259.3	5,4	17.7	4,1	13.4	1475/2040	2	2	4400/1350	17,5/9	1/105	1/4.1	8		
Rainbow	1930	79,04	259.3	5,4	17.7	3,9	12.7	1475/2030	2	2	4400/1320	17,5/9	1/105	1/4.1	8		
Porpoise	1932	82,5	270.7	7,7	25.2	4,5	14.7	1500/2053	2	2	3300/1630	15/8,7	1/105	1/4.1	6		
Severn	1934	98,8	324.1	8,5	27.8	4,1	13.4	1850/2723	2	2	10000/2500	22,2/10	1/105	1/4.1	6		
Triton	1937	83,6	274.2	8,05	26.4	3,6	11.8	1090/1575	2	2	2500/1450	15,2/9	1/100	1/3.9	10		
Classe S	1943	65,9	216.4	7,2	23.6	3,1	10.1	715/1000	2	2	1900/1300	14,5/10	1/76	1/3	7		
Classe T	1944	83,1	272.7	8,05	26.4	3,6	11.8	1090/1575	2	2	2500/1450	15,2/9	1/100	1/3.9	11		
Classe A	1946	85,6	280.9	6,7	21.9	5,1	16.7	1385/1620	2	2	4300/1250	19/8	1/100	1/3.9	10		
Oberon	1961	90	295.2	8,5	27.8	5,4	17.7	2030/2410	2	2	3680/6000	12/17			8		
Dreadnought	1963	80,7	264.9	9,7	31.8	7,9	25.9	3500/4000		N					6		
Valiant	1966	86,6	284.2	10,1	33.1	8,2	26.9	4000/4900		N	15000	28			6		▮
Resolution	1967	129,5	424.8	10,1	33.1	9,1	29.8	7500/8400		N	15000	20/25			6	16	▮
Swiftsure	1973	82,9	271.9	9,8	32.1	8,2	26.9	4000/4500	D	N	4000/15000	-/30			5		
FRANCE																	
Gymnote	1888	17,2	56.4	1,8	5.9	1,7	5.5	30/-		1	-/55	-/8			2		
Narval	1900	34	111.5	3,8	12.6			117/202	1 R	1	250/80	9,8/5,3			4		
Triton	1901	33,8	111.1	3,7	12.2	3,9	12.7	106/200	1 R	1	250/-	12/8			4		
Pluviôse	1907	51	167.3	5	16.4	3,1	10.1	400/550	2 R	2	700/460	12,5/8			7		
Papin	1907	41,9	137.6	4,01	13.1	3,04	9.9	398/550	1	1	700/-	12/7,5			7		
Circé	1908	46,8	153.5	5,01	16.4	3,04	9.9	351/490	2	2	450/-	11/8			6		
Ampère	1910	41,9	137.6	4,01	13.1	3,04	9.9	398/550	2	2	700/460	12,5/8			7		
Brumaire	1911	50,5	165.9	5,01	16.4	3,1	10.1	398/505	2	2	840/560	13/9	1	1	7		
Zedé	1913	73,8	242.3	5,9	19.3	3,7	12.2	740/1000	2T	2	2400/1700	19/10	2	2	8		
Daphné	1915	67,7	222.4	5,6	18.3	3,7	12.2	640/945	2	2	1800/1400	15/11	1	1	10		
Dupuy de Lôme	1915	75	246	6,3	20.6	3.9	12.7	833/1100	2T	2	4000/1600	18/11	2	2	8		
Joessel	1915	73,7	241.7	7,09	23.2	4,3	14.1	900/1250	2	2	2900/—	16,5/11	2/57	2/2.3	8		
Romazzotti	1917	75	246	6,3	20.6	4,01	13.1	840/1317	2	2	2600/—	16,5/11	2/57	2/2.3	8		
Jean Autric	1917	71,4	234.2	6,2	20.3	3,8	12.6	744/1053	2	2	2400/—	16/8,5	1/105	1/4.1	6		
Lagrange	1917	73,8	242.3	5,9	19.3	3,7	12.2	836/1317	2	2	2600/—	16,5/11	2	2	8		
Fulton	1917	73,7	241.7	5,9	19.3	4,1	13.4	915/1203	2	2	2900/—	16,5/11	2	2	8		
Pierre Chailly	1922	69,8	229	7,9	25.9	3,9	12.7	798/1182	2	2	1800/1200	14/9	1/100	1/3.9	4		
Requin	1924	77,8	255.3	6,5	21.3	5,4	17.7	974/1410	2	2	2900/1800	16/10	1/100	1/3.9	10		
Redoutable	1924	91,9	301.6	9,2	30.1	4,7	15.4	1384/2080	2	2	6000/2000	18/10	1/100	1/3.9	11		
Tourquoise	1928	65,8	215.9	7,06	23.1	4,1	13.4	669/925	2	2	1300/—	12/9	1/76	1/3	4		
Saphir	1928	65,8	215.9	7,1	23.2	4,8	15.7	669/925	2	2	1300/1000	12/9	1/76	1/3	5		
Surcouf	1929	119,6	392.4	8,9	29.1	7	22.9	2880/4300	2	2	7600/3400	18/10	2/203	2/8	12		▮
La Creole	1938	73,5	241.1	6,5	21.3	4,2	13.7	893/1170	2	2	3000/1450	15/9,3	1/100	1/3.9	9		
Morillot	1938	91,9	301.6	8,2	26.9	4,2	13.7	1810/2417	2	2	12000/2300	23/10	1/100	1/3.9	10		
Aurore	1938	73,5	241.1	6,5	21.3	4,2	13.7	893/1170	2	2	3000/1400	17/9	1/100	1/3.9	9		
Narval	1954	77,8	255.3	7,1	23.2	5,4	17.7	1640/1910	2	2	4000/5000	16/18			8		
Daphné	1959	57,9	189.9	6,7	21.9	4,7	15.4	869/1043			1300/1600	13,5/16			12		
Le Redoutable	1969	128,7	422.2	10,6	34.7	10	32.8	8045/8940		N	16000	20/25			4	16	▮
Le Foudroyant	1973	128,7	422.2	10,6	34.7	10	32.8	8045/8940	2	N	1306/16000	20/25			4	16	▮
Agosta	1974	67,5	221.4	6,8	22.3	5,4	17.7	1450/1725			3600/4600	12/20			4		
Rubis	1982	72,1	236.2	7,6	24.9	6,4	20.9	2385/2670		N	65000	25			4	1	
GERMANY																	
U 1	1906	42,3	139	3,7	12.3	3,1	10.1	238/283	2 G	2	400/400	8/8,7			1		

Name	Year	Length		Beam		Draft		Displacement	Engine		H P	Speed	N. Guns/mm	N. Guns/in	TT	ML	C
		m	ft	m	ft	m	ft	t	D	El		in Knots					
GERMANY (cont'd.)																	
J 9	1910	57,3	188.2	6	19.6	3,1	10.1	493/611	2	2	1000/1160	14,2/8,1			4		29
J 21	1913	64,1	210.4	6,1	20	3,5	11.4	650/837	2	2	1700/1200	15,4/9,5	1/88	1/3.5	4		35
J 91	1915	65,8	215.8	6,2	20.3	2,8	9.4	757/998	2	2	2400/1200	15,6/8,6	1/88	1/3.5	6		36
JB 3	1915	28,1	92.2	3,1	10.1	3,03	9.9	127/142	1	1	60/120	6,5/5,5			2		14
J 43/50	1916	65	213.2	6,2	20.3	3,7	12.2	725/940	2	2	2000/1200	15,2/9,7	2/88	2/3.5	4		36
J 55	1916	65,2	213.9	6,4	21.1	3,6	11.8	715/902	2	2		17,1/9,1	2/88	2/3.5	4		36
JB 48-249	1916	55,3	181.4	5,8	19	3,6	11.8	516/651	2	2	1100/788	13,6/8	1/88	1/3.5	5		34
J 117	1918	81,5	267.4	7,4	24.3	4,2	13.7	1164/1512	2	2	2400/1200	14,7/7	1/88	1/3.5	4		40
J 126	1918	82	269	7,4	24.3	4,2	13.7	1163/1468	2	2	2400/1235	14,7/7,2	1/88	1/3.5	4		40
JC 90-118	1918	56,5	185.3	5,5	18.1	3,7	12.2	491/571	2	2	660/770	11,5/6,6			3		32
JC 3	1918	33,9	111.5	3,1	10.1	3,04	9.9	168/183	1	1	90/175	6,2/5,2					14
J 140-141	1918	92	301.8	9,1	29.9	5,2	17	1930/2483	3	2	3950/1703	15,3/7,6	2/88	2/3.5	6		62
J F		44,6	146.3	4,4	14.5	3,9	12.7	364/381	2	2	600/720	11/7	1/88	1/3.5	5		30
J 25-26	1936	72,3	237.4	6,2	20.3	4,3	14.1	862/983	2	2	2900/1000	18/8	1/105	1/4.1	4		43
J 55	1939	66,5	218.1	6,2	20.3	4,7	15.4	753/857	2	2	2800/750	17,2/8			5		44
J 45-54; 69-71	1938	66,5	218.1	6,2	20.3	4,7	15.4	753/857	2	2	2800/750	17,2/8			5		44
J 56-63	1938	42,7	140	4,08	13.3	3,9	12.7	279/330	2	2	700/360	13/7			3		25
J 37-44; 64-68	1939	76,5	250.9	6,7	21.9	4,7	15.4	1051/1178	2	2	4400/1000	18,2/7,3	1/105	1/4.1	6		48
II C-42		67,3	220.7	6,8	22.3	5	16.4	999/1050	2	2	2700/750	16,7/7,5	1/88	1/3.5	5		45
XXI	1944	76,7	251.6	8	26.2	6,2	20.3	1620/1820	2	3	4000/4565	15,6/17,5			6		58
XXIII	1945	36,4	119.6	4	13.1	3,6	11.8	232/256	1	1	630/550	9,7/12,5			2		14
J 1 - U 12 (Tipo 205)	1961	43,9	144	4,6	15	4,3	14.1	419/450			1500	10/17			8		22
J 13 - U 30 (Tipo 206)	1972	48,6	159.4	4,6	15	4,5	14.7	450/498			1800	10/17			8		22
ITALY																	
Glauco	1903	36,8	120.7	4,3	14.1	2,5	8.2	160/243	2 G	2	600/170	13,5/6,5			3		15
Foca	1908	42,5	139.4	4,3	14.1	2,5	8.2	185/280	3	2	800/160	12,8/6,5			2		17
Medusa	1912	45,1	148.1	4,2	13.7	3	9.8	250/305	2	2	650/300	12,5/8,2			2		21
Pacinotti	1916	65	213.2	6,05	19.8	4,1	13.4	710/869	2	2	2000/900	14,6/9	2/76	2/3	5		39
Classe F	1916	45,6	149.6	4,2	13.7	3,1	10.1	262/319	2	2	700/500	12,5/8	1/76	1/3	2		26
N 3	1917	45,8	150.2	4,6	15	3,7	12.2	360/474	2	2	490/600	12/11	1/76	1/3	4		27
Pietro Micca	1918	63,2	207.3	6,2	20.3	4,2	13.7	842/1244	2	2	2600/1300	14,5/11	2/76	2/3	6		40
Barbarigo	1918	67	219.8	5,9	19.3	3,8	12.6	762/924	2	2	2600/1400	17/10	2/76	2/3	6		40
Balilla	1928	86,7	284.6	7,8	25.5	4,7	15.4	1450/1904	3	2	4425/900	17,5/8,9	1/120	1/4.7	6		77
Sirena	1933	60,2	197.5	6,4	20.9	4,2	13.7	681/842	2	2	1350/800	14/7,7	1/100	1/3.9	6		44
Perla	1936	60,1	197.4	6,4	20.9	4,7	15.4	695/855	2	2	1400/800	14/7,5	1/100	1/3.9	6		44
Brin	1939	72,5	237.8	6,7	21.9	4,5	14.7	1016/1266	2	2	3000/1100	17,3/8	1/100	1/3.9	8		54
Saint Bon	1944	87,9	288.3	7,7	25.2	5,8	19	1703/2164	3	2	5100/1800	16,8/8,5	2/100	2/3.9	14		78
Platino	1941	60,1	197.4	6,4	20.9	4,7	15.4	710/870	2	2	1400/800	14/7,7	1/100	1/3.9	6		44
Classe CB	1942	15	49.2	3	9.8	2,1	6.8	36/45	1	1	90/100	7,5/7			2		4
Romolo	1943	87	285.4	7,8	25.5	6,1	20	2220/2616	2	2	2600/900	14/6,5					63
Piomarta	1952	87,4	286.7	8,3	27.2	6,2	20.3	2050/2700			4500/5600	15,5/16			8		75
Toti	1968	46,2	151.6	4,7	15.4	3,9	12.7	524/582			2000	8,3/13,5			4		22
Sauro	1980	63,9	209.6	6,8	22.3	5,7	18.7	1456/1631			3210/3650	11/20			6		45
SPAIN																	
Perla	1888	22	72.1	2,8	9.1	1,9	6.2	87/-		2	-/120				1		
Monturiol	1917	45,4	149	4,1	13.4	3,09	10	260/382	2	2	700/500	13/8,5			2		17
PORTUGAL																	
Foca	1917	44,8	147.2	4,1	13.4	3,3	10.8	260/389	2	2	600/450	13/8,5			2		20
Delfim	1934	69,05	226.5	6,4	20.9	3,8	12.6	813/1125	2	2	2300/1000	16,5/9,2	1/100	1/3.9	6		36
NORWAY																	
Tipo Ula	1964	45,1	148	4,5	14.7			400/435			1200	10/17			8		17
SWEDEN																	
Uttern	1921	56,3	184.9	5,6	18.3	3,04	9.9	429/640	2	2	2800/-	15/9	1/47	1/1.8	4		28
Delfinen	1962	69	226.3	5,1	16.7	4,6	15	835/1100			1660	17/20			4		36
Sjöormen	1967	51	167.3	6,1	20	5,8	19	1130/1400			2200	15/20			6		23
Näcken	1980	49,5	162.3	5,6	18.3	5,6	18.3	1030/1125				20/20			8		19
FINLAND																	
Vetehinen	1931	63,5	208.4	6,1	20	3,1	10.1	490/710	2	2	1060/600	14/8			4		27
HOLLAND																	
Classe K 2 - K 7	1917	64,2	210.9	5,6	18.3	3,4	11.1	550/800	2	2	1740/630	16/9,5			6		

SUBMARINES–TECHNICAL DATA

Name	Year	Length m	Length ft	Beam m	Beam ft	Draft m	Draft ft	Displacement t	Engine D	Engine El	H P	Speed in Knots	N. Guns/mm	N. Guns/in	TT	ML	C
HOLLAND (cont'd.)																	
K XI	1924	73,1	239.9	6,2	20.3	3,8	12.6	670/820	2	2	2400/725	15/8,8	1/90	1/3.6	6		3
O 19	1938	80,4	263.9	7,06	23.1	3,8	12.6	967/1468	2	2	5300/1000	20/9	1/90	1/3.6	8		4
O 21	1940	77,5	254.3	6,4	20.9	3,9	12.7	962/1195	2	2	5200/1000	19,5/9	1/90	1/3.6	6		5
Potvis	1961	79,2	260.1	7,8	25.5	4,7	15.4	1494/1826	2	2	3100/4200	14,5/17			8		6
Zwaardvis	1972	66,2	217.1	10,3	33.7	7,1	23.2	2350/2640				13/20			6		6
Walrus	1982	67	219.8	8,4	27.5	7	22.9	2350/2640							6		4
DENMARK																	
Flora	1918	47,4	155.5	4,4	14.4	2,8	9.1	301/369	2	2	1000/650	15/10,5			4		2
Delfinen	1956	53,9	176.9	4,7	15.4	4,5	14.7	595/643	2	2	1200/1200	16/16			4		3
Narhvalen	1970	44,3	145.3	4,6	15	4,2	13.7	420/450	1	1	1500/1500	12/17			8		2
ESTONIA																	
Kalev (Lembit)	1936	57,9	183.9	7,4	24.2	3,4	11.1	600/820	2	2	1200/450	13,5/8,5	1/40	1/1.5	4		3
LATVIA																	
Ronis	1926	54,8	180	4,5	14.7	3,04	9.9	390/514	2	2	1300/700	14/9,2	1/76	1/3	6		2
AUSTRIA																	
U 3	1908	42,3	138.7	3,7	12.2	2,9	9.5	237/300	2P	2	600/300	12/9			2		1
GREECE																	
Nordenfelt N° 1	1885	19,5	63.9	3,6	11.8	3,2	10.4	60/64	1 R	1 R	100/100				1		3
Glavkos	1927	68,4	224.4	5,6	18.3	4,1	14.4	700/930	2	2	1420/1200	14/9,5	1/100; 1/76	1/3.9; 1/3	6		4
Glavkos	1971	54,5	178.8	6,2	20.3	5,5	18	1100/1210			5032	11/23			8		3
TURKEY																	
Atilay	1975	56	183.7	6,2	20.3	5,5	18	980/1290			5000	10/22			8		3
RUSSIA–USSR																	
Ossetyr	1901	20,5	67.2	4,2	13.7	3,4	11.1	136/174	2 G	2		10/7			3		
Bolshevik (Ryss)	1915	69,7	228.8	4,5	14.7	3,8	12.6	650/784	2	2	500/900	10/9	2/76	2/3	12		5
Metallist	1918	45,7	150	4,7	15.4	4,6	15	375/467	2	2	480/320	12/8	1/57	1/2.3	4		
Dekabrist	1929	84,8	278.2	6,9	22.6	5,01	16.4	896/1318	2	2	2500/1200	15/8	1/100	1/3.9	8		4
Yakobinetz	1935	84,8	278.2	6,9	22.6	5,01	16.4	959/1370	2	2	2500/1200	15/8	1/100	1/3.9	8		4
Chuka (SHCH)	1935	57,8	189.7	5,9	19.3	3,9	12.7	620/738	2	2	1600	15,5/8,5	2/45	2/1.7	6		
Malodki (M)	1935	37,6	123.6	3,1	10.1	2,5	8.2	168/202	2	2	685/240	13/7	1/45	1/1.7	2		
Quebeck	1954	54,6	179.1	5,5	18	4,1	13.4	450/530			2000/2000	17/16			4		40
Zulu	1955	90	295.2	7,4	24.2	6,1	20	1950/2300	3	3	6000/5000	18/16			10		7
November	1958	110,9	363.8	9,1	29.8	6,7	21.9	4200/5000		N	30000	-/30			10		8
Romeo	1958	76,8	251.9	7,3	23.9	5,5	18	1400/1800	2	2	4000/4000	17/14			8		5
Juliett	1960	86,7	284.4	10,1	33.1	7	22.9	3000/3800			8000/6000	19/14			6	4	7
Echo I	1960	114	374	9,1	29.8	7,3	23.9	4300/5200		N	30000	-/28			8		9
Alfa	1960	79,3	260.1	10	32.8	7,6	24.9	-/3800		N	40000	-/42			6		6
Hotel	1962	115,2	377.9	9,1	29.8	7,6	24.9	-/5500		N	30000	-/26			8	3	9
Whiskey (Long Bin)	1963	83,8	274.9	6,5	21.3	5	16.4	1200/1500			4000/2700	18/12			4	4	
Echo II	1963	117,3	384.8	9,2	30.1	7,8	25.5	4800/5800		N	22500	-/25			8	8	10
Yankee	1967	129,5	424.8	11,6	38	7,8	25.5	7800/9300		N	40000	-/30			6	16	12
Golf II	1967	98	321.5	8,5	27.8	6,4	20.9	2300/2800	3	3	6000/12000	17/14			6	3	8
Foxtrott	1971	91,5	300.1	8	26.8	6,1	20	1950/2500	3	3	6000/6000	18/16			10		7
Papa	1971	109	357.6	11,5	37.7	7,6	24.9	-/7000		N	40000	-/35				10	9
Tango	1972	90,5	296.9	8,6	28.2	6,4	20.9	2100/2500	3	3	6000/6000	20/16			6		6
Charlie II	1972	102,9	337.5	9,9	32.4	7,8	25.5	4400/5500		N	20000	-/28			6	8	9
Delta II	1975	152,7	500.9	11,8	38.7	10,2	33.4	-/11000		N	30000	-/25			6	16	13
Delta III	1976	150	492.1	12	39.3	10,2	33.4	11000/13250		N	60000	-/24			6	16	13
Typhoon	1982	183	600.3	22,9	75.1			-/30000		N	120000	-/24			8	20	15
UNITED STATES																	
American Turtle	1775			2,2	7.2	1,8	5.9										1
Hunley	1863	12,1	39.6	1,06	3.4	1,2	3.9					2,5/2,5					9
Holland H7	1899	16,4	53.8	3,1	10.1	2,5	8.2	64/75	1 G	1		6/5			1		7
Adder SS 3	1901	19,3	63.3	3,6	11.8	3,2	10.4	135/175	1 G	1	160/70	8,5/7,3			1		7
Fulton	1904	19,3	63.3	3,5	11.4	3,3	10.8	122/150	1 G	1	160/70	8,5/7			1		14
Narwhal (D)	1910	40,8	133.8	4,2	13.7	3,4	11.1	280/345	1 G	1	600/330	13/9			2		15
Carp (E)	1911	42,5	139.4	4,5	14.7	3,6	11.8	330/400	2	2	480/350	12/10,5			4		18
L	1914	51,3	168.3	31,7	104	3,8	12.6	450/720	2	2	1200/750	12/10,5	1/76	1/3	4		
Classe AA	1917	82,08	269.2	6,9	22.6	4,2	13.7	1100/1490	4	2	4000/1350	20/12	2/76	2/3	4		54
S 45	1923	68,7	225.3	6,2	20.3	4,8	15.7	906/1126	2	2	1200/1500	14,5/11	1/100	1/3.9	4		38

Name	Year	Length m	ft	Beam m	ft	Draft m	ft	Displacement t	Engine D	El	H P	Speed in Knots	N. Guns/mm	N. Guns/in	TT	ML	C
U.S. (cont'd.)																	
4 - V 6	1925	103,8	340.5	8,3	27.2	4,7	15.4	3000/4000	2	2	4500/2000	19,5/8	2/152	2/6	6		86
gonaut	1927	115,8	379.9	10,1	33.1	4,6	15	2710/4080	2	2	5000/2500	14,5/8	2/152	2/6	4		89
rwhal	1930	112,7	369.7	10,1	33.1	4,6	15	2730/3960	2	2	5450/2540	17/8,5	2/152	2/6	6		88
ttlefish	1933	82,6	270.9	7,6	24.9	3,8	12.6	1120/1650	2	2	3400/800	17/9	1/76	1/3	6		45
lmon	1937	90,5	296.9	7,9	25.9	4,4	14.4	1450/2198	2	2			1/76	1/3	8		55
to	1942	93,3	306	8,2	26.9	4,2	13.7	1815/2425			6500/2750	21/10	1/76	1/3	10		74
lao	1942	94,7	310.6	8,3	27.2	5,1	16.7	1816/2425			6500/2750	21/10	1/76	1/3	10		75
nita	1952	59,5	195.2	7,6	24.9	4,9	16	765/—			1050/1050	13/13			4		49
utilus SSN 571	1954	96,9	317.9	8,5	27.8	7,7	25.2	3180/3747		N	15000	20/23			6		104
a Wolf SSN 575	1955	102,7	336.9	8,8	28.8	6,6	21.6	3260/4110		N	15000	20/22			6		105
ate SSN 578	1957	81,5	267.3	7,6	24.9	6,7	21.9	2360/2570		N	6600	20/25			8		87
ipjack SSN 585	1959	79,6	261.1	9,7	31.8	8,5	27.8	3075/3513		N	15000	16/35			6		90
iton SSN 586	1959	136	446.1	11,2	36.7	7,2	23.6	5900/7750		N	34000	-/27			6		170
libut	1960	106,4	349	8,9	29.1	6,5	21.3	3650/5000		N	6600	18/25			4		97
ashington	1960	116,1	380.9	10	32.8	8,8	28.8	6019/6888		N	15000	20/31			6	16	112
resher	1962	84,9	278.5	9,6	31.4	8,7	28.5	3750/4300		N	15000	20/30			4	2	103
han Allen	1961	125	410.1	10,1	33.1	9,8	32.1	6955/7880		N	15000	20/30			4	16	142
anklin	1965	129,5	424.8	10,1	33.1	9,6	31.4	6650/7250		N	15000	20/30			4	16	168
urgeon	1967	89	291.9	9,5	31.1	7,9	25.9	3640/4640		N	15000	20/30			4	2	107
rwhal	1969	95,9	314.6	11,5	37.7	8,2	26.5	4450/5350		N	17000	20/30			4	2	107
oscomb	1974	111,3	365.1	9,7	31.8	9,5	31.1	5813/6480		N		25/25			4	2	120
s Angeles	1976	109,7	359.9	10,1	33.1	9,9	32.4	6000/6900		N	35000	-/30			4	12	127
io	1981	170,7	560	12,8	41.9	10,8	35.4	16600/18700		N	60000				4	24	133
BRAZIL																	
moio	1937	60,1	197.1	6,3	20.6	3,9	12.7	615/853	2	2	1350/800	14/7,5	1/100	1/3.9	6		37
CANADA																	
ibwa	1965	90	295.2	8,1	26.5	5,5	17.7	2030/2410	2	2	3680/6000	12/17			8		65
AUSTRALIA																	
ley	1967	90	295.2	8,1	26.5	5,5	18	2030/2410			3680/6000	16/17			8		62
JAPAN																	
8	1908	42,2	138.4	4,1	13.4	3,4	11.1	286/321	1	1	600/300	12/8,5			2		26
lland N° 1-5	1905	20,3	66.6	3,6	11.8	3,3	10.8	103/124	1 G	1	180/70	8/7			1		13
10	1911	43,2	141.7	4,1	13.4	3,4	11.1	291/326	1	1	600/300	12/8,5			2		25
13	1911	38,5	126.3	4,1	13.4	3,04	9.9	304/340	1	1	1000/300	10,8/8			2		26
15	1917	26,5	86.9	5,1	16.7	3,09	10	410/665	2	2	2000/850	17/10	1/57	1/2.3	4		30
11-12	1917	69	226.3	6,3	20.6	3,4	11.1	720/1035	2	2	2600/1200	18/9,7	1/76	1/3	6		45
18-21	1920	65,3	214.2	6,05	19.8	4,1	13.4	689/1047	2	2	2800/1200	12/8			5		43
3	1921	66,5	218.1	6,1	20	4,1	13.4	689/1950	2	2	2600/1200	18/9,5	1/76	1/3	5		40
16-24	1922	69,9	229,3	6,08	19.9	3,6	11.8	740/1050	2	2	2600/1200	17/8	1/76	1/3	4		45
idai 44	1924	91,4	299.8	8,9	29.1	4,5	14.7	1390/2430	4	4	5200/2000	20/10	1/120	1/4.7	8		60
	1924	97,5	319.8	8,9	29.1	4,8	15.7	1955/2500	2	2	6000/2600	17,5/8	2/130	2/5.1	6		92
3-64	1929	97,2	318.8	7,7	25.2	4,8	15.7	1635/2300	2	2	6000/1800	20/8	1/120	1/4.7	8		63
nsen I 1	1929	96,9	317.9	9,1	29.8	5,3	17.3	1970/2791	2	2	6000/2600	18/8	2/150	2/5.9	6		92
nsen 1 M	1932	93,8	307.7	9,01	29.5	5,3	17.3	2080/2921	2	2	6000/2600	18/8	2/130	2/5.1	6		93
idai I 68-73	1938	102,3	335.6	8,1	26.5	4,5	14.7	1400/2440	2	2	9000/1800	23/8,2	1/101	1/4	6		84
12-15	1943	108,1	354.6	12,8	41.9	5,8	19	2620/4762	2	2	4400/600	16,7/5,5	1/130	1/5.1	6		
shio	1965	87,7	287.7	8,2	26.9	3,7	12.2	1600/-	2	2	2900/6300	14/18			8		80
ushio	1971	72	236.2	9,9	32.4	7,5	24.6	1850/-			6800/7200	12/20			6		80
ushio	1981	76	249.3	9,9	32.4	7,5	24.6	2200/-			7800/7200	12/20			6		75

D = Diesel
El = Electric
TT = Torpedo tubes
ML = Missile launcher
C = Complement

The year given is the year of commissioning.

Under the heading "engine" various letters sometimes appear after the number: "R" stands for reciprocating, "G" for gasoline engine, "T" for turbine, "P" for petroleum engine, and "N" for nuclear.

Under the headings "Displacement," "Horsepower," and "Speed" there are two numbers separated by a stroke: The first refers to the unit when on the surface and the other when submerged.

CRUISERS–TECHNICAL DATA

Name	Launch Year	Length m	Length ft	Beam m	Beam ft	Draft m	Draft ft	Displacement t	Engine RE	Engine T	Horsepower	Speed in Knots	Range in Miles
GREAT BRITAIN													
Incostant	1868	106,4	349	15,2	49.8	7	22.9	5782	1		7364	16,5	4300
Volage	1869	85,1	279.1	12,8	41.9	5,7	18.7	3078	1		4655	15,1	900
Shah	1872	106	247.7	15,8	50.8	7,2	23.6	6075	1		6868	16,2	1470
Boadicea	1875	91	298.5	13,7	44.9	6,6	21.6	4140	1		5130	14,8	1270
Shannon	1875	79,2	259.8	16,4	53.8	6,4	20.9	5439	2		3542	12,6	
Northampton	1876	85,3	279.8	18,2	59.7	7,3	23.9	7230	2		6060	13,1	5000
Comus	1878	68,5	224.7	13,5	44.2	5,3	17.3	2383	1		2460	13,8	
Terrible	1895	162	531.4	21,6	70.8	8,6	28.2	14400	2		25900	21,9	25000
Pelorus	1896	95,5	313.3	11,1	36.4	5,1	16.7	2167	2		7000	20	8000
Hermes	1898	113,3	371.7	16,4	53.8	6,6	21.6	5600	2		10000	18	
Cressy	1899	143,8	471.7	21,1	69.2	7,6	24.9	12000	2		21000	21	2600
Amethyst	1903	109,4	358.9	12,1	39.6	4,4	14.4	3000		2	13000	23	
Minotaur	1906	160	524.9	22,7	74.4	8,5	27.8	14600	2		27000	23	
Invincible	1907	172,8	566.9	23,9	78.4	7,8	25.5			4	44875	26,5	3000
Boadicea	1908	123,1	403.8	12,4	40.6	4,1	13.4	3300		2	18000	25	
Bristol	1909	138,06	452.9	14,3	46.9	6,6	21.6	4800		2	22000	25	
Queen Mary	1912	213,4	700.1	27,1	88.9	8,8	28.8	27000		4	70000	28	
Cambrian	1916	135,9	445.8	12,5	41	4,1	13.4	3750		4	40000	28,5	
Repulse	1916	242,7	796.2	27,4	89.8	8,2	26.9	32074		2	120000	32	3650
Courageous	1916	239,6	786	24,7	81	7,1	23.2	22690		4	90000	31	
Hood	1918	262,2	860.2	31,7	104	8,9	29.1	44700		4	144000	31	4000
Frobisher	1920	184,4	604.9	15,4	50.5	5,3	17.3	10000		8	65000	30,5	54000
Kent	1926	192	629.9	20,8	68.2	5,01	16.4	9850		4	80000	31,5	10400
Leander	1931	169	554.4	16,8	55.1	5,5	18	7140		4	72000	32,5	7000
Arethusa	1934	154,3	506.2	15,5	50.8	5	16.4	5220		4	64000	32,2	5000
Southampton	1936	180,2	591.2	18,7	61.3	5,9	19.3	12200		4	75000	32	7000
Dido	1939	156,1	512.1	15,5	50.8	4,8	15.7	7200		4	62000	33	5000
Fiji	1939	169,3	555.4	18,9	62	5,5	18	10600		4	72500	31	8000
C 20 Tiger	1945	172,8	566.9	19,5	63.9	7	22.9	12080		4	80000	31,5	6500
D 02 Devonshire	1960	158,7	520.6	16,5	54.1	6,1	20	6200		2	60000	30	4500
CAH 1 Invincible	1977	206,6	677.8	27,5	90.2	7,3	23.9	19500		4	112000	28	5000
FRANCE													
Victorieuse	1875	78,6	257.8	14,8	48.5	6,5	21.3	4504	1		2214	12,7	2740
Duquesne	1876	106,7	350	15,5	50.8	6,8	22.3	5522	2		7500	17	5000
Duguay-Trouin	1877	89,8	294.6	13,2	43.3	5,2	17	3189	2		3740	16	5000
Eclaireur	1877	77,2	253.2	10,8	35.4	4,5	14.7	1643	2		2050	15	4500
Villars	1879	76	249.3	11,6	38	5,9	19.3	2268	1		2760	15,5	7000
Duguesclin	1883	81,06	265.9	17,3	56.7	8,5	27.8	5869	2		4100	14	
Tage	1886	118,9	390	16,3	53.4	6,9	22.6	7590	2		12000	19	
Algier	1889	105,9	347.4	13,8	45.2	5,5	18	4300	2		8000	19,5	
Dupuy de Lôme	1890	114,6	375.9	15,7	51.5	7,07	23.1	6400	3		14000	20,5	
Chasseloup-Laubat	1893	97	318.2	13,2	43.3	5,8	19	3740	2		9500	19,5	
Amiral Pothuau	1895	113	370.7	15,3	50.1	6,5	21.3	5365	2		10200	19,2	4500
Jeanne d'Arc	1899	145,3	476.3	19,4	63.6	7,5	24.6	11270	3		28500	23	13500
Léon Gambetta	1901	148,3	486.5	21,4	70.2	8,2	26.9	12416	3		29000	23,1	12000
Duquesne	1925	191	626.6	18,9	62	6,3	20.6	11900		4	120000	33	3000
Algérie	1932	188	616.7	20	65.6	6,2	20.3	13900		4	84000	31	
La Galissonière	1933	178,9	586.9	18,5	60.6	5,2	17	9120		2	84000	31	6800
De Grasse	1946	188,09	617	18,5	60.6	5,5	18	10225		2	105000	33,5	5000
Colbert	1956	180,8	593.1	19,7	64.6	7,7	25.2	11300		2	86000	32,4	4000
GERMANY													
Sachsen	1877	98,2	322.1	18,3	60	6	19.6	7400	2		5600	14	
Gefion	1893	110,4	362.2	13,2	43.3	6,4	20.9	4300	2		9000	19	6500
Fürst Bismarck	1897	127	416.6	20,4	66.3	8,4	27.5	11281	3		13500	18	2400
Lübeck	1904	111,1	364.4	13,3	43.6	5,6	18.3	3815		2	14400	23	5000
Scharnhorst	1906	144,6	474.4	21,6	70.8	8,3	27.2	12985	3		26000	22,5	7500
Blücher	1908	161,8	530.8	24,5	80.3	8,8	28.8	17500	3		43000	25,8	
Kolberg	1908	130,7	428.8	13,01	42.6	5,3	17.3	4350		2	20000	25,5	
Von der Tann	1909	171,7	563.3	26,6	87.2	9,2	30.1	21082		2	42000	24,8	4400

Number of Guns/mm	Number of Guns/in	Machine guns/mm	TT	ML	Belt Protection mm	Belt Protection in	Turret Protection mm	Turret Protection in	Airplanes Helicopters	C
229; 6/178	10/9; 6/7		1							605
178	6/7									300
230; 16/181; 8/160	2/9; 16/7; 8/6.3		1							600
178	14/7		1							375
254; 7/229	2/10; 7/9		1		229	9.01				450
254; 8/229	4/10; 8/9	8	1		229	9.01				560
178; 12/160	2/7; 12/6.3		1							250
234; 12/152; 16/76	2/9.2; 12/6; 16/3	9	4							890
102	8/4	3	2							224
152; 9/90	11/6; 9/3.6	2	2							450
234; 12/152; 14/76	2/9.2; 2/6; 14/3	8	2		152	6	152	6		760
101; 8/76	12/4; 8/3	2	2							296
230; 10/190; 14/90; 2/76	4/9; 10/7.5; 12/3.6; 2/3		5		152	6	203	8		843
305; 16/102	8/12; 16/4		5		152	6	178	7		784
101	6/4		2							264
152; 10/101	2/6; 10/4		2							376
343; 14/102	8/13.5; 14/4		2		229	9.01	229	9.01		997
152; 2/76	4/6; 2/3	2	6		76	3				323
381; 15/102	6/15; 15/4		2		152	6	279	10.9		1181
381; 18/102; 2/76	4/15; 18/4; 2/3		2		76	3	330	12.9		842
381; 12/140; 4/102; 4/76	8/15; 12/5.5; 4/4; 4/3	15	6		305	12	381	15		1477
190; 8/101; 4/76	7/7.5; 8/4; 4/3	2	6		76	3				774
203; 4/102; 4/76	8/8; 4/4; 4/3	4/40; 12	8				51	2	4	679
152; 4/102; 4/76	8/6; 4/4; 4/3	18	8		76	3	25	0.9	1	550
152; 4/102; 4/76	6/6; 4/4; 4/3	14	6		70	2.7	25	0.9	1	450
152; 8/102; 4/76	12/6; 8/4; 4/3	18	6		114	4.4	51	2	2	750
133	10/5.7	8/40; 8/12,7	6		76	3	38	1.5		550
152; 8/102	12/6; 8/4	8/40; 16/12,7	6		110	4.3	51	2	2	730
152; 2/76	2/6; 2/3			2	89-83	3.5-3.2			4	885
115	4/4.5	2/20		10					1	441
				2					12 + 6	
240; 1/190; 4/140	6/9.5; 1/7.5; 6/5.5				150	5.9				352
190; 14/140	7/7.5; 14/5.5									550
190; 5/140	5/7.5; 5/5.5									322
140	8/5.5									194
140	15/5.5									264
240; 1/190; 6/140	2/9.5; 1/7.5; 6/5.5				254	9.9				400
164; 10/138	8/6.5; 10/5.4		7							530
164; 6/138	4/6.5; 6/5.4		4							390
194; 6/154	2/7.6; 6/6.1		4		92	3.6	100	3.9		526
164; 4/100	6/6.5; 4/3.9		4							328
194; 10/139	2/7.6; 10/5.5	4	5		60-32	2.3-1.2	190	7.5		463
194; 14/139	2/7.6; 14/5.5		2		150-56	5.9-2.2	200	7.8		651
194; 16/164	4/7.6; 16/6.5		5	1	170-90	6.6-3.5	203	7.9		728
203; 8/76	8/8; 8/3	8/37	6						2	605
203; 12/100	8/8; 12/3.9	8/37	6		110	4.3	100	3.9	3	605
152; 8/100	9/6; 8/3.9	8/37	4		105-76	4.1-3	100	3.9	4	540
127	16/5				120	4.7				966
127	16/5				80-50	3.1-1.9			1	800
260	6/10.2									317
105	10/4.1	8	2							300
240; 12/150; 10/88	4/9.5; 12/5.9; 10/3.5	14	6		200	7.8	200	7.8		529
105	10/4.1		2							288
120; 6/150; 20/88	8/8.3; 6/5.9; 20/3.5		4		150	5.9	170	6.6		764
210; 8/152;16/88	12/8.3; 8/6: 16/3.5		3		180-100	7-3.9	180	7		856
105;	12/4.1	4	2							362
280; 10/150; 18/88	8/11; 10/5.9; 18/3.5		4		250	9.8	230	9		998

CRUISERS—TECHNICAL DATA

Name	Launch Year	Length		Beam		Draft		Displacement	Engine		Horsepower	Speed	Range
		m	ft	m	ft	m	ft	t	RE	T		in Knots	in Miles
GERMANY (*cont'd.*)													
Goeben	1911	186,5	611.8	29,5	96.7	9,2	30.1	24999		2	52000	25,5	4120
Derfflinger	1913	210,4	690.2	29	95.1	9,6	31.4	30707		2	63000	26,5	5300
Koenigsberg	1927	174	570.8	15,3	50.1	6,2	20.3	8130	2D	2	68000	32	10000
Nürnberg	1934	176,7	579.9	16,4	53.8	4,3	14.1	8380	4D	2	60000	32	7000
Admiral Hipper	1937	205,9	675.5	21,3	69.8	7,7	25.2	18200		3	132000	32	6800
ITALY													
Cristoforo Colombo	1875	75,7	248.3	11,3	37	5,2	17	2362	1		3782	17	
Amerigo Vespucci	1882	84,5	277,2	12,8	41.9	5,9	19.3	2892	1		3340	14	300
Piemonte	1888	97,8	320.8	11,6	38	5,1	16.7	2780	2		12000	22	7000
Liguria	1893	84,8	278.2	12,03	39.4	4,7	15.4	2460	2		7000	17	4000
Vettor Pisani	1895	105,7	346.7	18	59	7,5	24.6	7242	2		13000	18,6	6000
Giuseppe Garibaldi	1899	111,7	366.4	18,2	59.7	7,3	23.9	8100	2		14000	19,7	9300
San Giorgio	1908	140,8	461.9	21,02	68.9	8	26.2	11300	2		18200	23,2	6200
Libia	1912	111,8	366.7	14,5	47.5	5,5	18	4465	2		12500	22	3150
Trento	1927	196,9	643.9	20,6	67.5	6,8	22.3	13548		4	150000	35	4160
Bartolomeo Colleoni	1930	169,3	555.4	15,5	50.8	5,3	17.3	6954		2	95000	37	3800
Zara	1930	182,8	599.7	20,6	67.5	7,2	23.6	14530		2	95000	32	5360
Eugenio di Savoia	1935	186,9	613.1	17,5	57.4	6,5	21.3	10843		2	110000	36,5	3900
Garibaldi	1936	187	613.5	18,9	62	6,7	21.9	11335		2	85000	30	4500
Etna	1942	153,8	504.5	14,4	47.2	5,9	19.3	6000		2	40000	28	
Andrea Doria	1963	149,3	489.8	17,2	56.4	4,9	16	6500		2	60000	31	6000
Vittorio Veneto	1967	179,6	589.2	19,4	63.6	6	19.6	8850		2	73000	32	6000
Giuseppe Garibaldi	1983	179	587.2	23	75.4			10043		4	80000	29	7000
SPAIN													
Reina Victoria Eugenia	1920	140,8	461.9	15,2	29.8	4,7	15.4	5502		2	25500	25,5	4500
Principe Alfonso	1925	176,6	579.3	16,4	53.8	5,01	16.4	9237		4	80000	33	5000
Canarias	1931	193,8	635.8	19,4	63.6	5,2	17	12230		4	90000	33	8000
HOLLAND													
Giava	1921	154,8	507.8	15,9	52.1	5,4	17.7	7050		3	65000	30	5000
De Ruyter	1935	173,1	567.9	15,6	51.1	5,01	16.4	7548		2	66000	32	5000
De Ruyter	1944	187,2	614.1	17.2	56.4	5,6	18.3	11926		2	85000	32	
Kaiserin und Koenigin Maria Theresia	1893	114	274	16,2	53.1	6,5	21.3	5270	2		9800	19,4	
Kaiser Franz Josef	1889	103,7	340.2	14,8	48.5	5,6	18.3	4000	2		9800	19	3000
Sankt Georg	1903	124,3	407.8	19	62.3	6,8	22.3	8070	2		15000	22	
Saida	1912	130,6	428.4	12,8	41.9	5,3	17.3	4417		2	25000	27	1600
GREECE													
Giorgios Averoff	1910	140,5	460.9	21,1	69.2	7,4	24.2	10600	2		19000	22,5	7125
Helli	1912	97,8	320.8	11,8	38.7	4,2	13.7	2600		3	6000	20	5250
RUSSIA													
General Admiral	1873	87,1	285.7	14,6	47.8	6,4	20.9	4650	1		6300	15	5900
Admiral Nakimoff	1885	101,5	333	18,6	61	7,8	25.5	7780	2		9000	18,5	
Rurik	1892	130	426.5	20,4	66.9	9,1	29.8	10920	4		13500	18,8	
Svietlana	1896	101	331.3	13	42.6	5,7	18.7	3850	2		8500	20	
Gromovoi	1899	146,5	480.6	20,9	68.5	7,9	25.9	12367	3		18000	20	
Aurora	1899	124,9	409.7	16,7	54.7	6,4	20.9	6630	3		11600	20	
Borodino	1915	221,9	728	29,8	97.7	8,7	28.5	32500		4	68000	26,5	
Krasni Krim	1915	154,7	507.5	15,3	50.1	5,5	18	8050		2	50000	29,5	3700
Admiral Greig	1916	154,3	506.2	15,3	50.1	5,5	18	6800		4	50000	29,5	
Krasni Kavkaz	1916	161,5	529.8	15,3	50.1	6,1	20	9650		2	55000	30	3700
Kirov	1936	191,5	628.2	18	59	6,1	20	11500	2D	2	11000	35	3500
Chapaev	1940	208	682.4	19,5	63.9	7,1	23.2	15500	2D	2	130000	35	4500
Sverdlov	1951	210	688.9	22	72.1	7,5	24.6	19200		2	130000	34	8700
Admiral Fokin	1961	142	465.8	15,8	51.8	5,3	17.3	6000		2	100000	35	
Vize Admiral Drodz	1965	155	508.5	17	55.7	5,5	18	7500		2	100000	35	5500
Moskwa	1965	196,6	645	23	75.4	7,6	24.9	18000		2	100000	30	

Number of Guns/mm	Number of Guns/in	Machine guns/mm	TT	ML	Belt Protection mm	in	Turret Protection mm	in	Airplanes Helicopters	C
0/280; 12/150; 14/88	10/11; 12/5.9; 14/3.5		4		270	10.6	230	9		1053
/305; 12/150; 8/88	8/12; 12/5.9; 8/3.5		4		300	11.8	270	10.6		1182
/150; 4/88; 8/76	9/5.9; 4/3.5; 8/3	10	12		50	1.9	30	1.1	1	514
/150; 8/88; 8/76	9/5.9; 8/3.5; 8/3	4	12		50	1.9	30	1.1	2	656
/203; 12/105	8/8; 12/4.1	12/37; 8/20	12		80	3.1	105	4.1	3	1600
/120	8/4.7									207
/150; 3/76	8/5.9; 3/3	4								268
/152; 6/120	6/6; 6/4.7		3							257
/152; 6/120	4/6; 6/4.7	2	3							257
2/152; 6/120	12/6; 6/4.7	2	5		110-150	4.3-5.9				504
/254; 2/203; 14/152; 10/76	1/10; 2/8; 14/6; 10/3	2	4		150-80	5.9-3.1	150	5.9		555
/254; 8/190; 18/76	4/10; 8/7.5; 18/3	3	3		200-60	7.8-2.3	180	7		699
/152; 8/120	2/6; 8/4.7		2							310
/203; 16/100	8/8; 16/3.9	4/40; 8/13	8		70	2.7	100	3.9	3	723
/152; 6/100	8/6; 6/3.9	8/37; 8/13,2	4		24	0.9	23	0.9	1	507
/203; 16/100	8/8; 16/3.9	4/37; 8/13,2			150	5.9	150	5.9	2	140
/152; 6/100	8/6; 6/3.9	8/37; 12/13,2	6		70	2.7	90	3.5	2	578
/135; 8/76	6/5.3; 8/3			6	100 + 30	3.9 + 1.1	100	3.9		665
/135	6/5.3	12/20			60	2.3				
/76	8/3		6	2					4	478
/76	8/3		6	2					9	530
		6/40	6	10					16	500
/152; 4/76;	9/6; 4/3	4	2		76	3				404
/152; 4/102; 2/76	8/6; 4/4; 2/3	1	12		76	3				564
/203; 8/100	8/8; 8/3.9	8/40	12		51	2	25	0.9	2	765
0/150; 4/88	10/5.9; 4/3.5	4			76	3				474
/150	7/5.9	10/40; 8/12,7; 8			76	3	102	4	2	485
/152	8/6	8/40			76	3	101	4		964
/240; 8/150	2/9.5; 8/5.9	2	2		100	3.9				450
/240; 6/150	2/9.5; 6/5.9		4							367
/235; 5/185; 4/150; 8/88	2/9.3; 5/7.3; 4/5.9; 8/3.5	2	2		210	8.2	127	5		628
/100; 2/76	9/3.9; 2/3		4		63	2.4				368
/254; 8/190; 16/76	4/10; 8/7.5; 16/3	2	3		203	8	152	6		600
/152; 4/101; 2/76	2/6; 4/4; 2/3		2							232
/203; 2/152	4/8; 2/6				152	6				480
/203; 10/152	8/8; 10/6		4		254	10				567
/203; 16/152; 6/120	4/8; 16/6; 6/4.7		6		254	10				727
/152	6/6		4							360
/203; 16/152; 20/76	4/8; 16/6; 20/3		4		152	6				877
/152; 22/76	8/6; 22/3		4							570
2/305; 24/155; 4/101	12/12; 24/6.1; 4/4	4	6		310	12.2				
5/130; 4/100; 4/76	15/5.1; 4/3.9; 4/3	4	9		76	3	76	3		700
5/130; 4/101; 4/76	15/5.1; 4/4; 4/3	4	2		76	3				
/180; 4/100	4/7; 4/3.9		12		76	3			1	850
/180; 8/100	9/7; 8/3.9	6/37	6		76	3	102	4	2	734
2/152; 8/101	12/6; 8/4	28/37			90	3.5	100	3.9		834
2/152; 12/100	12/6; 12/3.9	32/37	10		100-125	3.9-4.9	127	5		1050
/76	4/3		6	10						390
			10	8					1	400
			10	6					18	800

CRUISERS – TECHNICAL DATA

Name	Launch Year	Length m	ft	Beam m	ft	Draft m	ft	Displacement t	Engine RE	T	Horsepower	Speed in Knots	Range in Miles
RUSSIA (*cont'd.*)													
Admiral Isakov	1970	158,5	520	17	55.7	6	19.6	7500		2	100000	33	5500
Nikolayev	1971	173,8	570.2	18,3	60	6,2	20.3	10000		4GT	120000	34	
Kiev	1972	274,4	900.2	41,2	135.1	9	29.5	42000		4	180000	32	13500
Kirov	1977	247	810.3	27	88.5	7,5	24.6	23000	4GT	4+1R	155000	34	
UNITED STATES													
Atlanta	1884	86,3	283.1	12,8	41.9	5,1	16.7	3189	2		4030	15,6	
Olympia	1892	106,3	348.7	16,1	52.8	6,5	21.3	5870	2		17000	21	12000
CA 3 Brooklyn	1895	122,7	402.5	19,5	63.9	7,3	23.9	10068	4		16000	21	6216
C 22 Charleston	1904	129,5	424.8	19,7	64.6	6,6	21.6	9700	2		21000	21,5	
CL 3 Salem	1907	128,9	422.8	14,3	46.9	5,8	19	3750		2	16000	24	6850
C 16 Chattanooga	1913	93,9	308	13,3	43.6	5,2	17	3100	2		4700	16,5	7000
CL 4 Omaha	1920	169,5	556	16,8	55.1	6,1	20	9190		4	90000	33,9	10000
CA 24 Pensacola	1929	178,4	585.2	19,8	64.9	4,9	16	12200		4	107000	32,7	13000
CA 33 Portland	1932	186,2	610.8	20,1	65.9	5,3	17.3	12600		4	107000	32,7	10000
CL 40 Brooklyn	1936	185,4	608.2	18,7	61.3	7,3	23.9	12500		4	100000	32,5	14500
CL 51 Atlanta	1941	164,8	540.6	16,2	53.1	7,9	25.9	8100		2	75000	33	7500
CL 55 Cleveland	1941	186,2	610.8	20,1	65.9	6,1	20	13755		4	100000	33	10000
CA 69 Boston	1942	205,3	673.5	21,6	70.8	7,9	25.9	17500		4	120000	34	9000
CB 1 Alaska	1943	246,6	809	27,7	90.8	10,4	34.1	34250		4	150000	33	
CLG 3 Galveston	1945	185,9	609.9	20,2	66.2	7,6	24.9	14600		4	100000	31,5	10000
CG 10 Albany	1945	205,3	673.5	21,6	70.8	8,2	26.9	17500		4	120000	34	9000
CL 144 Worcester	1947	207,1	679.4	21,5	70.5	7,6	24.9	18500		4	120000	32	12000
CA Des Moines	1946	218,4	716.5	23,3	76.4	7,9	25.9	21500		4	120000	33	8000
CGN 9 Long Beach	1959	220	721.7	22,3	73.1	8,8	28.8	17350		2	80000	25	
CG 16 Leahy	1961	162,5	533.1	16,6	54.4	7,9	25.9	7800		2	85000	34	8000
CGN 25 Bainbridge	1961	172,5	565.9	17,6	57.7	9,5	31.1	8580		2	60000	30	
CG 26 Belknap	1963	166,7	546.9	16,7	54.7	8,7	28.5	7930		2	85000	34	8000
CGN 35 Truxtun	1964	117,9	386.8	17,7	58	9,4	30.8	9127		2	60000	30	
CGN 36 California	1971	181,7	596.1	18,6	61	9,6	31.4	10150		2		30	
CGN 38 Virginia	1974	177,3	581.6	18,9	62	9	29.5	11000		2		30	
BRAZIL													
Tamandaré	1890	89,6	293.9	14	45.9	6,2	20.3	4537	2		7500	17	
Almirante Barrozo	1896	100,5	329.7	13,3	43.6	6,1	20	3450	2		7500	20	
25 de Mayo	1890	100,3	329	13,2	43.3	5,01	16.4	3200	2		13000	22	
25 de Mayo	1929	162,5	533.1	17,6	57.7	4,9	16	8600		2	85000	32	
CHILE													
Esmeralda I	1883	82,08	269.2	12,7	41.6	5,5	18	2920	2		6803	18	2200
Esmeralda II	1894	140,7	461.6	16,1	52.8	6,5	21.3	7000	2		16000	22,2	
General O'Higgins	1897	124,05	406.9	19.09	62.6	6,7	21.9	8500	2		16500	21,2	
Melbourne	1912	138,9	455.7	12,4	40.6	4,7	15.4	5400		4	25000	25	
Sydney	1934	169,1	554.7	17,2	56.4	5,5	18	9275		4	72000	32,5	7000
JAPAN													
Amagi	1877	65,1	213.5	10,8	35.4	4,3	14.1	1030	1		720	11	
Yamato	1885	62,8	206	10,6	34.7	4,6	15	1478	1		1622	13	
Ibuki	1907	147,8	484.9	23	75.4	7,9	25.9	14600		2	25000	22	
Hirato	1911	144,4	473.7	14,1	46.2	5,1	16.7	5040		2	25000	26,8	10000
Nachi	1927	203,5	667.6	17,3	56.7	5,8	19	12374		4	128000	35,5	8000
Mogami	1934	197,9	646.3	18	59	5,4	17.9	11169		4	152000	37	8150
Mogami	*	201,6	661.4	18,2	59.7	5,9	19.3	13440		4	152000	34	8500
Katori	1939	133,5	437.9	15,9	52.1	5,7	18.7	6700		2	80000	18	
Agano	1941	174,03	570.9	15,1	49.5	5,7	18.7	8534		4	100000	35	6900

Number of Guns/mm	Number of Guns/in	Machine guns/mm	TT	ML	Belt Protection mm	in	Turret Protection mm	in	Airplanes Helicopters	C
		8/30	10	10					1	500
4/76	4/3	4	10	10					1	500
4/76	4/3		10	13					35	2500
2/100	2/3.9	8/30	10	34					4	8500
2/203; 6/152	2/8; 6/6	2								289
4/203; 10/127	4/8; 10/5	4	6				102	4		446
8/203; 12/127	8/8; 12/5	4	5		76	3	380	15		561
14/152; 18/76	14/6; 18/3	4			101	4				673
2/127; 6/76	2/5; 6/3		2		51	2				359
10/127; 8/76	10/5; 8/3	2								293
12/152; 2/76	12/6; 2/3		4		76	3				458
10/203; 4/127	10/8; 4/5		6		76	3	38	1.5	4	1200
9/203; 8/127	9/8; 8/5	2/47; 10/12,7			76-102	3-4	76	3	4	850
15/152; 8/127	15/6; 8/5	4/47; 8/12,7			100	3.9	127	5	4	1200
16/127	16/5	32/40; 8/20	8		90	3.5	38	1.5		810
12/152; 12/127	12/6; 12/5	28/40; 24/20			127	5	127	5	3	1400
6/203; 10/127; 8/76	6/8; 10/5; 8/3			4	152	6	152	6		1223
9/305; 12/127	9/12; 12/5	56/40; 34/20			229	9	325	12.7	4	2251
6/152; 6/127	6/6; 6/5		1	2	127	5	127	5		1200
2/127	2/5		6	7	152	6			1	1010
12/152; 20/76	12/6; 20/3	12/40			152	6	152	6	3	1800
9/203; 12/127; 24/76	9/8; 12/5; 24/3				203	8	152	6	4	1860
2/127	2/5		6	7					1	1010
4/76	4/3		6	5						413
4/76	4/3		6	5						470
1/127; 2/76	1/5; 2/3		6	4					1	418
1/127; 2/76	1/5; 2/3		4	2						492
2/127	2/5		4	3						540
2/127	2/5		6	4					2	442
10/152; 2/120	10/6; 2/4.7	8								450
6/152; 4/120	6/6; 4/4.7	4								366
2/203; 8/120	2/8; 8/4.7		3							300
6/190; 12/100	6/7.5; 12/3.9	6/40	6		70	2.7	50	1.9		600
2/254; 6/152	2/10; 6/6	7	3							300
2/203; 16/152; 8/90; 9/76	2/8; 16/6; 8/3.6; 9/3	8	3		152	6				500
4/203; 10/152; 4/120	4/8; 10/6; 4/4.7		2		178	7	190	7.4		500
8/152; 1/76	8/6; 1/3	4	2		76	3				392
8/152; 4/102; 4/76	8/6; 4/4; 4/3	17	8		76	3	25	0.9	1	550
1/170; 4/120; 3/76	1/6.7; 4/4.7; 3/3	3								159
2/170; 5/120; 1/76	2/6.7; 5/4.7; 1/3	4								231
4/305; 8/203; 12/152; 4/76	4/12; 8/8; 12/6; 4/3			5	178	7	178	7		817
8/152; 4/76	8/6; 4/3	2	3							392
10/200; 6/120	10/7.9; 6/4.7	8/25; 2	12		100	3.9	76	3	2	773
15/155; 8/127	15/6.1; 8/5	6	12		127	5	25	0.9	3	850
10/203; 8/127	10/8; 8/5	30/20	12		127	5	76	3	11	850
4/140; 2/127	4/5.5; 2/5	4/25	4						1	
6/150; 4/80	6/5.9; 4/3.2	32/25	8		60	2.3	25	0.9	2	730

RE = Reciprocating engines   T = Turbines   TT = Torpedo tubes   ML = Missile launchers   C = Complement

*after modifications

Under the heading "Engine" various letters sometimes appear after the number: "GT" stands for gas turbine, "R" for reactor, and "D" for diesel.

TORPEDO BOATS—TECHNICAL DATA

Name	Year	Length		Beam		Draft		Displacement	Engine		HP	Speed	N. Guns/mm	N. Guns/in	TT	Mg.	C
		m	ft	m	ft	m	ft	t	RE	T		in Knots					
GREAT BRITAIN																	
Lightning	1877	25,6	83.9	3,3	10.8	1,1	3.6	27	1		390	18,7			3		15
N 2-12 Th	1878	26,5	86.9	3,3	10.8	0,8	2.6	27	1		425	20			1		15
N 51-54 Th	1879	17,1	56.1	2,1	6.8	0,9	2.9		1		180	14,7			2		
N 64 Th	1880	19,2	62.9	2,2	7.2				1		170	17,3			2		10
N 17 Ya	1880	25,9	84.9	3,3	10.8	1,4	4.5	33	1		450	20,7			1		8
N 81 W (Swift)	1844	45,7	149.9	5,3	17.3	1,9	6.2	125	1		1387	20,8	6/47	1/1.8	3		25
N 22 Th	1885	34,4	112.8	3,8	12.4	1,7	5.5	63	1		736	20			2	1	15
N 24 Ya	1886	36,5	119.7	4,02	13.1	1,6	5.2	67	1		600	19,5			2	2	15
N 25 Th-41 Th	1886	38,8	127.2	3,8	12.4	1,9	6.2	68	1		670	20			4	3	16
N 80 Ya	1887	41,1	134.8	4,2	13.7	1,8	5.9	105	1		1540	23	4/47	4/1.8	3		21
N 38 Ya	1889	18,2	59.7	2,8	9.1	1,1	3.6	16,5	1		230	16,5			2	1	10
N 91 Th	1894	43,4	142.3	4,7	15.4	2,2	7.2	130	2		2500	23,5	3/47	3/1.8	3		18
N 98 Th	1900	48,7	159.7	5,1	16.7	2,5	8.2	180	1		2900	25	3/47	3/1.8	3		32
Caroline	1904	47	154.1	4,6	15	2,4	7.8	130	1	2	2250	26	2/47	2/1.8	2		
N 1-24	1906	55,4	181.7	5,4	17.7	1,8	5.9	259		4	4000	25	2/76	2/3	3		35
N 25-36	1909	53,9	176.8	5,4	17.7	1,8	5.9	263		4	4000	25	2/76	2/3	3		35
FRANCE																	
N 33	1878	27,4	89.8	3,6	11.8	1,7	5.5	34		1	500	18			2		11
N 30	1878	19,2	62.9	2,2	7.2	0,9	2.9	11,8	1		120	16			2		9
N 1	1878	38,6	126.6	4,2	13.7	1,6	5.2				120				2		
N 65-125	1883	35	114.8	3,3	10.8	2,5	8.2	58	1		525	19			2		16
N 126	1887	36,8	120.7	3,9	12.7	2,6	8.5	79,4	1		900	21			2	2	21
Coureur	1888	45,3	148.6	4,3	14.1	1,6	5.2		2		1500	23,5	2/47	2/1.8	2		28
Avant Garde	1889	45,4	148.9	4,5	14.7	2,4	7.8	130	2		1250	20,5	2/47	2/1.8	2		27
Ouragan	1889	47,2	154.8	4,8	15.7	2,9	9.5	180	1		1600	25	2/47	2/1.8	4		32
N 152	1890	37,8	124	3,9	12.7	2,5	8.2	79	1		1000	21			2	2	22
N 130-144	1891	34	111.5	3,5	11.4	2,1	6.8	53	1		720	21			2	2	18
Turco	1892	42,06	137.9	4,5	14.7	2,1	6.8	124,5	2		1800	21	2/47	2/1.8	2		28
Lansquenet	1894	52,6	172.5	5,3	17.3	2,4	7.8	138	2		2800	26			2	2	30
Forban	1895	44	144.3	4,6	15	1,4	4.5	152	2		3985	31			2	2	27
Aquilon	1896	43,2	141.7	4,5	14.7	2,4	7.8	120	1		2000	26	2/47	2/1.8	2		27
N 201-292	1897	39,1	126.2	4,1	13.4	2,6	8.5	84,2	1		1500	23			2		23
N 293	1903	39,5	129.5	4,2	13.7	2,3	7.5	95,6		3	2000	26			2		23
Mistral	1903	46,5	152.5	5,1	16.7	2,5	8.2	185	2		4200	25	2/47	2/1.8	3		30
N 295-369	1903	40,1	131.5	4,4	14.4	2,6	8.5	102	1		2000	26			3	2	23
N 294	1904	39,5	129.5	4,09	13.4	2,2	7.2	102		3	4200	26			2	2	23
Libellule	1905	36,2	118.7	3,4	11.1	1,9	6.2	58	1		1000	15			1		14
La Pomone	1936	89,9	294.9	9,3	30.5	2,5	8.2	994		2	22000	34,5	2/100	2/3.9	2	4	23
GERMANY																	
Th 1	1884	37,2	122	3,8	12.4	2,07	6.7	81	1		653	17,8			2	2	6
Th 2	1884	19,2	62	2,2	7.2	1,3	4.2	14,5	1		164	15,4			2	2	6
XII-XVII (W 1-6)	1884	34,9	114.4	3,8	12.4	2,3	7.5	91	1		910	19,8			2	2	14
XVIII-XXVII (V 1-10)	1884	32,7	107.2	3,7	12.1	1,8	5.9	61	1		590	17,9			1	2	14
XXVIII-XXXIII (S 1-6)	1884	37,7	123.6	4,8	15.7	2,2	7.2	99	1		900	17			2	2	16
Y	1885	36,5	119.7	4,02	13.1	1,6	5.2	83	1		599	18,3			2	2	14
G	1885	36,2	118.7	4	13.1	2,3	7.5	86	1		722	18,8			2	2	14
S 7-57	1886	37,7	123.6	4,8	15.7	2,1	6.8	103	1		831	20			3	2	16
D 1-10	1887	56,5	185.5	6,6	21.6	3,4	11.1	300	1		2036	20,6			3	6	45
S 58	1892	44,3	145.3	5	16.4	2,5	8.2	152	1		1332	20,5	1/50	1/1.9	3		16
S 125	1904	64,7	212.2	7	22.9	3,1	10.1	454		7	6600	28	1/88; 2/50	1/3.5; 2/1.9	3		57
G 137	1907	71,5	234.5	7,6	24.9	3,2	10.4	693		7	10800	33,9	1/88	1/3.5	3		81
V 161	1908	72,5	237.8	7,8	25.5	2,9	9.3	687		2	14800	33	2/88	2/3.5	3		84
G 197	1911	74	242.7	7,9	25.9	3,2	10.4	810		2	19130	33,9	2/88	2/3.5	4		84
V 105	1915	62,6	205.3	6,2	20.3	2,5	8.2	421		2	5670	29,4	2/88	2/3.5	4		60
A 56	1917	61,1	200.4	6,4	20.9	2,2	7.2	381		2	6008	28,2	2/88	2/3.5	1		50
A 26	1918	50	164	5,3	17.3	2,3	7.3	250		1	3506	25,8	2/88	2/3.5	1		29
Möwe	1927	87	185.4	8,4	27.5	3,6	11.8	1290		2	22100	32	3/105	3/4.1	6	4	120
Wolf	1928	92,6	303.8	8,6	28.2	3,5	11.4	1320		2	25160	34,6	3/105	3/4.1	6	4	120
T 37-51	1943	106	347.7	10,7	35.1	3,7	12.1	2155		2	40000	31	4/105	4/4.1	6	4	206

Name	Year	Length		Beam		Draft		Displacement	Engine		HP	Speed	N. Guns/mm	N. Guns/in	TT	Mg.	C
		m	ft	m	ft	m	ft	t	RE	T		in Knots					
ERMANY (cont'd.)																	
1-21	1943	84,3	276.5	8,6	28.2	2,9	9.5	1088		2	31000	35,5	1/105	1/4.1	6	8	206
ITALY																	
bbio	1878	24,2	79.3	3,05	10	0,9	2.9	26	1		250	18			2		10
terpe	1883	19,2	62.9	2,3	7.5	1,1	3.6	13,5	1		150	17,3			2	1	10
debaran	1883	30,5	100	3,5	11.4	1,6	5.2	39	1		430	21			2	1	10
po S	1886	39	127.9	4,8	15.7	2,1	6.8	80	1		1000	22			1	2	16
-79 Ya	1887	42,7	140	4,2	13.7	1,5	4.9	110	2		1600	25			4	2	20
lgore	1887	56,7	186	6,3	20.6	2,2	7.2	370	2		2100	17	2/57	2/2.3	3	4	55
quila	1888	47,6	156.1	5,1	16.7	2	6.5	139	2		2200	23,5			2	2	23
T	1888	31,03	101.8	3,5	11.4	1,7	5.5	44	1		350	18			2	1	11
tum	1892	30,8	101	3,5	11.4	2,3	7.5	42	1			19					
ndore	1900	48	157.4	5,5	18	1,2	3.9	140	2		2400	25,7			2	2	30
llicano	1900	48,7	159.7	5,7	18.7	1,5	4.9	184	2		2680	23			2	2	30
rio	1905	51,3	168.3	6	19.6	1,9	6.2	215	2		3000	25,3	3/47	3/1.8	3		38
gaso 2°	1905	50,3	165	5,3	17.3	1,7	5.5	210	2		3000	25	3/47	3/1.8	3		42
bbiano 2°	1907	49,6	162.7	5,9	19.3	1,4	4.5	174	2		2200	22	2/47	2/1.8	3		32
lo	1915	73	239.4	7,3	23.9	2,7	8.8	806		2	16000	30	2/76	2/3	4		69
RM	1916	42,5	139.4	4,6	15	1,4	4.5	140	2	1	3200		1/57	1/2.3	2		30
-75 OLT	1918	45,7	149.9	4,6	15	1,7	5.5	195		2	3500	27	2/76	2/3	2		31
-69 PN	1918	42,5	139.4	4,6	15	1,6	5.2	156	2		3200	27	2/76	2/3	2		30
lestro	1922	80,4	263.7	8,02	26.3	3,1	10.1	1180		2	22000	32	4/102	4/4	4		106
ica	1935	80,3	263.4	8,2	26.9	2,8	9.1	901		2	19000	34	3/100; 2/76	3/3.9; 2/3	4	8	99
clone	1942	87,7	287.7	9,9	92.4	3,7	12.1	1652		2	16000	25	3/100	3/3.9	4	6	177
iete	1943	83,5	273.9	8,6	28.2	3.1	10.1	1127		2	22000	31,5	2/100	2/3.9	6	10	150
SPAIN																	
iete N 3	1887	44,9	147.3	4,3	14.1	1,4	4.5	97	2		1600	26			2	2	
abana N 8	1887	34,8	114.1	3,8	12.4	1,8	5.9	67	1		780	21,2			2	2	17
1 - N 7	1910	50	164	5	16.4	1,6	5.2	190		3	3750	26	3/47	3/1.8	3		31
8 - N 22	1919	50	164	5	16.4	1,6	5.2	190		2	3750	26	3/47	3/1.8	3		31
NORWAY																	
eipner	1937	74,3	243.7	7,8	25.5	2,1	6.8	708		2	12500	30	3/102	3/4	2	1	100
HOLLAND																	
dra	1900	40	131.2	4,1	13.4	2,2	7.2	103	1		1500	24,3			3	2	20
1 - G 4	1905	47	154.1	4,7	15.4	2,4	7.1	142	1		2100	24,7	2/50	2/1.9	1		26
5 - Z 8	1914	58,8	192.9	6	13.6	1,6	5.2	310	2		5700	27	2/76	2/3	4		46
1 - Z 4	1915	62,6	205.3	6,2	20.3	2,5	8.2	421		2	5500	27	2/76	2/3	4		39
DENMARK																	
aerdfisken	1881	33,5	109.9	3,6	11.8	1,8	5.9	49	1		695	20			2	1	14
lfinen	1883	45,1	147.9	5,1	16.7	2,1	6.8	187	2		3500	26	1/76	1/3	2		30
vhesten	1888	42,03	137.8	4,2	13.7	2,1	6.8	94	1		1200	22,8			4	2	20
ridderen	1912	56,3	184.7	5,5	18	1,9	6.2	271		2	5300	28,2	2/76	2/3	3		33
agen	1930	60,5	198.4	5,9	19.3	2,3	7.5	290		2	6000	27,5	2/76	2/3	6	4	51
itfeld	1943	86	282.1	8,4	27.5	3,4	11.1	890		2	24000	35	2/105	2/4.1	6	3	100
per	1896	44,8	146.9	4,5	14.7	2,4	7.8	126	1		2000	26	2/47	2/1.8	3	2	21
1-6	1910	43,3	142	4,3	14.1	1,4	4.5	110	1		2600	26	2/47	2/1.8	2	2	20
- 63 T	1910	56	183.7	5,5	18	2,7	8.8	200	1		3000	27	4/47	4/1.8	3	4	31
M	1915	60,3	197.8	5,6	18.3	1,5	4.9	250		2	5000	28,5	2/66	2/2.5	4	2	38
GREECE																	
gli	1913	45	147.6	5	16.4	1,2	3.9	125	2		2400	25	2/57	2/2.3	3		30
TURKEY																	
scher	1890	49	160.7	5,6	18.3	2,2	7.2	150	2		2500	24			2	5	
dul Mezid	1902	50,6	166	5,6	18.3	1,2	3.5	145	2		2400	27			2	2	
RUSSIA																	
tum 251	1880	30,4	99.7	3,8	12.4	1,5	4.9	40	1		500	20			2	1	12
chum - 257	1883	34,4	112.8	3,8	19.4	1,8	5.9	65	1		730	19,5			2	2	12
ler - 259	1885	47,6	156.1	5,1	16.7	2,0	6.5	139	2		2200	27,4			2	2	
borg - 102	1886	45,1	147.9	5,1	16.7	2,3	7.5	140	2		1400	21,9			3	2	
tha 105	1887	39	127.9	4,8	15.7	2,1	6.8	74	1		550	19			2	2	
rnov - 103	1893	44,2	145	4,5	14.7	2,4	7.8	129	2		2000	25,4			3	2	

TORPEDO BOATS–TECHNICAL DATA

Name	Year	Length m	Length ft	Beam m	Beam ft	Draft m	Draft ft	Displacement t	Engine RE	Engine T	HP	Speed in Knots	N. Guns/mm	N. Guns/in	TT	Mg.	C
RUSSIA *(cont'd.)*																	
N 214 - 223	1901	46,5	152.5	4,9	16	2,5	8.2	152	2		4200	30	2/47	2/1.8	1		
Shtorm	1932	72,5	237.8	7,3	23.9	3,04	9.9	740		2	13200	25	2/100	2/3.9	3	6	7
Dzerzhinsky	1934	89	291.9	8,2	26.9	5,08	16.6	810	3D		4800	20	3/100	3/3.9			12
Yastreb	1939	85,03	278.9	8,2	26.9	4,8	15.7	1250		2	23000	35	3/102	3/4	3	4	9
Albatros	1944	85,03	278.9	8,3	27.2	5,04	16.5	1300		2	23000	34	1/100	1/3.9	3	2	9
UNITED STATES																	
Cushing N 1	1889	42,05	137.9	4,2	13.7	1,4	4.5	150	2		1800	22,5			2	3	2
Winslow N 5	1897	48,7	159.7	4,9	16	1,5	4.9	165	2		2000	28,6			3	3	
Gwin N 15	1898	30,4	99.7	3,8	12.4	0,9	3.2	46,5	1		850	20			2	1	
Porter N 6	1898	53,3	174.8	5,4	17.7	1,4	4.5	165	2		3400	28,7			3	3	
Levant N 23	1898	18,2	59.7	2,5	8.2	0,7	2.2	16	1		250	17,5					
Stringham N 19	1900	69,5	228	6,7	21.9	2	6.5	340	2		3600	30	7/57	7/2.3	2		
BRAZIL																	
Araguary	1892	45,7	149.9	4,4	14.4	1,6	5.2	106	2		1750	25,8	2/47	2/1.8	4		
Panne	1892	47,6	156.1	5,1	16.7	2	6.5	130	2		2200	28			3	2	
ARGENTINA																	
Commodoro Py	1891	45,7	149.9	4,4	14.4	1,5	4.9	110	2		1860	25	3/47	3/1.8	4		
CHINA																	
Chang N 1	1895	39	127.9	4,8	15.7	2,1	6.8	89	1		1200	24			3	2	
THAILAND																	
Puket	1935	68	223	6,4	20.9	2,1	6.8	470		2	9000	31	3/76	3/3	6	2	
JAPAN																	
Kotaka	1886	50,6	166	5,7	18.7	1,5	4.9	190	2		1217	19	4/47	4/1.8	6		
N 15 - 24	1891	34	111.5	3,5	11.4	2,1	6.8	53	1		720	21			2		
N 22 - 23	1894	39	127.9	4,8	15.7	2,1	6.8	85	1		1000	22,5			3	3	
N 31 - 38	1899	39	127.9	4,8	15.7	2,1	6.8	89	1		1200	24			3	3	
Shirataka	1900	46,5	152.5	5,1	16.7	1,2	3.9	127	2		2600	28	3/42	3/1.6	3		
Hayabusha	1900	46,3	151.9	4,9	16	2,5	8.2	152,4	2		4200	29	1/57	1/2.3	3		
N 50 - 59	1902	34	111.5	3,5	11.4	2,1	6.8	152	1		1200	32	2/47	2/1.8	3		
N 67 - 75	1902	46,3	151.9	4,9	16	2,5	8.2	152	1		1200	32	2/47	2/1.8	3		
Tidori	1933	81,9	268.6	7,3	23.9	2,4	7.8	737		2	17000	30	3/127	3/5	4		1
Otori	1937	88,5	290.3	8,1	26.5	2,7	8.8	1040		2	19000	30,5	3/47	3/1.8	3	1	1

RE = Reciprocating engines
T = Turbines
TT = Torpedo tubes
Mg. = Machine guns
C = Complement

*after modifications

Under the heading "Engine," the letter "D," which sometimes appears after the number, stands for diesel.

Name	Year	Length m	Length ft	Beam m	Beam ft	Draft m	Draft ft	Displacement t	Engine RE	Engine T	HP	Speed in Knots	N. Guns/mm	N. Guns/in	TT	ML	C
GREAT BRITAIN																	
avoc	1893	54,8	179.7	5,6	18.3	1,6	5.2	240	2		3550	26	1/66; 3/57	1/2.5; 3/2.3	2		43
aring I	1894	56,5	185.3	5,7	18.7	2,1	6.8						1/66; 3/57	1/2.5; 3/2.3	3		45
rret	1895	59,4	194.8	5,8	19	1,5	5.1	280	2		4582	27	1/66; 5/57	1/2.5; 5/2.3	3		50
rly	1895	60,9	199.8	5,9	19.3			280	2		4188	27	1/76; 5/57	1/3; 5/2.3	2		45
ontest	1895	63,5	208.3	5,8	19			290	2		4503	27	1/76; 5/57	1/3; 5/2.3	2		50
rdent	1895	60,9	199.8	5,7	18.7			265	2		4543	28	1/76; 5/57	1/3; 5/2.3	2		45
arger	1895	58,1	190.6	5,6	18.3			250	2		3216	26	1/76; 5/57	1/3; 5/2.3	2		50
rago	1896	64,9	212.9	6,5	21.3	1,6	5.2	395	2		7004	30	1/76; 5/57	1/3; 5/2.3	2		60
per	1900	64,09	210.2	6,4	20.9	2,2	7.2	393		4	11500	33	1/76; 5/57	1/3; 5/2.3	2		62
obra	1901	68,1	223.4	6,2	20.3	2,2	7.2	430		4	12000	36	1/76; 5/57	1/3; 5/2.3	2		62
elox	1902	64,02	210	6,4	20.9	2,2	7.2	462		4	7000	27	1/76; 5/57	1/3; 5/2.3	2		68
erwent	1903	67,1	220.1	7,2	23.6	2,4	7.8	540	2		7230	25	1/76; 5/57	1/3; 5/2.3	2		70
ridi I	1905	76,2	249.9	7,4	24.5	2,2	7.2	855		3	21300	33	3/76	3/3	2		70
wift	1909	105,1	344.8	10,4	34.1	3,9	12.7	2390		2	30000	36	4/102	4/4	2		162
eagle	1909	81,9	268.6	8,2	26.9	2,5	8.2	953		3	14300	27	1/102; 3/76	1/4; 3/3	2		96
risk	1911	74,9	245.7	7,7	25.2	2,5	8.2	765		2	14600	27	2/102; 2/76	1/4; 2/3	2		72
rrett	1912	74,9	245.7	7,8	25.5	2,6	8.5	778		2	17000	30	2/102; 2/76	2/4; 2/3	2		72
dger	1912	75,06	246.2	7,8	25.5	2,7	8.8	810		2	17700	30	2/101; 2/76	2/4; 2/3	2		72
ewellyn (L)	1914	81,9	268.6	8,4	27.5	2,6	8.5	1142		2	26326	31	3/102; 1/37	3/4; 1/1.4	4		77
ansfield (M)	1915	82,7	271.3	8,2	26.9	3,2	10.4	1055		2	28255	35	3/102; 1/37	3/4; 1/1.4	4		76
alentine	1917	-95,08	311.9	8,9	29.1	3,5	11.4	1523		2	27000	34	4/101; 1/76	4/4; 1/3	6		115
enturous	1917	95,08	311.9	8,9	29.1	2,7	8.8	1339		2	27000	34	4/101; 1/76	4/4; 1/3	4		110
ruce	1919	101,3	332.4	9,6	31.4	3,2	10.4	1801		2	40000	36	5/120; 1/76	5/4.7; 1/3	6		164
itshead	1919	95,08	311.9	8,9	29.1	2,7	8.8	1325		2	27000	34	4/120	4/4.7	6		127
eppel	1920	100,2	328.7	9,6	31.4	3,2	10.4	1740		2	40000	36	5/120; 1/76	5/4.7; 1/3	6		164
casta	1930	98,4	322.8	9,8	32.1	3,6	11.8	1330		2	34000	35	4/120	4/4.7	8		138
rvis	1939	106,06	347.9	10,6	34.7	2,7	8.8	1690		2	40000	36	6/120	6/4.7	10		183
ridi II	1939	108,3	355.3	11,1	36.4	2,7	8.8	1870		2	44000	36,5	8/120	8/4.7	4		190
veley	1940							2500		2	45000	36,5	6/120	6/4.7	8		
gincourt	1947	115,5	378.9	12,3	40.3	3,8	12.4	3300		2	50000	31	5/101	5/4	10		268
attleaxe	1948	111,2	364.8	11,5	37.7	3,8	12.4	3000		2	40000	31	4/101	4/4	10		234
aring II	1952	118,8	389.7	13,1	42.9	5,1	16.7	2600		2	54000	34,7	6/120	6/4.7	5	1	297
ampshire	1963	158,6	520.6	16,4	54	6,1	20	6200		2	60000	32,5	4/115	4/4.5		3	440
effield	1975	125	410.1	14,3	46.9	5,8	19	4500	4GT		56000	29	1/115; 2/20	1/4.5; 2/0.7	6	2	268
roadsword	1979	131,2	430.4	14,8	48.5	6	19.6	4000	4GT		56000	30	2/40	2/1.5	6	6	223
FRANCE																	
amée M.4	1900	58,2	190.9	6,3	20.6	3,02	9.9	348	2		5200	27	1/65; 6/37	1/2.5; 6/1.4	2		58
atagan	1901	58,2	190.9	6,3	20.6	3,02	9.9	348	2		5200	27	1/65; 6/47	1/2.5; 6/1.8	2		58
arabine	1904	58,2	190.9	6,3	20.6	3,2	10.4	318	2		6300	28	1/65; 5/47	1/2.5; 5/1.8	2		60
laymore	1906	58	190.2	6,5	21.3	2,9	9.5	356	2		7200	30	1/65; 6/47	1/2.5; 6/1.8	2		70
hasseur	1909	67,6	221.7	6,5	21.3	2,8	9.1	450		3	8600	30	6/65	6/2.5	3		58
ameluck	1910	69,3	227.3	6,6	21.6	3	9.8	540	2		7760	29	6/65	6/2.5	3		65
oltigeur	1910	67,6	221.7	6,8	22.3	2,6	8.5	445	1	3	2900 + 8500	31	6/65	6/2.5	3		65
railleur	1910	67,6	221.7	6,4	20.9	2,9	9.5	414	1	3	3000 + 7800	29	6/65	6/2.5	3		65
ansquenet	1910	67,6	221.7	6,8	22.3	2,8	9.1	540	2		7000	28	6/65	6/2.5	3		58
outefeu	1910	77,2	253.2	7,7	25.2	3,05	10	760		2	18000	31	2/100; 4/65	2/3.9; 4/2.5	4		81
uclier	1911	72,3	237.2	7,8	25.5	2,9	9.5	780		3	14000	31	2/100; 4/65	2/3.9; 4/2.5	4		81
anissaire	1911	67,6	221.7	6,5	21.3	2,8	9.1	450		3	7000	29	6/65	6/2.5	3		65
antassin	1911	67,6	221.7	6,6	21.6	2,8	9.1	450		2	8600	31	6/65	6/2.5	3		65
lgérien	1917	82,8	271.6	8,2	26.9	2,3	7.5	690	3		10000	29	1/120; 4/76	1/4.7; 4/3	4		87
Adroit	1927	112	367.4	9,8	32.1	3,7	12.1	1810		2	34000	33	4/130; 2/37	4/5.1; 2/1.4	6		
uépard	1929	131	429.7	11,8	38.7	5,07	16.6	3080		2	64000	36	5/138; 4/37	5/5.4; 4/1.4	6		220
auban	1931	131,01	429.8	11,7	38.3	4,7	15.4	3080		2	64000	36	5/138; 4/37	5/5.4; 4/1.4	6		220
e Fantasque	1934	132,4	434.3	11,9	39	4,2	13.7	3230		2	74000	37	5/138; 4/37	5/5.4; 4/1.4	9		220
ogador	1938	137,4	450.7	12,4	40.6	4,4	14.4	3760		2	90000	38	8/138; 4/37	8/5.4; 4/1.4	10		238
urcouf	1956	128,6	421.9	12,7	41.6	6,3	20.6	3740		2	63000	32	6/57	6/2.3	6	1	277
uffren	1967	157,6	517	15,5	50.8	6,1	20	6090		2	72500	34	2/100; 4/20	2/3.9; 4/0.7		10	355
uquesne	1970	157,6	517	15,5	50.8	6,1	20	6090		2	72500	34	2/100; 4/20	2/3.9; 4/0.7		10	355
ourville	1974	152,8	501.3	15,3	50.1	5,7	18.7			2	54400	32	1/100	1/3.9		8	292
eorges Leygues	1979	139	456	14	45.9	5,7	18.7		2D	2GT	42000	30	1/100	1/3.9		7	216

DESTROYERS–TECHNICAL DATA

Name	Year	Length m	Length ft	Beam m	Beam ft	Draft m	Draft ft	Displacement t	Engine RE	Engine T	H P	Speed in Knots	N. Guns/mm	N. Guns/in	TT	ML	C
GERMANY																	
S-90 - S 101	1898	63	206.6	7	22.9	2,8	9.1	394	2		5900	27	3/50	3/1.9	3		5
S 125	1905	73,9	242.4	7	22.9	3,1	10.1	454		3	6600	27	3/50	3/1.9	3		6
G 137	1907	71,5	234.5	7,6	24.9	3,2	10.4	693		3	10800	30	1/88; 3/52	1/3.5; 3/2	3		8
V 161	1908	72,5	237.8	7,8	25.5	2,9	9.5	687		2	14800	33	2/88	2/3.5	3		8
V 162	1909	73,9	242.4	7,8	25.5	3,1	10.1	739		2	16000	32	2/88	2/3.5	3		8
G 172	1909	74	242.7	7,9	25.9	3,2	10.4	777		3	16600	32	2/88	2/3.5	3		8
V 25	1914	78,5	257.5	8,3	27.2	3,6	11.8	975		2	24800	33,5	3/88	3/3.5	6		8
S 36	1915	79,6	261.1	8,3	27.2	3,6	11.8	971		2	24000	33,5	3/88	3/3.5	6		8
Maas	1937	119	390.4	11,3	37	4,2	13.7	3156		2	70000	38	5/127; 4/37	5/5; 4/1.4	8		32
Von Roeder	1940	123,2	404.1	11,8	38.7	4,5	14.7	3415		2	70000	38	5/127; 4/37	5/5; 4/1.4	8		32
Hamburg	1964	133,7	438.6	13,4	43.9	6,2	20.3	4680		2	68000	34	3/100; 8/40	3/3.9; 8/1.5	4	4	2
Bayern	1965	133,7	438.6	13,4	43.9	6,2	20.3	4680		2	68000	34	3/100; 8/40	3/3.9; 8/1.5	4	4	2
Lütjens	1969	132,2	433.7	14,3	46.9	6,1	20	4500		2	70000	30	2/127	2/5		1	33
ITALY																	
Fulmine	1900	62,1	203.7	6,4	20.9	2,08	6.2	342	2		4700	26	5/57	5/2.3	3		4
Lampo	1901	62,05	203.5	6,5	21.3	2,6	8.5	354	2		6000	30	1/76; 5/57	1/3; 5/2.3	2		5
Nembo	1905	63,4	208	5,9	19.3	2,1	6.8	330	2		5200	30	5/57	5/2.3	4		5
Alpino	1910	65,07	213.4	6,1	20	2,1	6.8	415	2		6000	28,5	4/76	4/3	3		5
Indomito	1913	73	239.4	7,3	23.9	2,6	8.5	720		2	16000	30	1/120; 4/76	1/4.7; 4/3	2		6
Pilo	1915	73	239.4	7,3	23.9	2,7	8.8	806		2	16000	30	6/76	6/3	4		6
Audace II	1916	87,5	287	8,4	27.5	2,8	9.1	1364		2	22000	30	7/102	7/4	4		11
Sirtori	1917	73,5	241.1	7,3	23.9	2,8	9.1	865		2	16000	30	6/102; 2/40	6/4; 2/1.5	4		7
La Masa	1917	73,5	241.1	7,3	23.9	2,9	9.5	875		2	16000	30	4/102; 2/76	4/4; 2/3	4		7
Leone	1924	113,4	372	10,3	33.7	3,6	11.8	2203		2	42000	31	8/120; 2/76	8/4.7; 2/3	6		20
Sauro	1926	90,1	295.6	9,2	30.1	3,7	12.1	1580		2	38000	35	4/102; 2/40	4/4; 2/1.5	6		14
Navigatori	1929	107,2	351.7	10,2	33.4	3,6	11.8	2599		2	55000	38	6/120; 2/40	6/4.7; 2/1.5	6		17
Dardo-Freccia	1931	96,1	315.2	9,7	31.8	4,3	14.1	1890		2	44000	38	4/120; 2/40	4/4.7; 2/1.5	6		15
Oriani	1937	106,7	350	10,2	33.4	4,3	14.1	2320		2	48000	39	4/120	4/4.7	6		17
Impavido	1963	130,9	429.4	13,6	44.6	4,4	14.4	3940		2	70000	34,4	2/127; 4/76	2/5; 4/3	6	1	33
Ardito	1973	136,6	448.1	14,2	46.5	4,6	15	4400		2	73000	33	2/127; 4/76	2/5; 4/3	6	1	35
SPAIN																	
Terror	1896	68,2	223.7	6,7	21.9	2,9	9.5	458	2		6000	28	2/57; 8/37	2/2.3; 8/1.4	2		7
Almirante Anteguera	1934	101,4	333	9,6	31.4	5,1	17	2036		2	42000	36	4/100; 3/37	4/3.9; 3/1.4	6		17
NORWAY																	
Drang	1908	69,1	226.7	7,2	23.6	2,7	8.8	580	2		7500	37	6/76	6/3	3		7
SWEDEN																	
Mode	1901	68,4	224.4	6,2	20.3	1,5	5.1	450	2		6500	31	6/57	6/2.3	2		6
Göteborg	1936	94,6	310.3	9	29.6	3,8	12.4	1300		2	32000	39	3/120; 4/40	3/4.7; 4/1.5	6		13
Halland	1956	121	396.9	12,6	41.3	5,5	18	3400		2	58000	35	4/120; 2/57	4/4.7; 2/2.3	8	20	29
Ostergötland	1959	112	367.4	11,2	36.7	3,7	12.1	2600		2	40000	35	4/120; 4/40	4/4.7; 4/1.5	6	4	24
HOLLAND																	
Wolf	1911	70,1	229.9	6,5	21.3	2,06	6.7	507	2		8000	30	2/75	2/2.9	2		
Tromp	1976	138,2	453.4	14,8	48.5	4,6	15	4580		4GT	58000	30	2/120	2/4.7	2	17	24
Regele Ferdinand I	1928	101,9	334.3	9,5	31.1	3,5	11.4	1900		2	75000	34	5/120; 1/76	5/4.7; 1/3	6		
Huszar	1905	68,4	224.4	6,2	20.3	2,5	8.2	400	2		6000	28,5	6/70	6/2.7	2		6
Tatra	1912	84	275.5	7,8	25.5	2,5	8.2	850		2	20680	32	2/100; 6/70	2/3.9; 6/2.7	2		10
GREECE																	
Aspis	1907	67,1	220.1	6,2	20.3	1,8	5.9	350	2		6700	30	2/76; 4/57	2/3; 4/2.3	2		7
Thyella	1907	67,2	220.4	6,2	20.3	1,8	5.9	400	2		6000	30	2/76; 4/57	2/3; 4/2.3	2		7
Aetos	1912	89,3	292.9	8,4	27.5	2,5	8.2	1175		2	19750	32	4/102; 1/57	4/4; 1/2.3	4		10
Vasileus Georgios I	1939	97,5	319.8	10,05	32.9	2,5	8.2	1350		2	34000	36	4/127; 4/37	4/5; 4/1.4	8		15
TURKEY																	
Samsun	1908	58,2	190.9	6,3	20.6	3,2	10.4	303	2		6300	28	1/65; 6/47	1/2.5; 6/1.8	2		6
Artemiz	1967	115,5	378.9	12,3	40.3	5,3	17.3	3360		2	50000	31	4/115; 2/40	4/4.5; 2/1.5		2	27
RUSSIA																	
Sokol (Pritkij)	1896	59,7	195.8	5,8	19			220	2		4400	30	1/75; 3/47	1/2.9; 3/1.8	2		6
Kit (Bditelnyj)	1900	61	200.1	7	22.9	3	9.8	350	2		6000	27	1/75; 5/47	1/2.9; 5/1.8	3		5

Name	Year	Length m	ft	Beam m	ft	Draft m	ft	Displacement t	Engine RE	T	HP	Speed in Knots	N. Guns/mm	N. Guns/in	TT	Mg.	C
RUSSIA (*cont'd.*)																	
Jastreb	1901	57,9	189.9	5,8	19.02	1,8	5.9	240	2		4000	27	1/75; 3/47	1/2.9; 3/1.8	2		52
Iskusuyj	1906	58,2	190.9	6,3	20.6	1,8	5.9	345	2		5200	26	2/75	2/2.9	2		69
Emir Bucharskij	1906	72,5	237.8	8,2	26.9	2,3	7.5	650	2		6500	26	2/75; 6/57	2/2.9; 6/2.3	3		99
Vsadnik	1907	71,9	235.8	7,4	24.2	2,3	7.5	750	2		6500	25	2/75; 6/57	2/2.9; 6/2.3	3		97
Stereguszyj	1907	73,2	240.1	7,2	23.6	2,3	7.5	630	2		7000	27	2/75; 6/57	2/2.9; 6/2.3	2		85
Nowick	1913	102,4	335.9	9,5	31.1	2,3	7.5	1280		3	39000	35	4/100	4/3.9	8		130
Bespokojnyj	1914	98	321.3	9,3	30.5	2,7	8.8	1450		2	25500	30	3/100; 2/47	3/3.9; 2/1.8	10		93
Isyaslav	1920	92,7	304.1	9,5	31.1	2,9	9.5	1350		2	32700	35	5/101; 1/47	5/4; 1/1.8	9		
Leningrad	1936	127,3	417.6	11,6	38	3,9	12.8	3500		2	66000	36	5/130; 2/76	5/5.1; 2/3	8		
Svetly	1936	127,5	418.3	12,9	42.3	4,6	15.1	3800									
Stremitelny	1936	112,8	369	10,2	33.4	3,8	12.4	2039		2	48000	38	4/130; 2/76	4/51; 2/3	10		250
Taskent	1937	139,7	458.3	13,7	44.9	3,7	12.1	3200		2	110000	42	6/130; 6/45	6/5.1; 6/1.7	6		250
Skory	1949	121,5	398.6	12	39.3	4,5	14.7	2246		2	60000	36	4/130; 2/88	4/5.1; 2/3.5	10		207
SAM Kotlyn	1956	127,5	418.3	12,9	42.3	4,6	15.1	3600		2	84000	34	2/138; 4/45	2/5.4; 4/1.7	5	2	360
Neulovimy (Kildin)	1958	126,5	415.02	13	42.6	4,9	16	3600		2	72000	35	4/76; 16/57	4/3; 16/2.3		4	300
Zhguchy	1962	139	456	14,7	48.2	5	16.4	4700		2	84000	34	8/57; 8/30	8/2.3; 8/1.1		2	350
Obraztsovyi (Kashin)	1964	143,3	470.1	15,8	51.8	4,7	15.4	4500		4GT	96000	35	4/76; 4/30	4/3; 4/1.1	4	8	280
Kanin	1968	139	456	14,7	48.2	5	16.4	4700		2	84000	34	8/57; 8/30	8/2.3; 8/1.1	10	2	350
UNITED STATES																	
Bainbridge DD 1	1902	76,2	249.9	7,1	23.2	2,3	7.5	420	2		8000	28	2/65; 6/57	2/2.5; 6/2.3	2		73
Hopkins DD 6	1903	75,8	248.6	7,4	24.2	1,8	5.9	408	2		7200	29	2/65; 6/57	2/2.5; 6/2.3	2		73
Smith DD 17	1910	89,5	293.6	8,2	26.9	2,4	7.8	700		3	10000	28	5/76	5/3	3		73
Perkins DD 26	1910	89,5	293.6	8,2	26.9	2,7	8.8	740		2	12000	29,5	5/76	5/3	6		89
DD 22 - 31	1910	89,5	293.6	8,2	26.9	2,7	8.8	740		3	12000	29,5	5/76	5/3	6		89
Walke DD 34	1911	89,5	293.6	8,2	26.9	2,7	8.8	890		2	12000	29,5	5/76	5/3	6		83
Cassin DD 44	1913	93,04	305.2	9,4	30.8	2,8	9.1	1139	1	2	16000	29	4/102	4/4	8		97
Mac Dougal DD 54	1914	93,04	305.2	9,4	30.8	2,8	9.1	1139	2	2	27000	35	4/127; 1/76	4/5; 1/3	12		122
Wainwright DD 62	1915	96,08	315.2	9,3	30.5	2,9	9.5	1265		2	17000	29,5	4/102	4/4	8		99
Brooks DD 232	1920	95,8	314.3	9,4	30.8	2,9	9.5	1308		2	27000	35	4/127; 1/76	4/5; 1/3	12		122
Ellet DD 398	1938	104,1	341.6	10,5	34.6	3	9.8	1500		2	42800	36,5	4/127	4/5	16		172
Anderson DD 411	1939	103,9	341	10,6	35	3,05	10	1570		2	44000	36,5	5/127	5/5	12		250
Craven DD 382	1939	104,1	341.5	10,5	34.4	2,9	9.5	1500		2	42800	36,5	4/127	4/5	16		172
Livermore DD 429	1940	106,2	348.4	10,9	35.7	3,05	10	2450		2	50000	37	4/127	4/5	5		250
Sims DD 409	1941	106,06	347.9	10,9	35.7	3,05	10	1570		2	44000	36,5	5/127	5/5	5		250
Benson DD 421	1942	106,2	348.4	10,9	35.7	3,05	10	1630		2	50000	36	4/127	4/5	5		250
Fletcher DD 445	1943	114,7	376.3	9,4	30.8	3,7	12.1	2750		2	60000	36	5/127	5/5	5		353
A.M. Sumner DD 692	1944	114,7	376.3	12,4	40.6	3,8	12.4	3900		2	60000	36	6/127; 6/76	6/5; 6/3	5		350
W.C. Lawe DD 763	1946	119,03	390.5	12,4	40.6	5,8	19	3479		2	60000	35	6/127	6/5	5		350
Hyatt DD 712	1945	119,03	390.5	12,4	40.6	5,7	18.7	3480		2	60000	35	4/127; 4/76	4/5; 4/3		4	296
Gearing DD 710	1946	119	390.4	12,6	41.3	5,8	19	3479		2	60000	32,5	6/127; 6/76	6/5; 6/3	5		307
Morton DD 948	1959	127,5	418.3	13,7	45	5,9	19.5	4200		2	70000	33	3/127; 4/76	3/5; 4/3	6		276
Preble DLG 15	1960	158,4	520	16	52.5	6	20	5600		2	85000	34	1/127; 4/76	1/5; 4/3	6	1	355
Buchanan DDG 14	1962	133,1	437	14,3	47	6	20	4500		2	70000	35	2/127	2/5	6	1	333
Spruance DD 963	1975	171,7	563.3	16,8	55.1	8,8	28.8	7810		4GT	80000	33	2/127	2/5	6	3	296
Kidd DDG 993	1983	171,6	562.9	16,8	55.1	9,1	29.8	8300		4GT	80000	33	2/127	2/5	6	2	338
BRAZIL																	
Amazonas	1909	73,1	239.8	7,1	23.2	2,4	7.4	650	2		8000	27	2/102; 4/47	2/4; 4/1.8	2		75
ARGENTINA																	
Santa Fé	1896	57,9	189.9	5,9	19.3	2,2	7.2	280	2		4000	27	1/76	1/3	3		54
Santissima Trinidad	1976	125	410.1	14,3	46.9	5,8	19	4100		4GT	56000	30	1/120	1/4.7	6	5	300
Almirante Brown	1982	125,9	413	14	45.9	5,8	19	3600		4GT	66680	30,5	1/127	1/5	6	16	198
CHILE																	
Capitan Orella	1897	69,9	229.3	6,5	21.3	2,5	8.2	311	2		6500	30	1/76; 5/57	1/3; 5/2.3	3		65
Almirante Riveros	1980	122,5	401.8	13,1	42.9	4	13.1	3300		2	54000	34,5	4/102	4/4	6		266
COLOMBIA																	
7 de Agosto	1958	121,1	397.5	12,4	40.6	3,5	11.5	3100		2	55000	35	6/120	6/4.7	4		260
CANADA																	
Iroquois	1972	129,8	425.8	15,2	49.8	4,4	14.4	4700		4GT	50000	29	1/127	1/5	6	8	235
AUSTRALIA																	
Perth	1965	134,3	440.6	14,3	46.9	6	20	4618		2	70000	30	2/127	2/5	6	3	333

DESTROYERS–TECHNICAL DATA

Name	Year	Length		Beam		Draft		Displacement	Engine		HP	Speed	N. Guns/mm	N. Guns/in	TT	ML	C
		m	ft	m	ft	m	ft	t	RE	T		in Knots					
CHINA																	
Hai-Lung	1898	59	193.5	6,4	20.9	2,5	8.2	284	2		6500	32	6/47	6/1.8	2		
Ansan	1941	112,8	370	10,2	33.4	4	13.1	2040		2	48000	32	4/130	4/5.1	4		2
Luda	1971	131	495.4	13,7	44.9	4,6	15	3500		2	72000	36	4/130; 8/37	4/5.1; 8/1.5		6	2
INDIA																	
Rajput (Kashin)	1966	146,5	480.6	15,8	51.8	4,8	15.7	4950		4 GT	96000	35	2/76	2/3	8	8	3
JAPAN																	
Ikazuchi	1900	68,4	224.4	6,2	20.3	1,5	4.9	410	2		6000	31	2/76; 4/57	2/3; 4/2.3	2		
Murakumo	1900	65,6	215.2	5,9	19.3	1,7	5.5	351	2		5940	30	2/76; 4/57	2/3; 4/2.3	2		
Akatusuki	1902	60,04	196.9	5,6	18.3	2,2	7.2	440	2		3800	27,5	1/76; 3/47	1/3; 3/1.8	2		
Satsuki	1902	63,9	209.6	6,3	20.6	1,7	5.5	356	2		5700	26,5	1/76; 5/47	1/3; 5/1.8	2		
Harusame	1905	71,3	233.9	6,5	21.3	1,8	5.9	435	2		6000	29	2/76; 4/57	2/3; 4/2.3	2		
Asakaze	1909	71,3	233.9	6,5	21.3	1,8	5.9	450	2		6000	29	6/88	6/3.5	2		
Umikaze	1911	97,8	320.8	8,5	27.8	2,7	8.8	1150		3	20500	33	2/120; 5/76	2/4.7; 5/3	3		14
Kaba	1915	83,5	273.9	7,3	23.9	2,3	7.5	850	3		9500	30	1/130; 3/80	1/5.1; 3/3.1	4	92	
Momo	1917	85,8	281.4	7,7	25.2	2,3	7.5	1080		2	16000	31,5	3/120; 2/76	3/4.7; 2/3	6		1
Amatsukaze	1917	99,3	325.7	8,4	27.5	2,8	9.1	1570		3	27000	34	4/120; 2/76	4/4.7; 2/3	6		12
Kamikaze	1924	102,5	336.2	9,1	29.8	2,9	9.5	1720		2	38500	37	4/120; 2/76	4/4.7; 2/3	6		14
Fubuki	1926	115,2	377.9	10,3	33.7	3,1	10.1	2090		2	50000	38	6/127	6/5	9		19
Kagero	1941	118,4	388.4	10,7	35.1	3,7	12.1	2490		2	52000	35	6/127	6/5	8		24
Takatsuki	1967	136	446.1	13,4	43.9	4,4	14.4	3100		2	60000	32	1/127	1/5	6	2	27
Yamagumo	1967	114,9	376.9	11,8	38.7	4	13.1	2150		6 D	26500	27	4/76	4/3	6		2
Haruna	1974	153	501.9	17,5	57.4	5,1	16.7	4700		2	70000	32	2/127	2/5	6	1	3
Takikaze	1976	143	469.1	14,3	46.9	4,6	15	3850		2	60000	33	2/127	2/5	6	1	2
Shirane DD 143	1980	159	521.6	17,5	57.4	5,3	17.3	5200		2	70000	32	2/127	2/5	6	1	3
Hatsuyuki DD 122	1982	126	413.3	13,6	44.6	8,5	27.8	2950		4 GT	45000	30	1/76	1/3	6	9	
DD 145	1986	143	469.1	15,6	51.1	5,8	19	4500		4 GT		32	2/127	2/5	6	9	

RE = Reciprocating engines
T = Turbines
TT = Torpedo tubes
ML = Missile launchers
C = Complement

The year given is the year of launching.

Under the heading "Engine," the letter "D," which sometimes appears after the number, stands for diesel.

Name	Year	Length m	Length ft	Beam m	Beam ft	Draft m	Draft ft	Displacement t	Engine D	Engine T	H P	Speed in Knots	N. Guns/mm	N. Guns/in	TT	ML	C
GREAT BRITAIN																	
ML 54-542	1915	24,3	80	3,8	12.5	0,9	3.1		2 G		440	19	1/76	1/3			9
Flowers	1915	80,0	262.5	10	33	3,6	11.8	1200	1 R		1800	17	2/101; 1/76	2/4; 1/3			77
P. Boats	1917	74,5	244.5	7,2	23.8	2,3	7.8	613		2	3500	20	1/101	1/4			50
P.C. Boats	1917	75,2	247	7,7	25.5	2,5	8.3	682		2	3500	20	1/101	1/4			55
Flowers	1917	79,9	262.3	10,6	35	3,8	12.4	1290	1 R		2500	17	1/101; 2/57	1/4; 2/2.3			93
Kil	1918	55,4	182	9,1	30	3,5	11.4	890	1 R		1400	13					
Sir Hugo	1919	84,2	276.5	10,6	35	3,6	11.8	1320	1 R		2500	17	2/101	2/4			82
Leith	1933	81,0	266	10,3	33.7	2,6	8.7	990		2	2000	16,5	2/120; 1/76	2/4.7; 1/3			100
Bittern	1934	81,0	266	11,2	36.8	2,5	8.3	1085		2	3300	18,7	4/105; 4/76	4/4.1; 4/3			125
Kingfisher	1935	74,1	243.2	8	26.5	1,8	6	530		2	3600	20	1/101	1/4			60
Egret	1938	84,1	276	11,4	37.5	2,5	8.5	1200		2	3600	19,2	8/101; 7/57	8/4; 7/2.3			188
Flowers	1940	62,4	205	10	33	4,4	14.4	925	1 R		2750	16	1/101	1/4			85
River	1942	91,8	301.3	11,1	36.4	3,6	11.8	1460	2 R		5500	20	2/101	2/4			140
Hunt III	1942	85,3	280	9,6	31.5	2,3	7.8	1620		2	19000	29	4/101	4/4	2		168
Castle	1943	76,8	252	11,1	36.4	4,1	13.5	1100	1 R		2880	16	1/101	1/4			85
Loch	1944	93,5	307	11,7	38.5	3,6	11.8	1435	2 R		5500	19,5	1/101	1/4			103
Bay	1944	93,6	307.3	11,7	38.5	3,9	12.8	1600	2 R		5500	19,5	4/101	4/4			157
Blackwood	1957	94,4	310	10	33	4,7	15.4	1456		1	15000	29,8					111
Leopard	1957	103,5	339.8	12,2	40	4,8	15.7	2520	8		12380	25	4/115	4/4.5			195
Salisbury	1957	100,6	330	12,2	40	3,6	11.8	2408	8		14400	24	2/115	2/4.5			237
Rothesay	1961	112,8	370	12,5	41	5,3	17.3	2800		2	30430	31	2/120	2/4.7		1	235
Tribal (Zulu)	1964	109,7	360	12,8	41.9	5,3	17.3	2700	1GT	1	12500	28	4/120	4/4.7		1	253
Leander	1963	113,4	372	12,5	41	4,5	14.7	2860		2	30000	30	2/115	2/4.5		1	260
Amazon	1974	118	387.1	12,7	41.6	6	19.6	3250		4 GT	64500	30	1/115	1/4.5	6	5	175
FRANCE																	
Agile	1916	60,1	197.5	6,8	22.6	2,4	8.2	350	1 R		1800	17,1	2/90	2/3.6			55
Aisne	1916	78	256.2	8,0	26.4	2,6	8.7	680	2 R		4000	20,5	4/100	4/3.9			97
Aldébaran	1916	68,6	225.3	10,2	33.4	3,7	12.1	1470	1 R		2500	17	2/130	2/5.1			92
Conquérante	1917	64,3	211	6,8	22.6	2,4	8.2	457	2		1800	17	2/100	2/3.9			65
Diligente	1917	60,8	199	6,8	22.6	2,4	8.2	355	2		1800	15	2/100	2/3.9			50
Arras	1918	74,9	246	8,7	28.8	2,8	9.5	700		2	5000	20,5	2/140	2/5.5			105
Dubourdieu	1918	64,2	210.8	7,9	26.2	2,6	8.7	500		2	2000	17,4	1/130; 1/90	1/5.1; 1/3.6			72
Ailette	1918	78	256.2	8	26.5	2,4	8.2	650	2 R		5000	21	4/100	4/3.9			65
Normand C	1921	43,2	142	5,2	17.2	1,2	4.3	133	1 R		1300	16,5	2/75	2/2.9			32
Clan	1938	78	256.2	8,4	27.8	2,3	7.8	700	2		4000	20	2/100	2/3.9			88
Chamois	1938	78	256.2	8,4	27.8	2,3	7.8	700	2		4000	20	2/100	2/3.9			
Le Corse	1955	99,8	327.5	10,1	33.3	3	10	1702		2	20000	27	6/57	6/2.3	12		198
Le Normand	1956	99,8	327.5	10,1	33.3	3	10	1702		2	20000	27	6/57	6/2.3	12		200
Commandant Rivière	1962	103,7	340.2	11,7	38.3	4,8	15.7	2250		2	16000	25	3/100	3/3.9	6		180
D'Estienne D'Orves	1976	80	262.4	10,3	33.7	5,3	17.3	1170		2	11000	24	1/100	1/3.9	4	2	79
GERMANY																	
	1935	75,9	249.3	8,7	28.8	2,5	8.5	800		2	9000	28	2/105	2/4.1			124
Köln	1961	109,9	360.5	11	36	5,1	16.7	2700	2	2GT	36000	28	2/100	2/3.9	4		210
Bremen	1982	130,5	428.1	14,4	47.2	6	19.6	3415	2	2GT	62000	30	1/76	1/3	4	3	199
ITALY																	
Albatros	1934	70,5	231.2	6,8	22.6	2,2	7.3	499		2	4300	24,5	2/100	2/3.9			52
Pegaso	1938	89,2	292.6	9,6	31.4	3,7	12.1	1600		2	16000	28	2/100	2/3.9	4		154
Gabbiano	1942	64,4	211.2	8,7	28.8	2,8	9.5	728	2		3500	18	1/100	1/3.9	2		110
Albatros	1955	76,3	250.3	9,6	31.4	2,6	8.7	950	2		4000	20	2/76	2/3			117
Centauro	1957	103,1	338.2	12	39.3	3,8	12.4	2200		2	22000	26	4/76	4/3	2		235
Bergamini	1961	93,9	308	11,3	37	3,1	10.2	1650	2		16800	26	3/76	3/3	6		157
Alpino	1966	113,3	371.7	13,3	43.6	3,7	12.1	2689	2	2GT	31800	29	6/76	6/3	6		164
De Cristofaro	1966	80,2	263.1	10,2	33.4	2,7	8.8	940	2		8300	23,5	2/76	2/3	6		128
Lupo	1977	106	347.7	12	39.3	3,7	12.1	2500	2	2GT	12700	35	1/127	1/5	6	1	185
Maestrale	1981	122,7	402.5	12,8	42.3	8,4	27.5	3040	2	2GT	61000	32	1/127	1/5	6	5	232
SPAIN																	
Pizarro	1946	95,3	312.6	12	39.3	5,4	17.7	2246	2		6000	18,5	6/120	6/4.7			250
Atrevida	1954	75,5	247.7	10,2	33.4	3	10	1135	2		3000	18,5	1/105	1/4.1		2	113
Navarra	1984	135,6	444.8	13,7	44.9	7,5	24.6	3605		2GT	41000	30	1/76	1/3	6	2	163

FRIGATES and CORVETTES–TECHNICAL DATA

Name	Year	Length m	ft	Beam m	ft	Draft m	ft	Displacement t	Engine D	T	H P	Speed in Knots	N. Guns/mm	N. Guns/in	TT	ML	C
HOLLAND																	
Van Speijk	1967	113,4	372	12,5	41	5,5	18	2735		2	30000	30	2/115	2/4.5		2	25
Kortenaer	1978	130,5	428.1	14,4	47.2	6,2	20.3	3630		4 GT	58000	30	1/76	1/3	4	2	16
DENMARK																	
Triton	1955	76,3	250.3	9,6	31.4	2,8	9.5	950	2		4400	20	2/76	2/3			11
Hvidbjornen	1962	72,6	238.1	11,6	38	4,9	16	1650	2		6400	18	1/76	1/3			8
Peder Skram	1966	112,6	369.4	12	39.3	3,6	11.8	2720	2	2GT	41800	30	2/127	2/5		3	11
Niels Juel	1980	84	275.5	10,3	33.7	4	13.1	1320	2	2GT	18400	30	1/76	1/3	4	3	9
BELGIUM																	
Wielingen	1978	106,4	349	12,3	40.3	5,6	18.3	2283	2	1GT	28000	29	1/100	1/3.9	2	5	16
LIBYA																	
Dat Assawari	1973	100,6	330	11	36	3,4	11.1	1625	2	2GT	49900	37,5	1/115	1/4.5	6	4	
Wadi M'Ragh	1979	61,7	202.4	9,3	30.5	2,2	7.3	670	4		18000	33	1/76	1/3	6	4	5
NIGERIA																	
Aradu	1981	125,6	412	15	49.2	4,3	14.1	3630	2	2 GT	60000	30,5	1/127	1/5	6	3	20
IRAN																	
Saam	1971	94,4	309.7	11,1	36.4	4,3	14.1	1400	2	2GT	49800	39	1/115	1/4.5		2	12
MALAYSIA																	
Rahmat	1971	93,9	308	10,4	34.1	4,5	14.7	1600	2	1GT	23350	26	1/115	1/4.5		1	14
RUSSIA																	
Cheka	1935	61,8	203	7,1	23.3	2,2	7.3	540	2		2800	18	1/101	1/4			5
Riga	1955	91,5	300	10,1	33.3	3,2	10.4	1320		2	20000	28	3/100	3/3.9	2		17
Kola	1960	92,9	305	9,9	32.8	3,5	11.4	2000		2	30000	31	4/100	4/3.9			19
Petya	1960	82,3	270	9,1	29.8	3,2	10.4	1100	1	2 GT	36000	35	4/76	4/3	5		9
Mirka	1964	81	265.7	9,1	29.8	3	10	1100	2	2 GT	42000	36	4/76	4/3	5		9
Grisha 1	1969	73	239.4	9,7	31.8	3,7	12.1	1100	2	1GT	18000	36	2/57	2/2.3	4	1	8
Krivak	1970	122,5	401.8	14	45.9	4,7	15.4	3800		4 GT	72000	32	4/76	4/3	8	6	22
UNITED STATES																	
Eagle Boats	1918	60,9	200	7,7	25.5	2,2	7.3	615		1	2500	18	2/101; 2/76	2/4; 2/3			6
PC 564 Chadron	1941	52,9	173.7	6	20	2,2	7.2	450	2		2560	20	1/76	1/3			8
PCS 1387 Beaufort	1942	41,4	136	7,4	24.5	2,5	8.5	338	2		800	14	1/76	1/3			6
PCE 852 Battleboro	1942	56,2	184.5	10	33	2,8	9.5	903	2		2400	16	1/76	1/3			9
DE 445 Fletcher	1942	114,7	376.5	11,9	39.1	5,4	17.7	2940		2	6000	35	2/127; 4/76	2/5; 4/3	4		35
DE 129 Edsall	1943	93,2	306	11,2	36.8	3,3	11	1850	2		6000	21	3/76	3/3	6		14
DE 224 Rudderow	1943	93,2	306	11,2	36.8	3,2	10.4	1780		2ET	12000	28	2/127	2/5			22
DE 51 Buckley	1943	93,2	306	11,2	36.8	3,2	10.7	1720		2ET	12000	28	3/76	3/3			22
PF 21 Bayonne	1943	92,6	304	11,4	37.5	4,1	13.7	1430	2R		5500	20	3/76	3/3			19
PF 16 Bangor	1943	92,6	304	11,4	37.5	4,1	13.7	1430	2R		5500	20	3/76	3/3			19
DE 339 J.C. Butler	1943	93,2	306	11.1	36.4	3,9	12.8	2100		2	12000	24	2/127	2/5			22
DE 5 Evarts	1943	88	289	10,6	35	3,2	10.4	1350	2DE		6000	20	3/76	3/3			20
DE 103 Bostwick	1943	93,2	306	11,2	36.8	4,2	13.8	1900	2DE		6000	19	3/76	3/3			15
DDE 871 Damato	1945	119	390.5	12,4	40.8	5,7	19	3300		2	60000	35	4/127; 6/76	4/5; 6/3	5		35
DDE 825 Carpenter	1949	119	390.5	12,4	40.8	5,7	19	3300		2	60000	35	4/76	4/3			35
DE 1006 Dealey	1954	95,8	314.5	12,2	40	4,2	13.8	1914		1	20000	25	4/76	4/3	6		14
DE 1033 C. Jones	1959	95	312	11.8	39	4.3	14.1	1750	1			21	2/76	2/3	6		17
DLG 9 Coontz	1960	158,4	520	15,9	52.3	6	19.6	5600		2	85000	34	1/127; 4/76	1/5; 4/3	6	1	35
FF 1040 Garcia	1964	126,3	414.3	13,5	44.2	4,6	15	3403		1	35000	27,5	2/127	2/5	6	1	24
FFG 1 Brooke	1966	126,3	414.3	13,5	44.2	4,6	15	3426		1	35000	27,5	1/127	1/5	6	1	24
FF 1052 Knox	1969	133,5	437.9	14,3	46.9	4,6	15	4200		1	35000	27	1/127	1/5	4	1	24
FFG 7 O.H. Perry	1977	135,6	444.8	13,7	44.9	4,5	14.7	3605		2GT	41000	29	1/76	1/3	6	1	16
BRAZIL																	
Niteroi	1976	129,2	423.8	13,5	44.2	5,5	18	3800	2	2 GT	56000	30	2/117	2/4.5	6	5	20
ARGENTINA																	
King	1945	77	252.6	8,8	29.1	2,3	7.8	1000	2		2500	18	3/105	3/4.1			13
PERU																	
Meliton Carvajal	1979	113,2	371.3	11,3	37	3,7	12.1	2500	2	2 GT	57800	35	1/127	1/5	6		18
ECUADOR																	
Esmeraldas	1982	62,3	204.3	9,3	30.5	2,5	8.5	685	4		18000	34	1/76	1/3	6	5	5
VENEZUELA																	
Mariscal Sucre	1979	113,2	371.3	11,3	37	3,7	12.1	2500	2	2 GT	57800	35	1/127	1/5	6	2	18

me	Year	Length m	Length ft	Beam m	Beam ft	Draft m	Draft ft	Displacement t	Engine D	Engine T	H P	Speed in Knots	N. Guns/mm	N. Guns/in	TT	ML	C
CANADA																	
napolis	1964	113,1	371	12,8	41.9	4,4	14.4	3000		2	30000	28	2/76	2/3	6		246
Laurent	1956	111,6	366.1	12,8	41.9	4,3	14.1	2800		2	30000	28,5	2/76	2/3	6		250
AUSTRALIA																	
ealide	1980	135,6	444.8	13,7	44.9	7,5	24.6	3678		2 GT	40000	29	1/76	1/3	6	2	186
CHINA																	
eng-Du	1959	91,5	300.1	10,1	33.3	3,2	10.4	1320		2	20000	28	3/100	3/3.9		1	175
ng-Nan	1967	90,8	297.8	10	33	3,9	12.7	1600	2		24000	28	3/100	3/3.9	2		175
ng-Dong	1977	103	337.9	12	39.3	4	13.1	2000	2		24000	26,5	2/100	2/3.9	2	2	190
ng-Hu	1978	103	337.9	12	39.3	4	13.1	2000	2		24000	26,5	2/100	2/3.9	2	2	195
JAPAN																	
1	1934	64,0	210	3,2	10.5	1,4	4.8	280	2		3400	24					45
orofu	1942	77,7	255	8,8	29.1	3	10	1020	2		4200	19,7	3/120	3/4.7			147
kura	1942	78,8	258.6	9	29.7	2,1	7.1	1020	2		4200	19,5	3/120	3/4.7			150
	1943	67,5	221.5	8,4	27.7	2,9	9.6	810	2		1900	16,5	2/120	2/4.7			136
	1943	69,4	228	8,6	28.3	3	10	940		1	2500	17,5	2/120	2/4.7			168
uru	1944	78,7	258.5	8,8	29.1	3	10	1020	2		4200	19,5	3/120	3/4.7			150
B	1945	48,4	159.1	5,4	17.9	2,4	8.2	282	2		800	15	1/40	1/1.5			
azuki	1955	87,4	287	8,6	28.3	3,1	10.2	1300	2		12000	25	2/76	2/3			150
zu	1961	94,3	309.3	10,4	34.1	3,5	11.4	1700	2		16000	25	4/76	4/3	6		180
ikugo	1970	93,1	305.4	10,8	35.4	3,5	11.4	1470	2		16000	25	2/76	2/3	6	1	165
ikari	1981	84	275.5	10,6	35	5,9	19.3	1250	2	1 GT	27200	25	1/76	1/3	6	2	

D = Diesel
T = Turbines
TT = Torpedo tubes
ML = Missile launchers
C = Complement

The year given is the year of launching.

Under the heading ''Engine'' various letters sometimes appear after the number: ''R'' stands for reciprocating, ''G'' for gasoline engine, ''ET'' for electric turbines, ''DE'' for diesel-electric and ''GT'' for gas turbines.

BIBLIOGRAPHY

Alden, J.D., *The fleet submarine in the U.S. Navy*. Annapolis: U.S. Naval Institute, 1979.

Archibald, E., *The fighting ship in the Royal Navy*. Poole: Blandford, 1984.

Bagnasco, E., *Submarines of World War Two*. Annapolis: U.S. Naval Institute, 1978.

Baker, A.D. III, and J. Labayle-Couhat, *Combat fleets of the world*. Annapolis: U.S. Naval Institute, various years, latest 1984.

Brown, D.K., *A century of naval construction: The history of the Royal Corps of Naval Constructors*. London: Conway Maritime Press, 1983.

Brown, J.D., *Aircraft carriers*. London: Macdonald & Jane's 1977.

Bulkley, R.J., *At close quarters: PT boats in the United States Navy*. Washington: U.S. Navy, 1962.

Buxton, I., *Big gun monitors*. Annapolis: U.S. Naval Institute, 1980.

Campbell, N.J.M., *Naval weapons of the Second World War*. London: Conway Maritime Press, 1985.

Chapelle, H.I., *The American sailing navy*. New York: W.W. Norton, 1949.

Chesneau, R., *Aircraft carriers of the world*. Annapolis: U.S. Naval Institute, 1984.

Compton-Hall, R., *The underwater war, 1939–45*. Poole: Blandford Press, 1982.

Croizat, V., *Brown water navy*. Poole: Blandford, 1985.

Dittmar, F., and J.J. Colledge, *British Warships 1914–1919*. London: Ian Allan, 1972.

Dousset, F. *Les navires de guerre français de 1850 a nos jours*. Paris: Editions de La Cité, 1975.

————, *Les porte-avions français*. Paris: Editions de la Cité, 1978.

Dulin, R.O., and W.H. Garzke, *Battleships*. Annapolis: U.S. Naval Institute; 3 vols., 1976, 1980, 1985.

Elliott, P., *Allied escort ships of World War II*. London: Macdonald & Jane's, 1977.

————, *Allied minesweeping in World War Two*. Annapolis: U.S. Naval Institute, 1979.

Fock, H., *Fast fighting boats, 1870–1945*. Annapolis: U.S. Naval Institute, 1973.

Fraccaroli, A., *Italian warships of World War II*. London: Ian Allan, 1968.

————, *Italian warships of World War I*. London: Ian Allan, 1970.

Friedman, N., *Battleship design and development*. London: Conway Maritime Press, 1978.

————, *Modern warship design and development*. London: Conway Maritime Press, 1979.

————, *Carrier air power*. London: Conway Maritime Press, 1980.

————, *Naval radar*. Annapolis: U.S. Naval Institute, 1981.

————, *U.S. destroyers: An illustrated design history*. Annapolis, U.S. Naval Institute, 1982.

————, *U.S. aircraft carriers: An illustrated design history*. Annapolis: U.S. Naval Institute, 1983.

————, *U.S. naval weapons*. Annapolis: U.S. Naval Institute, 1983.

————, *Submarine design and development*. Annapolis: U.S. Naval Institute, 1984.

————, *U.S. cruisers: An illustrated design history*. Annapolis: U.S. Naval Institute, 1984.

————, *U.S. battleships: An illustrated design history*. Annapolis: U.S. Naval Institute, 1985.

Gardiner, R. (ed.), *Conway's all the world's fighting ships*. Five vols., covering, respectively, 1860–1905, 1906–1921, 1922–1946, and 1947–1982, the last divided into 2 vols; Annapolis: U.S. Naval Institute, 1979, 1985, 1980, 1983, 1984.

Greger, R., *The Russian Fleet 1914–1917*. London: Ian Allan, 1972.

————, *Austro-Hungarian warships of World War I*. London: Ian Allan, 1976.

Gröner, E., *Die deutsche Kriegsschiffe*. Munich: Bernard & Graefe, 6 vols., 1982–9.

Hartmann, G.K., *Weapons that wait: Mine warfare in the U.S. Navy*. Annapolis: U.S. Naval Institute, 1979.

Hodges, P., and N. Friedman, *Destroyer weapons of World War 2*. Annapolis: U.S. Naval Institute, 1979.

Hodges, P., *The big gun: Battleship main armament*. Annapolis: U.S. Naval Institute, 1981.

Hovgaard, W., *Modern history of warships*. London: Conway Maritime Press; reprint of 1920 edition.

Howard, F., *Sailing ships of war, 1400–1860*. London: Conway Maritime Press, 1979.

Jentschura, H., D. Jung, P. Mickel, (transl. A. Preston and J.D. Brown), *Warships of the Imperial Japanese Navy, 1869–1945*. Annapolis: U.S. Naval Institute, 1977.

King, J.W., *The war-ships and navies of the world*. London: Conway Maritime Press, 1982, reprint of 1880 book.

Labayle-Couhat, J., *French warships of World War II*. London: Ian Allan, 1971.

————, *French warships of World War I*. London: Ian Allan, 1974.

Ladd, J.D., *Assault from the sea, 1939–1945*. London: David & Charles, 1976.

Lambert, A., *Battleships in transition*. Annapolis: U.S. Naval Institute, 1984.

Lambert, J., *Anatomy of the ship: The Fairmile "D" type motor torpedo boat*. Annapolis: U.S. Naval Institute, 1985.

Lavery, B., *The ship of the line*. Annapolis: U.S. Naval Institute, 1984.

Le Masson, H., *The French Navy*. London: Macdonald, 1969; 2 vols in series "Navies of the Second World War."

Lenton, H.T., and J.J. College, *Warships of World War II*. London: Ian Allan, 1964; British warships.

Lenton, H.T., *Royal Netherlands Navy*. London: Macdonald, 1968, in series "Navies of the Second World War."

————, *German warships of the Second World War*. New York: Arco, 1976.

Longridge, C.N., *The anatomy of Nelson's ships*. Annapolis: U.S. Naval Institute, 1980.

Macintyre, D., and B.W. Bathe, *Man of war*. New York: McGraw-Hill, 1969.

March, E., *British destroyers*. London: Seeley Service, 1966.

Meister, J., *Soviet warships of the Second World War*. London: Macdonald & Jane's, 1977.

Parkes, O., *British battleships*. London: Seeley Service, 1957.

Phelan, K., and M. Brice, *Fast attack craft*. London: Macdonald & Jane's, 1977.

Polmar, N., *Aircraft carriers*. Garden City: Doubleday, 1969.

————, *The ships and aircraft of the U.S. Fleet*. Annapolis: U.S. Naval Institute, various years, latest, 1984.

————, *Guide to the Soviet Navy*. Annapolis: U.S. Naval Institute, various years, latest, 1983.

————, *The American submarine*. Annapolis: Nautical & Aviation, 1981.

Preston, A., *Battleships of World War I*. London: Arms & Armour, 1972.

Raven, A.L., and J. Roberts, *British battleships of World War Two*. Annapolis: U.S. Naval Institute, 1976.

————, *British cruisers of World War Two*. Annapolis: U.S. Naval Institute, 1980.

Reilly, J.C., and R.L. Scheina, *American battleships 1886–1923*. Annapolis: U.S. Naval Institute, 1980.

Reilly, J.C., *United States navy destroyers of World War Two*. Poole: Blandford, 1983.

Roberts, J., *Anatomy of the ship: The aircraft carrier Intrepid*. Annapolis: U.S. Naval Institute, 1982.

————, *Anatomy of the ship: The battlecruiser Hood*. Annapolis: U.S. Naval Institute, 1982.

Rodgers, W.L., *Greek and Roman naval warfare*. Annapolis: U.S. Naval Institute, 1937.

————, *Naval warfare under oars*. Annapolis: U.S. Naval Institute, 1967.

Roessler, E., *The U-boat*. Annapolis: U.S. Naval Institute, 1981.

Ross, A., *Anatomy of the ship: The destroyer escort England*. Annapolis: U.S. Naval Institute, 1985.

Royal Institution of Naval Architects, *British warship design in World War II*. Selected papers, originally published 1947; Annapolis: U.S. Naval Institute, 1983.

Sapolsky, H.M., *The Polaris system development*. Cambridge: Harvard University Press, 1972.

Scheina, *U.S. Coast Guard cutters and craft of World War II*. Annapolis: U.S. Naval Institute, 1982.

Showell, J.P.M., *The German Navy in World War Two*. Annapolis: U.S. Naval Institute, 1979.

Silverstone, P.H., *U.S. warships of World War II*. London: Ian Allan, 1962.

————, *U.S. warships of World War I*. London: Ian Allan, 1970.

Taylor, J.C., *German warships of World War II*. London: Ian Allan, 1966.

————, *German warships of World War I*. London: Ian Allan, 1970.

Ufficio Storico Marina Militare, *Le navi di linea italiane*. Rome, 1962; first of a series of official histories listed below:

————, *Gli incrociatori italiani*. Rome, 1971.

————, *I sommergibili italiani*. Rome, 1971.

————, *I cacciatorpediniere italiani*. Rome, 1971.

————, *Le torpediniere italiane*. Rome, 1974.

————, *Esploratori, fregate, corvette e avvissi italiani*. Rome, 1974.

————, *Le MAS italiane*. Rome, 1974.

U.S. Navy, Office of Naval Intelligence, *Allied landing craft*. Annapolis: U.S. Naval Institute, 1985; reprint of 1944–1945 manuals.

Watton, R., *Anatomy of the ship: The cruiser Belfast*. Annapolis: U.S. Naval Institute, 1985.

Westwood, D., *Anatomy of the ship: Type VII U-boat*. Annapolis: U.S. Naval Institute, 1984.

Whitley, M.J., *Destroyer!* Annapolis: U.S. Naval Institute, 1984.

Periodicals

Brassey's naval annual. London: Brassey's; published 1886–1949, then as *Brassey's defence annual;* 1913 edition has been reprinted.

Combat fleets of the world. Annapolis: U.S. Naval Institute; every other year since 1976–1977; translation and considerable addition to the French *Flottes de combat*.

Jane's fighting ships. London: Jane's Publishing Company: annual since 1898; issues for 1898, 1905–1906, 1906–1907, 1914, 1919, 1924, 1931, 1939, 1944–1945, and 1950–1951 have been reprinted.

Proceedings of the U.S. Naval Institute. Annapolis; monthly.

Ships of the world. Tokyo; monthly.

Warship. London: Conway Maritime Press; quarterly.

Warship international. Toledo, Ohio: International Naval Research Organization; quarterly.

INDEX OF SHIPS ILLUSTRATED

BY COUNTRY

GENERAL INDEX

(the numbers in bold type indicate illustrated entries)

DATE DUE

DEMCO 38-296